SIR NICHOLAS HARRIS NICOLAS was born in 1799, and served in the Royal Navy in the Mediterranean from 1808 to 1816 under Admiral Duckworth and Lord Exmouth. Retired on half-pay at the end of the Napoleonic Wars, he turned to antiquarian and literary pursuits after a brief legal career, compiling and editing a large number of scholarly works. This seven-volume annotated compilation of Nelson's correspondence was originally published by Henry Colburn between 1844 and 1847, and was to be followed by his ambitious *A History of the British Navy, from the Earliest Times to the Wars of the French Revolution*, but when he died in France in 1848, only the first two volumes, covering up to the year 1422, had been completed.

THE

DISPATCHES AND LETTERS

OF

VICE ADMIRAL

LORD VISCOUNT NELSON

WITH NOTES BY

SIR NICHOLAS HARRIS NICOLAS, G.C.M.G.

" The Nation expected, and was entitled to expect, that while Cities vied with each other
in consecrating Statues in marble and brass to the memory of our NELSON, a Literary Monu-
ment would be erected, which should record his deeds for the immortal honour of his own
Country, and the admiration of the rest of the World." — QUARTERLY REVIEW.

THE SIXTH VOLUME.

MAY 1804, TO JULY 1805.

CHATHAM PUBLISHING

LONDON

Published in 1998 by
Chatham Publishing,
1 & 2 Faulkner's Alley, Cowcross Street,
London EC1M 6DD

Chatham Publishing is an imprint of
Gerald Duckworth and Co Ltd

First Published in 1846
by Henry Colburn

ISBN 1 86176 053 1

PREFACE.

A PERIOD of fifteen months of the life of NELSON is illustrated by his Correspondence in this Volume; and as his career approached its close, his Letters increased in interest and importance.

These Letters extend from May 1804 to July 1805, during the whole of which time he was Commander-in-Chief in the Mediterranean, watching the French Squadron in Toulon, until it sailed, in April 1805, to the West Indies, whither it was pursued by LORD NELSON with a very inferior force.

Besides showing NELSON'S unabated energy, his unwearied attention to the minutest details of his Command, his constant regard for the comfort of the Crews of his Ships, as to their provisions and clothing; his continual efforts to prevent any waste of stores, and the Government from being imposed upon by Contractors, the most remarkable parts of his Letters in 1804 are, perhaps, those relating to Vice-Admiral La Touche Tréville, the Commander-in-Chief of the French Squadron in Toulon, whose premature death, according to Monsieur Thiers, was the principal cause of England's not having been invaded!—to the refusal of Artillery Officers embarked on board of Bombs to submit to Naval discipline, which led to the formation of the Corps of Royal Marine Artillery—those to the Lord Mayor, on receiving the thanks of the Corporation of London for " blockading Toulon," when he assured the Lord Mayor, that instead of having " blockaded" that Port, he had, on the contrary, afforded the French Fleet every opportunity of putting to sea, and expressed his determination not to be separated in Thanks from the two Admirals under his orders, whom he considered to have been unjustly neglected by the Corporation—and the Letters in which he denounced the Gibraltar Privateers as a " horde of sanctioned robbers," whose piratical proceedings were " disgraceful to the character of the British Nation."

His Letters respecting Vice-Admiral La Touche Tréville, are, however, so characteristic, as to justify particular attention being drawn to them. On the 1st of June 1804, LORD NELSON said he had sent Rear-Admiral Sir Richard Bickerton to another station; and that he was himself close off Toulon with five Sail of the Line, " in hopes to tempt Mr. La Touche out of Port." On the 7th, he said, " Do not think I am tired of watching Mr. La Touche Tréville. I have now taken up a method of making him angry. I have left Sir Richard Bickerton, with part of the Fleet, twenty leagues from hence,

and, with five of the Line, am preventing his cutting
capers, which he had done for some time past, off Cape
Sicie.   Mr. La Touche has several times hoisted his topsail yards up; and on the 4th of June, we having hoisted
the Standard and saluted, he sent outside Sepet, about
one mile, five Sail of the Line and two Frigates, and kept
three Sail and three Frigates with their yards aloft, himself one of them, and the Rear-Admiral another, therefore I did not believe him in earnest; however, we run as
near as was proper, and brought to.   They formed a
pretty line at sunset, and then stood into the Harbour.
A Ship of the Line and Frigate every morning weigh,
and stand between Sepet and La Malgue.   Some happy
day I expect to see his eight Sail, which are in the
Outer Road, come out; and if he will get abreast of
Porquerolle, I will try what stuff he is made of."

In the afternoon of the 14th of June, eight Ships of
the Line of the Enemy came out of Toulon, and LORD
NELSON, with only five Sail of the Line, formed in Order
of Battle to receive them; but they returned into Port.
He attached no importance to this proceeding; and
writing, on the 18th of June, merely said, " We are as
usual.   The French Fleet safe in Toulon; but upon the
14th, Monsieur La Touche came out with eight Sail of the
Line and six Frigates, cut a caper off Sepet, and went in
again. I was off, with five Sail of the Line, and brought
to for his attack, although I did not believe that anything was meant serious, but merely a gasconade."

It is not difficult, from NELSON'S chivalric sense of

honour, and deep love of truth, to understand the surprise and indignation with which he read Vice-Admiral
La Touche Tréville's official report, wherein he ventured
to assert that, on the 14th of June, the English Admiral
" recalled his Ship and his two Frigates, which were
among the Islands, and bore away. I pursued him until
night; he ran to the South-East. In the morning, at
daylight, I saw no more of him." The insult sank deep
in NELSON's mind. To the Admiralty he merely said,
that " Although I most certainly never thought of writing
a line upon Monsieur La Touche's having cut a caper
a few miles outside of Toulon on the 14th of June,
where he well knew I could not get at him without
placing the Ships under the batteries which surround
that Port, and that, had I attacked him in that position, he could retire into his secure nest whenever he
pleased, yet as that gentleman has thought proper to
write a letter stating that the Fleet under my command ran away, and that he pursued it, perhaps it
may be thought necessary for me to say something,
but I do assure you, Sir, that I know not what to say,
except by a flat contradiction; for if my character is
not established by this time for not being apt to run
away, it is not worth my time to attempt to put the
world right;" but in his Private Letters he used the
most emphatic language on the subject. " You will have
seen Monsieur La Touche's letter," he said to his brother,
" of how he chased me, and how I *ran*. I keep it;
and, by God, if I take him, he shall *Eat* it;" while to

his friend Davison, he observed, " I am expecting Monsieur La Touche (as he has wrote a letter that I ran away) to come out of his nest. The whole history was too contemptible for my notice, but I have thought it right, not upon my own account, but for the satisfaction of the Admiralty, &c. to send a copy of the Victory's Log: for if my character for *not* running away, is not fixed by this time, it is not worth my trouble to put the world right at my time of life; and if any Englishman has believed for one moment the story, I may, to my friend, say, without fear of being thought arrogant, that they do not deserve to have me serve them; but I have kept Monsieur La Touche's letter; and if I take him, I shall either never see him, or, if I do, make him *eat* his letter. Perhaps sovereign contempt is the best." Similar expressions occur in many other letters; but as the French Admiral died early in August following, the meeting never took place, and the command of the French Squadron was given to Vice-Admiral Villeneuve.

In August 1804, LORD NELSON'S state of health obliged him to apply for leave to go to England, which reached him in December; but the War with Spain, and the great probability that the Enemy would put to sea, induced him to remain, and he kept the authority to give up his Command a profound secret. At this period his feelings were greatly mortified by his Command being divided, and the Ships off Cadiz formed into a separate Squadron, under Vice-Admiral Sir John Orde, his senior

Officer, whose jealousy of NELSON had shown itself some
years before. " I almost begin to think that he is sent
off Cadiz to reap the golden harvest," he said, " as
Campbell was sent off Cadiz by Cornwallis (by orders
from England) to reap my sugar harvest. It's very odd,
two Admiralties to treat me so: surely, I have dreamt
that ' I have done the State some service.'"

While the Squadron was at the Madalena Islands for
water and refreshments, intelligence was brought to him,
in the afternoon of the 19th of January, 1805, that the
Enemy, consisting of eleven Sail of the Line, under Vice-
Admiral Villeneuve, had put to sea; and as it was steering South, or S. by W., he concluded that it was bound
round the Southern end of Sardinia, whereas its real destination was out of the Straits, and thence to the West Indies.
LORD NELSON's Squadron, likewise consisting of eleven
Sail of the Line, immediately got under weigh, ran through
the Passage between Biche and Sardinia, and then bore
away, round the East side of that Island, for Cape Carbo-
naro, its South-Easternmost point. A heavy gale of wind
forced the Enemy back to Toulon, on the 21st; but LORD
NELSON, impressed with the belief that they had either returned to Port, crippled in the gale, or that they had gone
to Egypt, passed the Faro of Messina with a foul wind,
(being the first Fleet that was ever known to have
" beaten" through,) and proceeded to Egypt. His Letters show that his anxiety was not less, and his exertions
to obtain information as great, as when in a similar
pursuit in 1798; and it was not until his return from

Alexandria, on the 19th of February, that he knew the French Fleet was in Toulon.

Towards the end of March, the Squadron went to Sardinia; and on the 4th of April, the day after LORD NELSON sailed from Pula Roads, in the Gulf of Cagliari, he received information that the French had quitted Toulon in the night of the 31st of March, when he used every effort to get to the Westward, supposing that they intended to make the Island of Galita.

Our Annals afford no instance in which a man was more entirely devoted to the service of his Country, than NELSON during his pursuit of the French Fleet in 1805. It was well said, soon after the event, that " in this part of his glorious career of Public duty, this was perhaps the most glorious;" and that " few great characters in our History were capable of adopting, and none have ever put so great and noble a measure into execution."[1] From the moment he heard of the departure of the French Squadron from Toulon, until it was beyond his reach, the ardour of pursuit, the aspirations of valour, the responsibilities of command, the eager desire to meet the Enemy, and the bitterness of his disappointment at having missed them, are powerfully described in his Letters. No one can read these genuine expressions of his feelings without emotion; and to Officers they are animating examples in their career of professional fame. While ignorant of the destination

---

[1] Annual Register, 1805, p. 226.

of the Enemy, NELSON said, " I have nothing to wish
for but to meet them"—" I am, in truth, half dead; but
what man can do to find them out, shall be done;"
" I can neither eat, drink, or sleep.   It cannot last long
what I feel"—" Under the severe affliction which I feel
at the escape of the French Fleet."—Impeded by a foul
wind, he said, " My good fortune seems flown away.
I cannot get a fair wind, or even a side wind.   Dead
foul!—dead foul! . . . I believe this ill luck will go near
to kill me."   Yet even when his mind was thus a prey
to care and anxiety, his usual goodness of heart displayed itself in kind feelings and good offices.

He learnt, at last, that the Enemy had passed the
Straits.   To follow them, "either to the West Indies, or
to the Antipodes," was to NELSON a simple act of duty.
Accordingly, on the 11th of May 1805, he pursued, with
only ten Sail of the Line, the Combined Fleet composed of eighteen; and all he thought it necessary to
say to his dearest friend of the immense responsibility
he incurred, or of the risk which so great a disparity of
force involved, was, " My lot is cast, and I am going to
the West Indies, where, although I am late, yet chance
may have given them a bad passage, and me a good
one: I must hope the best."   He certainly need not have
supposed that the world would (as he seems to think the
Admiralty might) " imagine he was on a party of pleasure, running after eighteen Sail of the Line with ten, and
that to the West Indies."   During his voyage he drew
up a Plan of Attack, remarkable alike for its terseness,

and for its great professional truths. " The business of an English Commander-in-Chief," was, he said, " first to bring an Enemy's Fleet to Battle, on the most advantageous terms to himself, (I mean that of laying his Ships close on board the Enemy, as expeditiously as possible;) and secondly, to continue them there, without separating, until the business is decided." .... " If the two Fleets are both willing to fight, but little manœuvring is necessary; the less the better;—a day is soon lost in that business." .....
" Signals from these moments are useless, when every man is disposed to do his duty. The great object is for us to support each other, and to keep close to the Enemy, and to leeward of him. If the Enemy are running away, then the only signals necessary will be to engage the Enemy as arriving up with them." On the success of his Plan depended, he truly added, " not only the honour and glory of our Country, but possibly its safety, and with it, that of all Europe, from French tyranny and oppression."

On the 4th of June, the Squadron arrived at Barbadoes, and finding it to be the general opinion that the Enemy intended to attack Tobago and Trinidad, and being informed by General Brereton that they had passed St. Lucia in the night of the 28th of May, he accepted Lieutenant-General Sir William Myers's offer to embark two thousand troops for the relief of those Islands, and sailed on the following day, in the full confidence of a Battle. " I hope," he observed, " that my

next letter will be worth all I have hitherto wrote."
On approaching Tobago the Squadron prepared for
Battle, but the Enemy were not there; and a Vessel
having, by mistake, made the signal for their being
at Trinidad, LORD NELSON hastened thither. He was,
however, again disappointed; for the Combined Fleet
had never been off St. Lucia, but had gone to Martinique, whence they returned to Europe. Information of the arrival of the Enemy at Martinique reached
LORD NELSON on the 8th of June; the troops were
disembarked at Antigua; and in the forenoon of the
13th, the Squadron was on its way towards the Straits
of Gibraltar.

LORD NELSON'S vexation at having been misled by
General Brereton's report, was unbounded. To the
Duke of Clarence he said—" Your Royal Highness will
easily conceive the misery I am feeling at having hitherto
missed the French Fleet. . . . But for that false information, I should have been off Fort Royal as they were
putting to sea, and our Battle, most probably, would
have been fought on the spot where the brave Rodney
beat De Grasse." In his other Letters, which are nearly
filled with the subject, he said—" I have no reason to
blame Dame Fortune: if either General Brereton could
not have wrote, or his look-out man had been blind,
nothing could have prevented my fighting them on the
6th of June."—" There would have been no occasion
for opinions, had not General Brereton sent his d—d
intelligence from St. Lucia; nor would I have received

it, to have acted by it, but I was assured that his information was very correct.   It has almost broke my
heart, but I must not despair."—" I am, as you may
readily believe, very, very unhappy at not having got at
the Enemy: they were missed by General Brereton's
unlucky information; but I shall be close after them in
Europe, and when I have housed them, I shall certainly
instantly return to England: I want rest."—" You will
lament the unfortunate intelligence from General Brereton, which led me a wrong road, or June 6th would have
been a fighting day for me, and, I trust, a glorious one for
our Country.   However, I must not despair of getting
up with them before they enter the Straits."—" Saw
three planks, which I think came from the French Fleet.
Very miserable, which is very foolish!"   On reaching
Cape Spartel, he wrote in his Diary—" Cape Spartel
in sight, but no French Fleet, nor any information about
them: how sorrowful this makes me; but I cannot help
myself!"   To his friend Vice-Admiral Collingwood, off
Cadiz, he said—" I am, as you may suppose, miserable
at not having fallen in with the Enemy's Fleet, and I
am almost increased in sorrow in not finding them.
The name of General Brereton will not soon be forgot:
but for his false information, the Battle would have been
fought where Rodney fought his, on June 6th.   I must
now only hope that the Enemy have not tricked me,
and gone to Jamaica.   The moment the Fleet is watered,
and got some refreshments, of which we are in great
want, I shall come out and make you a visit—not, my

dear friend, to take your Command from you, (for I
may probably add mine to you,) but to consult how
we can best serve our Country, by detaching a part of
this large force."—" I am, my dear Mr. Marsden, as
completely miserable as my greatest enemy could wish
me; but I neither blame fortune, or my own judgment.
Oh, General Brereton! General Brereton!" But it was
to his confidential friend Mr. Davison, that he expressed his feelings most fully:—" I am as miserable as
you can conceive. But for General Brereton's d—d
information, NELSON would have been, living or dead,
the greatest man in his Profession that England ever
saw. Now, alas! I am nothing—perhaps shall incur
censure for misfortunes which may happen, and have
happened. When I follow my own head, I am, in general, much more correct in my judgment, than following
the opinion of others. I resisted the opinion of General
Brereton's information till it would have been the height
of presumption to have carried my disbelief further.
I could not, in the face of Generals and Admirals, go
N.W., when it was *apparently* clear that the Enemy
had gone South. But I am miserable."

The Squadron arrived at Gibraltar on the 19th of
July, and the next day LORD NELSON went on shore,
which was, he says, "the first time since the 16th of
June, 1803, and from having my foot out of the Victory,
two years wanting ten days." He sailed on the 23rd of
July; and being informed in the morning of the 25th,

that the Combined Fleet had been seen steering to the Northward, he instantly bent his course for Ushant.

No other observations are necessary in explanation of the contents of this Volume, except to remark that the " Letter-Book" and " Order-Book," from which so many documents have been taken, end—the former on the 6th of October, and the latter on the 15th of November, 1804. That there were similar Books of a much later date, is certain; but they have not fallen into the Editor's hands.

He has the pleasure of being able to add, that LORD NELSON'S Letters to the first Earl Spencer have been obligingly communicated to him by the present Earl, to whom he begs leave to offer his best thanks for so valuable a contribution. Those Letters, with numerous others (and some of them of the highest interest) that reached him too late for insertion in their proper places, will be found in the Seventh and last Volume, which will be published about the beginning of April.

Torrington Square,
21st February, 1846.

CONTENTS.

LETTERS.

1804.

1804, *continued.*

1804, *continued.*

b 2

1803, *continued.*

1804, *continued.*

1804, *continued.*

1804, *continued.*

xxiv

CONTENTS.

1804, *continued.*

CONTENTS. XXV

1804, *continued.*

1804, *continued.*

1805.

CONTENTS.   xxvii

1805, *continued.*

1805, *continued.*

1805, *continued.*

xxxii   CONTENTS.

1803, *continued.*

ANALYSIS

OF THE

LIFE OF NELSON,

FROM MAY 1804 TO JULY 1805.

YEAR.	MONTH.	FACTS.

1804. — May { VICE-ADMIRAL OF THE WHITE, Commanding in Chief in the Mediterranean, with his Flag in the *Victory*, off Toulon.

— — 11th............Anchored at the Madalena Islands.

— — 19th............Proceeded off Toulon.

— July to 30th { Off Toulon. On the 14th of June, the French Fleet came out, but returned to Port.

31st............Anchored in Palma Bay, Sardinia.

— August 7th............Sailed.

— — 8th............Anchored in Pula Roads, in the Gulf of Cagliari.

— — 10th............Proceeded off Toulon.

— October to 17th { Off Toulon.

— — 18th............Anchored at the Madalena Islands.

— — 27th........ ...Proceeded off Toulon.

— December to 12th } ...Off Toulon.

— — 13th............Anchored in Pula Roads, in the Gulf of Cagliari.

— — 17th............Sailed.

— — 18th............Anchored in Palma Bay.

— — 19th............Proceeded off Toulon.

1805. January to 11th } ...Off Toulon.

12th ....Anchored at the Madalena Islands.

YEAR.	MONTH.		FACTS.

1805, *continued* .... Vice-Admiral of the White.

— January 19th ....Received information that the French Fleet had sailed on the 18th from Toulon, and immediately proceeded with the Squadron, on the East side of Sardinia, to the Southern end of that Island.

— — 22nd .... Sixteen leagues East of Cape Carbonara.

— — 25th .... In the Gulf of Cagliari.

— — 29th .... Passed the Faro of Messina, and, supposing that the Enemy had gone to Egypt, proceeded to Alexandria.

— February 8th .... Off Alexandria.

— — 12th .... Off Candia. Hearing nothing of the French Fleet, proceeded back to Sardinia.

— — 19th .... Off Malta. Learnt that the French Fleet had returned to Toulon.

— — 28th .... Anchored in Pula Roads, Sardinia.

— March 4th .... After two attempts to put to sea, sailed from Pula Roads.

— — 7th .... Anchored.

— — 8th .... Sailed, and anchored in Palma Bay.

— — 9th .... Proceeded off Toulon.

— — to 26th } ... Off Toulon.

— — 27th .... Anchored in the Gulf of Palma.

— — 30th .... Sailed.

— — 31st .... Anchored in Pula Roads.

— April 3rd .... Sailed.

— — 4th .... Received intelligence that the Enemy's Fleet was at sea, having left Toulon on the 30th or 31st of March. Proceeded to the Westward, between Galita and Sardinia.

— — 18th .... Off Toro. Learnt that the French Fleet had passed Gibraltar on the 8th, and proceeded to Gibraltar.

— May 4th .... Anchored at Tetuan.

— — 5th .... Sailed from Tetuan.

— — 6th .... Anchored at Gibraltar, and sailed in the evening.

— — 9th .... Anchored in Lagos Bay.

— — 11th .... Proceeded to the West Indies, in pursuit of the Combined Fleet.

— June 4th .... Anchored in Carlisle Bay, Barbadoes, and having heard that the Enemy's Fleet had gone to Tobago and Trinidad, embarked 2000 Troops.

— — 5th .... Sailed.

YEAR.	MONTH.	FACTS.

1805, *continued* .... VICE-ADMIRAL OF THE WHITE.

— June 6th .... Off Tobago.

— — 7th .... Anchored in the Gulf of Paria, Trinidad.

— — 8th .... Sailed. Heard that the French Fleet had arrived at Martinique on the 4th, and was erroneously informed that it was to sail for an attack on Grenada and Dominica.

— — 9th .... In St. George's Bay, Grenada.

— — 11th .... Off Guadaloupe.

— — 12th .... Anchored at St. John's, Antigua; disembarked the Troops, and determined to proceed towards the Mediterranean, believing that the Enemy had returned to Europe.

— — 13th .... Sailed from Antigua.

— July 8th .... Off the Azores.

— — 18th .... Off Cape Spartel.

— — 19th .... Anchored at Gibraltar.

— — 22nd .... Sailed from Gibraltar, and anchored at Tetuan.

— — 23rd .... Sailed from Tetuan, and having heard that the Enemy had been seen on the 19th, steering for the Northward, proceeded for Ushant.

LETTERS.

1804—ÆT. 45.

TO REAR-ADMIRAL SIR EDWARD PELLEW, BART.[1]

[From Clarke and M'Arthur, vol. ii. p. 362.]

May 1st, 1804.

You have always, my dear Sir Edward, proved yourself so equal to command a Fleet, that it would be a sin to place you in any other situation, and my services are very nearly at an end; for, in addition to other infirmities, I am nearly blind: however, I hope to fight one more Battle. I am, &c.,

NELSON AND BRONTE.

TO J. B. GIBERT, ESQ., HIS MAJESTY'S VICE-CONSUL, BARCELONA.

[Autograph draught in the possession of Earl Nelson, and Letter-Book.]

Sir,   Victory, at Sea, 1st May, 1804.

I am much obliged by your letter of the 25th ultimo, respecting the Hindostan;[2] but I am afraid that little of value except anchors is unburnt, and, therefore, that it would hardly answer the expense of sending for Neapolitan divers. However, if any person save any of the effects, I am perfectly ready to allow them a most liberal salvage; but, as I said before, unless it is the people who live in the Bay, and watch the opportunity of fine weather, I much doubt if it would pay the expenses of the undertaking. Captain Le Gros certainly

---

[1] Afterwards Admiral Viscount Exmouth, G.C.B., who had then expressed his desire to serve under Lord Nelson.

[2] Vide vol. v. p. 503.

ought to have directed his letter to you : it would have gone more regularly to the Captain-General. I can only suppose that Mr. Gayner did what he thought for the best. Captain Le Gros has spoken of his kind attention in terms of great praise. I am, Sir, with great respect, &c.,

NELSON AND BRONTE.

TO J. B. GIBERT, ESQ., HIS MAJESTY'S VICE-CONSUL, BARCELONA.

[Autograph draught in the possession of Earl Nelson, and Letter Book.]

Victory, at Sea, 1st May, 1804.

Sir,

I am much obliged by your letters of the 25th and 27th ultimo. The Englishmen belonging to the Cutter[3] have behaved very ill, in not going on board the Juno; and I desire that you will not, upon any account, forward them to Gibraltar, or pay them, after their refusal to embark, unless they are lodged in gaol, to be delivered to the first King's Ship. I am, &c.,

NELSON AND BRONTE.

TO CAPTAIN SIR WILLIAM BOLTON, H.M. SLOOP CHILDERS.

[Order Book.]

Victory, at Sea, 3rd May, 1803.

Having received information that there are three French Privateers (two of them Brigs) who have taken their station off Tunis, for the purpose of intercepting and capturing our Trade, You are hereby required and directed to take His Majesty's Sloop named in the margin[4] under your command, and proceed immediately in quest of them, passing the Southwest end of Sardinia in your way ; and if the weather be favourable, send a Boat into St. Pierres, in order to obtain information respecting them. Having so done, you will make the best of your way to the Island of Galita, and run close round it, where it is probable you may fall in with the said Privateers. Should you not, you will proceed inside the Cannes, passing between

[3] The Swift.   [4] Cameleon.

Plane Island and the Point of Porto Farino, to the Island of
Zimbra; from which place, the French Privateers, last year,
made several captures of our Ships, as mentioned in the Memorandum which accompanies this, to which, I desire you
will particularly attend, in order that, if possible, these Privateers may be captured or destroyed, strictly consistent with
the Neutrality of Tunis, should you fall in with them at the
Island of Zimbra, or near the Rocks called the Cannes, or in
fact, any way near those places without gun-shot of the Bey
of Tunis' forts or batteries. Not falling in with them at either
of these places, you will stand over to Pantellaria, and from
thence to Maritimo, where you will make every inquiry
respecting them, and also, at Trepani. In the event of your
capturing these Privateers or any of them, you will proceed
with them to Malta, giving particular directions that neither
the Captains nor Officers of them are to be liberated on any
account whatever. After having seen them in safety to Valetta
Harbour, and completed your provisions and water, &c., to
the usual time, (which is to be done with the utmost dispatch,)
you will return and join me without loss of time on Rendezvous
No. 102, where you will find me, or orders for your further
proceedings; but, should you not fall in with the Privateers
before-mentioned, or receive certain information respecting
them at Pantellaria, Maritimo, or Trepani, you will return
and join me immediately on the said Rendezvous.

NELSON AND BRONTE.

MEMORANDUM FOR CAPTAIN SIR WILLIAM BOLTON.

[Autograph draught, in the possession of Earl Nelson, and Order Book.]

Victory, at Sea, 3rd May, 1804.

In looking for these Privateers mentioned in my order of
this date, I would recommend, if the wind is favourable, sending a Boat into St. Pierres, South-West end of Sardinia, for
information, as last year that was their place of great resort;
but it is possible they may lay under the Isle of Vache or
Toro, and keep people on the top to give them information.

From St. Pierres, or Toro, I would advise making Galita,
running close round it. This Island I do not consider as

belonging to any State which can give it Neutrality. From thence, passing under the Cannes, and either pass between Plane Island, and the Point of Porto Farino, or outside of it, steer for the Islands of Zimbra, from which place last year one of these Captains of French Privateers made captures of our Ships passing, using the Tunisian flag, and dressing their men with turbans &c.; and on representing the capture to the Bey of Tunis, his answer was, that the Islands of Zimbra were Rocks in the sea, from which the English might look out, as well as the French, but that Prizes must not be taken within gun-shot of his Coast. It is therefore evident that the Bey did not consider the Zimbras as part of his Coast, and therefore that you may take Vessels close to Zimbra, and you may do the same close to the Rocks called Cannes, which are several miles from the shore; but you will be very careful not to infringe the Neutrality of Tunis, by making captures *within cannon* shot of the shore.

Should you gain no information of the Privateers, you will stand over to Pantellaria, and from thence to Maritimo, inquiring at those places, and Trepani, for information; and not being able to get such information as may lead you to suppose it in your power to get at them, you will return and join me.

I would recommend disguising both the Brigs from the moment of separation, and I rely upon your exertions in getting hold of these gentry; and if you do, take them to Malta, and take care the Captains and Officers of the Privateers are not liberated upon any account.

TO THE RIGHT HONOURABLE LORD HOBART, SECRETARY OF STATE FOR THE WAR DEPARTMENT.

[Autograph, in the Colonial Office.]

Victory, May 3rd, 1804.

My dear Lord,

In addition to what I have formerly said about Sardinia, I have only to add, that such is its present state, that an offer will generally be made of it to the French, if we will not take it, by treaty, or some other way; for under the present Government the Inhabitants do not wish to live. Having, in former letters, stated its immense importance, I only now presume to bring the subject forward to your Lordship's most serious consideration. The question is not, shall the King of Sardinia keep it? that is out of the question; he cannot, for any length of time. If France possesses it, Sicily is not safe an hour; and the passage to the Levant is completely blocked up. Pardon me, my Lord, for bringing this important subject again before you: but I really think that I should not do my duty to my Country if I did not. I am, &c.,

NELSON AND BRONTE.

TO J. B. GIBERT, ESQ., HIS MAJESTY'S VICE-CONSUL, BARCELONA.

[Letter Book.]

Victory, at Sea, 3rd May, 1804.

Sir,

In answer to your letter of the 1st instant, I herewith enclose you a list of the late Swift Cutter's crew, received by his Majesty's Ship Juno, and Cameleon Sloop.[4] I am happy to find that our two Countries still continue in amity, though I have very much to complain of the limited supplies of bullocks and fresh beef at Rosas, as contrary to the subsisting treaties between them, and request you will officially mention this to his Excellency, the Captain General at Barcelona. I am, with much respect, &c.,

NELSON AND BRONTE.

TO LADY HAMILTON.

[From " Lord Nelson's Letters to Lady Hamilton," vol. ii. p. 37.]

Victory, May 5th, 1804.

I find, my dearest Emma, that your picture is very much admired by the French Consul at Barcelona; and that he has not sent it to be admired—which, I am sure, it would be—by Buonaparte. They pretend, that there were three pictures

---

[4] On the 3rd of May 1804, Lord Nelson signed an acknowledgment to have received from J. B. Gibert, Esq., his Britannic Majesty's Vice-Consul at Barcelona, by the Juno and Cameleon, Mr. Isaac Watson, Master, the Gunner, Boatswain, and fifteen Seamen, late belonging to the Swift Cutter.—*Letter-Book.*

taken. I wish I had them; but they are all gone, as irre-
trievably as the dispatches—unless we may read them in a
book, as we printed their correspondence from Egypt.[5] But,
from us, what can they find out? That I love you most
dearly; and hate the French most damnably. Dr. Scott
went to Barcelona, to try to get the private letters; but, I
fancy, they are all gone to Paris. The Swedish and American
Consuls told him, that the French Consul had your picture,
and read your letters; and, the Doctor thinks, one of them
probably read the letters. By the Master's account of the
Cutter, I would not have trusted a pair of old shoes in her.
He tells me, she did not sail, but was a good Sea-boat.

I hope, Mr. Marsden will not trust any more of my
private letters in such a conveyance; if they choose to trust
the affairs of the Public in such a thing, I cannot help it.
I long for the Invasion being over; it must finish the War,
and I have no fears for the event. . . . .

TO CAPTAIN CRACRAFT, H.M. SHIP ANSON.

[Order-Book.]

Victory, at Sea, 6th May, 1804.

Whereas, it has been represented to me that the Private
Marine named in the margin, had for some particular reasons
entered into the service by that name, but is, in reality, a
young man of genteel family, with good expectations, and his
discharge having at the same time been solicited, you are
hereby required and directed to discharge the said Charles
Taylor from his Majesty's Ship under your command, into the
first Ship of War going to England, directing the Commander
of such Ship to state to the Admiralty the particulars of his
case, in order that their Lordships may grant him his discharge from the Service, in such manner as may appear to
them proper.

NELSON AND BRONTE.

---

[5] Vide vol. v. p. 503, note 4.

TO CAPTAIN MOUBRAY, H.M. SHIP ACTIVE.

[Order-Book.]

Victory, at Sea, 10th May, 1804.

Whereas, it is my intention to proceed immediately with the Squadron to the Madalena Islands, for the purpose of completing the wood and water of the different Ships, and procuring the necessary refreshments for their Companies, which will not detain me more than five or six days at that anchorage; You are, therefore, hereby required and directed to take his Majesty's Ships named in the margin [6] under your command, and remain on Rendezvous No. 102, for the purpose of watching the Enemy's motions at Toulon, and acquainting any of his Majesty's Ships or Vessels in search of the Squadron where I am gone to. You will take an early opportunity of reconnoitring the Enemy's force at the above mentioned place, and as they are occasionally in the habit of sending out two or three of their Frigates, (sometimes under cover of a Ship of the Line), you will perform this service with proper caution, so as to enable you to ascertain their real situation, without the risk of being captured. And as it will be desirable for me to know the Enemy's motions, you will on the first examination of Toulon, after my leaving you, send a Frigate to Madalena with an account thereof, and continue frequently with the rest of your Ships to reconnoitre them, during my absence as above mentioned; taking particular care that some Vessel of War is left upon Rendezvous No. 102, in order to acquaint anything in search of the Fleet where it is gone to, calculating from the time I leave you, when the Squadron may be able to gain the anchorage at Madalena, and bearing in mind that it will only remain there five or six days for the purpose before mentioned; and afterwards, if the wind is from the Eastward, the Squadron will proceed on the West side of Corsica, but if from the Westward on the East side of that Island, to Rendezvous No. 102, where you will keep a good look-out for my return, in order that I may be joined by the Frigates the moment I arrive on the said Rendezvous. Should the Enemy in the meantime

[6] Active, Seahorse, Phœbe, Amazon.

put to sea, you will be governed in communicating an account
thereof to me, from the circumstances above stated, sending
a Vessel on the East and West side of Corsica to fall in with
me, in case the Squadron should have left the Madalena
Islands,

NELSON AND BRONTE.

TO WILLIAM MARSDEN, ESQ., ADMIRALTY.

[Original, in the Admiralty.]

Victory, at Sea, 10th May, 1804.

Sir,

I have received your letter of the 4th ultimo, with a copy
of the letter therein mentioned, which has been written by
the Secretary of State to Sir Alexander Ball, respecting the
appropriation of the Palace of Bugia for the service of a
Naval Hospital; and you will please to acquaint the Lords
Commissioners of the Admiralty that I have sent Doctor Snipe
to Malta to consult with Sir Alexander Ball, and to assist in
forming an estimate of the expense attending the same for Lord
Hobart's information. You will, at the same time, acquaint
their Lordships, that the additional building to the said Palace
mentioned by Doctor Snipe is absolutely necessary, for the
convenience and comfort of a Naval Hospital, and that a
certain space of ground attached to the said building is also
indispensably necessary for a garden, a place for the con-
valescent Seamen and Marines to enjoy a little exercise and
fresh air. I am, &c.,

NELSON AND BRONTE.

TO WILLIAM MARSDEN, ESQ., ADMIRALTY.

[Original, in the Admiralty.]

Victory, at Sea, 10th May, 1804.

Sir,

I have received your letter of the 16th March, together
with a copy of the one therein mentioned from the Secretary
to the Board of Ordnance, respecting the negotiation for arms
at Vienna having failed, and signifying their Lordships' direc-

tion to me to recall the Ships named in the margin[7] from
the Adriatic ; In answer thereto, you will please to acquaint the
Lords Commissioners of the Admiralty, that the Monmouth
proceeded direct for England, and that I have ordered the Agincourt, after receiving her guns at Gibraltar, and escorting the
Argo and such Trade as may be under her protection, twenty
or twenty-five leagues to the Westward of Cadiz, to return to
Malta (calling in her way at Gibraltar for any Vessels which
may be desirous of proceeding with her to Valetta Harbour)
for the purpose of being joined by the Thisbe, and convoying
our Trade from the Archipelago and Adriatic to England.　I
am, Sir, &c.,

NELSON AND BRONTE.

TO THE PRINCIPAL OFFICERS AND COMMISSIONERS OF HIS
MAJESTY'S NAVY, LONDON.

[Letter-Book.]

Victory, at Sea, 10th May, 1804.

Gentlemen,
　　I have received your letter of the 14th February last,
acquainting me that his Majesty's Store-ship Diligent is
ordered to be loaded at Woolwich with stores for Gibraltar.
As my letters of the 10th January last have reached your
Board, as acknowledged by yours of the 6th March, I must
request that you will reply to my letter under the first-mentioned date, inclosing a copy of one from Commissioner Otway,
together with Vouchers for caulking his Majesty's Ship Victory,
as therein set forth, in order that the Carpenter of the said
Ship, and people employed on the occasion, may be satisfied
that the discontinuing this necessary remuneration (should
such be the case) for their extra labour, does not remain with
me.　It is to be lamented that the Carpenters and their Crews
are not apprised of any circumstance of this nature, to prevent
murmur or discontent amongst them.　I am, &c.,

NELSON AND BRONTE.

---

[7] Monmouth, Agincourt.　Vide vol. v. p. 358.

TO CAPTAIN GORE, H. M. SHIP MEDUSA.

[Letter-Book. Friday, 11th May, 1804. " At 10 A.M., shortened sail, and
came to [in the Madalena Islands.] Superb, Triumph, Leviathan, Niger, and the
Bombs with their Tenders, anchored here. Royal Sovereign, Canopus, Belleisle,
and Donegal anchored in the Eastern Bay; ~Renown and Excellent in the Western
Bay."—*Victory's Log.*]

Victory, Madalena Islands, 12th May, 1804.

Sir,

I have received your letter of the 20th ultimo, and copies
of the ones therein-mentioned, addressed to the Captains of
the Orpheus and Amphion, which, from the reasons stated in
your said letter, I very much approve of. I am sorry to find
that the main-keel of the Medusa is so much injured, and
hope an opportunity may soon offer for heaving down that
Ship, and effectually repairing the damages she has sustained.
It is rather unfortunate that the Maidstone should at this time
have sprung her foremast and bowsprit; but I am satisfied
that every exertion will be used in making good her defects,
after the Halcyon is ready for sea. You have done perfectly
right in anchoring the Maidstone off the Mole-Head: her
apparent readiness for sea may check the Privateers from any
depredation on our Trade. I must request, the moment
the Halcyon is ready for service, that you will keep Captain
Pearse[8] on the alert, as I am sorry to observe that the Service
has not derived that benefit from her which might have been
expected from so fine a Vessel. I am, &c.,

NELSON AND BRONTE.

TO CAPTAIN GORE, H.M. SHIP MEDUSA.

[Letter-Book.]

Victory, Madalena Islands, 12th May, 1804.

Sir,

I have received your letter of the 12th ultimo, acquainting
me with the loss of the Apollo, and Merchant-vessels therein
mentioned, on the Coast of Spain. I approve of the order
you have given Captain Pearse to proceed to Gibraltar for

---

[8] In a subsequent Letter, Lord Nelson said he was mistaken on this point, and
expressed himself fully satisfied with Captain Pearse's exertions. Vide p. 137, post.

the purpose of being repaired, but am sorry to find that the Halcyon is constantly in want of something done to her. It is unpleasant that any differences between our Boats' Crews and L'Aigle's[9] should have taken place; but I am glad to find the circumstance should have been so amicably settled between you and the French Captain, and that their Seamen in future are prevented from wearing arms. I am, &c.,

NELSON AND BRONTE.

TO SIR ALEXANDER JOHN BALL, BART., MALTA.

[Letter-Book.]

Victory, Madalena Islands, 12th May, 1804.

Sir,

I beg leave to enclose you a copy of a letter from Mr. Secretary Marsden, dated the 4th of April, together with a copy of the one therein referred to, from Mr. John Sullivan, communicating Lord Hobart's directions on the subject of converting the Palace of Bughay, in Malta, to a Naval Hospital, lest the original of the last-mentioned letter should not have reached you. I have also thought it proper to send Doctor Snipe, Physician to the Fleet under my command, to Malta, on this occasion, in order that he may consult with you, as to the necessity of wings being built to the intended Naval Hospital at Bughay, or any other circumstance which may relate thereto, and assist in forming the estimate alluded to in the said letter. I am, &c.

NELSON AND BRONTE.

TO CAPTAIN PHILIP LAMB, AGENT FOR TRANSPORTS, MALTA.

[From a Copy in the Admiralty.]

Victory, Madalena Islands, 12th May, 1804.

Sir,

I herewith transmit you a copy of a letter from Mr. Secretary Marsden, together with the lists No. 1 and 2, therein referred to, directing that the Transports on the highest terms of hire may be sent home as soon as possible after the arrival

---

[9] The French Line-of-Battle Ship at Cadiz.

of those which are now about to sail, according to the last-mentioned list. I must, therefore, refer you to my letter of the 20th March, with its inclosure, on the subject of sending all the Transports to England without delay, except those absolutely wanted for the service of Malta and the Fleet under my command; and desire that the most strict attention is paid to their Lordships' instructions contained in the copy of Mr. Secretary Marsden's letter above-mentioned, as well on the present as on all future occasions, that Government may not be put to unnecessary expense by the detention of Transports in the Mediterranean, which may not be wanted.

The moment the two coppered Transports, under the charge of Lieutenant Woodman, return from the Black Sea, (provided neither of them are wanted to bring the residue of the provisions or Naval stores purchased by Mr. Eaton at Odessa for the Fleet in these seas,) you will send them also to England, under the first Convoy.

I must also desire that you will communicate to Major-General Villettes the orders you have received to send all the Transports which are not wanted for the immediate service of this Country to England; and, at the same time, beg of the General to inform you whether the Transports now at Malta ready to embark Troops, are wanted for that service? otherwise, that you will include them in the number for England. I am not aware that there are Troops at Malta intended for distant service at this moment; but should that hereafter be the case, I trust the transportation of them will not be difficult, as I presume a sufficient number of Vessels will soon be procured to answer the purpose. I am, &c.,

NELSON AND BRONTE.

TO CAPTAIN STEPHEN PETER MOUAT, AGENT FOR TRANSPORTS ETC., MALTA.

[Letter-Book.]

Victory, Madalena Islands, 12th May, 1804.

Sir,

I have received your letter of the 21st ultimo, with the list of Transports that arrived at Gibraltar, under convoy of the Leviathan therein mentioned, and a daily account of Prisoners

of War, from the 8th to the 21st of April, acquainting me also
that the Harmony and Ibbetson are laden with coals for the
Fleet—that the former was sent to Malta, and the latter
detained at Gibraltar, by order of the Senior Officer, to supply
the Ships that may want coals, until further directions should
be given respecting her. In answer thereto, I have to acquaint
you that the Harmony arrived under convoy of the Leviathan,
and has supplied the different Ships of the Squadron with the
coals that were wanted, and proceeded to Malta with the
residue, for the use of his Majesty's Yard, at that place. I
approve of the Senior Officer's having detained the Ibbetson,
for the purpose of supplying the different Ships ; and must
desire that the remainder is received into his Majesty's Stores
at Gibraltar, for the use of the Yard, and to answer any
future emergency of service. I am glad that the postscript of
your letter takes notice of the quantity of coals which were on
board the Harmony on Government account, and am rather
surprised that there was not a regular Bill of Lading sent out
with them from England, that it might have been ascertained
what quantity the Master had actually to deliver, independent
of his private consumption, and that, from comparing the
whole issues with such Bill of Lading, it might have appeared
how far the Pursers, and stores at Malta, had been done justice
by. I am, &c.,

NELSON AND BRONTE.

TO CAPTAIN THOMAS BRIGGS, H. M. SHIP AGINCOURT.

[Letter-Book.]

Victory, Madalena Islands, 12th May, 1804.
Sir,
I received a letter from his Majesty's Vice - Consul at
Cagliari, in the Island of Sardinia, acquainting me that he
had supplied his Majesty's Ships named in the margin,[1] with six
bullocks each, when they were last in the Bay of Palma, which
were not paid for, and requesting that I would remit him the
amount. It appears very extraordinary that no mention was
made to me of this circumstance, when the Agincourt was last

---

[1] Argo, Agincourt.

in company with the Fleet, or that the Purser of that Ship did not transmit the Agent-Victualler an account thereof, as well as of their produce, the same as Captain Hallowell of the Argo. I must, therefore, desire you will immediately acquaint me with the particulars of this transaction, that I may be governed in the payment of the said cattle, and, at the same time, transmit me a regular account of their produce, signed by all the Signing Officers. I am, &c.,

NELSON AND BRONTE.

TO WILLIAM MARSDEN, ESQ., ADMIRALTY.

[From a Copy in the Admiralty.]

Sir,   Victory, Madalena Islands, 13th May, 1804.

I have received your letter of the 6th ultimo, together with a list of all the regular Transports now in the Mediterranean, and of those under orders to proceed hither, signifying their Lordships' directions to send home the Transports on the highest terms of hire, as soon as possible after the arrival of those which are now about to sail, according to the last-mentioned list, reserving in preference, if necessary, the lowest-priced coppered Ships.

In answer thereto, I herewith transmit you a copy of my letter of the 20th of March last, to Captain Lamb, Agent for Transports at Malta, with a copy of the one therein alluded to; also copy of my letter, of the 15th April, to Captain Mouat, Resident Agent for Transports at Gibraltar, together with a copy of my letters of yesterday's date to those Agents, which you will please to lay before the Lords Commissioners of the Admiralty, for their information; and, at the same time, acquaint their Lordships that, aware of the great expense incurred by the Transport Service, every means in my power has been taken to prevent the detention of Transports in this Country, except those absolutely wanted for the Island of Malta, and the Fleet under my command. The Transports mentioned in the last part of my letter of yesterday to Captain Lamb, it appears, were thought necessary by General Villettes and Sir Alexander Ball to be held in readiness to convey Troops from Malta to Sicily. I have, however, not conceiving the immediate want of them, directed their return to England. I am, &c.,

NELSON AND BRONTE.

TO THE COMMANDERS OF H. M. BOMB-SHIPS ETNA, THUNDER,
AND ACHERON.

[From a Copy in the Admiralty.]

Victory, Agincourt Sound, 13th May, 1804.

Memorandum.

It is my directions that the Artillery embarked on board
the Bomb-Ships do, when in Port, keep watch as sentinels,
and, when at sea, in the same manner as the Ship's Company.

NELSON AND BRONTE.

TO THE RESPECTIVE OFFICERS OF HIS MAJESTY'S YARD AT
MALTA.

[Letter-Book.]

Victory, Madalena Islands, 14th May, 1804.

Gentlemen,

The Lords Commissioners of the Admiralty having directed
the Niger to be put on the establishment of a twenty-eight
gun Ship, it is my intention to send her to Malta, in the
course of a few days, for the purpose of getting carronades
fitted in the room of her guns. I therefore desire you will
have everything ready for mounting the Madras's carronades,
and such as may have been moved from the late Raven on
board the Niger, on her arrival in Valetta Harbour. I have
wrote to Captain Schomberg on this subject, who will order
the carronades to be sent you from the Madras, and assist in
facilitating the Niger's equipment as far as may depend upon
him. I am, &c.,

NELSON AND BRONTE.

TO MAJOR-GENERAL VILLETTES.

[Autograph, in the possession of J. B. Heath, Esq.]

Victory, May 14th, 1804.

My dear General,

Nothing particular has happened in the Fleet since I had
the pleasure of writing you some time ago ; the French Fleet
I am satisfied have an object in view, and the longer it is
deferred the nearer must be its attempt at accomplishing it ;

some day we shall have them, and then we must try and make them make us amends for all our toils. I am, in my Command, deriving as much pleasure as a man can do who is always at sea, for the health and cheerfulness of every individual in this Fleet cannot be exceeded.

I have the Papers from Paris of May 1st—not one word of Moreau; on the 30th of April a motion was proposed to be discussed in three days afterwards, and those who intended to speak for or against it, were to inscribe their names. The question was, ' shall Buonaparte be declared Emperor of the Gauls?' Fourteen inscribed their names for the appointment to the Imperial Purple, and Carnot, of famous memory, hoping that liberty of speech would be allowed, declared that he should argue against the appointment; the result may bring great events to pass. From Rosas, in Spain, of May 11th, the Spanish funds have suddenly fell ten per cent., and the people fear a War with England, but I hope that will be avoided. I want not riches at such a dreadful price; Peace for our Country is all I wish to fight for,—I mean, of course, an honourable one, without which, it cannot be a secure one. We have, via Paris, London news to April 21st. I should rather think the Ministry are not very firm. The almost entire union of Pitt and Fox—in all general questions they have declared their union—has in some questions relative to the Irish Militia been hard run; with 300 members, the Minister has only had a majority of 25—that is, nothing in these times. I think I have given you all my news.

Captain Lamb, the Agent for Transports, will call upon you officially to know whether the Transports, fitted and victualled when the Argo returned from Egypt, are wanted by you, as I am ordered to send all home which are not wanted. The embarkation of the 2000 men for Sicily—a voyage of twenty-four, or forty-eight hours—cannot want many Transports, or much fitting, and the Ships of War which may be at the moment at Malta, would of course take on board as many as possible. I am ever, my dear General, with the sincerest esteem and regard, your most obliged and faithful friend,

NELSON AND BRONTE.

TO NATHANIEL TAYLOR, ESQ., NAVAL OFFICER, MALTA.

[Letter-Book.]

Sir,　　　　　　　Victory, Madalena Islands, 14th May, 1804.

Conceiving, from the loss of his Majesty's late Ship Hindostan, that Seamen's bedding, canvas, and cordage, would be much wanted, I directed Captain Ryves, previous to his leaving Naples, to procure a sample of a Seaman's bed complete, together with the price thereof, and number which might be had on a short notice, and also of the price and quality of canvas and cordage which might be procured at that place for the use of the Fleet under my command, should such measure become necessary. I therefore send you the copy of a letter from Mr. John James, Pro-Consul at Naples, to Captain Ryves, on the above subject, in case our wants should oblige us to apply to that quarter; but it is, at the same time, to be observed, that I do not think it would be safe to trust Mr. James with any money in advance, and only to *receive* and *pay* for such articles as may be purchased from him. I must therefore desire, if you have not entered into an agreement with any person to supply bedding, cordage, and canvas, that you will proceed to Naples as early as possible, and purchase of the said Mr. James, Pro-Consul, the number of Seamen's beds complete, coils of ropes, and bolts of canvas under-mentioned, for the use of the Fleet, applying to Captain Schomberg, or the Senior Officer at Malta, for a conveyance to Naples; and on your arrival there, I would recommend the preference to be given to the said Mr. James for the articles before-mentioned, as the samples herewith sent appear good of their kind, and fit for his Majesty's Service, and no doubt the procuring of them has been attended with some considerable trouble. The beds, cordage, and canvas, which may be purchased at Naples, you will put on board his Majesty's Ship Kent, to be taken care of till I shall think proper to send for them to the Fleet, or order them to Malta; and for the payment thereof, you will draw bills on the Commissioners of his Majesty's Navy, taking care to transmit to their Board regular Vouchers for the same accordingly. I am, &c.

NELSON AND BRONTE.

TO DR. ALLOTT,[2] DEAN OF RAPHOE.

[From Clarke and M'Arthur, vol. ii. p. 363.]

14th May, 1804.

I remember you, dear Sir, most perfectly at Burnham, and I shall never forget the many little kindnesses I received from your worthy brother, with whom I was always a great favourite. Most probably I shall never see dear, dear Burnham again; but I have a satisfaction in thinking that my bones will probably be laid with my Father's, in the Village that gave me birth. Pardon this digression; but the thought of former days brings all my Mother into my heart, which shows itself in my eyes. May Heaven, my dear Sir, long preserve you in health, for the sake of your family and friends; and amongst the latter allow me to place the name of your very faithful servant,

NELSON AND BRONTE.

TO SIR ALEXANDER JOHN BALL, BART., MALTA.

[Autograph, in the possession of Sir William Keith Ball, Bart.]

Victory, May 14th, 1804.

My dear Ball,

Captain Keats will tell you all our news, therefore it will be superfluous in me to detail it to you. Keats is going again to Algiers, as our Government wish to avoid, if possible, a quarrel with the Dey; but as I have reason to believe that Mr. O'Brien[3] is not quite a faithful interpreter of our communication with the Dey, I wish you could find a proper person for that office at Malta, and, of course, if any money is necessary to be paid him, do you say the sum, and I will either repay you (if you pay him) or send the money to Malta. Captain Ryves is just arrived from Naples; by Mr. Elliot's letters, General Acton is certainly on the eve of quitting his

---

[2] Doctor Richard Allott, Dean of Raphoe, was brother of Reverend Brian Allott, Rector of Burnham, in Norfolk, who died in September, 1803. The Dean of Raphoe died at Beaurivage, near Lausanne, in 1832, aged 87. Vide the "Gentleman's Magazine," vol. cii. p. 373.

[3] The American Consul at Algiers.

employments; the new *Emperor* will insist upon it: he is to be divorced from Madame B. and married to a Blood Royal of Germany. Mr. Elliot thinks, it is possible the French may attack Malta, and the French papers say, they have more friends in that Island than we think. Great events are certainly near, and I only hope they will tend to give a secure, and of course, honourable Peace. Believe me ever, my dear Ball, your most obliged and affectionate friend,

NELSON AND BRONTE.

TO CAPTAIN SIR ROBERT BARLOW, H.M. SHIP TRIUMPH.

[Letter-Book.]

Victory, Madalena Islands, 15th May, 1804.

Sir,

I have received your letter of the 13th instant, representing to me that the thirty-seven men named on the other side hereof, are afflicted with an inveterate scurvy, and requesting that an additional allowance of sugar may be ordered them in consequence; and the Physician of the Fleet having acquainted me, that it is necessary, in order to remove an inveterate scurvy, to give each man so afflicted six ounces of lemon juice, and two ounces of sugar, daily, in addition to the present quantity issued by the Purser, for the space of twelve days, I am, therefore, to desire you will order the Purser of his Majesty's Ship under your command to issue to the Surgeon of the said Ship, six ounces of lemon juice and two ounces of sugar to each of the before-mentioned thirty-seven men, in addition to what is usually supplied them, for the space of twelve days from the date hereof, when it is to be discontinued, and report made to the Physician of the Fleet, by the Surgeon of the Triumph, of the effect this mode of treatment has in removing an inveterate scurvy. I am, &c.,

NELSON AND BRONTE.

TO CAPTAIN RICHARD GOODWIN KEATS, H. M. SHIP SUPERB.

[Order-Book.]

Victory, Madalena Islands, 15th May, 1804.

You are hereby required and directed to proceed immediately, with his Majesty's Ship Superb, under your command
to Malta; and on your arrival there, endeavour to procure an
intelligent Interpreter, who is perfectly acquainted with the
language spoken by the Dey of Algiers, that you may be able,
with exactitude, to communicate through him with the Dey,
on the different objects of your instructions, which are herewith transmitted. So soon as you have procured an Interpreter, you will proceed immediately from Malta (taking with
you the Renard Schooner, or any of the Sloops of War which
may be at that place) to the Bay of Algiers, and endeavour to
put in execution the purport of my letter, which accompanies
this. When the object of your instructions is settled with the
Dey, you will send the Renard, or such other Vessel as may
be with you, to Malta, with an account of the result thereof,
to Sir Alexander Ball at that place, and join me in his Majesty's Ship Superb, on Rendezvous No. 102, without a
moment's loss of time.

NELSON AND BRONTE.

TO CAPTAIN LEWIS SHEPHEARD, H. M. SHIP THISBE.

[Letter-Book.]

Victory, Madalena Islands, 16th May, 1804.

Sir,

I am to desire you will proceed with his Majesty's Ship
Thisbe, together with the Victuallers under your charge, and
join me on Rendezvous No. 102, as communicated to you by
Captain Donnelly of the Narcissus, where you will find the
Squadron, or orders for your further proceedings. In joining
me on the said Rendezvous, I must recommend you will proceed through the Straits of Bonifaccio, passing on the West
side of the Island of Corsica, and not attempt to go round
Cape Corse, as in the event of the wind coming strong from
the N.W., it would be an awkward passage for a stranger,
particularly with Victuallers under his charge. I am, &c.,

NELSON AND BRONTE.

TO WILLIAM MARSDEN, ESQ., ADMIRALTY.

[Letter-Book. "Thursday, 17th May.—At 5, P.M. weighed, as did the Squadron. Made sail into the Eastern Bay. At 6·10, anchored: Squadron anchored here. Friday, 18th May, A.M. At 6·30, weighed and made sail to the Eastward, through the Biche Channel, as did the Squadron for Terranova Bay. At 1, P.M. shortened sail and anchored: Squadron anchored here. Saturday, 19th May, A.M. At 5·30, weighed and made sail out of Terranova Bay. Stood to the Eastward, as did the Squadron. Termagant rejoined. Three Algerine Cruizers in the N.W.; showed our Colours to them. At 8, P.M. a Ship in the S.W. made the signal of distress, and wanting immediate assistance. Sent the Phœnix to her assistance. The Ship that wanted assistance proved to be the Excellent, which struck on an unknown reef in the Eastern passage to the Madalena Islands."—*Victory's Log.*]

Victory, Madalena Islands, 17th May, 1804.

Sir,

I have received your letter of the 4th ultimo, together with a copy of a memorandum from Captain Bligh, respecting the variance in the two Charts, made by Captain Ryves, of the Madalena and Barelino Islands, and also the copies of them, signifying their Lordships' direction to transmit such remarks as may contribute to the perfection of the said Charts. In answer thereto, you will please to acquaint the Lords Commissioners of the Admiralty, that Captain Ryves, and the Masters of the Gibraltar and Victory, have strictly examined the said two copies, and cannot discover any material difference, except the soundings marked in red ink, taken by the Victory, and a few small rocks, which are visible above water, in what is called Agincourt Sound, but of no consequence whatever. Captain Ryves's Chart is, therefore, as perfect in its original state as can be made, except by the nice and accurate hand of an expert Surveyor, and then it would not be more useful. I am, &c.,

NELSON AND BRONTE.

P.S.—On passing by the East entrance of the Madalena Islands, on the 20th instant, his Majesty's Ship Excellent struck on a reef of rocks, which is not laid down in Captain Ryves's Chart. She received no hurt whatever, being perfectly smooth water when she struck. The bearings, &c., of this reef, taken by Mr. Atkinson, Master of the Victory, are herewith inclosed.

N. AND B.

TO CAPTAIN GEORGE COCKS, H.M. BOMB-VESSEL THUNDER.

[From a Copy in the Admiralty.]

Victory, Madalena Islands, 17th May, 1804.

Sir,

I have received your letter of yesterday's date, acquainting me that you had confined James Braid of the Royal Artillery, agreeably to the tenour of your instructions from the Lords Commissioners of the Admiralty, dated the 28th March 1804, for disobedience to your orders in replying to your command, ' that he was ordered neither to pull nor haul till he received ' that order from his own Officer.' In reply thereto, I must express my surprise that you have not either communicated my order of the 13th instant to the Officer of Artillery on board the Thunder, or, if you have, that he has been guilty of so much neglect of his duty, as not to have informed, in a regular manner, the Artillerymen that they must, upon every occasion, be obedient and respectful to all commands of the Officers of the Ship; and that, if they have any cause of complaint, they will report it to their Officer, who will represent it in a respectful manner to the Commander of his Majesty's Bomb, that any real grievance may be immediately redressed. If the man confined has not been informed of my order of the 13th instant, he may have erred through ignorance; but if the Officer of Artillery, being informed of my order, has neglected to inform the Artillerymen of it, you will acquaint him that he has been guilty of a great neglect of his duty. I am, &c.,

NELSON AND BRONTE.

TO THE RESPECTIVE OFFICERS OF THE NAVAL YARD AT MALTA.

[Letter-Book.]

Secret.   Victory, Madalena Islands, 17th May, 1804.

Gentlemen,

There being reason to suppose that the coals supplied by Mr. ———, Master of the Harmony Transport, from improper measure in the hold of that Vessel, have been delivered to the respective Pursers of the Squadron nearly an eighth short, I therefore transmit you a copy of a letter from the Transport Office, stating the quantity of coals shipped on board the Harmony for the use of the Navy, and desire you will, the moment that Transport arrives in Valetta harbour, take her alongside the wharf, and see the coals, which may be remaining on board her, measured with the strictest attention; and in order to ascertain the exact quantity supplied the Pursers, you will call upon the Master of the Harmony for the receipts from them respectively, which you will tottle up and add to the quantity you may find remaining, which, consequently, when compared with the original quantity shipped, will show what may have been defrauded by improper delivery, which overplus quantity I am to desire you will seize and detain, as the right and property of the Pursers of the Ships supplied from the Harmony at this anchorage. You will take into account (if it does not appear that Mr. ———— has purchased private coals for the use of his Transport) the quantity he may reasonably have used from the time of his leaving England, and furnish me with the particulars of your proceedings by the first opportunity. I am, &c.,

NELSON AND BRONTE.

N.B.—The deficiency of coals is supposed to have arisen from the Master of the Harmony not having acquainted the Officers attending the delivery, that the basket ought to be *heaped*, which, consequently was not done.

TO CAPTAIN GEORGE COCKS, H. M. BOMB-VESSEL THUNDER.

[Autograph draught in the possession of the Reverend Henry Girdlestone, and a Copy in the Admiralty.]

Victory, at Sea, 19th May, 1804.

Sir,

From representations made to me, it appears that the Officers of Artillery embarked on board his Majesty's Bombs Thunder, Etna, and Acheron, are entirely ignorant of the Act of Parliament for the regulation of his Majesty's Ships, Vessels, and Forces by Sea; it is, therefore, my directions that you deliver to the Officer of Artillery embarked to serve on board his Majesty's Bomb Thunder, under your command, the Act of Parliament inclosed in a letter, in order that in future, he may not plead ignorance of the Act above mentioned, as he will be made answerable for a breach of it.

You will direct the Officer of Artillery to muster, when you think necessary, the clothes of the Artillery, and direct him to take care that the men are kept in cleanliness and discipline, becoming such a fine body of men. You will give directions that the mortars and Artillery-stores are examined occasionally, in order that they may be always fit for service, and direct the Officer of Artillery to report to you any defect in them, that such directions may be given as the case shall require. And in every respect you will pay the same attention to the Artillery embarked on board the Bomb under your command, as is paid to Officers and Men of the Navy of like rank. I am, &c.,

NELSON AND BRONTE.

N.B.—A letter of the above tenour and date was delivered to the Commanders of the Etna and Acheron Bomb-Vessels.

NELSON AND BRONTE.

TO CAPTAIN THE HONOURABLE COURTENAY BOYLE, H. M. SHIP SEAHORSE.

[Letter-Book.]

Victory, at Sea, 19th May, 1804.

Sir,

Should this, contrary to my expectation, find you at the Madalena Islands, I am to desire you will join the Squadron (who is proceeding by Cape Corse to Rendezvous No. 102) without a moment's loss of time. I am, &c.,

NELSON AND BRONTE.

TO WILLIAM MARSDEN, ESQ., ADMIRALTY.

[Letter-Book.]

Victory, 19th May, 1804.

Sir,

I herewith transmit you a letter from Mr. Bauguier, Purser of his Majesty's Sloop Termagant, which you will please to lay before the Lords Commissioners of the Admiralty for their consideration; and, at the same time acquaint their Lordships that I have not thought proper to comply with his request without their direction, as it is not possible for me to judge how far the necessary attention has been paid to the preservation of the provisions and stores committed to his charge, since his appointment to that Sloop. I am, &c.,

NELSON AND BRONTE.

TO CAPTAIN RYVES, H. M. SHIP GIBRALTAR.

[Letter-Book.]

Victory, at Sea, 19th May, 1804.

Sir,

On examining the Vouchers for the purchase of provisions for the Company of his Majesty's Ship Gibraltar, under your command, between the 21st September 1803, and the 6th instant, at Naples, there appears a charge of upwards of a hundred pounds sterling, for onions, cabbages, leeks, and pumpkins, for the people during the said time. I must therefore desire, as it was the duty of the Purser of the said Ship to have purchased a sufficient quantity of vegetables for the Ship's Company's soup, the fresh meat days, which ought not to have been included in the vouchers, that you inform me with the reason of this very extraordinary charge. I am, &c.,

NELSON AND BRONTE.

TO WILLIAM MARSDEN, ESQ., ADMIRALTY.

[Letter-Book.]

Victory, at Sea, 19th May, 1804.

Sir,

In answer to your letter of the 6th ultimo, I request you will be pleased to inform the Lords Commissioners of the Admiralty, that although Mr. Thomas Pearse[4] did not produce documents for having served his time, yet the Passing Captains were satisfied that he had done so, and that he had taken out

_____

[4] Query, if the present Lieutenant Thomas Pearse, who obtained that rank on the 1st of August 1807?

his time at the Navy Office, which, by some mistake, he had
left behind. It also comes within my certain knowledge, that
Mr. Pearse has been upwards of six years in his Majesty's
Service. I am, &c.,

NELSON AND BRONTE.

TO WILLIAM MARSDEN, ESQ., ADMIRALTY.

[Original, in the Admiralty, and "London Gazette" of June 1804.]

Victory, at Sea, 19th May, 1804.

Sir,

I herewith transmit you for the information of the Lords
Commissioners of the Admiralty a copy of a letter[4] from
Captain Pettet, commander of his Majesty's Sloop Termagant,
giving an account of the Boats of that Sloop having, on the
15th instant, taken possession of the French Xebeck Privateer,
Felicité, off Port Favona, in Corsica, which, it appears the
Enemy had scuttled previous to leaving her, as she soon afterwards sank. I am very much pleased with Captain Pettet's
exertions in having destroyed this Vessel, as she was one of
the finest Privateers in this Country, and had captured two of
our Merchantmen last year off Tunis. I am, &c.,

NELSON AND BRONTE.

TO WILLIAM MARSDEN, ESQ., ADMIRALTY.

[Original, in the Admiralty.]

Victory, at Sea, 19th May, 1804.

Sir,

I have received the duplicate and triplicate of your Secret
Letter, dated the 9th March last, signifying their Lordships'
direction to govern myself in conformity with the instructions
contained in Lord Hobart's letter, with respect to the Dey of
Algiers, so far as the same can be done consistently with the
due attention to the more important object of watching the
French force in Toulon. In answer to which, you will please
to acquaint the Lords Commissioners of the Admiralty, that
I have sent the Superb to Algiers and given Captain Keats

---

[4] This letter was published in the London Gazette.

the necessary instructions for his government, conformably with the spirit of those received from Lord Hobart, and shall transmit the result of his mission for their Lordships' information the moment the Superb returns from Algiers. I am, &c.,

NELSON AND BRONTE.

TO WILLIAM MARSDEN, ESQ., ADMIRALTY.

[Original, in the Admiralty.]

Victory, at Sea, May 22nd, 1804.

Sir,

On being joined by the Bomb-Vessels named in the margin,[5] I was informed that on coming to sea, the Artillerymen were ordered to keep watch the same as the people composing their Companies, (the Bomb-Vessels at that time being on no particular service ;) but were prevented from it by their Officers, who had directed them not to keep watch. The Commanders of these Vessels not judging it prudent to enforce their compliance, in consequence, I presume, of their Lordships' instructions to them respecting the Artillery, allowed this measure, so subversive of discipline, to remain for my directions; and, in consequence of such communication, I gave out an order, dated the 13th instant, a copy of which (No. 1) is herewith transmitted. On the 16th following, I received a letter from Captain Cocks of the Thunder, a copy of which (No. 2) also accompanies this, together with a copy of my answer thereto, and also, a copy of my letter (No. 4),[6] which I found necessary from the conduct of the Artillery Officers to give to the respective Commanders of the said Bomb-Vessels, which I desire you will please to lay before the Lords Commissioners of the Admiralty for their information ; and, at the same time, acquaint their Lordships, that I have read their instructions which have been given to the Commanders of the Bombs, which may be interpreted as not rendering the Officers and Soldiers embarked in the Bomb-Vessels liable to be tried by Court-Martial. I am, however, decidedly of opinion that nothing short of an Act of the Legislature can lay aside the Acts of Parliament by which our Naval Service is directed to

---

[5] Thunder, Ætna, Acheron.   [6] Vide pp. 22, 23, ante.

be governed; and as these Acts clearly point out that Soldiers are (with the exception only of their being embarked in Trans-port-Ships) as liable to the regulations of that Act of Parliament as any Seaman, and as it is impossible that two Commanders can exist in the same Ship, and the very salvation of our Navy, perhaps of our Country, depends upon the perfect subordina-tion of every individual to the Commander thereof,—I have to request their Lordships will take this most important subject into their serious consideration, that such directions may be given thereupon as the wisdom of Parliament shall think proper; for, until the Act of Parliament is altered, I shall hold it my indispensable duty to enforce obedience from the Artillery Officers before-mentioned to the orders of their respective Commanders, be it by Court-Martial or otherwise, and communicate the result to the Commander-in-Chief of the Army in the Mediterranean, in order that it may be laid before the King.

I lament that it is necessary for me to call their Lordships' attention to this very recent circumstance of the Army serving on board his Majesty's Fleet: the Sea-Lords, to whom I par-ticularly address myself on this most serious subject, are well aware of the dangerous tendency of insubordination, and of the consequences which would result from placing the Army, who serve in the different Ships, independent of the Officers who command them. I am, &c.,

NELSON AND BRONTE.

TO JOHN JULIUS ANGERSTEIN, ESQ., CHAIRMAN TO THE COM-MITTEE FOR THE PATRIOTIC FUND, LLOYD'S COFFEE-HOUSE, LONDON.

[Letter-Book.]

Victory, at Sea, 24th May, 1804.

Sir,

I received your letter of the 6th of March last, requesting that I would transmit you the name and family of a Seaman who was killed on board his Majesty's Sloop Morgiana, that the Committee for the Patriotic Fund may take the same into consideration. In answer to which, you will please to acquaint the Committee that I have given a general order to return the names and families of all the Officers and men who have been, or may be, killed or wounded, on board the different Ships under my command, which shall be transmitted agreeably to your request. I am, &c.,   NELSON AND BRONTE.

TO ADMIRAL LUTWIDGE.

[Autograph, in the possession of Major Lutwidge.]

Victory, May 24th, 1804.

My dear Admiral,

Many, many thanks for your kind letter of April 3rd, and I beg you will thank good Mrs. Lutwidge for hers ; for in truth, by one conveyance, I can only write to one in a house ; and both your letters arrived the same day, by the Leviathan. You are sure that I shall always be happy in paying attention to your recommendations, and shall certainly see Mr. Baker, but I have not the smallest chance of being useful to him ; for, it is not *two* French Fleets that will clear the way of what are on the Admiralty, and my list. I think the Admiralty has had a hard run, and if Pitt goes on,[7] I do not think my friend Addington can stand the united parties of Pitt and Fox. Our dear Lady Hamilton for ever speaks of your and Mrs. L.'s kindness to her : her good heart is feelingly alive to such acts.

Our Ships have been very unfortunate, latterly ; the loss of Apollo[8] and Convoy is shocking, off Brest ; I am only surprised more are not lost, or rather, that any are saved. I am truly sorry for your nephew,[9] for I see no prospect of an exchange of Prisoners with the Republic, but the new Emperor may think differently, and I should not be surprised if

[7] On the 15th of March, 1804, Mr. Pitt brought forward a motion on the state of the Naval Defence of the Country ; and, in a long speech, censured the Admiralty for not increasing the Navy, and especially for not having prepared a Flotilla to resist that of the Enemy. The debate on that occasion is very fully reported in the " Naval Chronicle," (vol. xi. p. 316, *et seq.*) with editorial comments in support of the Admiralty.

[8] The Apollo Frigate, Captain J. W. T. Dixon, with forty sail of her Convoy, bound to the West Indies, was wrecked near Cape Mondego, on the Coast of Portugal, on the 1st of April 1804. Captain Dixon and many of his Officers and crew perished. An interesting narrative of the circumstances is given in the " Naval Chronicle," vol. xi. p. 392.

[9] Lieutenant Henry Lutwidge, who was shipwrecked on the Saints', in the Hussar Frigate, in February 1804, taken prisoner, and detained in France till the end of the War. Vide vol. v. p. 2.

we have a speedy Peace, for he must want to settle firmly his new dignity; *brave Corsican!* When you write to Kingsmill,[1] remember me kindly to him, and make acceptable my most sincere good wishes to Mrs. Lutwidge, and that she may never be ill; and believe me, my dear Admiral, that I am for ever, your most grateful and obliged friend,

NELSON AND BRONTE.

I have sent Dalton his letter, and have since seen him.

TO REAR-ADMIRAL CAMPBELL.

[From Clarke and M'Arthur, vol. ii. p. 366.]

24th May, 1804.

I am more obliged to you than I can express, for your not allowing the very superior force of the Enemy to bring you to Action.[2] Whatever credit would have accrued to your own and your gallant Companions' exertions, no sound advantages could have arisen to our Country; for so close to their own harbour they could always have returned, and left your Ships unfit, probably, to keep the sea. I again, my dear Admiral, thank you for your conduct. Some day, very soon, I have no doubt but an opportunity will offer of giving them fair Battle; and that it may arrive very, very soon, is the most sincere wish of, my dear Campbell, your most obliged friend,

NELSON AND BRONTE.

[1] Admiral Sir Robert Kingsmill, Bart., so frequently mentioned. Vide vol. i. p. 40.

[2] " On the 24th of May, in the forenoon, as the Canopus, Donegal, and Amazon, having been detached from the Fleet, then out of sight in the offing, were standing upon the larboard tack, with a light air from the South-West, close to the Eastward of Cape Sepet, for the purpose of reconnoitering the Fleet in Toulon, a French Line-of-Battle Ship and Frigate were observed under sail between the Capes Sepet and Brun, which form the entrance to the harbour. At half-past noon, when about three miles from the shore, the Amazon, Donegal, and Canopus tacked in succession. No sooner had the Canopus put about, than several French Gun-boats swept from under Cape Sepet, and, profiting by the calm state of the weather, opened a distant fire upon her and the Amazon. The Canopus, in return, discharged a few of her lower-deck guns, and stood on to the South-East by East, with the wind, now a moderate breeze from the West-North-West. On hearing the firing, two French Ships of the Line, and two Frigates had slipped their cables, and made sail, to assist the Line-of-Battle Ship and Frigate already outside. At 2h. 30m. P.M., two more Sail of the Line slipped, and followed the others; making now five Sail of the Line and three Frigates that were in chase of the reconnoitring Ships. Shortly afterwards the French Van-Frigate, being on

TO HIS EXCELLENCY SIR JOHN ACTON, BART.

[From a Copy, in the Elliot Papers.]

Victory, ce 25 Mai, 1804.

Mon cher Chevalier,

Actuellement je ne pense pas vous incommoder, puisque je sens que vous aurez un vrai plaisir à rendre service à la chère Lady Hamilton.

Le Chevalier, lors de son mariage, lui assigna 800 livres sterling par an, et comme il avoit destiné exactement la meme somme à sa première femme, l'an 1752, il croyoit avoir agi avec beaucoup de libéralité. Mais les temps ont si fort changé, que 800 livres sterling ne suffisent plus pour une dame dans la position de veuve du Chevalier Hamilton, et ne donnent guères de quoi acheter du pain et du fromage. Monsieur Addington est, je le sais, trés bien intentionné envers Milady, mais les frais de la guerre, et probablement le manque de quelqu'un qui pousse l'affaire, le rendent un peu difficile, quand il s'agit d'accorder une pension, quoiqu'il doit avouer, avec tout le monde, que cette pension est due, et a été bien méritée.

La Reine de Naples est, j'en suis convaincu, aussi sincèrement attachée à Lady Hamilton qu'elle le doit, puis qu'Elle n'a jamais eu une amie aussi sincère et aussi désinteressée. Ainsi si Sa Majesté vouloit avoir la condescendance d'écrire une ligne à Monsieur Addington, sans que cela passe par le canal de Castelcicala, mais directement à Monsieur Addington, je suis sûr, que l'on ne réfuseroit plus la pension. Je ne dis rien de plus, excepté que je serai aussi très obligé à la Reine, si Elle veut écrire cette lettre à Monsieur Addington, et je suis persuadé que le cœur de la Reine est trop généreux pour oublier son Emma. Je suis à jamais, mon cher Chevalier, &c.,

NELSON AND BRONTE.

the weather-quarter of the Canopus, opened a fire upon her and the Donegal, which these Ships immediately returned. With so superior a force it was in vain to contend, and Rear-Admiral Campbell directed his little Division to make sail. At 3h. 30m. P.M., finding pursuit useless, the French Ships tacked, and stood back to their Port; and at 9h. 30m. P.M., and not before, the Canopus and her two companions joined the Victory and the Fleet."—*James's Naval History*, vol. iii. pp. 236, 237. See also *Naval Chronicle*, vol. xii. p. 242.

TO THE RIGHT HONOURABLE GEORGE ROSE.

[Autograph, in the possession of the Right Hon. Sir George Rose, G.C.H.]

Victory, May 25th, 1804.

My dear Sir,

Many thanks for your good wishes. I bear your friends in mind; but, alas! I see no prospect of being useful to them during the probably short stay my health will allow me to serve in the Mediterranean without some rest; and I expect to eat my Christmas dinner in England, and much sooner if the French Fleet will come out. I only serve to meet them. That done, I feel the great demand of my Country is complied with.

I have read with attention Mr. Pitt's speech[3] respecting the Admiralty. My mind has been long formed upon that subject; and with all my personal regard for Lord St. Vincent, I am sorry to see that he has been led astray by the opinion of ignorant people. There is scarcely a thing he has done since he has been at the Admiralty that I have not heard him reprobate before he came to the Board. I do not mean but that the attempt to prevent the gross abuses in our Dockyards, &c. &c., was laudable ; but it is the mode of reforming those abuses which I disapprove of: but this is too long a subject for me to enter into upon paper.

I had wrote a Memoir, many months ago, upon the propriety of a Flotilla. I had that command at the end of last War, and I know the necessity of it, even had you, and which you ought to have, thirty or forty Sail of the Line in the Downs and North Sea, besides Frigates, &c. ; but having failed so entirely in submitting my thoughts upon three points, I was disheartened. They were upon the speedy Manning the Navy at the commencement of a War[4]—the inducing the Seamen to fly into the Naval Service instead of from it—and for the better payment of Prize-money.[5] I have not the vanity to think that any of my plans were perfect; but they were intended, by contradicting my plans, to bring forth better:

---

³ Vide p. 29, ante.   ⁴ Vide vol. v. p. 44.
⁵ Vide vol. v. p. 53.   The Memoir on the Flotilla has not been found.

but nothing has been done, and something was and is necessary.

Upon the accession of the new Emperor, either the Invasion
will take place, or we shall have Peace. Hoping soon to take
you by the hand, I am ever, my dear Sir, your much obliged
friend,

NELSON AND BRONTE.

The Reverend Mr. Scott desires me to present his best
respects; and I cannot let this opportunity slip of telling you
that his abilities are of a very superior cast, and he would be
a most useful person to you, or any one high in Office, for
Foreign matters and languages : he lives with me, and, therefore, I can speak confidently of his abilities.

TO ADMIRAL THE EARL OF ST. VINCENT, K.B.

[From Clarke and M'Arthur, vol. ii. p. 364.]

25th May, 1804.

There is no real happiness, my dear Lord, in this world :
with all content and smiles around me, up start these Artillery
boys;[6] I understand they are not beyond that age, and set us
all at defiance—speaking in the most disrespectful manner of
the Navy and its Commanders, &c. I know you, my dear
Lord, so well, that with your quickness, the matter would
have been settled, and perhaps some of them been broke. I
am perhaps more patient, but I do assure you not less resolved, if my plan of conciliation is not attended to. You
and I are on the eve of quitting the theatre of our exploits;
but we owe it to our successors, never, whilst we have a
tongue to speak, or a hand to write, to allow the Navy to be
in the smallest degree injured in its discipline by our conduct.
If these continued attacks upon the Navy are to be carried on
every two or three years, it would be much better for the
Navy to have its own Corps of Artillery :[7] the present case is
indeed with lads; but they are set on by men, I can see

---

[6] Vide pp. 22, 23, ante.
[7] This was afterwards done by the establishment of a branch of the Royal
Marines, called the " Royal Marine Artillery."

that very clearly. The new Emperor (bravo, Corsican!) will, I hope, begin his reign by ordering his Fleet to come out; for if they do not very soon, they will wear us out, and most particularly myself. My health has suffered very much, but I am as happy in the command as man can be. I am, &c.,

NELSON AND BRONTE.

TO ADMIRAL SIR CHARLES POLE, BART.[8]

[From Clarke and M'Arthur, vol. ii. p. 365.]

[About 25th May, 1804.]

I am sure Lord St. Vincent ought to feel grateful for your zealous support of his measures ;[9] and I hope, my dear Pole, you will stand by the Navy against all attempts to have Soldiers placed in our Ships, independent of the Naval Act of Parliament, from whatever quarter it may be attempted : when that takes place, there is an end of our Navy,—there cannot be two Commanders in one Ship. We are all as happy as a set of animals can be, who have been in fact more than a year at sea, or rather without going ashore : for, with the exception of anchoring under the Northern end of Sardinia, not a Ship has been to a Naval Yard to refit during that time. Hope keeps us up. I am, &c.,

NELSON AND BRONTE.

TO CAPTAIN SIR THOMAS TROUBRIDGE, BART., ADMIRALTY.

[From Clarke and M'Arthur, vol. ii, p. 364.]

[About 25th May, 1804.]

My dear Troubridge,

You will see that I have been obliged to write a letter to the Admiralty, on the subject of Soldiers embarked on board Ships of War ; and I have written it strong, as I know it must go further than your Board. It is the old history—trying to do away the Act of Parliament; but I trust they will never succeed—for when they do, farewell to our Naval supe-

---

[8] Vide vol. i. p. 37.

[9] Sir Charles Pole had spoken in the House of Commons, on the 24th of March in defence of the Admiralty.

riority! We should be prettily commanded! You may say, 'they are not intended to command the Navy, but that the Navy is not to command Soldiers on board a Ship.' Let them once gain the step of being independent of the Navy on board a Ship, and they will soon have the other, and command us. It may be said, 'if the Soldiers behave improperly, they would be tried by a Court-martial on shore:' were that possible, of what Members would that Court be composed? Mostly Subalterns, I fancy, who, although we might think the Officer had behaved very improperly, might, and probably would think that he had behaved very properly to us Seabrutes. But, thank God, my dear Troubridge, the King himself cannot do away the Act of Parliament. Although my career is nearly run, yet it would embitter my future days and expiring moments, to hear of our Navy being sacrificed to the Army. I can readily conceive the attempts of the Army at this moment, when they think themselves of such great importance. The Admiralty order might lead those wrong who do not know that nothing but an Act of Parliament can do away an Act of Parliament. Ever, my dear Troubridge, yours most faithfully,

NELSON AND BRONTE.

TO CAPTAIN RICHARD HUSSEY MOUBRAY, H. M. SHIP ACTIVE.

[Order-Book.]

Victory, at Sea, 27th May, 1804.

You are hereby required and directed to take his Majesty's Ship named in the margin[1] under your command, and proceed immediately to the head of the Gulf of Lyons, where you will take a sweep for the space of forty-eight hours, in order to obtain intelligence of the Enemy's intended movements at Toulon, and to capture or destroy any of their numerous Privateers, which I understand are fitting out at Marseilles; and at the expiration of eight days from the date hereof, you will join me on Rendezvous No. 102, where you will find the Squadron, or orders for your further proceedings.

NELSON AND BRONTE.

[1] Seahorse.

D 2

TO LADY HAMILTON.

[From " Lord Nelson's Letters to Lady Hamilton," vol. ii. p. 39.]

Victory, May 27th, 1804.

My dearest Emma,

Yesterday, I took' Charles Connor on board, from the Phœbe, to try what we can do with him. At present, poor fellow, he has got a very bad eye—and, I almost fear, that he will be blind of it—owing to an olive-stone striking the eye : but the Surgeon of the Victory, who is by far the most able medical man I have ever seen,[2] and equally so as a Surgeon, [says] that, if it can be saved, he will do it. The other complaint, in his head, is but little more, I think, than it was when he first came to Deal; a kind of silly laugh, when spoken to. He always complains of a pain in the back part of his head; but when that is gone, I do not perceive but that he is as wise as many of his neighbours. You may rely, my dear Emma, that nothing shall be wanting, on my part, to render him every service. Capel,[3] although, I am sure, very kind to younkers, I do not think, has the knack of keeping them in high discipline ; he lets them be their own masters too much. I paid Charles's account, yesterday ; since he has been in the Phœbe, £155 14s. However, he must now turn a new leaf; and I sincerely hope, poor fellow, he will yet do well.

I wrote you on the 22nd, through Rosas, in Spain ; and I shall write, in a few days, by Barcelona : this goes by Gibraltar. I have wrote Admiral Lutwidge; Mrs. Lutwidge must wait, for I cannot get through all my numerous letters : for, whoever writes, although upon their own affairs, are offended if they are not answered. I have not seen young Bailey : I suppose, he is in the Leviathan. By the parcel, I see, he is in the Canopus ; and I can, at present, be of no use to him. Charles is very much recovered. I write you, this day, by Barcelona. Your dear phiz—but not the least like you—on the cup, is safe ; but I would not use it, for the world ; for, if it was broke, it would distress me very much. Your letters, by Swift, I shall never get back. The French Consul,

---

[2] Doctor, now Sir George Magrath, K.H.

[3] Captain, now Vice-Admiral, the Honourable Sir Thomas Bladen Capel, K.C.B. Vide vol. iii. pp. 7, 103,

at Barcelona, is bragging that he has three pictures of you
from the Swift. I do not believe him; but, what if he had a
hundred! . . . . . I see, Lord Stafford is going to oppose Mr.
Addington; the present Ministry cannot stand. I wish Mr.
Addington had given you the pension; Pitt and hard-hearted
Grenville, never will. What a fortune the death of Lord
Camelford gives him! Everything you tell me about my dear
Horatia charms me. I think I see her, hear her, and admire
her; but she is like her dear, dear mother . . . .
    Mr. Falcon is a clever man. He would not have made such
a blunder as our friend Drake and Spencer Smith. I hear the
last is coming, viâ Trieste, to Malta. Perhaps, he wants to
get to Constantinople; and, if the Spencers get in, the Smiths
will get anything. Mr. Elliot, I hear, is a candidate for it.
He complains of the expense of Naples, I hear; and, that he
cannot make both ends meet, although he sees no company.
The histories of the Queen are beyond whatever I have heard
from Sir William. Prince Leopold's establishment is all
French. The Queen's favourite, Lieutenant-Colonel St. Clair,
was a subaltern; La Tour, the Captain in the Navy; and,
another! However, I never touch on these matters; for, I
care not how she amuses herself. It will be the upset of
Acton; or, rather, he will not, I am told, stay. The King is
angry with her; his love is long gone by. I have only one word
more—Do not believe a syllable the newspapers say, or what
you hear. Mankind seems fond of telling lies. Remember
me kindly to Mrs. Cadogan, and to all our mutual friends,
and be assured that I am, &c.   NELSON AND BRONTE.

    George Campbell[4] desires me always to present his best
respects; and make mine to good Mr. Yonge. What can I
write him? I am sure he must have great pleasure in attending you: and when you see Sir William Scott,[5] make my
best regards acceptable to him. There is no man I have a
higher opinion of, both as a public and private character.
You will long ago have had my letter, with one to Davison,
desiring he will pay for the alterations at Merton. I shall send
you a letter for the hundred pounds a month to the Bank.[6]

---

    [4] Rear-Admiral George Campbell.   [5] Afterwards Lord Stowell.
    [6] After the death of Sir William Hamilton, Lord Nelson made Lady Hamilton
an annual allowance of £1200.

TO WILLIAM MARSDEN, ESQ., ADMIRALTY.

[Letter-Book. " Monday, 28th May, A.M. At 6, Cape Sicie bore N. b W. ½ W., distant 7 or 8 leagues. Light breezes and clear. Cleared Ship. Observed the Enemy's Ships coming round Cape Sepet. At Noon, Cape Sicie bore N ½ W., distant 6½ leagues. Excellent and Leviathan in company. P.M., moderate breezes and clear. ½ past 12, hauled our wind on the Larboard Tack, and made sail. Hove to, and tried the current, and found it set nearly 1 mile in 6 hours, W.N.W. by compass. At 3·30, filled, and exercised great guns. At 4, hove to. The Enemy's Ships still standing to the Eastward alongshore, consisting of 4 Ships of the Line, 3 Frigates, and 2 Brigs, with some Gun-boats. Light breezes. Enemy's Ships tacked and stood in for Sepet."—Tuesday, 29th May, at Noon. Two of the Enemy's Ships under sail off Cape Sepet. Cape Sicie bore N. ¼ W., distant 4 leagues. Excellent and Leviathan in company. Moderate breezes and hazy. ¼ past 12, hauled our wind on the Larboard tack, and made all sail in chase of a French Ship of the Line. At 1, bore up; at 2, hauled to S. b E. Fresh breezes and hazy. At 4·30, saw the Fleet, S.E. b S. At 5·45, joined ditto, consisting of Royal Sovereign, Canopus, Donegal, Belleisle, Renown, Gibraltar, Triumph, Ætna, Thunder, and Acheron."—*Victory's Log.*]

Victory, at Sea, 28th May, 1804.

Sir,

I herewith transmit you, for the information of the Lords Commissioners of the Admiralty, a copy of my order of this day to Captain Ryves, of the Gibraltar; and also, of my letter to Commissioner Otway, respecting the refit of that Ship, which you will please to communicate to their Lordships; and also, acquaint them that the Kent will be ordered to proceed to England in July next—being the most moderate season of the year; and, fearful of any accident happening to her, I shall direct a Transport to accompany her on the passage. The Renown will take her place at Naples, but she ought to proceed to England before the winter, and the Superb must also be sent to England before that period arrives, as her stem, and the knees of her head, are loose and broke; nothing but the great exertions of Captain Keats has kept her at sea this last season. The Triumph will go to Gibraltar to get a new foremast, and probably be careened before the winter, if their Lordships do not think proper that she should proceed to England. I am, &c.,

NELSON AND BRONTE.

TO CAPTAIN GEORGE FREDERICK RYVES, H. M. SHIP
GIBRALTAR.

[Order-Book.]

Victory, at Sea, 28th May, 1804.

The Lords Commissioners of the Admiralty having ordered
Commissioner Otway to refit his Majesty's Ship Gibraltar,
under your command, as signified to me in Sir Evan Nepean's
letter, dated the 21st December, 1803, You are, in obedience to
their Lordships' direction, hereby required and directed to proceed with his Majesty's said Ship to Gibraltar, and put her
into the hands of the Naval Yard Officers at that place; but
should Commissioner Otway, after examining the Gibraltar,
find that she cannot be made an efficient Ship, I have directed
him to state the same to you officially by letter, upon receipt
of which, you are to proceed, without a moment's loss of time,
to Rendezvous No. 97, under Cape St. Sebastians, where
there is a Frigate stationed to acquaint any of his Majesty's
Ships of my Rendezvous; and upon your joining me, I shall
direct the Gibraltar to proceed to Malta, for the purpose of
taking the Trade which may be collected there from the
Archipelago and Adriatic to England.   Commissioner Otway
is furnished with a copy of this order, that no delay may
attend its being put into immediate execution.

NELSON AND BRONTE.

Memorandum.

It is my directions that you receive Doctor Scott and the
Agent Victualler of the Fleet on board the Gibraltar; and if
in passing Rendezvous No. 97, under Cape St. Sebastians,
you should fall in with the Juno, you will deliver the accompanying letter to Captain Richardson, and afterwards land
Doctor Scott with my dispatches at Barcelona.

TO CAPTAIN SUTTON, H. M. SHIP AMPHION.

[Autograph, in the possession of Captain Ives Sutton.]

My dear Sutton,   Victory, May 29th, 1804.

If by any chance a Ship of the Line should become vacant,
would you like to have her?   I have been told that you
would; and you will believe that I shall, upon every occasion,
be happy to meet your wishes, being most truly, your much
obliged,   NELSON AND BRONTE.

TO WILLIAM MARSDEN, ESQ., ADMIRALTY.

[Original in the Admiralty.]

Victory, at Sea, 29th May, 1804.

Sir,

You will please to acquaint the Lords Commissioners of
the Admiralty, that his Majesty's Ship Victory, on her passage
to the Mediterranean, captured the Ambuscade French Frigate, manned her with a sufficient number of Officers and
Seamen, and directed her to proceed to Gibraltar. On her
way there, and after she had parted company with the Victory,
she fell in with and captured the Marie Therese, a French
Merchantman, and carried her with her to that place. On
the Ambuscade's arrival off the Mole with her Prize, as above,
the Revolutionaire and Bittern, who were lying there, sent
out their Boats to the said Merchant-Ship, (knowing her to
be the Ambuscade's Prize,) and afterwards laid in their claim
as joint captors in the Vice-Admiralty Court at Gibraltar;
but upon trial of the said Vessel, their claim was thrown out,
and the Marie Therese condemned as sole and legal prize to
the Victory. The Agent, consequently, (after keeping the
proceeds a considerable time in his possession to meet the
claims of those Ships, in the event of any having been
established by them in England,) not hearing of any claim
being made, sent the Prize-money to the Victory for distribution; but has since acquainted the Captain of that Ship
that the Marie Therese is claimed as a Droit of Admiralty.
I therefore request you will be pleased to lay this particular
case before the Lords Commissioners of the Admiralty, and
move their Lordships, under the circumstances before mentioned, to order the Admiralty claim (if any has been made)
to be withdrawn, as I consider it a very great hardship upon
the Officers and Seamen of the Victory.[6] I am, &c.,

NELSON AND BRONTE.

---

[6] Lord Nelson repeated this inquiry on the 1st of August, 1805, and the Admiralty, having referred to their Proctor, Mr. Gosling, they forwarded his Report to
Lord Nelson on the 22nd of that month. It stated that the Lords of Appeal had,
on the 5th of April 1805, reversed the sentence by which the Marie-Therese had
been adjudged a Prize to the Victory, and condemned the Ship and Cargo as a

TO DR. BAIRD.

[From " The Athenæum," and Clarke and M'Arthur, vol. ii. p. 367.]

Victory, May 30th, 1804.

My dear Sir,

I have many thanks to give you for your truly kind letter of January 24th. From what we hear about Buonaparte's being Emperor, perhaps it will bring about a Peace; and if we give up Malta, it will be unnecessary to make a Naval Hospital. I have sent Dr. Snipe to look at the place, with Sir Alexander Ball, and to take care that we have the ground with the house; for, with the ground, it is the most healthy and eligible situation in Valette Harbour; without it, confined with four bare walls, it would be the very worst place in the place, for the heat would be intolerable.

The health of this Fleet cannot be exceeded; and I really believe that my shattered carcase is in the worst plight of the whole Fleet. I have had a sort of rheumatic fever, they tell me; but I have felt the blood gushing up the left side of my head, and the moment it covers the brain, I am fast asleep: I am now better of that; and with violent pain in my side, and night-sweats, with heat in the evening, and quite flushed. The pain in my head, nor spasms,[7] I have not had for some time. [Mr. Magrath, whom I admire for his great abilities every day I live, gives me excellent remedies; but we must lose such men from our Service, if the Army goes on in encouraging Medical men, whilst we do nothing. I am sure much ought to be done for our Naval Surgeons, or how can we expect to keep valuable men? I look to you not only to propose it, but to enforce it, to Lord St. Vincent, who must be anxious to preserve such a valuable set of men to the Navy.[8]]

With every kind wish for your health and happiness, I am always, my dear doctor, your much obliged friend,

NELSON AND BRONTE.

Droit of Admiralty, taken by the Non-Commissioned Ship Ambuscade; and the Lords assigned the accounts of sales and proceeds to be brought in."—*Original Letter* in the Croker Papers.

[7] " The pain in my heart, not spasms," in the copy in Clarke and M'Arthur.

[8] The passage within brackets is supplied from the copy in Clarke and M'Arthur.

I wish it may be in [my] power to be useful to your friend
Mr. Hammick,[9] on board the Renown ; but I see no prospect
at present.

ORDERS FOR REAR-ADMIRAL SIR RICHARD BICKERTON, BART.

[Autograph draught in the possession of the Reverend Henry Girdlestone, and
Order-Book.]

Victory, at Sea, 31st May, 1804.

I am going off the Port of Toulon with the Van Division
of the Fleet. You are to remain with the Lee Division and
Bombs, South of Porto Cross ; but on no account to come to
the Northward of 42 : 20 N., as nearer than that distance
Ships are seen from the Hières Islands. And as the Victuallers are hourly expected from Malta, you will direct the Ships
with you to complete to five months. You will send me an
account when the Victuallers arrive, that I may return and
clear them.

Should the Childers join, you will send her to me, and also
the Narcissus ; and should anything particular happen, so as
to make a communication for other purposes necessary, you
will send a Ship to me, directing her Commander to approach
Toulon, or the Ships off that place, with great caution.

NELSON AND BRONTE.

TO HIS EXCELLENCY COUNT WORONZOW.

[From Clarke and M'Arthur, vol. ii. p. 368.]

31st May, 1804.

These gentlemen,[1] being lads, must be treated in a different
manner to the grown-up Officers we have formerly had. The
allowance made them from the Emperor, is, I understand,

---

[9] Mr. Stephen Love Hammick, Surgeon of the Renown, was for many years
Surgeon to the Royal Hospital at Plymouth. He was created a Baronet in July
1834.

[1] Some young Russian gentlemen, who were placed in our Ships in the Mediterranean, that they might learn our Naval system, (vide vol. v. p. 448.) The policy
of our having taught Foreigners to become Naval Officers seems incomprehensible.

£40 a year, which sum is very well after the youngsters are
fitted out, and the Ship they are in has sailed; but to fit them
out and keep them a year, it is by no means a sufficient sum.
I would, therefore, propose, that the twelve lads who came out
in the Royal Sovereign, should have all their outfit paid, and
passage to Plymouth, and that the £40 a year should not
commence until the day the Royal Sovereign sailed from
Plymouth. It costs an English lad from 70 to £100 to fit him
out, besides his yearly stipend; and these very fine lads must
have hats, shoes, &c., and money for their mess. I do not
think they will have many opportunities of spending their
money ashore. I shall cause inquiries to be made into their
little wants, and shall advance the money. They are most exceedingly good boys, and are very much liked in the Ships
they are placed in. I am, &c.,

NELSON AND BRONTE.

TO THE RIGHT HONOURABLE LORD HOBART.

[Autograph, in the Colonial Office.]

Victory, May 31st, 1804.

My Lord,
　　I have been honoured with your Lordship's duplicate letter
of March 8th[2]—the original, I presume, taken in the Swift

---

[2] " Secret.

" Downing Street, 8th March, 1804.

" My Lord,—I have received your Lordship's letters referred to in the margin,
(22nd December, 1803; 4th January, 1804; 6th ditto; 19th ditto; 20th ditto;
20th ditto,) and I have great pleasure in expressing the approbation of his Majesty's
confidential servants, of the energy and spirit which have marked your Lordship's
conduct, in the measures that you have taken with respect to the Dey of Algiers,
as well as the discretion and good sense with which your orders have been executed by
Captain Keats. The instructions of the 9th January, which by his Majesty's commands, I communicated to your Lordship, will have reached you shortly after the
date of your last Dispatches, and your Lordship will have observed that they perfectly accord with the determination you had previously taken, to forbear proceeding to actual hostilities, until you can strike an effectual blow against the Algerine
Cruizers. But as your Lordship has mentioned the latter end of the month of
April, as the period which you would fix for the commencement of operations, it
has appeared advisable to his Majesty's Ministers that another communication
should be made to the Dey of Algiers, in the hope that means may yet be found for
procuring due satisfaction for the honour of this country, without having recourse

Cutter. Expecting your Lordship's answer, I did not, of course, commence hostilities against the Dey's Cruizers. I meant that the 28th of April was about the time of their sailing, and when an effective blow might be struck. I do not think the Dey has ventured to send his Cruizers to sea·

to measures of decided hostility. By personal communication with Mr. Falcon, the fact of the Moorish women having been found in his house, is clearly established ; but from the representation of that gentleman, no doubt can be entertained of their having been introduced without his knowledge. As, however, it is understood that the women themselves, as well as a French servant belonging to Mr. Falcon, have been induced to declare that Mr. Falcon and his Secretary, were the persons on whose account they were admitted into the house of the Consul, the conduct of the Dey, with reference to the prejudices of the Moorish people, may admit of some degree of palliation, although it is not possible for him to justify the insult offered to his Majesty's Representative, by the abrupt manner in which he was sent away from Algiers. Under this impression, and in consequence of Mr. Falcon's representation since his return to England, intimating that many circumstances had occurred, which were calculated to render him peculiarly obnoxious to the Dey ; and as the Dey has signified his readiness to receive any other person whom his Majesty might think proper to nominate as his Consul at Algiers, his Majesty's Ministers are of opinion that your Lordship should, with the least possible delay, take such measures as shall appear to you most proper, for causing it to be signified to the Dey that your Lordship might be induced to interpose your good offices with his Majesty's Government, for the purpose of having the appointment of Consul conferred upon some other person, provided the Dey shall, in the first instance, express his concern for the disrespect which had been shown to the accredited Agent of his Majesty, in the person of Mr. Falcon ; and provided, likewise, that the Maltese inhabitants captured by the Algerine Cruizers, and held in slavery at Algiers, be restored, as also their Vessels and cargoes, or a pecuniary compensation made for the damages sustained by their detention. If the communication of such a favourable disposition on the part of your Lordship, should fail to produce the effect that might reasonably be expected from it, it will then become necessary that the Dey should be made to feel that the power of punishment for the insult offered by him, is equal to the moderation and forbearance that have been observed towards him ; and I have an entire confidence that your Lordship will so regulate your proceedings, as to be able to take the most effectual measures for that purpose. Inclosed I send your Lordship a copy of the Treaty of the 19th of March, 1801, entered into by his Majesty's Agent and Consul-General, Mr. Falcon, and his Highness Mustapha Dey, Bashaw and Governor of Algiers, by which your Lordship will observe that, from the 7th of December 1800, the inhabitants of the Island of Malta are to be treated upon the same footing as the rest of his Majesty's subjects. I have the honour to be, &c.—HOBART."—*Original.*

Copy of the Treaty enclosed in the preceding Letter :—

" Whereas the Island of Malta, in the Mediterranean Sea, has been conquered by his Britannic Majesty's arms, it is now hereby agreed, and fully concluded, between John Falcon, Esquire, his Britannic Majesty's Agent and Consul-General for the City and Kingdom of Algier, and his Highness Mustapha Dey, Bashaw and Governor, &c. &c. of Algier, that from the seventh day of December last, 1800, the inhabitants thereof shall be treated upon the same footing as the rest of his

I have sent Captain Keats to Algiers; and, unless the Dey is set on, and supported by the French against us, I have every hope, that now Mr. Falcon is out of the question, matters will be amicably settled. As for three Bombs going against Algiers, I could as soon whistle the walls down. If force is to be used, not less than ten or twelve Sail of the Line, and as many Bombs as possible, could, in my opinion, produce the proper effect of humbling him; and I feel that a Fleet is not, at this moment, to be crippled on such a service.

The moment Captain Keats returns, I shall write to your Lordship the result of his mission; and I am, &c.,

NELSON AND BRONTE.

TO SPIRIDION FORESTI, ESQ., CORFU.

[From Clarke and M'Arthur, vol. ii. p. 365.]

[About 31st May, 1804.]

The only place to guard against a *coup de main* from, was Toulon, where 12,000 Troops are ready for embarkation : this I have taken effectual care to prevent, by a perseverance at sea never surpassed in the annals of the world—not a Ship in this Fleet has been into any Port to refit since the War, and to this moment I never have had my foot out of the Ship.[3] I am, &c.,   NELSON AND BRONTE.

TO . . . . ., MANAGER OF THE ESTATE OF BRONTE.

[From Clarke and M'Arthur, vol. ii. p. 366.]

[About May, 1804.]

I am so little versed in business, that I hardly know how to answer your letter. Ungrateful as the Brontese have behaved,

Britannic Majesty's subjects; and the said Island shall be considered in all respects like the other places subject to the Crown of Great Britain, and agreeable to the Convention made with his Britannic Majesty by Bracen Rais, Ambassador from his Highness the Dey. Confirmed and sealed in the warlike City and Kingdom of Algier, in the presence of Almighty God, the 19th day of March, 1801, and in the year of the Hegira 1216, and the 6th day of the moon Gelip.—JOHN FALCON.

[3] Clarke and M'Arthur state, in a note to this letter, on the authority of the Duke of Clarence, (vol. ii. p. 362,) that "Lord Nelson never went out of the Victory but three times, and then on the King's service, from his leaving England in 1803, to his return in August 1805; and none of these absences from his Ship exceeded an hour."

yet the Prince . . . . . . shall never, upon any consideration, be their master for an hour. In Sicily, I suppose, they have certain forms and customs as we have in England. The gentry may forget that I am master. I consider that we deal on the strictest honour, *our words are our bonds.*[4] You may assure the Brontese, that I shall never consent to anything which can oppress them. At this moment I can only think of the French Fleet. I am, &c.,

NELSON AND BRONTE.

TO GEORGE MATCHAM, ESQ.

[From Clarke and M'Arthur, vol. ii. p. 366.]

I fear my-friends think, that I neglect those I ought to be attentive to; but be assured, my dear Mr. Matcham, that whether I write or not, my heart always stands in the right place to you, my dear Sister, and her family. I am, &c.,

NELSON AND BRONTE.

TO CAPTAIN HENRY RICHARDSON, H.M. SHIP JUNO.

[Letter-Book.]

Victory, at Sea, 31st May, 1804.

Sir,

As the Enemy at Toulon are in the habit of sending their Frigates several leagues from Cape Sepet, under the cover of two or more Ships of the Line, I am to desire that you will acquaint the Captain or Commander of any of his Majesty's Ships or Vessels, in search of me, thereof, and recommend the greatest caution to them in passing that place, on their way to join me, on my Rendezvous No. 102. Should Mr. Ford, the Agent-Victualler, join the Juno, you will land him at Palamos, or as near the Bay of Rosas as you may judge prudent, consistent with the service you are employed on. I am, &c.,

NELSON AND BRONTE.

---

[4] " In a letter afterwards to a noble Spaniard, his Lordship said, ' I can assure you, Sir, that the word of honour of every Captain of a British Man-of-War is equal, not only to mine, but to that of any person in Europe, however elevated his rank.' "—*Clarke and M'Arthur*, vol. ii. p. 366.

TO CAPTAIN ROBERT PETTET, H. M. SLOOP TERMAGANT.

[Order-Book.]

Victory, at Sea, 1st June, 1804.

You are hereby required and directed to receive my public dispatches on board his Majesty's Sloop Termagant, under your command, and proceed with them to Naples with as little delay as possible ; and on your arrival there, you will deliver them to his Excellency Hugh Elliot, Esq., his Majesty's Minister at that Court, acquainting him that you are directed to wait for his answers, and such dispatches as he may have to forward to me (which I hope will not detain you long). Having received Mr. Elliot's answers to my letters, you will return and join me on Rendezvous No. 102, without a moment's loss of time, where you will find the Squadron, or orders for your further proceedings.

NELSON AND BRONTE.

Memorandum.

If the weather permits, you have my permission to pass on the East side of the Island of Corsica, in your way to Naples, in order to intercept a French twenty-gun Ship, which I have received information is cruizing on that coast.

NELSON AND BRONTE.

TO HIS EXCELLENCY HUGH ELLIOT, ESQ.

[Autograph, in the Elliot Papers. " Friday, 1st June. At 6 A.M., Cape Sicie bore N. b W. ½ W., distant 5 leagues. At 11, a Ship of the Line and one Frigate of the Enemy's under sail, near Cape Sepet."—*Victory's Log.*]

Victory, June 1st, 1804.

My dear Sir,

I was honoured by the Gibraltar with your Excellency's letters of May 6th, and I have read with much interest (now and then with sorrow) their contents. The politics of Europe will probably so completely turn upon a Monarchical Government being again formed in France, that I believe no one can guess what the two Emperors of Russia and Germany will do. If they acknowledge Napoleon as their brother, there is no great honour in being allied to their family; but I think in that case it will give us peace. If they will not call him

brother (Gracious Heaven! thy ways are hid from man!)
Jack Coroo brothor to two Emporors! then I suppose we shall
have a general War. Either way, it must benefit both England
and Naples. The French papers tell us of the great probability of a change of Ministry.[5] It is certain they cannot
carry on the business of the Nation with only a majority of
thirty-seven in the House of Commons; and I rather think
in the House of Lords they will be in a minority. But
most likely you know these matters sooner than we do. I had
a line from Mr. Frere of May 2nd. In answer to mine
respecting the probability of a Spanish War, he says—viz.,
' Not having my cipher at hand, I can only say that I think
you need not be influenced by the apprehensions which you
mention:' therefore, I should think that Mr. Frere would
hardly wilfully lead me into a blind security. He would take
a severe responsibility if he did.

I observe what you say about 888. You may safely rely
that I never trust a Corsican or a Frenchman. I would give
the devil ALL the good ones to take the remainder. I
am close off Toulon, with Victory, Canopus, Donegal, Belleisle, and Excellent, in hopes to tempt Mr. La Touche out
of Port. Sir Richard Bickerton I have sent to another
station. The French have eight Sail of the Line in the
Outer Road, and six Frigates, and two or three of the Line in
the Inner Road. I must try and finish my career before
winter; for I have not an idea of being able to encounter such
another as the last. You may be assured his Sardinian
Majesty shall want no support in my power to give him.
The answer of Russia is unworthy a great Emperor to a little
King, whom he pretends to protect; but such things are. [Be-
lieve] at least, that I am, with the truest respect and esteem,
your Excellency's most obedient and faithful Servant,

NELSON AND BRONTE.

[5] A change of Administration had taken place on the 12th of May, when Mr.
Pitt succeeded Mr. Addington as Prime Minister; Earl Camden became Secretary
of State for the War Department; and the new Board of Admiralty consisted of
Viscount Melville (First Lord); Sir Philip Stephens, Bart.; Vice Admiral James
Gambier; Captain Sir Harry Burrard Neale, Bart.; Admiral Sir John Colpoys, K.B.;
Vice-Admiral Philip Patton; and William Dickenson, Esq. Of these Members,
Sir Philip Stephens and Sir Harry Burrard Neale had belonged to the preceding
Board; and the former had been a Lord of the Admiralty since March 1795.

TO HIS EXCELLENCY HUGH ELLIOT, ESQ.

[Autograph, in the Elliot Papers.]

My dear Sir,   Victory, June 1st, 1804.

I have taken your son William[6] out of the Gibraltar, and Captain Parker of the Amazon has been so good as to take him in that Ship, when she next joins. The Gibraltar is too large for him. I am sure he will make a Seaman : his bent lays that way, and his real good sense is rarely met with in any age of life. Captain Ryves sailed yesterday for Gibraltar —I am sure, fully impressed with the kindness of their Majesties, your Excellency, and Sir John Acton towards him. With respect to the conduct of the Gibraltar, I trust every English Ship of War will conduct herself equally well. I wonder that General Acton should for one moment believe the professions of General St. Cyr, more especially coming through the mouth of Micheroux, who I know of old. Did the French ever appear friendly, but for the purpose of more readily destroying those whom they can *cajole?* This word is English, although it writes very bad. I have more fears for Naples and Sicily than Malta.

I have not mentioned any time in Captain Pettet's orders, but I rely that your Excellency will not keep him many days. I am so distressed for Small Craft, that I do not know which way to turn to send a letter. I am ever, my dear Sir, your much obliged friend,   NELSON AND BRONTE.

When your Excellency sees the Prince Trebbia, pray tell him that I thank him for his polite letter, and that I would have wrote to him, but that my *Italian* writer (Doctor Scott) is gone to Spain. I beg my respectful compliments to Mrs. Elliot.

TO LADY HAMILTON.

[From " Lord Nelson's Letters to Lady Hamilton," vol. ii. p. 48.]

Victory, June 6th, 1804.

Since I wrote you, my dearest Emma, on the 30th and 31st May, nothing new has happened; except our hearing the

---

[6] Mr. William Elliot, so frequently mentioned, obtained the rank of Lieutenant, and died young.

feu-de-joie at Toulon, for the declaration of Emperor.[6] What
a capricious Nation those French must be! However, I
think, it must, in any way, be advantageous to England.
There ends, for a century, all Republics! By Vessels from
Marseilles, the French think it will be a Peace ; and they say,
that several of their Merchant-Ships are fitting out. I earnestly
pray, that it may be so; and, that we may have a few years
of rest. I rather believe my antagonist at Toulon begins to
be angry with me : at least, I am trying to make him so; and
then, he may come out, and beat me, as he says he did, off
Boulogne. He is the Admiral that went to Naples in December
1792 [1793], La Touche Tréville, who landed the Grenadier.[7]
I owe him something for that.

I am better, my dear Emma, than I have been, and shall get
through the summer very well ; and I have the pleasure to tell
you, that Charles is very much recovered. There is no more
the matter with his intellects than with mine! Quite the
contrary ; he is very quick. Mr. Scott, who has overlooked
all his things, says his clothes, &c. are in the highest order he
has ever seen. I shall place him in the Niger, with Captain
Hillyar, when he joins; but, all our Ships are so full, that it is
very difficult to get a berth for one in any Ship. Would you
conceive it possible! but, it is now from April 2nd, since I
have heard direct from Ball. The average time for a Frigate
to go and return, is from six to seven weeks. From you, I
had letters, April 5th, and the papers to April 8th, received
May 10th, with a Convoy. This goes through friend Gayner.
Sir William Bolton joined last night; and received his letters,
announcing his being called papa. He is got a very fine
young man and good Officer. Lord St. Vincent has desired
he may have the first Admiralty vacancy for Post; but nobody
will die or go home. *Apropos!* I believe, you should buy a
piece of plate, value fifty pounds, for our god-daughter of
Lady Bolton ; and something of twenty or thirty pounds'
value, for Colonel Suckling's......

---

[6] Sunday, 3rd June, 7 P.M. " The Ships in Toulon fired a salute."—*Victory's
Log.*

[7] " The last visit the King of Naples had, was from a French Grenadier belonging to Monsr. Truguet's Fleet, threatening him with War if he did not, within
an hour, disavow his remonstrances against the reception of Monsieur Sémonville
at Constantinople." Vide Nelson's Letter, 7th—11th September, 1798, vol. i. p. 223.

TO CAPTAIN ROBERT CORBET, H.M. SLOOP BITTERN.

[Letter-Book.]

Victory, off Toulon, 7th June, 1804.

Sir,

Captain Schomberg of his Majesty's Ship Madras has transmitted to me your letter[8] of the third ultimo, giving an account of your having captured the Hirondelle French Privateer, and re-captured the two English Merchantmen named in the margin,[9] her prizes; I therefore beg to assure you, that your conduct and perseverance in the capture of the said Privateer, and her Prizes, merit my entire approbation, and I must request that you will be pleased to receive, and to express my thanks to the Officers and Company of the Bittern, for their great exertions[1] on the occasion. I am, &c.,

NELSON AND BRONTE.

TO SIR ALEXANDER JOHN BALL, BART., MALTA.

[Autograph, in the possession of Sir William Keith Ball, Bart.]

Victory, June 7th, 1804.

My dear Ball,

I have been so unwell for this last fortnight, although not sick, that I cannot do more than run over hastily an answer to your letter, and write a line to General Villettes, for I am likewise anxious to get the Thisbe to Malta, as I hope the Agincourt is by this time arrived to take the Convoy to England. I should not think them safe if they have proceeded in any numbers with the Maidstone, who Captain Bayntun ordered to Malta with our Convoy, and to bring down another; but the passages are very different at this season when the Westerly winds so constantly prevail. The going on in the routine of a station, if interrupted, is like stopping a watch—the whole machine gets wrong. If the Maidstone takes the Convoy, and when Agincourt arrives, there is none for her or Thisbe,

---

[8] Captain Corbet's letter is in the "London Gazette," of August 1804.

[9] Mentor, Catherine.

[1] The Crew of the Bittern "were at the Sweeps for thirty-six hours without intermission, even to meals, in which time they swept the Ship 60 miles, without an air of wind."—Captain Corbet's Letter.

it puzzles me to know what orders to give them. If they chace the Convoy to Gibraltar, the Maidstone may have gone on with them to England, and in that case, two Ships, unless I begin to give a new arrangement, will either go home without Convoy, or they must return in contradiction to the Admiralty's orders to send them home ; I am sure you see it in its true point of view. I am thankful you did not allow that General to come to me—I would not have seen him; I answered his letter to Smyrna, and wrote Mr. Werry that everything he had to propose he might send to England, or to some of Her Ministers, for that I neither could or would have anything to do with him or his plans. Mr. Elliot wanted to send me a *good* Frenchman, that I might land and take on board occasionally. My answer was, *No!* I knew the force at Toulon, and that nothing would be of any use to me but a copy of the French Admiral's sailing orders.[2]

The dispatches taken in the Swift, Captain Keats will tell you, related only to Algiers, and thank God, there was none of any consequence! The loss of the King George Packet[3] I am sincerely concerned at, and I would give you at least two more Sloops if I had them, but in the event of having dispatches to send to either you, Naples, or Gibraltar, I have only the two brigs Cameleon and Childers. I send you some intercepted papers from Egypt; I cannot·make out the ciphers ; they were hid in a Ragusa Vessel from Alexandria; except what may be in cipher they do not appear of much consequence ; when read, pray take a copy of them, and enclose the originals to Lord Hobart, and let me know the cipher if you can make it out. I send you our last Paris papers; in addition to their contents, the French Fleet in Toulon fired a *feu-de-joie*, dressed Ship, &c. on the 3rd, for his taking upon himself the title of Emperor. At Marseilles they talk of Peace, and you will see the probability of a change of Administration. I have nothing from Madrid later than May 2nd, all was then quiet, and I do not believe that the reports of Mr. Frere being on the eve, in April, of leaving Madrid, had any foundation beyond the fancy of the Neapo-

---

[2] Vide vol. v. p. 238.

[3] The King George, Malta Government Brig, was captured on the 27th of April, 1804, by L'Hirondelle French Privateer, of Cape Passaro.

litan Minister at Madrid. The Victory in June, 1803, captured a French Tartan; and, to avoid being put into quarantine, he sunk her, and, as the Captain conceived, French
property to the amount of several thousand pounds; it was so
truly disinterested a measure that it met my most sincere
approbation. My head is so bad that I must finish. I have
wrote to Mr. Elliot and General Acton my surprise that they
should believe any declaration made by General St. Cyr,
especially a verbal one, passing through the mouth of Micheroux,
who is, in my opinion, *always* in the French service. Acton
now finds I am right: he is probably out of the Ministry by
this time. *Gallo* wants to be in his place. I am ever, my
dear Ball, &c.,

NELSON AND BRONTE.

TO MAJOR-GENERAL VILLETTES, MALTA.

[Autograph, in the possession of Samuel Simpson, Esq.]

Victory, June 7th, 1804.

My dear General,
I sincerely hope that the Convoy brought up by the Maid-
stone has relieved your anxiety about letters. By the papers I
have sent Ball, you will not be surprised at a change of
Ministry; it's reported to be a coalition between the
Prince of Wales and Mr. Pitt. The names seem to mark
it as such to the exclusion of the Grenvilles: Pitt, Chief;
Fox, Lord Moira, and Grey, Secretaries of State;[4] Lord
Melville, Admiralty; Erskine, Attorney-General; the other
places filled up alternately. I rather think this change, with
Buonaparte being Emperor, may bring about a Peace. The
change, however, from a Republic, must be advantageous to
England; and, if the *two* Emperors like Brother Napoleon,
we cannot object.
I agree with you about the fatal security which the Cabinet
of Naples so readily falls into; General St. Cyr only meant
to deceive them, for within a few days the French Minister
held the most insulting language. General Acton is probably
out before this time. I am truly sensible of all your kindness,

---

4 Lord Nelson's information was not correct.

my dear General, and good wishes : they are reciprocal in
the truest sense of the word. I have been but very so so,
but I hope to last the summer, or at least till Mr. La Touche
pleases to come out of his nest which, if it is as hot as it is
outside, must be very warm ; but, perhaps, he fancies he
should find it hotter outside. But out he must come, some
day or other, and, as he says, he beat me at Boulogne, it is,
I think, my turn now ; and, that it shall be so, nothing shall
be wanting on the part of, my dear friend, your much
obliged,

NELSON AND BRONTE.

TO SIR ALEXANDER JOHN BALL, BART., MALTA.

[Autograph, in the possession of Sir William Keith Ball, Bart.]

Victory, June 7th, 1804.

My dear Ball,

I do most earnestly desire that you will not fail saying
anything to me that you please, I can never take it amiss ;
but, as you see, the jumble which will be about Maidstone
and Agincourt, upsets my arrangements. Do not think I am
tired of watching Mr. La Touche Tréville. I have now
taken up a method of making him angry. I have left Sir
Richard Bickerton, with part of the Fleet, twenty leagues
from hence, and, with five of the Line, am preventing his
cutting capers, which he had done for some time past, off
Cape Sicie. Mr. La Touche has several times hoisted his
topsail-yards up ; and on the 4th of June, we having hoisted
the Standard and saluted,[5] he sent outside Sepet, about one
mile, five Sail of the Line and two Frigates, and kept three
Sail and three Frigates with their yards aloft, *himself* one of
them, and the *Rear*-Admiral another, therefore I did not
believe him in earnest ; however, we run as near as was proper, and brought to. They formed a pretty line at sunset,
and then stood into the Harbour. A Ship of the Line and
Frigate every morning weigh, and stand between Sepet and
La Malgue. Some happy day I expect to see his eight Sail,
which are in the Outer Road, come out ; and if he will get

---

[5] In honour of the King's birthday.

abreast of Porquerolle, I will try what stuff he is made of; therefore you see, my dear Ball, I have no occasion to be fretful; on the contrary, I am full of hopes, and command a Fleet which never gives me an uneasy moment.

[A page of the letter is missing.]

If by the Nimble the Agincourt is gone with the Convoy, without waiting for Thisbe, I have directed her to remain under Captain Schomberg's orders. From the accounts I have heard, I am sorry to have mentioned the names of Mr. and Mrs. L.:[6] send them to Tripoli. ......

———

TO CAPTAIN CHARLES MARSH SCHOMBERG, H.M. SHIP MADRAS.

[Letter-Book.]

Victory, off Toulon, 7th June, 1804.

Sir,

In the event of the Agincourt's having sailed from Malta, with the Trade for England, previous to the arrival of the Thisbe, and you should judge that the Convoy is too far on its passage for the Thisbe to overtake, I am to desire that you will detain Captain Shepheard at Malta, for the purpose of accompanying the next Convoy from the Adriatic and Archipelago, employing the Thisbe in such manner as you shall judge best for the service of the Island, and collecting the Trade until I shall think proper to appoint a Convoy to proceed to England. Captain Shepheard has received my orders in the event of the Agincourt's having proceeded from Malta, to put himself under your command. I am, &c.,

NELSON AND BRONTE.

N.B.—You will render every assistance in your power to fit the Hirondelle for actual service, and lend her men to assist in navigating her.

———

[6] Mr. and Mrs. Longford.

TO THE RESPECTIVE OFFICERS OF HIS MAJESTY'S YARD AT MALTA.

[Letter-Book.]

Victory, off Toulon, 7th June, 1804.

Gentlemen,

Captain Schomberg of his Majesty's Ship Madras, having transmitted to me the valuation of the French Cutter L'Hirondelle captured by his Majesty's Ship Bittern, by which it appears that she is in good condition; and if you consider her in every respect fit for his Majesty's service, I am to desire you will mention it to Sir Alexander Ball, and submit to him (as she is intended for the service of Malta) the propriety of her being made a Schooner, as a more handy Vessel for the said service; and upon his approbation being signified, you will use every exertion in completing her for immediate service. The necessary orders for your proceedings herein shall be sent to Malta by the Transports, together with answers to your several letters, &c., as there is only time for the present to say they are received. I am, &c.,

NELSON AND BRONTE.

N.B.—Since writing the above, I understand that L'Hirondelle is not a Cutter, and therefore it is probable she will answer the service she is intended for better in her present state. But you will act in this as Sir Alexander Ball may think proper.

N. & B.

TO CAPTAIN RICHARD HUSSEY MOUBRAY, H.M. SHIP ACTIVE.

[Letter Book.]

Victory, off Toulon, 7th June, 1804.

Sir,

I herewith transmit you a letter which I have received from the Governor of St. Pierres, respecting two Sardinian Vessels employed in the Tunny Fishery, which, as their names are not mentioned, I cannot comply with his request; but in order to remove the evil as far as it is practicable, I have enclosed two blank Certificates, which you will see properly filled up, with the Vessels' names, and those of their

Commanders, and explain to the Governor the reason of his letters not being answered in Italian is owing to Doctor Scott's being absent. I am, &c.,

NELSON AND BRONTE.

TO CAPTAIN VINCENT, H. M. SLOOP ARROW.

[Letter-Book.]

Victory, off Toulon, June 8th, 1804.

Sir,

I have received your letter of the 11th ult., addressed to Captain Cracraft, of the Anson, together with the defects of his Majesty's Sloop Arrow, under your command; and I must desire, on your return into Valetta harbour, that you will put her in a state for being hove down, or otherwise, as the Builder may think necessary, to repair her defects. If the tanks cannot be repaired, water casks must be substituted in their room. I have sent an order to the Master Shipwright for this purpose; and must desire that every exertion which depends upon you, to facilitate her equipment, may be used, that the service of this Country may be deprived of so fine- a Vessel but for as short a time as possible. I am, Sir, &c.

NELSON AND BRONTE.

TO CAPTAIN VINCENT, H. M. SLOOP ARROW.

[Letter-Book.]

Victory, off Toulon, June 8th, 1804.

Sir,

I have received your letter of the 6th of April last, acquainting me with your return from Smyrna on the 5th of that month, with such Trade as were ready to accompany you to Malta; and that you were about to proceed again to Smyrna, with two English Vessels and Transports, under the charge of Lieutenant Woodman, which you mean to escort into the Dardanelles, and afterwards bring the Trade from Smyrna to Valetta harbour. In answer to which, I approve of the line of conduct you mean to pursue in the execution of your orders, and also of your correspondence with his Excellency,

Mr. Stratton, our Minister at Constantinople, relative to the
conduct of the Governor of the Castle on the European side,
on entering the Dardanelles; and make no doubt that the
Ottoman Government will sufficiently account for the conduct
of the Castle's firing upon the Arrow and Convoy, and make
the necessary reparation to our Minister for the insult. The
two letters, &c. from Mr. Thomas M'Gill, mentioned in yours
of the 6th April, have also been received, and I observe, with
some degree of surprise, the protection afforded the French
at Ancona, contrary to the laws of Neutrality. You have
done perfectly right in circulating the information of the Privateers and Corn Vessels to all the Captains on your station,
and hope they may be intercepted. I have also to acknowledge the receipt of your letter of the 7th April, with the list
of Vessels captured and detained, as therein mentioned. I
am, Sir, &c.

NELSON AND BRONTE.

TO WILLIAM MARSDEN, ESQ., ADMIRALTY.

[Original in the Admiralty, and " London Gazette," August 1804.]

Victory, off Toulon, 8th June, 1804.

Sir,

I herewith transmit you, for the information of the Lords
Commissioners of the Admiralty, a copy of a letter dated the
3rd ultimo, from Captain Corbet, of his Majesty's Sloop Bittern, to Captain Schomberg, Senior Officer at Malta, giving
an account of his having, on the 28th of April last, captured
the French Privateer L'Hirondelle, and recaptured the two
English Merchant Ships named in the margin,[7] her prizes.
The conduct of Captain Corbet, the Officers and Company of
the Bittern, entitles them to my warmest thanks for their
very great perseverance and exertions in the capture of the
above Privateer, which, I understand, is a remarkably fine
Vessel, and had greatly annoyed our Trade in this Country.
I am, &c.

NELSON AND BRONTE.

[7] Mentor, Catherine.

TO WILLIAM MARSDEN, ESQ., ADMIRALTY.

[Original, in the Admiralty.]

Victory, off Toulon, 8th June, 1804.

Sir,

In addition to my letters of the 10th January and 15th March last, and in further compliance with their Lordships' direction, contained in Sir Evan Nepean's duplicate letter to me of the 9th November last, respecting the conduct of Lieutenant Shaw, of the Spider Brig,[a] I herewith transmit you the copy of a letter from Captain Schomberg, of the Madras, which I request you will be pleased to lay before the Lords Commissioners of the Admiralty for their information, and acquaint their Lordships that I consider Lieutenant Shaw's conduct on this occasion very meritorious and praiseworthy; and I have to hope that their Lordships' approbation of his conduct will be signified to him ; for while the Sicilian Government, and that of the Republic of the Seven Isles, as mentioned in my letter to you of this date, hold forth such retreats, and allow such piratical proceedings by the Enemy's Privateers, from their Ports, in violation of the laws of Neutrality, it certainly becomes the duty of every British Officer to capture or destroy any Enemy's Vessel that attacks him, wherever the attack is made. Enclosed are the copies of a letter and note which I gave the Captains of the Anson and Thisbe on this subject. I am, &c.

NELSON AND BRONTE.

P.S.—Enclosed are affidavits from the Masters of the Vessels carried into Girgenti by a French Privateer.

TO WILLIAM MARSDEN, ESQ., ADMIRALTY.

[Original, in the Admiralty.]

Victory, off Toulon, 8th June, 1804.

Sir,

I herewith transmit you a copy of a letter from Captain Shepheard of his Majesty's Ship Thisbe, dated the 1st ultimo, and of the one therein mentioned from Lieutenant Robert

[a] Vide vol. v. p. 205.

Corner of that Ship, giving an account of his having taken possession of La Veloce Privateer, bearing the colours of the Italian Republic, and retaken a Brig, one of the Thisbe's Convoy, captured by the above Privateer, or rather Pirate, close in with a Bay in Great Cephalonia. I also transmit you a copy of Captain Shepheard's letter to me, dated at Corfu, 6th May, together with copies of the letters therein alluded to, and also a copy of one from Spiridion Foresti, Esq., his Majesty's Minister to the Seven Islands, on the subject of the said capture, in consequence of an Official Note from Count Moncenigo, the Russian Minister to the said Republic, a copy of which, with Mr. Foresti's answer, also accompanies this, which I request you will lay before the Lords Commissioners of the Admiralty, for their information; and, at the same time, acquaint their Lordships, that I very fully approve of every part of Captain Shepheard's conduct on the above occasion. The piratical conduct of the Enemy's Privateers, which are allowed to use the Harbours, Bays, Creeks, &c., of the Republic of the Seven Isles, from whence they capture our Trade, and, when attacked, complain of a violation of the Neutrality, is so notoriously practised, to the great annoyance and destruction of our Trade, that I submit to their Lordships the necessity of a very strong remonstrance being made to the Government of the Seven Islands, in order to prevent those Privateers the use of their Harbours and Ports, &c., for such piratical purposes. I am, Sir, &c.,

NELSON AND BRONTE.

TO CAPTAIN SCHOMBERG, H. M. SHIP MADRAS.

[Letter-Book.]

Victory, off Toulon, 8th June, 1804.

Sir,

I have received your letter of the 10th ultimo, inclosing one from Captain Corbet of his Majesty's Sloop Bittern, giving an account of his having captured L'Hirondelle French Privateer, and recaptured the two Merchant-vessels named in the margin,[9] her Prizes. I am very much pleased with Captain

⁹ Mentor, Catherine.

Corbet's exertions on this occasion, and have expressed my
sentiments of approbation to him, his Officers, and Company.
And I have also to acknowledge your watchful attention to
the capture of the said Privateer, and am very much pleased
with your having sent the Bittern in search of her. Your
letter of the 15th ultimo, with the valuation of L'Hirondelle,
has also been received; and I am very much obliged by your
anticipating my wishes, as it appears she will answer the
service of Malta. I am, &c.,

NELSON AND BRONTE.

TO CAPTAIN SCHOMBERG, H. M. SHIP MADRAS.

[Letter-Book.]

Victory, off Toulon, 8th June, 1804.

Sir,

I have received your letter of the 7th April last, together
with the several letters and papers therein referred to, on the
subject of Lieutenant Shaw's late conduct at the Port of
Girgenti, and I am very fully and most perfectly satisfied with
your proceedings on the occasion, and have no hesitation in
believing that the Admiralty will equally approve of Lieutenant Shaw's conduct; but as they desire that it may be left
for them to determine, on receiving my report, I cannot take
upon me officially to express my approbation to Lieutenant
Shaw. I am, &c.

NELSON AND BRONTE.

TO CAPTAIN CRACRAFT, H. M. SHIP ANSON.

[Letter-Book.]

Victory, off Toulon, 8th June, 1804.

Sir,

I have received your letter of the 12th ultimo, together
with a copy of a letter from Captain Corbet, Commander of
his Majesty's Sloop Bittern, requesting a Court-Martial on
the five men named in the margin, for having deserted from
the said Sloop, at Messina on the 14th April last. In answer
thereto, I am to acquaint you that Captain Corbet's original
letter ought to have been sent to me, and not a copy, as a

Court-Martial cannot be ordered upon the latter. But I am inclined to think that Captain Corbet, from the said men's long confinement, and their late exertions in capturing L'Hirondelle, French Privateer, may be inclined to forgive them. You will, therefore, signify the purport of this letter to Captain Corbet, that if he is disposed to forgive them, I have no objections, under the present circumstances. I am, &c.,

NELSON AND BRONTE.

TO THE RIGHT HONOURABLE LORD HOBART.

[Autograph, in the Colonial Office.]

Victory, off Toulon, 8th June, 1804.

My Lord,

I have the honour to transmit, for your Lordship's information, a letter from Captain Schomberg of his Majesty's Ship Madras, together with a letter from the Bey of Tunis, and papers therein referred to; and beg to observe to your Lordship, that the disgraceful conduct of the Privateer in question calls loudly for redress, and may involve unpleasant consequences between our Country and the Bey of Tunis, who very justly demands redress, and considers that my power is not only equal to this measure, but to prevent similar conduct in these Pirates in future. I have exceedingly to lament that this line of conduct, so disgraceful to the character of the British Nation, is practised by the Gibraltar Privateers in these seas every day, as complaints are constantly laid before me from the Government of Sardinia of their nefarious conduct, which I have transmitted to the Governor of Gibraltar for his interference, as Naval Commanders have no authority whatever over those Pirates. I have the honour to be, &c.,

NELSON AND BRONTE.

TO CAPTAIN PHILIP LAMB, RESIDENT AGENT OF TRANSPORTS, MALTA.

[Letter-Book.]

Victory, off Toulon, 8th June, 1804.

Sir,

I have received your letter of the 17th ultimo, with the list of Transports therein mentioned, and must desire, on the

return of the Transports from Odessa, &c., that you will pay
due attention to my instructions on the subject of sending
them to England, provided they are not wanted for the immediate service of this Country. With respect to sending Prisoners of War, to England in Ships charged with Convoys, or
in unoccupied Transports, as mentioned in your said letter, I
must desire to observe, that but very few could be sent in the
Ships of War; and certainly a very small number of determined Prisoners, on board of any Transport, might at pleasure,
by taking advantage of the night, rise upon her Company
and run away with her. It therefore strikes me as a very
improper way of sending them to England, and I do not feel
justified in acquiescing in it without directions from the Admiralty for that purpose. But should Sir Alexander Ball
wish to have any of the Officers sent from Malta to England,
in the manner before mentioned, I have no objections to your
doing so, as there cannot be any consequences apprehended
from two or three, under strict watchfulness, being sent in
any of the Ships of War or Transports. The Senior Officer
at Malta will give the necessary direction for their being
received and victualled at two-thirds allowance during their
passage. I am, &c.,

NELSON AND BRONTE.

TO WILLIAM MARSDEN, ESQ., ADMIRALTY.

[Letter-Book.]

Victory, off Toulon, 8th June, 1804.

Sir,
    I herewith transmit you an extract of a letter from Captain
Philip Lamb, Resident Agent for Transports, &c., at Malta,
together with an extract of my letter of this date, in answer
thereto, which you will please to lay before the Lords Commissioners of the Admiralty, for their consideration; and
acquaint their Lordships, that although the Agent for Transports at Gibraltar is in the habit of sending Prisoners of War
from thence to England, in the manner mentioned in the extract of Captain Lamb's said letter, yet I conceive there is a
wide difference; for before any plan could be devised by the
Prisoners for the purpose of running away with the Transport

they might be on board of, the Convoy from Gibraltar is in the ocean; but from Malta to Gibraltar the case is different, and the frequent calms, and uncertain changes of weather in those seas, would afford an opportunity for bad intentions. Their Lordships will, therefore, give such directions on this subject as may appear to them proper. I am, &c.,

NELSON AND BRONTE.

TO CAPTAIN WILLIAM EDWARD CRACRAFT, H.M. SHIP ANSON.

[Letter-Book.]

Victory, off Toulon, 8th June, 1804.

Sir,

I have received your letters of the 13th, 14th, and 15th ultimo, acquainting me with your arrival at Malta, after having made a circuit of the Adriatic, that you left at Corfu three Russian Frigates, and that a much larger force was expected at that place. I am sorry to find that the Arrow is in so defective a state, and very much surprised that a vessel of her description cannot be repaired at Malta; surely the Master Shipwright cannot have weighed his report maturely. I shall, however, send him an order to take her into hand, and repair her defects. I hope the Anson's being docked at Constantinople, as communicated in your said letter, will not be attended with any heavy expense. The arrangement you have made with the Sloops named in the margin[1] will, I trust, sufficiently protect our Trade from the Enemy's Privateers, and prevent them from making any movement with Troops till your return. Your letter of the 15th ultimo, enclosing a list of three Vessels detained by the Jalouse, has also been received, with the State and Condition of that Sloop. I am, &c.,

NELSON AND BRONTE.

[1] Arrow, Bittern, Morgiana, Jalouse.

TO NATHANIEL TAYLOR, ESQ., NAVAL OFFICER, MALTA.

[Letter-Book.]

Victory, off Toulon, 8th June, 1804.

Sir,

I have received your letter of the 17th ultimo, acquainting me that as there was very little rope for sale in the Island of Malta, you had written to the proprietor of the Syracuse manufactory, to know on what terms he will make rope, and at the same time requested him to send ten ton of, from five to three-inch, to be forwarded to the Fleet, in order to judge if its quality will answer. In answer to which, I approve of your having ordered the cordage from Syracuse; and request you will furnish me with the particulars of the purchase, and the terms upon which the said Proprietor of the Manufactory will agree to supply any future demand for rope, which the exigency of the Service may render necessary. The sails, &c. sent on board the Narcissus and Thisbe, have been received, as acknowledged by the Captain of the Fleet, and also Mr. Leard's letter, with an account of the cordage sent from Fiume. On the subject of the appointment of two Foremen to the Master Shipwright and Master Attendant, I must desire to refer you to my letter of the 7th October, 1803, and to acquaint you that I should deem it excessively improper to make any addition or alteration whatever in the establishment of his Majesty's Yard at Malta, as the Navy Board must be perfectly aware of the propriety of their appointment; and therefore you must make your application to them on the present, and on all future occasions. I am, &c.,

NELSON AND BRONTE.

TO SIR JOHN ACTON, BART., NAPLES.[2]

[From Clarke and M'Arthur, vol. ii. p. 369.]

[About June 8th, 1804.]

The following observations naturally arise from looking at Europe at this moment. The restoration of a Monarchy in

[2] Though not mentioned in Mr. Elliot's correspondence with Lord Nelson, the following letter from the Queen of Naples (apparently) to Sir John Acton, would show that a report prevailed at Naples, towards the end of May 1804, that Nelson

France, although it may be of disadvantage to the Bourbons, must be beneficial to Europe—the reign of Republics is over for a century; and in particular, both Great Britain and Naples must feel the immediate consequence. If the two Emperors of Russia and Germany, do not acknowledge Buonaparte as Emperor, then, if there be a grain of spirit left in them, they will go to war; and if it be prosecuted with vigour in Italy, I think that all the Italian Republic and Piedmont may be restored. We have both, my dear Sir, lived long enough in the world to know, that Nations are like individuals—make it their interest to do what is right, and they will do it; with very few exceptions of any man, or Nation, being so devoid of principle as to act the part of a villain without an interest. Therefore, if the Italian Republic were to be changed, and submit to a Monarch, I am sure, if the Emperor of Germany, with a large Army, promises his former Subjects more privileges than they have enjoyed under Buonaparte, and also a *quietus* for their purchases of land, &c., they would return to their obedience, and probably behave better than ever.

I feel much obliged for all the particulars you have given me, of the honourable reasons that induced you to retire to Palermo. I well know, that upon every occasion you sacrifice your own feelings, for the benefit of our dear good Sovereigns; and that same feeling induces you not to desert them at this critical moment. I beg that your Excellency will say, that I have received the honour of their Majesties' letters; and although in doing my very utmost I only perform my duty, yet that it shall be done with cheerfulness, and to the full extent of my abilities: the more their Majesties may want my exertions to serve them, the more they shall be given, to the last drop of my blood. I have only to be told their wants and

had been killed in an Action with the French Fleet; but as this letter was originally indorsed " 27th May, 1805," the Queen may have misdated it, in which case and more probably, the rumour was prevalent in the latter year, when Nelson was in pursuit of the Enemy's Fleet:—

" Je suis dans la plus vive inquiétude pour les nouvelles qui se repandent, que dans un combat notre heros sauveur et bienfaiteur Nelson a peri; je vous prie de me vouloir tranquiliser, sur ces nouvelles, qui me tiennent dans les plus vives alarmes, et croyez moi, mon digne Chevalier, avec les constants sentimens qui chez moi sont invariables, votre bien affectionée, CHARLOTTE.—Le 27 Mai, 1804."

wishes, and as far as I am able they shall be complied with. I am in hopes to shame La Touche out of his nest; and when I reflect on his insult [3] to my Sovereigns, at Naples, in 1793, it will add vigour to my attack. My first object must ever be to keep the French Fleet in check; and if they put to sea, to have force enough with me to *annihilate* them; and that, with God's blessing, I have no fear of being able to perform. That would keep the Two Sicilies free from any attack from sea. If the French Fleet could carry 12,000 men into the Bay of Naples, whilst their Army was marching by land, the consequences would be fatal to that Capital. The 2000 Troops are ready at Malta, and it was only on the 7th, that I prayed General Vilettes to keep them in readiness; and if your Excellency were to think it proper to write a confidential letter to the General, I am sure he would be much flattered. I am glad to find Russia thinks properly, and, I trust, there will be no jealousies, but that both Countries will try who can best serve and save the Two Sicilies. Temporizing may be necessary in small States; in large ones it ought not to happen —it is humiliating. Either Peace, or 100,000 Russians and as many Austrians, in Italy; but I cannot help thinking that Buonaparte will wish for Peace rather than a War with two Empires. Again and again, my dear Sir John, you may rely upon me. I am &c.,　　　　　NELSON AND BRONTE.

TO ADMIRAL SIR JOHN BORLASE WARREN, K.B.,
AMBASSADOR AT ST. PETERSBURG.

[From Clarke and M'Arthur, vol. ii. p. 370.]

[About 10th June, 1804.]

The events which are daily happening through the ambition of Buonaparte, are much better known to you than they can be to me, who have now been at sea from the first day of the War, and never had my foot outside the Ship. I hope Russia and Austria will assist the good cause, and Piedmont be restored to the King of Sardinia; but Courts very seldom draw together; and it is the more sincerely to be regretted at this time, when a common interest ought to unite them

closely—but I am touching on a subject out of my depth.
Monsieur La Touche Tréville seems inclined to try his hand
with us, and by my keeping so great an inferiority close
to him, perhaps he may some day be tempted. I am, &c.,

NELSON AND BRONTE.

TO LADY HAMILTON.

[From " Lord Nelson's Letters to Lady Hamilton," vol. ii. p. 53.]

Victory, June 10th, 1804.

My dearest Emma,

I wrote to you, on the 6th, *viâ* Rosas : this goes by Barcelona; to which place I am sending Sir William Bolton, to
fetch Dr. Scott, who is gone there, poor fellow, for the benefit
of his health. I have just had very melancholy letters from
the King and Queen of Naples, on account of General Acton's
going to Sicily. The insolence of Buonaparte was not to be
parried without a War; for which they are unable, if unassisted. I have letters from Acton, May 28, on board the
Archimedes, just going into Palermo. He will probably
return to Naples, unless new events arise : and that may be ;
for a Minister, once out, may find some difficulty in renewing
his post. He has acted with great and becoming spirit.

I am better, but I have been very unwell. It blows, here,
as much as ever. Yesterday, was a little hurricane of wind. I
dare say, Prince Castelcicala knows it by express; if not, you
may tell him, with my best respects. He, and every one else,
may be sure of my attachment to those good Sovereigns.
By this route, I do not choose to say more on this subject.

With my kindest regards to Horatia, and your good mother,
Charlotte, Miss C., and all our friends, believe me, &c.,

NELSON AND BRONTE.

I fear Sardinia will be invaded from Corsica before you get
this letter. I have not small Ships to send there, or anywhere
else; not in the proportion of one to five. You may communicate this to Mr. Addington, if you think that he does
not know it ; but, to no one else, except Castelcicala, of what
relates to Naples. I have very flattering letters from the Grand
Vizir, in the name of the Sultan; and from Cadir, now Capitan
Pacha.

TO NATHANIEL TAYLOR, ESQ., NAVAL OFFICER, MALTA.

[Letter-Book.]

Victory, off Toulon, 12th June, 1804.

Sir,

As it is essentially necessary that the Captain of the Fleet under my command should know the exact remains of every description of stores in his Majesty's magazines under your charge,—I am therefore to desire that you will transmit me an account of the remains of every article of stores by the first opportunity, and continue to do so monthly, that it may at all times be known in case of exigency what dependence may be had upon the stores under your charge. I am, &c.,

NELSON AND BRONTE.

TO THOMAS WARRINGTON,[3] ESQ., NAPLES.

[Letter-Book.]

Victory, off Toulon, 12th June, 1804.

Sir,

I received your letter of the 2nd instant by the Maidstone, acquainting me that Colonel M'Neil, previous to his leaving Malta, transmitted you my acceptance of his proposals to supply the Fleet under my command with one hundred oxen, at a stated price and weight; that you had, in consequence, purchased that number of cattle, which was ready to embark whenever I shall think proper to send for them. In answer to which, I have to acquaint you that Colonel M'Neil delivered Captain Keates of the Superb, when that Ship was at Naples, in July last, proposals for supplying bullocks, &c. to the Squadron—that in September following he offered to supply one or two hundred head of oxen at Naples; in consequence of which I wrote him a letter dated the 1st November, a copy of which is herewith enclosed; and at the same time ordered Transports in readiness to proceed to Naples for a hundred head of oxen, mentioned in the copy of my said letter, which were kept in that state for a considerable time; but not hearing more of this business, the Transports were

[3] Afterwards British Consul at Messina.

sent away, and I considered the matter as entirely gone past, till I received a letter from Colonel M'Neil, dated at Malta, 19th January last, extract of which accompanies this, by which, it appears, that previous to his leaving Naples in November, he had directed you to acquaint me with the earliest time the bullocks in question would be ready, and hoped even at that time, (January,) you had done so: therefore, after such a lapse of time (notwithstanding so many opportunities of communication between Naples and the Squadron) I considered that you had totally relinquished the idea; and Government having in the intermediate time appointed an Agent-Victualler to the Fleet, I have now nothing at all to do with purchases. But as it appears by your said letter that you have purchased a hundred head of cattle for the Squadron, I shall direct the Kent to receive sixty of them from you at Salerno, upon the terms mentioned in Colonel M'Neil's letter of the 26th of July last, a copy of which is herewith enclosed, and shall order the Agent-Victualler to pay you the amount agreeably thereto. The other forty I shall order to be taken from you, as soon after as possible, upon the same terms. I am, &c.,

NELSON AND BRONTE.

TO CAPTAIN PULTENEY MALCOLM, H. M. SHIP KENT.

[Letter-Book.]

Victory, off Toulon, 12th June, 1803.

Sir,

I herewith transmit you a copy of a letter from Mr. Warrington, dated the 2nd instant, together with a copy of my answer, and the several papers therein referred to; and must desire that previous to your leaving Naples, you will give the said Mr. Warrington sufficient notice to bring sixty head of oxen to Salerno, where you will proceed and embark them, for the use of the Fleet, together with a sufficient quantity of fodder to last them during the passage, directing your Purser to draw bills on the Commissioners for Victualling his Majesty's Navy, for the amount, at thirty days. And I must desire to recommend that the sixty bullocks so purchased from Mr. Warrington are of the weight, and not exceeding the price,

mentioned in the copy of Colonel M'Neil's letter to Captain
Keats, dated the 26th July last, by which you will particularly
govern yourself in this transaction, that Government may not
be put to an unnecessary expense on the present occasion, or
the bullocks be inferior in weight or quantity to what is considered an agreement.   I must also desire that you will
transmit the whole of these papers, from No. 1 to 5, to the
Officer who I shall think proper to send to Naples, together
with a copy of this letter, in order that he may proceed to
Salerno, and bring with him the other forty bullocks from
Mr. Warrington, who is hereby directed to pay for them in the
same manner, and to govern himself agreeably to the said
instructions.   I am, &c.,

                                   NELSON AND BRONTE.

                  TO THE GRAND VIZIR.

            [From Clarke and M'Arthur, vol. ii. p. 371.]

                                      13th June, 1804.

  Buonaparte, by whatever name he may choose to call himself—General, Consul, or Emperor—is the same man we have
always known, and the common disturber of the human race;
it is much more dangerous to be his friend than his enemy.
With the appearance of friendship he deceives; to be on the
latter terms, the hand should be always on the sword.   May
God grant his Imperial Majesty health and length of days,
and may your Highness for many, many years, guide his
councils with your wisdom.   I beg of your Highness to assure
his Imperial Majesty, that I am penetrated with his condescension in remembering my former exertions in the execution of my duty: whilst my health remains, they shall never
cease.   Other Admirals will readily be found of probably
more abilities, but none with more zeal to cement the harmony
and perfect good understanding between our two good Sovereigns.   The French Fleet is quite safe in Toulon, and for
the summer they cannot readily escape without a Battle.
May God give the victory to the just cause.   I am, &c.

                                   NELSON AND BRONTE.

TO MR. STODDARD, GENOA.[1]

[From Clarke and M'Arthur, vol. ii. p. 363. " Friday, 15th June, 1804" (*i. e.*, the afternoon of Thursday, the 14th of June.) "At 4·30, bore up for the Grand Pass of the Hières Islands; set studding-sails and royals. At 5, observed the Enemy's Ships coming out of Toulon: in studding-sails and royals, and hauled in Line of Battle on the starboard tack, the Enemy's Ships consisting of eight Sail of the Line and four Frigates. Wore Ship. At 7·35, tacked; in 1st and 2nd reefs topsails. Moderate and clear. Cape Sicie, bore N.W..b N., dist. 7 leagues, and the S.E. end of Porquerolle bore N.E. b E. ½ E., distant 7 miles. Fresh breezes; in 3rd reefs topsails, down jib and handed the mainsail. At 12·20, wore Ship. At 1·30 [A.M. of Friday, 15th], wore and hove-to. At 3·45, out 3rd reef topsails; set the foresail. 4, wore, and set the mainsail and spanker. Out 2nd reefs; set top gallant sails and royals. In royals and stay-sails. Cape Sicie bore N. ½ W., dist. 7 or eight leagues. Tacked; moderate and clear. Out 1st reef topsails, and set the royals. Bore up to the E.N.E. At noon, the N.W. end of Porquerolle bore E. by N. ¼ N., dist. 11 miles. Squadron in company."

. . . . " Sunday, 17th June, 1804. Saw the detached Squadron bearing N.E. b E. Set studding-sails and royals. Out launch. Shortened sail, and joined all the Squadron—viz., Royal Sovereign, Triumph, Leviathan, Renown, Active, Seahorse, Maidstone, Thunder, Acheron, Etna, and three Transports. Employed getting on board bread from the Chatham Transport."—*Victory's Log.*]

16th June, 1804.

I am blockading Genoa, &c., and am continuing it in the way I think most proper. Whether modern law or ancient law makes my mode right, I cannot judge; and surely of the mode of disposing of a Fleet, I must, if I am fit for my post, be a better judge than any landsman, however learned he

---

[4] Clarke and M'Arthur, vol. ii. p. 362, give fragments of two other Letters from Lord Nelson to Mr. Stoddard, at Genoa, one written in March, 1804; but no date is assigned to the other:—" In writing, during the month of March, to Mr. Stoddard, at Genoa, his Lordship thus answered some objections that had been made respecting the blockade of that Port, and the seizure of Vessels: ' It is my bounden duty, Sir, to make these seizures, and they will be continued until the Admiralty order the contrary. Whether the Admiralty be right, or wrong, in giving these orders, is not my business: *obedience* is my duty. . . . . . Eleven years' experience has taught me how to blockade Genoa, or any other Port in the Mediterranean, and the capture of Vessels breaking the blockade, is, I believe, a full proof of it.' In a subsequent letter, he added: ' In my humble opinion, Vessels of War never ought to be seen from Genoa; and if I knew of forty Sail intending to leave Genoa for Cadiz or Lisbon, for instance, I should order a look out to be kept for them more particularly in the Gut of Gibraltar, than any other place; and, from my knowledge of Genoa and its Gulf, I assert, without fear of contradiction, that the nearer Ships cruise to Genoa, the more certain is the escape of Vessels from that Port, or their entrance into it insured.' "

may appear. It would be the act of a fool to tell Europe where I intend to place the Ships, for the purpose of effectually obeying my orders; not a Captain can know it, and their positions will vary, according to information I may receive: therefore, if I were so inclined, I cah assure you, upon my word, that I cannot at any one moment tell the most likely spot to intercept the commerce of Genoa and Especia. I endeavour, as well as I am able, to obey my orders, without entering into the nice distinctions of lawyers I will not further take up your time on a subject which, without being a lawyer, merely as a man, could have admitted of no dispute. I am, &c.

NELSON AND BRONTE.

TO THE CAPTAIN OR COMMANDER OF ANY OF HIS MAJESTY'S SHIPS OR VESSELS IN THE ADRIATIC.

[Letter-Book.]

Victory, at Sea, 18th June, 1804.

Sir,

Should his Excellency Thomas Jackson, Esq., his Britannic Majesty's Minister to the King of Sardinia, judge it necessary, from the Political circumstances of that Country, to leave Rome, it is my directions, upon this letter being produced, that you immediately receive Mr. Jackson, his suite, and baggage, on board his Majesty's Ship or Vessel under your command, and proceed with them to Trieste, Venice, or any other Port in the Adriatic where his Excellency may desire, and you shall think perfectly consistent with the safety of his Majesty's Ship [to go.] Having performed this service, you are immediately to return to the execution of your former orders. I am, &c.

NELSON AND BRONTE.

TO THE COMMISSIONERS FOR VICTUALLING HIS MAJESTY'S
NAVY, LONDON.

[Letter-Book.]

Victory, at Sea, 18th June, 1804.

Gentlemen,

As the substitution of rice for cheese is not in general
liked by the Ships' Companies, who do not take up near their
allowance of that species of provisions, it may, therefore,
shortly be expected that lists of the savings of rice as cheese,
will be delivered to me, by the respective Captains of the
Fleet under my command, for payment. I must, therefore,
desire to acquaint you therewith; and that as it has been the
custom of this Country to pay the Ships' Companies their
savings of oil as butter and cheese, and the measure appearing to me so just and reasonable, that the savings of rice as
cheese should be paid for as savings of the latter, that I can
have no doubt of its propriety. But as the quantities may be
considerable, it is my wish that the payment of such savings
should have the approbation and authority of your Board,
and, therefore, I request that you will furnish me with your
regulations on this subject accordingly. I am, &c.

NELSON AND BRONTE.

TO CAPTAIN PULTENEY MALCOLM, H.M. SHIP KENT.

[Autograph, in the possession of Rear-Admiral Sir Charles Malcolm.]

Victory, June 18th, 1804.

Dear Sir,

I am much obliged by your letter of June 3rd, by the
Maidstone. If the French do stop our supplies from Naples,
we shall do very well. I have always looked too far forward,
ever to be really distressed; but I dare say anything may be
got off from Naples, with prudent management. When you
come away, which will be in about a month, if Mr. Warrington has, on account of Colonel M'Neil, bought 100 head of
cattle for the Fleet, you will have to go to Salerno, to take
them on board; and you will take care that all impediments
are removed, before you proceed there. The price, weight,

&c., is fixed, and will be sent you with the order. I approve very much of Mr. Taylor's return to Malta. It never was my intention that he should [go] further than to arrange matters, and that the articles were not to be paid for, until delivered to the Kent, or other King's Ship. I thank you for your letter of May 24th, and for the newspaper, which was very interesting. I am, dear Sir, your obliged and obedient servant,

NELSON AND BRONTE.

TO HIS EXCELLENCY HUGH ELLIOT, ESQ.

[Autograph, in the Elliot Papers.]

Victory, June 18th, 1804.

My dear Sir,

By the Maidstone I was favoured with your truly interesting letters respecting the removal of. Sir John Acton. The General must, I think, possess more than ever the confidence of both our, and the Russian Ministry, from the very circumstance of his being so much hated by the French. Gallo and Micheroux never can. They have shown, on all occasions, too evident a partiality to the French, or, to say no worse, dislike to us. I am obliged by your sending me the letter from Sir John Warren, which your Excellency did most perfectly right in reading. I beg to trouble you with an answer, which the Russian Minister will forward. I was in hopes to hear of 100,000 Russians, and as many Austrians, coming into Italy—that would do everything which we could wish. The changes of Ministry can make none in our connexions with Foreign Powers; but I still think it may bring about a Peace.

We are as usual: the French Fleet safe in Toulon; but, upon the 14th, Monsr. La Touche came out with eight Sail of the Line and six Frigates, cut a caper off Sepet, and went in again. I was off with five Ships of the Line, and brought to for his attack, although I did not believe that anything was meant serious, but merely a gasconade. I wrote to General Acton, by the Fame[4] on the 10th; but he desired me to answer

<hr>

[4] A Neapolitan Corvette, which had brought Lord Nelson dispatches off Toulon.

the King and Queen's letter by a Corvette of my own, which I have not been able to do till last night. Doctor Scott is translating my letters into Italian for the King, and French for the Queen.

My health has been, latterly, but very so-so, and I wish the French Fleet would give me an early opportunity of finishing my career; for I do not believe it possible for me to stand the hard service of another winter. I am ever, with the highest respect and esteem, your Excellency's most obedient servant,

NELSON AND BRONTE.

Pray keep the Bomb as short a time as possible; for I am distressed enough by the non-arrival of the Termagant. You will, I am sure, take care that my letters get to the King and Queen without being opened. There is one for Acton in the King's, as he desired. William is very well on board the Amazon.

TO SIR JOHN ACTON, BART., NAPLES.

[From Clarke and M'Arthur, vol. ii. p. 372.]

18th June, 1804.

The great change of Ministry cannot, unless it gives us Peace, which I think by no means improbable, make any alterations respecting Russia, and the assistance which our Country is in duty and honour bound to give Naples. I trust that Austria will also assist in preventing this new Charlemagne from possessing the old Empire. Monsr. La Touche came out on the 14th. I was off the Hières with five Ships; he had eight of the Line and six Frigates. In the evening he stood under Sepet again; and, I believe I may call it, we chased him into Toulon the morning of the 15th. I am satisfied he meant nothing beyond a gasconade; but am confident, when he is ordered for any service, that he will risk falling in with us, and the event of a Battle, to try and accomplish his orders. I am, &c.

NELSON AND BRONTE.

TO NATHANIEL TAYLOR, ESQ., NAVAL OFFICER, MALTA.

[Letter-Book.]

Victory, at Sea, 18th June, 1804.

Sir,

As it is impossible that any general order can apply itself to all circumstances, or shut the door of purchases when they are, from unforeseen causes, absolutely necessary, I must therefore desire that you will regard my order and letter of the 20th March last, as meant only to preclude the unnecessary purchase of stores, and to prevent any Senior Captain arriving at Malta, from giving orders to purchase stores, either for his own Ship, or general service, to which there would be no end. But I wish it to be perfectly understood, that whilst I desire the utmost regard to be had to prevent the unnecessary purchase of stores, his Majesty's Ships or Vessels arriving at Malta in want of repairs must not be delayed on any account. You will, consequently, after having acquainted the Senior Officer with the deficiency of the Stores under your charge, procure his approbation for the purchase of such articles as may be absolutely wanted for the particular service of the moment, till the arrival of Store Ships, which order I will approve of, upon its being transmitted to me for that purpose. I am, &c.,

NELSON AND BRONTE.

N.B.—If you will specify the quantity of canvas purchased for the repairs of sails, as mentioned in your letter of the 17th March, an order shall be transmitted you for that purpose.

TO NATHANIEL TAYLOR, ESQ., NAVAL OFFICER, MALTA.

[Letter-Book.]

Victory, at Sea, 18th June, 1804.

Sir,

For the very great want of slops for the different Ships of the Fleet under my command, I must desire, as there is none in the stores under your charge, that you will purchase a sufficient quantity of Malta cotton, of the quality and width of the enclosed pattern, to make five thousand banyans, and five thousand pairs of trowsers. The quantity required to make each banyan and pair of trowsers to be cut out at Malta, and the necessary quantity of thread, with four moulds for each, put up with them ; and I must also desire that you will send a particular account of the price of each banyan and pair of trowsers, including thread, (of which plenty must be sent,) and moulds, to me, that the distinct charge of each article may be entered on the respective Ship's Books. It must be remembered, that if the cotton so purchased is not agreeable to the pattern, it will be returned, without any allowance being made for it. I am, &c.

NELSON AND BRONTE.

TO WILLIAM MARSDEN, ESQ., ADMIRALTY.

[Letter-Book.]

Victory, at Sea, 20th June, 1804.

Sir,

As there is doubt that the late Private Signals, established for his Majesty's Brigs, Cutters, Luggers, &c., on this station, commanded by Lieutenants, were taken in the Swift Cutter, I herewith transmit you a Sheet of Signals altered on the 10th instant, and issued to the different Ships under my command, which you will please to lay before the Lords Commissioners of the Admiralty, in order that their Lordships may direct Lieutenants commanding Vessels of the above description sent to this Country, to be furnished with them previous to their leaving England. I am, &c.

NELSON AND BRONTE.

TO CAPTAIN RICHARD HUSSEY MOUBRAY, H.M. SHIP ACTIVE.[5]

[Order-Book.]

Victory, at Sea, 20th June, 1804.

Whereas it is my intention to intercept and cut off all commerce between Italy and the Enemy's Ports at Marseilles

[5] On the 23rd of June, Captain Donnelly, in the Narcissus, was ordered to relieve the Active on this service ; and that Ship was directed to join Lord Nelson immediately.—Order Book.

and Toulon, You are hereby required and directed to take his Majesty's Ships named in the margin[6] under your command, and proceed with them immediately to the Hières Islands, where you will anchor, or cruise between that and Cape Taillat, as you may from circumstances judge most likely to fall in with and destroy the Enemy's commerce, or any of their Vessels of War which may accompany it. The strictest attention, however, must be paid, and a good look-out kept on all occasions upon the Enemy, that you are not surprised by a superior force ; and I must also desire that you endeavour to keep the Squadron, which I am about to proceed with off Toulon, as much as possible in sight, and endeavour to communicate with me by Boat, or otherwise send a Brig, once in forty-eight hours, at least ; and should the Enemy come out in force, and you judge that they intend to bring on an Action, you will immediately join me with the Ships under your command.

NELSON AND BRONTE.

TO HIS EXCELLENCY MR. JACKSON.

[From Clarke and M'Arthur, vol. ii. p. 373.]

[About 20th June, 1804.]

I have been favoured with your account of what had passed at Cività Vecchia, respecting a Spanish Vessel detained by an English Privateer. The conduct of all Privateers is, as far as I have seen, so near piracy, that I only wonder any civilized Nation can allow them. The lawful as well as unlawful commerce of the Neutral flag is subject to every violation and spoliation ; but I do not believe that any Foreign Power can make itself a judge, whether the detention be legal or not. The Spanish Consul, if he thought the conduct of the English Privateer wrong by an unjust detention, had only to apply to the Court of Vice-Admiralty at Gibraltar or Malta. You know, my dear Sir, that no person in our Country can interfere with the laws. I am always sorry when unpleasant circumstances arise. You will see by the enclosed papers, the supposed improper conduct of the Papal

---

[6] Amazon, Maidstone, Thunder, Childers, Cameleon.

Government at Ancona; but I do not enter into the subject, for I cannot be a judge by only hearing one side. I admit the very unpleasant situation of the Papal Government; for I am well aware, if they were just in their Neutrality, that Buonaparte would take Rome from his Holiness, as he has done before: I have always directed the Neutrality of the Papal State to be attended to. I am, &c.

NELSON AND BRONTE.

DISPOSITION OF HIS MAJESTY'S SHIPS AND VESSELS ON THE MEDITERRANEAN STATION, UNDER THE COMMAND OF THE RIGHT HONOURABLE LORD NELSON, K.B., DUKE OF BRONTE.

[Letter-Book.]

Victory, off Toulon, 21st June, 1804.

Victory, Royal Sovereign, Canopus, Donegal, Belleisle, Triumph, Leviathan, Renown, Seahorse, Active, Amazon, Maidstone, Childers, Cameleon, Thunder-Bomb—Cruizing with the Commander-in-Chief off Toulon.

Medusa, Amphion—Cruizing outside the Straits for the protection of our Trade bound into the Mediterranean, and the destruction of the Enemy's Privateers and Cruisers, to continue on this service until further orders, under Captain Gore.

Halcyon, La Sophie—Ordered to cruize between Ceuta and Cape Spartel for the protection of our Trade in the Straits of Gibraltar, and destruction of the Enemy's Privateers and Cruisers—affording Lieutenant-General Sir Thomas Trigge every assistance he may require for the health and comfort of the Garrison. To continue on this service till relieved, under the Senior Officer's orders.

Anson, Arrow, Bittern, Morgiana, Jalouse—Cruising from the mouth of the Archipelago along the Adriatic, as far as Ancona, for the purpose of keeping the Adriatic open to the Trade of his Majesty's Subjects, and to prevent the Enemy from sending Troops into the Morea: to afford every protection to our Trade, and to appoint Convoys, not only from Malta up the Adriatic, but also to bring the Trade from

Trieste, Venice, Fiume, Patras, Zante, &c., to Valetta Harbour, and to render every assistance to our commerce.

Juno—Cruizing off Cape St. Sebastian, for the purpose of communicating occasionally with Barcelona, and of obtaining intelligence of the intentions of Spain : also to inform any of the Ships ordered to that Rendezvous, where I may be found with the Squadron.

Agincourt, 19th April, 1804—Ordered to proceed to Gibraltar, in company with the Argo, to receive her lower-deck guns on board, and to escort that Ship, and the Convoy which may be under her protection, twenty or twenty-five leagues to the Westward of Cadiz. After having so done, to return to Gibraltar, and take such Trade as are bound up the Mediterranean to Valetta Harbour, where Captain Briggs will be joined by the Thisbe, and proceed from thence, with our Levant Ships, &c., to Gibraltar and England.

Kent—26th April, Ordered to proceed to Naples for the purpose of relieving the Gibraltar, and to remain there till the arrival of the Renown, in July next, (to execute my secret order, in the possession of our Minister at that Court, should the political circumstances of that Country render it necessary,) when I shall order her to England, most probably attended by a Transport—her hull being in so bad a state as makes it unsafe to trust her, even at this season of the year, as mentioned in my letter of the 28th May.

Superb—16th May, Ordered to proceed to Malta, for the purpose of partially repairing her defects—afterwards to procure from Sir Alexander Ball, a person perfectly acquainted with the Lingua Franca, spoke at Algiers, to which place he is to proceed with the utmost dispatch, and endeavour to accomplish the object of his mission to the Dey. Captain Keats is directed to take a Cutter, or Vessel of War, with him from Malta, and to return her from Algiers to Valetta Harbour, with an account of the result to Sir Alexander Ball, and to join me in the Superb without loss of time.

Niger—19th May, Ordered to Malta, to get carronades from the Madras in lieu of her nine-pounders, and to be otherwise completed as a 28-gun Frigate, agreeably to the Admiralty establishment. Having so done, to join me without loss of time.

Gibraltar—28th May, Ordered to Gibraltar to repair her masts and rigging only, agreeably to their Lordships' directions; but from the excessive bad state of her hull, I have directed Commissioner Otway, if she cannot be made an efficient Ship for a winter's cruize in these seas, not to enter upon her repairs, but to signify the same officially by letter to Captain Ryves, who I have ordered, in such case, to return and join me immediately, for the purpose of proceeding to Malta as a Convoy to our Trade from the Archipelago and Levant bound to Gibraltar and England.

Termagant—1st June 1804, Ordered to Naples with my public dispatches for his Excellency Mr. Elliot, and to return and join me with his answer without delay.

Narcissus—11th June, Ordered to the Madalena Islands to repair her bowsprit, and complete her wood and water; afterwards to join me with all dispatch.

Excellent—19th June, Ordered to take the Chatham Victualler, with empty water-casks from the Fleet, and proceed to Porto Conte, in the Island of Sardinia, for the purpose of filling them, and completing her own wood and water, with the utmost dispatch; and afterwards to join me without delay, bringing as many live bullocks for the Fleet as the Excellent can conveniently stow.

Phœbe—19th June, Ordered to the Bay of Rosas, with the Thetis Transport, for the above purpose, and to join me immediately after.

Acheron Bomb—19th June, Ordered to Naples with my public dispatches for his Majesty's Minister, and to join me immediately after.

Ætna Bomb—19th June, Ordered to proceed to Malta, with two empty Victuallers, and to bring a Transport, loaded with bread, back to the Fleet.

Madras—Prison-ship *pro tempore* at Malta.

Spider Brig, and Renard Schooner—Ordered to protect the Trade at Malta, and to proceed with dispatches to wherever Sir Alexander Ball may require.

L'Hirondelle—Ordered to be purchased into his Majesty's Service at Malta, and to be considered as attached to that Island, under the immediate directions of Sir Alexander Ball, as above.

NELSON AND BRONTE.

TO THE RIGHT HONOURABLE LORD MELVILLE, FIRST LORD
OF THE ADMIRALTY.

[From Clarke and M'Arthur, vol. ii. p. 373.]

21st June, 1804.
My dear Lord,

In case Earl St. Vincent and Sir Thomas Troubridge
should not send you my letters to them, respecting the conduct of Soldiers embarked to serve in his Majesty's Ships, I
think it of great consequence to the Naval Service, you should
be informed of my sentiments upon that subject. It requires
not the gift of prescience to assert, if Soldiers embarked in
Ships of War are not, as heretofore, left subject to the Act of
Parliament for the government of his Majesty's Ships, Vessels,
and Forces by Sea, whereon, as our forefathers said, 'the safety,
wealth, and prosperity of the Kingdom chiefly depend,' that
the Navy, which we have all heretofore looked up to, will be
ruined. The absolute power must remain; there cannot be
two Commanders in one Ship, nor two sets of laws to regulate
the conduct of those embarked in the same bottom. I will
not, my Lord, take up your time in debating, whether it
would be better for the Navy to be subject to the same
Articles of War as the Army; but we may take a lesson from
the epitaph, 'I was well; I would be better, and here I am:'
my opinion is, 'Let well alone.' I am, &c.,
                                NELSON AND BRONTE.

TO LORD HAWKESBURY.

[From Clarke and M'Arthur, vol. ii. p. 374.]

22nd June, 1804.

His Majesty was supported by the Russian Minister, and
your Lordship's words were quoted to me: the consequence
will be the loss of Sardinia—either France or England must
have it. The loss to us will be great indeed. I do not think
that the Fleet can then be kept at sea. From Sardinia we
get water and fresh provisions; the loss of it would cut us off
from Naples except by a circuitous route, for all the purposes
of getting refreshments, even were Naples able to supply us.

I have hitherto watched Sardinia ; but at this moment, when from the bad condition of many of the Ships under my command, I can barely keep a sufficient force at sea to attend to the French Fleet, I have not Ships to send to Madalena: not less, my Lord, than ten Frigates, and as many good Sloops, would enable me to do what I wish, and what, of course, I think absolutely necessary. But I am aware of the great want of them in England, and that other services must be starved to take care of home. If I were at your Lordship's elbow, I think I could say so much upon the subject of Sardinia, that attempts would be made to obtain it ; for this I hold as clear, that the King of Sardinia cannot keep it, and, if he could, that it is of no use to him ; that if France gets it, she commands the Mediterranean; and that by us it would be kept at a much smaller expense than Malta: from its position, it is worth fifty Maltas. Should the War continue, the blockade of Marseilles is a measure absolutely essential, and the points necessary for us to occupy are to be considered, and I think I could satisfy your Lordship of the probability of holding those positions : nothing could distress France so much, and make her wish for Peace with us at present. Not less than forty Sail a week go into Marseilles . . . . . I will not trouble your Lordship with a longer letter on the various objects well worthy of consideration within the Mediterranean, and which the experience of eleven years has made me turn my thoughts to. I am, &c.,

NELSON AND BRONTE.

TO THE RIGHT HONOURABLE LORD MELVILLE.

[From Clarke and M'Arthur, vol. ii. p. 374.]

22nd June, 1804.

It is to redeem the solemn pledge I have made, never to omit, upon any change of Administration, stating the just claim which I consider the Battle of Copenhagen has to the reward of Medals, such as have been given for other great Naval victories: I therefore inclose for your Lordship's perusal a statement of facts, and the letters which passed between me and Earl St. Vincent upon that occasion;[8] and when your Lordship has leisure time, I request your perusal of them ..... I am aware, my Lord, that his Majesty has the most undisputed right to bestow Medals, or to withhold them, as he pleases. No man admits it more fully than myself; but, my Lord, I turn back to the 1st of June 1794; from that moment I have ever considered, that his Majesty, by implication, pronounced these words to his Fleet, holding forth the Medal ‘This, my Fleet, is the great reward which I will bestow for great and important Victories like the present!’ Considering this as a solemn pledge, his Majesty gave it as the reward for the Battles of St. Vincent, of Camperdown, and the Nile: then comes the most difficult achievement, the hardest-fought battle, the most glorious result that ever graced the Naval Annals of our Country : the Medal is withheld, for what reason Lord St. Vincent best knows. Could it be said that the Danes were not brave ? the contrary has always been shown. Was our force so superior that there was no merit in gaining the Victory? If guns made the superiority, the Danes were very superior. If it be said, ‘Ay, but your Ships were superior:’ to that I can answer, that the force placed by the Danes for the preservation of their Arsenal, their Fleet, and the City of Copenhagen, was such, and of that description of Vessels, which they thought inexpugnable by any force that could be brought against it. I have no more to say, but beg to refer your Lordship to the papers sent herewith; and I hope, in the name of those brave Commanders who were under my orders on the glorious 2nd of April 1801, for your recommendation to his Majesty, that he may be pleased to bestow that mark of honour on the Battle of Copenhagen, which his goodness has given to the Battles of St. Vincent, the 1st of June, of Camperdown, and the Nile. I am, &c.,

NELSON AND BRONTE.[9]

[8] Vide vol. iv. p. 526.
[9] Lord Melville's answer to this letter is printed in vol. iv. p. 527.

TO CAPTAIN ROSS DONNELLY, H. M. SHIP NARCISSUS.

[Autograph, in the possession of the late Adam Bromilow, Esq. Sunday, 24th June, about Noon.—" The French Ships in Toulon fired a salute."—*Victory's Log.*]

Victory, 27th June, 1804.

My dear Sir,

I am glad that the Narcissus did not suffer the other day, and I am sure you will do all you can to annoy the Enemy. I really am of opinion that it will force La Touche out, therefore, be prepared to join me. I send the Termagant for her men, and I wish you to send the Childers with Termagant to join me, as I want their services. We have nothing new. When we have, you shall know it. Ever, my dear Sir, yours faithfully,

NELSON AND BRONTE.

Compliments to all around you, and may success attend you!

TO THE RIGHT HONOURABLE LORD HAWKESBURY.

[Autograph, in the Colonial Office.]

Victory, June 29th, 1804.

My Lord,

In my letter of May 31st, I acquainted Lord Hobart that I had sent Captain Keats to Algiers, &c., and that the moment he returned I should inform his Lordship of the result of Captain Keats' mission. The Superb returned yesterday; and I transmit your Lordship Captain Keats' very intelligent letters and papers, by which you will see that things at Algiers are better than they were, but not so well as we could wish.

With great deference, from giving the papers all the attention in my power, and from the very intelligent explanations of Captain Keats, I venture to lay my opinion before your Lordship—that the Ape, being *bonâ fide* the property of an English Merchant, and with a cargo belonging to Government, although the Master and crew were actually Neapolitans and Sicilians, must be given up, with her whole crew; for we must never allow the principle of their interpretation of that part of our Treaty, and we are bound in honour not to leave those poor people in slavery. Had the Dey yielded this point, and granted a further remuneration for a Maltese Vessel which was sold, and the amount paid to the Maltese, although a further sum is demanded, and, I believe, admitted by the Dey's Ministers to be just, I should have had no difficulty in placing a Pro-Consul at Algiers, and left the other points for discussion, or to be given up as his Majesty might think proper to direct.

I am of opinion that the four Vessels recently taken in April 1803, and May the same year, are, although with British Passes, not entitled to any protection from us. Allowing the Dey's to be a legitimate warfare, what would Sir William Scott say to a French Ship, French crew, French cargo, with the Dey's Passport?—Condemn. The other small Vessels, taken four or five years past, are, I believe, hopeless ; the crews have been restored; even Mr. Falcon gives them up as a lost case. Therefore, the Dey having for him made fully the *amende honorable* for his conduct to Mr. Falcon, there is only the Ape and a further remuneration for the Maltese Vessel, which prevents perfect harmony being restored. Mr. M'Donough, who has been our Pro-Consul at Tripoli, and who was so good as to attend Captain Keats, is going to England, therefore I shall direct the Vessel which carries him to Gibraltar to put into Algiers, in order that your Lordship may be informed, whether the Dey still continues to refuse our just demand about the Ape, on which, probably, will depend his Majesty sending another Consul to Algiers.

Had all matters been amicably settled, I should have appointed Mr. M'Donough Consul *pro tempore*, as, from all accounts I have heard of him for several years past at Tripoli, he strikes me as being most perfectly qualified for the office of Consul. I never saw the gentleman, but shall when the weather moderates; I am therefore perfectly disinterested, except for the public good.

The more I hear of Mr. Falcon, the more I have reason to be satisfied of his being a gentleman qualified for a far superior situation to that of Consul at Algiers. Upon the whole, it appears that the mode of conduct which I have pursued towards Algiers, has given them great uneasiness. Not a Cruiser has been at sea this year; and I ought not to conclude my letter without assuring your Lordship that I con-

sider Captain Keats' conduct to have been such, through the
whole of this very delicate mission, as to merit his being
mentioned to the King. I have, &c.

NELSON AND BRONTE.

TO THE RIGHT HONOURABLE LORD HAWKESBURY.

[Autograph, in the Colonial Office.]

Victory, June 30th, 1804.

My Lord,

I send your Lordship a translation of the Dey of Algiers'
letter to me, and my answer, which I hope your Lordship
will approve. Should my reasonable demands be complied
with, it is my intention to place Mr. M'Donough in the situation of Consul at Algiers; and from my former knowledge of
his abilities, and from the conversation I have held with him
this day, I really think him a gentleman every way qualified
to be Consul at Algiers, or any other of the Regencies of
Barbary. I much wish that Mr. Longford, the Consul sent
out to Tripoli, may answer our purpose with the Bashaw of
Tripoli; but I more than fear, whatever abilities Mr. L. may
possess, that the situation of Consul to a Barbary Power, is
not suited to either his abilities or disposition. Your Lordship will be informed that, both in the last and present War,
the Bashaw of Tripoli has consented, if it is necessary, in the
event of the French getting to Egypt, to allow of our occupy-
ing Derne, a most important station, to prevent the French
having a communication with Egypt. I have sent Mr.
M'Donough in a Sloop of War, with my letter to the Dey of
Algiers. If it answers my wishes, Mr. M'Donough will
return to me, and I shall send Captain Keats to place him in
his Office; if not, he will present your Lordship with this
letter. Your Lordship will find him very equal to give you
much information. Mr. M'Donough has had no remuneration from me; that I leave to your Lordship's liberality and
justice. I have, &c.

NELSON AND BRONTE.

TO THE RIGHT HONOURABLE HENRY ADDINGTON.

[Autograph, in the Sidmouth Papers.]

Victory, 30th June, 1804.

My dear Sir,

Friend I may call thee now, without the suspicion of adulation to a Minister; but believe me, that my opinion of your honourable abilities as a Minister, and your constant friendship for me as a man, have ever held the same place in my heart. I feel pride in avowing it, now you are a private gentleman. I will not say too much, because when a change takes place, if honourable men are to take the helm, I am sure amongst the foremost will be placed one Henry Addington, whose sincere friend is ever his attached and obliged,

NELSON AND BRONTE.

I shall see you before Christmas; for I am almost worn out and blind.

TO COMMISSIONER OTWAY, GIBRALTAR.

[Letter-Book.]

Victory, at Sea, 30th June, 1804.

Sir,

As many of the Ships in the Squadron are in want of caulking, I am to desire you will be so good as order twenty barrels of pitch, and ten of rosin, to be sent by the first opportunity for the above purpose; but should there not be any rosin in store, you will send thirty barrels of pitch. You will also order the lower masts to be kept in the greatest state of preparation, and a foremast for the Triumph, which ought to have been put in when she was last at Gibraltar. That Ship will be sent to the Rock as soon as circumstances of service will admit. I am, &c.,

NELSON AND BRONTE.

TO WILLIAM MARSDEN, ESQ., ADMIRALTY.

[Letter-Book.]

Victory, at Sea, 30th June, 1804.

Sir,

Commissioner Otway having informed me that by the present plan of having the Mail brought from Lisbon to Faro, by land, the letters become liable to a very heavy postage, and that there are now many letters in the Post-Office, for the Seamen and Petty Officers of the Fleet, unredeemed; I therefore request you will please to communicate to the Lords Commissioners of the Admiralty, that from the very high charge of postage from Lisbon, it is impossible that the Seamen and Petty Officers can redeem their letters, and submit to their Lordships the propriety of directing the postage thereof, being paid by Government, as I understand has been done on some former occasions. I am, &c.

NELSON AND BRONTE.

TO B. M'DONOUGH, ESQ., BRITISH CONSUL AT ALGIERS.

[From a Copy in the Colonial Office.]

Victory, June 30th, 1804.

Sir,

I beg leave to return you many thanks for your readiness in attending Captain Keats to Algiers, and for your conduct in transacting the business between Captain Keats, the Dey, and his Ministers.

I have now to request your further services, which may prove of great National importance, and in the execution of them, that you will be guided by the instructions transmitted herewith for your guidance. I have not offered you any pecuniary recompence for your services, as I am sure Lord Hawkesbury will have the greatest pleasure in doing the thing in a handsome manner. Accept again, Sir, my sincere thanks, and believe me, &c.

NELSON AND BRONTE.

TO B. M'DONOUGH, ESQ.

[Autograph Draught, in the possession of James Young, Esq., of Wells.]

1st July, 1804.

Sir,

You will herewith receive my letter to his Highness the Dey of Algiers, and proceed in his Majesty's Sloop Termagant to Algiers, the Commander of her having my orders to receive you on board. On your landing at Algiers you will go to the Ministers, and tell them that you have a letter from me to his Highness, which you desire they will deliver to him.

They will naturally inquire of you what are the contents of my letter, and if everything is amicably settled; to which you will reply in such a manner as the occasion calls for, and according to the purport of my letter, a copy of which is hereunto annexed. You will give them to understand that you are merely a passenger on your way to Gibraltar, and that unless the Dey wishes to see you, that you have no business with him. You may safely assert from your knowledge of me, and from what you have heard me say, that the British Sloop Ape, and her whole crew, is a point which never will be given up; and you may express my astonishment at her capture and detention, and much more that she should not have been given up directly to Captain Keats.

Should my demands in respect to the Ape and her crew be complied with, you will state the loss at 5000 hard dollars; and with respect to the other case of further remuneration for the St. Antonio de Padua, that shall be settled amicably; and that until these two points are settled, that I never will send an English Consul to Algiers, but that the moment these just demands are complied with, that I will send a Consul to arrange amicably the other matters.

Should the business terminate favourably, you will return to me from Gibraltar with all expedition, as I wish to place you as Consul to Algiers, and transmit my letter to the Right Honourable Lord Hobart; but should matters, contrary to my wishes and just expectations, not be *amicably settled*, in that case you will give *his Lordship an account of your proceedings*, deliver my letter to Lord Hawkesbury, and explain

to him your opinion upon the present state of affairs, not only
in Algiers, but also in Tripoli. Wishing you every success, I
am, Sir, with great respect, your most obedient servant,

NELSON AND BRONTE.

TO THE DEY OF ALGIERS.

[Autograph draught, in the possession of James Young, Esq., of Wells.]

Victory, at Sea, 1st July, 1804.

Sir,

I have received your Highness's letter of June 15th, by
Captain Keats ; and he has explained to me your Highness's
solemn declaration, that, in future, you never will commit
such an indignity to his Majesty, as sending off his Agent and
Consul-General to the Regency of Algiers. Captain Keats
has also informed me, that he had, according to your wishes,
talked over with your Ministers the precise situation of the
several Vessels taken with Passes from the Governor of
Malta.

Upon several of them much may be said on both sides,
and time might be allowed for serious and deliberate discussion, that strict justice might be done without endangering
the harmony which ought ever to subsist between his Majesty
and the Regency of Algiers, and which I have done everything in my power to preserve, in interesting myself for the
removal of Mr. Falcon, who it appears was not a pleasant
Consul to your Highness. Your Highness' utmost wishes
being gratified in these respects, it is with no small degree
of surprise I observe that your Highness should by your own
act prevent a Consul being placed at Algiers, by the detention
of a bonâ fide English Vessel called the Ape, with an English
cargo, under the pretence that the Vessel was not navigated
with one-third of her crew English. Such a pretence (where
the two first and only real objects for detention were perfectly
clear—viz., the Ship and cargo being English) ought to have
subjected the Rais who seized her to your Highness's severest
punishment; and I did expect that my worthy friend Captain
Keats would have brought me an account of your Highness's
having delivered up the Ape and her whole crew, wherever
they may have happened to be born, with many apologies for

her unjust detention; and also, promised such further remuneration as to justice should belong, in the case of the St. Antonio de Padua. When your Highness shall have complied with these just claims, I will then send a Consul to Algiers: therefore, from this moment, if an English Consul is not at Algiers, the cause rests entirely with your Highness.

NELSON AND BRONTE.

TO B. M'DONOUGH, ESQ.

[From a Copy in the Colonial Office.]

Victory, July 1st, 1804.

Sir,

Should the Dey of Algiers have settled all my just demands, and wrote me word so, in that case you will deliver to Captain Pettet the enclosed letter, in order that he may return to the Fleet, and enable me to place you at Algiers as soon as possible. But as Captain Pettet is charged with all my Public dispatches, you will not deliver him the letter, unless you are sure, from under the Dey or his Minister's hands, that everything is finally settled, and ready for Captain Keats' conclusion. I am, &c.

NELSON AND BRONTE.

TO CAPTAIN ROBERT PETTET, H. M. SHIP TERMAGANT.

[Order-Book.]

Victory, at Sea, 1st July, 1804.

You are hereby required and directed to receive Mr. M'Donough on board his Majesty's Sloop Termagant under your command, and proceed with him as expeditiously as possible to Algiers, where you will remain in the Bay for the space of three days, (should that time be necessary for the accomplishment of his mission with the Dey,) but on no account longer. You will then proceed with Mr. M'Donough to Gibraltar, when, after having landed him, you will cause every possible exertion to be used in refitting the Termagant, (which must not exceed more than seven days.) Having so done, and com-

pleted your provisions, water, and necessaries, to the usual
time, you will return and join me on Rendezvous No. 97,
under Cape St. Sebastians, where you will find me, or orders
for your further proceedings, taking care to bring with you
any Transports which may be loaded for the Fleet.

NELSON AND BRONTE.

TO CAPTAIN PETTET, H. M. SLOOP TERMAGANT.

[Autograph, in the possession of Thomas Garwood, Esq.]

Victory, July 1st, 1804.

Sir,

If Mr. M'Donough delivers you this letter, and informs
you that everything is settled at Algiers, ready to receive our
Consul, in that case, notwithstanding any former orders, you
will proceed and join me, without one moment's loss of time,
on Rendezvous No. 102; and should you meet with any of
his Majesty's Ships going to Gibraltar, you will put my
dispatches on board of them. I am, Sir, &c.

NELSON AND BRONTE.

TO THE RIGHT HONOURABLE LORD HAWKESBURY.

[Autograph, in the Colonial Office, and Autograph Draught.]

Victory, at Sea, 1st July, 1804.

My Lord,

I send you a translation of a letter from the Bey of Tunis,
respecting the Passports for his Vessels coming from Hol-
land with his presents. I hope Mr. Clarke, English Pro-Consul
at Tunis, has made all the explanations I directed him to do
to the Bey; but I much fear, by the Bey's letter, that he has
neglected my instructions, and that, from so great a delay,
doubts will arise in the mind of the Bey, as to our readiness
to comply with his just desires.

The effect of their being obliged to ask us for permission to get their presents across the seas, is attended with
very good effects. I understand the Dey of Algiers means,
when we have settled our matters, to ask for Passports to get
over his French presents. I send your Lordship extracts of

my letter to Mr. Clarke, and his answer, therefore I have done everything; but the want of proper and little attentions to these gentry, do us much harm. I have, &c.

NELSON AND BRONTE.

TO LADY HAMILTON.

[From " Lord Nelson's Letters to Lady Hamilton," vol. ii. p. 56.]

Victory, July 1st, 1804.

. . . . . . Your letters of April 13th, 22nd, and May 13th, through Mr. Falconet, came safe, a few days ago. Mr. Falconet is the French banker;[1] and he dare not buy a little maccaroni for me, or let an Englishman into his house. Gibbs is still at Palermo : I fancy he will make a good thing of my estate ; however, I wish it was settled. He wrote me, a short time since, that he wished I would give him a hint (but without noticing that it came from him) that I thought Mrs. Græfer and her child had better go to England, on pretence of educating her daughter, &c. But I would have nothing to do with any such recommendation: it would end in her coming to me, in England ; and saying, that she could not live upon what she had, and that I advised her to come to England, or she should not have thought of it. In short, Gibbs wants to remove her. He is afraid of his pocket, I fancy ; and the daughter is, I fancy, now in some seminary at Palermo, at Gibbs's expense. I wrote him word, fully, I would advise no such thing ; she was to form her own judgment. What our friends are after at Naples, they best know. The poor King is miserable at the loss of Acton. The Queen writes me about 'honest Acton,' &c., &c., and I hear, that she has been the cause of ousting him : and they say (her enemies) that her conduct is all French. That, I do not believe ; although she is likely to be the dupe of French émigrés, who always beset her. I doubt much, my dear Emma, even her constancy of real friendship to you; although, in my letter to Acton, which Mr. Elliot says he read to her, I mentioned the obligations she was under to you, &c. &c., in very strong terms. What could the name of the Minister signify ! It was

---

[1] At Naples.

the letter which was wanted to the Prime Minister. But,
never mind; with prudence, we shall do very well. I have
wrote to Davison, by land: who, I am very sorry for; but, he
never would take a friend's caution, and he has been severely
bit.[2] Your accounts of Merton delight me; and you will long
ago have known that I have directed the bills for the alterations to be paid. I never could have intended to have taken
it from the hundred pounds a month.

You will not hear of my making Prize-money. I have not
paid my expenses these last nine months. I shall expect to
eat my Christmas dinner at Merton; unless those events
happen which I can neither foresee nor prevent. I am not
well: and must have rest, for a few months, even should the
Country [want me], which, very likely, they will not. News,
I can have none.

April 9th, Leviathan sailed; so Government don't care
much for us. Kiss my dear Horatia, for me! I hope you will
have her at Merton; and believe me, &c.,

NELSON AND BRONTE.

_____

TO CAPTAIN PULTENEY MALCOLM, H.M. SHIP KENT.

[Letter-Book.]

Victory, at Sea, 1st July, 1804.

Sir,

Having thought proper to appoint Captain White to supersede you in the Kent, I am to desire that you will, immediately
after taking command of the Renown, order the Kent to proceed to Salerno, for the purpose of receiving on board the
sixty head of bullocks (or more if they can be stowed, for the
use of the Fleet) from Mr. Thomas Warrington, with hay
sufficient to last them during the passage, as mentioned in my
letter to you, dated the 12th ultimo, by which you will govern
yourself, in the payment of the said sixty bullocks &c., and
also the other forty bullocks from Mr. Warrington, either
when the Renown leaves Naples, or by such Vessel, as I
may judge proper to send for them. I have to observe,
for your information, that the twenty coils of rope sent by
the Termagant, run upwards of six hundred fathoms *short*,

_____

[2] Vide vol. v. p. 143.

and it is perfectly clear that none has been cut off, as the mark of the hooks is distinctly seen on each end of the rope. A survey has been ordered upon the said rope; and if it is practicable, the reports will be sent to you. At any rate, it will become necessary to state this uncommon deficiency to Mr. James, that an equal quantity may be sent in lieu, and that every inch on board the Kent which may have been received from him, is measured most strictly, before your Boatswain grants receipts for it. You will consider the Renown as employed on the same service as Kent, and remain at Naples with her until you shall be relieved, or receive my further directions, as mentioned in my order to you, dated the 26th April last. I am, &c.

NELSON AND BRONTE.

TO NATHANIEL TAYLOR, ESQ., MALTA.

[Letter-Book.]

Victory, at Sea, 1st July, 1804.

Sir,

I have received your letter of the 28th May, acquainting me that it would be necessary to make some purchases of stores, to complete the Niger; in answer thereto, I must desire you will send me an account of the stores, which it may be found necessary to purchase on the above occasion, approved of in the manner mentioned in my letter to you of the 18th ultimo, and continue to do so on all future occasions, where purchases may become absolutely necessary. With respect to lodgings for the Artificers, the Senior Officer can have nothing at all to do with it. You must, therefore, write to the Navy Board on the subject. I am, &c.

NELSON AND BRONTE.

TO CAPTAIN DONNELLY, H. M. SHIP NARCISSUS.

[Autograph, formerly in the possession of the late Adam Bromilow, Esq.]

Victory, July 2nd, 1804.

My dear Sir,

I believe your orders are to cruise or anchor, as you may judge best for carrying on the service entrusted to you;

therefore, you will act as you see best. Your Boats can be
inside, at night, in moderate weather, and in day-time you
can work between the Islands ; but I should wish you not to
be out of the reach of the Fleet in case Monsieur La Touche
should come out of his nest. I am obliged by your accounts of Hières Bay. When our Fleets occupied it, the
Islands were not fortified. The Enemy, I am sure, want to
get some small Ships of War to the Eastward, probably for
the invasion of Sardinia ; and by disappointment for some
time, I think the Fleet will be ordered out to fight close to
Toulon, that they may get their crippled Ships in again,
and that we must then quit the Coast to repair our damages,
and thus have the Coast clear ; but my mind is fixed not to
fight them, unless with a Westerly wind, outside the Hières,
and, with an Easterly wind, to the Westward of Sicie. I am
sure, one of these days they will come out ; for, besides their
degradation to all Europe, Marseilles must suffer for want of
her usual commerce. I have only again to repeat, that you
will keep under sail, or anchor, as you please ; and I am sure
you will always be upon your guard against a surprise from a
superior force. We have nothing new. Algiers is rather better
than it was, but not quite so well as we could wish. Phœbe
not joined. With my best regards to all your Squadron,
be assured, I am ever, my dear Sir, yours most faithfully,

NELSON AND BRONTE.

TO HIS EXCELLENCY HUGH ELLIOT, ESQ.

[Autograph, in the Elliot Papers.]

Victory, July 7th, 1804.

Private.
My dear Sir,

Your son William is on board the Amazon, and, I am sure,
very happily placed with his *money*, &c. &c. She is one of
the Squadron stationed in Hieres Bay, which, for a few weeks
in summer, will stop all their Coasting trade. We have
nothing but incessant gales of wind, and I am absolutely worn
out. From Gantheaume's having hoisted his Flag at Brest,
I have no doubt but that an attempt will be made to get

a superiority of force into the Mediterranean. However, our force is diminishing daily. Kent, Renown, and Gibraltar are gone for any further use; Superb and Triumph must go. Several of the Ships want to go into Port to refit; and if I was to do as they do in the Channel, I have not, by that mode of judging, four Sail fit to keep the sea. I absolutely keep them out by management; but the time must come when we shall break up, unless the new Admiralty act very differently from the old, and send out six Sail of the Line, and fifteen Frigates and Sloops; and I do not believe that the late Admiralty have left them *one* to send. But I must not indulge these thoughts, or I should say much more; but I *pay it* off with thinking. I am ever, my dear Sir, yours most faithfully,

NELSON AND BRONTE.

With respect to the Queen's writing to this Minister or that, whether Addington or Pitt, it cannot matter. It depends upon her Majesty's feelings towards the best friend she ever had, and Lady Hamilton has had opportunities of serving her Country which can fall to the lot of very few; and therefore has those claims for personal services which, as I said before, few can have. As Sir William's wife, I believe (indeed am sure) they will give her not one farthing.

TO HIS EXCELLENCY HUGH ELLIOT, ESQ.

[Autograph, in the Elliot Papers.]

Victory, July 8th, 1804.

My dear Sir,

I was honoured by the Termagant with your Excellency's letter of June 15th. If Russia goes to war with France, I hope it will be her own War, and not joined with us. Such Alliances have never benefited our Country. If the Emperor of Germany joins against France, something good may arise. If not, Russia's going to war in the way I am sure she will, will cause the loss of Naples and Sardinia; for that Court will not send 100,000 men into Italy, and less are useless for any grand purpose. *No;* Russia will take care of the Ionian

H 2

Republic, the Morea, and, in the end, Constantinople. The views of Russia are perfectly clear.

The French Navy is daily increasing, both at Toulon and Brest, whilst ours is as clearly going down-hill. It will require all Lord Melville's abilities to get our Fleet a-head of that of the French. We made use of the Peace, not to recruit our Navy, but to be the cause of its ruin. Nothing but a speedy Battle, a complete annihilation of the Enemy's Fleets, and a seven years' Peace, can get our Fleet in the order it ought to be; therefore I, for one, do not wish to be shackled with Allies. I am for assisting Europe to the utmost of our power, but no Treaties, which England only keeps.

I hope, my dear Sir, your next letters from Naples will give me news to alter my opinion of degenerate Europe; for I am sick at heart at the miserable cringing conduct of the great Powers. But I have done. I wish Acton had followed your advice; but being once gone, will he ever be able to come back again? Not without Naples is actually at War. What could have had no ill effects to resist, may, by bringing Acton back again, cause a War, or rather a pretence for taking Naples; but I am no politician, and have done. I have had nothing from England since April 5th; and if we did not get the French papers, we should be left in total ignorance. The Fleet is as healthy as usual; but if the Admiralty do not very largely reinforce this Fleet, so as to enable me to send some Ships home, and others into Port to refit, it cannot be kept at sea another winter. I am ever, with the greatest respect, your Excellency's most obedient servant,

NELSON AND BRONTE.

TO CAPTAIN DONNELLY, H. M. SHIP NARCISSUS.

[Autograph, formerly in the possession of the late Adam Bromilow, Esq.]

Victory, July 8th, 1804.

My dear Sir,

I send the Seahorse to relieve the Amazon, who must go for water, but before she goes I would have her complete the Thunder-Bomb, (if she has as much on board.) If you have no immediate prospect of doing much where you are,

leave Boyle with directions what to do, and come to me with
the Cameleon Brig, as I have a little service for you to perform. I send not Amazon's orders, as I want to see Parker
before he goes off. We have nothing new; ever yours most
faithfully,

NELSON AND BRONTE.

TO CAPTAIN DONNELLY, H.M. SHIP NARCISSUS.

[Autograph, formerly in possession of the late Adam Bromilow, Esq.]

Victory, July 8th, 1804, 7 P.M.

Dear Sir,

I was sending the Seahorse to relieve Amazon, and to desire
you and Cameleon to come to me ; but as I find the Thunder
so short of water, and it blows fresh, I fear that she may not
beat up to windward, therefore I send her to get water:
therefore, you will remain in your command, which you so
ably fill, and send the Cameleon to me without a moment's
loss of time, and also, the Amazon. I am, dear Sir, most
faithfully yours,

NELSON AND BRONTE.

TO CAPTAIN PULTENEY MALCOLM, H.M. SHIP KENT.

[Autograph, in the possession of Rear-Admiral Sir Charles Malcolm.]

Victory, July 8th, 1804.

My dear Sir,

You may be sure that when I can I shall always be glad
to meet your wishes, in respect to your changing into a Line-
of-Battle Ship, likely to remain in this Country. You will see
by my joint-letter to you and Captain White, that I have given
my consent to all convenient changes ; but, with respect to
men, you will be glad of my refusal ; for, I never knew a
Captain to take followers, but that he took so many ungrateful people, and always troublesome ones.

It is possible that it may be *very* inconvenient for Mr.
Frisilique[4] to go to England: if so, and that you are inclined
to receive him into the Renown, I can have no objection.

4 Query, Froessolecque ?

The Rope sent by Termagant was received from the Kent, I understand, but that the Boatswain of the Sloop gave a receipt to Mr. James[5] for it, when he ought to have given it to the Boatswain of the Kent; then, unless the Contractor makes up the deficiency, it would have been properly charged against the Boatswain of the Kent's wages, for receiving it without measuring. This must be very carefully done in future; and if Mr. James does not make up the deficiency of the last, I desire that nothing more of any kind or sort may be taken of him; for Government must not be defrauded. You will, I am sure, take care that nothing is got off publicly, which can in the least bring on difficulty with the French and the King of Naples. I am ever, my dear Sir, your most obedient and faithful Servant,

NELSON AND BRONTE.

TO CAPTAIN PULTENEY MALCOLM, H.M. SHIP KENT.

[Order-Book.]

Victory, at Sea, 8th July, 1804.

Should any political change of affairs at Naples render it necessary for his Majesty's Subjects to leave that place, his Excellency Mr. Elliot will, of course, give due notice thereof to the Merchants and others residing at Naples. You are, therefore, hereby required and directed, upon receiving such intimation from his Excellency Mr. Elliot, to take all the Merchant-Vessels, with the persons, property, and effects of his Majesty's Subjects at Naples, under the cover of your guns, and afford them every assistance and protection in your power for their safety.

NELSON AND BRONTE.

TO HIS EXCELLENCY HUGH ELLIOT, ESQ.

[Autograph, in the Elliot Papers.]

Victory, July 9th, 1804.

My dear Sir,
    The Acheron last night brought me your Excellency's letter of June 28th, with the inclosure from the Queen. I

* Pro-Consul at Naples.

hardly see what I can answer to her Majesty, for her continued good opinion of me, except that it shall be my study to continue to deserve it. There is but little in your Excellency's letters to comfort any well-wisher for the honour of Europe; and the arrival of Russian Troops at Corfu and the Morea may hasten the attack upon Naples.

I had a letter yesterday from Rear-Admiral Cochrane,[6] who commands off Ferrol. The French Fleet at Brest, Rochford, and Ferrol, are perfectly ready for sea; and we know they are ready at Toulon; and I have no doubt but that the Mediterranean will be the scene of Action. I only hope that it will very soon happen, or I shall have nothing to do with it; for I do assure you that every part of my constitution is broke up.

I never hear from England, but as we manage to get the Paris papers regularly through Spain. From ten days to a fortnight we get them from their date at Paris : therefore, we know the very great events which are passing in Europe—at least, as much as the French people. A great expedition seems fitting out. I fear it is to send abroad, when I think it might be much more usefully employed in the Mediterranean, and in taking Belleisle. I send you our Pro-Consul's letter from Barcelona. I very seldom hear from Mr. Frere, although Cochrane's letter must have passed through his hands, yet I have not a scrap of a pen. The Renown goes to replace the Kent, who goes direct for England. Gibraltar is absent. Belleisle leaves me to-night; for she cannot keep the sea even these summer gales : therefore, I shall be left with only seven to ten, and that I expect reduced by the miserable state of the hulls and rigging, &c., of the Ships. Adieu, my dear Sir, and believe me ever your Excellency's most obedient and obliged servant,

NELSON AND BRONTE.

[6] Afterwards Admiral the Honourable Sir Alexander Forrester Inglis Cochrane, G.C.B.; he died in June 1832.

TO CAPTAIN THE HONOURABLE T. B. CAPEL, H.M. SHIP PHŒBE.

[Order-Book.]

Victory, at Sea, 9th July, 1804.

Whereas I have received information that the Enemy are collecting troops and stores at Porto Ferraio, in the Island of Elba, with an intent of making a descent on the Island of Sardinia, You are, therefore, hereby required and directed to take his Majesty's Sloop named in the margin[7] under your command, and proceed, without a moment's loss of time off Porto Ferraio, where you will cruise very diligently for the space of ten days, between that place and Leghorn, and endeavour to capture or destroy any of the Enemy's Vessels of War or Transports which you may fall in with. You are at liberty, during the said period of time, to extend your cruising ground as far as Port Specia, if, from information, you should judge it more likely to fall in with the Expedition before mentioned, taking care to join the Squadron by the 25th instant on Rendezvous No. 102, where you will find me, or orders for your further proceedings.

NELSON AND BRONTE.

TO CAPTAIN MALCOLM, H.M. SHIP KENT.

[Autograph, in the possession of Rear-Admiral Sir Charles Malcolm.]

Victory, July 9th, 1804.

Many, many thanks for your Papers, which are very interesting.

My dear Sir,

The Acheron joined me last night with your letter of June 28th. I am glad you have stopped the making of beds. I had not an idea that there was a single bed at Malta till Captain Keats's arrival a week ago. I wrote you yesterday about the rope. I, for one, am glad at Monarchy, under any shape, being restored in France. It may be better for us—cannot be worse. I am much obliged by your kind offers of service. The Renown will part the moment the weather moderates that I can get water from her. I am ever, dear Sir, your most obliged servant,

NELSON AND BRONTE.

[7] Cameleon.

TO THE QUEEN OF NAPLES.

[From " The Life of the Reverend Doctor Scott," p. 114.]

Victory, 10th July, 1804.

Madam,

I have been honoured by your Majesty's gracious and condescending letter of June 28th. I have no other reply to make to such flattering expressions of confidence, than to offer my most devoted thanks, and my assurances of always studying to merit your Majesty's favourable sentiments, and those of my benefactor, the King.

It would be presumptuous on my part to venture to speak of political matters in a letter to your Majesty; but I cannot help wishing that Europe was like a handful of rods against France. If it be proper to give way to the times, let us temporise : if to make War, let us all make it. On this principle, I could have wished that Russia had avoided War, unless she had been joined by Austria. Then, acting honourably side by side, there would have been some hope from such a coalition.

If Russia sends men and Vessels to the Ionian Republic, and into the Morea only, I have no hesitation in saying, that she compromises Naples much more than if she had, for the moment, bent to the storm. At least, 50,000 troops (it should be 100,000) are necessary to answer for the safety of Italy. To say the truth, I do not believe we had in the last War, and, according to all appearance, we shall not have in the present one either, plans of a sufficiently grand scale to force France to keep within her proper limits. Small measures produce only small results. I dare not let my pen run on. The intelligent mind of your Majesty will readily comprehend the great things which might be effected in the Mediterranean. On this side Buonaparte is the most vulnerable. It is from here that it would be most easy to mortify his pride, and so far humble him, as to make him accept reasonable conditions of Peace. I entreat your Majesty's pardon for having expressed my sentiments with such boldness.

Mr. Elliot has informed me, by writing, of what your Majesty wished to say on the subject of writing to the Minister, respecting the pension for your Emma. Poor Sir William Hamilton believed that it would have been granted, or it would have been unpardonable in him to have left his widow with so little means. Your Majesty well knows that it was her capacity and conduct which sustained his diplomatic character during the last years in which he was at Naples. It is unnecessary for me to speak more of it. It only remains for me—begging pardon for having occupied your Majesty's time so long—to subscribe myself your Majesty's faithful and devoted servant,

NELSON AND BRONTE.

TO THE REVEREND DAVID EVANS,[8] H. M. SHIP SUPERB.

[Autograph, in the possession of Mrs. Evans, his widow.]

Victory, July 10th, 1804.

Dear Sir,

I feel very much obliged by your kind offer of translating any pieces for me in case of Dr. Scott's ill health or absence. I have no doubt but that the translation was a perfect good one ; and should I want your kind assistance in future, you have encouraged me to apply without hesitation, which very much obliges, dear Sir, your very faithful servant,

NELSON AND BRONTE.

TO CAPTAIN KEATS, H. M. SHIP SUPERB.

[Autograph, in the possession of the Reverend Richard Keats.]

Victory, July 10th, 1804.

My dear Sir,

If your nephew, Mr. Buck,[9] can effect an exchange into the Kent, I will do the needful ; but if an exchange cannot be effected, and you wish your nephew to go home a passenger, had he not better remain in the Kent, and go home a passenger in her ? Will you dine here to-morrow, and we will talk more upon the subject. Be assured whatever you wish I shall be happy in doing, being ever your most obliged and faithful,

NELSON AND BRONTE.

---

[8] Then Chaplain of the Superb, and afterwards Secretary to Admiral Sir George Martin, G.C.B., G.C.M.G.

[9] Lieutenant Richard Buck, son of George Stucley Buck, Esq., by Martha, daughter of the Rev. Richard Keats, and sister of Admiral Sir Richard Goodwin Keats, G.C.B.: he died a Post-Captain in July 1830.

TO SIR JOHN ACTON, BART.

[From Clarke and M'Arthur, vol. ii. p. 376.]

[About 10th July, 1804.]

Admiral Gantheaume, I see, has hoisted his Flag at Brest; a sure indication to my mind, that at least a part of that Fleet is destined for the Mediterranean. It is in this Country that Buonaparte wishes to make himself great, and, therefore, this is the Country where large Armies and Fleets should be placed. I trust our Government will take care not to allow a superiority, beyond my power of resistance, to get into the Mediterranean. I calculate upon no joint exertion of the Russian Fleet, even should the Emperor go to war; and if it is only a War of manifestoes, as Catherine's War, and sending Troops to the Morea, and Ionian Republic, I do not see any good either to Naples or England from it; indeed, I fear such a War would much endanger both Naples and Sardinia. I am, &c.,

NELSON AND BRONTE.

TO EDWARD GAYNER, ESQ., ROSAS.

[Letter-Book.]

Victory, at Sea, 11th July, 1804.

Sir,

I have received your letter of the 1st instant, acquainting me that the Captains of some of his Majesty's Ships frequenting Rosas have requested you to pay the sum of eight dollars for the apprehending any Seamen, &c., who may desert from their Ships, and that, in consequence, you had paid the sum of sixteen dollars for two Seamen that had been apprehended as deserters from the Phœbe, and eight for one from the Victory, which you intend putting into the general account. In answer to which, I feel very much obliged by your kind attention to this circumstance of Service; but must beg to observe, that as those sums are charged respectively against the Deserters on the Ship's Books, and paid by the Captain's certificate, I can have nothing at all to do with it, nor must it appear in the general account you allude to. The Captains, on such occasions, pay for apprehending Deserters from their Ships, and are reimbursed by the certificate before mentioned.

I must beg you will be good enough to send me an account of your expenses for the Hindostan's people, as mentioned in my letter of the 26th April, in order that I may direct its being paid immediately, as in the event of Captain Le Gros's accounts being closed previous to yours arriving in England, it is more than probable it will be charged against me. I am, &c.   NELSON AND BRONTE.

TO ADMIRAL SIR PETER PARKER, BART.

[From Clarke and M'Arthur, vol. ii. p. 353.]

[About July, 1804.]

I most sincerely condole with you, on the premature death of my dear friend and contemporary, your son.[1] In your grandson Peter, you possess everything which is amiable, good, and manly—an Officer and a gentleman. He is sure of my warmest and affectionate interest for his welfare, as long as I live. Never whilst I breathe shall I forget your kindness to me, to which I owe all my present Honours. May God bless you, my dear Friend, and keep you in health many, many years. I am, &c.,

NELSON AND BRONTE.

TO CAPTAIN ROSS DONNELLY, H. M. SHIP NARCISSUS.

[Autograph draught, and Order-Book.]

Victory, at Sea, 12th July, 1804.

Memorandum.

Lord Nelson has received with much satisfaction the report of Captain Donnelly, of the gallant conduct of the Officers and Men employed in destroying the Enemy's Vessels at La Vendura.[2] The judicious arrangement of Lieutenant Thomp-

---

[1] Vice-Admiral Christopher Parker, who died on the 26th of May, 1804, leaving a son, Peter, who succeeded his grandfather in the Baronetcy, in December 1811, and was killed while Captain of the Menelaus, in storming an American camp at Bellaire, near Baltimore, in August 1814.

[2] Captain Donnelly's and Lieutenant John Thompson's letters, describing the successful attack by the Boats of the Narcissus, Seahorse, and Maidstone, on some Enemy's Vessels at La Vandour, in Hières Bay, in the night of the 10th of July,

son merits my praise, for without that, bravery would be useless; and the example of Lieutenants Parker, Lumley, and
Moore, was such as to ensure the bravery of the inferior Officers
and Men; for I never knew the superior Officers to lead
on well but that they were always bravely supported by the
men under their orders. Wounds must be expected in fighting the Enemy. They are marks of honour, and our grateful
Country is not unmindful of the sufferings of her gallant de-
fenders. A regular list will be sent to the Patriotic Fund at
Lloyd's, and the Captains are to give each man a certificate
before he leaves the Ship, describing his wound, signed by
the Captain and Surgeon. The wounded men to be sent to
the three Flag-Ships, as they will probably find better accommodation than in a Frigate.

NELSON AND BRONTE.

TO CAPTAIN HARGOOD, H.M. SHIP BELLEISLE.

[Order-Book.]

Memorandum.   Victory, at Sea, 12th July, 1804.

You will be on your guard against a surprise of the Enemy,
during your stay in Agincourt Sound, as it's by no means
improbable but they will make a descent on the Madalena
Islands; in which case, you will render the Governor and Inhabitants every assistance in your power, and endeavour to
destroy the Enemy's Vessels and Troops.

NELSON AND BRONTE.

TO CAPTAIN ROSS DONNELLY, H.M. SHIP NARCISSUS.

[Order-Book.]

Victory, at Sea, 14th July, 1804.

Having received information that the Enemy are in the
habit of sending their Privateers and other Vessels of War

1804, were published in the London Gazette of August following. Lieutenant
John Thompson's subsequent career has not been ascertained. [Query if he were
the Lieutenant of those names who died in 1809.] Lieutenant John Richard Lumley
died a Post Captain, about 1821: Lieutenant Ogle Moore died in that rank, about
1816; and Lieutenant Hyde Parker is now a Rear Admiral of the Blue, and a
Companion of the Bath.

from Corsica to the Port of Genoa, You are hereby required
and directed to take his Majesty's Ship named in the margin[n]
under your command, and proceed immediately off the above-
mentioned Port, where you will cruize very diligently, and
endeavour to fall in with any Vessels of the above description,
or Transports with Troops on board; upon doing so you will
use your utmost exertions to capture or destroy them. In the
execution of this service, should any intelligence be obtained
necessary for my immediate information, you will join me
forthwith on Rendezvous, No. 102. At all events, you must
not be longer absent from the Squadron, which you will find
on the said Rendezvous, than the 10th of next month, August.
It is my intention to send the Thunder Bomb-Vessel on this
service, the moment she joins; you will, therefore, take her
under your orders, and employ the whole as you may find
best for the execution of the said service.

                                    NELSON AND BRONTE.

The closer you cruize off the Mole Head the better, and
send your Boats out at night.   N. & B.

TO CAPTAIN ARTHUR FARQUHAR, H.M. BOMB-VESSEL ACHERON.

[Order-Book.]

Victory, at Sea, 15th July, 1804.

Having ordered the two Transports named in the margin [4]
to be loaded with empty water-casks from the different Ships,
You are hereby required and directed to take the said Transports under your charge, and proceed immediately with them
to Porto Conte in the Island of Sardinia; and on your arrival
there you will cause the utmost exertion to be used in filling
the same empty water-casks, directing the Officers super-
intending that service, to see that the greatest care is taken of
the casks, in rolling them to and from the spring, that no injury
may be done them. You will also instruct the Officers so
employed not to suffer the casks to be filled at high water, as
the surface of one of the wells at those times is level with the
sea, consequently impregnated with salt water. A Corporal's

party of Marines will be sent in each of the Transports, for the
purpose of attending the watering parties to prevent the casks
from being stolen by the Inhabitants, and the men from getting
drunk, or deserting, to which the utmost attention must be
paid, as these people are very much in the habit of bringing
down quantities of wine. To all and each of these circumstances I must desire to call your particular attention. During
your stay at Porto Conte you will purchase as many live
bullocks as may be necessary for the Bomb's Company, and
you will also procure a hundred quintals of good onions, for
the use of the Squadron. For the payment thereof the Agent-
Victualler will supply you with dollars, upon your granting
the usual receipt for the same, and returning the proper and
regular vouchers for the disbursement thereof. Having completed the service above mentioned, which is to be done with
the utmost possible expedition, you will return and join the
Squadron on Rendezvous No. 102, where you will find me,
or orders for your further proceedings.

NELSON AND BRONTE.

TO CAPTAIN MOUBRAY, H. M. SHIP ACTIVE.

[Order-Book.]

Victory, at Sea, 16th July, 1804.

You are hereby required and directed to take the Vessel
named in the margin[5] under your command, and after the
close of day, you will proceed, with as much dispatch as possible off Marseilles, for the purpose of intercepting any of the
Enemy's Frigates, Vessels of War, or Merchant-Ships, which
may be going into that Port. You will afterwards stretch
over to Cette, for the above purpose, taking care to join me
on Rendezvous No. 102, with the first Westerly wind, and
not to be longer absent from the Squadron than four or five
days from the date hereof.

NELSON AND BRONTE.

[5] Thunder.

TO REAR-ADMIRAL CAMPBELL.

[From Clarke and M'Arthur, vol. ii. p. 376.]

17th July, 1804.

The French Ships have either altered their anchorage, or some of them have got to sea in the late gales: the idea has given me half a fever. I am, &c.,

NELSON AND BRONTE.

TO REAR-ADMIRAL SIR RICHARD BICKERTON, BART.

[From Clarke and M'Arthur, vol. ii. p. 376.]

17th July, 1804.

I have been in a little alarm at the idea of Mons. La Touche having given me the slip, and it is not quite cleared up. I am sending Active and Thunder off Marseilles for informa-tion; for I am sure if that Admiral were to cheat me out of my hopes of meeting him, it would kill me much easier than one of his balls. Since we sat down to dinner Captain Moubray has made the signal, but I am very far from being easy. I shall place Seahorse and Amazon close in shore, in order to examine Toulon every way to-morrow. I am, &c.,

NELSON AND BRONTE.

TO CAPTAIN MOUBRAY, H.M. SHIP ACTIVE.

[Letter-Book.]

Victory, July 17th, 1804.

My dear Sir,

I believe you mistook our signal this morning—it was to reconnoitre Toulon. After dark, you will part company, and I wish you good luck. Put 'Thunder' in the margin of your order. As I am still inclined to believe that a part of the Enemy's Fleet have put to sea, I request you will be very inquisitive for information from any Vessels coming from Marseilles; and indeed from all others, as somebody must fall in with them.   Vessels from Tunis and the Levant, if they are bound to the Levant,[1] are most likely to meet them, and if you get any information which may be useful to me, I beg that you will join me directly.   Ever, dear Sir, yours faithfully,

NELSON AND BRONTE.

TO LIEUTENANT H. B. LANE, ROYAL ARTILLERY, SERVING ON
BOARD HIS MAJESTY'S BOMB-VESSEL THUNDER.

[Letter-Book.]

Victory, at Sea, 17th July, 1804.

Sir,

I have this moment received your letter of the 15th instant, stating, 'that finding it totally impossible from the difference of orders sent to you by command of the Right Honourable the Earl of Chatham, Master-General, and the Honourable Board of Ordnance, with the approval of the Lords Commissioners of the Admiralty, and those given by me to the Commanding-Officer of the Thunder, Bomb-Vessel, to agree with him on your different branches of duty, and to be responsible for the mortars and stores placed in your charge, by the Board of Ordnance, and comply with their orders in every respect;' in return, I beg leave to inform you that it is not in my power to allow any Officer under my command to quit his duty on any pretence.   The orders to which you allude as given by me, were to enforce due obedience to Superior Officers, and the greater care of the mortars, stores, and artillerymen : I cannot comprehend that it is possible any disagreement can take place between you and the Commander of the Thunder-Bomb, under whose command you are, as you have only to obey.   I have directed Captain Cocks to order you, when he thinks the service and weather will admit of it, to examine the mortars and stores under your charge, in order that they may always be kept in good condition, and fit for immediate service.   I am, &c.,

NELSON AND BRONTE.

[1] Sic.

TO CAPTAIN GEORGE COCKS, H. M. BOMB THUNDER.

[From a Copy in the Admiralty.]

Victory, at Sea, 17th July, 1804.

Sir,

I herewith transmit you a copy of a letter from Lieutenant
Lane, of the Royal Artillery, serving on board his Majesty's
Bomb-Vessel Thunder, under your command, together with
a copy of my answer thereto ; and I must desire that you will
cause the mortars and Artillery stores to be examined, when
the weather and Service will admit, as mentioned in the copy
of my said letter, and transmit me a report thereof for my information. I am, &c.,

NELSON AND BRONTE.

TO WILLIAM MARSDEN, ESQ., ADMIRALTY.

[Original, in the Admiralty.]

Victory, at Sea, 18th July, 1804.

Sir,

I herewith transmit you the copy of a letter from Lieutenant
Lane of the Royal Artillery, serving on board his Majesty's
Bomb-Vessel Thunder, together with a copy of my answer
thereto ; and also, of my letter to Captain Cocks, Commander
of the said Bomb-Vessel, which I request you will be pleased
to lay before the Lords Commissioners of the Admiralty for
their consideration.

It is painful for me to consider their Lordships' orders
alluded to in Lieutenant Lane's letter, as in any degree
sanctioning that Officer, and the others embarked on board
the Ætna and Acheron, to act or hold themselves independent
of the Commanders of these Bombs, particularly so, as every
day's experience more fully convinces my mind of the indispensable necessity of there being but *one* Commander in a
Ship, and that every Land Officer (whatever his rank may be)
if embarked to serve on board Ship, should most implicitly
conform to, and comply with, the orders of the Captain or
Commander of such Ship or Vessel.

Having so fully wrote you on this subject in my letter

dated 22nd of May,[6] with the papers therein referred to for their Lordships' information; I have only to hope that their Lordships will see the immediate necessity of having this business fully cleared up, if any doubts can be entertained as to the construction of the Act of Parliament for the Government of his Majesty's Ships, Vessels, and Forces by Sea. I am, &c.,

NELSON AND BRONTE.

TO THE NAVAL STOREKEEPER, MASTER SHIPWRIGHT, AND MASTER ATTENDANT OF MALTA YARD.

[Original, in the Record Office in the Tower of London.]

Victory, at Sea, 28th July, 1804.

Gentlemen,

I have received your letter of the 5th instant, acquainting me with the circumstances attending the unloading and measuring the coals from the Harmony Transport, and that there were sixty chaldrons detained and received into His Majesty's Stores at Malta, for my further directions; also, submitting your opinion that there did not appear any fraud, or intention to defraud, to be imputed to Mr. ——, Master of the Harmony, in the delivery of the coals to the Fleet under my command, as from his report there was great hurry and inattention in delivering them. In answer to which, I conceive it was improper to give a receipt for the sixty chaldron of coals which the Pursers were defrauded of by Mr. ——'s short measurement; and that it was extremely wrong in you, and not consistent with my order, to have offered an opinion exculpating the fraud of the said Mr. ——, which you have taken upon yourselves to do from his own *ipse dixit;* and imputed blame to *those* who received the coals, and of course were concerned to have just measure. I shall transmit a copy of your said letter to the Transport Board, that the conduct of Mr. —— may meet its deserts. I am, &c.,

NELSON AND BRONTE.

[6] Vide p. 27, ante.

TO CAPTAIN RICHARD BUDD VINCENT, H. M. SLOOP ARROW.

[Original, in the Admiralty.]

Victory, at Sea, 28th July, 1804.

Sir,

I have received your letter of the 5th June, giving an account of your having, on the 3rd of that month, destroyed, and set fire to a French Privateer under the Island of Fano. The destruction of the Enemy's Privateers, who are so numerous in these seas (and contrary to all known laws of Neutrality, shelter themselves, and make a convenience of the Neutral Territory of the Powers at amity with Great Britain, from whence they commit the most unwarrantable depredations on our Commerce), becomes an object of serious consideration, and certainly justifies an attack upon these Pirates.

I therefore feel pleased with your conduct in the destruction of the Privateer before mentioned, and shall write Mr. Foresti, his Majesty's Minister at Corfu (if necessary) to remonstrate against the conduct of those unprecedented and sanctioned Pirates, as I did in the instance of the Thisbe; for certainly the Neutral Territory that does not afford protection, cannot be allowed to give it to the original breaker of the Neutrality, and therefore, from the offensive state of the Privateer in question, and her firing upon the Arrow's Boats, I cannot but approve of your having destroyed her; but I must beg to be perfectly understood, that I would on no account have the Neutrality broken or disturbed by his Majesty's Ships or Vessels, &c., under my command, firing upon any of the Enemy's Privateers or endeavouring to destroy them under the protection of a Neutral Port, unless such Privateers shall first use such offensive measures, and fire upon his Majesty's Subjects; in which case, they forfeit the protection of the Neutral Port, and ought to be destroyed, if possible.

I am sorry for the Arrow's loss in killed and wounded on the occasion, as stated in the list which accompanied your said letter. The paper of instructions saved from the Privateer before alluded to, has been received. I am, &c.,

NELSON AND BRONTE.

TO CAPTAIN VINCENT, H.M. SLOOP ARROW.

[Letter Book.]

Victory, at Sea, July 28th, 1804.

Sir,

I yesterday received your letter of the 13th ult., acquainting me with your proceedings, in consequence of the orders you received from Captain Cracraft, of his Majesty's Ship Anson; that you had visited Zante, Corfu, Valona, and Otranto, agreeable to his directions; and that on your arrival at Corfu, you had received a letter, with an enclosure from Mr. Foresti, acquainting you with the loss of the Merchant Brig, General Moore, near Valona, on the 18th of November last; and also, with the treatment the Master and Crew of the said Vessel had received from the Bey and Vizir of Burat. In answer thereto, I am very much pleased with the whole of your conduct, and hope that your remonstrances will not only induce the Vizir to deliver up the English Subjects, but also make sufficient reparation for his treatment to the Master and Crew of the said Vessel, as well as for having detained them and others of His Majesty's Subjects. I am very much obliged for your communication of the different circumstances that are passing in the Adriatic, mentioned in your said letter and Log-book, which have been received, together with copies of Mr. Foresti's letter, and the paper which accompanied it; also, the list of Vessels boarded by the Arrow as stated therein.
I am, &c.,

NELSON AND BRONTE.

TO LIEUTENANT HARDING SHAW, COMMANDING HIS MAJESTY'S BRIG SPIDER.

[Letter-Book.]

Victory, at Sea, 28th July, 1804.

Sir,

I have received your letter of the 12th instant, acquainting me with your having, on the preceding day, captured the Conception French Privateer, mounting two brass guns, and manned with forty-seven men. In answer to which, I am very much pleased with your success on this occasion, and

hope your future exertions may soon enable you to capture or
destroy more of those piratical Privateers, who so much annoy
our Coasting trade.   Your log and weekly account have been
delivered me by the Captain of the Fleet.   Let them in future
be transmitted to me.   I am, &c.,

NELSON AND BRONTE.

TO PATRICK WILKIE, ESQ., AGENT VICTUALLER, MALTA.

[Letter-Book.]

Victory, at Sea, 28th July, 1804.

Sir,

I have received by the Ætna, your letter of the 6th instant,
and observe, by the abstract of the remains of provisions therein
mentioned, the state of his Majesty's stores under your charge,
which will meet with due attention, and I trust be soon re-
cruited with every species of provisions from England, by the
first Convoy, which it is to be presumed is at no great distance
from its arrival.   I observe what you say respecting the five
hundred pipes of wine, contracted for at Marsala, and, consequently, shall approve of such steps as the Senior Officer
may take to send the said wine to England.   I am sorry to
observe that the wine supplied his Majesty's Ships from the
stores under your charge, is excessively bad of its kind, and
very much inferior to what we receive from Gibraltar, or purchase in the vicinity of Rosas, and I presume higher priced.
I therefore desire that you will write the Contractor on the
subject, and insist upon good sound wine being sent, as I am
satisfied that the Faro wine is excellent.   You will, at the same
time, transmit me a copy of the said contract, that I may
judge how far a public remonstrance to the Victualling Board
may be necessary to remedy this serious evil.   I am, &c.

NELSON AND BRONTE.

P.S.—In future, let your Returns, or Remains of provisions,
&c. in the stores under your charge, be transmitted to me.

TO NATHANIEL TAYLOR, ESQ., NAVAL OFFICER, MALTA.

[Letter-Book.]

Victory, at Sea, 28th July, 1804.

Sir,

I have to acknowledge the receipt of your letter of the 6th instant, with a copy of the list of cordage undertaken to be found by Mr. Dyson of Syracuse, also a list of canvas and timber which you have ordered from Fiume, for the use of his Majesty's stores at Malta, together with a list of canvas purchased at Malta with the approbation of the Senior Officer. In answer thereto, I herewith transmit you an order for the payment of the canvas purchased at Malta, and desire to observe, that as stores are now arrived in the Mediterranean, it's of little consequence whether the cordage you have ordered from Syracuse is received or not. As canvas was to be had at Naples, I cannot account for your having ordered such a quantity of it, and other stores, from Fiume, on your return to Naples from Malta, as there appears no necessity for such a measure; and my instructions only justify your making inquiry where Naval stores may be had in case of emergency, and not to purchase, except small quantities, and that in cases only of absolute necessity, with the concurrence and authority of the Senior Officer. I hope your conduct on this occasion will meet the approbation of the Navy Board, and that the disbursement of the Public money in your department for every article purchased may be perfectly correct, and entirely to their satisfaction.

In future, it is my directions, that previous to the purchase of any description of stores, you consult with the Senior Officer on the necessity thereof, as well as to the exact quantity of every article wanted; and upon his being perfectly and fully satisfied of the absolute and indispensable necessity of such temporary purchase, you are to obtain from him an order for that purpose, which must specify the particular quantity of every article intended to be procured; a copy of which order, &c., you will transmit to me immediately, (in the event of there not being time to make application to me in the first instance, which is always to be done when practicable,) and also an account from the person of whom the purchase is made, setting forth the quantity and price of every article, in order that I may, on any future occasion, satisfy myself with the correctness thereof.

I approve L'Hirondelle's being fitted in her present state, and hope she will soon be ready for active service. Her valuation, and a list of the remains of stores under your charge, have also been received. I am very much surprised that directions were not given to the Master of the Louisa, to receive the lime for the use of the Fleet. Your application ought to have been to the Senior Officer, who would have taken the necessary steps for this purpose. I shall, however, direct the Agent of Transports to attend to your request on all future occasions. The Jolly-boat for the Childers has been received, and also the Victory's hammock-cloths; but I am extremely concerned to observe the inattention which they have met with in Malta Yard. They have been badly painted (if it may be called painting), as it is all run in flecks, and peels off with the least touch. In addition to this, a considerable part of one of them is entirely rotten. The want of these hammock-cloths will be severely felt, and there is none on board to cover the men's bedding. A survey shall be ordered upon them, and a report thereof sent to the Admiralty for their Lordships' consideration. I am, &c.

NELSON AND BRONTE.

P.S.—In future, let the monthly return of the stores under your charge be transmitted to me. Your letter of the 14th July, acquainting me that the Jalouse had sprung her mainmast, has been received.

TO CAPTAIN SCHOMBERG, H. M. SHIP MADRAS.

[Letter-Book.]

Victory, at Sea, 28th July, 1804.

Sir,

I have received your letters of the 29th June, and 6th instant, acquainting me that the Bittern had landed Mr. Longford and suite at Tripoli, on the 26th June; transmitting me a list of Convoy under the protection of the Agincourt and Thisbe; and that it was your intention, if the Agincourt had not arrived, to have sent the Niger to Gibraltar with the

Convoy, on account of their perishable cargoes; also, that it
is the opinion of Sir Alexander Ball, and the Officers of the
Yard at Malta, that the Hirondelle will answer better in her
present state, than as a Schooner. In answer to which, I am
perfectly satisfied with the orders you gave Captain Corbet,
and am very glad that Mr. Longford and suite are at last safe
arrived at Tripoli. The list of Convoy which accompanied
your last-mentioned letter has been received; and your intentions of sending the Niger to Gibraltar with the Convoy,
under the circumstances stated in your said letter, would
have met my approbation, although it would very much
[have] interfered with my arrangement, as, in the event of
the Agincourt not arriving, I had intended the Maidstone to
have taken the Convoy from Malta to England. I am perfectly satisfied with the Hirondelle's remaining in her present
state, and hope she may soon be actively employed for the
service of Malta. I must desire you will direct the Masters
of any of the Transports coming to the Fleet with stores or
provisions, to receive such articles as the Naval Storekeeper
or Agent-Victualler may have to send to the Squadron. Mr.
Taylor mentions his having applied to one of the Transports
to receive twelve barrels of lime, which he declined doing,
notwithstanding he had previously spoken to Captain Lamb.
I am, &c.   NELSON AND BRONTE.

TO CAPTAIN SCHOMBERG, H. M. SHIP MADRAS.

[Letter Book.]

Victory, at Sea, 28th July, 1804.

Sir,

As it is my intention to appoint the Maidstone to convoy
the Trade bound from Malta to England, about the middle
or latter end of September next, I must request you will inform
me as early as possible if the Trade (which, I suppose, cannot
be many) will be ready by that time, or whether a fortnight
later will answer better, in order that the Maidstone may be
at Malta by the period you may judge proper to fix for their
sailing; and you will, in the interim, use every possible exertion to collect the Merchant-Vessels from Fiume, and other
Ports in the Adriatic and Archipelago, and have them in
readiness to proceed at the time appointed.

The Agent-Victualler having applied to me for a Transport, or Transports, to carry five hundred pipes of wine from Marsala to England, I request you will be pleased to order such Vessels as the Agent of Transports may be sending home to proceed to the above place for the said wine, and join the Convoy before mentioned. And I must also desire that you will in future, (in case there should not be sufficient time to obtain my order for that purpose,) cause the Naval Storekeeper to furnish you with the particular articles he may want to purchase : and after your being fully satisfied with the indispensable necessity of such purchase, you will direct it to be made, enumerating every article most strictly on the said order—a copy of which, together with the stores so ordered for purchase, you will transmit to me for my information, as I am by no means satisfied with the loose manner these purchases are made by the Storekeeper. I trust the stores that are arrived in this Country from England will preclude the necessity of any purchase whatever for a considerable time. The stores ordered from Fiume, by the Naval Officer, appears to me a very extraordinary measure. I am, &c.,   NELSON AND BRONTE.

TO CAPTAIN PHILIP LAMB, AGENT FOR TRANSPORTS, MALTA.

[Letter-Book.]

Victory, at Sea, 28th July, 1804.

Sir,

I have received your letter of the 7th instant, acquainting me that you had ordered the Ellice to England, under convoy of the Agincourt, and transmitting a state of the Prisoners of War and Transports on this station. In answer to which, I approve of your having sent the Ellice to England, as mentioned in your said letter. As the Naval Storekeeper, and other Officers of the Yard, have frequently occasion to send things to the Fleet, you will be good enough to direct the Master of any of the Transports leaving Malta for the Squadron, to receive such articles as either of those Officers may have to send, if it can be stowed; and not to object, as was lately the case, on the Naval Storekeeper's applying for twelve barrels of lime being received for conveyance to the Fleet. I am, &c.,

NELSON AND BRONTE.

TO WILLIAM MARSDEN, ESQ., ADMIRALTY.

[Original, in the Admiralty.]

Victory, at Sea, 29th July, 1804.

Sir,

You will please to acquaint the Lords Commissioners of the Admiralty, that his Majesty's Ship Ambuscade joined the Squadron this morning, and that I have taken Captain Durban and the said Ship under my command, agreeably to their Lordships' order of the 16th May. The Ambuscade has brought six Victuallers and two Store-ships under her Convoy to the Fleet, and as it has blown a gale of wind for these two days past, and still continues, with every appearance of its doing so, I shall proceed immediately with the Squadron to the Gulf of Palma, in order to complete the provisions and water of the different Ships, and furnish them with such a proportion of stores as the quantity sent out will admit of. I am, &c.   NELSON AND BRONTE.

TO MAJOR-GENERAL VILLETTES.

[From Clarke and M'Arthur, vol. ii. p. 376.]

[About July, 1804.]

I am of no party: I hope and believe that any Administration would ever act to the best of their judgment, for the power and advantage of their Country. I am not one of those who think, that the safety of the State depends on any *one*, or upon one hundred men; let them go off the stage, and others would ably supply their places. I am, &c.,

NELSON AND BRONTE.

TO MR. R. WILBRAHAM.

[From Clarke and M'Arthur, vol. ii. p. 379.]

[About July, 1804.]

The coalition of parties the most opposite in principles ought not to surprise us. Windham and Fox may again meet at Holkham, and Pitt join the party—such things are. Politicians are not like other men; and probably all other men would be politicians, if they had the sense. I am, &c.,

NELSON AND BRONTE.

124   LETTERS.   [1804.

TO JAMES DUFF, ESQ., CONSUL AT CADIZ.

⌊From Clarke and M'Arthur, vol. ii. p. 379.⌋

[About July, 1804.]

I live in hopes yet to see Buonaparte humbled, and Spain resuming her natural rank amongst the Nations, which that clever scoundrel prevents: he wants to have her revolutionized, or that he should have more money for preserving the name of the Spanish Monarchy. I sincerely hope England and Spain will long remain at peace. I am, &c.,

NELSON AND BRONTE.

TO THE CAPTAIN OR COMMANDER OF ANY OF HIS MAJESTY'S SHIPS OR VESSELS PROCEEDING FROM GIBRALTAR TO ENGLAND.

[Order-Book.]

Victory, at Sea, 31st[6] July, 1804.

Whereas Mr. M'Donough, his Majesty's late Consul at Tripoli, intends proceeding to England by the first opportunity from Gibraltar, You are hereby required and directed to receive the said Mr. M'Donough, his servant, and baggage, on board his Majesty's Ship under your command, and give them a passage to England, with such accommodation as his situation entitles him to, bearing them on a supernumerary list for victuals, at whole allowance of all species, during their continuance on board.

NELSON AND BRONTE.

TO THE RIGHT HONOURABLE THE LORD MAYOR.

[From "The Annual Register," vol. xlvi. p. 415. "Tuesday, 31st July. P.M. At 7·40, shortened sail and came to in Palma Bay. Squadron anchored here. . . . . . Changed the Right Honourable Lord Viscount Nelson's Flag, Blue at the Fore to White."[7] "Wednesday, 1st August, A.M. Rear-Admiral Sir Richard Bickerton changed from White at the Mizen, to Red; and Rear-Admiral Campbell from Blue at the Mizen, to White."]

Victory, August 1st, 1804.

My Lord,

This day, I am honoured with your Lordship's letter of April 9th, transmitting me the Resolutions of the Corporation

---

[6] *Sic*, but more probably the *first* of July, as it follows the order to Captain Pettet, of that date, in p. 93, ante.

[7] Vide vol. v. p. 513.

of London, thanking me as commanding the Fleet blockading Toulon. I do assure your Lordship that there is not a man breathing who sets a higher value upon the thanks of his Fellow-Citizens of London than myself; but I should feel as much ashamed to receive them for a particular service marked in the Resolution, if I felt that I did not come within that line of service, as I should feel hurt at having a great Victory passed over without notice. I beg to inform your Lordship that the Port of Toulon has never been blockaded by me : quite the reverse—every opportunity has been offered the Enemy to put to sea, for it is there that we hope to realize the hopes and expectations of our Country, and I trust that they will not be disappointed.

Your Lordship will judge of my feelings upon seeing that all the Junior Flag-Officers of other Fleets, and even some of the Captains, have received the thanks of the Corporation of London, whilst the Junior Flag-Officers of the Mediterranean Fleet are entirely omitted. I own it has struck me very forcibly; for, where the information of the Junior Flag-Officers and Captains of other Fleets was obtained, the same information could have been given of the Flag-Officers of this Fleet and the Captains; and, it is my duty to state, that more able and zealous Flag-Officers and Captains do not grace the British Navy, than those I have the honour and happiness to command.

It likewise appears, my Lord, a most extraordinary circumstance, that Sir Richard Bickerton should have been, as Second in Command in the Mediterranean Fleets, twice passed over by the Corporation of London: once after the Egyptian Expedition, when the First and Third in Command were thanked, and now again! Conscious of high desert, instead of neglect, the Rear-Admiral resolved to let the matter rest until he could have an opportunity personally to call upon the Lord Mayor, to account for such an extraordinary omission ; but from this second omission, I owe it to that excellent Officer not to pass it by. I do assure your Lordship, that the constant, zealous, and cordial support I have had in my Command, from both Rear-Admiral Sir Richard Bickerton and Rear-Admiral Campbell, has been such as calls forth all my thanks and admiration. We have shared together the constant attention of being fourteen months at sea, and are ready to share the dangers and glory of a day of Battle ; therefore, it is impossiblè that I can ever allow myself to be separated in Thanks from such supporters. I have the honour to remain, with the very highest respect, your Lordship's most faithful and obedient servant,

NELSON AND BRONTE.[8]

TO THE MASTERS OF HIS MAJESTY'S SHIPS VICTORY, AMAZON, AND PHŒBE.[9]

[Order-Book.]

Victory, Gulf of Palma, Sardinia, 2nd August, 1804.

Captain Bayntun, of his Majesty's Ship Leviathan, having represented to me by letter of this date, that in receiving bread from the Amity Transport, a bag of it, said to contain 112lbs, by accident fell overboard into the sea, and that in consequence of the great swell and the Boats pitching considerably, the said bag of bread was completely wet, and thereby rendered unfit to issue, and requested a survey thereon ; You are hereby required and directed to repair on board his Majesty's Ship Leviathan, and strictly and carefully survey the bag of bread complained of as above, taking care to see every particle of it particularly picked, and the dust wiped off, in order that as much as possible of it may be saved for further use, reporting to me, from under your hands, a very correct and distinct account of your proceedings herein, stating the quantity that may be fit for issuing, which you will leave in charge of the Purser for that purpose, and also, the unserviceable bread to be dried, and returned into his Majesty's Store ; and you are further hereby directed strictly to inquire whether blame is to be attached to any individual for the said loss, in order that it may be charged against his growing wages.

NELSON AND BRONTE.

[8] "As soon as this letter was made public, Mr. Dixon, Common Councilman, sent to all the newspapers an explanation, which stated that the ' Vote of Thanks' to Admirals Cornwallis and Thornborough, proposed by himself, was amended by Alderman Curtis, with a Vote of Thanks to Lord Nelson. The worthy Alderman, it seems, whose good motives cannot be doubted, did not happen to recollect the names of the Officers next in command."—*Annual Register*, vol. xlvi. p. 415.

[9] This, and some similar Orders are inserted because they show the attention which Lord Nelson paid to the minutest details of his Command, and his extreme care of the Public stores.

TO CAPTAIN ROSENHAGEN, H. M. SLOOP LA SOPHIE.

[Letter-Book.]

Victory, Gulf of Palma, 2nd August, 1804.

Sir,

I have received your letter of the 7th July, with a Journal of La Sophie's proceedings from 15th April to 31st May last: also, a list of a Vessel detained, and since condemned in the Vice-Admiralty Court, at Gibraltar. Your letter of the 8th ultimo has also been received, together with a Log of your proceedings since your leaving the Fleet. In answer to which, I am very much pleased with your success in the detention of the Vessel above alluded to, and hope the sentence of condemnation may be confirmed in England. Your indefatigable exertions for the protection of our Commerce, and destruction of the Enemy's Privateers has my entire approbation ; and I trust on your return from Malta, that your endeavours for the destruction of those Pirates may be more successful. I am, &c.,

NELSON AND BRONTE.

TO COMMISSIONER OTWAY, GIBRALTAR.

[Letter-Book.]

Victory, Gulf of Palma, 2nd August, 1804.

Sir,

Lieutenant Lloyd commanding the Guerrier Prison-Ship having for the greater protection of our Trade, and destruction of the Enemy's Privateers, requested that I would place a Gun-Boat under his immediate command,—as his request appears to have the good of his Majesty's Service for its object, I have no objections to a Gun-Boat being placed under his orders, provided they are under your directions, and no reason remains with you to the contrary. Enclosed is an extract of my letter on this subject to Lieutenant Lloyd, for your further information. I am, &c.,

NELSON AND BRONTE.

TO CAPTAIN GORE, H. M. SHIP MEDUSA.

[Letter-Book.]

Victory, Gulf of Palma, August 2nd, 1804.

Sir,

I have received your letter of the 11th July, with the
Report of Survey, and two letters, therein mentioned. In
answer thereto, I am very sorry for the hurt Mr. Noot has
received; and perfectly satisfied with your having taken Mr.
Bridges, the Boatswain intended for the Phœbe; and herewith
transmit you a Warrant appointing him to the Medusa. With
respect to Mr. Ford, the Gunner, whom you represent as a
worthless man, and incapable of doing his duty, I have only
to observe that if you can invalid him, I will appoint either
the Gunner of Halcyon or Sophie, if you particularly desire
it,—otherwise send you a Gunner from the Squadron the
moment you apply to me for that purpose: and I should
suppose so worthless a character would be glad of getting
away with his Warrant, sooner than risk a Court-Martial. I
am, &c.,

NELSON AND BRONTE.

TO CAPTAIN HENRY W. PEARSE, H. M. SLOOP HALCYON.

[Letter-Book.]

Victory, Gulf of Palma, 2nd August, 1804.

Sir,

I have received your letters of the dates and purport under-
mentioned, viz. :—

Of the 24th of May, acquainting me with your having, on
the 16th of that month, proceeded to Faro, with the Mails for
Gibraltar, and that on your return, on the 24th, near Tarifa,
you fell in with three Settees, under Spanish colours, whose
conduct and manœuvres soon proved to you they were
French Privateers; that after firing upon them they pulled
towards the shore; and that two of them, in attempting their
escape, were drove on the reefs, one of which was entirely
lost, and the other got off by the Spaniards, and transmitting a
Log of your proceedings on the occasion, for my information.
And of the 9th of July—transmitting a Log of the Halcyon's

proceedings, from 1st March to 30th June, enclosing two lists of Vessels detained by the said Sloop. In answer to which, I am very much pleased with your conduct against the Enemy's Privateers, or rather Pirates, before-mentioned, as well as with your detention of the two Vessels, and hope they may answer your expectations. Your future exertions for the protection of our Trade, and destruction of the Enemy's Privateers, within the limits of your Station, will, I trust, be unremitting, and attended with success. I am, &c.,

NELSON AND BRONTE.

TO COMMISSIONER OTWAY, GIBRALTAR.

[Letter-Book.]

Victory, Gulf of Palma, 2nd August, 1804.

Sir,

I have received your letter of the 20th June last, together with a copy of your letter to Captain Ryves, and his answer thereto, on the subject of the impossibility of refitting the Gibraltar, agreeable to their Lordships' direction, in consequence of which, you had recommended Captain Ryves's proceeding immediately to England. In answer to which, I am very much pleased with your having sent her to England, as I never approved of the partial and inefficient refit intended by the late Admiralty order to you. I am, &c.,

NELSON AND BRONTE.

TO LIEUTENANT ROBERT LLOYD, COMMANDING HIS MAJESTY'S PRISON-SHIP GUERRIER.

[Letter-Book.]

Victory, Gulf of Palma, 2nd August, 1804.

Sir,

I have received your letter of the 10th July, acquainting me, that on the 28th May last, you assisted with the Guerrier's Boat at the capture of a Polacca Ship, part of whose cargo has since been condemned as French property, in the Vice-Admiralty Court of Gibraltar, and that you considered your joint assistance in the said capture as entitling you to share for the Prize. In answer to which, notwithstanding the

Privateer's Boat, mentioned in your said letter, boarded the
Polacca Ship first, there can be no doubt that the presence of
the Guerrier's Boat intimidated, and most probably induced,
the people on board that Vessel, to give her up without resistance; and therefore, if the Judge has not decided against
you, I should most certainly have considered you entitled
to share, from the circumstances stated in your said letter; but
judgment having passed, I must give full credit to the sentence,
satisfied that the purity of our laws embrace, and maturely
weigh, all circumstances before sentence is given. In further
answer to your letter on the subject of placing a Gun-Boat
under your order, for the greater benefit of his Majesty's
Service, I have no objections to this measure, provided Commissioner Otway (under whose charge I presume they are,
and to whom I have written on the subject) sees no impropriety therein; and therefore, should the Commissioner
deem it proper to do so, you are to receive his instructions
on all services when it may be necessary to employ the Gun-
Boat alluded to. I am, &c.,

NELSON AND BRONTE.

TO COMMISSIONER OTWAY, GIBRALTAR.

[Letter-Book.]

Victory, Gulf of Palma, 2nd August, 1804.

Sir,

I have received your several letters of the dates and purport under mentioned—viz., [here follow the dates and purport
of the numerous letters alluded to.] In answer to your several
above-mentioned letters, I am perfectly satisfied with your
inquiry into Mr. ——'s neglect of duty, in refitting the Phœbe;
but by no means with his conduct, either on that occasion, or
in the valuation of the Ambuscade. So fine a Frigate, and so
lately repaired as she was, to be only in value *equal* to the
Halcyon, is extraordinary indeed, and leaves upon my mind
no very favourable opinion of Mr. C——'s judgment, particularly as the masts of the said Frigate were considered by the
Officers at Portsmouth Yard more than one-third under their
real value. I am very much obliged by the enclosures which
accompanied your several letters. The abstracts made of the

Musters, as mentioned in yours of the 10th ultimo, do not take any notice of Mr. Ross, Boatswain of the Halcyon, being absent without leave. Although it appears, by Captain Pearse's letter, that he left that Sloop on the 23rd day of February last, the said Mr. Ross does not either appear chequed on the abstract for March last. The Prevoyante's bill of lading was very properly sent, as it will enable me to know what dependence can be had on your stores. I am, &c.

NELSON AND BRONTE.

TO SIR ALEXANDER JOHN BALL, BART., MALTA.

[From Clarke and M'Arthur, vol. ii. p. 378.]

3rd August, 1804.

I have received, my dear Ball, your sketch of the views of the French in the Mediterranean, on the whole outline of which I perfectly agree with you, and on the smaller part there are only shades of difference. My opinion of the views of Russia has long been formed, and to this moment I see everything she does works to the same end—the possession of all European Turkey. I have delivered my opinion when in England, how this plan of Russia might be turned to much advantage for us, and how it would operate against France. I know the importance of Malta; but, my friend, I fancy, I also know how far its importance extends: on this point we may differ, but we both agree that it never must be *even risked* falling into the hands of France....... Look at the position of Sardinia; I have touched, I recollect, before upon that subject, and you should be Viceroy. I have *warned* the folks at home, but I fear in vain. Algiers will be French in one year after a Peace: you see it, and a man may run and read; that is the plan of Buonaparte. Respecting Egypt, I agree with you most perfectly. And now, my dear Ball, I will not plague you with my nonsensical ideas any more; and have only to hope Monsieur La Touche, who says, in his letter to Paris,[8]

[8] Of this Letter, which naturally gave great offence to Lord Nelson, and to which he very frequently alluded, the following is a copy:—

"Abord du Bucentaure, en rade de Toulon,
"Général,　　　　　　　　le 26 Prairial an 12.

"J'ai l'honneur de vous rendre compte de la sortie de toute l'escadre à mes ordres. Sur l'avis que j'avais reçu que plusieurs corsaires Anglais infestaient la

that I ran away from him on June 14th, will give me an
opportunity of settling my account before I go home, which
cannot be much longer deferred, or I shall never go. I
am, &c.,

NELSON AND BRONTE.

TO LAMBTON ESTE, ESQ., MALTA.

[Autograph, in the possession of Dr. Lambton Este. Dr. Este states that,
" When proceeding up the Mediterranean, in July 1804, I found at the Post Office
at Gibraltar, several letters for persons in high situations, detained on account of
some trifling postage, which I caused to be properly forwarded. I did the same at
Port Mahon and at Malta. At Malta there were several for Lord Nelson, then off
Toulon. One letter, especially, excited my attention; it was from La Touche Tréville, the French Admiral then opposed to his Lordship, which I forwarded to Lord
Nelson, with some remarks on the Post Offices, and I afterwards received the following answer:]

Victory, August 3rd, 1804.

Dear Sir,

I feel very much obliged by your letter of July 7th, and
for Monsieur La Touche's letter,[9] who, I suppose, not knowing
where to find me, he directed to Malta. I most perfectly
agree with you on the great irregularity of our Post Offices
in this Country, but the mending them does not only not
rest with me, but, probably, if I was to meddle or recommend, it might make *bad worse*. I hope you left your
worthy father well : do little wonder that you are not at your
post in Egypt. I had a line from Mr. Lock[1] from Naples:
reports say that he is going first to Constantinople. With
every good wish, I am, dear Sir, your much obliged servant,

NELSON AND BRONTE.

côte et les îles d'Hières, je donnai l'ordre, il y a trois jours, aux frégates l'Incor-
ruptible et la Syrène, et le brick le Furet, de se rendre dans la baie d'Hières. Le
vent d'est les ayant contrariées, elles mouillèrent sous le château de Porqueroles.
Hier matin, les ennemis en eurent connaissance. Vers midi, ils détachèrent deux
frègates et un vaisseau, qui entrèrent par la grande passe, dans l'intention de couper
la retraite à nos frégates. Du moment où je m'aperçus de sa manœuvre, je fis
signal d'appareiller à toute l'escadre ; ce qui fut exécuté. En 14 minutes, tout
était sous voiles, et je fis porter sur l'ennemi pour lui couper le chemin de la petite
passe, et dans le dessein de l'y suivre, s'il avait tenté d'y passer ; mais l'Amiral
Anglais ne tarda pas à renoncer à son projet, rappela son vaisseau et ses deux
frégates engagés dans les îles et prit chasse. Je l'ai poursuivi jusqu'à la nuit ; il
courait au sud-est. Le matin, au jour, je n'en ai eu aucune connoissance. Je
vous salue avec respect, LA TOUCHE TREVILLE."

[9] Vide vol. v. p. 459.   [1] Vide vol. iii. p. 420, and iv. pp. 127, 128.

TO COUNT MOCENIGO, AT CORFU.

[From Clarke and M'Arthur, vol. ii. p. 381.]

[About 4th August, 1804.]

In Sea affairs, nothing is impossible, and nothing improbable. I am, &c.,

NELSON AND BRONTE.

TO JOHN PALMER, ESQ.

[Autograph, in the possession of Mrs. Palmer.]

My dear Sir,   Victory, August 4th, 1804.

I am favoured with your kind letter of May 17th, and if it
had been in my power, I should have readily kept your good
son[2] in the Mediterranean; but we have no Sloops here. I
congratulate you upon the Earl's promoting him before he
quitted. I wish he had thought of my nephew. I hope the
Ministry will get us an honourable Peace: we want one for
many reasons; and for none more than for an opportunity of
getting our Navy in order again. When you see Lord Lans-
downe, I beg my kindest respects to him, and believe me ever,
my dear Sir, your most obliged servant,

NELSON AND BRONTE.

TO ADMIRAL SIR ROBERT KINGSMILL, BART.

[Autograph, in the possession of Sir John Kingsmill.]

My dear Kingsmill,   Victory, August 4th, 1804.

It gave me a twitch of pleasure to see your handwriting
again; and believe me, my dear friend, that there is nothing
that you can desire me to do, that I should not fly to do with
the greatest pleasure. Can I forget all your former kindness
to me? No, Horatio Nelson is (all that is left of him) the
same as you formerly knew him; nor do I forget all Mary's
goodness to me.

Bastard[3] is a very fine young man, and I will remove him

---

[2] Afterwards Captain Edmund Palmer, C.B. Vide vol. ii. p. 440.

[3] Lieutenant John Bastard, second son of Edmund Bastard of Kitley, in Devonshire, Esq.: he died a Post Captain, in January 1835.

out of the Bomb. Independent of your friendship, Mr. Bastard,[4] Member for Devon, is a character that we must all respect for his high worth and principles. I can readily believe the pleasure you must have had, in meeting some of my friends at good Admiral and Mrs. Lutwidge's. I am sorry to tell you that my health, or rather constitution, is so much shook, that I doubt the possibility of my holding out another winter, without asses' milk, and some months' quiet; then I may get on another campaign or two; but, my dear Kingsmill, when I run over the under-mentioned wounds—Eye in Corsica, Belly off Cape St. Vincent, Arm at Teneriffe, Head in Egypt—I ought to be thankful that I am what I am. If Monsieur La Touche will give me the meeting before I go home, it will probably finish my Naval career. He is ready, and, by their handling their Ships, apparently well manned; but I command, for Captains and Crews, such a Fleet, as I never have before seen; and it is impossible that any Admiral can be happier situated. *Rotten Ships* neither rests with me nor them. God bless you, my dear Kingsmill, and believe me ever your most faithful and affectionate friend,

NELSON AND BRONTE.

TO SIR EVAN NEPEAN, BART.

[From Clarke and M'Arthur, vol. ii. p. 381.]

August 4th, 1804.

You will, I am sure, see with regret, that my shattered carcase requires rest. The leaving this Fleet, where every one wishes to please me, and where I am as happy as it is possible for a man to be in a Command, must make me feel; but I owe to my King and Country, and to myself, not to let the Service suffer upon my account. I have not interest, nor can I expect to be permitted to return in the Spring to this Command. Yet is this place, perhaps, more fitted for me than any other—but I submit. All my wishes now rest that I may meet Monsieur La Touche before October is over. I am, &c.

NELSON AND BRONTE.

---

[4] John Pollexfen Bastard, Esq., uncle of Lieutenant Bastard.

TO SIR ALEXANDER JOHN BALL, BART.

[Autograph, in the possession of Miss Collinson.]

Victory, August 5th, 1804.

My dear Ball,

This will be delivered to you by Mr. Curtis,[3] who goes Acting-Captain of the Jalouse, during Captain Strachey's going on shore for the recovery of his health. Curtis will be confirmed, therefore, you may safely call him Captain Curtis. He is Sir Roger's only son, and I think Sir Roger the most likely person to take my place; and I think him the fittest for it. He is an able Officer and conciliating man. Captain Parker of the Amazon I believe you know: he is only to be known to be loved, both as an Officer and a Gentleman. Ever, my dear Ball, yours most faithfully,

NELSON AND BRONTE.

TO CAPTAIN WILLIAM PARKER, H. M. SHIP AMAZON.

[Order-Book.]

Victory, Gulf of Palma, Sardinia, 5th August, 1804.

Memorandum.

It is my directions that you receive on board the Amazon, the crew of a Vessel detained by the Donegal, and give them a passage to Malta, that they may share the fate of their Vessel. You will also receive a French gentleman, who was found a passenger in the said Vessel; and on your arrival in Valetta Harbour, you will carry him to Sir Alexander Ball for examination, and if there does not appear anything suspicious or improper in his conduct, he may be allowed to proceed to Corfu, agreeable to his intentions. It is not my wish that he, or the people above-mentioned, should be treated as Prisoners, but that care should be taken of them. You will also receive the Officers named in the margin, on board the Amazon, together with such other persons as may be going to Malta from the different Ships, victualling the crew and French gentleman found on board the detained Vessel

---

[3] Now Rear-Admiral Sir Lucius Curtis, Bart., C.B., eldest son of the late Admiral Sir Roger Curtis, Bart., G.C.B.

before mentioned, at two-thirds, and the others at full allowance of all species of provisions, during their passage to Malta.

NELSON AND BRONTE.

TO CAPTAIN RICHARD HUSSEY MOUBRAY, H.M. SHIP ACTIVE.

[Order-Book.]

Victory, Gulf of Palma, Sardinia, 6th August, 1804.

You are hereby required and directed to take his Majesty's Ships named in the margin,[5] under your command, and proceed immediately with them to Rendezvous No. 102, where you will find the Niger, and most probably the Acheron, and two Transports with water for the Squadron. You will, as early after as possible, reconnoitre the Enemy at Toulon, leaving the Niger and Bombs with the Transports on the said Rendezvous; and you will deliver my letter, herewith transmitted, together with a copy of this order, to Captain Hillyar, that he may give them to Captain Hargood, on the Belleisle's joining him, in case she should not have done so previous to your getting there. You will also desire Captain Hillyar to acquaint the Captains of the Belleisle and Kent, or any Vessel that may be in search of me, to remain on Rendezvous No. 102, as I shall proceed with the Squadron to that place this evening, or to-morrow morning early, should the wind continue from the Eastward; but if from the Westward, I shall go to Pula, in order to complete the Squadron with water. You will, therefore, in the event of the Enemy having put to sea from Toulon, take these circumstances into account, and dispatch a Vessel, without a moment's loss of time, with directions to her Commander to look into this anchorage, and at Pula. Not finding the Squadron at either of those places, he must judge from the wind and weather, where it is most likely to fall in with it, in its way to the before-mentioned Rendezvous, and proceed in search of it with the utmost dispatch.

NELSON AND BRONTE.

[5] Phœbe, Seahorse.

TO CAPTAIN GORE, H.M. SHIP MEDUSA.

[Letter-Book.]

Victory, Gulf of Palma, August 6th, 1804.

Sir,

I have received your letter of the 12th ult., with copies of your two letters to his Excellency the Marquis de Solano, Governor of Cadiz, and to Mr. Frere, his Majesty's Minister at Madrid; also, the several documents which accompanied them, setting forth the enormities and unlicensed outrages of the French Privateers, together with the papers transmitted you by Sir Thomas Trigge on the same subject. In answer thereto, I beg to say, how sensible I am of the interest you have taken on this occasion, for the good and protection of the Trade of his Majesty's Subjects against the unprincipled conduct of the French Pirates; and hope it may in some degree check them in future, though I much fear while Spain and Portugal remain in their present state of quiet and fearful subjection to the tyrannical yoke of France, little else but similar depredations can be expected. Your persevering conduct, however, on this, and on every other occasion, has my entire approbation. I am, &c.,

NELSON AND BRONTE.

TO CAPTAIN GORE, H.M. SHIP MEDUSA.

[Letter-Book.]

Victory, Gulf of Palma, 6th August. 1804.

Sir,

I have to acknowledge the receipt of your letter of the 1st ult., with copies of the several orders, and Log-Book, &c., therein mentioned, and to express my full approbation thereof. I am glad to find the Halcyon is completely repaired, and particularly so, that Captain Pearse's conduct meets your approbation. The inactivity of that Sloop reached me through different channels;[6] but I am satisfied, from your account of the state of the Halcyon, that blame is not imputable to her Commander, and I request you will tell him so. I am very

---

[6] Vide p. 10, ante.

much pleased with your having carried Captain Layman to Lisbon, and that he and Captain Whitby were so fortunate as to get a passage to England in the Fisgard, as well as with your exertions to procure men at Lisbon and Oporto; and hope, on some future occasion, you will be more fortunate. You were perfectly right in taking the fifteen supernumeraries from the Poulette, as her Commander will be able to pick up some men, while he is waiting for the Convoy from Lisbon. The station you occupied with the Medusa, La Sophie, and Halcyon, for the protection of the Ambuscade and Convoy, was a very proper one, and such as would not fail to insure their safety. Your intentions to destroy the Enemy's Privateers and other Vessels in the Gut, I hope may be attended with success. At any rate much credit is due for the attempt; and I feel much pleasure in acknowledging the very great service your unwearied exertions and perseverance have rendered to the Trade of his Majesty's Subjects, as well as to the destruction of the Pirates who infest the vicinity of Gibraltar. I am, &c.,

NELSON AND BRONTE.

TO THE COMMISSIONERS OF THE TRANSPORT BOARD, LONDON.

[Original, in the Record Office of the Tower of London. " Tuesday, 7th August, 1804. At 4·30 A.M., weighed, as did all the Squadron, and made all sail. At 10 P.M., anchored. Wednesday, 8th August, weighed and made sail. At 7·30, anchored in Pula Roads, in the Gulf of Cagliari, with the Squadron. At 1·15, saluted his Majesty's Consul at Cagliari with nine guns, on his coming on board, and again, at 7·15, on his going away."—*Victory's Log.*]

Victory, at Sea, 7th August, 1804.

Gentlemen,

It having been represented to me by the Captains of the Squadron, that the coals supplied their respective Ships from the Harmony Transport at the Madalena Islands in May last, were nearly one-eighth short of their measure, I wrote to the Officers of Malta Yard, a copy of which letter is herewith enclosed, together with the Report, and my answer thereto, by which it appears that sixty chaldrons of coals were short of the quantity which ought to have been delivered to the respective Pursers of the Squadron before-mentioned, by the fraudulent conduct of Mr. ——, Master of the said Transport; I therefore desire to observe the propriety of a severe example being made of this man, for such a dishonest practice; and of the very great necessity of giving the most positive instructions to the Masters of all future Transports, sent out to the Fleet with coals, to give just measure in the delivery of them to the respective Ships, and not avail themselves of any false pretence, or the pressing necessity of quick dispatch to rob the individual of his property. I consider Mr. ——'s conduct the more reprehensible, as the weather was fair, the water smooth, and his Vessel taken alongside each Ship at the Madalena Islands for delivery.

The coals are in store at Malta, and I have written the Commissioners for Victualling on the subject, that they may give the respective Pursers credit for the quantity they have been so defrauded of; and have at the same time, directed the Officers of Malta Yard to consider them as Government's and use them accordingly, transmitting to your Board and to the Commissioners for Victualling an account thereof. I am, &c.,

NELSON AND BRONTE.

TO WILLIAM MARSDEN, ESQ., ADMIRALTY.

[Original, in the Admiralty.]

Victory, at Sea, 7th August, 1804.

Sir,

Your letter of the 15th May, with the Commissions therein mentioned, appointing me Vice-Admiral of the White Squadron; Sir Richard Bickerton, Bart., Rear-Admiral of the Red; George Campbell, Esq., Rear-Admiral of the White; and George Murray, Esq., Rear-Admiral of the Blue: also a Commission continuing Rear-Admiral Murray Captain of the Fleet under my command, together with one promoting the Honourable Josceline Percy[6] to be Lieutenant of the Medusa. In answer thereto, you will please to acquaint their Lordships, that the Commissions to the Flag-Officers above mentioned have been delivered, and that the Honourable Lieu-

---

[6] Fourth son of Algernon, first Earl of Beverley, now a Rear-Admiral of the Blue, and Companion of the Bath.

tenant Percy's shall be sent to him the first opportunity going to Gibraltar. My Secretary has been directed to receive the Fees marked on them respectively, and to account to your Office for the same. I am Sir, &c.,

NELSON AND BRONTE.

TO WILLIAM MARSDEN, ESQ., ADMIRALTY.

[Original, in the Admiralty.]

Victory, at Sea, 7th August, 1804.

Sir,

I have received your letter of the 15th May, inclosing a copy of a representation from the Underwriters at Lloyd's Coffee-House respecting the captures made by the Enemy's Privateers in the Adriatic: also inclosing an extract of a letter from a gentleman at Trieste, stating that the Ship Betsy had been captured by a French Privateer off the Island of Chiozza, in consequence of her having been incautiously left at the entrance of the Gulf by her Convoy, directing me to make inquiry into this circumstance, and report the same to you, for their Lordships' information, and further directions.

In answer thereto, you will please to acquaint the Lords Commissioners of the Admiralty that the utmost attention has been paid to the protection of our Commerce in the Adriatic and Archipelago, as far as the number of Frigates and Sloops under my command has enabled me, (which their Lordships will observe by the Disposition of the Squadron;) and I can say, that there never was known, at any one time, so great a number of Vessels of War in the Adriatic as is at this moment under the orders of Captain Cracraft; but certainly, if two small Frigates or large Sloops could be spared, I would place one at Trieste, and another at Venice. Such arrangement is not, however, in my power at present; and to reduce Captain Cracraft's Squadron would leave the entrance to the Adriatic without a sufficient force to prevent the Enemy conveying Troops into the Morea at pleasure.

The protection afforded the Enemy's Privateers and Row-boats in the different Neutral Ports in these seas, so contrary to every known law of Neutrality, is extremely destructive to our Commerce, and will certainly prove so in spite of all the force which can be brought against these Pirates. The most strict orders have and shall be given to the Commanders of Convoys bound from Malta up the Adriatic and Archipelago, to see the Ships and Vessels under their charge in safety to their destination, and inquiry made into the circumstances attending the capture of the Ship Betsy, before mentioned, and report made accordingly. I am, &c.,

NELSON AND BRONTE.

TO THE COMMISSIONERS FOR VICTUALLING HIS MAJESTY'S NAVY, LONDON.

[Letter-Book.]

Victory, at Sea, 7th August, 1804.

Gentlemen,

I have received your letter of the 26th March, respecting the claims of Mr. Gibert, Vice-Consul at Barcelona, for his losses, in endeavouring to supply the Fleet under my command with wine; stating, at the same time, that you consider the investigation into the said losses may be more efficiently accomplished under my authority. In answer thereto, I offered to take the said wine from Mr. Gibert at an advanced price, previous to the arrival of Mr. Ford, the Agent Victualler to the Fleet, and have since, through him; but Mr. Gibert will not fix any price, and only wishes us to take the wine, which has been since kept in store at Rosas, and I presume by this time is entirely sour. I shall make another official offer, and endeavour to bring the business to issue, the result of which shall be transmitted to your Board. I am, &c.

NELSON AND BRONTE.

TO WILLIAM MARSDEN, ESQ., ADMIRALTY.

[Original, in the Admiralty.]

Victory, at Sea, 7th August, 1804.

Sir,

I herewith transmit you a copy of a contract entered into by Doctor Snipe, Physician of the Fleet, and Mr. Gray, Surgeon of the Naval Hospital at Malta, with Mr. John Broadbent, Merchant at Messina, for supplying thirty thousand gallons of lemon juice, for the Sick and Hurt Board, which you will please to lay before the Lords Commissioners of the Admiralty for their information, as it appears to me, from the low price contracted for, to be an object of great consideration in the Victualling Department, and by which immense sums might be saved by that Board in their future purchase of this article, which I understand from the Physician of the Fleet, may be had in any quantity.

I must here beg to observe, that Doctor Snipe went from Malta (where he was on service) to Messina, for the purpose of accomplishing this contract: and when it is considered that lemon juice in England (if so it may be called) costs eight shillings per gallon, and in the contract before-mentioned only one shilling for the real juice, it will, I am sure, entitle Doctor Snipe to their Lordships' approbation for his conduct and perseverance on the occasion; and I understand from him, that Mr. Broadbent's profits are still very fair. I judge it proper to remark that two Pursers, who have been dismissed their situations for improper conduct, are both employed at Malta; one, Mr. ———, as Agent to the Hospital, and the other, Mr. ———, as Agent to the Contractor for Prisoners of War. The conduct of the former has already been extremely improper, as represented by Doctor Snipe to the Sick and Hurt Board; and it will naturally occur to their Lordships the impropriety of appointing such characters to Public situations abroad.

I am informed it is the intention of the Agent to the Contractor for Prisoners of War, to discontinue giving them fresh beef, and to supply them with salt in lieu, on account of the latter being so much more reasonable than the former. I must, therefore, beg to observe to their Lordships, that as Prisoners of War are not allowed wine, the giving them salt beef instead of fresh, will, from their long and close confinement, naturally produce disease and very dangerous consequences; and it is with much deference I take the liberty of mentioning to their Lordships (that as Frenchmen are in the habit of drinking small wine in their own Country) the propriety of allowing Prisoners of War a certain quantity each per day. I am, &c.

NELSON AND BRONTE.

TO THE COMMISSIONERS FOR SICK AND WOUNDED SEAMEN,
LONDON.

[Letter-Book.]

Victory, at Sea, 7th August, 1804.

Gentlemen,

I have received your letter of the 27th April, acquainting me that, in consequence of directions from the Lords Commissioners of the Admiralty, you had dismissed Mr. ——— from the situation of Dispenser at Gibraltar Hospital, and appointed Mr. Christie in his room. In answer thereto, I am extremely happy that a character so dangerous, not only to the individual, but also to the Public Service, is dismissed from it with disgrace ; and I hope it may be a warning to all in subordinate situations, and prevent them from attempting, by such infamous means, to succeed in their advancement, at the expense of sacrificing the upright and honest man. I am, &c.

NELSON AND BRONTE.

TO CAPTAIN JOHN GORE, H.M. SHIP MEDUSA.

[Letter-Book.]

Victory, at Sea, 7th August, 1804.

Sir,

As no General Order can, on all occasions, embrace the good of the individual, and at the same time prevent his Majesty's Service from being imposed on, by the invaliding improper objects, (too frequently done to get clear of bad and worthless characters,) my order of the 10th May, directed to the Senior Officer, was meant, as much as possible, to do away this last-mentioned custom ; and to prevent every Senior Officer from ordering Surveys at Gibraltar Hospital, when they thought proper, and by no means intended to preclude discreet Officers from holding Surveys on proper objects. You will, therefore, order such men to be examined as may appear to you proper objects for invaliding, and continue to do so on all future occasions when you may deem it necessary ; but I have desired the Surgeon of the Hospital to consider my said order still in force, except when you might think proper to direct it otherwise, so that this service is entirely at your discretion, and I must desire that no other Officer may interfere with it. I am, &c.

NELSON AND BRONTE.

TO WILLIAM MARSDEN, ESQ., ADMIRALTY.

[Letter-Book.]

Victory, at Sea, 7th August, 1804.

Sir,

I have received your letter of the 14th May, acquainting me that their Lordships had ordered Captain Durban to be furnished with two Time-keepers, and that he has provided himself with instruments necessary for making observations and surveys, their Lordships intending that he should be employed in the Black Sea, for the further purposes communicated in your said letter. In answer to which, you will please to acquaint their Lordships that with Sir Evan Nepean's letter to me, of the 28th September last, was transmitted a copy of a letter from Count Woronzow, the Russian Minister at our Court, to Lord Hawkesbury, and of one from Count Alexander Woronzow, at St. Petersburg, prohibiting, in the strongest manner, the navigation of the Black Sea, by any description of Armed Vessels. Under such instructions, it is impossible that their Lordships' intentions, communicated to me in your letter before-mentioned, can for the present be put in force; and I am also informed that there is an objection, on the part of the Porte, to any Ships passing beyond the Seven Towers, without a particular convention. On this subject I have wrote to Mr. Stratton, our Minister at Constantinople. I am, &c.

NELSON AND BRONTE.

TO WILLIAM MARSDEN, ESQ., ADMIRALTY.

[Letter-Book.]

Victory, at Sea, 7th August, 1804.

Sir,

I have received your letter of the 9th April, with the inclosure therein mentioned, from the Spanish Minister to

Lord Hawkesbury, complaining of the conduct of the Commander of the British Privateer Les Deux Frères, in capturing a Spanish Vessel close off the Port of Palamos, in Catalonia, and signifying to me their Lordships' direction to make the necessary inquiry into the circumstances therein stated, and take such steps as the case may require. In answer thereto, you will please to acquaint the Lords Commissioners of the Admiralty, that if I had the least authority whatever in controlling the Privateers, whose conduct is so disgraceful to the British Nation, I would instantly take their Commissions from them; but as Naval Commanders have no power over them whatever, I am obliged to hear from the Sardinian Government and others, of their daily depredations, without being able either to check, or put a stop to it. The only thing I can, therefore, do in the present instance (as I have in several other similar ones) is to transmit your letter, and its enclosure to the Governor of Gibraltar, that he may take such steps as may appear to him proper, to put a stop to the piratical proceedings of such a hoard of sanctioned robbers. I am, &c.

NELSON AND BRONTE.

TO CAPTAIN GEORGE RYVES, H.M. SHIP GIBRALTAR.

[Letter-Book.]

Victory, at Sea, 7th August, 1804.
Sir,

I have received your letter of the 15th June, together with a copy of the one therein-mentioned from Commissioner Otway; and I am very much pleased, and extremely happy that you proceeded to England with the Gibraltar, instead of re-joining me, as I have long seen the necessity of that Ship's being in dock. I am, &c.

NELSON AND BRONTE.

TO HIS EXCELLENCY SIR THOMAS TRIGGE, K.B.

[Letter-Book.]

Victory, at Sea, 7th August, 1804.

Sir,

I beg leave to enclose a copy of a letter from Mr. Secretary Marsden, dated the 9th April last, together with a copy of the one therein-mentioned, from the Spanish Minister at our Court to Lord Hawkesbury, respecting the conduct of the Commander of Les Deux Frères, Privateer, in capturing a Spanish Vessel, as therein stated. It is not necessary for me to point out the disgraceful conduct of the Gibraltar Privateers in these seas, as so many circumstances must long ago have satisfied you with this truth. I shall, therefore, say no more on the subject; and only beg to express a hope that the most exemplary punishment may be inflicted upon the delinquents, when the enormity of their crimes can be proved to conviction, in order to deter them from future depredations. I am, &c.

NELSON AND BRONTE.

TO CAPTAIN SIR EDWARD BERRY.

[From a Copy in the Nelson Papers.]

Victory, August 8th, 1804.

My dear Sir Edward,

You must think that I took your offer of not answering your kind letter of March, (which I take to mean March 1st,) but I only received it by the Ambuscade, which only arrived ten days ago. I sincerely hope now a change has taken place, that you will get a Ship. I attribute none of the tyrannical conduct of the late Board to Lord St. Vincent. For the Earl I have a sincere regard, but he was dreadfully ill-advised, and I fear the Service has suffered much from their conduct. Mrs. Faddy[7] has the impudence of the devil: however, I have made her son a Lieutenant. He seems a smart young man, and is full-grown. I do assure you, my dear Sir Edward, that your letters always give me much pleasure; and I have no great

---

[7] Vide vol. iii. pp. 7, 8, 127, and vol. iv. p. 463.

cause for anxiety, for I certainly command as fine a portion
of Ships as are in the Service.   Hardy is very well and desires
his kind remembrances.   Sutton[8] is stationed at Gibraltar: I
have not seen him for a year past.   I am ever, my dear Sir
Edward, your much obliged friend,

NELSON AND BRONTE.

TO THE REVEREND DR. NELSON.

[Autograph, in the Nelson Papers.]

Victory, August 8th, 1804.

My dear Brother,

Mr. C. B. Yonge[9] had joined the Victory long before your
letter was wrote, and he is a very good, deserving young
man, and when he has served his time, I shall take the earliest
opportunity of putting him into a good vacancy; but that will
not be until October, the very finish, I expect, of my remaining
here, for my health has suffered much since I left England,
and if the Admiralty do not allow me to get at asses' milk
and rest, you will be a Lord before I intend you should.
I am glad the wine was good and acceptable.   I have been
expecting Monsieur La Touche to give me the meeting
every day for this year past, and only hope he will come out
before I go hence.   Remember me kindly to Mrs. Nelson
and believe me ever, your most affectionate brother,

NELSON AND BRONTE.

You must excuse a short letter.   You will have seen
Monsieur La Touche's letter[1] of how he chased me and how I
ran.   I keep it; and, by God, if I take him, he shall *Eat* it !

---

[8] Captain Samuel Sutton, of the Amphion.

[9] Mr. Charles B. Yonge, a distant relation of Mrs. (afterwards Countess) Nelson:
he was appointed Acting Lieutenant of the Seahorse, on the 12th of October following, and appears to have died between 1806 and 1809.

[1] Vide p. 131, note, ante.

TO ALEXANDER DAVISON, ESQ.

[Autograph, in the possession of Colonel Davison.]

Victory, August 9th, 1804.

My dear Davison,

What can be the reason that since the Leviathan, I have never received a scrap of a pen from you; but as I know that I have a box missing sent me by dear Lady Hamilton, I hope that there are some letters from you in it; for I should, my dear friend, be sorry, could I either think that you take to heart your present uncomfortable situation[2] beyond what a man must naturally feel,` or that you could forget for a moment the sincerest of your friends. We all know, that if it was brought forth, that I am sure all the House of Commons, and I dare say, every Freeholder in the United Kingdom, would be with you; for 'directly or indirectly, every man has his price.' So said Sir Robert Walpole. Never mind. Do not take it to heart. It will soon pass away, and I shall come and see you in the Christmas holidays, and we shall laugh at the event.

I have on former occasions wrote to you all about my Merton improvements, that I am sure you will order everything to be paid. If the new building is finished, I shall have a very comfortable house; and I hope the Architect has made the passage from the kitchen to the servants' hall. I would not have one farthing taken from the hundred pounds a month[3] for any of these improvements; and, as I before wrote you, I wish to have them in a separate account, that I may know the cost. I am expecting Monsieur La Touche (as he has wrote a letter that I ran away) to come out of his nest. The whole history was too contemptible for my notice, but I have thought it right, not upon my own account, but for the satisfaction of the Admiralty, &c. &c., to send a copy of the Victory's Log: for if my character for *not* running away, is not fixed by this time, it is not worth my trouble to put the world right at my time of life; and if any Englishman has believed for one moment the story, I may, to my friend, say, without fear of being thought arrogant, that they do not deserve to have me serve them; but I have kept Monsieur La Touche's letter; and if

---

[2] Vide vol. v. p. 143.   [3] His allowance to Lady Hamilton.

I take him, I shall either never see him, or, if I do, *make him
Eat* his letter—perhaps, sovereign contempt is the best.

This conveyance will carry my letter for returning, for the
re-establishment of my health, for a few months. I expect
that the Admiralty will give this Command to some other
Officer, and not allow of my return, if I am able, in the Spring.
But I may say, as the famous De Witt said, ' my life I will
freely risk for my Country, but my health I must take care of.'
If the mind is not strong from good health, depend on it the
other faculties are in unison with it. Asses' milk and a few
months rest may do much for me. But, my dear Davison,
believe me for ever, at all times, your most sincere and
affectionate friend,

NELSON AND BRONTE.

TO JAMES SYKES, ESQ.[4]

[Autograph, in the possession of Rear-Admiral Sykes. " Friday, 10th August.
At 11 A.M., weighed and made sail. At 5·45 P.M., anchored. Saturday, 11th
August. At 5 A.M., weighed and made sail."—*Victory's Log.*]

Victory, August 9th, 1804.

Dear Sir,

I am favoured with your letter of May 18th, regarding
your nephew; it was hardly possible for a young man to
come to a worse station for promotion than the Mediterranean,
for we have no deaths. If the French Fleet come out during
my stay, we may have a chance for promotion, when I will do
my best for your nephew, if our success is equal to the wishes
of, dear Sir, your very obedient Servant,

NELSON AND BRONTE.

---

[4] Mr. Sykes was a respectable Navy Agent, whose business devolved upon Messrs.
Stilwell and Son, of 22, Arundel Street, Strand, to whose professional ability, integrity, and personal worth the Editor has sincere pleasure in bearing testi-
mony. Mr. Sykes' nephew is the present Rear-Admiral Sykes, mentioned in the
Preface.

TO WILLIAM MARSDEN, ESQ., ADMIRALTY.

[Original, in the Admiralty, and autograph draughts in the possession of the Rev. Henry Girdlestone, and of James Young, Esq., of Wells.]

Victory, at Sea, 12th August, 1804.

Sir,

Although I most certainly never thought of writing a line upon Monsieur La Touche's having cut a caper a few miles outside of Toulon, on the 14th of June, where he well knew I could not get at him without placing the Ships under the batteries which surround that Port, and that, had I attacked him in that position, he could retire into his secure nest whenever he pleased, yet as that gentleman has thought proper to write a letter stating that the Fleet under my command ran away, and that he pursued it, perhaps it may be thought necessary for me to say something. But I do assure you, Sir, that I know not what to say, except by a flat contradiction; for if my character is not established by this time for not being apt to run away, it is not worth my time to attempt to put the world right. It is not, therefore, I do assure their Lordships, with any such intention that I stain my paper with a vaunting man's[6] name, and, therefore, I shall only state, that the Fleet I have the honour and happiness to command is in the highest state of discipline, good order, good humour, and good health, and that the united wishes of all are, I am sure, to meet Monsieur La Touche at sea: then I ought not to doubt that I should be able to write a letter equally satisfactory to my King, my Country, and myself.

I send you a copy of the Ship's Log.[7] I observe that even the return of Monsieur La Touche into Toulon is not noticed—so little must have been thought of the French returning into Port that day, more than any other. I send

[6] Lord Nelson originally wrote "coxcomb's," but altered the word to "man's."

[7] "Which I have never seen till this day. I observe that so little was thought of Monsieur La Touche's return to Toulon harbour more than any other time, that it is not even noticed, *although, by the bearings at Noon, and latitude, that we were but four miles outside* the Port, where he was snug at anchor, and that at one o'clock we attempted to get at the Swiftsure, which was the only Ship outside the harbour."—*Autograph draught.*

you the bearings of the land for the 14th and 15th,[8] and the
movements of the Squadron on the evening of the 14th June.
I am, &c.,   NELSON AND BRONTE.

French Fleet under Monsieur La Touche—Eight Sail of
the Line, and four Frigates, two Frigates and a Brig in Hières
Bay, who joined in the night.

British Fleet—Five Sail of the Line, and two Frigates, one
of which, the Excellent 74, and two Frigates, did not join till
the middle of the night, having been sent into Hières Bay.

From 6·10 to 7·28 P.M., the British formed in 〔 Canopus.
a line to receive Monsieur La Touche, main- ⎱ Belleisle.
topsail to the mast.   ⎰ Donegal.
                                            〔 Victory.

Movements of the Squadron on the evening of the 14th
June 1804.

At 5·43 P.M.—Prepared for Battle.
    5·49 . . . . Recalled the Excellent.
〔 6·10 . . . . Formed the Line of Battle.
Laying to〔 7·28 . . . . Came to the wind together on the
〔   larboard tack.
    7·45 . . . . Tacked together.
    7·59 . . . . Formed the Order of Sailing.
                    NELSON AND BRONTE.

ᵗ " And also of the inclosed Signals made."—*Ibid.*

            103
            96 〕. . . . Tack together . . . . **7·45.**
            96 〕
(*Sic.*)   86 . . . . . Reef topsails.
            80 . . . . Alter course to Port.
            103 . . . . Keep in the Admiral's Wake.
            70 . . . . . Form Order of Sailing . . **7·59.**

        Movements of the Squadron, evening of June 14th:—
    H. M.
    5 43 13 . . . . Prepared for Battle.
    5 59   . . . . Recalled the Excellent.

    6 10 44 . . . . Formed Line of Battle.
    7 28 102 . . . . Came to the Wind together on the Larboard Tack.
    7 45 96 . . . . Tacked together.
    7 59 72 . . . . Formed the Order of Sailing.
(*Sic.*) N.B.—At 7·43, Monsieur La Touche tacked and stood for Toulon."—

This list of Signals is from the *Autograph*, in the possession of Earl Nelson.

TO WILLIAM MARSDEN, ESQ., ADMIRALTY.

[Original, in the Admiralty, and " London Gazette."]

Victory, at Sea, 12th August, 1804.

Sir,

Herewith I transmit you for the information of the Lords Commissioners of the Admiralty, a copy of a letter from Captain Donnelly, of his Majesty's Ship Narcissus, with a copy of one to him from Lieutenant Thompson of the said Ship, detailing the destruction of several of the Enemy's Coasting-vessels. The importance of this service may be but little, but the determined bravery of Lieutenants Thompson, Parker, Lumley, and Moore, and the Petty-Officers, Seamen, and Marines employed under them, could not be exceeded. I am concerned to observe that Lieutenant Lumley has been obliged to suffer amputation at the shoulder; but I have much pleasure in adding, that this fine young man is fast recovering. His sufferings, I am sure, will meet their Lordships' consideration.

I have placed Lieutenant Moore in the Seahorse, and given Mr. Bedingfield,[9] who was shot through the hand, a Commission for the Maidstone, which is going to England with the first Convoy. I am, &c.,

NELSON AND BRONTE.

TO LADY HAMILTON.

[From " Lord Nelson's Letters to Lady Hamilton," vol. ii. p. 62.]

Victory, August 12th, 1804.

Although, my dearest Emma, from the length of time my other letters have been getting to you, I cannot expect that this will share a better fate, yet, as the Childers is going to Rosas, to get us some news from Paris—which is the only way I know of what is passing in England—I take my chance of the post: but I expect the Kent will be in England before this letter, and by which Ship I write to the Admiralty relative to my health. Therefore, I shall only say, that I hope a little of your good nursing, with asses' milk, will set me up

[9] Vide vol. v. p. 488.

for another campaign, should the Admiralty wish me to
return, in the spring, for another year; but, I own, I think we
shall have Peace.

The Ambuscade arrived this day fortnight with our Victuallers, &c., and very acceptable they were. By her, I
received your letters of May 14th, 22nd, and 30th, *viâ* Lisbon;
and of April 9th, 18th, 25th, May 10th, 18th, 29th, June 1st,
5th, through, I suppose, the Admiralty. The box you mention is not arrived ; nor have I scrap of a pen from Davison.
The weather in the Mediterranean seems much altered. In
July, seventeen days the Fleet was in a gale of wind. I
have often wrote to Davison, to pay for all the improvements at Merton. The new building the chamber over the
dining-room, you must consider. The stair window, we settled, was not to be stopped up. The under-ground passage
will, I hope, be made ; but I shall, please God, soon see it all!
I have wrote you, my dear Emma, about Horatia; but, by
the Kent, I shall write fully. May God bless you, &c.

TO WILLIAM MARSDEN, ESQ., ADMIRALTY.

[Original, in the Admiralty.]

Victory, at Sea, 12th August, 1804.

Sir,

You will please to acquaint the Lords Commissioners of
the Admiralty, that the Diligent Transport has brought out
frocks and trowsers for the use of the Fleet under my command ; but instead of their being made of good Russia duck,
as was formerly supplied the Seamen of his Majesty's Navy,
the frocks at 4s. 8d. each, and the trowsers at 4s. per pair,
those sent out are made of coarse wrapper-stuff, and the price
increased—the frocks two-pence each, and the trowsers three-
pence per pair, which makes the former 4s. 10d. and the latter
4s. 3d. I therefore think it necessary to send you one of each,
in order that their Lordships may judge of their quality and
price; and at the same time beg to observe, for their information, that the issuing such coarse stuff to the people, who have
been accustomed to good Russia duck cheaper, will no doubt
occasion murmur and discontent, and may serious conse-

quences. I therefore am most decidedly of opinion, that the Contractor who furnished such stuff ought to be hanged; and little less, if anything, is due to those who have received them from him. I shall say no more on the subject, as their Lordships will naturally see the propriety of this evil being remedied as early as possible. I am, &c.,

NELSON AND BRONTE.

P.S.—Enclosed is a letter from Captain Hardy of the Victory on the subject of the frocks and trowsers. The Malta cotton therein alluded to is sent in a box, with a sample of the Slops lately received by the Diligent Store-ship.

TO COMMISSIONER OTWAY, GIBRALTAR.

[Autograph, in the possession of Rear-Admiral Inglefield, C.B.]

Victory, August 14th, 1804.

My dear Sir,

I have been favoured with your letter of July 14th: the whole of your conduct is so correct, that I can have no doubt but it must always give me satisfaction. With the various species of Stores which we have been able to get at Naples, and in the Adriatic, the Fleet is not badly supplied. The canvas and cordage at Naples is excellent, and I believe much cheaper than in England; but I rather doubt that the Naval Storekeeper at Malta did not like purchasing at Naples so well as in the Adriatic; and therefore doing the thing publicly, occasioned a complaint from the French Minister. Now I am upon the subject of purchasing Stores, I feel it my duty (if you think you are authorized by anything I can say) to urge your visiting the Naval Yard at Malta, and to examine into the expenditure of the Public money. *All* may be correct there, but there does appear to me very great irregularity. I can have no doubt but that the Admiralty consider you as eligible to overlook both Yards. If you have not that power, you either should have it, or another Commissioner be sent to Malta.

I approve most fully of the Gibraltar's being sent home. She ought to have gone years ago. The Kent is in a miserable state. Superb cannot keep the sea this winter. Renown and

Triumph ought also to go home : it would be saving five Ships instead of destroying them.   I shall see Ganges and Terrible, and also my friend Otway,[1] with great pleasure, although from my state of health, it will probably be under another Commander-in-Chief they will have to serve.   The Maidstone goes to Malta for any straggling Merchant-Ships, and from thence to England.   We have nothing new here : seventeen days' gale of wind in July.   I am always, my dear Sir, with the highest esteem, your much obliged Servant,

NELSON AND BRONTE.

TO THE REV. ROBERT ROLFE, SAHAM WATTON, NORFOLK.

[Autograph, in the possession of the Reverend Robert Rolfe.]

Victory, August 15th, 1804.

My dear Rolfe,

Your recommendation, Mr. Bedingfield,[2] has been wounded in the hand, which the Surgeons say will go off with only a stiff finger ; in order to complete the cure I have given him a Lieutenant's commission ; he is a fine young man and bears an excellent character.   Remember me kindly to your good mother, my aunt, and your sister, and believe me ever, my dear Rolfe, your affectionate Cousin,

NELSON AND BRONTE.

TO CAPTAIN SAMUEL SUTTON, H.M. SHIP AMPHION.

[Autograph, in the possession of Captain Ives Sutton.]

Victory, August 15th, 1804.

My dear Sutton,

I have received your letters of June 17th and 27th.   I thought it possible you might wish a good Seventy-four, and one at that time I thought very probable to be vacant.   For your own sake and good Hardy's, I wish you success ; but for myself, I had rather hear of your destroying two Privateers than taking a Merchant-Ship of £20,000 value.   I am not a

---

[1] The present Admiral Sir Robert Waller Otway, Bart., G.C.B.

[2] Mr. Bedingfeld was wounded in the boats of his Ship, the Narcissus, in an attack on some Settees on the night of the 11th July, 1804.

money-getting man, for which I am probably laughed at. I am but very so-so, and probably you will soon see another Commander-in-Chief in the Mediterranean. But wherever I am, believe me always, dear Sutton, your much obliged friend,

NELSON AND BRONTE.

TO HIS ROYAL HIGHNESS THE DUKE OF CLARENCE.

[From Clarke and M'Arthur, vol. ii. p. 381.]

15th August, 1804.

If anything the least new was to occur here, your Royal Highness is sure that I should have written to you; but we have an uniform sameness, day after day, and month after month—gales of wind for ever. In July, we had seventeen days very severe weather; the Mediterranean seems altered. However, with nursing our Ships, we have roughed it out better than could have been expected. I have always made it a rule never to contend with the gales; and either run to the Southward to escape its violence, or furl all the sails and make the Ships as easy as possible. Our friend Keats is quite well; in his own person he is equal in my estimation to an additional Seventy-four; his life is a valuable one to the State, and it is impossible that your Royal Highness could ever have a better choice of a Sea friend, or Counsellor, if you go to the Admiralty. Keats will never give that counsel which would not be good for the Service. I am, &c.,

NELSON AND BRONTE.

TO WILLIAM MARSDEN, ESQ., ADMIRALTY.

[Original, in the Admiralty, and autograph draught in the possession of the Rev. Henry Girdlestone.]

[No date; but about the 15th August, 1804.]

Sir,

It is with much uneasiness of mind that I feel it my duty to state to you, for the information of their Lordships, that I consider my state of health to be such as to make it absolutely necessary that I should return to England to re-establish it. Another winter, such as the last, I feel myself unable to stand against. A few months of quiet may enable me to serve again next spring; and I believe that no Officer is more anxious to serve than myself. No Officer could be placed in a more enviable Command than the one I have the honour to be placed in, and no Command ever produced so much happiness to a Commander-in-Chief, whether in the Flag-Officers, the Captains, or the good conduct of the Crews of every Ship in this Fleet; and the constant marks of approbation for my conduct which I have received from every Court in the Mediterranean, leave me nothing to wish for but a better state of health.

I have thought it necessary to state thus much, that their Lordships might not for a moment suppose that I had any uneasiness of mind upon any account. On the contrary, every person, of all ranks and descriptions, seem only desirous to meet my wishes, and to give me satisfaction. I must, therefore, intreat their Lordships' permission to return to England for the re-establishment of my health, and that their consent may reach me as soon as possible, for I have deferred my application already too long. I have the honour, to be, &c.,

NELSON AND BRONTE.

TO VISCOUNT MELVILLE.

[Autograph draught, in the possession of the Reverend Henry Girdlestone.]

Victory, [about August 15th, 1804.]

My dear Lord,

Nothing but what I think an absolute necessity, your Lordship will, I trust, believe, could have induced me to write to the Board, desiring permission to return home in order to re-establish my health, and which, I flatter myself a few months' quiet, and asses' milk, will restore to me in a certain degree, and enable me to serve again next spring, either here, where I have served nine years, or wherever the Board may think fit to employ me. I therefore request your Lordship's influence with the Board, that they may grant me their permission, before the winter gets too far advanced.

I know there are many Admirals desirous of this Command, with better health, and probably with greater abilities than myself, but none, my dear Lord, allow me to say, without being thought vain, who will serve with more zeal; therefore I can hardly expect, should even my health be perfect, to be allowed to return to this, my favourite Command: but should any such plan occur to your Lordship, it is my duty to state, and it is well known to the Board, that the Second in Command here, who has held that post, and the Command of the Fleet, for four years, Sir Richard Bickerton, is an Officer of not only distinguished merit, but also a most perfectly correct and safe Officer, and fit to command any Fleet.

The Superb, from the state of the knee of her head, cannot be kept at sea this winter, without being docked; therefore, if it suited the Board's arrangements, I should prefer going home in her, to any other of the Ships who ought to go home. Six weeks in dock, will enable that Ship to run for two or three years. The same I may say of the Triumph and Renown. They are certainly amongst our finest Ships, and absolutely going to ruin for want of a few weeks in dock. The state of the Kent will show what would have been saved, had she gone home last year, as I ventured to propose; but as it is not my intention to criticise, I shall not touch upon these subjects, but conclude by assuring you of the respect with which I am, my dear Lord, your most faithful,

N. & B.

TO VISCOUNT MELVILLE.

[From Clarke and M'Arthur, vol. ii. p. 382.]

[About 16th August, 1804.]

I am sure that your Lordship will allow me to present to you Lieutenant Lumley, of the Seahorse, who had almost a miraculous recovery from his severe wounds.[3] The arm is not only taken out of the shoulder-joint, but much of the shoulder-bones has been extracted. His general conduct as an Officer has, from the report of the Honourable Captain Boyle, been such as always to merit approbation; and his conduct upon the occasion of losing his arm, has been such as to claim all our regard and esteem, and I am sure his good behaviour and sufferings will attract your Lordship's notice. I am, &c.

NELSON AND BRONTE.

[3] Vide p. 109, ante.

TO CAPTAIN JOHN CHAMBERS WHITE, H.M. SHIP KENT.

[Order-Book.]

Victory, at Sea, 16th August, 1804.

You are hereby required and directed to receive my Public dispatches on board his Majesty's Ship Kent, under your command, and proceed with them immediately to Gibraltar, where you will deliver those for that place to Commissioner Otway, and inform yourself, without a moment's loss of time, whether the Merchants have any money to send home, and if there are any Ships perfectly ready to accompany you to England. Should there be any Trade (which I rather suppose not) ready and willing to avail themselves of your protection, you will take them under your convoy) but not to wait longer than forty-eight hours, as a Convoy will soon arrive there from Malta,) and proceed with them, with all convenient dispatch, consistent with their safety; and in order the more effectually to enable you to take the Trade from Gibraltar and Cadiz, I have directed the Senior Officer at Gibraltar to accompany you, or send a Sloop of War to escort the Kent, and such Trade as may be under her protection, from Gibraltar to Cadiz, twenty or twenty-five leagues to the Westward of the last-mentioned place, where you will call for such Vessels as may be ready, and also receive such money as the Merchants may have to send home. Having so done, you will proceed with the whole, as expeditiously as possible, to Spithead, dropping such as are bound to Ports in the Channel on your way up ; and on your arrival at that place, you will deliver my Public dispatches for the Admiralty to Admiral Montagu, or the Commanding Officer at Portsmouth, who will forward them without delay. You will acquaint the Secretary of the Admiralty with your arrival, and transmit to him an account of your proceedings for their Lordships' information, and remain at the above anchorage for their further orders.

NELSON AND BRONTE.

TO WILLIAM MARSDEN, ESQ., ADMIRALTY.

[Original, in the Admiralty. " Thursday, 16th August. H.M. Ships Belleisle, Kent, Active, Seahorse, Narcissus, Phœbe, Maidstone, and Niger, and Acheron, with the Transports, rejoined.   H.M. Ship Fisgard, from England, joined com·pany."—*Victory's Log.*]

Victory, at Sea, 16th August, 1804.

Sir,

You will please to acquaint the Lords Commissioners of the Admiralty, that on the Squadron's return from Palma this morning, I was joined by the Fisgard, and as the Kent is just proceeding to England, I have only a moment to acknowledge your several letters, &c., which shall be duly attended to, and answered by the first opportunity.

The Fleet is complete in provisions and water to five months, and in stores as far as we have been able, and I have the pleasure to add, is in most perfect health.   Nine Sail of the Enemy's Line-of-Battle Ships, and seven Frigates, came out on the 14th instant a few miles from Sepet, and returned into Port in the evening.   I am, &c.,

NELSON AND BRONTE.

TO THOMAS TYRWHITT, ESQ.[4]

[Additional MSS. 12,102 in the British Museum.]

Victory, August 16th, 1804.

Sir,

The box left by Mr. A'Court for H. R. H. the Prince of Wales must have gone home in either the Argo or Agincourt, as they were the only large Ships that left the Fleet, and I was fearful that in a small Vessel they would get wet.   I hope they are, long before this time, safe arrived.   I beg to present my humble duty to his Royal Highness.   I have the honour to remain, &c.,

NELSON AND BRONTE.

---

[4] Keeper of the Privy Seal, Private Secretary to H. R. H. the Prince of Wales, and Lord Warden of the Stannaries.   He was appointed Gentleman Usher of the Black Rod, and Knighted in 1812 ; and died at Calais, on the 24th of February 1833.

TO CAPTAIN JOHN CHAMBERS WHITE, H. M. SHIP KENT.

[Order-Book.]

Victory, at Sea, 16th August, 1804.

Having received a letter from the Honourable Captain
Boyle of his Majesty's Ship Seahorse, which is herewith
transmitted, respecting James Reynolds, alias James Clarke,
a native of Mullingar, who acknowledges himself the murderer
of a Mr. Rochfort, and the said man having delivered himself
up to the Civil Law, You are hereby required and directed
to receive him on board his Majesty's Ship Kent, under your
command, and keep him in confinement, as a person guilty of
the crime he has acknowledged, until your arrival in England,
when you will deliver him up to the Civil Power, with the
before-mentioned letter, acquainting the Commanding-Officer
at Portsmouth of the circumstances, previous to your doing so.
You will victual the said man the same as your Ship's Company during the passage.

NELSON AND BRONTE.

TO CAPTAIN JOHN GORE, H. M. SHIP MEDUSA.

[Letter-Book.]

Victory, at Sea, 18th August, 1804.

Sir,
I have received your letter of the 22nd ultimo, and very
much approve of your having sent the Fisgard direct to me,
as well as of your ordering the Termagant to Malta with the
Convoy. I am glad it was convenient for you to take Mr.
M'Donough and my dispatches to Lisbon, and sincerely
hope you may join the Amphion, and fall in with the French
Frigates mentioned in the enclosure which accompanied your
said letter. You did perfectly right in detaining the Fisgard,
for the purpose of bringing the Public money to the Fleet. I
am, &c.

NELSON AND BRONTE.

TO SIR ALEXANDER JOHN BALL, BART., MALTA.

[Autograph, in the possession of Sir William Keith Ball, Bart.]

My dear Ball,   Victory, August 19th, 1804.

Since the Amazon left us, except the arrival of the Fisgard,
which you know of, but little has occurred. She is a fine
Frigate ; but both Maidstone and Narcissus must go home—
therefore, I am still reducing. Except some Public letters of
no consequence, I have not a scrap of a pen from any one in
Office. The French Ships have been out a few miles; but
they see so far that the Coast is clear, that there is but very
little prospect of getting at them: they are now reported
nine Sail of the Line in the Outer Road, and seven or eight
Frigates. I am keeping as many Frigates as possible round
me; for I know the value of them on the day of Battle : and
compared with that day, what signifies any Prizes they might
take ?

I yet hope to get hold of them before my successor arrives,
then ten years will be added to my life. Although I have no
particular complaint, my general constitution has suffered
much the last winter, and I ought not, in justice to myself, to
encounter another. I think either Sir Roger Curtis or Young[3]
are likely to come here: either will do well ; but they may
leave the command with Sir Richard Bickerton. Sir John
Orde (Lord Mark Kerr[4] says) is gone to succeed Young at Plymouth. If so, he is either coming here, or going, instead of
Pellew, to command in India; but I can only guess, for none
of them write me news. Your sister Emma,[5] was very well
June 23rd, and always desires to be remembered to you and to
Macaulay; say so to him. I send you, in confidence, a copy
of my letter to the Admiralty about Monsieur La Touche :
they may do as they please, I care not. Such a liar is below
my notice, except to thrash him, which will be done, if in the
power of, my dear Ball, your sincere friend,

NELSON AND BRONTE.

I am so much pleased with Mr. M'Donough's conduct at

[3] Afterwards Admiral Sir William Young, G.C.B. Vide vol. i. p. 88.
[4] Third son of William John, fifth Marquis of Lothian, K.T. ; and Captain of
the Fisgard, which had lately joined Lord Nelson from England : he died a Rear-
Admiral of the Red, in September 1840.
[5] Lady Hamilton.

Algiers in the Termagant, that I have recommended him for Tripoli in the room of *your friend*, who, I am sure, is unfit for that place.   I shall write the Dey of Algiers a trimmer.[6]

TO CAPTAIN WILLIAM PARKER, H. M. SHIP AMAZON.

[Letter-Book.]

Sir,   Victory, at Sea, 19th August, 1804.

His Majesty's Ship Amazon, under your command, being sent to Malta, for the purpose of refitting with all dispatch, and as the different Port duties might materially interfere with your constant attention to the more important service of completing the Amazon for sea, I would recommend your allowing Captain Schomberg to carry on the Port duty, and not give yourself the trouble of interfering with it, as your own concerns will afford you sufficient employment.   I am, &c.

NELSON AND BRONTE.

TO CAPTAIN THE HONOURABLE GEORGE ELLIOT, H.M. SHIP MAIDSTONE.

[Order-Book.]

Victory, at Sea, 19th August, 1804.

Whereas it is my intention that his Majesty's Ship Maidstone, under your command, shall proceed to England with the Convoy from Malta, about the middle, or 20th September next, or earlier, should Captain Schomberg signify to you officially, that they are ready for that purpose.   You are hereby required and directed (when Captain Schomberg shall signify to you, as above, that the Trade are ready to proceed to the United Kingdom,) to make the signal for, and take the whole which may be collected from the different Ports in the Adriatic, Archipelago, and Sicily, under your convoy and protection, and proceed with them as expeditiously as possible, consistent with their safety, to Gibraltar, taking care on your passage to that place that you do not keep too near to Algiers, as the intentions of the Dey towards us may not be friendly.   On your arrival at Gibraltar, you will consult with

6 Vide p. 170, post.

the Senior Officer on the probability of getting our Trade from Cadiz, should the French have a superior force in that Port, and be governed by his instructions on the subject of calling for them on your way to England, as it is impossible for me, at this distance, to fix a line of conduct for that particular service. I must, therefore, leave it to the discretion of the Senior Officer to act as circumstances may render necessary.

You will take such Trade as may be at Gibraltar, whose Masters are ready and willing to avail themselves of your protection, and proceed with the whole of them, without a moment's loss of time, to England, (governing yourself with respect to our Trade at Cadiz, as above-mentioned) paying the most particular attention to every Vessel under your charge, and regulate your rate of sailing with that of the worst going Ship of your Convoy, in order that none of them may separate from the Maidstone, or fall into the hands of the Enemy's Privateers. On your arrival off Plymouth, you will order the Trade bound for Ireland, or the Bristol Channel, to put into Cawsand Bay, and apply to the Commanding Officer at that place for convoy, proceeding with the Ships bound for London to the Downs, dropping such as are destined to the Ports in the Channel on your way to that place. On your arrival in the Downs, you will immediately acquaint the Secretary of the Admiralty, and transmit to him an account of your proceedings, for their Lordships' information, and remain there for further orders.

NELSON AND BRONTE.

TO RICHARD BULKELEY, ESQ.[7]

[From Clarke and M'Arthur, vol. ii. p. 367.]

[Apparently about August 20th, 1804.]

You will have read of my running away from Mons. La Touche; but, as I have written to the Admiralty, if my character is not established by this time for not being apt to run away, it is not worth my while to put the world right. I never was more surprised than to see the fellow's letter; but the next French paper makes a sort of apology. I am, &c.

NELSON AND BRONTE.

[7] Vide vol. ii. p. 445.

TO CAPTAIN SUTTON, H. M. SHIP AMPHION.

[From Clarke and M'Arthur, vol. ii. p. 367.]

[About August 20th, 1804.]

I have every reason to think, that if this Fleet gets fairly up with Mons. La Touche, his letter, with all his ingenuity, must be different from his last. We had fancied that we had chased him into Toulon; for blind as I am, I could see his water-line when he clued his topsails up, shutting in Sepet; but from the time of his meeting Captain Hawker in the Iris, I never heard of his acting otherwise than as a poltroon and a liar.[4] Contempt is the best mode of treating such a miscreant. I am, &c.

NELSON AND BRONTE.

---

[4] In the Memoir of Vice-Admiral La Touche Treville, published in the Moniteur of the 1st of September, 1804, after his death, (which took place at Toulon on the 18th of August,) it is said that he commanded the Hermione Frigate, on the Coast of America, in 1780, when he attacked the English Frigate Iris, of equal force, and that the Iris only owed her safety to superior sailing, which enabled her to take refuge in New York. The *facts*, however, are thus stated in the Log of the Iris:—

"June 1780, Wednesday 7th, Sandy Hook, West, distance 28 Leagues. Fresh breezes and cloudy weather. At 2 P.M., saw a strange Sail, and gave chase. Fired several shot at her. At 4 ditto, she ran ashore on Long Island. Out Boats, and sent them on board the Snow. At 9, shortened sail for the Snow. ½ past A.M. (?) saw a strange Sail to the Southward: gave chase. At 6, left off chasing the Brig. Chased a Sloop, and Schooner Privateer, to the Northward. At 7, saw a Frigate bearing N.W. Left off chasing the above Vessels, and chased the Frigate. Soon after, she tacked, and stood towards us. Cleared Ship for Action. At about a musket shot she hoisted French colours. Proved to be the La Hermione, of 36 guns. At 9, we began a close Action, which continued an hour and twenty minutes, when the French Frigate made sail from us, with all the Sail she could make. We followed her for three-quarters of an hour, when another Sail was seen ahead, and we were obliged to haul our wind, when our fore-topsail-yard went away, and being very much damaged in our sails and rigging. We had 7 men killed and 9 wounded, and among the latter is Lieutenant Bourne, of the Marines. Employed knotting, splicing, and reeving running rigging." "Thursday, 8th, Fresh breezes, &c., &c." "Friday, 9th, Ditto." "Saturday, 10th. Inside the Hook. Unbent sails, and moored Ship."

Captain James Hawker's official report of the Action has not been found: he distinguished himself in command of the Hero, of 74 guns, in the Action with Admiral Suffrein, in Porto Praya Bay, in April 1781, and died in 1787.

TO CAPTAIN ROSS DONNELLY, H.M. SHIP NARCISSUS.

[Order Book.]

Victory, off Cape St. Sebastians, 20th August, 1804.

Whereas it is my intention to try every possible means to induce the French Fleet at Toulon to put to sea, You are hereby required and directed to take his Majesty's Ships named in the margin[5] under your command, and proceed off the West end of Porquerolle, in order to induce the Enemy to get to the Eastward, as it is my intention to get into the Gulf of Lyons, and to push round Cape Sicie the first favourable wind. Your appearance may, therefore, tempt them to come out and stand to the Eastward, or to anchor in Hières Bay, which may afford the Squadron under my command an opportunity of bringing them to Action.

NELSON AND BRONTE.

TO LADY HAMILTON.

[From " Lord Nelson's Letters to Lady Hamilton," vol. ii. p. 65.]

Victory, August 20th, 1804.

My dearest Emma,

The Kent left us three days ago; and, as the wind has been perfectly fair since her departure, I think she will have a very quick passage, and arrive long before this letter. But, as a Ship is going to Rosas, I will not omit the opportunity of writing through Spain; as, you say, the letters all arrive safe. We have nothing but gales of wind; and I have had, for two days, fires in the cabin, to keep out the very damp air.

I still hope that, by the time of my arrival in England, we shall have Peace. God send it! I have not yet received your muff; I think, probably, I shall bring it with me. I hope, Davison has done the needful, in paying for the alterations at Merton. If not, it is now too late; and we will fix a complete plan, and execute it next summer. I shall be clear of debt,

---

[5] Fisgard, Ambuscade, Niger.

and what I have will be my own.   God bless you! Amen.
Amen.   George Elliot goes to Malta, for a Convoy to
England, this day.   If you ever see Lord Minto, say so.

                                        NELSON AND BRONTE.

———————

TO WILLIAM MARSDEN, ESQ., ADMIRALTY.

[Original, in the Admiralty.]

Victory, at Sea, 22nd August, 1801.

Sir,

You will please to acquaint the Lords Commissioners of
the Admiralty, that agreeably to their order of the 27th June,
I have taken Captain the Right Honourable Lord Mark
Robert Kerr, and his Majesty's Ship Fisgard, under my command; and in further obedience to their Lordships instructions
communicated to me in your letter of the 29th of the said
month, I have sent the Maidstone (being very much in want
of repairs) to Malta, to take the Trade from thence and
Gibraltar to England; and as the Narcissus's Gover's gun-car-
riages are almost rendered useless, and she cannot be supplied
with others in this Country, a considerable quantity of copper
being also off her bottom, and otherwise in want of repairs,
it is my intention to send her in a few days to Gibraltar, to
cruize in the Gut for the protection of our Trade, and destruction of the Enemy's Privateers, until the arrival of the
Maidstone and Convoy from Malta, when I shall direct
Captain Donnelly to take the said Trade, together with such
as may be at Gibraltar and Cadiz, under his protection, and
proceed with them, in company with the Maidstone, to
England.

I am extremely happy that their Lordships intend sending
out Ships of the Line to relieve such of those under my
command as are in want of repairs, and I hope they may
arrive time enough to enable me to send home the three
Ships named in the margin,[6] before the winter sets in, as
they are certainly not equal to meet another season of bad
weather, without very great injury to their hulls.   The Officers
of Malta-Yard having informed me that the Arrow cannot

———————

[6] Superb, Renown, Triumph.

be repaired in this Country on account of her tanks and other defects, (which they interfere with,) it is my intention to send her to England in the Autumn, with the next Convoy after the Narcissus and Maidstone, which I hope will meet their Lordships' approbation. I am, &c.,

NELSON AND BRONTE.

TO ALEXANDER DAVISON, ESQ.

[Autograph, in the possession of Colonel Davison.]

Victory, August 22nd, 1804.

My dear Davison,

By the Spencer yesterday I had dear Lady Hamilton's letters to July 19th, and she tells me that you have wrote ; but not a scrap of a pen comes to me. I have not heard from you these six months. However, I shall see you soon, and then all these things will be explained, and my only hope is to make a finish before I leave this truly fine Fleet. I dare say, Monsieur La Touche will have a different sort of letter to write, if I can once get a shake at him. Whether the world thinks that I ran away or no, is to me a matter of great indifference. If my character is not fixed by this time, it is useless for me to try to fix it at my time of life. There will be many trying for this Command, and as I see I have voted against the Ministry, I can have no right to expect that they will allow me to return to it. I hope my house will be finished, and I rely that you have done the needful. If not, I shall arrange it all for next year. God bless you, my dear Davison, and believe me ever, your most attached and affectionate friend,

NELSON AND BRONTE.

I hope Mr. Marsden will take care that I am not kept in Quarantine whenever I may arrive. When you see or communicate with Lord Moira, remember me kindly to him ; and from my heart I wish him every felicity of which the marriage[7] state is capable—particularly children to inherit his virtues.

[7] Francis, second Earl of Moira, married, on the 11th of July, 1804, Flora Muir Campbell, Countess of Loudon in her own right.

I cannot venture to write anything public by the Post
through Spain. Tell Mr. Marsden the Spencer joined me the
19th day.

TO REAR-ADMIRAL SUTTON.[8]

[From Clarke and M'Arthur, vol. ii. p. 382.]

24th August, 1804.

The Spencer joined the 19th, from Plymouth. I was very
glad to see so fine a Ship, and so good a man as Captain
Stopford.[9] I have long, my dear Friend, made up my mind
never to be tired; the longer the happy day is deferred, still
every day brings it nearer, and we all feel that the day will
arrive ; the sooner the better certainly, or I shall not be in at
the death; for I have every reason to think if this Fleet gets
fairly at Monsieur La Touche, that his letter, with all his
ingenuity, must be different from his last. I have sent
White, who is a treasure, to the good Commissioner. I
am, &c.,

NELSON AND BRONTE.

TO THE EARL OF CARYSFORT.

[From Clarke and M'Arthur, vol. ii. p. 384.]

August 24th, 1804.

Granville,[1] my dear Lord, is a very fine young man, and
now you must try and get him the two next steps, Commander and Post, for until that is done, nothing substantial
is effected ; then the whole glory of our Service is opened to
him. As an Officer, I am of no party, and from my heart I
believe that all the different parties are composed of honourable
men, and men of great abilities. I do not understand the

---

[8] Afterwards Admiral Sir John Sutton, K.C.B., so frequently mentioned: he died
in August 1825.

[9] The present Admiral the Honourable Sir Robert Stopford, G.C.B., G.C.M.G.,
Governor of Greenwich Hospital.

[1] The Honourable Granville Leveson Proby, third son of John Joshua, first
Earl of Carysfort, was made an Acting Lieutenant of the Royal Sovereign, by Lord
Nelson, on the 1st of August 1804, and in October exchanged into the Narcissus :
he is now (1845) a Rear-Admiral of the Blue.

least of the Defence Bill, further than that it is good to have
as large a regular Army as possible, and in the quickest way;
and I hope Lord Moira thought so too. I have the very
highest opinion of his honour and abilities as a Soldier. Mr.
Pitt is a host of strength in himself. The Powers on the
Continent are a set of dirty fellows; and I do not believe, if
every person of all parties were in Administration, that they
would be able to move those Powers to either assist us, or
support their own honour. If they do ever go to war with
France, I hope it will be for themselves, and not to involve us
in their quarrels. I am, &c.,

NELSON AND BRONTE.

TO HIS HIGHNESS THE DEY OF ALGIERS.

[From a Copy, formerly in the possession of the late Adam Bromilow, Esq.
" Saturday, 25th August. Noon. Royal Sovereign, Triumph, Excellent, and Belleisle parted. Three Men-of-War, bearing E. b S., which proved French, close in
with Cape Sicie. . . . . . These Ships rejoined in the evening."—*Victory's Log.*]

Victory, August 26th, 1804.

Sir,

I have received your Highness's letter of July 6th, and as it
appears that my great attentions to your Highness seem not
to have made all the impression they ought to have done, I
therefore, now state to your Highness my unalterable sentiments and determination, which must be complied with before
I ever send an English Consul to Algiers.

The English Vessel the Ape, or her value, shall be restored
before any Consul lands. With respect to El Veloce, your
Highness knows that it has been proved that her whole cargo
was French property, and that not one farthing of its value
belonged either to you, or any of your Subjects, and if any one
has told your Highness to the contrary, they have told you a
falsehood. His Britannic Majesty, my Royal Master, con-
descended to write you, that the cargo was condemned by the
acknowledged laws of all Nations for being Enemy's property.
I am, therefore, much surprised at your Highness renewing
this subject.

No Consul will ever enter into this matter; it is finished,

and the legal captors have received the amount. I have done all in my power to please your Highness, but I must now inform you that I shall never send to Algiers again about the Consul, for I do not understand being trifled with; your Highness may send me your sentiments when and how you please. I am, your Highness's most obedient Servant,

NELSON AND BRONTE.

TO CAPTAIN ROSS DONNELLY, H. M. SHIP NARCISSUS.

[Order-Book.]

Victory, at Sea, 27th August, 1804.

You are hereby required and directed to receive my dispatches for the Dey of Algiers, and proceed with them to that place in his Majesty's Ship under your command, without a moment's loss of time; and as the intentions of the Dey are very doubtful, and may be hostile towards us, you will take the necessary precaution to anchor the Narcissus well out of reach of their guns and batteries, until you have sent a Boat with an Officer on shore, and are assured of their peaceable disposition. You will then land, and send my letter to the Dey immediately through his Ministers, who I desire you will acquaint with my astonishment at the Dey's conduct after all the conciliatory measures I have taken on his account with our Government. In the event of the Dey's wishing a personal interview, you will wait upon him, but by no means on your part desire it; and in such case, you will express to him in the strongest manner, my astonishment at his conduct, as before-mentioned. I herewith transmit you a copy of my letter to the Dey, for your guidance in this mission, and desire you will govern yourself agreeably to the spirit of the said letter. Having remained at Algiers twenty-four hours, you will proceed immediately, with such letter or other information as you may receive from the Dey, to Gibraltar, and deliver them to Commissioner Otway, to be transmitted to me by the first opportunity; and afterwards put yourself under the command of Captain Sir Robert Barlow of the Triumph, and follow his orders for your further proceedings.

NELSON AND BRONTE.

TO CAPTAIN SIR ROBERT BARLOW,[2] H. M. SHIP TRIUMPH.

[Order-Book.]

Victory, at Sea, 27th August, 1804.

You are hereby required and directed to proceed immediately, with his Majesty's Ship Triumph under your command, to Gibraltar; and on your arrival there, you will use
every dispatch in woolding and securing the foremast, and
also in strengthening the mainmast, if necessary to put them
in a proper state for a short period of service; but you are on
no account whatever to take out either your fore or main
mast at Gibraltar; or to give the Triumph any kind of refit,
which may take the stores from that Arsenal, but such as may
be absolutely necessary for temporary service. Having secured
your foremast, &c. you will proceed outside the Straits (taking
care, previous to your leaving Gibraltar, to acquaint the
Merchants at Cadiz and Malaga, that a Convoy will sail for
England very early in October, in order that they may be
ready to avail themselves of its protection,) and cruize in such
a situation as you may think most likely to insure the safety
of a Convoy hourly expected from England. But should you
judge that the Triumph's presence in Cadiz would more
effectually protect them from L'Aigle, or any of the Enemy's
small Cruizers which may be there, you are at liberty to put
in there, and remain until you shall learn, or are satisfied, that
the said Convoy has entered the Straits, and safe arrived at Gibraltar, when you will return to that place, bringing with you
the Trade, and such money as the Merchants at Cadiz may
have to send to England, if they are ready to accompany you.
Having directed the Captains of the Narcissus and Maidstone
to follow your orders for their further proceedings, you will
take them under your command accordingly; and it is my
positive directions that the former is not allowed to take out
her bowsprit, or get any repairs whatever at Gibraltar, but
such as may really be wanted; and you will be very careful
not to take any more stores or provisions in the Ships under

---

[2] Sir Robert Barlow died an Admiral of the Red, and a Knight Grand Cross of
the Bath, in May 1843.

your orders than may be necessary for the passage; and so
soon as the Maidstone arrives with the Trade from Malta,
(which I expect will be about the latter end of next month,
or early in October,) you will proceed with the whole Convoy
from Malaga, Gibraltar, Malta, and Cadiz, as expeditiously
as possible, consistent with their safety, through the Straits,
and accompany them till they are round Cape St. Vincent,
and clear of L'Aigle, when you will direct Captain Donnelly
to continue on with the whole of them (taking care to regulate his rate of going with that of the worst sailing Vessel in
his Convoy,) till it shall be deemed proper for the Trade
bound to Ireland and the Bristol Channel to part company,
when you will order him to make the signal for that purpose ;
and as the Maidstone is in a very bad state, and not equal to
encounter a winter's gale, direct Captain Donnelly to proceed
with the before-mentioned Trade in the Narcissus, and send
the Maidstone on with the rest of them to the Downs ; in-
structing the Honourable Captain Elliot to drop such as are
bound to Ports in the Channel on his way up, and to inform
the Secretary of the Admiralty with his arrival and proceedings, and wait at that anchorage for their Lordships' further
orders. And when the Narcissus shall have seen the Trade
under her protection, for Ireland and the Bristol Channel, in
safety to their destination, you will order him to proceed to
Spithead, and acquaint the Admiralty, as above-mentioned.
With respect to the mode of getting the Trade from Cadiz, and
such money as the Merchants may have to send to England
by the Triumph, I must leave it entirely with you to determine upon, and act as circumstances may render necessary,
as it is impossible for me to give an opinion, and therefore I
must desire you will adopt the most advisable measure for this
purpose ; and after having seen the whole of the Convoy safe
round Cape St. Vincent, and given the necessary orders to
Captain Donnelly, as before mentioned, you will proceed with
the utmost possible dispatch, in his Majesty's Ship Triumph
under your command, to Spithead ; and on your arrival there,
acquaint the Secretary of the Admiralty, and transmit to him
an account of your proceedings, for their Lordships' information, and remain at that anchorage for their further orders.

NELSON AND BRONTE.

TO CAPTAIN SIR ROBERT BARLOW, H. M. SHIP TRIUMPH.

[Order-Book.]

[Apparently about 27th August, 1804.]

Memorandum.

Having received information that the Enemy have two large Row-boat Privateers at Malaga, which have done considerable destruction to our Trade, it is my directions that you send the Narcissus, immediately on her arrival at Gibraltar, to cruize off that place and Cape de Gatte, until the arrival of the Maidstone and Convoy from Malta, for the purpose of their greater security, and the destruction of the said Rowboats, calling occasionally at Europa Point, to obtain information of the Maidstone's arrival, or any orders you may leave for him.

NELSON AND BRONTE.

TO WILLIAM MARSDEN, ESQ., ADMIRALTY.

[Original, in the Admiralty.]

Victory, at Sea, 27th August, 1804.

Sir,

I herewith transmit you copies of Acting Orders which I have given to the two gentlemen named in the margin,[3] in the room of the Lieutenants therein mentioned, who have been invalided, which I request you will be pleased to lay before the Lords Commissioners of the Admiralty, for their information; and, at the same time, acquaint their Lordships that Mr. Woodin[4] is the son of a very old and faithful servant of the Country, who was Master with Lord Hood for a considerable time, and has since been appointed Master-Attendant at Gibraltar. He is a very worthy, good man, and his services will, I trust, induce their Lordships to promote his son (who was in the Vanguard with me in the action of the Nile, and has always conducted himself with great propriety) to the rank of Lieutenant. In consequence of the Purser of the

---

[3] Mr. Alexander Dixie, Mr. John Woodin.

[4] Lieutenant John Woodin was appointed to the Belleisle, and was killed in that Ship at Trafalgar.

Narcissus being invalided, I have appointed Mr. Chenoweth of the Cameleon to that Ship, and Mr. John M'Arthur of the Victory to supersede him in the last mentioned Ship, which I hope will meet their Lordships' approbation.   I am, &c.

NELSON AND BRONTE.

TO LORD HAWKESBURY.

[From Clarke and M'Arthur, vol. ii. p. 384.]

August 27th, 1804.

The deplorable state of the finances in the Island of Sardinia, has been represented to me not only by the Viceroy, but also by all the Governors, &c.   Not one of their few Soldiers has been paid for years, nor a Governor or Officer. The Forts are going to ruin ; there is not a gun-carriage fit to bear a gun, and their Gallies are to be laid up, from the impossibility of even purchasing provisions for them.   In short, my Lord, Sardinia is gone, if the French make a landing; not from their regard to the French, for I am sure the greater part hate them, but the Islanders must be released from their present miserable condition.   I wrote to Lord Hobart fully upon the necessity of keeping the French out of it ; for even should they take a temporary possession, how is Toulon to be watched ? and great difficulty would be found in getting a Convoy either to or from Malta.   I have said enough to your Lordship's intelligent mind ; and if it is not lost before I have the honour of seeing you, I think I can satisfy your Lordship of the absolute necessity of having Sardinia open to us.   I am, &c.,

NELSON AND BRONTE.

TO HIS EXCELLENCY HUGH ELLIOT, ESQ.

[Autograph, in the Elliot Papers.]

Victory, August 28th, 1804.

My dear Sir,

Since I received your letter, by the Kent, we have had a severe gale of wind, and have been blown under St. Sebastians, from whence I only got back on Saturday the 26th, on which day I examined Toulon myself.   Twenty Ships of War are in

the Outer Road of Toulon: nine certainly—I believe ten—
are of the Line ; the rest Frigates and large Corvettes, besides
Brigs, &c. &c.   In the Inner Harbour, one Ship of the Line
and a Frigate.   Monsieur La Touche's flag was not flying on
board Ship, but we suppose he was up on Cape Sepet with
his flag, directing any movements which he might think necessary.   The Kent left me for England on the 17th, and
yesterday the Triumph and Narcissus for the same place.
Maidstone is gone to Malta for a Convoy, and from thence to
carry them to England.   The Spencer seventy-four has joined
me from Plymouth, and the Fisgard Frigate.   The Renown
is ordered to be sent home, and then Superb : indeed, I
expect every day the Ships to relieve them.

   It is not upon my own account, but that I may be able to
answer for my conduct to the Admiralty, that I must ask this
question of the King of Naples[2]—viz., do you think your
situation requires the constant presence of an English Ship of
the Line at Naples ?   His Majesty and the Queen know that
I would sooner fight the Enemy's Fleet with an inferior force,
than have them in the least uneasy ; but Ministers may not
always think as their attached Nelson and Bronté does :
therefore, my dear Sir, you will see the necessity I am under
of repeatedly asking the same question; and I beg that the
answer may be direct to the point, that if I go (and if I do not
go before next winter, I shall never go) to England, that my
successor may not have the power of taking the Ship from
Naples, without the King's consent first obtained.

   I have wrote to Lord Melville my desire to return to this
Command in March, or April, if I am removed; but the
Administration may have so many other Admirals looking to
them, that I may very possibly be laid upon the shelf.   I
dare not presume to think that with all my zeal and attachment to their Sicilian Majesties, that I am of sufficient importance for the King to express his wish *to England* for my
return.   That must be for him to consider; and if he thinks
proper to do it, nothing, I suppose, but a letter to his brother
George can do it, and that must not go through me, but
through his Minister Castelcicala.   I have to thank your Ex-

2 Vide p. 219, post.

cellency for news from Berlin, &c. &c. I yet hope that Europe will be roused. On August 11th, I see Buonaparte was upon the Coast, and it was thought the attempt upon England would no longer be deferred. We have reports from Leghorn; but I believe no credit is to be given to them of an Action in the Channel, destruction of Gun-Boats, &c. &c.

August 30th, Noon.—Close in with Toulon : all safe, and looking very smart. I am ever, my dear Sir, your Excellency's most faithful and obliged Servant,

NELSON AND BRONTE.

TO HIS EXCELLENCY HUGH ELLIOT, ESQ.

[Autograph, in the Elliot Papers.]

Victory, August 28th, 1804.

My dear Sir,

Before our friend Dr. Scott leaves the Mediterranean, he is very anxious to pay his respects in the hot-bed of diplomacy, and, joking apart, to pay his respects to you. He is very much in my friendship, and confidence, to a certain extent. He has heard so much of the King and Queen of Naples and the Royal Family, that if he could be presented to them in private, as belonging to me, the Doctor would be very much gratified, and I own it would please me. Both Admiral Murray and good Captain Hardy have suffered by this constant being at sea : they are neither of them in good health. I beg my best respects to Mrs. Elliot, and believe me ever, my dear Sir, your Excellency's most faithful and obliged Servant,

NELSON AND BRONTE.

TO CAPTAIN PARKER, H.M. SHIP AMAZON.

[From a Copy in the Nelson Papers. This letter was written while the Amazon was refitting at Malta.]

Victory, August 28th, 1804.

My dear Parker,

I hope you are making haste to join me, for the day of Battle cannot be far off, when I shall want every Frigate; for the French have nearly one for every Ship, and we may as well have a Battle Royal—Line-of-Battle Ships opposed to Ships of the Line, and Frigates to Frigates; but I am satisfied of your exertions; and be assured that I am ever faithfully yours,

NELSON AND BRONTE.

TO . . . . . .

[From Clarke and M'Arthur, vol. ii. p. 383, who state that Lord Nelson, being much hurt at an insinuation which had been thrown out by some Mercantile men, of his having favoured some Merchants more than others, sent the following letter to one of their Chairmen.]

August, 1804.

I can imagine no circumstance that could possibly influence me, as a British Admiral, to grant more particular protection to one British Merchant, in preference to another; all are equally entitled to the protection of his Majesty's Ships, and if my own brother were in your situation, I should scold him most sincerely for venturing to suppose that any influence would make me unjust. I am, &c.,

NELSON AND BRONTE.

TO NATHANIEL TAYLOR, ESQ., NAVAL STOREKEEPER, MALTA.

[From a Copy in the Nelson Papers.]

Victory, at Sea, 28th August, 1804.

Sir,

On my directing you, by letter of the 14th May last, to proceed to Naples, for the purpose of purchasing canvas and cordage, &c. for the Fleet under my command, it is perfectly clear that the instructions therein contained, authorized and directed you to procure these articles upon the best and most reasonable terms, (giving a preference to Mr. James, for the reasons therein mentioned) and to draw bills for the payment thereof on the Navy Board. This I took for granted you had done, until I received a letter, a few days ago, from Mr. James, wherein he charges two and a half per cent. upon the amount of the whole purchase. This being a measure so very extraordinary and unusual, (as I consider you the purchaser, and him, Mr. James, the Merchant of whom the articles were procured,) that I must desire you will transmit copies of the agreement you may have made with Mr. James, as well as of every paper relative thereto, as I cannot suppose you went to Naples without settling a fixed price upon every article, and the mode of payments by bills upon the Navy Board, as directed; and therefore the charge of two and a half per cent. appears to me an imposition on Government, which I cannot submit to. The Captain of any of his Majesty's Ships could have purchased Stores for the Fleet (if I had not thought you the most proper person for that service) without a charge of any per centage whatever being made ; and I do venture to assert, that in every instance where purchases are made on Government account, the bills given for the payment thereof include every charge. I must, therefore, desire your answer to this by the very first Vessel coming from Malta, with a copy of the agreement and papers before mentioned. I am, &c.

NELSON AND BRONTE.

TO JOHN JAMES, ESQ., HIS MAJESTY'S PRO-CONSUL, NAPLES.

[From a Copy in the Nelson Papers.]

Victory, at Sea, 29th August, 1804.

Sir,

Rear-Admiral Murray having transmitted to me your letter of the 26th ultimo, with the duplicate account of stores therein mentioned, purchased by Mr. Taylor from you, and sent in the Termagant for the use of the Fleet under my command, and as I consider Mr. Taylor, his Majesty's Store-keeper at Malta, the purchaser, and you the Merchant of whom the Stores before alluded to were bought, I cannot help expressing my astonishment at observing in the said accounts, not only a Custom-House charge and agio on the ducat, but also a commission of two and a half per cent. on the whole amount. I must, therefore, request that you will transmit me a copy of the agreement or contract, which Mr. Taylor may have entered into with you, and other papers relative thereto, in order that I may most fully understand the transaction, which at present I do not ; for my idea of purchases is, that if I agree with a Merchant to deliver me a cer-

N 2

tain quantity of goods on board any Ship, or otherwise, at a
certain price, I consider that that price includes everything,
and, therefore, I protest against the two and a half per cent.,
and desire the business may be put a stop to for the present.
I am, &c.

NELSON AND BRONTE.

P.S.—As the cordage of every description is charged to the
Board of his Majesty Navy, in fathoms, the rope you sent on
Board the Kent and Termagant ought also to have been in
fathoms.

TO SIR WILLIAM BOLTON, COMMANDER OF H. M. SLOOP
CHILDERS.

[Order-Book.]

Victory, at Sea, 30th August, 1804.

You are hereby required and directed to proceed to Barcelona in his Majesty's Sloop Childers, under your command,
with all dispatch (using the necessary precaution in communicating with the shore, previous to your anchoring the said
Sloop) and deliver my letter to Mr. Gibert, his Majesty's Pro-
Consul at that place, and receive from him such letters, papers,
&c. as he may have for me.   Having so done, you will make
the best of your way to Rosas, and deliver my letter, herewith
transmitted, to Mr. Edward Gayner, Merchant at that place,
who will give you such letters and papers, as he may have for
me, with any Political information he may be able to obtain,
with which you will return and join the Squadron on Rendezvous No 102, where you will find me, or orders for your
further proceedings; and as I am exceedingly anxious for information from England, and also with respect to the Political
state of Spain, I must desire that this service is performed
without a moment's loss of time.

NELSON AND BRONTE.

TO LADY HAMILTON.

[From " Lord Nelson's Letters to Lady Hamilton," vol. ii. p. 67.]

Victory, August 31st, 1804—say 30th, at Evening.　Therefore I
wrote, in fact, this day, through Spain.

My ever dearest Emma,

Yesterday, I wrote to you, through Spain; this goes by
Naples. Mr. Falconet, I think, will send it; although, I am
sure, he feels great fear from the French Minister, for having
anything to do with us. Mr. Greville is a shabby fellow! It
never could have been the intention of Sir William, but that
you should have had seven hundred pounds a year, neat
money; for, when he made the Will, the Income Tax was
double to what it is at present; and the estate which it is
paid from is increasing every year in value. It may be law,
but it is not just; nor in equity would, I believe, be considered as the will and intention of Sir William. Never mind!
Thank God, you do not want any of his kindness; nor will
he give you justice!

I may fairly say all this; because my actions are different,
even to a person who has treated me so ill. As to ——, I
know the full extent of the obligation I owe him, and he may
be useful to me again; but I can never forget his unkindness
to you. But, I guess, many reasons influenced his conduct,
in bragging of his riches, and my honourable poverty; but,
as I have often 'said, and with honest pride, what I have is
my own; it never cost the widow a tear, or the Nation a
farthing. I got what I have with my pure blood, from the
Enemies of my Country. Our house, my own Emma, is built
upon a solid foundation; and will last to us, when his house
and lands may belong to others than his children. I would not
have believed it, from any one but you! But, if ever I go
abroad again, matters shall be settled very differently. I am
working hard with Gibbs about Bronté, but the calls upon me
are very heavy. Next September, I shall be clear; I mean,
September 1805. I have wrote to both Acton and the Queen
about you. I do not think she likes Mr. Elliot; and, therefore, I wish she had never shown him my letters about you.
We also know that he has a card of his own to play. Dr.
Scott, who is a good man—although, poor fellow! very often

wrong in the head—is going with Staines, in the Cameleon,
just to take a peep at Naples and Palermo. I have introduced him to Acton, who is very civil to everybody from me.
The Admiralty proceedings towards me, you will know much
sooner than I shall. I hope they will do the thing handsomely, and allow of my return in the Spring; but I do not
expect it. I am very uneasy at your and Horatia being on
the Coast; for you cannot move, if the French make the
attempt; which, I am told, they have done, and been re-
pulsed. Pray God, it may be true!

I shall rejoice to hear you and Horatia are safe at Merton.;
and happy shall I be, the day I join you. *Gannam Justem.*
Gaetano is very grateful for your remembrance of him. Mr.
Chevalier is an excellent servant. William says, he has wrote
twice: I suppose he thinks that enough. This is written
within three miles of the Fleet in Toulon, who are looking
very tempting. Kind regards to Mrs. Cadogan, Charlotte,
&c. and compliments to all our joint friends; for they are
no friends of mine, who are not friends to Emma. God bless
you, again and again! Captain Hardy has not been very
well; and I fancy, Admiral Murray will not be sorry to see
England, especially since he has been promoted..... he expects his flag may be up. God bless you, my dearest Emma,
and be assured I am, &c.

TO CARDINAL DESPUIG.

[From Clarke and M'Arthur, vol. ii. p. 385.]

August, 1804.

Having always paid the greatest attention to your Brother
Cardinals, and to the Sovereignty of the Pope, particularly in
1798, when I saved them from Naples, and in 1799, when a
British Naval Officer under my orders hoisted the Papal
colours, and hauled down the French, upon the Castle of St.
Angelo, I therefore send (although I am sure no British
Officer requires such an order) an order for every Officer
under my command to pay your Eminence all the respect
due to your high rank, and also to give you every facility in
their power to forward the successful termination of your

voyage : and if I can be useful in sending your Eminence to
Italy, only tell me so, and I shall be happy in the opportunity
of assuring your Eminence with what respect I am, your most
obedient servant,

NELSON AND BRONTE.

TO CAPTAIN THOMAS STAINES, ESQ., H.M. SLOOP CAMELEON.

[Order-Book.]

Victory, at Sea, 1st September, 1804.

Most secret.

You are hereby required and directed to proceed without
a moment's loss of time in his Majesty's Sloop Cameleon,
under your command, through the Faro of Messina into the
Adriatic, and cruise and search for the numerous French
Privateers which infest that sea, as you will observe by the
enclosed list.   You will call occasionally at Trieste, Pirano,
Fiume, Ragusa, and, in short, at any place not occupied
by the French, where you may possibly gain information,
except Ancona and Manfredonia : both these last-mentioned
places appear to require great caution in approaching their
harbours, you will, therefore, act with respect thereto as from
circumstances may be proper.   As the object of the service
you are to be employed on, is secret and confidential, you
will conceal it from any Senior Officer you may fall in with,
and also from our Consuls, acquainting them that you expect
dispatches either for me, or orders to meet you at the place,
&c. &c., which will regulate your future conduct ; consequently,
your stay in the Adriatic and time of leaving it, will also
remain with yourself.   In the event of your being applied to
take Convoy, except from Trieste to Venice, or a similar
distance, which will only employ the Cameleon for a few
hours, you will on no account do so, stating, as a reason, that
you are employed on a particular service, and expect orders
or dispatches for me, and therefore cannot divert from it a
moment ; but in this your judgment will point out what may
be most proper ; and I am led to hope from your disguising
the Cameleon, added to the known abilities and perseverance
which has on all occasions marked your conduct, that your
present visit to the Adriatic will clear that place of the
Privateers before alluded to.

The Enemy's Vessels which you may capture can be sent into any of the Austrian Ports, or certainly into Corfu, until you return to Malta, when you will take any Convoy from the Adriatic, which may be ready to proceed to Valetta Harbour, under your protection. I herewith transmit you a copy of a letter from Captain Raynsford, of the Morgiana, which will enable you to form a judgment how to act, together with an order to prevent any Senior Officer from interfering with you, or to demand a sight of this, which is most secret.

I hope the state of the Cameleon, in every respect, will enable you to continue on this service in the Adriatic until the end of October, when you will return to Malta, and deliver the accompanying order to the Officers of that Yard, which will enable you to make her complete, and fit for any future service. In the execution of these instructions I rely with confidence on your judgment and exertions, and must leave it for you to act as from circumstances of information you may judge best for the destruction of the Enemy's Privateers.

NELSON AND BRONTE.

TO THE CAPTAIN OR COMMANDER OF ANY OF HIS MAJESTY'S SHIPS OR VESSELS WHO MAY FALL IN WITH HIS MAJESTY'S SLOOP CAMELEON.

[Order-Book.]

Victory, at Sea, 1st September, 1804.

You are hereby required and directed on no account to interfere with Captain Staines, or to demand a sight of his Orders, which are *most secret*, unless from particular circumstances it may be judged necessary, in which case you are to keep them most inviolably secret.

NELSON AND BRONTE.

TO CAPTAIN ROBERT PETTET, H. M. SLOOP TERMAGANT.

[Order-Book.]

Victory, at Sea, 1st September, 1804.

You are hereby required and directed to proceed without a moment's loss of time in his Majesty's Sloop Termagant,

under your command, to Palermo, and deliver my secret
dispatches herewith transmitted to Captain Staines of the
Cameleon, passing through the Straits of Bonifaccio, on your
way to the above mentioned place (but on no account to
anchor at Madalena). Should the Cameleon not have
arrived at Palermo, you will wait there for Captain Staines,
and receive from him such letters, &c. as he may have
brought from Naples; and afterwards, remain at Palermo
three days for such dispatches as Sir John Acton and Mr.
Gibbs may have to send to me. Having waited at Palermo,
and received the letters, &c., as above mentioned, you will
return and join me with all possible expedition, passing to
the Southward of Sardinia, in order to get your Westing, and
join me on Rendezvous No. 102, where you will find the
Squadron, or orders for your further proceedings. Should
you be forced to the Westward as far as Minorca, and as Cape
St. Sebastians is not far out of your way, it is possible the Fleet
may be there: you will, consequently, judge the propriety of
passing through Rendezvous No. 97.

NELSON AND BRONTE.

TO CAPTAIN ROBERT RAYNSFORD, H.M. SLOOP MORGIANA.

[From a Copy in the Admiralty.]

Victory, at Sea, 2nd September, 1804.

Sir,

I have received your letters of the 29th and 30th July, together with the several inclosures which accompanied them,
and I have great satisfaction in expressing my full and entire
approbation of every part of your conduct, as mentioned in
your foresaid letters. With respect to the line of conduct
necessary to be observed with the Enemy's Privateers, under
similar circumstances, it is impossible for me to name any
precise mode of proceeding; for if the laws of Neutrality are
not adhered to, and enforced by the Powers in amity with all
the world, it will, I fear, if remonstrances are not attended to
by those Powers, become necessary to destroy the Enemy's
Privateers wherever they may be found. But this measure
must not be resorted to until proofs of misconduct on the part

of our Enemies have been made manifest. In that case, I am
clearly of opinion, that on the spot where the breach of
Neutrality has been committed by the French, the Enemy has
no right to claim the protection of Neutrality, if he should be
overpowered. I am sure it is the furthest from the wish of our
Government to break the Neutrality of any State, although the
French may; but it is no longer a Neutral spot, if the French
are permitted to commit hostilities against us. I am, &c.

NELSON AND BRONTE.

TO CAPTAIN VINCENT, H. M. SLOOP ARROW.

[From " The Naval Chronicle," vol. xvii. p. 278.]

Sir, Victory, at Sea, 2nd September, 1804.

I have received your letter of the 8th of August last, with
the several enclosures therein mentioned, and very highly approve of your complying with Mr. Foresti's request in conveying his dispatches to Venice, and landing the Russian courier
at that place. I am very much obliged by the information
contained in your said letter and enclosures; and particularly
satisfied with the whole of your proceedings. With respect
to the line of conduct necessary to be observed in the destruction of the Enemy's Privateers, I must beg to remark to
you the same as I have done to Captain Raynsford—viz., " It
is impossible for me," &c. [Vide p. 185, ante.] I am, &c.,

NELSON AND BRONTE.

TO CAPTAIN PHILIP LAMB, RESIDENT AGENT OF TRANSPORTS,
MALTA.

[Letter-Book.]

Sir, Victory, at Sea, 2nd September, 1804.

I have received your letter of the 20th ultimo, transmitting, for my information, the state of the Transports and
Prisoners of War, under your charge. I am perfectly satisfied with your ready acquiescence in every point of service,
and I am equally so, that your future attention to the good
and interest of his Majesty's Service in your department, will
be unremitting. I am, &c.,

NELSON AND BRONTE.

TO LIEUTENANT HARDING SHAW, COMMANDING H. M. BRIG
SPIDER.

[Letter-Book.]

Victory, at Sea, 2nd September, 1804.

Sir,

I have received your letters of the 9th July and 20th
ultimo : the former acquainting me with the detention of the
Ragusa Brig, Madonna del Rosario, from Canea, Island of
Candia, bound to Marseilles, with oil; and the latter ques-
tioning the existence of a British Consul at Canea, by the
name of Bertrand, who it appears had signed some of the
said Vessel's papers as such, observing, at the same time, that
it might be to the advantage of our Cruizers to ascertain this
fact, and to permit your going there for that purpose. In
answer thereto, I hope the concealed papers you mention,
and other circumstances, may determine the Judge of the
Vice-Admiralty Court at Malta to deem her a legal prize ;
but I cannot see the necessity of your proceeding to Canea,
for the purpose stated in your said letter, as there is no doubt
that you will be able to ascertain the fact from Sir Alexander
Ball, who must know all the British Consuls, and from any
Vessel arriving at Malta from that place, or Merchant who
may have correspondents at Canea. I am, &c.,

NELSON AND BRONTE.

TO CAPTAIN CHARLES MARSH SCHOMBERG, H.M. SHIP MADRAS.

[Letter-Book.]

Victory, at Sea, 2nd September, 1804.

Dear Sir,

I am sorry to observe that his Majesty's Ship Madras,
under your command, bears a Lieutenant more than her
established complement, in consequence of Lieutenant Isaac
Strutt's[9] being invalided as belonging to that Ship, and from
the report of survey on the said Lieutenant, stating him as one
of her proper Officers, I appointed Mr. Charles Royer in his
room, without adverting to the circumstance of Lieutenant

---

[9] He died a Lieutenant, about 1823.

Strutt's having belonged to the Donegal, and exchanged duties with Mr. Seymour,[1] who was appointed to the Madras in the room of Lieutenant Coltman, invalided from that Ship on the 14th January last, and afterwards succeeded by Lieutenant Adderley,[2] appointed by the Admiralty. This late appointment of Mr. Adderley's, led, in the first instance, to the mistake; and the suffering Lieutenant Strutt, of the Donegal, to be invalided from the Madras, when in fact he ought to have been returned to his proper Ship, or discharged from the Service on Lieutenant Adderley's joining, has led to a subsequent one. But we must endeavour to get rid of it the best way we can, and, therefore, I have enclosed an Acting-Order for Mr. Royer, in the room of Lieutenant Waller, and request you will be so good as date the said order the day after Mr. Waller may be invalided, and acquaint me therewith, that I may also date the copy in my possession. I am, with much regard, dear Sir, &c.,

NELSON AND BRONTE.

TO CAPTAIN CHARLES MARSH SCHOMBERG, H. M. SHIP MADRAS.

[Letter-Book.]

Victory, at Sea, 2nd September, 1804.

Sir,

Lord Elgin having requested through Sir Alexander Ball that I would allow a Ship to call at Cerigo, to bring from thence to Malta some marble antiquities,[3] and as I am perfectly disposed to meet his Lordship's wishes on this occasion, I am to desire you will send a small Transport to Cerigo, with the first Convoy going up the Levant, and leave her there, for the purpose of receiving the antiquities before-mentioned on board (provided it is a safe place for her to remain at) till the return of the Convoy, when you will direct the Officer in charge thereof to call at Cerigo, and bring the Transport with his Lordship's antiquities on board, safe under his protection to Malta, when Sir Alexander Ball will direct the disposal of them; and if it is intended to send them to England, you will give the necessary orders accordingly. I am, &c.

NELSON AND BRONTE.

[1] Vide vol. v. p. 415.   [2] Now Captain Arden Adderley.
[3] The Elgin Marbles, now in the British Museum.

TO MAJOR LOWE.

[Autograph, in the possession of Josiah French, Esq.]

Victory, September 6th, 1804.

Dear Sir,

I have been favoured with your letter of August 21st, and Stephano Scapero shall be sent to Comte Revel, who I have also wrote to upon the subject, assuring him that it was undesignedly Captain Morati enlisting him; but Captain M. has trusted, as Comte Revel writes me, unfaithful people in the environs of Sapire to recruit for him. Considering upon what tender ground the recruiting is upon everywhere, we should be very guarded in our conduct, and not commit the only Power who overlooks our recruiting in their Dominions. I am sure your orders have been correct. I am, dear Sir, wishing you every success in completing your Corps, your very faithful servant,

NELSON AND BRONTE.

TO MAJOR-GENERAL VILLETTES,[4] MALTA.

[Autograph, in the possession of Mr. M. M. Holloway.]

Victory, September 6th, 1804.

My dear General,

Scapero is received, and I have wrote to Comte Revel, that if the man is not really a deserter, he may be returned. But, in fact, the Sardinian Government allowing our recruiting at Madalena, is such an act of kindness in them (when none of the Great Powers will permit it) as demands all our attention with respect to the consequences of giving up this Sardinian; it is but an act of common justice, as they give up all ours. And, to say the truth, I had rather that not one Corsican or Italian was raised, if it is to be at the expense of perhaps losing double the number of English Seamen; for such is the love for roaming of our men, that I am sure they would desert from heaven to hell, merely for the sake of change.

[4] Of this Officer, some account will be found in vol. i. p. 378. He died a Lieutenant-General, while commanding the Forces in Jamaica, on the 13th of July 1808, aged 54. A Memoir of him is given in the Gentleman's Magazine, vol. lxxix. part i. p. 297, and part ii. p. 798.

I should be very sorry if the few Recruits we get for the Marines, should interfere with recruiting for the Army. I never wish to see an Italian recruit. If they come, I must receive them; but I give no encouragement to the raising Italians. Good Germans I cannot have any objections to. If the Russians continue increasing their Naval Force in this Country, I do not think the French will venture to the Eastward; therefore, I rather expect they will, as the year advances, try to get out of the Straits; and should they accomplish it with 7000 Troops on board, I am sure we should lose half our West India Islands, for I think they would go there, and not to Ireland. Whatever may be their destination, I shall certainly follow, be it even to the East Indies. Such a pursuit would do more, perhaps, towards restoring me to health than all the Doctors; but I fear this is reserved for some happier man. Not that I can complain; I have had a good race of glory, but we are never satisfied, although I hope I am duly thankful for the past; but one cannot help, being at sea, longing for a little more. La Touche has given me the slip—he died of the colic; perhaps Buonaparte's, for they say he was a rank Republican. Dumanoir is the Rear-Admiral at present in Toulon. God bless you, my dear General, and believe me ever, your much obliged friend,

NELSON AND BRONTE.

TO REAR-ADMIRAL SIR RICHARD BICKERTON, BART.

[From Clarke and M'Arthur, vol. ii. p. 386. " Thursday, 6th September. 6 A.M. Parted H. M. Ships Royal Sovereign, Spencer, Leviathan, Excellent, Belleisle, Thunder, and Acheron. . . . . Out all reefs of the topsails. At 9·45, wore and stood in for Toulon under all sail with the Starboard Division, except the Spencer. Niger rejoined. Mustered at quarters : Larboard Division in the offing. Squadron in Company. At Noon, Cape Sicie North, eight leagues. P.M. At 1·45, shortened sail, tacked, and hove to. At 2·45, made sail on the larboard tack. At 5·10, set royals. Joined H.M. Ships Royal Sovereign, Spencer, Belleisle, Excellent, Leviathan, Thunder, and Acheron."—*Victory's Log*,]

Victory, September 6th, 1804.

I shall stand inshore with the Starboard Division, and I therefore desire you to keep your present position. I shall come back again in the evening, merely wishing to take a look who are out; for I think they will now push to the

Westward, and if they should get out of the Straits, I am of
opinion they will try for the West Indies, and then, with
7000 Troops, farewell our Islands.   I am, &c.

NELSON AND BRONTE.

TO SIR ALEXANDER JOHN BALL, BART., MALTA.[5]

[Autograph, in the possession of Sir William Keith Ball, Bart.]

My dear Ball,   Victory, September 6th, 1804.

Many thanks for your kind letter of August 20th.   I am
sensible of your partiality for me ; but I cannot bring myself

[5] Of this able Officer, the following brief notice will probably be read with interest. After seeing much service, including Lord Rodney's Action in 1782, Captain
Ball obtained Post Rank in 1783 ; and having gone to France during the Peace, he
met Nelson at St. Omer's, in November of that year, where, as has been already
observed, they imbibed a mutual dislike for each other. (Vol. i. p. 88.)   The
remarkable manner in which, after an interval of many years, their friendship
commenced, has also been stated, (vol. iii. p. 21,) and it has been shown that
Captain Ball greatly distinguished himself at the Battle of the Nile, in command of
the Alexander.   In October 1798, he was placed by Lord Nelson in command of the
Squadron blockading Malta, and " at the request of the Chief of the contending fac-
tions in that Island, he mediated between them, succeeded in restoring harmony, and
by his wise and conciliatory conduct, secured the confidence of the Maltese people.
He presided over their councils, organized the government, and, with singular zeal
and energy, directed the operations of the native battalions." At the request of the
Maltese, his Sicilian Majesty appointed him Governor of Malta; and though he
joined Lord Nelson in the Alexander, in May 1799, he soon after returned to the
government of Malta, at the earnest desire of the inhabitants.   In March 1801,
Captain Ball was superseded at Malta by Major-General Pigot, the Commander of
the Forces; and, in June following, his eminent services were rewarded by a
Baronetcy, previously to which he had obtained permission to wear the Cross of
Commander of the Order of St. Ferdinand and Merit, and of the Order of
Malta.   By the Treaty of Amiens, the Island of Malta was to revert to the Order
of St. John of Jerusalem, and Sir Alexander Ball was sent to Malta as British
Plenipotentiary, where he was received, on his arrival in August 1802, with the
strongest demonstrations of gratitude and affection.   Soon after, the Civil Government of the Island was temporarily placed in his hands; and, in 1803, he was
confirmed as his Majesty's Commissioner for the Civil Affairs of Malta.   In 1805,
he obtained the rank of Rear-Admiral, and in 1807, was ordered to hoist his
Flag, and carry on the Naval duties of the harbour of Valetta, in conjunction with
those of Civil Governor.   Sir Alexander Ball died at Malta, a Rear-Admiral of the
White, on the 25th of October 1809, aged 52, deeply lamented by all to whom he was
known ; and more especially by the Maltese, who, from his paternal care, and kindness of heart, had bestowed upon him the appellation of their " father."   The high
opinion which Nelson entertained of his talents, is shown by his correspondence ;
and a publication of a Memoir of his Services, including a selection from his Letters,
would establish his right to an elevated position among the Naval Worthies of his
Country.   To his only son, Sir William Keith Ball, Bart., the Public are indebted
for some of the most interesting Letters in this Work.

to suppose but that one half of the Admirals on the list will perform the duty of the Mediterranean Command as well, at least, as myself; and if the other half of the Admirals' list was to hear of my vanity they would think me a fool; but be that as it may, I am very far from well. At the same time if I was to get better, nothing could please me so much as returning to this Command; but I have no interest and another will come, and I think very probably Orde, or Curtis—Young seems fixed at Plymouth. With respect to Mr. Fagan, you sent me Admiral Murray's letter instead of his, (but I can assure you I have not read it.) I have heard Mr. Fagan well spoken of by several of our travelling gentry, and I carried him from Naples, and returned him to Leghorn; but if I had interest, I must know more of his services than I can recollect at present, and what remuneration an Artist can claim from Government I know not. He wants, I fancy, to be Consul and Agent at Città Vecchia and Rome, which Mr. Dennis has been long appointed to. The Vice-Consul at Girgenti has much greater claims upon the Government than Mr. Fagan, and both you and I ought to exert ourselves to get him a small pension as Vice-Consul; but of his merits you know even more than I do. I have read the account of the Marquis Dasserto. I never intended to hold any communication with him. I considered him as a French spy, and for that reason referred him to Diplomatic characters, if he had anything to communicate. Mr. Elliot wanted to send me some good Frenchmen, to go ashore, and to get me information. My [answer] to all these offers [is], 'I can be told nothing of any consequence to me; but a copy of the French Admiral's orders; when he is to put to sea, and where he is destined to, is the only useful information I can care about. I can see the number and force at Toulon any day I please, and as for the names of the Captains or Admirals, I care not what they are called;' therefore, as you may suppose, I have none of these 'good Frenchmen' about me. I will direct the Agent of Transports to send a Vessel to Cerigo with the first Convoy destined into the Levant for Lord Elgin's things, if she will lay in safety there, and one of our Ships shall call for her upon her return. I wish I had any Sloops of War; but you have them all to the Eastward, and at Gibraltar the Childers is the only one I can call upon.　The Termagant is going to Gibraltar to be hove down.　I wrote to the Admiralty until I am tired, and they have left off answering those parts of my letters.　The late Admiralty thought I kept too many to the Eastward of Sicily; the Smyrna folks complain of me, so do the Adriatic, so they do between Cape de Gatte and Gibraltar.　But all I have are to the Eastward, as by list.

Bittern, Arrow, Halcyon, Sophie—Gibraltar.

Morgiana, Termagant—going to heave down.

Seahorse, Childers—between the Fleet and Spain.

Renard—September 20th, found bad; gone to Gibraltar to heave down.

Spider, Hirondelle, Cameleon—gone to the Adriatic.

If I had them, I do assure you not one of them should go Prize hunting : that I never have done ; and to this day, I can solemnly assure you, that I am a poorer man than the day I was ordered to the Mediterranean Command, by upwards of £1000 ; but money I despise, except as it is useful, and I expect my Prize-money is embarked in the Toulon Fleet.　I should think, now the Russians are getting so large a Naval Force into the Mediterranean, that the Toulon Fleet will not think of going to the Eastward.　I should rather think the West Indies more likely for them to succeed in.　Suppose this Fleet escapes, and gets out of the Straits, I rather think I should bend my course to the Westward ; for if they carry 7000 men —with what they have at Martinico and Guadaloupe—St. Lucia, Grenada, St. Vincent, Antigua, and St. Kitts would fall, and, in that case, England would be so clamorous for Peace, that we should humble ourselves.　What do you think ? Tell me.　I have weighed Ireland against the West Indies. With me the latter throws the beam up to the ceiling ; but I may be wrong.　It is at best but a guess, and the world attaches wisdom to him that guesses right.　I wish I could see you in Sardinia ; for if we do not manage to have it, France will ; and what shall we do then ?　I have wrote a last letter upon the importance of it ; but I dare say my opinions are thrown aside, as either ignorant or impertinent : so be it.　God bless you, my dear Ball, and ever be assured that I am your most faithful friend,

NELSON AND BRONTE.

TO JOHN TURNBULL, ESQ., CHAIRMAN OF THE BRITISH
MERCHANTS TRADING TO THE MEDITERRANEAN.

[From a Copy in the Nelson Papers.]

Victory, at Sea, 7th September, 1804.

Sir,

I have received through Mr. Higgins, Merchant at Malta,
your letter without date, stating that some little delay has
been experienced at that place, by the Merchant Vessels
arriving from England, bound to Ports in the Adriatic and
Levant, being obliged to wait in Valetta Harbour for Convoy. In answer to which, I herewith transmit you a letter
from Captain Schomberg, of the Madras, dated the 7th October 1803, which will show my general desire that every possible protection is to be afforded the Trade bound to and
from the Adriatic and Levant, &c. I might also transmit
you several extracts of my letters and orders to Captain Cracraft of the Anson, and other Officers employed in the
vicinity of Malta, on the same subject, but do not judge it
necessary, as I am satisfied that my instructions on that head
have been as fully executed as possible ; and it will ever be my
particular desire to expedite our Trade to its destination, and
protect it to the utmost of my power from falling into the
hands of the Enemy.

I have to observe on the subject of the Enemy's numerous
Privateers and Row-Boats, who, in violation of every known
law of Neutrality, capture our Trade under the very forts
which ought to protect them, that the conduct of those Pirates
has been fully stated to the Lords Commissioners of the Admiralty, and that I have, in the meantime, adopted the most
effectual measures in my power for their destruction. Mr.
Higgins's application to the Senior Officer at Malta, respecting
Convoys, will always meet with due attention. I am, &c.

NELSON AND BRONTE.

TO WILLIAM MARSDEN, ESQ., ADMIRALTY.

[Original, in the Admiralty.]

Victory, at Sea, 8th September, 1804.

Sir,

I herewith transmit you copies of two letters from Captain Raynsford of the Morgiana, dated the 29th and 30th of July last, together with copies of his letter of the 27th June, and a list of Privateers alluded to in his first-mentioned letter, which you will please to lay before the Lords Commissioners of the Admiralty for their information ; and also a copy of my answer thereto, dated the 2nd instant, which also accompanies this. Their Lordships will observe, by Captain Raynsford's before-mentioned letters, the piratical proceedings of the Enemy's Privateers in the Adriatic, and the necessity of making such remonstrances with the Imperial Court, as may prevent similar robberies under their forts in future. I must here beg to observe that the conduct, not only of the Morgiana, but also of all the Vessels of War employed in the Adriatic and Levant, has been such as merits my warmest thanks, and will, I hope, entitle them to their Lordships' approbation. I am, &c.

NELSON AND BRONTE.

TO CAPTAIN THE HONOURABLE COURTENAY BOYLE, H. M. SHIP SEAHORSE.

[Order-Book.]

Victory, at Sea, 8th September, 1804.

Whereas it is my intention to proceed immediately with the Squadron to Rendezvous No. 97, under Cape St. Sebastians, You are hereby required and directed to take his Majesty's Ship named in the margin,[7] under your command, and station yourself between Rendezvous No. 102 and Toulon, in such position as you may judge best for watching the Enemy's motions in that Port, and for ascertaining with correctness their putting to sea, in case they should do so. In reconnoitring and watching the Enemy as above-directed, the

¹ Niger.

greatest care must be taken that you do not approach Toulon so as to render yourself liable to being becalmed, and consequently to an attack from a superior force of Ships and Gunboats in such situation. You will occasionally proceed to Rendezvous No. 102, in order to acquaint any of his Majesty's Ships that the Squadron is gone to Rendezvous No. 97, where they will find me, or intelligence where I am gone to. The moment the Active joins from Port de Torres, you will desire Captain Moubray to follow me immediately to Rendezvous No. 97, and also order the Amazon (daily expected from Malta) to join me at that place. Should any other of his Majesty's Ships arrive on Rendezvous No. 102, you will direct their Captains to join me forthwith; and in the event of the Enemy's putting to sea, or any important intelligence obtained respecting them, you will join me yourself, or send the Niger to Cape St. Sebastians, with all dispatch.

NELSON AND BRONTE.

TO J. B. GIBERT, ESQ., PRO-CONSUL, BARCELONA.

[Letter-Book.]

Victory, at Sea, 10th September, 1804.

Sir,

I have received the copy of your letters dated the 14th and 22nd ultimo, the former acquainting me that you had forwarded some letters from Madrid and England, by the Master of a Vessel leaving Barcelona, who was good enough to say that he would deliver them to some of the Fleet, and the latter on the subject of Mr. Ford's offer for your wine at Rosas. I have likewise received your two letters of the 1st instant, acquainting me that an epidemical disease had again broke out at Malaga—that you had determined not to send any more letters to me by casual Vessels, from the great uncertainty of their delivery, and enclosing a letter from Mr. Hunter from Madrid. In answer to your said letters, I am extremely obliged by your kindness in forwarding my letters, but request, as mentioned in my last letter by Sir William Bolton, that no more of my Public dispatches or private letters are sent out, unless by a Vessel directed to

cruize till she shall fall in with some Ship of War belonging
to the Fleet. It is, however, strange that the Vessel you
mention to have taken out my letters, should have missed the
Fleet, or some of the look-out Frigates, which are constantly
cruizing in the vicinity of Toulon.

I have [to offer you] many thanks for your forwarding my
letters to England, and very much obliged by your sending
me Mr. Hunter's letter, the answer to which, herewith transmitted, I shall beg you to forward. On the subject of the
wine, I have sent Mr. Ford, the Agent-Victualler, to make a
final settlement, with respect to the quantity at Rosas which
may be fit for his Majesty's Service; and you will judge from
the sentiments communicated in my private letter to you of
this date, the propriety of making a statement of the loss sustained from its being so long kept, &c., in order that I may
use my influence with the Victualling-Board for such remuneration being made you as may appear proper. Mr. Ford,
being perfectly acquainted with these matters, will assist you
in the arrangement. I am, &c.,

NELSON AND BRONTE.

TO CAPTAIN WILLIAM DURBAN, H. M. SHIP AMBUSCADE.

[Autograph draught, in the possession of Miss Bolton, of Burnham, and Order-
Book.]

Victory, at Sea, 11th September, 1804.

Whereas I wish very much to be made acquainted with the
Anchorage and Gulf of Palma, in the Island of Majorca, and
as a most favourable opportunity now presents itself by the
circumstance of the Cardinal Despuig wanting a passport
from me, and as he is brother to the Vice-Roy, the Marquis
de Monte Negro, You are therefore hereby required and
directed to proceed to Palma, and first by offering to salute
the place upon the assurance of an equal number of guns
being returned, deliver my letter to the Cardinal, and personally assure his Eminence of my earnest desire to meet his
wishes; so much so, that even should he wish to go to Italy
in the Ambuscade, that you are at liberty to carry him to
either Cività Vecchia or Naples, without any further order
from me, provided his Eminence is ready to embark in forty-

eight hours, to which time I must limit your stay; during which time you are to examine not only everything laid down in the printed orders of the Admiralty, but examine the general state of the Island, its forts, and the probability of its being taken, in case of a Spanish war. You will examine in the environs of Palma, the best place for landing Troops, the situation of the forts or towers which are in the Gulf, the best mode of approaching the Town, the strength of its fortifications, both on the land and sea side ; whether there is a ditch ; how deep ; and what is the probable height of the wall ; whether Ships could approach near enough to batter the fortifications; how Bomb-Vessels could act; what is the general Garrison : in short, everything which my opinion of your good sense and abilities leads me to expect from you. Whether, if the Fleet was to anchor there, that it would be ill or well received ; the cattle or other refreshments it could obtain. Having made the observations, &c., at Palma, as before-mentioned, which must not detain the Ambuscade more than two or three days, you will leave that place, and return and join the Squadron on Rendezvous No. 97, under Cape St. Sebastians, with all possible dispatch, where you will find me, or orders for your further proceedings. But should Cardinal Despuig express a desire to be conveyed to Italy in the Ambuscade, you will receive his Eminence and suite on board, and proceed with them, with all convenient expedition, either to Città Vecchia or Naples, where you will land them, and afterwards return and join me on Rendezvous No. 97, without delay, as before directed. You are not to wait for his Eminence at Palma, in the event of his going with you, longer than the time above-mentioned.

NELSON AND BRONTE.

TO WILLIAM MARSDEN, ESQ., ADMIRALTY.

[Original, in the Admiralty.]

Victory, at Sea, 12th September, 1804.

Sir,

I herewith transmit you for the information of the Lords Commissioners of the Admiralty, a copy of a Survey held on Lieutenant Thomas Vol, of his Majesty's Ship Niger, and request you will be pleased to acquaint their Lordships that I have removed Lieutenant Nicholas[5] (at his own request) to the Niger, and have appointed Mr. Edward Flin,[6] of the Victory, to act in the Bittern, in consequence thereof; a copy of whose Acting-Order is also herewith transmitted. I must beg to observe that Mr. Flin's conduct very justly merits my approbation as stated in the margin of the said Acting-Order,[7] and that his general conduct since he has been in the Victory, has been very meritorious. I therefore hope their Lordships will approve of my having placed him in this invaliding vacancy, and confirm the appointment. I am, &c.

NELSON AND BRONTE.

TO CAPTAIN HENRY RICHARDSON, H. M. SHIP JUNO.

[Order-Book.]

Victory, at Sea, 14th September, 1804.

You are hereby required and directed to proceed immediately to Barcelona, for the purpose of landing the passengers found on board the Vessel detained by his Majesty's

[5] Mr. Vol died a Lieutenant, between 1816 and 1820. Lieutenant Robert Nicholas was made a Commander in 1805, and was lost in command of the Lark Sloop, off Cape Causada, in August 1809.

[6] The circumstance is thus noticed in the Victory's Log:—"Tuesday, 11th September. P.M. At 9·55, James Archibald, seaman, fell overboard: down Cutter, and got him in safe, being saved by Mr. Flin, Master's Mate, who jumped overboard after him." In the "Recollections of Dr. Scott," p. 125, where the accident is erroneously stated to have occurred "one bright morning", while Mr. Flin "was sitting on the deck, comfortably sketching," and where the man is said to have been Mr. Flin's servant, the following anecdote is added:—"On Lord Nelson's presenting Mr. Flin with his Commission, a loud huzza from the Midshipmen, whom the incident had collected on deck, and who were throwing up their hats in honour of Flin's good fortune, arrested Lord Nelson's attention. There was something significant in the tone of their cheer, which he immediately recognised, and putting up his hand for silence, and leaning over to the crowd of Middies, he said, with a good-natured smile on his face—' Stop, young gentlemen! Mr. Flin has done a gallant thing to-day, and he has done many gallant things before, for which he has got his reward. But mind, I'll have no more making Lieutenants for servants falling overboard!'" Mr. Flin died a Post Captain, and a Companion of the Bath, in May 1819.

[7] The Marginal Note was as follows:—"Appointed, in consequence of his having jumped overboard, on the night of the 11th instant, then very dark, and at the risk of his life, saved James Archibald, a Seaman belonging to the Victory, who had by accident fallen overboard, and certainly would have been drowned. Mr. Flin's conduct, independent of this, is very meritorious. NELSON AND BRONTE."

Ship Juno, under your command, a few days ago. And, whereas it is my intention to proceed with the Squadron the first strong Westerly wind off Toulon, for the purpose of reconnoitring the Enemy at that Port, and from thence pass through Rendezvous No. 102, to receive any information the Ships there may have obtained of them, You are hereby required and directed, the moment you have landed the passengers before-mentioned at Barcelona, to return to your station, and inform any of his Majesty's Ships, Vessels, or Transports arriving on Rendezvous No. 97 thereof, and direct their Commanders to remain on the last-mentioned Rendezvous, under Cape St. Sebastians, until my return, whatever may be the importance of their orders, as the Squadron will only take the route above-mentioned, and return immediately to Rendezvous No. 97, where the strictest look-out is to be kept for arrivals from England, Malta, &c., daily expected.

NELSON AND BRONTE.

TO CAPTAIN JOHN GORE, H. M. SHIP MEDUSA.

[Letter-Book.]

Victory, at Sea, 15th September, 1804.

Sir,

As no Return has been made by the Ships that have lately joined the Squadron, of any men being sent by you to the Victory, to complete the complements of the different Ships, as I may judge proper, I must desire, in future, whether the men are sent by a Senior or Junior Officer to the Victory, that you transmit me a regular list of their names, entries, and charges, &c., in order that they may be discharged to the different Ships in want of them, and not detained on board the Ship bringing them from Gibraltar, at the pleasure of the Captain. I am, &c.

NELSON AND BRONTE.

TO CAPTAIN GEORGE COCKS, H. M. BOMB-VESSEL THUNDER.

[Letter-Book.]

Victory, at Sea, 17th September, 1804.

Sir,

As I intend proceeding from hence with the Squadron very shortly, and probably before the return of the Juno, I am to desire you will remain on Rendezvous No. 97, under Cape St. Sebastians, till you are joined by his Majesty's Ship Juno, when you will deliver the accompanying letter to Captain Richardson, and put yourself under his command. In the meantime, should any of his Majesty's Ships arrive on the above Rendezvous in search of me, you will detain them till the return of the Juno, who has my directions for their further proceedings. I am, &c.

NELSON AND BRONTE.

TO CAPTAIN RICHARDSON, H. M. SHIP JUNO.

[Letter-Book.]

Victory, at Sea, 20th September, 1804.

Sir,

Having transmitted to Captain Cocks of the Thunder, a letter for you, dated the 17th instant, directing you to take that Bomb-Vessel under your command, and cruize off Cape St. Sebastians, and on Rendezvous No. 97, for the reasons therein mentioned, I am to desire you will make the signal for the Thunder to accompany the Juno, and proceed immediately, (without regard to the motions of the Squadron) to Rendezvous No. 97, for the purpose of acquainting any of his Majesty's Ships or Vessels which may be there in search of the Squadron, where I am, as when the weather comes fine, we have to clear the Transport with water. I am, &c.

NELSON AND BRONTE.

TO DR. BAIRD.

[From "The Athenæum."]

Victory, September 22nd, 1804.

My dear Sir,

I feel truly sensible of all your kindness and good wishes, for which I hope soon to thank you in person. We have been very near losing Dr. Snipe, in appearance by a consumptive complaint, but he is getting better. He is indefatigable in his duty, to which, and to his trip to Sicily about the lemon-juice for England, we attribute his very serious complaint, spitting blood, &c. My complaints have not been so violent, but are sufficient to make me require a few months' rest. Since the 16th June 1803, I have never set my foot outside the Ship. Experience teaches us that this climate is the worst in the world for hectic complaints—at least, it is so at sea. Of the few men we have lost, nine in ten are dead of consumption. Upon the best mode of keeping a Fleet healthy, much may be said, and much must be done— there are various opinions; suffice it for me, that although other places may be better, yet that we have no sick. We shall talk of this, and many other matters, before any great length of time. When you see the Earl,[8] remember me kindly to him, and believe me, my dear Doctor, yours most faithfully,

NELSON AND BRONTE.

TO EDWARD CAREY, ESQ., MASTER SHIPWRIGHT, GIBRALTAR.

[From a Copy in the Nelson Papers.]

Victory, at Sea, 22nd September, 1804.

Sir,

I have received your letter of the 28th July last, with the enclosures therein alluded to, and in answer desire to acquaint you, that no endeavour to impress my mind with an unfavourable idea of your conduct has been attempted. The opinion of Captain Capel was honourable and public, and as such transmitted, that you might be made acquainted with it.

[8] Earl St. Vincent.

With respect to your complying with the orders you receive for the repairs of any of his Majesty's Ships or Vessels sent to Gibraltar for that purpose, I take it for granted that every Officer and person under Government exert themselves to the utmost of their abilities in the faithful performance of the duty and trust imposed on them; and therefore have only to recommend to you the same line of conduct, which cannot fail to give satisfaction to Commissioner Otway, and the Commander-in-Chief of his Majesty's Ships and Vessels on this station. I am, &c.,

NELSON AND BRONTE.

TO WILLIAM MARSDEN, ESQ., ADMIRALTY.

[Autograph, in the Admiralty.]

Victory, September 22nd, 1804.

Sir,

Herewith I transmit you a letter from Captain Hardy of H. M. Ship Victory. The measure of paying for such provisions which the Seamen do not either take up, or, which is not issued to them, either from scarcity, or from its not being in the Fleet, is so just that it cannot be controverted; but upon the present case there seems doubts whether the men have a right to be paid for the half allowance of oatmeal, when no molasses is to be procured. I am sure their Lordships will see the justness of the case as plainly as I do. Each man was formerly allowed a pint of oatmeal on certain days. As it was found that generally a man could not get a pint of dry oatmeal down his throat, and, I suppose, thinking it no longer necessary to present this saving to the Purser, half-a-pint of oatmeal was issued instead of the pint, and, in lieu of the other half-pint, a proportion of molasses. It has sometimes occurred in the Channel Fleet that no molasses could be procured, nor was there any allowance made for such temporary omissions. In the West Indies cocoa and sugar are allowed; in the Channel, I hear, tea and sugar: in the Mediterranean we have no molasses, nor any substitute; nor is our want of molasses temporary, but lasting.

I beg, therefore, with all due respect, to call their Lordships' attention to the circumstance, and to propose that when molasses cannot be obtained, a proportion of sugar should be allowed to be mixed with the oatmeal, in lieu of molasses; and that if sugar cannot be obtained, the men having no substitute in lieu, should be paid the saving, as in all other species of provisions. It is not necessary to enter more at large upon this subject: their Lordships' wisdom will direct their proceedings. I am, &c.

NELSON AND BRONTE.

TO WILLIAM MARSDEN, ESQ., ADMIRALTY.

[Original, in the Admiralty.]

Victory, at Sea, 22nd September, 1804.

Sir,

Finding it necessary from the defects of his Majesty's Ship Childers, to send her to Gibraltar to have them made good, I avail myself of the opportunity to acquaint you for the information of the Lords Commissioners of the Admiralty, that no news or intelligence of any kind has reached me since the sailing of his Majesty's Ship Triumph, on the 27th ult., as there have been no arrivals from Gibraltar, Malta, or Naples. I am, however, in daily expectation of something joining me from those places.

As the Triumph was directed to cruise outside the Straits, for the greater security of any Convoy arriving from England, until the Maidstone (who was to sail about the middle of this month from Valetta Harbour) might be expected with the Trade from Malta, I therefore feel confident that L'Aigle will be prevented from making any attempt to intercept the said Convoy. I am, &c.

NELSON AND BRONTE.

TO J. B. GIBERT, HIS MAJESTY'S PRO-CONSUL AT BARCELONA.

[Letter-Book.]

Victory, at Sea, 25th September, 1804.

Sir,

As it is more than probable the four Seamen named in the margin, who deserted from his Majesty's Bomb-Vessel

Acheron, in the Bay of Rosas, on the 17th instant, have, or will, come the way of Barcelona, I am to request you will give the most strict orders for their being apprehended as deserters from the said Bomb-Vessel; and you will be so good as pay the person who shall apprehend them the sum of eight dollars for each, which I shall cause to be reimbursed. Those men having most audaciously left their duty, cannot be considered as straggling; and, therefore, the greatest care is to be taken to prevent their escape. You will please to send them on board the first Ship, or Vessel of War, calling at Barcelona, that they may be brought to the Fleet. I am, &c.

NELSON AND BRONTE.

TO LADY HAMILTON.

[From " Lord Nelson's Letters to Lady Hamilton," vol. ii. p. 73.]

Victory, September 29th, 1804.

This day, my dearest Emma, which gave me birth, I consider as more fortunate than common days, as, by my coming into this world, it has brought me so intimately acquainted with you, who my soul holds most dear. I well know that you will keep it, and have my dear Horatia to drink my health. Forty-six years of toil and trouble! How few more the common lot of mankind leads us to expect; and, therefore, it is almost time to think of spending the few last years in peace and quietness! .By this time, I should think, either my successor is named, or permission is granted me to come home; and if so, you will not long receive this letter before I make my appearance; which will make us, I am sure, both truly happy. We have had nothing for this fortnight, but gales of Easterly winds and heavy rains; not a Vessel of any kind or sort joined the Fleet. I was in hopes Dr. Scott would have returned from Naples, and that I could have told you something comfortable for you, from that quarter; and it is now seven weeks since we heard from Malta, therefore I know nothing of what is passing in the world. I would not have you, my dear Emma, allow the work of brick and mortar to go on in the winter months. It can all be finished next summer; when I hope

we shall have Peace, or such an universal War as will upset
that vagabond Buonaparte. I have been tolerably well, till this
last bad weather, which has given me pains in my breast; but,
never mind, all will be well when I get to Merton. Admiral
Campbell, who is on board, desires to be remembered to you.
He does not like much to stay here, after my departure. Indeed, we all draw so well together in the Fleet, that I flatter
myself the sorrow for my departure will be pretty general.
Admiral Murray will be glad to get home ; Hardy is as good
as ever; and Mr. Secretary Scott is an excellent man. God
bless you, my dearest Emma! and be assured I am ever your
most faithful and affectionate,

N. & B.

Kiss dear Horatia.   I hope she is at Merton, *fixed*.

TO CAPTAIN CHARLES MARSH SCHOMBERG, H.M. SHIP MADRAS,
OR SENIOR OFFICER AT MALTA.

[Letter-Book.]

Victory, at Sea, 29th September, 1804.

Sir,

Having ordered his Majesty's Bomb-Vessel Thunder to proceed immediately to Malta, for the purpose of convoying the
Victuallers, mentioned in my letter to the Agent-Victualler of
the 20th August last, to the Madalena Islands, it is my directions that you afford every facility in your power for their quick
dispatch ; and as their safe and speedy arrival at the Madalena
Islands is of the utmost consequence, (as you will observe by
Captain Cocks's order,) I am to desire, should there be any
of his Majesty's Ships or Vessels in Valetta Harbour ready
for sea, that you will direct the Commander thereof, to accompany the Thunder and Victualler to the Madalena
Islands; and after having seen them to that anchorage in
safety, to return, (if belonging to Captain Cracraft's Squadron,
or under Sir Alexander Ball's directions,) and follow their
former orders. You will also direct Captain Cocks to receive
on board the Thunder such stores, &c., as the Naval Officer
may have to send to the Fleet, provided there is not sufficient

room for them on board the Victuallers, and cause every possible expedition to be used for their immediate dispatch to the Madalena Islands, as before mentioned. I am, &c.

NELSON AND BRONTE.

TO CAPTAIN GEORGE COCKS, H. M. BOMB-VESSEL THUNDER.

[Order-Book.]

Victory, at Sea, 29th September, 1804.

Having directed the Agent-Victualler at Malta, by letter of the 20th August last (a triplicate of which is herewith transmitted) to have Transports laden with provisions for the Fleet, and ready to sail from Valetta harbour by the middle of October, under the protection of any Ship of War which might be leaving Malta to join me about that time, or such Convoy as I should think proper to send for them ; and whereas I am apprehensive that no opportunity is likely to offer for that purpose, You are hereby required and directed to proceed in his Majesty's Bomb-Vessel Thunder, under your command, to Malta, with the utmost possible dispatch ; and on your arrival there, you will deliver my aforesaid letter to the Agent-Victualler, and also the inclosed one to Captain Schomberg, or the Senior Officer at that place, who is directed to send such Ship, or Vessel of War, as may be there, to accompany you to the Madalena Islands.   But should there not be any Vessel of War at Malta, you will take the Victuallers under your protection, and proceed with them without a moment's loss of time, to the Madalena Islands, passing on the East side of Sardinia to the anchorage in Agincourt Sound; and as it is possible that the Enemy may have possessed themselves of those Islands, and the Victuallers being of the utmost consequence to the Fleet under my command, you are to approach the said Islands with great caution, until you have fully satisfied yourself that the Enemy have not taken possession of them; when you will moor the Victuallers in safety in Agincourt Sound, and hold them and the Thunder in momentary readiness to leave that place, on the appearance of an Enemy of superior force; and in order the more effectually to discover their approach, you are to keep a constant watch on Point Leche by day, and a Guard-boat rowing in such situation during night, as may be most likely to inform you thereof, and have the Thunder per-fectly prepared to defend them, or proceed to sea, should it become necessary. In the execution of this service, the utmost dispatch is to be used, in order that the Victuallers may be at the Madalena Islands by the 20th October, where you will remain (observing the above instructions) till my arrival, or you receive orders for your further proceedings.

NELSON AND BRONTE.

TO CAPTAIN RICHARDSON, H.M. SHIP JUNO.

[Order-Book.]

Victory, at Sea, 29th September, 1804.

Whereas it is my intention to proceed with the Squadron, the first Westerly wind, off Toulon, for the purpose of recon-noitring the Enemy at that Port, and from thence pass through Rendezvous No. 102, to receive any information the Ships there may have obtained of them, You are hereby required and directed to keep on your station, Rendezvous No. 97, and inform any of his Majesty's Ships, Vessels, or Transports arriving on the said Rendezvous thereof, and direct their Commanders to remain there, under Cape St. Sebastians, until my return, as the Squadron will only take the route before-mentioned, and return immediately to Rendezvous No. 97, where the strictest look-out is to be kept for arrivals from England, Malta, &c., daily expected. Having ordered the Thunder Bomb-Vessel to Malta, you will take the Acheron in her room, under your command, and employ her on the service mentioned in my letter to you of the 17th instant.

NELSON AND BRONTE.

TO CAPTAIN LORD MARK ROBERT KERR, H. M. SHIP FISGARD.

[Order-Book.]

Victory, off Toulon, 1st October, 1804.

Whereas I am proceeding with the Squadron to Rendezvous No. 97, under Cape St. Sebastians, You are hereby required and directed to take his Majesty's Ship named in the margin[9] under your command, and station yourself between Rendezvous No. 102 and Toulon, in such position as you may judge best for watching the Enemy's motions in that Port, and for ascertaining with correctness their putting to sea, in case they should do so. In reconnoitring and watching the Enemy as above directed, the greatest care must be taken that you do not approach Toulon, so as to render yourself liable to being becalmed, and consequently to an attack from a superior force of Ships and Gun-boats in such situation. You will occasionally proceed to Rendezvous No. 102, in order to acquaint the Commander of any of his Majesty's Ships or Vessels that the Squadron is gone to Rendezvous No. 97, where they will find me, or intelligence where I am gone to. You will therefore direct them to join me under Cape St. Sebastians with the utmost dispatch. In the event of the Enemy putting to sea, or any important intelligence obtained respecting them, you will join me yourself, or send the Niger to Rendezvous No. 97, with all dispatch.

NELSON AND BRONTE.

TO CAPTAIN RICHARD HUSSEY MOUBRAY, H. M. SHIP ACTIVE.

[Order-Book.]

Victory, off Toulon, 1st October, 1804.

You are hereby required and directed to take his Majesty's Ship named in the margin[1] under your command, and steer into the Gulf towards Marseilles, and take a sweep of that place, for the purpose of falling in with any of the Enemy's Vessels of War or Trade, which may be cruizing in that vicinity, and join me in three or four days' time from the date hereof, on Rendezvous No. 97, under Cape St. Sebastians, where you will find me, or orders for your further proceedings.

NELSON AND BRONTE.

---

[9] Niger.　　　　[1] Ambuscade.

TO THE CAPTAINS OR COMMANDERS OF ANY OF HIS MAJESTY'S
SHIPS OR VESSELS EMPLOYED IN THE ADRIATIC.

[Letter-Book.]

Victory, at Sea, 4th October, 1804.

Sir,

Captain Leake, of the Royal Artillery, who is directed by
Government to proceed to Corfu, and may, from the nature
of his instructions, find it necessary to remove to the Morea,
or Albania, it is my particular directions, should his Majesty's
Ship or Vessel under your command be in the environs of
either of the before-mentioned places, and Captain Leake
make application to be removed, that you comply with his
request, provided the more important service which you
may be then employed on, will admit of your so doing. I
am, &c.

NELSON AND BRONTE.

TO CAPTAIN SCHOMBERG, H.M. SHIP MADRAS.

[Letter-Book.]

Victory, at Sea, 4th October, 1804.

Sir,

As Vessels of very valuable cargoes may soon be expected
at Malta from England, under the convoy of the Hydra and
other Ships of War, for the Levant, Constantinople, and the
Adriatic, it is my particular directions that you appoint sufficient Convoys for the protection of any Merchant Ship or
Vessel destined to either of the above-mentioned places, in
order that they may not be in danger of capture by the
Enemy. And I am to desire, on the arrival of the Hero from
England, which is freighted by Government, and bound to
Constantinople, that you will give the most strict orders to
the Officer charged with that Vessel, to see her in safety to
her destination. It perhaps may not be necessary to convoy
the Ships bound to Constantinople further than the Dardanelles, but of this you will be the best judge, having been
more recently there. You will give strict orders to the Officers
charged with these Convoys to bring all the Trade from the
Ports in the Archipelago in safety to Malta. I am, &c.

NELSON AND BRONTE.

TO LIEUTENANT HARDING SHAW, COMMANDING HIS MAJESTY'S
BRIG SPIDER.

[Letter-Book.]

Victory, at Sea, 4th October, 1804.

Sir,

I have received your letter of the 6th ultimo, acquainting
me with the circumstance of your having flogged John Carter,
Seaman, belonging to the Spider, on the 5th of that month;
that soon after, a shot was flung from forward by some of the
people, which fell close by you, and Mr. Langdon, the Master;
and, in order to discover the offender, you judged it necessary
to threaten them with individual punishment, which, as they
would not confess, you had inflicted upon each of your company, by calling them over by the watch-bill, and giving them
a dozen each. In answer to which, I cannot approve of a
measure so foreign to the rules of good discipline and the accustomed practice of his Majesty's Navy, and therefore caution
you against a similar line of conduct. Had you fixed upon
one or more guilty individuals, and punished them severely,
it might have had the desired effect, or put them into confinement, and brought them to a Court-Martial. I trust your
watchful conduct will prevent any such confusion, or disposition to riot, from happening again. I am, &c.

NELSON AND BRONTE.

TO CAPTAIN SCHOMBERG, H.M. SHIP MADRAS.

[Letter-Book.]

Victory, at Sea, 4th October, 1804.

Sir,

I have received your letter of the 1st ultimo, together with
the one therein mentioned from Lieutenant Spencer, of the
Renard, stating the circumstance of his having chastised the
French privateer as therein mentioned. In answer thereto I
herewith transmit you a letter[2] for Lieutenant Spencer, on
the subject, which you will be so good as seal and deliver. I
cannot here omit observing how desirable the destruction of
the Enemy's Privateers is, when they commit any act of hos-

---

2 Vide p. 214, post.

tility; but in the present instance, it does not appear that the Enemy fired a shot. I have to acknowledge the receipt of your letter of the 1st September, with its enclosure, from Captain Raynsford, of the Morgiana, respecting the circumstances of the capture of the Betsy Merchant Vessel, one of his Convoy, in March last; and you will be pleased to acquaint Captain Raynsford that I shall transmit his letter to the Admiralty for their information. Your letter of the 19th September, with the enclosures therein mentioned, respecting the purchase of Stores, has been received, and I very much approve of the order which you gave the Naval Officer on that occasion, and which you will desire him to consider as sufficient authority for the payment thereof, and settling his accounts for that particular service. I am, &c.

NELSON AND BRONTE.

TO CAPTAIN CRACRAFT, H. M. SHIP ANSON, OR SENIOR OFFICER
AT MALTA.

[Letter-Book.]

Victory, at Sea, 4th October, 1804.

Sir,

Captain Leake, of the Royal Artillery, being employed by Government, and directed to proceed to Corfu as early as possible, I am to desire you will order him a passage to that place, by the very first Vessel of War going there, or which can be spared for that service; and as Captain Leake may, from the nature of his instructions, find it necessary to proceed to the Morea, or Albania, it is my directions, whenever any of his Majesty's Ships or Vessels under your command may be in the environs of Corfu, &c., if consistent with the more important service they are there employed on, that you will give the necessary directions to their Commanders to receive Captain Leake on his application for that purpose, and give him a passage to or from either of the before-mentioned places. I am, &c.

NELSON AND BRONTE.

TO LIEUTENANT HARDING SHAW, COMMANDING HIS MAJESTY'S
BRIG SPIDER.

[Letter-Book.]

Victory, at Sea, 4th October, 1804.

Sir,

I herewith transmit you a copy of a letter from Mr. Langdon, Master of his Majesty's Brig Spider, under your command, and am to desire that you will immediately transmit me an account of all the certificates you have granted the Master of the said Brig for Pilotage, since you commanded her: and also account to me for your very extraordinary conduct in demanding from Mr. Langdon the one-half of the said Pilotage, that I may judge the propriety of ordering a public inquiry into your conduct on this occasion. I desire to caution you against giving certificates for Pilotage in future, unless under particular circumstances, as I conceive, from the length of time you have been in this country, that you are perfectly acquainted with any Port in those seas. I am, &c.

NELSON AND BRONTE.

TO CAPTAIN RICHARD BUDD VINCENT, H. M. SLOOP ARROW.

[Letter-Book.]

Victory, at Sea, 4th October, 1804.

Sir,

I have received your letter of the 10th ultimo, acquainting me with your return to Malta from the Adriatic, for the purpose of completing your provisions, and putting the Arrow in a condition for further service. In answer to which, I am perfectly satisfied with the necessity of your return to Valetta harbour, and am led to hope, from the Master Shipwright's Report, that the Arrow will answer for the service of this country, during the winter season, and that the repairs she has had will enable you to keep her actively employed during that time; it will then be taken into consideration the propriety of sending her to England to be docked. I am, &c.

NELSON AND BRONTE.

TO SIR ALEXANDER JOHN BALL, BART., MALTA.

[From Clarke and M'Arthur, vol. ii. p. 387.]

October 4th, 1804.

Captain Leake,[2] who I believe has letters for you, if not, I know he is instructed to correspond and communicate with you, is, as you will see, a person perfectly in the confidence of Government; and he is very highly spoken of. From the little I have seen of him in one day, I think he merits their confidence by his good sense. He has begged me to present him to you. I sincerely hope, my dear Ball, that the Russians will not act so as to have the Austrians united with the French and Turks against them and us; but Russia must be careful how she conducts herself in the Ionian Republic and the Morea. I have great fears; I think I see much too close a connexion between France and Austria, and we know the Turks would jump to join such an alliance. The times are big with great events. I wish my health was better. I have mentioned to Lord Melville what you have thought about Sir Richard Bickerton, in case I should be able to return; but I do not expect such a compliance—time will show. Toulon was safe on Sunday last, as Boyle will tell you. No Admiral has hoisted his Flag in the room of La Touche;—he is gone, and all his lies with him. The French papers say he died in consequence of walking so often up to the Signal-post, upon Sepet, to watch us: I always pronounced that that would be his death. I am, &c.

NELSON AND BRONTE.

TO LIEUTENANT ROBERT SPENCER, COMMANDING HIS MAJESTY'S SCHOONER RENARD.

[From a Copy in the Nelson Papers.]

Victory, at Sea, 4th October, 1804.

Sir,

I have received your letter of the 30th July, acquainting me that, on account of the weather, you judged it necessary to

---

[2] Colonel Leake was English Resident in the Morea, and from 1805 to 1809, resided chiefly at the Court of Ali, Pacha of Yannina. His interesting account of his travels in Morea, Northern Greece, Asia Minor, &c., is well known.

let the four small Vessels under your convoy on the 28th of
that month, anchor to the Southward of Cape Moro di Porco,
and took that occasion to reconnoitre a Vessel to leeward; in
the meantime a strange Vessel came round the Cape from
Syracuse, which the Masters of those four Vessels judging to
be a Privateer, cut their cable, and ran down to you; that on
the said Privateer observing you stand towards her, she ran
upon the rocks, and landed her men; and that, from the frequent violations of Neutrality which the Enemy's Privateers
had been guilty of, you judged it a good occasion to chastise
them. In answer to which, however much the destruction of
the Enemy's Privateers under the violation of the laws of
Neutrality may be desired, I cannot, in the present instance,
justify your leaving the Vessels under your Convoy exposed
to the risk of capture, under any circumstances whatever.
Had you been in company with your Convoy, a legal opportunity might have offered for capturing or destroying the
Privateer alluded to. The instructions for Officers charged
with Convoys, are so strict and well known, that I am sorry
it becomes necessary for me to call your most strict attention
to them in future. I am, &c.

NELSON AND BRONTE.

TO LAMBTON ESTE, ESQ., PRIVATE SECRETARY TO CHARLES
LOCK, ESQ., CONSUL-GENERAL IN EGYPT.

[Autograph in the possession of Dr. Lambton Este. He had been appointed
Secretary and Physician to Mr. Lock's mission to Egypt and the Levant.]

Victory, October 4th, 1804.

My dear Sir,

I am much obliged by your obliging letter of August 20th,
and in your note of September 16th, announcing the death of
Mr. Lock,[3] which I am most sincerely sorry for, unless you
can get his appointment, which I am sure Sir Alexander Ball
thinks would be a wise measure of Government; and I wish
it was so, for we want men fit for places, and not places for

------

[3] Mr. Lock, formerly Consul at Naples, who has been often mentioned, died of
the plague, in the Lazaretto, at Malta, on the 12th of September 1804, together
with two of his suite. They were assiduously attended by Mr. (now Dr.) Este,
who placed himself in the Lazaretto with them for that purpose.

men who are too often unfit for them.   I shall see, most probably, your worthy Father before you; but, at all events, be
assured, dear Sir, that I shall be happy in being useful to you,
on his account, and your own merit, and that I am your much
obliged and humble servant,

NELSON AND BRONTE.

TO LIEUTENANT THE HONOURABLE HENRY DUNCAN,[4] H.M. SHIP
ROYAL SOVEREIGN.

[Autograph, in the possession of Alexander Haldane, Esq.]

Victory, October 4th, 1804.

My dear Sir,

There is no man who more sincerely laments the heavy
loss you have sustained than myself:[5] but the name of Duncan
will never be forgot by Britain, and, in particular, by its
Navy, in which service, the remembrance of your worthy
father will, I am sure, grow up in you.   I am sorry not to
have a good Sloop to give you; but still an opening offers,
which I think will insure your confirmation as a Commander.
It is occasioned by the very ill state of health of Captain
Corbet of the Bittern, who has requested a few weeks leave to
reside on shore at the Hospital.   You will be confirmed
before he resumes his command.   You had better get your
things on board the Seahorse this afternoon, as she will go to
Malta in the morning.   I am ever, my dear Sir, with every
kind wish, most faithfully yours,

NELSON AND BRONTE.

TO MAJOR-GENERAL VILLETTES, MALTA.

[Autograph, in the possession of Josiah French, Esq.]

Victory, October 4th, 1804.

My dear General,

Many thanks for your kind letter and good wishes, but
home I ought to go, if they will let me.   I think that appear-

---

[4] Second son of Admiral Viscount Duncan, afterwards Captain the Hon. Sir
Henry Duncan, C.B., K.C.H.: he died in November 1835.

[5] This Letter was accompanied by a newspaper, which announced the sudden
death of Admiral Viscount Duncan, on his way to Scotland, on the 4th of August,
1804.

ances are such, that you may be soon called upon for the Troops to garrison Messina. I only write from what I hear is passing, for when Russia goes to war, I consider it very probable that Naples will be taken by the French. My orders are repeated to take care of Sicily; but I know that you are always ready. I have nothing later than Hydra will bring you; but believe me ever, my dear General, yours most faithfully,

NELSON AND BRONTE.

TO CAPTAIN CRACRAFT, H.M. SHIP ANSON.

[From a Copy in the Nelson Papers.]

Victory, at Sea, 4th October, 1804.

Sir,

I have received your letter of the 30th August last, acquainting me with the return of his Majesty's Ship Anson, under your command, from Constantinople with the Convoy, and that the Sublime Porte had not made any charge for the repairs of the said Ship, except fees, which you had drawn for on the Navy Board, amounting to £41 sterling. I am very happy that the Anson has again resumed her station, and hope that the Sloops under your command will soon be in a state to join you. The active and unwarrantable conduct of the Enemy's Privateers in the Adriatic, will require the most watchful and alert conduct on the part of our Cruizers in that sea; but your indefatigable zeal for his Majesty's service leads me to hope that those Pirates will be kept in pretty good check, and destroyed the moment they attempt to proceed without the protection of Neutrality.

I shall, as soon as a reinforcement of Small Vessels arrive, send you more force, as it may be necessary to order the Arrow to England with the next Convoy. Your letter of the 30th August, respecting the Bittern's five men being forgiven by Captain Corbet,[6] and also that of the 31st, inclosing a list of sails, have been received. I am, &c.,

NELSON AND BRONTE.

⁶ Vide p. 62, ante.

TO MAJOR-GENERAL VILLETTES.

[Autograph, in the possession of J. Bullock, Esq.]

Victory, October 5th, 1804.

My dear General,

Captain Leake, a gentleman most fully in the confidence of Government, is going to Albania, Morea, &c. &c., to look about him, and give opinions; and as I find he is not personally known to you, I beg leave to present him to your kind attention. He is most strongly recommended to me by Government. I am ever, dear General, most faithfully yours,

NELSON AND BRONTE.

TO COMMISSIONER OTWAY, GIBRALTAR.

[Letter-Book.]

Victory, at Sea, 6th October, 1804.

Sir,

I have received your several letters of dates and purports undermentioned. [Here follow the dates and purport of the several letters.] In answer to your above-mentioned letters, I am very much obliged by the Spanish 'Naval Occurrences at Cadiz,' as well as by the list of arrivals and sailings to and from Gibraltar, and the account of the Stores unloading from the William Storeship at that place. I very much approve of the inquiry you have made into Mr. Pownall's omission in not checking the Boatswain of the Halcyon, on mustering that Sloop, and trust his attention in future to that part of his duty will render such a measure unnecessary. I am, however, sorry to observe that the Ships in the vicinity of Gibraltar are prevented from delivering in their Muster-Books from want of muster-paper, and beg you will be good enough to write the Navy Board again on that subject. The Woollen slops, which you very properly directed the Storekeeper to [send to] the Fleet, will be very acceptable indeed. I am, &c.

NELSON AND BRONTE.

TO HIS EXCELLENCY HUGH ELLIOT, ESQ.

[Autograph, in the Elliot Papers.]

Victory, October 7th, 1804.

My dear Sir,

An English Ship of War shall always remain at Naples, as long as his Sicilian Majesty may think it necessary. You will know that it is necessary for me, now and then, to ask the question.[7]

Your Excellency's summary account of the situation of Naples since the negotiations with Russia, and of your very interesting communication with the King in person, are perfectly clear; and [even] if I did not know Naples, and the men who move the wheels of Government, so well as I do, would make the situation of the affairs of that Kingdom perfectly clear to any person. I was in hopes Circello would before this time have been in the place of Chevalier Micheroux. Our Government, nor any English Minister or Officer, dare place confidence in him. I hope he is loyal and true to his King, but much more is required for a Foreign Court to trust its plans of operations and ultimate views to. *Implicit confidence must be placed*, and, with the Chevalier Micheroux, so far from *confidence*, the greatest *distrust* must prevail. This, I assert, is my opinion, of which your Excellency will make a proper use.

The new Ministry seem to have honoured me with unbounded confidence, and I understand that your letters relative to all the affairs of Naples, both as to its safety and pecuniary assistance, are to the same tenour as mine. (I have wrote to General Villettes to keep the two thousand men ready to embark for Messina.) The regret of General Acton's leaving

---

[7] In reply to this question in Lord Nelson's letter to Mr. Elliot on the 28th of August, (vide p. 176, ante,) that Minister informed him on the 8th of September, that the King of Naples had desired him, " to acquaint your Lordship, officially, that in no period since the commencement of hostilities, has the presence of a British Ship of War been more necessary for the protection of this Capital, and the security of his Family, than at the present critical conjuncture. His Sicilian Majesty therefore trusts that your Lordship will not find it incompatible with the other objects of your important command, to leave a British Ship of force in this road, until some favourable change shall have taken place in the unfortunate situation of this Kingdom."—*Original*, in the Elliot Papers.

the helm at such an important moment is most strongly expressed. We none of us can have equal confidence in any other man. Circello, I believe, is sincerely attached to Acton and the King. Our great and good Queen sometimes, I fear, allows herself to be guided by people not possessed of one half of her excellent head and heart. But the times are such that Kingdoms must not be played with ; for it is not difficult to see that if Austria joins with France, so will the Turks, and then Russia will have her hands full; and so far from Russia assisting Naples, it may involve her, without the greatest care and circumspection, in total ruin. Naples must not be hastily involved in a war with France. Sicily must be saved. The Calabrians must be kept from the entrance of French Troops. If we are consulted, we must assist Naples in keeping off the blow as long as possible, and of giving up as little as possible every time she may be pushed too hard, and that a crisis arrives.

It is certainly most important that the King's person should not fall into the power of the French ; but the exact time when he should retreat to Sicily should be well weighed. If he goes too soon, it may be said that he leaves his Subjects in distress : if he stays too long, he may be forced to sign things that may lose him his Kingdom. There are times when a King should put himself at the head of his Troops, and defend his Kingdom. Naples has not the means of resisting the enormous power of France unassisted. How far it might be right to leave the Queen and Prince Royal, I really feel, without much more information than I could obtain—without talking to your Excellency and Sir John Acton confidentially—unable to give an opinion; and I ought to beg your pardon for having ventured to say so much as I have done ; but independent of my duty to protect their Sicilian Majesties, I feel naturally,[8] having before seen them in the depth of adversity, that my heart feels[8] for their situation. What I can do, shall be done ; and perhaps my being in England, and conversing with the Ministers, if I am to be in their confidence, will be of more real use to the Kingdom of Naples, than my being here the winter, completely done up, and in the spring be obliged to retire for ever. I sincerely hope that your Excellency's

news is correct from Berlin; but I have my doubts. It would
be too much happiness for *Europe*, which seems bent upon
destroying itself. I am ever, with the highest respect, your
Excellency's most obedient humble Servant,

NELSON AND BRONTE.

TO HIS EXCELLENCY HUGH ELLIOT, ESQ.

[Autograph, in the Elliot Papers.]

Victory, October 7th, 1804.

My dear Sir,
I am truly sensible of the kind concern you express for the
state of my health;[9] but you might be sure that if I had not
found it indispensably necessary, that I should not have made
the application for a few months' rest. If I am able, it is my

---

[9] On the 8th of September, 1804, Mr. Elliot wrote the following letter to Lord
Nelson:—

"My Lord,—I cannot sufficiently express the infinite regret with which their
Sicilian Majesties have learnt your determination of quitting your Command in the
Mediterranean, and of going to England this winter for the re-establishment of
your health. Their Sicilian Majesties are in this not more concerned for your in-
disposition, than they are anxious from the evil effects which they apprehend must
ensue to their interest, in consequence of your Lordship's absence from the Mediterranean. I know it is the King's intention to write to the Prince of Castelcicala,
to apply to the British Government for your Lordship's speedy return to these seas,
in order to resume the high Command you have hitherto exercised, with no less
credit to yourself than advantage to the many Countries, whose future security rests
entirely upon the skill by which a British Admiral may be enabled to maintain the
superiority of the British Fleet over that of the Enemy in the Mediterranean.
When such great interests are concerned, I shall not presume to dwell upon my
own feelings, although I cannot but recall to your Lordship, that I only consented
to depart as abruptly as I did from England, to undertake this arduous and ruinous
Mission, from the expectation that my efforts to direct the councils of this Kingdom
would have been seconded by your pre-eminent talents and judgment. Allow me,
however, my Lord, in this emergency, to propose to your consideration a plan, con-
cerning which I have already had much conversation with the Queen, and which,
if it can be adopted, will obviate many of the misfortunes to which we should be
exposed by your absence. As your Lordship's health requires that you should not
be exposed to the rigours of another winter's cruize in the Gulf of Lyons, it is the
sincere wish of this Court that you would spend the severe months of the year,
either here or at Palermo, without abandoning your chief Command in the Mediterranean. I only do my duty in suggesting this idea to your Lordship, without
venturing to press upon you the many arguments by which, I think, I could prove
its expediency. You must be sensible, my Lord, that no Admiral who is not as
well acquainted as yourself with the political state of these Kingdoms, or other

wish to return ; for where such unbounded confidence is placed, I should feel a beast not to exert myself. Long before this time, Lord Melville has fixed upon whether I am to return ; or another Admiral is, most probably, at this moment upon his passage. Being on shore, either in Sicily or Naples, would not relieve my mind of the charge entrusted to me ; for my thoughts would always be off Toulon, and I should feel answerable for measures which I do not direct. If the Admiralty choose to leave Sir Richard Bickerton, the Mediterranean cannot be left in the hands of a more correct and discreet Officer. I beg you will express to their Majesties my true sense of all their gracious goodness towards me ; and believe me ever, my dear Sir, your most obliged and faithful servant,

NELSON AND BRONTE.

TO THE CHEVALIER MICHEROUX.

[From a Copy, in the Elliot Papers.]

Victory, October 7th, 1804.

Sir,

I have been honoured with your Excellency's letters of August 28th, with the several inclosures respecting the conduct of the Boat of his Majesty's Sloop Bittern, in the Mole of Naples, and of the conduct of his Majesty's Schooner Renard, on the Coast of Sicily, in destroying a Privateer belonging to the Italian Republic. Your Excellency having wrote officially to his Excellency Mr. Elliot upon those subjects, which he has transmitted to me, I have sent my answers to his Excellency, who will regularly communicate them to you. But with your Excellency's leave, I will reply to such parts of your letter as his Majesty's good opinion of my conduct

Eastern Countries, and of Russia can possibly act with the same effect that you can do, when there is every reason to expect that the Emperor of Russia, and perhaps even the Ottoman Porte, will utimately co-operate with us in our endeavours to set bounds to the lawless ambition of France. May my representations upon this subject not come too late, as I am certain that your departure from the Mediterranean will not less tend to encourage our Enemies, than to diminish the confidence of those friendly Powers, who look towards your Lordship's abilities as to the surest means of success. I have the honour to be, &c.—H. ELLIOT."—*Original* in the Elliot papers.

demands—that I should express that it still, and ever will be, my pride, to deserve his Majesty's continued good opinion, and I shall venture to do it with that openness, which a mind void of offence is able to do ; and I rely that your Excellency will approve of what I shall say, and acquiesce in the justness of some of the observations.

The trivial, although certainly irregular conduct of the Bittern's Boat, was not worth the time of your Excellency to write to a Public Minister. In the first instance, if the Captain of the Port, or Naval Officer, had gone with the complaint to Captain Malcolm, he would, in the first instance, have not only disapproved the proceeding, but reprimanded the Officer, as he has done when communicated to him, for his conduct. The searching for Deserters, or for men absent from their Ships, has in all Countries been tolerated. If improper conduct is pursued, certainly it is cause for just offence ; but none is stated to have happened. All Vessels in the Mole of Naples are Neutrals, as far as relates to any of the belligerent Powers ; therefore no offence could be given to either French or Dutch. It may be an irregularity, searching for absent Seamen, but it is tolerated by all Nations. Do not other Nations look for their men every day at Naples? Certainly they do. But it is my wish to have our conduct so correct, that envy and malice itself should not be able to find fault with us, and to contrast our conduct with that of French Armed Vessels, in the Mole of Naples, to the British Officers and Men.

I have sent Mr. Elliot the Officer's Report of his destroying the Privateer upon the Coast of Sicily, and I have already directed a strict inquiry into the transaction; for although the conduct of the Enemy's Privateers is so infamous, and in defiance of all laws of Neutrality, yet their doing wrong is no rule why we should. There is a general principle which I have laid down for the regulation of the Officers' conduct under my command—which is never to break the Neutrality of any Port or place. But never to consider as Neutral any place from whence an attack is allowed to be made,—the attacker forfeits all Neutrality.

The result of this inquiry shall be sent to Naples as soon as possible ; and I beg leave to request that your Excellency

will assure his Sicilian Majesty, that the strictest justice shall
be done, as far as is in the power of your Excellency's most
obedient, humble servant,

                                        NELSON AND BRONTE.

TO HIS EXCELLENCY HUGH ELLIOT, ESQ.

[Autograph, in the Elliot Papers.]

                                        Victory, October 7th, 1804.
    My dear Sir,
    As I send you my answer to Chevalier Micheroux's letter,
it will not be necessary to enter into any detail of my opinions
to your Excellency. The fault of the Bittern's Officer[1] was
nothing, if he conducted himself properly. It is an irregularity committed by all Nations, every day, in every Port.
But certainly Captain Malcolm's reprimand was full and
ample for every hurt which the foot of a British Officer could
do, in trampling upon the deck of a French or Dutch Ship.
I certainly wish nothing to be done, which could in any
manner commit the good King of Naples with the French.
They wish for nothing better. I send your Excellency Lieutenant Spencer's letter. I have not approved of his conduct ;
for although I have no doubt but that this Vessel would have
committed herself, yet as she does not appear to have done it,
under that presumption Mr. Spencer was hasty.[2] This Privateer has before, I dare say, broke the Neutrality ; at least, I
hope, for Mr. Spencer's sake, that it will appear so in the
inquiry I have ordered. The conduct of the French in
Sicily, and of many of the Governors, has been shameful.
Nothing would prevent their being complained of, but the
consideration of the very delicate situation of his Sicilian
Majesty. I am, my dear Sir, your most faithful servant,

                                        NELSON AND BRONTE.
    With respect to the Neapolitan Vessels taken near Especia,

---

[1] In the afternoon of the 23rd of August, 1804, an Officer and Boat's crew, armed
with cutlasses, belonging to the Bittern, went on board of three Dutch Vessels in
the Mole at Naples, in search of four deserters ; but not finding them, they proceeded
to a French Brig, the Master of which having positively refused to allow his Vessel
to be examined, without an order from the French Ambassador, the Officer returned
to the Bittern for further orders. Nothing more, however, took place.

[2] Vide p. 215, ante.

it is not the direct road to Barcelona; and how little must the Chevalier know of our just laws, to think that either you, or I, or even the King, dare to communicate with a Judge. Justice will be done, be it for or against the captor of these Vessels.

TO HIS EXCELLENCY HUGH ELLIOT, ESQ.

[Autograph, in the Elliot Papers.]

Private.　　　　　　　　　Victory, October 7th, 1804.

My dear Sir,

Doctor Scott is delighted with your kind attention to him. He joined us, October 3rd. The wind blows [so] strong Easterly, that nothing can leave me. I am very anxious to send your dispatches from the Secretary of State. I have been better than I am, but at this moment I am very unwell. We shall see what the Admiralty will do with me. I beg my respectful compliments to Mrs. Elliot, and believe me ever, yours most faithfully,

NELSON AND BRONTE.

Turn over.

Your son is very well; the Amazon is with us. Pray, forward my letter to Mr. Jackson.

TO HIS EXCELLENCY HUGH ELLIOT, ESQ.

[Autograph, in the Elliot Papers.]

Victory, October 8th, 1804.

My dear Sir,

Captain Leake, Royal Artillery, who has wrote to you upon the subject of a Draftsman, is anxious that I should write you a line to mention him to your Excellency. Captain L. is very high in the confidence of Government, and employed on a Military mission, and to *look about him*, that we may know what is really going forward with the Russians, &c. &c. I am ever, my dear Sir, most faithfully yours,

NELSON AND BRONTE.

TO THE RIGHT HONOURABLE THE EARL CAMDEN, K.G.

[Autograph, in the Colonial Office.]

Victory, at Sea, 10th October, 1804.

My Lord,

I had the honour to receive your Lordship's letter of the
17th August, on the subject of a Tunisian Vessel having been
carried into Palermo by a Privateer supposed to be belonging
to Gibraltar. In answer thereto, I have the honour to acquaint your Lordship that the business respecting the detention of the said Tunisian Vessel is settled; and, I have the
pleasure to add, without any subsequent bad consequences.
I have, &c.

NELSON AND BRONTE.

TO THE RIGHT HONOURABLE EARL SPENCER, K.G.

[From Clarke and M'Arthur, vol. ii. p. 387.]

Victory, 10th October, 1804.

I do assure you, my dear Lord, that not one of all your
Naval friends, and you ought to have many, loves, honours,
and respects you more than myself, or is more grateful for all
your kindness. Circumstances may have separated us: but
my sincere respect and attachment can never be shaken by
either political or other considerations; and it will always give
me pleasure, in showing my regard for the Father by attentions to the Son.[4] The sight of your letter called forth feelings of which I have reason to be proud, but which cannot be
readily expressed; therefore I shall only say for myself, that
Nelson never has, nor can change. I am, &c.

NELSON AND BRONTE.

[4] The Honourable Robert, afterwards Captain Sir Robert Spencer, K.C.H., who
died on the 4th of November, 1830.

TO VISCOUNT MELVILLE, FIRST LORD OF THE ADMIRALTY.

[From Clarke and M'Arthur, vol. ii. p. 388, who state that " the Admiral expressed himself as being satisfied with the arrangements that had been made by the Board of Admiralty, as to Line-of-Battle Ships, yet lamented the manner in which the Service continued to be cramped for want of Frigates. A deficiency of them in the Mediterranean allowed the Enemy's Privateers to increase, and considerable depredations to be made on our valuable Trade in that sea;" and he added:]

10th October, 1804.

But I am sure, my Lord, from your wise beginning, that a full crop of credit, and I believe of glory, will accrue to the Board of Admiralty. I am, &c.

NELSON AND BRONTE.

TO WILLIAM MARSDEN, ESQ., ADMIRALTY.

[Original, in the Admiralty.]

Victory, at Sea, 10th October, 1804.

Sir,

You will please to acquaint the Lords Commissioners of the Admiralty that I have received their order, dated the 31st July last, directing me to hold in readiness, in such Port as may be agreed upon by Mr. Jackson, his Majesty's Minister to the King of Sardinia, and myself, one of the Ships under my command, for the purpose of conveying his Sardinian Majesty to such Port in the Mediterranean as he may appoint; and to adopt such measures for the Naval defence of the Island of Sardinia as may be best calculated for that purpose, and consistent with the other services entrusted to my care. In answer to which, you will please to acquaint the Lords Commissioners of the Admiralty that, in the very early part of my communication with Mr. Jackson, the removal of his Sardinian Majesty was a principal consideration; and that I have frequently wrote to that Minister on the same subject, and have constantly had the safety of his Sardinian Majesty in view.

I wrote on the 7th instant to Mr. Jackson, and the moment he signifies his Sardinian Majesty's pleasure to me, a Ship of War shall be sent agreeably to his wish, to remove his Majesty to any Port in the Mediterranean which he may think proper.

The defence of the Island of Sardinia shall be constantly kept in view, and the necessary measures adopted for that purpose, as far as may be compatible with the other services entrusted to my care.   I am, &c.

NELSON AND BRONTE.

TO WILLIAM MARSDEN, ESQ., ADMIRALTY.

[Original, in the Admiralty.]

Victory, at Sea, 10th October, 1804.

Sir,

I herewith transmit you a letter from the Reverend Mr. Hughes,[5] Chaplain to the Naval Hospital at Gibraltar, which you will please to lay before the Lords Commissioners of the Admiralty for their consideration ; and at the same time acquaint their Lordships that Mr. Hughes is a very respectable Clergyman, and appears to me deserving of some relief. A former application from Mr. Hughes was transmitted in my letter to Sir Evan Nepean, dated the 18th August, 1803. I am, &c.

NELSON AND BRONTE.

TO WILLIAM MARSDEN, ESQ., ADMIRALTY.

[Original, in the Admiralty.]

Victory, at Sea, 10th October, 1804.

Sir,

I have received your letter of the 28th August last,[6] acquainting me that it is the wish of his Majesty's Confidential

---

[5] Mr. Hughes' letter stated that he had performed the duty in the Gibraltar Naval Hospital and Yard for fourteen years, with no remuneration but burial fees ; and he therefore requested to be allowed a salary.

[6] The letter referred to has not been found ; but Lord Nelson then received the following letters from Earl Camden, Secretary of State for the War Department, and from Lord Harrowby, Secretary of State for Foreign Affairs, (to some of which he afterwards alludes,) which show the high value the Government attached to his opinions, especially respecting Sardinia :—

FROM EARL CAMDEN TO LORD NELSON.

" Most private and confidential.

" My Lord,   " Downing Street, 29th August, 1804.

" His Majesty having been graciously pleased to place in my hands the Seals of the Colonial and War Department, the letters which your Lordship addressed to

Servants that I should keep a watchful look over any motions
of the Enemy that may have a tendency to injure any of the
rights and possessions of the Allies of Great Britain in this
Country, and signifying to me their Lordships' direction to

Lord Hobart on political subjects, have been delivered to me. In this dispatch I
propose to confine myself to the communications received from your Lordship on
the great importance which you attach to the Island of Sardinia, both as its possession regards the object to which this Country must always look in the Mediterranean,
or as its occupation by France would enable that Power to counteract these objects,
and assist her own views in that part of the world.

" This letter, as well as one of this date which your Lordship will receive from
Lord Melville, will apprise your Lordship how much weight is justly given to your
remarks and reasoning upon the subject of the Island of Sardinia. Lord Melville's
letter, which his Lordship has communicated to me, makes it unnecessary for me to
address you on the Naval part of this subject, as connected with that Island; but
in addition to the observations contained in that letter, and the instructions which
are conveyed to you in it, your Lordship will naturally expect to receive from me
an intimation of the probability of our being enabled to detach from this Country
Troops to be employed in the Mediterranean.

" The extensive preparations of the Enemy on the opposite Coasts of France,
render it absolutely inexpedient to advise a present reduction of the force in Great
Britain and Ireland, by detaching any part of it upon distant expeditions; and until
the season of the year shall render the proposed attempt of the Enemy less probable, or until the measures in progress for augmenting the Army shall have taken
place, no addition can be made to the force *now* in the Mediterranean.

" Whenever such addition can be made, the King's Ministers consider the
objects in that quarter as of the highest importance, and the preventing of the Island
of Sardinia from falling into the hands of France, amongst the very first objects to
be attended to. As far as the arrival of reinforcements bears upon that subject, I
cannot hold out to your Lordship any expectation of that event before the close of
the present year. Until such reinforcements may arrive, the instructions from
Lord Melville, to which I have alluded, point out the objects to which it is desired
your Lordship shall attend, as far as respects the Naval view of the subject. With
regard to the Military inquiries to be made, the Memorandum which Captain
Leake (who had before been instructed by Lord Harrowby to proceed to Corfu,
and the Coast of European Turkey) has received from his Lordship, makes it unnecessary for me to do more, than to desire your Lordship to afford whatever assistance
your situation enables you to the inquiries it is suggested that Officer shall make,
in case you should think it advisable that he should proceed to Sardinia for that
purpose. I entirely concur in the Memorandum alluded to, and to which I refer
your Lordship.

" Whenever, from Captain Leake's report, or from any other source on which
you may depend, your Lordship is enabled to give a more minute and detailed
account of the Island of Sardinia, both as the opportunity is afforded to take possession of it, as well as to retain it afterwards, you will give me the earliest information of these circumstances. In the meantime, your Lordship will not omit any
means within your power to prevent so serious a misfortune to this Country, as the
Islands of Sardinia or Sicily falling into the hands of France.

" I will not detain your Lordship further than to thank you for the communica-

afford his Majesty's Allies in the Mediterranean every protection in my power, consistent with a due attention to the
other important duties committed to my care. In answer to
which, you will please to acquaint the Lords Commissioners
of the Admiralty that due regard shall be paid to their instructions above mentioned. I am, &c.

NELSON AND BRONTE.

tions which have been received from you, and to request a continuance of that correspondence which my predecessor had the advantage of enjoying with your Lordship, on points so essential to his Majesty's interests in that quarter of the globe,
in which your Lordship is so desirably and so usefully employed. I have the
honour to remain, with great truth and regard, your Lordship's most sincere and
faithful, humble servant,—CAMDEN."—(*Original*, in the possession of the Right
Honourable John Wilson Croker.)

FROM EARL CAMDEN TO LORD NELSON.

" Private.   " Downing Street, August 29th, 1804.
" My Lord,

" I hope your Lordship will permit me to solicit a continuance of that most
useful and advantageous correspondence which Lord Hobart had the advantage of
possessing with your Lordship ; and I trust it is unnecessary to assure you that in
intrusting to me your Lordship's sentiments on the political subjects connected
with the Mediterranean, you repose them in a person who justly appreciates your
opinions, and has the highest admiration of your character. My letter of this date
will inform you how much weight the Government gives to your representations on
the subject of Sardinia, and I am very sorry to hold out to you only a distant
prospect of the arrival of reinforcements in the Mediterranean, as it regards the
particular subject of Sardinia, as well as other interesting objects in that quarter.

" Your Lordship's dispatches and their inclosures, on the subject of the points in
dispute with the Dey of Algiers, have arrived so lately in this country, that I am
not enabled to send, by the present conveyance, instructions on that subject. I beg
your Lordship, however, to be assured of the high opinion I entertain of your discretion and address in the orders you have given, and in the selection of the persons
you employed to execute them. I request your Lordship's permission to take this
opportunity to return you my thanks for the attention you were so good as to give
to my request about my nephew, Mr. James. I lament he did not accept your offer
to allow him to remain in the Mediterranean, and still more, that he has since
quitted the Sea for the Land Service. I have the honour to remain, with perfect
truth, your Lordship's most obedient, humble servant,—CAMDEN."—(*Autograph*,
in the possession of the Right Honourable John Wilson Croker.)

FROM LORD HARROWBY TO LORD NELSON.

" Downing Street, 29th August, 1804.
" My Lord,

" Having had the advantage of perusing the letters which your Lordship had
sent to Lord Hawkesbury, I beg to solicit the continuance of your Lordship's correspondence, upon such points as relate to the business of that department which
his Majesty has been graciously pleased to intrust to me.

" This letter will be delivered to you by Captain Leake, of the Royal Artillery,
an Officer of distinguished merit, who served with the Turkish Army in Egypt ;

TO WILLIAM MARSDEN, ESQ., ADMIRALTY.

[Original, in the Admiralty.]

Victory, at Sea, 10th October, 1804.

Sir,

I have received your letter of the 17th August, signifying to me their Lordships' direction to cause the Recruits raised by Captain Adair for the Royal Marines to be placed to the vacant Companies, in order to ascertain them. In answer thereto, I herewith transmit you a letter from Captain Adair, together with a Return of Recruits that have joined the Victory between the 1st September and 4th instant, which you will please to lay before the Lords Commissioners of the Admi-

he is directed to proceed upon a Military mission to Albania, and the Morea, for purposes fully detailed in instructions which he will communicate to your Lordship. He is also directed to put himself under your orders, in case you should think it advisable to ascertain with more precision, by the assistance of his professional knowledge, various points respecting the Island of Sardinia, that are specified in a Memorandum which I have put into his hands, or any other points on which you may think it desirable that further information should be obtained. You will, no doubt, be sensible that a mission of this nature will require considerable address and caution in the execution. As, for various reasons, which I cannot now detail, no communication has, or can well be made, to the King of Sardinia, or to his Minister here, upon such a subject, Captain Leake must be considered, in case you think it proper he should proceed, *as acting under your Lordship's orders only.* The frequent communications which you must necessarily have with different ports of the Island of Sardinia, will enable you to direct the conduct of Captain Leake, and of any Naval Officer whom he may accompany, in such a manner as to give the least possible occasion to jealousy or alarm. It is peculiarly important that no premature suspicion should arise of the occupation, in any contingency, of any part of Sardinia by British Troops, as such a suspicion would only serve to hasten the attack of the French. You will have seen, by Lord Camden's letter, that no sufficient force could at present be spared for that purpose; and the only hope of preserving it, in the meantime, rests upon the Naval defence, which the reinforcement now sent you, may enable you with less inconvenience to station near the Straits of Bonafaccio.

" Captain Leake is charged with the duplicates of some dispatches, which were sent by a Courier to Mr. Elliot two months ago, and with another dispatch of this date, which it is desirable should reach him without risk, or loss of time. I have directed them to be put under a flying seal, in order that your Lordship may be apprised of his Majesty's sentiments and instructions respecting an object which you have always near at heart, and to which your efforts have so essentially contributed—the preservation of the Persons and Dominions of their Sicilian Majesties. I have the honour to be, &c.—HARROWBY.

" As there is not time to have this letter copied, your Lordship will have the goodness to excuse the form in which it comes."—(*Autograph*, in the possession of the Right Honourable John Wilson Croker.)

ralty, for their information; and at the same time move their Lordships to give the necessary directions for Captain Adair's being allowed the sum of one guinea and a half for each of the Recruits he has so raised. It is but justice to mention that Captain Adair has, by the most indefatigable exertions, procured the men he has already enlisted without ever going out of the Ship, or sending an Officer for that purpose; consequently, as their Lordships will observe, he is obliged to give a certain pecuniary reward to the people who procure them for him. I must also beg to mention that the Recruits have all been raised from the different places in the Mediterranean, and not enlisted from the Squadron, as I believe was done in many instances by Colonel Flight, during Lord St. Vincent's Command in these seas.

If any Officer employed on this service is entitled to an additional consideration for inspecting Recruits, I must beg to recommend Captain Adair[6] as justly deserving it. I am, &c.

NELSON AND BRONTE.

TO WILLIAM MARSDEN, ESQ., ADMIRALTY.

[Original, in the Admiralty.]

Sir,　　　　　　　　　　　　Victory, at Sea, 10th October, 1804.

I have received your letter of the 4th August, with the inclosure therein mentioned from Mr. Stanley, Consul at Trieste, to the Master of Lloyd's Coffee-house, and signifying their Lordships' direction to call upon the Captain of his Majesty's brig Morgiana to account for his having left his Convoy. In answer thereto, I beg leave to refer you to my letter of the 8th ult.,[7] with its inclosure from Captain Raynsford of the said Brig, giving a very full and correct account of his proceedings on the occasion alluded to in Mr. Stanley's said letter, which I have, as their Lordships will observe, approved of, and trust his conduct will also meet their approbation.

I cannot here omit noticing the very indecent liberty which Mr. Stanley takes with the conduct of Captain Raynsford, which, not only on the present, but on all former occasions that have come within my knowledge, has been highly to that Officer's credit, and the good of his Majesty's Service. I am, &c.,

NELSON AND BRONTE.

---

[6] Captain Adair was killed in the Victory, at Trafalgar.　　　[7] Vide p. 195, ante.

TO THE RIGHT HONOURABLE THE EARL CAMDEN, K.G.

[Autograph, in the Colonial Office.]

Victory, October 11th, 1804.

My Lord,

I have been honoured with your Lordship's letter of August
29th, and having answered Lord Melville and Lord Harrowby
on the subject of Sardinia, it would be a waste of your Lordship's time to repeat again what I have wrote them, and which,
of course, will come to your Lordship; and as, from the state of
my health, I shall be in England nearly as soon as this letter, I
shall then be happy to give your Lordship all the information
which, you may suppose, I possess relative to Sardinia,
Naples, Sicily, Morea, Barbary States, &c. &c.

I send your Lordship the last return of French troops in
Corsica and Elba. Captain Leake is going to Malta and
Corfu, &c. &c., not thinking it proper he should go to Sar-
dinia, as we possess every information about it, and another
Officer's going would probably hasten the French views
upon it.

I shall always keep a constant watch upon the French in
Corsica, that they shall not get over if I can help it. I have, &c.

NELSON AND BRONTE.

TO THE RIGHT HONOURABLE THE EARL CAMDEN, K.G.

[Autograph, in the Colonial Office.]

Victory, October 11th, 1804.

My Lord,

I have the honour to transmit you my correspondence with
the Dey of Algiers, since Mr. M'Donough went there. I have
done with him. He wishes to be thought a Marabout. Next
Spring it will be thought necessary to turn the thoughts of
Ministers towards Algiers ; but the more we appear to give
way, the more insolent he is. The business of the Veloce
was the Ship he sent an Ambassador to England about, in
the year 1800, and everything was settled. The Jews who
have led him wrong, are now seriously alarmed, but nobody
can give your Lordship such correct information as his Ma-

jesty's late Consul, Mr. Falcon; and allow me to say that, in my humble opinion, Mr. F. would fill the place of the late Mr. Lock in Egypt, with great advantage to the State. I have, &c.

NELSON AND BRONTE.

TO THE RIGHT HONOURABLE LORD HARROWBY.

[From Clarke and M'Arthur, vol. ii. p. 389.]

11th October, 1804.

My Lord,

You must excuse that want of regularity and method in arranging the various subjects, so easy to Statesmen, but with which a man who has been all his life at sea cannot be supposed to be so well acquainted. I received Captain Leake with that openness, which was necessary to make myself as well acquainted with him in three days, as others might do in as many years. I have given him all the knowledge of the men, their views, &c. &c., as far as I have been able to form a judgment. We know everything respecting Sardinia which is necessary—that it has no money, no troops, no means of defence... I will only mention the state of one Town, Alghiera, fortified with seventy large cannon, and containing 10 or 12,000 inhabitants. It has forty Soldiers and a Governor, not one of whom has been paid any wages for more than three years. They levy a small tax upon what comes in or goes out of the Town. Guns honeycombed for want of paint, and only two carriages fit to stand firing; and the Governor shows this, and says, ' How long can we go on in this manner?' This place was intended to, and would, in our hands, possess the whole of the coral fishery; but for want of active commerce, grass grows in the streets. I could repeat the same miserable state of the City of Sassari, where there is a regular University established, now in misery. The French mean to make that the seat of Government; it is in a beautiful and fertile plain twelve miles from the sea, to which a river flows. I am, &c.,

NELSON AND BRONTE.

TO CAPTAIN CRACRAFT, H.M. SHIP ANSON.

[From a Copy in the Admiralty.]

Victory, October 12th, 1804.

My dear Sir,

As the Medusa will very shortly proceed to England, and as I do not see the necessity of keeping so large a Frigate to the Eastward, now the Ionian Republic and the Morea are so well secured by the Russians, and if there are no immediate indications of an embarkation from the Heel of Italy, for Sicily, I think, as you wish it, that you may as well take Gore's place, as the Medusa must go to England to be docked; therefore, if you see nothing necessary to keep you at Malta, or to the Eastward, you will give all the necessary directions relative to the protection of the Convoys, and proceed to take the Medusa's station outside the Straits—orders will be sent down for your guidance. I am ever, my dear Sir, with high respect, your most obedient servant,

NELSON AND BRONTE.

TO JOHN TYSON, ESQ.

[Autograph, in the possession of Edwin Beedell, Esq.]

Victory, October 12th, 1804.

My dear Tyson,

Many thanks for your letter of July 23rd, and for all the good things you have sent me by the William, which the Conqueror and Tigre brought me from Gibraltar. I am glad to see my account so far worked down; the balance I owe you, and much more, but that we will settle in the Christmas holidays, by which time I expect you will have settled the Genoa business. Forgive my short letter, and only believe me ever, your much obliged and faithful friend,

NELSON AND BRONTE.

P.S.—I am much obliged by your attention to the Toulon business[7]—it is likely to be a shameful business.

[7] Prize money for the capture of Ships and Stores at Toulon, in 1793.

TO VICE-ADMIRAL BLIGH.

[From Marshall's " Naval Biography," Supplement, part i. p. 431.]

Victory, October 12th, 1804.

Your kind present of Newspapers of August 13th and 21st arrived safe, for all which, accept my sincere thanks. Your son has never done wrong—that I can answer for, since he sailed in the Victory, and I wish I could promote him, but I see no prospect : the Admiralty fill all vacancies except *death*, and nobody will die ; therefore, I recommend you to ask Lord Melville to let him be put upon the Admiralty list, and then I may be able to give him the step, which will afford great satisfaction to, my dear Admiral, yours, &c.,

NELSON AND BRONTE.

TO LIEUTENANT CUTHBERT ADAMSON, R.N., NEWCASTLE-UPON-TYNE.

[Autograph, in the possession of his son, Lieutenant John Adamson, R.N.]

Victory, October 12th, 1804.

Dear Sir,

I have only just received your letter of June 26th, respecting your nephew Mr. Hathwaite,[9] on board the Canopus. Without a Battle and Victory complete, it may not be in my power, from the very few vacancies which occur in this healthy climate, and from the Admiralty List being so long, independent of those naturally looking up to me from serving in the same Ship; but I will place him upon my list, and in the event of such a Victory, as I may expect from the services of the Fleet under my command, I will not forget your relation. I remember you most perfectly well in the Racehorse,[8] and my wonder has often been excited at your remaining a Lieutenant, and when all your living shipmates have rose to high rank in the Service. I am, dear Sir, your most obedient servant, NELSON AND BRONTE.

[8] Lieutenant Cuthbert Adamson was Second Lieutenant of the Racehorse in the Expedition to the North Pole, in 1773, when Lord Nelson was a Midshipman of the Carcass, Captain Lutwidge, (vide vol. i. p. 2.) Failing to obtain promotion, Mr. Adamson retired on half-pay, and died in November 1804, a few days before this letter reached Newcastle.

[9] A Mr. William Haithwaite was made a Lieutenant in September 1806, and died in that rank, in 1814.

TO VISCOUNT MELVILLE, FIRST LORD OF THE ADMIRALTY.

[Original, in the Admiralty.]

Victory, at Sea, 12th October, 1804.

My Lord,

I have the honour to transmit your Lordship a Memorial from several of the Surgeons belonging to his Majesty's Ships under my command; and as the particular case of so valuable and so respectable a body of men is no doubt well known to your Lordship, it is not necessary for me to make any comments on the justness of their request as mentioned in the said Memorial. I am, &c.,

NELSON AND BRONTE.

TO HIS EXCELLENCY THE CAPTAIN-GENERAL, BARCELONA.

[Autograph draught, in the possession of Miss Bolton, of Burnham.]

Victory, October 12th, 1804.

Sir,

I have just received from Mr. Gibert, the English Vice-Consul at Barcelona, a letter, in which he states to me that your Excellency has received an account of a bad fever having broke out at Gibraltar since the 15th of September. I have this day, *viâ* Barcelona and Madrid, received letters from Gibraltar, in which no mention whatever is made of such a dreadful circumstance, nor will your Excellency give the smallest credit to the report. As far as we know yet, from what I am going to relate, his Majesty's Ships Conqueror and Tigre sailed from England September 2nd, arrived at Gibraltar September 21st, sailed from thence the 22nd, and joined the Fleet a few days ago. The Captains, before I allowed them to communicate, declared that Gibraltar was in perfect health; and I had letters from Sir Thomas Trigge, the Governor and Sir Robert Barlow, the Commanding Sea-Officer, not mentioning a word of any fever.

Since the Termagant joined this day, the Childers Brig, who I had sent with dispatches to Sir Robert Barlow, of His Majesty's Ship, Triumph, on the 22nd of September, arrived, with dispatches from Sir Robert Barlow, cruizing off Europa Point, dated October 1st, ten o'clock at night

—that since the 26th, all his Majesty's Ships had left Gibraltar, and only communicated through the Lazaretto— that a fever similar to that at Malaga had broke out and carried off a number of the lower class of people, but that the Troops were very healthy ; that they were all encamped, and that a Lazaretto camp was formed upon the Neutral Ground, and that from the precautions taken it was hoped that the disease would not spread. From the care which your Excellency takes of the health of the Province of Catalonia, and from your Excellency's liberal conduct towards his Britannic Majesty's Ships, I think it is right to inform you of every circumstance; and I therefore beg leave this day to inform your Excellency upon my *sacred word* of honour that not *one* man is confined in the whole Fleet, by either sickness or accident. And at the same time, I assure your Excellency, on the word of an Officer, that when the Fleet is sickly that I will inform you, for this sickness is in its nature the curse of Europe. I have the honour to be, with high respect, your Excellency's most obedient servant,

NELSON AND BRONTE.

TO CAPTAIN JOHN GORE, H. M. SHIP MEDUSA.

[Autograph, in the possession of the Right Honourable John Wilson Croker.]

Victory, October 13th, 1804.

Sir,

I am most exceedingly sorry for the bad account you give of the Medusa, and as Gibraltar is entirely out of the question, I have no alternative than, if it is necessary, that you must take the Medusa to England; and until I can get the Anson to relieve you, you must direct Captain Graham Moore to take your station ; for our Runners from Newfoundland, and Convoys from England, &c., must not be left at the mercy of the French Ships in Cadiz. This is the only order I can give you, for I can say nothing about either Gibraltar or Cadiz. I am, &c.

NELSON AND BRONTE.

TO WILLIAM MARSDEN, ESQ., ADMIRALTY.

[Autograph, in the possession of the Right Honourable John Wilson Croker.]

Victory, October 13th, 1804.

Sir,

Last night I received from Captain Gore of his Majesty's Ship Medusa, the inclosed letter and order from Admiral Cornwallis to Captain Graham Moore. I own myself filled with astonishment, for if the orders for Admiral Cornwallis's proceedings came from England, similar orders, it is natural to suppose, would have been sent to me ;[1] and if the proceeding of Admiral Cornwallis emanated from himself thinking it was a Spanish War, I should, with all deference for his better judgment, have expected that he would have rather thought of giving the information to the Commander-in-Chief of this Station, than to have sent a Frigate to cruize off Cadiz, for the purpose of intercepting money. I must leave the whole of the order and transaction for their Lordships' judgment.

I am most exceedingly puzzled how to act; for if Admiral Cornwallis acted by the orders of the Admiralty, I am confident that similar orders would have been sent to me; for it was much more necessary for me to know that the War was to commence upon the Station entrusted to my direction, than to send orders for an Admiral upon another Station, to send a Frigate to commence the War upon the Station under my direction, and no orders even to acquaint me with it.

I am this day sending to Captain Gore, the letter of which I inclose a copy, by which their Lordships will see that I could form no idea of a War being likely to break out with Spain. I have the honour to be, Sir, &c.

NELSON AND BRONTE.

---

[1] A copy of the Admiralty's Instructions to Admiral Cornwallis, with similar Orders for his own guidance, were sent to Lord Nelson, and reached him a few hours after this and the next letter were written. (Vide p. 241, post.) The above letters to Mr. Marsden and Captain Gore, were consequently not forwarded, and on the cover which enclosed it, Lord Nelson wrote, " N.B. John Bull Cutter arrived the same day, with orders similar to Admiral Cornwallis's."

TO CAPTAIN JOHN GORE, H.M. SHIP MEDUSA.

[From a Copy in the possession of the Right Honourable John Wilson Croker.]

Victory, October 13th, 1804

Sir,

Last night I received your letter of October 1st, with a copy of Captain Graham Moore's orders from Admiral Cornwallis, which has filled me with astonishment; but without presuming to set myself in opposition to the Honourable Admiral's orders, there is a duty which I owe my Country that, although I risk the most precious thing to me in the world— my Commission,—I feel it my duty to give you my full opinion of the line of conduct you ought to pursue on this most extraordinary occasion; and to enable you to form a complete judgment of the conclusion I shall draw for your guidance, I shall detail to you what I think may have led Admiral Cornwallis to have given this most extraordinary order of sending a Frigate to cruize upon this Station.

It is reported to me by Mr. Hunter, Consul-General at Madrid, that September　, the Spanish Squadron at Ferrol, dropped down the Harbour, having on board a number of Spanish Troops, intending to carry them to the Province of Biscay, then in insurrection. (N.B. The passes by land into Biscay are very difficult, and probably in the hands of the insurgents.) On the 14th September, Admiral Cochrane wrote the Spanish Admiral, that as the French openly declared that they should sail with the Spanish Squadron, that he should attack [them], and that he hoped nothing would happen to interrupt the Neutrality, &c. Admiral Cochrane, in his letter to Mr. Hunter, of the 15th [said], 'the pretext to carry Troops to Biscay, is too flimsy to go down,' (I use Mr. Hunter's own words.) Mr. Hunter goes on to say, in consequence of what he has written by the Naiad, and what, of course, Mr. Frere will represent personally, the Admiral expects instructions and a reinforcement. This letter is dated Madrid, September 22nd. On the 26th, Mr. H. writes 'Admiral Cochrane's letter seems to have had an almost instantaneous effect.' It was dated the 14th, and on the 17th the Ships returned to the Arsenal, or Inner Harbour, and the Troops were landed, and ordered to go by land. Now, supposing the Naiad left Ferrol the 14th, she could not have got to England, and orders be sent out to Admiral Cornwallis by the 22nd; therefore, it is my decided opinion that the orders emanated from Admiral Cornwallis, in consequence of Admiral Cochrane's letter; therefore, upon the whole proceedings of Spain, as far as have come to my knowledge, and from the best consideration which my abilities enable me to give to this most important subject, I am clearly of opinion that Spain has no wish to go to War with England, nor can I think that England has any wish to go to War unnecessarily with Spain. Therefore, unless you have much weightier reasons than the order of Admiral Cornwallis, or that you receive orders from the Admiralty, it is my most positive directions that neither you, or any Ship under your orders, do molest or interrupt in any manner the lawful commerce of Spain, with whom we are at perfect peace and amity. I am, Sir, &c.

NELSON AND BRONTE.

TO CAPTAIN SIR RICHARD JOHN STRACHAN, BART., H. M. SHIP DONEGAL.

[From a Copy in the Admiralty.]

Victory, at Sea, 13th October, 1804.

Most Secret.

Whereas I have this moment received a secret Admiralty letter, dated the 19th September,[9] together with the copy of

---

[9] The Letter and Orders alluded to, were as follow:—

" Secret.   " Admiralty Office, 19th September, 1804.

" My Lord,

" I have it in command from my Lords Commissioners of the Admiralty, to send you herewith a copy of their Lordships' order, of yesterday's date, to Admiral Cornwallis, respecting the blockade of the Port of Ferrol, and to signify their direction to you to take such measures of precaution as may be necessary for opposing or counteracting any hostile attempts of the Government or Subjects of Spain, against his Majesty's Dominions, or the Trade of his Majesty's subjects, within the limits of your command. Your Lordship is, however, not to suffer any act of hostility or aggression (with the exception of detaining for further orders Ships having treasure on board, belonging to the Spanish Government) to be committed by the Ships under your command, towards the Dominions or Subjects of Spain, until you receive further orders, or until your Lordship shall have received from unquestionable authority, positive information of hostilities having been committed by the

their Lordships' most Secret Order, dated the 18th of that month, addressed to Admiral Cornwallis, respecting the blockade of the Port of Ferrol, and opposing or counteracting any hostile attempts of the Government or Subjects of Spain against his Majesty's Dominions. And whereas I think this service of the highest importance, and that an Officer of your rank and experience should be employed therein:—You are therefore hereby required and directed to proceed immediately with his Majesty's Ship Donegal under your command, outside the Straits of Gibraltar, and take his Majesty's Ships and Vessels named in the margin[1] under your command, together with any other of his Majesty's Ships or Vessels which you may fall in with, and use your utmost exertions to carry their Lordships' instructions contained in the copy of Mr. Marsden's letter and Admiralty order above-mentioned (herewith transmitted) into effect, taking every measure and precaution

subjects of Spain against his Majesty's interests. I have the honour to be, &c.— WILLIAM MARSDEN."—*Original.*

" TO THE HONOURABLE WILLIAM CORNWALLIS, ADMIRAL OF THE WHITE, &C. OFF BREST.

" Most Secret.

" You are hereby required and directed to give immediate orders to Rear-Admiral Cochrane, to continue the blockade of the Port of Ferrol with the utmost vigilance, not only with the view of preventing the French Squadron from escaping from that Port, but likewise with a view of preventing any of the Spanish Ships of War from sailing from Ferrol, or any additional Ships of War from entering that Port; and if, in consequence of your correspondence with Rear-Admiral Cochrane, you should be of opinion that the force under the Rear-Admiral is not adequate to the purposes above mentioned, you are without delay to reinforce the Squadron under his command, and measures will be taken with all possible expedition to send out to you a sufficient number of Ships to replace the force which you may so detach. You are to send intimation to the Spanish Government, through Rear-Admiral Cochrane, of the instructions you have given to the Rear-Admiral, and of your determination, in consequence thereof, to resist, under the present circumstances, the sailing either of the French or Spanish Fleets, if any attempt for that purpose should be made by either of them. And whereas information has been received that some Frigates are speedily expected to arrive at Cadiz, loaded with treasures from South America, you are to lose no time in detaching two of the Frigates under your command, with orders to their Captains to proceed with all possible dispatch off Cadiz, and the entrance of the Straits, and to use their best endeavours, in conjunction with any of his Majesty's Ships they may find there, to intercept, if possible, the Vessels in which the above-mentioned treasure may be contained, and to detain them until his Majesty's pleasure shall be further known. Given under our hands, the 18th of September 1804.—J. GAMBIER, JNO. COLPOYS, PH. PATTON."—*Original.*

[1] Medusa, Amphion, Sophie, Halcyon.

in your power for opposing or counteracting any hostile attempts of the Government, or Subjects, of Spain against his Majesty's Dominions, or Trade of his Majesty's Subjects.

You are hereby required and directed not to commit any act of hostility or aggression (with the exception of detaining for further orders Ships having treasure on board belonging to the Spanish Government) towards the Dominions or Subjects of Spain, until you shall receive further orders, or until you have received from unquestionable authority, positive information of hostilities having been committed by the Subjects of Spain, against his Majesty's interests. You will use your best endeavours, in conjunction with any of his Majesty's Ships which the Honourable Admiral Cornwallis may have sent off Cadiz, to intercept, if possible, the Vessels in which the above-mentioned treasure may be contained, and detain them until his Majesty's pleasure shall be further known.

You are to continue on this service until further orders, and cruize most diligently between Cape St. Vincent and the Straits' Mouth, in such situation as you may judge best for the purpose mentioned above, paying the most strict obedience to the spirit of Mr. Marsden's letter and copy of the order therein alluded to; and on no account commit any act of hostility against the Spanish Government or Subjects, (the detention of the Treasure-Ships excepted,) until you shall have received the most satisfactory proof of their having committed hostilities against his Majesty's Subjects. In the event of your detaining any of the Spanish Treasure-Ships, you will send them to Plymouth, under the protection of a Frigate or Ship of the Line, as the case may require, and you judge best for his Majesty's Service.

NELSON AND BRONTE.

TO LADY HAMILTON.

[From " Lord Nelson's Letters to Lady Hamilton," vol. ii. p. 79.]

Victory, October 13th, 1804.

My dearest Emma,

The dreadful effects of the yellow fever, at Gibraltar, and many parts of Spain, will naturally give you much uneasiness, till you hear that, thank God, we are entirely free from it, and in the most perfect health, not one man being ill in the Fleet. The cold weather will, I hope, cure the disorder. Whilst I am writing this letter, a Cutter is arrived from England with strong indications of a Spanish War.

I hope, from my heart, that it will not prove one. But, however that is, my die is cast; and, long before this time, I expect, another Admiral is far on his way to supersede me. Lord Keith, I think a very likely man. I should, for your sake, and for many of our friends, have liked an odd hundred thousand pounds; but, never mind. If they give me the choice of staying a few months longer, it will be very handsome; and, for the sake of others, we would give up, my dear Emma, very much of our own felicity. If they do not, we shall be happy with each other, and with dear Horatia.....
... Tell my brother, that I have made Mr. Yonge a Lieutenant, into the Seahorse Frigate, Captain Boyle....... I have scrawled three lines to Davison, that he should not think I neglected him in his confinement. I have received the inclosed from Allen.[2] Can we assist the poor foolish man with a *character?*

TO WILLIAM MARSDEN, ESQ., ADMIRALTY.

[Original, in the Admiralty.]

Victory, at Sea, 13th October, 1804.

Sir,

I request you will be pleased to acquaint the Lords Commissioners of the Admiralty, that his Majesty's Ships and Vessels under my command are in momentary readiness for any service, and that their respective Companies are all in most perfect health, and scarcely a man in the Squadron confined to bed for any complaint whatever. I am, Sir, &c.

NELSON AND BRONTE.

---

[2] Formerly his servant. Vide vol. i. p. xxv.

TO MR. JOHN DEBRETT.

[From " The Naval Chronicle," vol. xv. p. 189.]

Victory, at Sea, October 13th, 1804.

Sir,

I am favoured with your letter of August 22nd. Your observation, with regard to the Dukedom of Bronte, in Sicily, I take to be perfectly just;[3] and I cannot, therefore, have any objection to your making what use of it you think proper. I will not fail sending the Gazette to Rome by the first opportunity; and desiring you will believe me thankful for your kind wishes, I remain your most obedient, humble servant,

NELSON AND BRONTE.

TO WILLIAM MARSDEN, ESQ., ADMIRALTY.

[Original, in the Admiralty.]

Victory, at Sea, 14th October, 1804.

Sir,

I received by the John Bull, Hired Armed Cutter, which joined the Squadron yesterday about noon, from Plymouth, your secret letter, dated the 19th September, and a copy of their Lordships' order, dated also the 18th of that month (therein mentioned), addressed to the Honourable Admiral Cornwallis, off Brest. And you will please to acquaint the Lords Commissioners of the Admiralty, that the most strict attention shall be paid to their Lordships' instructions therein contained.

As the Triumph is outside the Straits, with the Medusa and Amphion, I trust their vigilance will prevent the escape of the Treasure-Ships, coming from South America to Cadiz, and the reinforcement their Lordships have sent, has enabled

---

[3] Mr. Debrett, Editor of the well-known Peerage, bearing his name, had written to Lord Nelson, stating that, " when the King of the Two Sicilies conferred the title of Bronté upon his Lordship, he perhaps was not aware of its appropriate meaning. It is the Greek word for *thunder*. The name of the individual Cyclops, who, in poetic fable, is described as forging the thunder of Jove, was Bronte. His residence was, of course, at Ætna."—*Naval Chronicle*, vol. xv. p. 189.

me to dispatch the Donegal on this service, under the directions of Sir Richard Strachan, whose zeal for the Public Service is well known. I am, &c.

NELSON AND BRONTE.

TO LIEUTENANT KORTWRIGHT, COMMANDING HIS MAJESTY'S HIRED ARMED CUTTER JOHN BULL.

[Order-Book.]

Victory, at Sea, 14th October, 1804.

You are hereby required and directed to receive my public dispatches, addressed to Mr. Secretary Marsden, on board his Majesty's hired Armed Cutter under your command, and proceed with them immediately to Plymouth, with the utmost possible expedition. You are to keep a proper weight constantly affixed to the above-mentioned dispatches, and, in case of falling in with an Enemy of superior force, and seeing no probability of escaping capture, you are to throw them overboard, and sink them. You are carefully to avoid speaking with any Ship or Vessel which you may happen to meet with during your passage, particularly on your entering the Straits of Gibraltar, where you may expect to meet with some of the Enemy's Cruizers, on which account you are to keep the most vigilant look-out, and to be as much upon your guard as possible. You are on no account whatever to communicate with Gibraltar, or receive any letters, &c. from any Boat or Vessel coming from that place, on account of the dreadful malady which has broke out there. On your arrival at Plymouth, you will deliver my dispatches to Admiral Young, or the Commanding Officer for the time being at that place, who will forward them to the Admiralty. Having so done, you will remain at Plymouth for their Lordships' further orders.

NELSON AND BRONTE.

These are to certify that his Majesty's Fleet under my command is in most perfect health, and that, at this moment, there is not a man on board either of the Ships confined to bed, on account of sickness, or any complaint whatever.

NELSON AND BRONTE.

TO WILLIAM MARSDEN, ESQ., ADMIRALTY.

[Original, in the Admiralty.]

Victory, at Sea, 14th October, 1804.

Sir,

I herewith transmit you a letter from Captain Pearse, of His Majesty's Ship Halcyon, dated the 23rd September last, giving an account of his having captured L'Esperance, French Privateer, on the 20th of that month, which you will please to lay before the Lords Commissioners of the Admiralty for their information; and at the same time acquaint their Lordships that Captain Pearse's exertion on the present and several former occasions, for the protection of our Trade and destruction of the Enemy's Privateers in the vicinity of Gibraltar, very justly entitles him to my warmest approbation. I am, &c.

NELSON AND BRONTE.

TO CAPTAIN HENRY RICHARDSON, H. M. SHIP JUNO.

[Order-Book.]

Victory, 15th October, 1804.

Most Secret.

Whereas, from the recent conduct of the Spaniards at Ferrol, the greatest circumspection becomes necessary on the part of his Majesty's Ships, either in communicating with the Spanish Ports, or on falling in with any of their Ships or Vessels of War, You are therefore hereby required and directed in your future communications with Rosas, Barcelona, or any other Spanish Port, to do so with the utmost caution, taking care to anchor His Majesty's Ship under your command well out of reach of shot from their Forts or Batteries, and always to be on your guard against surprise.

NELSON AND BRONTE.

TO CAPTAIN ARTHUR FARQUHAR, HIS MAJESTY'S BOMB VESSEL
ACHERON.

[Order-Book.]

Victory, at Sea, 15th October, 1804.

You are hereby required and directed to take the Transport named in the margin[5] under your protection, and proceed with her immediately to the Bay of Rosas, where you will moor her in safety, and leave her in the execution of my orders. The Agent Victualler having ordered two hundred quintals of onions from Mr. Gayner for the use of the Fleet, you are to receive a sufficient number of empty bags from the Victory to hold that quantity; and the moment you have received them from Mr. Gayner, which will not require more than twenty-four or thirty hours after your arrival, you will proceed with all possible expedition to the Madalena Islands, where I expect the Fleet will arrive about the 20th instant, and remain there till you receive my further orders for your proceedings, taking care to anchor the Acheron free from the place occupied by the Ships of the Line. You are on no account to remain longer than the time above mentioned at Rosas, and be particularly careful in not suffering your people to communicate with the shore, or afford them any opportunity for desertion. NELSON AND BRONTE.

N.B.—This order is to be kept secret, and none of your Officers or other person made acquainted that the Fleet is going to the Madalena Islands. N. AND B.

TO CAPTAIN THE HONOURABLE COURTENAY BOYLE, H. M. SHIP
SEAHORSE.

[From the " Naval Chronicle," vol. xxx. p. 37. " Thursday, 18th October.
A.M. At 9·50, shortened sail, and anchored in Agincourt Sound. At Noon, the
Royal Sovereign, Conqueror, Belleisle, and Leviathan, anchored in the Eastern
anchorage. Active and two Transports at anchor here."—Victory's Log.]

(A hint: most secret.)   Victory, October 19th, 1804.

My dear Boyle,

If you knew what I *could* tell you,[6] you would think every moment an age till you joined me. Ever, my dear Boyle, yours faithfully, NELSON AND BRONTE.

---

[5] Chatham.   [6] *i. e.* The probability of a Spanish War.

TO LIEUTENANT HENRY FREDERICK WOODMAN.

[Autograph, in the possession of Robert Fitch, Esq., of Norwich.]

Victory, October 20th, 1804.

Sir,

I have read with much satisfaction your letter of October 8th, 1804, giving the account of the Black Sea, of its Ports, and what you think may be procured from thence; the clearness with which everything is stated, does you the greatest credit

I shall not fail to transmit your very interesting letter to Lord Melville; and from his Lordship's liberal way of thinking, I flatter myself he will be induced to notice, in a satisfactory manner, your indefatigable and important exertions. For myself, I selected you for this service of observation[7] from the character I had heard of you, and which your conduct has most fully justified, and I beg you will accept my sincere thanks for your services. As you must necessarily have been at some expenses, I desire you will send me an account of them, that they may be paid. In addition to your other interesting papers, I beg you will send me a copy of your Log-Book, that courses, distances, marks for anchorage, &c. &c. may be known, and I beg you to be assured that I am, Sir, your much obliged and faithful servant,

NELSON AND BRONTE.

TO MR. THOMAS ATKINSON, MASTER OF H. M. SHIP VICTORY.

[Order-Book.]

Victory, Madalena Islands, Sardinia, 20th October, 1804.

Memorandum.

Having directed Captain Cocks to receive you on board the Thunder, and to proceed with her to the Island of Cabrera, in order to afford you every assistance with Boats, &c. for the purpose of ascertaining correctly the soundings and bearings, &c. of the Shoal Rock, which his Majesty's Ship Excellent struck upon in May last,[8] I am therefore to desire you will proceed immediately on board the Thunder, and survey the said Shoal, taking the most correct soundings on every part of

[7] Vide vol. v. p. 470.   [8] Vide p. 21, ante.

it, and between that and the Isle of Biche, its bearings, and every particular remark necessary to prevent any accident to his Majesty's Ships in future, which I expect will not detain you more than forty-eight hours, when you will report to Captain Cocks, and return immediately to the Victory.

NELSON AND BRONTE.

TO SIR ALEXANDER JOHN BALL, BART., MALTA.

[Autograph, in the possession of Sir William Keith Ball, Bart.]

Victory, October 22nd, 1804.

My dear Ball,

Many thanks for your kind letter, and for all your continued kindnesses to me, and you may rely in every situation in life, I shall cherish your friendship. Hallowell thinks the Ministers will not name another Commander-in-Chief, but see if I am able to return. I do not think so, for they are so beset by Admirals. Sir John Orde, I am told, is likely. Lord Radstock is trying; so is Sir Roger Curtis: and if a Spanish War comes, Lord Keith loves a little money, and a great deal much better. Time will bring many strange things to pass, but I believe can never alter the sincere, affectionate regard of your most attached and sincere friend,

NELSON AND BRONTE.

TO THE MASTERS OF HIS MAJESTY'S SHIPS.

[Order-Book.]

Victory, Madalena Islands, 22nd October, 1804.

The Agent-Victualler at Malta having acquainted me, by letter of the 11th instant, that the provisions mentioned in the margin were put on board the Eliza and Brumgrove, Transports, in the River Lima, in July and August last, by William Eaton, Esq., for the Victualling Stores at Malta; and whereas this is a new mode of supplying his Majesty's Stores, it becomes necessary to be most correctly ascertained whether they are good of their kind, and fit for his Majesty's Service, You are therefore hereby required and directed to repair on board the said Transports (or to his Majesty's Victualling

Stores, if the Provisions before-mentioned are landed,) and take a most strict and careful survey on the pork, tongues, hog's-lard, pease, and wheat, before stated, to see whether they are all sound and good of their kind; and in order to judge of the meat when boiled, that it does not shrink more than the pork used in the Navy, you are hereby required to take a certain number of pieces, out of one or more of the casks promiscuously, as they come to hand, and boil them on board the Senior Officer's Ship. You will also take a bushel of pease, in the same way, from one or more of the bags, and see them also boiled, paying very particular attention that neither the pork or pease are too much done, or otherwise. With respect to the wheat, you will adopt such measures as may be judged proper to ascertain its quality and fitness for his Majesty's Service. And as this is a service of very great importance, as well for preventing complaints or discontent amongst the Seamen, from the issue of bad provisions, as to provide against the serious consequences which would result from having a quantity of supposed good provisions in store, when in fact it might be otherwise, it is my positive directions that the strictest attention is paid to every circumstance which may tend fully to ascertain the real quality of the before-mentioned provisions, and also the comparative quality between them, and those from England. I would, therefore, recommend your calling upon the Agent-Victualler to attend you on this service, as his experience in these matters will render his assistance very useful; reporting to me, from under your hands, a most full and particular account of your proceedings on this service, which you will deliver to the Senior Officer, in order that it may be transmitted to me by the very first opportunity.

NELSON AND BRONTE.

TO WILLIAM MARSDEN, ESQ., ADMIRALTY.

[Original, in the Admiralty.]

Victory, Madalena Islands, 24th October, 1804.

Sir,

I herewith transmit you a letter from Captain Pettet, of his Majesty's Sloop Termagant, of this date, together with

the one therein mentioned, dated the 1st August, addressed
to you, on the subject of an allowance for the expenses incurred by bringing Mr. Falcon, late Consul at Algiers, and
his suite, from Gibraltar to the Victory, which I request you
will be pleased to lay before the Lords Commissioners of the
Admiralty for their consideration; and at the same time
acquaint their Lordships that I have paid Captain Pettet the
sum of twenty pounds sterling, for his expenses in accommo-
dating Mr. M'Donough from the Fleet to Algiers on particular service, and from thence to Gibraltar, conceiving the sum
to be moderate, and actually required for that purpose.

I also beg to observe that I consider the sum of sixty
pounds for stock, &c. purchased at Gibraltar for the accommodation of Mr. Falcon and his suite, as mentioned in Captain Pettet's letter, to have been necessary for that purpose,
and that from the length of time they were on board the
Termagant, every article so purchased was expended. I must
also request you will acquaint their Lordships that Captain
Pettet is an Officer of confined circumstances, with a large
family. I am, &c.

NELSON AND BRONTE.

TO CAPTAIN GEORGE COCKS, H.M. BOMB-VESSEL THUNDER.

[Order-Book. Friday, 26th October. A.M. At 10, weighed and made sail out of
Agincourt Sound, to the Westward. At Noon, Squadron all under sail. P.M. Inclinable to calms. At 2·30, anchored. Squadron all anchored here. Thunder
parted at 5, P.M. Saturday, 27th. A.M. At 6, weighed and made sail to the Westward. At Noon, Squadron in company."]

Victory, Madalena Islands, 26th October, 1804.

Most Secret.

Whereas I have received information that the Enemy intend sending three Privateers from Ajaccio, with a hundred
men, to surprise and take possession of the Town of Madalena, You are therefore hereby required and directed to proceed, with his Majesty's Bomb-Vessel under your command,
close in with the said Town, and anchor her in such situation
as you may judge best for its protection against invasion by
the Enemy. You are to keep the Thunder in constant
readiness to act with effect under any circumstances, and

have Boats rowing guard, during the night, in such position as you shall judge best for discovering their approach ; and in the event of their attempt upon the Town or Island of Madalena, you will consult with the Governor thereof, and render him every assistance in your power for its protection and safety; but on no account let the object of your remaining behind be known, (except to the Governor and Mr. Brandi, who acts as English Consul,) but keep it a profound secret.

NELSON AND BRONTE.

TO THE RIGHT HONOURABLE VISCOUNT MELVILLE.

[From Clarke and M'Arthur, vol. ii. p. 390.]

30th October, 1804.

The weather was very thick when I looked into Toulon, but I believe a Vice-Admiral has hoisted his Flag ; his name I have not yet heard.[9] They now amuse themselves with night-signals, and by the quantity of rockets and blue lights they show with every signal, they plainly mark their position. These gentlemen must soon be so perfect in theory, that they will come to sea to put their knowledge into practice. Could I see that day, it would make me happy. I am, &c.

NELSON AND BRONTE.

TO CAPTAIN SIR RICHARD JOHN STRACHAN, BART., H.M. SHIP DONEGAL.

[From a Copy in the possession of the Right Hon. John Wilson Croker.]

Victory, at Sea, 30th October, 1804.

Sir,

Whereas I have reason to believe that the state of the Medusa's hull will soon make it necessary to send her to England for the purpose of being docked, I must therefore desire, upon Captain Gore's representing to you officially that his Majesty's Ship Medusa is in want of being docked, and unfit to remain longer in this Country, that you will order Captain Gore to proceed immediately to Rendezvous No. 97, as I intend the Medusa to take the Trade from

---

[9] Vice-Admiral Villeneuve, who commanded the French Fleet at Trafalgar.

Malta, which are now waiting there for protection to England; but unless the representation above-mentioned comes from Captain Gore, the Medusa is to remain on the service she is at present employed upon. I am, &c.

NELSON AND BRONTE.

TO CAPTAIN JOHN GORE, H. M. SHIP MEDUSA.

[Original, in the possession of the Right Hon. John Wilson Croker.]

Victory, at Sea, 30th October, 1804.

Sir,

I herewith transmit you the copy of a letter of this date, to Sir Richard Strachan, relative to the Medusa's being sent to Rendezvous No. 97, for the purpose of taking the Trade from Malta to England, upon your representing her as unfit to remain longer in this Country. I shall therefore only observe, that, as at this moment the service of a Frigate is very much wanted outside the Straits, you will judge the propriety of remaining as long on your present station as the state of the Medusa will permit, and afterwards make the necessary representations to Sir Richard Strachan, who will consequently comply with my before-mentioned letter. I am, Sir, &c.

NELSON AND BRONTE.

TO CAPTAIN GORE, H. M. SHIP MEDUSA.

[Original, in the possession of the Right Hon. John Wilson Croker.]

Victory, at Sea, 1st November, 1804.

Sir,

I have received your letter of the 19th September last, together with copies of the several orders, the Medusa's defects, Daily-progress, and Log-Book, &c., therein-mentioned, and very much approve of your not having a particular repair done to the Medusa, from the reasons communicated in your said letter.

I am sorry to find La Sophie in so bad a state, and shall, as soon as possible, take an opportunity of getting her repaired, and placed on service more adapted to her qualifications. Your ordering one of the Gun-Boats to be equipped, and given in charge to Lieutenant Lloyd, of the Guerrier, very fully meets my approbation, as well as every part of your conduct communicated in your said letter. Indeed, your zealous and prudent attention to the good of his Majesty's service, cannot fail to be always gratifying to, Sir, &c.

NELSON AND BRONTE.

TO CAPTAIN GORE, H. M. SHIP MEDUSA.

[Original, in the possession of the Right Hon. John Wilson Croker.]

Victory, at Sea, 1st November, 1804.

Sir,

I have received your letter of the 18th September, with a copy of a letter from Captain Pearse, of his Majesty's Sloop Halcyon, and of your letters to Mr. Frere, and to the Captain-General at Cadiz, relative to the capture of some Bullock-Vessels by a French Privateer, between Ceuta and Tetuan, and within the protection of Neutrality ; and also respecting some British Sailors confined in prison at Ceuta. In answer to which, I very much approve of the forbearance of Captain Pearse, and the steps you have taken to prevent similar acts of piracy being tolerated by the Spanish Government. I am, &c.

NELSON AND BRONTE.

TO WILLIAM MARSDEN, ESQ., ADMIRALTY.

[Original, in the Admiralty.]

Victory, at Sea, 1st November, 1804.

Sir,

I herewith transmit you a letter from Captain Gore, of his Majesty's Ship Medusa, dated the 18th September last, together with copies of his letters, &c., to Mr. Matra, Consul-General at Tangier, and that Consul's answer, which you will please to lay before the Lords Commissioners of the Admiralty for their consideration.

Captain Gore's representations and remonstrances to Mr. Matra, appear to me extremely proper, and to have been very necessary ; for if his Majesty's Ministers and Consuls abroad are not particularly attentive to the Ships of War using tho different Ports, and see that they receive every right and privilege of Neutrality, his Majesty's Flag will be insulted, and his Subjects deprived of the right they are entitled to. Their Lordships will, therefore, judge how far Mr. Matra's conduct has been consistent on the present occasion. I am, &c.

NELSON AND BRONTE.

TO THE RIGHT HONOURABLE EARL CAMDEN.

[From Clarke and M'Arthur, vol. ii. p. 391.]

3rd November, 1803.

Sardinia, if it be possible, becomes every day in greater misery. The Stamenti, which is formed of proportions of the Nobles, Clergy, and the People, have dismissed themselves. They were summoned to meet in June or July; the two first Classes met, but the number of the last Class did not arrive until the Viceroy had opened the Session; when, instead of conciliating and promising to assist them in the formation of such regulations as might benefit the Island, he stated at once the distresses of the Government, and asked for one million of dollars. The last Class, finding that nothing was wanted of them but money, never filled up the legal numbers. The Clergy and Nobles agreed to the demand; but the meeting not being legal, no money could be raised. Yet as the Clergy and nobles had consented to the supply, 50 or 60,000 dollars have been squeezed out of them, not one farthing of which has gone to the real wants of the Island. The Clergy and Nobles are now, I hear, very much disgusted at being forced to pay this money, whilst the people pay nothing. This is the present state of Sardinia; it cannot last. I am, &c.

NELSON AND BRONTE.

TO LAMBTON ESTE, ESQ.

[Autograph in the possession of Dr. Lambton Este, who has obligingly communicated the following particulars of Lord Nelson:—

" 4th November, 1804.

" On joining the Victory, in my first interviews with Nelson, he complained of frequent pains in his right side, from former injuries,—that many warnings and inabilities made him conscious of his shattered frame, and anxious for repose. The sight of his remaining eye was fast failing him; a thick opaque membrane had grown over and into a part of the transparent cornea, and, as far as it extended, was an obstacle to vision in the only eye left to him. His thoughts, his ambition, evidently tended to the Admiralty—to the management of the Naval Service of his Country. In his cabin, with his confidential friends, he occasionally alluded to ' what he would do if he were in power :' his anxiety, in either alternative, of retaining his command in the Mediterranean, or of returning to employment at home, seemed to be, to get all his known, tried, and experienced people around him. Addressing Dr. Scott, jocosely, as he generally did, and remarking on his knowledge of Spanish, and of Spanish affairs, he would exclaim, ' Ah, my dear Doctor ! give me knowledge practically acquired—experience ! experience ! experience ! and practical men !'

" In one of the early conferences with his Lordship, he told me he had been upwards of twenty months afloat, without putting a foot on shore ; that he had made all his arrangements to return to England in about two months from the time he spoke ; that the Superb, Captain Keats, would convey him home ; that he was glad I had joined him ; that he wished me to remain with him, and to return with him to England in the Autumn. His sentiments continued unaltered, in this respect, through September and part of October, when intelligence arrived of an approaching War with Spain.

" On the 1st of November he sent for me, after breakfast, and exclaimed, ' Oh, my good fellow ! I have abandoned the idea of going to England, at present. I shall not go yet, and when I may go is quite uncertain—must depend upon events, and upon my own precarious health ; at the same time, I am doing you an evident injustice, by detaining you here so long in uncertainty.' A little pause followed, and I commenced by saying, ' My Lord, if I could be of further use, I should prefer remaining in uncertainty with your Lordship, to——' Anticipating the remainder of my an-swer, he turned upon me, abruptly, and exclaimed, " But *my* wish is that you should go,—I am anxious that you should go, and go without further delay !' ' My Lord, I am ready to start at this moment's notice,' was my reply. From his short, sharp, emphatic manner, I was apprehensive I had given offence, and felt uneasy and embarrassed. ' Oh, not quite so soon as that ! I shall want a day or two, at least,' he said, ' to prepare for you ; but the point is settled, and being settled, we shall both know what to be at ; I shall set to work accordingly, and forthwith. To tell you the truth, I am not entirely disinterested in this wish of mine. Go home ; get confirmed in your appointment, according to my de-sire, and return to me as soon afterwards as you can. Should I retain my com-mand in the Mediterranean, with the powers already conceded to me, I shall demand your re-appointment, and require your assistance in Italy, Naples, Sicily, and in the Islands, and perhaps also in your former scenes of action to the East-ward, where there may be more occupation for us all hereafter than we just now foresee, or may expect. If, in the course of events, I should return to England, and realize my anticipations, you must let me see you at Merton as soon as you know of my arrival there. The Termagant Sloop will be going to Lisbon—she has had a long spell of service. I shall send you in her ; you will find Captain Pettet a very worthy, agreeable companion. He has risen from humble origin by his own merits, with a little of my assistance ; he has a family, too, to maintain from his pay.' The papers and states of the Fleet, which had been accumulating for some time, he had intended to take home himself. ' I shall send them by you,' he said, ' together with my dispatches and letters.' He then gave me the following letter, addressed to Mr. Chamberlain, the Agent at Lisbon. A signal was made for the Termagant to move up to the Victory, and Captain Pettet, repaired on board; having received his instructions, and dined with the Admiral, we, shortly after dinner, took leave, and removed from the Victory to the Termagant.

" Here a trifling incident occurred, illustrative of the character of Nelson, and of his modes of proceeding. After the death of Mr. Lock, at Malta, I found myself in charge of the Affairs, with a large outfit provided for the Levant. As soon as the message was transmitted to me in the Lazaretto at Malta, by Sir Alexander Ball, that I was to join Lord Nelson in the Fleet off Toulon, I began to consider what I could do that might prove useful or gratifying to Lord Nelson, and to his associates, who, I knew, were in want of Naval stores, and who had been during many months afloat, exposed to rough usage and privations, in a tedious blockade. These consisted of two large tierces of the finest English porter, in bottles, thirty-six dozen in each; tongues, Bayonne hams, and some India pickles, &c.; all of which I sent on board the Phœbe Frigate, as presents for the Victory. When Lord Nelson saw the packages, he exclaimed, ' What's all this lumber? What the devil have you got here ?' He seemed hurt at my explanation, ' Only a little ammunition for the Fleet, my Lord;' but directed them to be stowed away carefully; and he told old Gaetano, his Italian steward, to look well after them. Days and weeks passed away, without any of the porter or tongues or hams appearing, either on the Admiral's table, or in the Ward-room of the Victory. This seemed strange, but no remark was made. Soon after we got on board the Termagant, a boat arrived with a letter to Captain Pettet, and one to myself, of which I give the purport, if not the exact words, from memory :—' I have tasted and reserved some of your princely and delicious presents. Had we returned together in the Superb, these should have afforded consolation to all on board that Ship, on our homeward voyage. As our destinies are altered, I have taken the liberty of sending them to Captain Pettet, to whom they will prove highly acceptable; and before you have been long on board, I trust you will think with me, that they could not have been more worthily bestowed. I have added a few bottles of fine Marsala, lately sent me by Wood-house from Sicily, that you may have the pleasure of drinking my health in my absence,' &c. &c.

" Off Cadiz, we joined Admiral Sir John Orde, who, a martyr to the gout, was then in bed, and had not quitted his cabin since he left England, and could not see us, and I delivered to Captain Robinson the following letter to Mr. Chamberlain :]

TO H. CHAMBERLAIN, ESQ., AGENT FOR THE PACKETS AT LISBON.

Victory, November 4th, 1804.

Sir,

Mr. Este has charge of my dispatches for the Admiralty, I have therefore to request that you will get him on board the first Packet bound for England. As no fever or ill health is in the Fleet, I hope the Termagant being directed not to communicate with Gibraltar, or any Ships who have had any communication, since the sickness, with that place, will not be subject to Quarantine; but should she be subject to it, I then request that you will take the proper steps that Mr. Este and my dispatches may get on board the Packet destined for England. Captain Pettet will receive the Gibraltar and Malta mails. I am, Sir, &c.

NELSON AND BRONTE.

TO CAPTAIN ROBERT PETTET, H. M. SLOOP TERMAGANT.

[Order-Book.]

Victory, at Sea, 4th November, 1804.

Having charged Mr. Este (Secretary to the late Mr. Lock) with my Public dispatches for Government, You are hereby required and directed to receive him on board his Majesty's Sloop Termagant, under your command, and proceed with him direct to Lisbon, without calling at, or communicating with Gibraltar; and on your arrival in the Tagus, you will put Mr. Este on board any Packet which may be laying there for England, acquainting the Captain thereof, and also the Agent for Packets that he is charged with my Government dispatches. From the uncertainty of the present state of affairs, the greatest caution is necessary in entering the Tagus, and in communicating with Lisbon, as it is impossible to say what the intentions of the Portuguese may be; you will therefore do so with the utmost care and circumspection, that his Majesty's Sloop under your command may not be brought into any unpleasant situation, from want of a due regard to the necessary precaution. And as I would not, on any account, have you subject yourself to Quarantine, I herewith transmit you an order directed to all Captains and Commanders, not to communicate with the Termagant on any account, till after her return from Lisbon; and not *then*, if they have been at any place where the present dreadful malady is raging. You will therefore pay due regard to this, and regulate your conduct in these particulars accordingly.

Having put Mr. Este on board the Packet, or landed him at Lisbon, if there is none there, you will receive the Mails for Gibraltar and Malta, and return with them with all dispatch; and if you shall learn from any of his Majesty's Ships that the

inhabitants of Gibraltar are become healthy, and that it is perfectly safe to refit there, you will proceed into the Mole, and put
the Termagant in a state for being hove down, and her keel and
other defects in her bottom made good, and new-coppered if
necessary. In performing this service, the utmost dispatch is
to be used, and every means taken to expedite the perfect
equipment of the said Sloop ; but if on your return to Gibraltar, the health of that place is still doubtful, you will land my
Public dispatches through the Lazaretto Ship, and proceed
(without communicating in any other way with that place) to
Valetta Harbour, for the purpose of getting the defects of the
Termagant made good, and put in a perfect state for winter's
cruizing. Having so done, and completed your provisions to
the usual time, you will return and join the Squadron on
Rendezvous No. 97, where you will find me, or orders for
your further proceedings.

                                        NELSON AND BRONTE.

N.B. If the Mails from England for Gibraltar and Malta
are not ready to be delivered, you will on no account wait,
but return as before directed.

TO THE CAPTAINS OR COMMANDERS OF ANY OF HIS MAJESTY'S
    SHIPS OR VESSELS WHICH THE TERMAGANT MAY FALL IN
    WITH.

                        [Order-Book.]

                        Victory, at Sea, 4th November, 1804.

Having sent his Majesty's Sloop Termagant with my Public dispatches to Lisbon, in order that they may be forwarded
from thence with the utmost dispatch, and as the communicating with her previous to her having been to Lisbon, would
not only subject her to Quarantine, under the present dreadful circumstances, but prevent her from putting dispatches on
board the Packet, You are therefore hereby required and
directed, on no account or consideration whatever, to communicate with his Majesty's said Sloop, until her return from
Lisbon.

                                        NELSON AND BRONTE.

TO CAPTAIN GORE, H.M. SHIP MEDUSA.

[Autograph, in the possession of the Right Hon. John Wilson Croker.]

Victory, November 4th, 1804.

My dear Gore,

Esperance is passed on to Madalena, therefore I have not seen her. You will receive a satisfactory order, I hope, for your future movements of the Medusa. The Merchants are tearing me to pieces for Convoys, and I dare not send a Frigate home without one. Indeed, I am positively ordered not to do it. Anson was ordered down when I received your wishes, before the Spanish business. She will be a powerful reinforcement to the Squadron. I wish you could get hold of a First-rate, loaded with money ; not that you or I should get any of it, under the present circumstances, but a few millions would be useful to the State. I am very unwell to-day, and can hardly hold my head up. You will know before me who is my successor. May health and success attend you, my dear Gore, and believe me ever, your obliged and faithful friend,

NELSON AND BRONTE.

We are remarkably healthy as to fevers.

TO CAPTAIN GORE, H.M. SHIP MEDUSA.

[Original, in the possession of the Right Hon. John Wilson Croker.]

Victory, at Sea, 5th November, 1804.

Sir,

I have received your letter of the 9th September last, together with Mr. Frere's, dated the 31st July, and the one therein alluded to from the Spanish Government, relative to the excesses committed by the Enemy's Privateers between Cadiz and Algiers, &c., and I am sorry to find the tardiness with which all our just complaints are treated. I should hope our Minister most strongly demands redress.

The letters from Captains Sutton and Rosenhagen, giving you an account of their proceedings, have also been received ; and I hope Captain Rosenhagen has stated to the Admiralty the conduct of the Master of the Vessel which followed him, and afterwards fell into the hands of the Enemy, as mentioned in his said letter. If he has not, desire he may, and let this be the constant duty of all Officers charged with Convoys, when any of the Vessels improperly leave them. I am, &c.

NELSON AND BRONTE.

TO CAPTAIN RICHARD BUDD VINCENT, H.M. SLOOP ARROW.

[Order-Book.]

Victory, at Sea, 5th November, 1804.

Whereas by the Defects and Report of Survey of his Majesty's Sloop Arrow, under your command, transmitted to me in your letter of the 20th ultimo, there appears an absolute necessity of sending her to England immediately, to be docked; and whereas I have received application for a Convoy to the Ships named on the other side hereof,[1] bound to the United Kingdom, and also been informed that several others may be expected from the different Ports in the Levant and Sicily, about the middle or latter end of this month; You are therefore hereby required and directed to take his Majesty's Bomb-Vessel named in the margin[2] under your command, (whose Captain is directed by the enclosed order to follow your instructions for his further proceedings,) and make the signal for, and take under your convoy and protection, the Merchant-Ships before-mentioned, with such as may have, or shall arrive at Malta, from any Port in the Levant or Sicily, this season, together with any Merchant-Ship or Vessel that may be ready, and bound your way; and when the whole of the Trade from the Levant and Sicily which may be expected for this season shall have arrived, and Captain Schomberg signifies his approbation to your leaving Malta, it is my directions that you take the Acheron with you, and proceed immediately with the whole of the Trade from Valetta harbour, which may be bound to any part of the United Kingdom, with as much expedition as possible, consistent with their safety, direct to England; and on no account or consideration whatever, touch at or go near Gibraltar, or allow any of the Convoy

[1] Andromeda, Castle, Blades, William, Alert, Alert, Helen, bound to Lisbon; Bridget, bound to Hull; Lady Cotton, bound to Ireland; Elizabeth, bound to Leith; Pomona, bound to Liverpool.

[2] Acheron.

under your command, at their peril, to communicate with that
place, or with any Boat or Vessel belonging to it, but proceed
direct through the Straits, and make the best of your way off
Plymouth, where you will leave the Trade bound for Ireland
and the British Channel in safety, to be sent from thence
to their destination by the Commander-in-Chief at Plymouth,
as the Acheron is by no means equal to protect them, or
indeed herself, against a strong Privateer.

Having hove-to sufficient time off the Ram Head, to see the
Ships before-mentioned safe into the entrance of Cawsand Bay
or the Sound, you will proceed on with the Acheron and the
rest of the Convoy to the Downs, dropping such as are bound to
Ports in the Channel, on your way up ; taking care to proportion your rate of going to that of the worst sailing Vessel
under your protection, and on no account part from them, or
leave any of the Trade in danger of being captured by the
Enemy. On your arrival in the Downs, you will acquaint
the Secretary of the Admiralty thereof, and transmit an
account of your proceedings, for their Lordships' information,
and wait there, together with the Acheron, until you receive
their orders for your further government.[3]

NELSON AND BRONTE.

TO CAPTAIN HENRY RICHARDSON, H. M. SHIP JUNO.

[Order-Book.]

Victory, at Sea, 8th November, 1804.

Having received instructions[4] from the Lords Commissioners
of the Admiralty to send a Frigate to such place as may be

---

[3] The Arrow and Acheron never reached England, being, with the Convoy,
intercepted, off Cape Caxine, by two large French Frigates, on the 4th of February
1805, when both those Vessels were captured, after a most determined resistance.

[4] On the 31st of July, 1804, the Admiralty issued an Order to Lord Nelson,
directing him to " hold in readiness, in such Port as may be agreed upon by you
and Mr. Jackson, one of the Ships under your command, for the purpose of conveying his Sardinian Majesty to such Port in the Mediterranean as he may appoint ;
and to adopt such measures for the Naval defence of the Island of Sardinia as may
be best calculated for that purpose, and as may be consistent with the other services entrusted to your care."

agreed upon by me, and Mr. Jackson, his Majesty's Minister to the King of Sardinia, to remove His Sardinian Majesty from Gaeta, or any other place where his Majesty may be residing, to any place within the Mediterranean where the King may think proper, You are therefore hereby required and directed to receive my Public dispatches for his Sardinian Majesty and Mr. Jackson, and proceed with them, in his Majesty's Ship Juno, under your command, to Gaeta, and on your arrival there, you will deliver my letter to the King, and should his Sardinian Majesty desire to be removed to any part of Sicily, Malta, Corfu, or any other place within the Mediterranean, you will receive his Majesty, the Queen, and *suite*, on board the Juno, and proceed to such place as his Majesty shall direct, where you will land him, the Queen, and *suite*, and afterwards proceed to Malta, for the purpose of being refitted. Should his Majesty request you to wait at Gaeta for three or four days, in order to prepare for his embarkation, you will do so, and immediately write Mr. Jackson, at Rome, (when his Majesty's intentions are signified to you,) that his answer may arrive previous to your sailing; and you will also, the instant you anchor at Gaeta, forward my dispatches to Mr. Elliot, at Naples, by express. But should his Sardinian Majesty not desire the Juno to wait for the purpose before mentioned, and signifies the same to you officially, you will proceed immediately to Naples, and receive from his Excellency Mr. Elliot such dispatches as he may have for Sicily or Malta, with which you will proceed, and make the best of your way to Valetta harbour, where you will cause every exertion to be used in refitting and completing the Juno for immediate service, agreeable to the letter herewith transmitted addressed to Commissioner Otway. Having so done, and completed your provisions, &c., to the usual time, you will afterwards return, and join the Squadron on Rendezvous No. 97, where you will find me, or orders for your further proceedings. I must desire to recommend that you will keep a particular account of all your disbursements in the event of his Majesty the King of Sardinia accompanying you, in order that Government may take the same into consideration, and direct your being repaid.

NELSON AND BRONTE.

TO HIS EXCELLENCY HUGH ELLIOT, ESQ.

[Autograph, in the Elliot Papers.]

Victory, November 8th, 1804.

My dear Sir,

Your letters by the Ætna, of the 14th October, were duly
received, and I thank your Excellency for all the interesting
information you are so good as to give me. I can only add
one lamentation more to the uncomfortable situation, to say
no worse of it, of those good Sovereigns of Naples. I never
had but one opinion of Russia, for many years past. I am to
this moment ignorant, except by the French papers, of what
is passing in Spain. What can be expected from such communications to a Naval Commander-in-Chief? Pray return
them: I keep them as curiosities.

I have heard nothing from England since August 28th:
French papers give us the news to October 11th; therefore, I
am left in total ignorance. I shall send a Vessel to Naples the
first arrival from England. She will probably bring out my
successor. I am very unwell, and the wet weather we have
had has done my cough no good.

I have wrote to the Admiralty, and to Lord Melville about
your desire for a Vessel to carry your dispatches: I have
none. The Juno, who goes first to Gaeta, in case the King
of Sardinia should not feel himself safe, will, if his Majesty
does not use her, proceed to Naples, and take any letters you
may have for either Malta or Sicily. The fever has much
abated at Gibraltar and Cadiz. At Malaga it has certainly
ceased, and the Port is expected to be opened. The Fleet is
in most perfect health. Pray, present my humble duty to
their Majesties. They have none that feel for them more
than myself, and they may rely upon me to the last moment
of my breathing. I hope Mrs. Elliot is perfectly recovered,
and beg my respectful compliments. William is very well.
I am ever, my dear Sir, your most obliged and faithful servant,

NELSON AND BRONTE.

TO WILLIAM MARSDEN, ESQ., ADMIRALTY.

[Original, in the Admiralty.]

Victory, at Sea, 8th November, 1804.

Sir,

I herewith transmit you a copy of a letter and paper therein referred to, from Captain Gore, of his Majesty's Ship Medusa, dated the 6th October, (a copy of which, he acquaints me, has also been transmitted to you) giving an account of the capture of three Spanish Frigates with treasure on board, as therein mentioned,[4] which you will be so good as to lay before the Lords Commissioners of the Admiralty, for their information; and, at the same time acquaint their Lordships that I very highly approve of the meritorious conduct of that excellent Officer, Captain Gore, upon the present, as well as upon all former occasions, since he has been under my command, in the important trust of watching the Enemy outside the Straits, and for the great and perfect security which he has afforded with his little Squadron to our Trade to, and from, this Country; and when the very bad state of the Medusa is considered, his constantly keeping at sea previous to this, and after an opportunity offered for his returning to England, with the Spanish Frigate Fama, deserves particular approbation. I am, Sir, &c.

NELSON AND BRONTE.

---

[4] On the 5th of October, 1804, off Cape St. Mary's, near Cadiz, the Indefatigable, Captain Graham Moore; Medusa, Captain John Gore; Amphion, Captain Samuel Sutton; and Lively, Captain Graham Eden Hamond, fell in with the four Spanish Frigates La Medée, bearing the Flag of Don Joseph Bustamente; La Fama, La Clara, and La Mercedes, from South America, laden with treasure and valuable merchandize. Captain Moore communicated to the Spanish Admiral his orders to detain these Ships (vide p. 241, ante), and expressed a wish to do so without bloodshed; but not receiving a satisfactory answer, an Action commenced. In ten minutes, La Mercedes blew up, and the three other Ships soon after surrendered. As Spain was then at peace with England, this affair naturally excited the indignation of the Court of Madrid, and led immediately to a War.

TO CAPTAIN GORE, H.M. SHIP MEDUSA.

[Autograph, in the possession of the Right Hon. John Wilson Croker.]

Most private.   Victory, November 9th, 1804.

My dear Gore,

From my heart do I congratulate you on your share of the capture of the Spanish Frigates; but I own it is mixed with regret that you did not command. However, it [is] a good thing, and I hope before this time you have taken more of them. The *Lima* Ships are loaded with gold. Should you find that I am destined to be here a few months longer, and that the Medusa is in absolute want of going to England, you can apply to Sir Richard Strachan, who will send Medusa to me; and you are sure that, if I can, you shall go home without Convoy, unless[4] *your* rich Prizes. Be assured of my inclination to meet your wishes as much as is possible.

The secret of the capture was perfectly well kept, but one of your Mids wrote a letter to Mr. Williams,[5] and out it all came. I hope Gibraltar is perfectly free from sickness by this time; and that you may very safely send your Prizes, and communicate with the Garrison. The water, I thought, from the Navy tank, was perfectly clear from the Garrison, and you will have, before this time, Transports with provisions and stores. I am very far from well; and what, my dear Gore, are the mines of Peru, compared to health? God bless you, and believe me ever your sincere and obliged friend,

NELSON AND BRONTE.

Captain Moore had no business to take the Amphion;[6] but I dare [say] Sutton wished it. I am distressed for Frigates and Sloops.

[4] *i. e.*, Except.

[5] Lieutenant Edward Williams. Having been in the Victory at Trafalgar, he was made a Commander on the 24th of December, 1805; and he died in that rank in 1843.

[6] Captain Moore stated in a letter to the Admiralty, of the 19th of October, that he ordered the Amphion to England, "for the security of the two Spanish Frigates, La Medée and La Clara."

TO LIEUTENANT ROBERT LLOYD, H.M. SHIP GUERRIER, ON
BOARD L'ESPERANCE.

[Order-Book.]

Victory, at Sea, 9th November, 1804.

You are hereby required and directed to proceed immediately with my Public dispatches to Gibraltar, and on your
arrival there, you will deliver my letter to his Excellency
General Sir Thomas Trigge, and keep those (in case the disease still continues) for the Donegal and Medusa to be forwarded by La Sophie or Halcyon, as early as possible. On
your passage from hence to Gibraltar, I must desire you will
be particularly careful, and not allow the Esperance to be
boarded by any Spanish Ship or Vessel of War, or suffer her
to be placed in any situation under their Forts or Batteries,
or otherwise, that may subject her to detention or capture, as
the intentions of Spain are at this moment very uncertain
with respect to our Country. After having disposed of the
dispatches as above mentioned, you will return to the command of his Majesty's Prison-Ship Guerrier, taking particular
care of the people on board L'Esperance, till an opportunity
offers for joining their proper Ship, and deliver L'Esperance
into the charge of the Halcyon, or her Agents.

NELSON AND BRONTE.

TO SIR ALEXANDER BALL, BART., MALTA.

[Autograph, in the possession of Sir William Keith Ball, Bart.]

Victory, November 10th, 1804.

My dear Ball,

Captain Moore has thought fit to take home with him the
Amphion, and I think very probable he would Gore, had he
not separated from him in pursuit of one of the Spanish Frigates,[7] which, after striking, attempted to get away. Gore, in
a very leaky Ship, would not proceed to England, but sent
the Lively home with her; yet I have no accounts of a War,

_____

[7] La Fama.

and what is more curious, an English Ship from London, which came out under Convoy of the Lively, entered Cadiz, the day of the Action. The Merchants are pulling me to pieces for Convoy, and I have been obliged to order the Arrow (Captain Vincent having made such complaints of her), and the Acheron Bomb, to take charge of the Convoy from Malta. Sir Richard Strachan is gone outside the Straits, and a Frigate must go in the room of the Amphion. The Sophie has so many complaints, that I much doubt her being reparable; but if it is a Spanish War, these gentlemen may not be so anxious to get home. The Admiralty have directed me to keep a Frigate with the King of Sardinia, (I have sent Juno to Gaeta,) and to place a Naval Force for the protection of Sardinia. Sometimes I smile, sometimes I am angry; for in the same packet, Lord Melville says, ' We can send you nothing.' I have before wrote to General Villettes to keep the 2000 Troops ready for embarkation, and I shall touch upon it again.

The Milbrook arrived at Lisbon, October 9th—five days from Falmouth. Mr. Frere[9] received the ultimatum of our Government the 16th. It was to be decisive in twenty-four hours; but 20th he had an audience—no result; and he had the tertian ague. On the 27th he had not had a second audience, saying he was ill, and could not attend to business. Could you believe all this? But it is too true—*shame, shame!* therefore, here I am completely in the dark. I wonder my successor is not arrived: I shall have a winter's passage.

The fever abates at Gibraltar: 500 Troops have died—1612 Inhabitants. At Malaga it has ceased, and at Alicant. Mr. Price, our Pro-Consul at Carthagena, is dead. Deaths at Malaga—Clergy, 114; Friars, 81; Nuns, 76; Physcians, 20;

---

[9] On the 5th of November, Mr. Frere demanded his Passports: on the 27th, the Court of Madrid issued a Decree, stating that the English having attacked Spanish Ships of War, and detained Merchant Vessels, reprisals were to be made on British property; and on the 12th of December, Spain formally declared War against England. On the 19th of December, an Order in Council appeared, forbidding any British Ship to enter any Port of Spain, and directing a general Embargo to be laid on all Spanish Ships in the Ports of Great Britain, which was followed on the 11th of January, 1805, by a Declaration of War.

Troops in Garrison, 1206; African Corps, 101; Individuals, 19,843.

God bless you, my dear Ball; ever most faithfully your friend,

NELSON AND BRONTE.

TO CAPTAIN WILLIAM DURBAN, H.M. SHIP AMBUSCADE.

[Order-Book.]

Victory, at Sea, 12th November, 1804.

You are hereby required and directed to proceed immediately, with his Majesty's Ship Ambuscade under your command, off Barcelona, and send an Officer on shore with my Public dispatches, herewith transmitted to Mr. Gibert, his Majesty's Pro-Consul at that place, with directions to wait in his Boat until the Pro-Consul has answered my letters; and the moment he has received it, with such other letters, &c., as Mr. Gibert may have to send, you will direct his immediate return to the Ambuscade. In the meantime, you will send an Officer to an English Merchant-Vessel laying at Barcelona, who, I should suppose, from the late circular letter from Mr. Hunter, would be desirous of quitting that place; and in case the Master of her should be so disposed, it is my directions that you take the said Vessel under your protection, and convoy her to the Fleet: otherwise, you will demand his reasons for not accompanying you, in writing. As you are apprised of the doubtful intentions of Spain, it is not necessary to recommend the greatest caution in performing this service, which you will do with as much expedition as possible, and join me on Rendezvous No. 97 with all dispatch.

NELSON AND BRONTE.

TO WILLIAM MARSDEN, ESQ., ADMIRALTY.

[Autograph, in the Admiralty.]

Victory, off Barcelona, November 15th, 1804.

Sir,

The appearances of a rupture with Spain induced me to proceed off this place, in hopes of hearing from his Majesty's Minister at the Court of Madrid; or, should he not think it

proper to write to me, that I might be able to form a judgment
whether War or Peace was likely to take place, of the uncertainty which, for some weeks past, has prevailed. For this
purpose I sent the Fisgard to Rosas for the purpose of watching, and desiring water and refreshments. The Governor
seemed very anxious that he should anchor between the Forts,
when he told the Officer the Ship should be furnished with
whatever she wanted. In short, his conduct, from rudeness,
was so polite, that no doubt was entertained in Lord Mark
Kerr's mind of the views of the Spanish Governor, and he
joined me last night.

The Ambuscade, which I stationed off Barcelona, joined
me this morning, with a Merchant Brig which was lying in
Barcelona Roads. She was yesterday, on her attempting to
join the Ambuscade, fired at by the batteries, and very much
damaged, but she escaped. The enclosed letter from Mr.
Frere has made me give orders for the general seizure of all
Spanish Vessels, whether of War or Merchandize. I have the
honour to be, &c.

NELSON AND BRONTE.

The Fleet is perfection itself. We have just captured a
complete Regiment going to Minorca.[1]

TO THE RESPECTIVE CAPTAINS AND COMMANDERS OF HIS
MAJESTY'S SHIPS AND VESSELS ON THE MEDITERRANEAN
STATION.

[From a Copy in the Admiralty.]

Victory, at Sea, 15th November, 1804.

Whereas Hostilities[2] have commenced between Great Britain
and the Court of Spain ; You are hereby required and di-

---

[1] " Thursday, 15th November. A.M. Boarded an Imperial Ship from Barcelona.
At 7·15, Ætna boarded a Spanish Bark, having Troops onboard. At 9·30, Am-
buscade boarded a Vessel under Spanish colours, having troops onboard. At 10·30,
Spencer boarded a Ship, under Russian colours, having Spanish troops onboard."
—*Victory's Log.* " On the 18th of November, Lord Nelson sent the Officers, &c.
belonging to the Spanish Regiment onboard a Swedish Ship for Barcelona."—*Ibid.*
" Monday, 19th November. A.M. At 7·20, Excellent detained the Bona Adventura
Spanish Schooner of War."—*Ibid.*

[2] The Batteries of Barcelona having, as Lord Nelson supposed, fired on an English Brig ; but it appears, from his letter to Mr. Marsden, of the 23rd of November,
that he had been misinformed. Vide p. 277, post.

rected, on falling in with any Spanish Ship or Vessel of War,
or Merchantman belonging to the Subjects of his Catholic
Majesty, or which may have Spanish property on board, and
on doing so, you will use your utmost endeavour to capture,
seize, burn, sink, or destroy them. In the event of your capturing any of their Merchant Vessels, or which may have
Spanish property on board, I must desire that the strictest
orders are given to the Officers sent into Port with such Merchant Vessels, to see that their hatches are immediately locked
and sealed up, and also that all the Ship's papers are sealed
up and taken care of, that no embezzlement of any kind whatever do take place, as they will answer the contrary at their
peril. As condemnation cannot take place until his Majesty's
pleasure is signified, it is my most positive directions that all
Vessels having perishable cargoes on board are, immediately
on their arrival in Port, delivered into the hands of the Vice-
Admiralty Court, to be disposed of as the Judge shall think
proper to direct.

NELSON AND BRONTE.

———————

TO CAPTAIN HILLYAR, H.M. SHIP NIGER.

[From a Copy in the Admiralty.]

Victory, at Sea, 15th November, 1804.

You are hereby required and directed to proceed with the
utmost expedition, in his Majesty's Ship Niger, under your
command, through the Straits and off Cape Spartel, where
you may expect to meet his Majesty's Ship Donegal, or
between that and Cape St. Vincent, and on joining her, you
will deliver my letter, herewith transmitted, to Captain Sir
Richard John Strachan, Bart., put yourself under his command, and follow his orders for your further proceedings. In
the event of your falling in with any Spanish Ship or Vessel
of War, or Merchantman, on your way to join the Donegal,
you will detain her, and send her to Gibraltar or Malta, as
may be most convenient, agreeable to the copy of my general
order of this date, herewith delivered.

NELSON AND BRONTE.

If you see either Halcyon or Sophie, they will probably be

able to tell exactly the position Sir Richard Strachan may have taken. Keep company with the Tigre until you are past Cape de Gatte, and Captain Hallowell makes the signal to separate.

TO THE RESPECTIVE CAPTAINS AND COMMANDERS OF HIS MAJESTY'S SHIPS AND VESSELS ON THE MEDITERRANEAN STATION.

[From a Copy in the possession of Miss Bolton, of Burnham.]

Victory, at Sea, [about 15th] November, 1804.

Whereas I judge it proper, under the present uncertain state of affairs between Great Britain and the Court of Spain, that all Spanish Ships and Vessels of War, as well as the Trade of his Catholic Majesty, shall be detained till further orders, You are hereby required and directed to detain all Spanish Ships and Vessels of War, or Merchantmen (Vessels laden with corn excepted) belonging to the Subjects of his Catholic Majesty, which you may fall in with, and send them either to Gibraltar or Malta, as circumstances shall render necessary; but I must desire that the Masters and such of the Crews of the said Vessels as may be left on board and sent into Port, are treated with the utmost attention, and allowed to remain in their respective Vessels, under the necessary precaution, till further orders: and it is my most positive directions that the Officers sent into Port with such detained Vessels, see that their hatches are immediately locked and sealed up, and that all the Ship's papers are likewise sealed up, and kept in the Officer's possession, till orders are given for their being delivered up to their owners, or otherwise disposed of; and on no account or consideration whatever, to suffer any part of their cargoes to be taken away, or otherwise embezzled, as they will answer the contrary at their peril.

Vessels whether Neutral, or belonging to the Subjects of his Catholic Majesty, laden with corn, are not to be detained for the present, but suffered to proceed to their destination, (if to any Port in Spain,) as mentioned in their Lordships' order, dated the 24th August 1804, and issued to the Fleet on the 4th October following.

TO CAPTAIN BENJAMIN HALLOWELL, H. M. SHIP TIGRE.

[From a Copy in the possession of Miss Bolton, of Burnham.]

[About 15th November, 1804.]

You are, in consequence of the circumstances above stated,[3] hereby required and directed to take his Majesty's Ship named in the margin under your command, and proceed immediately with her off Cape de Gatte, and in the event of falling in with the Spanish Frigates above-mentioned[4] (as the object of their cruizing must certainly be with hostile intentions against the Trade of his Majesty's Subjects) you will use your best endeavours to capture them, should they attempt to resist ; otherwise you will detain and bring them with you to the Fleet, until such time as the result of the present misunderstanding between Great Britain and the Court of Spain shall be officially known. In the execution of this service, should you fall in with any Spanish Merchant-Ship or Vessel, (those laden with corn excepted,) it is my directions that you detain her, and send her to Gibraltar or Malta, as you may from circumstances find necessary ; but I must desire to recommend that the Masters and Crews of the said Vessels which may be left on board them and sent into Port, are treated with the utmost attention, and allowed to remain in their respective Vessels, under the necessary precautions until further orders. And you will give the most strict and positive orders to the Officers sent in with such detained Vessels, to see that their hatches are locked and sealed up, and on no account or consideration whatever, suffer any part of their cargoes to be taken away, or otherwise embezzled ; and likewise that all the Ship's papers are sealed up, and reserved in the Officers' possession till called for, as they will answer the contrary at their peril. Vessels, whether Neutral or belonging to the Subjects of his Catholic Majesty, laden with corn, are not to be detained for the present, but suffered to proceed to their destination, (if to any Port in Spain,) as mentioned in their Lordships' order, dated the 24th August 1804, and issued to the Fleet on the 4th October following.

Should you not find any Spanish Ships or Vessels of War

---

[3] The former part of this Order is not preserved.

[4] Vide p. 280, post.

cruizing off Cape de Gatte, you may proceed a few leagues
further to the Westward, and after having delivered my order,
herewith transmitted, to Captain　　　　　, you will return
and join the Squadron on Rendezvous No. 97, with all expedition, where you will find me, or orders for your further
proceedings.

NELSON AND BRONTE.

TO . . . . . .

[Autograph draught, in the possession of Miss Bolton, of Burnham.]

[About 15th November, 1804.]

Having, on November 10th, received from John Hunter,
Esq., H.M.Consul-General at Madrid, a letter, dated November
3rd, enclosing a copy of his circular letter to the Consuls in
all the Ports in Spain, stating that Mr. Frere had, on the 2nd
November, repeated his demands for satisfaction upon certain
points, and that if a satisfactory answer was not speedily returned, he is determined to leave this Court, and proceed on
his return to London, and that he should not fail to acquaint the Consuls when this important business is finally
decided; And not having received any accounts from Mr. H.
since his letter of November 3rd, I have every reason to believe that no further communication is permitted by the
Spanish Government, and from the recent conduct of the
Spaniards . . . [*Imperfect.*]

TO [THE COMMISSIONERS OF THE NAVY?]

[From a Copy in the possession of Mrs. Conway.]

Victory, at Sea, 20th November, 1804.

Gentlemen,

In further answer to your Letter of the 25th June last, relative to my opinion of the Guernsey jackets of a new manu-
facture, as therein-mentioned, (which were issued to the
Seamen on the 14th October,) and what further supply of
them may be necessary for the Squadron under my command,
I must beg leave to observe that the quality of the said

Guernsey jackets is most excellent, but that they are considerably too narrow and short to be tucked into the Men's trowsers.
It is, therefore, my opinion, that they ought to be at least three
inches wider, and six longer. Indeed, if they were ten inches
or a foot, it would be so much better, as they shrink very considerably in washing; and when the Seamen are on the yards,
reefing or furling sails, the jacket rubs out of their trowsers,
and exposes them to great danger of taking cold in their loins;
so that, with this alteration, which is particularly necessary,
they certainly would be the best and most valuable slops that
ever were introduced into the Service, and be the means of
saving many a good Seaman's life. With respect to the quantity required, it would not be too many to send out one for
every Seaman in the Fleet. Perhaps the Guernsey jacket,
in its present state, might answer the largest of the boys. I
am, Gentlemen, &c.

NELSON AND BRONTE.

TO WILLIAM MARSDEN, ESQ., ADMIRALTY.

[Original, in the Admiralty.]

Victory, at Sea, 20th November, 1804.

Sir,

You will please to acquaint the Lords Commissioners of
the Admiralty, that the Squadron under my command detained
the Spanish Schooner Ventura, off Barcelona, yesterday morning; and as she is a remarkably fine Vessel, well found,
mounting eight brass four-pounders, and in every respect calculated for the service of this Country, it is my intention to
send her to Malta to be surveyed; and if found in good condition, to be valued, and taken into his Majesty's Service, as
Vessels of this description are particularly wanted on this
station, which I hope will meet their Lordships' approbation.

You will also please to acquaint their Lordships that the
Squadron detained this forenoon a large Dutch-built Ship,
upwards of three hundred and eight tons, bound to Barcelona,
laden, with knees, floor, and compass timbers, for the Spanish
Navy, which I have sent to the Naval Yard at Malta, in order
that Commissioner Otway may keep such part of it as may be

wanted for his Majesty's Ships on this station, and send the rest to England (should he be required to do so) after he has seen and examined it.   I am, &c.

NELSON AND BRONTE.

TO WILLIAM MARSDEN, ESQ., ADMIRALTY.

[Original, in the Admiralty.]

Victory, at Sea, November 20th, 1804.

Sir,

In my letter of the 15th instant, I informed you that an English Brig that was laying at Barcelona, on attempting to join the Ambuscade, was fired upon by the batteries, and very much damaged: this was an information I received previous to that Ship's joining me; and there being an English Vessel at Barcelona, which I had directed Captain Durban to bring out with him, from the suspicious conduct of Spain, I gave full credit to the report. I have since, however, been informed otherwise, and that the English Vessel alluded to was sent from Barcelona to perform quarantine at Mahon, but on her attempting to enter that place, she was fired upon by the batteries, and very much damaged—perhaps from its being considered she had the plague aboard, or come from some place where it was raging. The said Vessel afterwards fell in with the Ambuscade, and joined the Squadron in company with her. I judge it proper to clear up this mistake, lest hereafter it may become a matter of public discussion with Spain.   I am, &c.

NELSON AND BRONTE.

TO ALEXANDER DAVISON, ESQ.

[Autograph, in the possession of Colonel Davison.]

Victory, November 23rd, 1804.

My dear Davison,

Why my successor is not arrived, I cannot guess. A Spanish War, I should have thought would have been a spur to him. I am likely to have the very coldest month (January) to arrive in; and in that case I am fearful that March or April would suit me better. I never did, or ever shall, desert the service of my Country; but what can I do more than serve till I drop. If I take some little care of myself, I may yet live to perform some good service. My cough is very bad, and it brings forth the effect of my blow of the 14th February.[4] We are a little alert at the prospect of the French Fleet putting to sea: I yet hope it will happen before my departure. How are you? Keep up your spirits. Remember me kindly to Nepean. He is at the Board, I suppose, long before this time. I am expecting a Vessel from England every moment. It is now two months since the John Bull sailed. God bless you, my dear Davison, and believe me ever your most faithful and affectionate friend,

NELSON AND BRONTE.

TO LADY HAMILTON.

[From "Lord Nelson's Letters to Lady Hamilton," vol. ii. p. 83.]

Victory, November 23rd, 1804.

As all our communication with Spain is at an end, I can now only expect to hear from my own dear Emma by the very slow mode of Admiralty Vessels, and it is now more than two months since the John Bull sailed. I much fear, something has been taken; for they never would, I am sure, have kept me so long in the dark. However, by management, and a portion of good luck, I got the account from Madrid, in a much shorter space of time than I could have hoped for; and I have set the whole Mediterranean to work, and think the Fleet cannot fail of being successful; and if I had had the spare Troops at Malta at my disposal, Minorca would at this moment have had English colours flying. . . . . . Where is my successor? I am not a little surprised at his not arriving! A Spanish War, I thought, would have hastened him. Ministers could not have thought that I wanted to fly the Service; my whole life has proved the contrary: and if they refuse me now, I shall most certainly leave this Country in March or April; for a few months' rest I must have, very soon. If I am in my grave, what are the mines of Peru to me! But, to say the truth, I have no idea of killing myself. I may, with

---

[4] The Battle of St. Vincent.

care, live yet to do good service to the State. My cough is
very bad; and my side, where I was struck on the 14th of
February, is very much swelled; at times, a lump as large as
my fist, brought on occasionally by violent coughing; but I
hope and believe my lungs are yet safe. Sir William Bolton
is just arrived from Malta. I am preparing to send him a
cruise, where he will have the best chance I can give him of
making ten thousand pounds. He is a very attentive, good,
young man.
    I have not heard from Naples this age. I have, in fact, no
Small Craft to send for news. If I am soon to go home, I
shall be with you before this letter...... As our means of
communicating are cut off, I have only to beg you will not
believe the idle rumours of Battles, &c......

TO COMMISSIONER OTWAY, GIBRALTAR.

[Autograph, in the possession of Rear-Admiral Inglefield, C.B.]

Victory, November 24th, 1804.
My dear Sir,
    Yesterday the Childers brought me your letter of the 5th,
and I have dispatched her to Gibraltar; for I have not heard
from that place since October 22nd. I had then a letter from
one of the great men of the Rock—Joe King.[5] He says all
the Clerks except one are dead; that he is fatigued with
burying the dead; and that they are all much obliged by
Mr. Pownall's[6] attention. I therefore am anxious to hear that
even the Rock is in our possession.
    I send Mr. Jones, Boatswain of the Victory. He is an in-
valuable man; and should you want a Builder, I can say as
much, or more, for Mr. Bunce, Carpenter of the Victory.
Nature, I am sure, has fitted him for such a place. Keats
dines here to-day, and I will see if he chooses to send his
man, which I thought he had arranged with you, when with
the Fleet. You are so attentive to all our wants, that I am
sure you will very soon procure canvas for us. Captain

---

[5] Boatswain of the Dock Yard at Gibraltar. Vide vol. i. p. 257.
[6] Mr. Edward Pownall, the Naval Officer at Gibraltar.

Hardy has a mizen-topsail made of Neapolitan canvas. It has been five months in wear, and as we have the custom of laying-to with that sail, it has had much wear, and we find it very excellent, and far preferable to English canvas; for as there is no gum or size to fill up the pores, it does not mildew. Captain Hardy desires me to say that our top-lining is of Neapolitan canvas, which bears the beating much better than the harsh English canvas. I fear Mr. James, at Naples has not been latterly so correct in the materials for making beds; but none of these people can be trusted.

Will you write about Mr. Lawson to the Navy Board? He must consider that he cannot be an Agent, if appointed Master-Attendant. I never saw Mr. Eaton, but my opinion of him was formed some years ago; and from all I hear, I have no reason to alter it. He is, as Burke said of a noble Marquis, ' a giant in promises, a pigmy in performances.' I have repeatedly wrote to the Navy Board about Muster-paper. How can they expect the regular Monthly Books? But I will renew the application, although, in general, they attend more to a Brother Commissioner than a Sailor-man.

I much fear, my dear Commissioner, that I did not pay you all that attention that I wished. Our weather was bad, and I had you not on board the Victory, (although our friend took more real care of you than I could,) which was wrong. We have a report of three Spanish Frigates being off Cape de Gatte. I have sent Hallowell to take them, with Fisgard and Niger; and if the report is true, he will do it. I congratulate you upon your very fortunate escape from Gibraltar; and that good fortune in every other way may equally attend you, is the very sincere wish of, my dear Sir, your much obliged,

NELSON AND BRONTE.

The Schooner, with the Boatswain, and working foreman of the Blacksmiths, will go to Malta in a few days.

TO SIR ALEXANDER JOHN BALL, BART.

[Autograph, in the possession of Sir William Keith Ball, Bart.]

Victory, November 25th, 1804.

Most Secret.

My dear Ball,

A Lieutenant, late of the Bittern, who came down in the Childers, told me, that in the Mouth of the Adriatic they fell in with the Algerine Fleet, consisting of three Frigates and nine Corvettes; but as Captain Corbet has not mentioned it, I should almost doubt it, but from the circumstantial account Lieutenant Nicholas[7] gave. Now, if this is really so, I should like to know it, and if they are still at sea, for I have the *very* greatest inclination, if I could lay my hands upon the whole Fleet, to way-lay them, for they have, in my opinion, insulted us beyond what we ought to have suffered. I never would have given up a single point, for it only encourages them in their more insolent demands. But if you can tell me that his Cruizers have this year taken a single Maltese Vessel, I will try and take or destroy his whole Fleet, for I can stretch over to the Coast of Barbary, between Tunis and Algiers; but I will not strike unless I can hit him hard, for I would sooner allow two or three of his small Cruizers to pass unmolested than to give the scoundrel an idea of my intentions. *All* or *none*, is my motto.

I shall send the Schooner in a few days; this Settee[8] is the Majorca Packet, and sails very fast. She would be, I should think, a more effectual Vessel for taking the small Privateers upon the Coast of Sicily than any of the Schooners, and would, with very little expense, make a proper Malta Government Vessel. I am ever, my dear Ball, most faithfully yours,

NELSON AND BRONTE.

Capel thinks the French Fleet is upon the point of sailing from Toulon. I am ready for them.

[7] Vide p. 199, ante.

[8] A Spanish Settee, which was captured by the Prize Schooner Bona Adventura, a few days before.

TO WILLIAM MARSDEN, ESQ., ADMIRALTY.

[Original, in the Admiralty.]

Victory, at Sea, 26th November, 1804.

Sir,

Having, in my letter of the 20th instant, acquainted you, for the information of the Lords Commissioners of the Admiralty, that the Squadron under my command had detained the Spanish Schooner Ventura, which appeared in every respect well calculated for the service of this Country, you will please to acquaint their Lordships that as Vessels of her description are particularly wanted for the service of Malta, I have ordered her to be commissioned, and placed under the immediate direction of Sir Alexander Ball; and as Officers who have been employed in such Vessels are best calculated to command them, I have, at his own request, and the particular recommendation of Captain Sotheron, appointed Lieutenant Edward Giles,[9] of the Excellent, who has been on this kind of service before; and have given Mr. Andrew Reddie,[1] of the Victory, an order to act as Lieutenant of the Excellent, in his room. I herewith transmit you copies of the said Acting Orders, which I request you will be so good as to lay before the Lords Commissioners of the Admiralty for their information, and move their Lordships to confirm them. I am, &c.

NELSON AND BRONTE.

TO COMMISSIONER OTWAY, GIBRALTAR.

[Autograph, in the possession of Rear-Admiral Inglefield, C.B.]

Victory, December 1st, 1804.

My dear Sir,

The Schooner is far too heavily gunned; therefore I beg the four eight-pounders may be taken from her, and if her barricado could be nearly all taken away, she would be much better for the service she is destined for, of sailing and rowing. When you get supplies of copper, I would have her

---

[9] Lieutenant Edward Giles obtained that rank in March 1799, became a Retired Commander in December 1830, and died about 1842.

[1] Mr. Andrew Reddie died a Lieutenant between 1809 and 1814.

coppered, or she would require a clean tallowed bottom every six weeks. Hallowell has not been very fortunate. Tigre, Fisgard, and Niger have taken, *in toto*, about £20,000. Admiral Campbell has been very unwell, but is better. I hope Malta agrees with you. Nothing from England for seventy-two days! I am, my dear Sir, ever your most obliged, humble servant,

NELSON AND BRONTE.

TO WILLIAM MARSDEN, ESQ., ADMIRALTY.

[Original, in the Admiralty.]

Victory, at Sea, 1st December, 1804.

Sir,

I herewith transmit you the copy of a letter from Captain Corbet, of his Majesty's Sloop Bittern, together with the one therein alluded to, addressed to Captain Cracraft, of the Anson, giving an account of the capture of a small Privateer, mounting one gun, by the Boats of the said Sloop, on the Coast of Ragusa, which you will please to lay before the Lords Commissioners of the Admiralty for their information. I am concerned to observe that piracy is so much sanctioned in these seas by the Neutral Powers, which nothing but the strongest remonstrances can prevent. I am, Sir, &c.

NELSON AND BRONTE.

TO CAPTAIN KEATS, H.M. SHIP SUPERB.

[Autograph, in the possession of the Rev. Richard Keats.]

Victory, December 3rd, 1804.

My dear Sir,

I suppose, by the arrival of Sir John Orde[2] in our vicinity, that I may very soon be your troublesome guest;[3] therefore, that I may not hurry your Ship too much, I shall, with your leave, send some of my wine to the Superb this morning—fourteen casks, and about eleven or twelve cases; but, my

---

[2] Vice-Admiral Sir John Orde, who has been frequently mentioned, was appointed Commander-in-Chief of a Squadron off Cadiz, which station had previously formed part of Lord Nelson's command, in October 1804.

[3] Lord Nelson intended to return to England in the Superb.

dear Sir, there are so many things that I have to intrude upon
your goodness for, that I hardly see how to make you any
amends for the trouble I shall give. We shall lay to; therefore, will you come on board this morning, and you will very
much oblige,

NELSON AND BRONTE.

TO REAR-ADMIRAL CAMPBELL.[3]

[From a Copy in the Admiralty.]

Victory, December 4th, 1804.

Sir,

It was with the sincerest sorrow that I received your letter
of yesterday's date, stating the melancholy account of your
bad state of health, and that in your opinion it was absolutely
necessary you should go immediately to England for its re-
establishment, of which opinion I find is also the Physician of
the Fleet and other Medical Gentlemen. I shall therefore
order the very first Frigate[4] that comes to the Fleet, to bear
your Flag, and to proceed with you to such Port in England
as you shall direct her Captain; and I do most sincerely hope
that your health will be soon re-established, and that you
will very shortly be again at sea, where you have so long
served with both honour and advantage to your King and
Country; and I beg you to be assured that my most sincere
good wishes will ever attend you, and that I am, with the highest
esteem and regard, Sir, your most faithful and affectionate
Servant,   NELSON AND BRONTE.

TO REAR-ADMIRAL GEORGE CAMPBELL, H.M. SHIP CANOPUS.

[From a Copy in the Admiralty.]

Victory, at Sea, 4th December, 1804.

Having directed the Captain of his Majesty's Ship Ambuscade to put himself under your command, and follow your
orders for his further proceedings, you are hereby required

---

[3] Rear-Admiral Campbell died an Admiral of the Red, and a Grand Cross of the
Bath, on the 23rd of January, 1821.

[4] The Ambuscade, Captain Durban, having rejoined the Squadron at Noon, on
the 4th, Lord Nelson ordered her to take Rear-Admiral Campbell home.

and instructed to shift your Flag from his Majesty's Ship
Canopus into his Majesty's Ship Ambuscade, and proceed
direct to any Port in England, which you may find most convenient; and on your arrival you will direct Captain Durban,
of the said Ship, to wait at such Port until he receives their
Lordships' orders for his further proceedings.

NELSON AND BRONTE.

TO WILLIAM MARSDEN, ESQ., ADMIRALTY.

[Original, in the Admiralty.]

Victory, at Sea, 4th December, 1804.

Sir,

You will please to acquaint the Lords Commissioners of
the Admiralty, that there has no particular occurrence happened in the Squadron, since my letter to you of the 15th
ultimo, only the detention of two or three Spanish Vessels,
which have been sent to Malta; one of them, the Pearl, from
Buenos Ayres and Monte Video, had upwards of 106,000
dollars on board, in gold and silver, and otherwise a valuable
cargo. By a letter from Minorca to Barcelona, detained by
the Squadron, it appears by some of the intercepted letters,
that they have been some time expecting a War with England,
and have been putting the Forts of that Island, and their
Gun-boats, &c. in a state for active defence; but I am perfectly satisfied that no succour of Troops has yet been landed
on that Island. I am, Sir, &c.

NELSON AND BRONTE.

TO SIR ALEXANDER JOHN BALL, BART., MALTA.

[Autograph, in the possession of Sir Willam Keith Ball, Bart.]

Victory, December 5th, 1804.

My dear Ball,

No Sir John Orde, no orders, no letters from England;
very extraordinary. I almost begin to think that he is sent
off Cadiz to reap the golden harvest, as Campbell was sent off
Cadiz by Cornwallis (by orders from England) to reap my
sugar harvest. It's very odd, two Admiralties to treat me so:
surely I have dreamt that I have ' done the State some ser-

vice.' But never mind; I am superior to those who could
treat me so. When am I to be relieved? Seventy-six days
since my last letter from the Admiralty. Poor Admiral
Campbell sailed yesterday for England, very ill with debility,
hectic fever, &c., but he cheered up on going away. I shall
not trouble you with all my conjectures about Sir John Orde's
never communicating with me for the three weeks he has
been off Cadiz. I am ever, my dear Ball, yours most faithfully,

NELSON AND BRONTE.

A Man of War is in sight, South.

TO WILLIAM MARSDEN, ESQ., ADMIRALTY.

[Original, in the Admiralty. "Wednesday, 13th December. P.M. At 10, shortened sail, and came to in Pula Roads, in thé Gulf of Cagliari. Squadron anchored
and moored per Signal."]

Victory, in Pula Bay, Sardinia, 14th December, 1804.

Sir,

I herewith transmit you a copy of an acting order which I
have this day given to Mr. George Magrath,[4] Surgeon of his
Majesty's Ship Victory, to be Surgeon of his Majesty's Naval
Hospital at Gibraltar, in the room of the late Mr. William
Burd, which you will be so good as lay before the Lords Commissioners of the Admiralty for their information; and I beg
that you will acquaint their Lordships, that the conduct and
very great professional abilities of this deserving Officer, merits
my most full and entire approbation; not only in the discharge of his duty as Surgeon of the Victory, which reflects
great credit on his knowledge, but also in several particular
Surgical cases which he has performed with infinite judgment
and skill. I therefore presume to hope their Lordships will
confirm the appointment, as none can fill his intended [situa-
tion] with more credit to himself and benefit to the Public
service. I am, Sir, &c.

NELSON AND BRONTE.

⁴ Now Sir George Magrath, K.H. Mr. Magrath was succeeded as Surgeon of
the Victory, by Mr. William (afterwards Dr. Sir William) Beatty, who was previously Surgeon of the Spencer.

TO COMMISSIONER OTWAY, GIBRALTAR.

[Autograph, in the possession of Rear-Admiral Inglefield, C.B.]

Victory, 14th December, 1804.

Sir,

Having thought it proper to appoint a Captain and Officers to the Spanish Frigate Amphitrite,[5] I have therefore to request that you will give such directions as may be necessary for surveying her hull, masts, and stores; and you will also be pleased to place her on the same establishment as the Endymion. I am, Sir, &c.

NELSON AND BRONTE.

TO CAPTAIN SAMUEL SUTTON, H.M. SHIP AMPHION.

[Autograph, in the possession of Captain Ives Sutton.]

Victory, December 14th, 1804.

My dear Sutton,

The Purser of the Niger will be appointed to the Amphion, and will go down the very first opportunity after his survey. I have had a letter from Lieutenant Gates, saying that he wishes to go to England, and that he is a supernumerary Lieutenant on board the Amphion, she being only allowed *three* in War. If that *is so*, you may discharge him, writing an account to the Admiralty of your reasons, and directing his attendance at the Admiralty. For your and Hardy's sake,[6] I wish you had been more fortunate; for my own, if you can destroy Privateers and Ships of War, I care not for Prizes. I do not think you will have a Spanish War. I rejoice you like the Amphion; so do I the Victory. Not a Ship here can beat her in moderate weather. We shall see and feel the French Fleet very soon. I am, dear Sutton, always your obliged and faithful friend,

NELSON AND BRONTE.

[5] The Amphitrite was detained, or rather captured, by the Donegal, off Cadiz, on the 23rd of October, vide p. 292, post. Lord Nelson promoted Sir William Bolton into the Amphitrite.

[6] Captains Sutton and Hardy had agreed to share Prize-money, by which arrangement the latter gained some thousand pounds.

TO VICE-ADMIRAL SIR JOHN ORDE, BART., COMMANDER-IN-CHIEF OF A SQUADRON OFF CADIZ.

[From a Copy in the Admiralty.]

Victory, in Pula Bay, Sardinia, 16th December, 1804.

Sir,

Yesterday I received the honour of your letter, dated November 17th, off Cadiz, by his Majesty's Ship Anson, in which you are pleased to inform me that you arrived off that Port, in the Chief Command of a Squadron of his Majesty's Ships, and shall probably continue on that station some time. I have, therefore, only to request that you will have the goodness to give me timely information when you are likely to leave the station off Cadiz, that I may, as I am directed by the Lords Commissioners of the Admiralty, place a proper Squadron on that part of the station, hitherto under my orders. I have the honour to be, &c.

NELSON AND BRONTE.

TO HIS EXCELLENCY HUGH ELLIOT, ESQ.

[Autograph, in the Elliot Papers. " Monday, 17th December. A.M. At 5, weighed and made sail out of Pula Roads, as did the Squadron. Termagant rejoined." " Tuesday, 18th December. P.M. At 1·30, anchored in the Gulf of Palma. Squadron anchored here." " Wednesday, 19th December. P.M. At 1, unmoored: at 4, weighed and made sail out of Palma."]

Victory, December 19th, 1804.

Sir,

I send your Excellency a letter from Captain Corbet, of his Majesty's Sloop Bittern, together with the account of the Master, taken upon oath; and your Excellency will not fail to acquaint the Chevalier Micheroux of my surprise, as I am sure it will be of yours, to find that no complaint was preferred against the Officer of the Bittern, from the Minister or Consul of any Nation, of the Vessels boarded, for no French Vessel was boarded ;[6] and the Chevalier will, I hope, be desired by your Excellency to be more circumspect in accusing his Majesty's Officers, and be sure that the French Minister speaks truth, before he makes his complaint to your Excellency. I have the honour to be, &c.

NELSON AND BRONTE.

[6] Vide p. 224, ante.

TO HIS EXCELLENCY HUGH ELLIOT, ESQ.

[Autograph, in the Elliot Papers.]

Victory, December 19th, 1804.

My dear Sir,

Since I wrote you last November, I have not had any Vessel with the Fleet which I could detach to Naples, and I have been the less anxious, as I heard from Captain Cracraft, of the Anson, that everything was as usual when he left it, November 7th. The Termagant is the first Vessel which has come to me, and I send Captain Pettet to inquire how you get on. Since the Spanish hostilities—for I hardly know whether I am to call it War—I have not had the smallest communication with the Continent; therefore I am in most total darkness. I received yesterday the enclosed from Sir John Orde. I have learnt not to be surprised at anything; but the sending an Officer to such a point, to take, if it is a Spanish War, the whole harvest, after all my toils (God knows unprofitable enough! for I am a much poorer man than when we started in the Amphion,[1]) seems a little hard; but *patienza.* I suppose Sir John, in the end, will command here. I am but very, very so-so. My cough, if not soon removed, will stay by me for ever. On the 12th, the French Fleet were safe in Toulon; but I am firmly of opinion before this day fortnight they will be at sea. What would I give to know their destination! But I must take my chance, and I hope my usual good fortune will attend me. On the 14th of January, I shall be at Madalena; therefore if you want to send over in a Neapolitan Corvette any dispatches, it will be sure to find me there for some days—perhaps, a fortnight or upwards. That position secures Sicily and Naples, and you will assure their Majesties that must be an object ever most near my heart. It is now ninety days since I have heard from England; it is rather long at these critical times. Sir John Orde has three Cutters, and four or five fine Brigs attached to his Squadron; but, no; not one for me. *Such things are.* I am ever, my dear Sir, your Excellency's most faithful and obedient servant,

NELSON AND BRONTE.

[1] Mr. Elliot accompanied Lord Nelson from England in the Victory and Amphion.

TO HIS EXCELLENCY HUGH ELLIOT, ESQ.

[Autograph, in the Elliot Papers.]

Victory, December 19th, 1804.

Private.

My dear Sir,

William is very well, and Captain Parker likes him very much. The Amazon has been so little with us, that I have not seen him; but I shall, very probably, before this letter goes off. Anything like complaints against the Sicilian Government vexes me very much; but the encouragement of what can be called nothing short of piracy in the Governor of Syracuse, is indeed of very serious import. You shall have the result of the Court of Inquiry upon Lieutenant Spencer[6] as soon as I get it; but I hear from a gentleman who was passenger in her, that the Privateer came out of the Neutral Port, and within the limits of the Neutral Territory, fired upon the Convoy. I sincerely hope it will turn out so. If so, the punishment was well merited; and Chevalier Micheroux will get a rebuke from you, for not maintaining the Neutrality in Sicily. I am ever, my dear Sir, with most sincere good wishes, your most faithful and obliged,

NELSON AND BRONTE.

Pray return me Mr. Hunter's letter from Madrid; and in case I should be superseded, desire the letter to be sent to England after me.

TO THE QUEEN OF THE TWO SICILIES.

[From Clarke and M'Arthur, vol. ii. p. 392.]

Gulf of Palma, 19th December, 1804.

Although I have addressed a letter to the King, to assure him of my unalterable attachment, yet I cannot resist declaring the same to your Majesty, for my obligations are equal to both, and so is my gratitude. Never, perhaps, was Europe more critically situated than at this moment, and never was the probability of universal Monarchy more nearly being

[6] Vide p. 214, ante.

realized, than in the person of the Corsican. I can see but little difference between the name of Emperor, King, or Préfet, if they perfectly obey his despotic orders. Your Majesty's illustrious Mother would not have so submitted. Prussia is trying to be destroyed last—Spain is little better than a Province of France—Russia does nothing on the grand scale. Would to God these great Powers reflected, that the boldest measures are the safest! They allow small States to fall, and to serve the enormous power of France, without appearing to reflect that every Kingdom which is annexed to France makes their existence, as independent States, more precarious. Your Majesty sees all this, and much more than I can; for your Majesty is the true daughter of the great Maria Theresa. Your good heart will forgive my free manner of writing, it may be the last I shall ever address to you; for if I do not very soon get quiet on shore, my thread of feeble life will break: but God's will be done. My last breath will be for the felicity of your Majesty, the King, and Royal Family. I am, &c.

NELSON AND BRONTE.

TO WILLIAM MARSDEN, ESQ., ADMIRALTY.

[Original, in the Admiralty.]

Victory, at Sea, 21st December, 1804.

Sir,

I herewith transmit you a copy of a letter and paper therein referred to, from Captain Sir Richard John Strachan, of his Majesty's Ship Donegal, dated the 23rd October last, acquainting me with his having on that day, in company with the Medusa, detained the Spanish Frigate Matilda, from Cadiz, bound to the Spanish West Indies, with quicksilver for their mines, and sent her to England, under the charge of Captain Gore, until his Majesty's pleasure shall be known respecting her, which I request you will be pleased to lay before the Lords Commissioners of the Admiralty, for their information; and acquaint their Lordships that under the circumstances existing between the two Countries at the time the Matilda was detained, and from the reasons mentioned in the copy of Sir Richard Strachan's letter, and paper which accompanies

U 2

it, I very much approve of the said Vessel having been detained, and sent to England under charge of the Medusa,
until his Majesty's pleasure shall be signified; and trust their
Lordships will also approve of Sir Richard Strachan's conduct on the occasion. I am, &c.

NELSON AND BRONTE.

TO WILLIAM MARSDEN, ESQ., ADMIRALTY.

[Original, in the Admiralty.]

Victory, at Sea, 21st December, 1804.
Sir,

I herewith transmit you copy of a letter from Captain Sir
Richard John Strachan, of the Donegal, dated the 26th November, acquainting me with his having, on the morning of
the 19th of that month, after a long chase, and an action of
eight minutes, captured the Spanish Frigate Amphitrite,
(whose Captain, it appears, refused to return with him to
Cadiz,) which you will be pleased to lay before the Lords
Commissioners of the Admiralty, for their information; and
acquaint their Lordships that I very fully approve of Sir
Richard Strachan's exertions and zeal on this occasion, and
hope it will also meet their Lordships' approbation. The
Donegal has not yet joined the Squadron, but I am hourly in
expectation of seeing her. I am, Sir, &c.

NELSON AND BRONTE.

TO CAPTAIN PARKER, H.M. SHIP AMAZON.

[From a Copy in the Nelson Papers.]

Victory, off St. Sebastians, December 23rd, 1804.
My dear Parker,

Neither Seahorse nor Active have been here, therefore I
am very uneasy about Toulon; for I very much fear that
Phœbe and Hydra are both so short of water, that they may
have been forced to leave the station; therefore I am going
off Toulon, to see that all is safe, and it is my present intention to return to 97; but should a heavy gale of N.W. wind
come on, I shall not allow myself to be driven to the South-

ward of the Straits of Bonifaccio (upon that side the water) but shall go to Madalena, at which place I shall certainly be before the 7th January ; therefore if you have no chance of getting hold of the Squadron, from the sketch I have given you of my intentions, and you have many bullocks for us, I would recommend your going to Madalena, and landing Mr. Ford and the cattle, that they may be taken care of. You must be very cautious in approaching Madalena, for it is very possible the French may be in possession. Should you have much spare time (in case you go to Madalena) between the time of your arrival and the 7th of January, I would recommend your cruizing off the Coast of Corsica, and try to get the Nourice, a Store-Ship, which loads timber in the Gulf of Savoni, a Gulf just to the Northward of the Lamprinare Islands. If she is there, you [may] either take or destroy her ; and the French have 4000 Troops ready, they say, for embarking at Ajaccio. I am ever, dear Parker, yours faithfully,

NELSON AND BRONTE.

TO CAPTAIN MARK ROBINSON, H. M. SHIP SWIFTSURE.

[Autograph, in the possession of Commander Robinson.]

Victory, December 25th, 1804.

My dear Sir,

I would not trouble you to come out of the Swiftsure[7] with this swell, not being sure that you are not in Quarantine, and therefore I might be deprived of the pleasure of seeing you on board the Victory; and also, hearing from Captain Cracraft that you have lately had the gout. I therefore have made the signal for a Lieutenant; and if you are in Pratique I shall be glad to see you when we get into smooth water, which will probably be to-morrow. I am very anxious at this moment to get off Toulon, for we have reports that the French Fleet are expected every moment to put to sea with Troops embarked ; and it would not surprise me to find them sailed. I hope you have had a great deal of success, and pleasant cruizing, off Cadiz. I am, my dear Sir, with great esteem, your most faithful humble servant,

NELSON AND BRONTE.

[7] " December 25. Swiftsure joined at 8 A.M."— *Victory's Log.*

TO WILLIAM MARSDEN, ESQ., ADMIRALTY.

[Original, in the Admiralty.]

Victory, at Sea, 26th December, 1804.

Sir,

I have received your letter, dated the 27th October, together with the copy of one from the Navy Board, on the subject of the frocks and trowsers sent out some time ago in the Diligent Store-ship for the Fleet under my command, and particularly note the Commissioners' observations thereon; and, as no further complaint has been made, I hope the frocks and trowsers may turn out better after washing, than there was reason to believe from their original appearance. I particularly remark, in your letter of the 17th October, their Lordships' displeasure at Captain Bayntun's style of writing against the Navy Board, and shall communicate the same to that Officer, whose conduct certainly, in every other respect, is extremely correct and proper. I am, sir, &c.,

NELSON AND BRONTE.

TO WILLIAM MARSDEN, ESQ., ADMIRALTY.

[Original, in the Admiralty.]

Victory, at Sea, 26th December, 1804.

Sir,

I have received your letter of the 1st November, acquainting me that their Lordships had directed the Navy Board to prepare, and send out to Gibraltar, the frames of four Gunboats, which are forwarded in the Prevoyante Store-Ship; and that directions will be sent out to Commissioner Otway to put the said frames together, when he shall receive instructions from me for that purpose, and dispose of them as I may find necessary to direct. I have also to acknowledge your letter of the 6th November, acquainting me that directions were given to the Victualling-Board, to send out immediately two Transports, laden with coals for the Fleet; but I much apprehend (if come out) that they are gone to Malta with the Convoy, instead of coming direct to the Fleet; by which means a delay of several months may take place, and the Squadron be considerably distressed in consequence. I am, Sir, &c.,   NELSON AND BRONTE.

TO WILLIAM MARSDEN, ESQ., ADMIRALTY.

[Original, in the Admiralty.]

Victory, at Sea, 26th December, 1804.

Sir,

I have received your letter of the 15th October, signifying to me their Lordships' direction to order a passage to be provided for his Excellency the Right Honourable Charles Arbuthnot, his Majesty's Ambassador at Constantinople, from Trieste to that place. In answer thereto, you will please to acquaint the Lords Commissioners of the Admiralty, that I have, some time ago, communicated with his Excellency at Vienna, and suggested that he would let me know the particular time he wished to proceed from Trieste to Constantinople, that a Frigate might be appointed for that service, but I have not yet heard from him. I am Sir, &c.,

NELSON AND BRONTE.

TO WILLIAM MARSDEN, ESQ., ADMIRALTY.

[Original, in the Admiralty.]

Victory, at Sea, 26th December, 1804.

Sir,

I have received your letter of the 30th October, together with a copy of one from Lord Camden[8] therein mentioned,

---

[8] The following letters were then received by Lord Nelson from Lord Camden:

" My Lord,   " Downing Street, 29th October, 1804.

" I have received and laid before the King your Lordship's dispatch to Lord Hawkesbury, under date 29th June last, with nine enclosures, containing the account of Captain Keats' mission to Algiers, the instructions your Lordship has furnished him with, the result of his able negotiation, together with statements of the claims upon which his Majesty has a right to demand redress from the Dey. I have also received and laid before his Majesty your Lordship's dispatch to Lord Hawkesbury, of the 30th of June, transmitting a copy of the Dey of Algiers' letter to your Lordship, of the 15th June, together with your Lordship's letter to the Dey, and at the same time giving an account of your Lordship's instructions to Mr. M'Donough, whom you had sent to Algiers. I have likewise seen Mr. M'Donough, who arrived here some time ago, and brought a copy of the Dey of Algiers' letter to your Lordship, under date 6th July, in answer to the points of Mr. M'Donough's mission, of which I inclose a copy, lest the letter which Mr. M'Donough wrote to your Lordship from Gibraltar, may not have reached you.

" These letters of your Lordship and the Dey, together with Captain Keats's intelligent and able account of his proceedings, having been taken into full considera-

communicating his Majesty's commands that no other form
of Passport be granted to any Vessel than a regular Mediterranean passport, and signifying their Lordships' direction to
me to take measures for carrying into execution the instructions
therein contained. In answer thereto, you will please to acquaint the Lords

tion of his Majesty's Ministers, and their opinion having been laid before the King,
I am commanded to signify to your Lordship his Majesty's pleasure thereupon.

" The Dey of Algiers having more than once expressed his concern to Captain
Keats for the offence he has given his Majesty by his conduct to Mr. Falcon, his
Consul-General, and having promised that in future, if he should have occasion to
be dissatisfied with any Consul, he would content himself by writing and making
representations of the Consul's conduct, and never again so far avail himself of his
authority as to commit a similar act of indignity, I am to desire your Lordship will
signify to the Dey that his Majesty accepts these declarations and assurances as
satisfactory, and as a pledge of the Dey's intentions to preserve a good understanding and friendship with his Majesty, which his Majesty is ever disposed, on his part,
to return with sincerity.

" I am to express his Majesty's approbation of your Lordship's prudence in
acquainting the Dey of Algiers that, in future his Majesty's Vessels in the Mediterranean shall be furnished with regular Mediterranean Passports, and I am happy
to find that this concession is received by the Dey in so satisfactory a manner.
There seems reason to believe that much of the late misunderstandings with the
Barbary Powers, has arisen from the introduction of new Passports in the Mediterranean, which, certainly, are not in conformity with the strict letter of Treaties
with those Powers. Orders, therefore, will be issued to his Majesty's Officers in
the Mediterranean, never to furnish any of his Majesty's Vessels with other Passports than the regular Mediterranean Passes, which regulations will, I make no
doubt, prevent in future those mistakes and inconveniences which have arisen by
the introduction of forms with which those Powers were unacquainted, and which
seem to have been much abused, by being granted to Vessels not belonging to any
of his Majesty's Subjects.

" His Majesty's Ministers entirely coincide with your Lordship's opinion, that
his Majesty's Mediterranean Passes can only protect those Vessels which belong to
his Majesty, or his Subjects, and that when granted to Vessels of this description,
they fully protect the Vessel, the cargo, and the crew. They conceive that the
letter and spirit of the Treaties with Algiers, and the uniform practice under them,
completely warrant this interpretation. The endeavours, therefore, of the Dey to
establish it as a principle, that no Vessel is to be considered as British, but when
one-third of the crew are British Subjects, must be held as inadmissible, and your
Lordship will persist, as a preliminary to all accommodation, in demanding the full
restitution of the Ape, its cargo, and crew—a right to which his Majesty is clearly
entitled by Treaty, and which he can neither yield nor compromise.

" It appears from the Dey's last letter to your Lordship, that he is willing to
restore the Ape and its cargo, but that he persists in retaining the crew; and he
even endeavours to make the restitution of the Vessel and cargo conditional, upon
satisfaction being made to him for goods which he states to have lost in the El
Veloce. But his Majesty is so entirely assured of his right with respect to the

Commissioners of the Admiralty, that strict obedience shall
be paid to their direction, and to the instructions contained in
the copy of Lord Camden's letter above mentioned. There has
been no Passport granted by me, as I was perfectly aware of
the consequences and inutility of such an instrument. I am,
Sir, &c.　　　　　　　　　　　　NELSON AND BRONTE.

Ape, its cargo, and crew, that I am to desire your Lordship will not permit any
condition whatever to be annexed to their full restitution.

" His Majesty's Ministers have felt much surprise that the Dey should have
revived his claims upon the subject of the El Veloce, which they conceived had
long been finally settled. The Dey must be sensible that every exertion had been
made to do him the fullest justice in the case of this Vessel. No proof appeared in
his Majesty's Court of Appeals, that the cargo, or any part of it, belonged to the
Dey, after a full hearing of the case. Your Lordship will, therefore, acquaint the
Dey that it is hoped, on the part of his Majesty, that he will not endeavour to
revive claims already settled and adjudicated, as nothing can tend so strongly to interrupt mutual good understanding, and revive irritating discussions. It is his
Majesty's wish that a line of conduct entirely different should be adopted, and that,
instead of bringing forward from time to time subjects of complaint already terminated, means should be found of throwing even those which are supposed to exist
into oblivion.

" With this view, his Majesty will consent no longer to press for full compensation in the case of the St. Antonio di Padona, nor urge the redress of many other
complaints on the parts of his Subjects, but will waive his demands respecting
them, upon the full assurance that the Dey will receive this conduct of his Majesty
with due satisfaction, and that all existing differences shall be considered as terminated, and never to be revived. His Majesty's Ministers have advised the line
of conduct stated in the last paragraph, in consequence of your Lordship's representation that you conceive it will be difficult to substantiate the existing claims
against the Dey, except for a fuller compensation for the Antonio di Padona, and
your Lordship conceives that even this claim, which you think cannot amount to
more than 5000 dollars, might be reserved for a negotiation, and not insisted on as
a preliminary. It should seem, therefore, that the wisest policy would be to ex-
tinguish at once all claims on all sides, and to leave no ground whatever for future
altercations.

" I think, from your Lordship's letters, it appears to be understood by the Dey,
that the new Consul is to be admitted without the usual presents, and certainly the
Dey's conduct seems to make a deviation from the usual practice necessary; but
upon this head your Lordship will make the arrangement which shall appear to you the
most eligible. It appears matter of the most serious concern that several Foreigners,
who have sailed in Foreign Vessels, under the supposed protection of British Passports
granted at Malta, should be left in captivity, but there seems no ground arising from
Treaty, by which their liberation can be made the subject of a regular demand on
the part of his Majesty. It is a circumstance, however, which shows the necessity
of restraining the grant of Passports to Vessels entitled to receive them, and of
taking measures for the prevention of such abuses by his Majesty's Officers. If
any relief can be afforded to these unhappy people, through your Lordship's media-

TO WILLIAM MARSDEN, ESQ., ADMIRALTY.

[Original, in the Admiralty.]

Victory, at Sea, 26th December, 1804.

Sir,

I have received your letter of the 12th September last, with the extract of a letter from Count Fröberg to Colonel Clinton, therein mentioned; relative to the difficulties the former gentleman has experienced in transporting his Recruits from the different Ports in the Adriatic, to Malta. In answer thereto, I herewith transmit you copy of my general order

tion and influence with the Dey, it will be matter of much consolation, and I am to regret that it is not possible to make their case the subject of a real claim. I have the honour to be, &c.,—CAMDEN."—*Original*.

" Private.   " Downing Street, 29th October, 1804.

" My Lord,

" Your Lordship will receive herewith a letter of Public Instructions for your Lordship's future conduct, in arranging a settlement with the Dey of Algiers, in which all your Lordship's suggestions are fully adopted, by which I trust you will be persuaded of the entire confidence which is placed in your Lordship's capacity and judgment. The proposals on the part of his Majesty are so fair and reasonable, that I cannot have any doubt of the Dey's accepting them, unless he has secret motives for prolonging the present misunderstanding.

" I should have much wished to have attended to your suggestions in favour of Mr. M'Donough, but the appointment of a successor to Mr. Magra, at Tunis, had been arranged in favour of Mr. Oglander, before my accession to Office, and I have reason to believe he is in every way qualified for his situation. Mr. Cartwright I had also recommended for the succession to Mr. Falcon, before I received any intimation of your Lordship's wishes. He had been recommended to me from various quarters, as a gentleman, not only versed in business, but conversant in the languages of the Mediterranean. I hope he will deliver to your Lordship this dispatch; and if the Dey of Algiers shall acquiesce in the proposals which have been transmitted to him, by the authority of his Majesty's Ministers, your Lordship will have the goodness to have him landed at Algiers.

" I shall attend to Mr. M'Donough's claim for remuneration, in consequence of your Lordship's having judged it right to employ him in the Public service. Your Lordship must feel assured that the conduct of Captain Keats in his Mission, and the reports of his proceedings, have given entire satisfaction to his Majesty, and you will be pleased to signify the same to Captain Keats.

" I have, as matter of official form, desired the Lords Commissioners of the Admiralty to instruct the Officer Commanding in the Mediterranean, not to grant any other Pass than a Mediterranean Pass, and only to grant Passes to British Vessels, and I have signified the same to the Lieutenant-Governor at Gibraltar, and his Majesty's Civil Commissioner at Malta. I have the honour to be, &c.— CAMDEN."—(*Original*, in the possession of the Right Honourable John Wilson Croker.)

issued to the different Ships, dated the 28th December, 1803, directing them to receive such Recruits as might be put on board their respective Ships for the Army at Malta, and to land them at that place ; and I must desire to observe that Count Fröberg's language is extremely indecent; and if the reports of the different Officers who have been constantly in the Adriatic are to be credited, (which I cannot doubt,) the Count's statement is altogether groundless ; but, perhaps, it may be a convenient circumstance for him to advance, particularly as he speaks of additional expenses ; and for their Lordships' further information, I beg leave to inclose you a letter from Captain Cracraft, of the Anson, who was the Senior Officer in the Adriatic for a very considerable time, and to observe that by Captain Cracraft's account, Count Fröberg appears to be a slippery gentleman. I am, Sir, &c.

NELSON AND BRONTE.

TO WILLIAM MARSDEN, ESQ., ADMIRALTY.

[Original, in the Admiralty.]

Victory, at Sea, 26th December, 1804.

Sir,

I yesterday evening received your letter of the 26th October, acquainting me, by direction of the Lords Commissioners of the Admiralty, that their Lordships had judged it expedient that a Squadron of Line-of-Battle Ships and Frigates should be employed to watch the Enemy's Ships and those of Spain, lying in Cadiz, and that they have appointed Vice-Admiral Sir John Orde to be Commander-in-Chief of the Squadron to be employed on this service; and, at the same time, that I am not to consider my command as extending without the Straits of Gibraltar : in answer thereto, the most implicit obedience shall be paid to confine the Ships under my command within the limits of the station, as above-mentioned, except such Vessel as I may have occasion to send to Lisbon with dispatches, being the only means of communicating with their Lordships. I am, Sir, &c.

NELSON AND BRONTE.

TO WILLIAM MARSDEN, ESQ., ADMIRALTY.

[Original, in the Admiralty.]

Victory, at Sea, 26th December, 1804.

Sir,

You will please to acquaint the Lords Commissioners of the Admiralty, that his Majesty's Ship Swiftsure joined the Squadron yesterday evening, off Cape St. Sebastians, in my way to reconnoitre the Enemy's force at Toulon, which from every information I have received, are embarking Troops, and preparing for some immediate Expedition.

I shall, agreeable to their Lordships' orders, take the said Ship under my command, and also the Tribune on her joining the Squadron from Malta, to which place she has proceeded with the Convoy from England. The Fleet is in perfect good health, and good humour, unequalled by anything which has ever come within my knowledge, and equal to the most active service which the times may call for, or the Country expect of them. I am, Sir, &c.

NELSON AND BRONTE.

P.S.—Half-past three o'clock, P.M.—I have reconnoitred Toulon, and find the whole of the Enemy's Fleet still in Port.

TO RICHARD CARTWRIGHT, ESQ., CONSUL-GENERAL AT ALGIERS.

[From a Copy in the Colonial Office.]

Victory, at Sea, December 28th, 1804.

Sir,

Earl Camden, one of his Majesty's Principal Secretaries of State, having wrote to send you in a Ship of War to the Bay of Algiers, and after having had a communication with his Highness the Dey, relative to the restitution of an English Vessel called the Ape, her cargo and crew, which, if restored, and satisfaction given for several other matters, in that case, you are to be landed—if not, you are to return to me; I have, therefore, appointed Captain Keats, of his Majesty's Ship the Superb, to proceed to Algiers, and then to enter into such negotiation with the Dey, as may, I hope, terminate the differences existing between his Majesty and the Regency of Algiers; in which case, Captain Keats has my directions to signify the same to you, and to land you with the attention due to your situation. I have, &c.

NELSON AND BRONTE.

TO HIS HIGHNESS THE DEY OF ALGIERS.

[From a Copy in the Colonial Office, and Autograph draught, in the possession of the Rev. Henry Girdlestone.]

Victory, at Sea, off Toulon, 28th December, 1804.

Sir,

I have transmitted regularly to his Majesty's Ministers all the correspondence I have had with your Highness, with such remarks and observations as the occasion required; and out of my own regard for your Highness, and a sincere wish that the harmony which has subsisted so many years between Great Britain and the Regency of Algiers should not be interrupted, I ventured to recommend the removal of Mr. Consul Falcon, as you had a personal dislike to him. These representations have induced his Majesty's Ministers to recommend to his Majesty the sending out another Consul, who is now on board his Majesty's Ship Superb, Captain Keats, *my friend*, who your Highness knows commands her; and Captain Keats is instructed by me, in obedience to the orders of my Royal Master, to state to your Highness,—

That by our Treaties with the Regency of Algiers, the crew of a Vessel entirely British (of whatever Nation they may be composed) are exempt from captivity; and therefore that the British Vessel .Ape, with its cargo and *crew*, must be restored to Captain Keats, before any Consul will be allowed to be landed at Algiers.

That it is with surprise his Majesty sees that your Highness refers back to things which have been considered as long settled; particularly the case of the El Veloce, which was proved in the Courts of Justice to be French property, and from which sentence there was no appeal to the Superior Tribunals. The revival of this claim could only tend to interrupt the harmony, which his Majesty wishes to subsist be-

tween himself and the Regency of Algiers, and it is the wish
of his Majesty rather to cement, by any means, the harmony
between the two Countries, by an entire oblivion of the past,
than by reverting to claims long ago considered as terminated.
Your Highness having expressed to Captain Keats your
concern for the offence given his Majesty, by your conduct to
Mr. Falcon, and that you promised never to give such an insult to his Majesty again, as sending away, upon any pretence,
his Agent and Consul-General, his Majesty is pleased to
accept of such declarations and assurances as satisfactory; and
as a pledge of your intentions to preserve a good understanding, and friendship with him, which his Majesty is ever disposed to return with sincerity.

Your Highness will perceive in the proceedings I have had
with his Majesty's Ministers, how very much I have interested
myself, that the friendship of his Majesty and the Regency of
Algiers should be as short a time interrupted as possible. I
am, your Highness's obedient Servant,

NELSON AND BRONTE.

TO CAPTAIN KEATS, H.M. SHIP SUPERB.

[Autograph draught, in the possession of Earl Nelson.]

Victory, at Sea, off Toulon, 28th December, 1804.

Sir,

His Majesty having sent out a Consul-General for Algiers,
with directions for my demanding certain conditions, and without they are complied with, he is not to be landed; and as I
have the very highest confidence, from experience, in your zeal
and ability for the performance of this mission with the Algerines, I think it right to entrust it to your management. I shall,
therefore, do very little more than merely deliver to you the
orders I have received from Earl Camden, one of his Majesty's
principal Secretaries of State.

The extreme ignorance of the Dey, and his not remaining
long enough quiet to hear reason, will make it, probably, the
likeliest mode of coming to an amicable accommodation to
see and converse with the Ministers of his Highness before
you demand an audience; and explain to them most clearly

and distinctly, that as a preliminary, before you can enter
upon any other subject, the restitution of the English Vessel,
the Ape, her cargo and crew must be complied with. You
will also impress upon their minds the folly of bringing forward as claims, things which have been long ago considered
as settled, particularly the case of the El Veloce, which was
proved to be entirely French property; and that therefore
whoever told the Dey that any Neutral property was in the
Veloce, could only have done it either to keep back property
which might belong to the Dey, or his Subjects, or to try and
create a misunderstanding between his Majesty and the
Regency.

You will also call their attention to the friendly conduct of
his Majesty in sending another Consul to Algiers, in the
room of Mr. Falcon, after the very improper treatment his
Agent and Consul-General had received ; but that his
Majesty relies upon the Dey's word, that such an insult shall
not be given again. You will endeavour to impress upon
their minds, the long and uninterrupted harmony which has
subsisted between Great Britain and Algiers, and which his
Majesty has always been so desirous to preserve, by every
act of friendship on his part; and that it is the earnest wish
of his Majesty ever to remain on the most friendly terms with
the Regency. You will also give them an instance of it, which
they must know, that an Armament at Toulon, and a large
Army, after the Peace with Great Britain, was intended to
land and plunder Algiers, which they would doubtless have
effected, had not a British Fleet been placed in Oristan Bay,
Sardinia, to watch their motions, and to prevent such a dia-
bolical scheme from being carried into execution ; and had his
Majesty not been the most friendly disposed towards the
Algerines, with what ease could I have taken the whole of
the Cruizers belonging to the Regency! but the sincere wish
of his Majesty is peace and friendship with Algiers, if it can
be kept with honour.

Should the Dey comply with the just demands of his Majesty, you may then, as a proof of his Majesty's earnest desire
to be on the most friendly footing with the Regency, and to
bury in oblivion all that is past, give up the idea of any further
claims, which he might justly demand, particularly indemni-

fication for the St. Antonio de Padua, &c. &c.; but his Majesty has a right to expect, as a return for such a proof of his friendship, that the Dey will give up the poor innocent sufferers who were taken in them. Although I have touched upon the several points to which I would wish you to draw the attention of the Ministers of the Regency, yet the mode and manner I leave entirely to your superior judgment and experience; and you will deliver my letter to the Minister to be delivered to the Dey, that he may have full time to reflect upon the conduct he means to pursue, before you have an audience of him. Should you not be able to obtain the restitution of the Ape, her crew, and cargo, you are not, upon any consideration, to land the Consul, but bring him back to me. Wishing you success, I am, Sir, with the highest respect, &c.

NELSON AND BRONTE.

P.S. You will herewith receive a copy of Earl Camden's letter to me,[1] and also of my letter to the Dey of Algiers.

TO EARL CAMDEN, K.G.

[Autograph, in the Colonial Office.]

Victory, December 29th, 1804.

My Lord,

On the 25th, I was honoured with your Lordship's letter of October 29th, by Mr. Cartwright, his Majesty's Consul-General to Algiers; and, in obedience to your Lordship's instructions, I have sent Mr. Cartwright to Algiers, and have instructed Captain Keats how to proceed upon the occasion. A copy of my letter to the Dey, and my instructions to Captain Keats shall be transmitted; and I trust your Lordship will think, with me, that, if such condescension on the part of his Majesty will not have the desired effect, that the Dey must be influenced by motives from our Enemies. I trust your Lordship will think that my letter to the Dey is as conciliating as possible, consistent with a due regard to the honour of his Majesty. I have, &c.,

NELSON AND BRONTE.

[1] Vide p. 295, ante.

TO VICE-ADMIRAL SIR JOHN ORDE, BART., COMMANDER-IN-
CHIEF OF A SQUADRON OF HIS MAJESTY'S SHIPS OFF CADIZ.

[From a Copy in the Admiralty.]

Victory, at Sea, 29th December, 1804.

Sir,

By the Swiftsure, which joined on the 25th instant, I
received an order from the Lords of the Admiralty, to consider
my station as only extending to the Straits' Mouth. It is,
therefore, unnecessary for me to point out to you, that the
Convoys, either to or from England, are not safe, unless
taken in charge from twenty leagues to the Westward of Cape
Spartel, and seen safe to an anchor in Gibraltar Bay; or from
Cape Spartel as far to the Westward. I have the honour to
be, &c.,

NELSON AND BRONTE.

P.S.—I reconnoitred Toulon on the 26th instant, and
found the Enemy's Fleet still in Port.

TO THE RIGHT HONOURABLE LORD WALPOLE.

[Autograph.]

Victory, off Toulon, December 29th, 1804.

My dear Lord,

On this day I received your favour of May last, or, you
may believe, it should not have been so long unanswered;
for I do assure you, that I have the very highest regard,
esteem, and, if I might be allowed the expression, affection
for you, and every part of your family. Young Neville[2] is a
very excellent young man, and his good conduct has not
escaped my observation; and you may rely, my dear Lord, not
only upon this, but upon any occasion which may offer, that
I shall be truly happy to meet your wishes; for I never shall
forget the many favours, kindnesses, and civilities you have

---

[2] The Honourable Ralph Neville, second son of Henry, second Earl of Abergavenny, K.T., then a Midshipman of the Victory: he died a Post Captain in May
1826. Lord Abergavenny's brother, the Honourable George Henry Neville, had
married a niece of Lord Walpole.

shown me, and many parts of our family; and believe me
ever, my dear Lord, your most faithful and obliged,

NELSON AND BRONTE.

I beg my respectful compliments to Lady Walpole, Miss
Walpole,³ and Mr. and Mrs. Hussey,⁴ if they are with you.

TO CAPTAIN KEATS, H. M. SHIP SUPERB.

[Autograph, in the possession of the Reverend Richard Keats.]

Victory, December 29th, 1804.

My dear Sir,

I am very troublesome, for I must now send to the Superb
for a few cases, which are wanted to keep me from starving.
If the weather continues moderate, I shall lay to for an hour
to get our letters, at present on board the Swiftsure; and I
should be glad to see you for five minutes on board the
Victory. I am ever, my dear Sir, your much obliged,

NELSON AND BRONTE.

Admiral Campbell passed the Straits the 14th.

TO ALEXANDER DAVISON, ESQ.

[Autograph, in the possession of Colonel Davison.]

Victory, December 29th, 1804.

My dear Davison,

I feel infinitely obliged by your truly kind and affectionate
letter of October 5th. I believe you could have hardly
thought it possible that any man could have been sent to take
the chance of a few pounds Prize-money from me, in return
for all my hard service. At this moment, I am as poor as
when I left you at Portsmouth; but my spirit is above riches,
and nothing can shake my firm resolution to do my duty to

---

³ The Honourable Katherine Walpole, eldest daughter of Horatio, second Lord
Walpole, of Wolterton, afterwards Earl of Orford, by Rachel, daughter of William,
Duke of Devonshire, died unmarried, in July 1831.

⁴ The Honourable Mary Walpole married, in 1777, Thomas Hussey, of Galtrim,
co. Meath, Esq., and died in March 1840.

my Country. I respect Lord Melville, and shall probably
give him my support, when the great Sir John Orde will not
thank him for his great favour. Lord Melville is a liberal-
minded man, and he may oblige me some other way, in giving
me something for some of my relations. God knows, in my
own person, I spend as little money as any man; but you
know I love to give away.

The pamphlets and newspapers you mention, are not yet
arrived. I fear your correspondent at Portsmouth is not very
correct, or does not understand sending them on board Ship.
A batch of six months' news came at one time : but, my dear
Davison, I never believed your inattention to my wishes.
I am very glad to find that all goes on well at Merton,
for which I most sincerely thank you. I count when the
days of your honourable imprisonment are over; and it is
some comfort that I shall be in England to shake you by the
hand in St. James's-square. The moment an Admiral arrives
in the room of Admiral Campbell, I shall sail; for although
this winter is hitherto so much milder than the last, yet I
feel it pretty severely. Remember me kindly to Sir Evan
when you see him; and believe me ever, and for ever, my
dear Davison, your much obliged and faithful friend,

NELSON AND BRONTE.

TO WILLIAM MARSDEN, ESQ., ADMIRALTY.

[Autograph, in the Admiralty.]

Victory, December 30th, 1804.

Sir,

I have been honoured with your letter of October 6th, on
Christmas day, acquainting me that their Lordships had been
pleased to comply with my request for permission to return to
England for the re-establishment of my health; and that I am
to leave Rear-Admiral Sir Richard Bickerton in the command
of the Squadron. I am much obliged by their Lordships'
kind compliance with my request, which is absolutely necessary from the present state of my health, and I shall avail
myself of their Lordships' permission, the moment another
Admiral, in the room of Admiral Campbell, joins the Fleet,

unless the Enemy's Fleet should be at sea, when I should not think of quitting my Command until after the Battle. I have the honour to be, &c.

NELSON AND BRONTE.

TO CAPTAIN WILLIAM PARKER, H. M. SHIP AMAZON.

[From a Copy in the Admiralty, and Autograph draught in the possession of Earl Nelson.]

Victory, at Sea, 30th December, 1804.

You are hereby required and directed to proceed with His Majesty's Ship Amazon under your command, to Lisbon, with the utmost expedition, taking care before your entering the Tagus that we are upon friendly terms with Portugal; and should there be no impediment in your communicating with that place, I desire you will deliver my dispatches to any Ship of War which may be there, bound to England, otherwise to the Agent of the Packets, taking his receipt for the same. In proceeding and returning from Lisbon, you are not to approach within fifty leagues of Cape St. Vincent, and on no account go near Cadiz, or in any manner interfere with the Squadron under Sir John Orde. You are, on no consideration whatever, to deliver my dispatches to any person, otherwise than above mentioned; and should you be prevented from proceeding with them to Lisbon, you are to bring them back to me. Having delivered my dispatches as before directed, you will return to Rendezvous No. 97, where you will find me, or orders for your further proceedings.

NELSON AND BRONTE.

PRIVATE INSTRUCTIONS FROM LORD NELSON TO CAPTAIN PARKER.

[Autograph draught. These Instructions were delivered to Captain Parker with the above Order of the 30th December, 1804.]

Do not interfere with anything at Gibraltar; neither with Sophie or Halcyon, going to Lisbon or elsewhere; pass Cape Spartel in the night, and get to the Southward and Westward. Bring to for nothing, if you can help it; hoist the signal of Quarantine, and that you are ' Charged with dispatches.' If

you are forced to speak by a Superior Officer, show him only
my order for his not interfering with you; and, unless he is an
Admiral superior to me, you will obey my orders instead of
any pretended order from him, from my Superior Officer.

TO VISCOUNT MELVILLE.

[From Clarke and M'Arthur, vol. ii. p. 397.]

[No date, probably towards the end of 1804.]

It is only with great deference to the superior judgment of
your Lordship, that I venture once more to touch upon the
subject of the great want of Frigates and Sloops on the Mediterranean station; for I am fully aware of the want you
have of them at home, and for other Commands: the more
stations are multiplied, the greater must be the demand for
small Ships. I have, in a former letter, stated my opinion
freely upon the stations of Gibraltar and of Cadiz being given
to the same Officer; for without that is done, our Convoys
can never be considered safe. It may be thought by some,
but I am confident your Lordship's liberal mind will not
think so, that a desire of more extensive Command for the
hope of Prize-money actuates me. Such people know me
not; let me be placed alongside of the French Admiral. Had
the station been continued to me, I should have appointed
that excellent Officer, Sir Richard Strachan, to the command
at Gibraltar and off Cadiz; with, if to be had, one other Ship
of the Line, four Frigates, and as many Sloops, and to have
covered our Convoys both from Carthagena and Cadiz: and
something of that kind your Lordship will find it still necessary to adopt, to insure our Convoys. There is also another,
although perhaps a minor consideration, why the Officer at
Gibraltar should be under the orders of the Admiral commanding the Mediterranean Fleet—which is, that any Admiral independent of that station, takes all the stores which
he chooses, or fancies he wants, for the service of his Fleet;
thereby placing the Fleet in the Gulf of Lyons in great distress for many articles. I again beg your Lordship's indul-
gence for the freedom of my remarks. I am, &c.

NELSON AND BRONTE.

TO LORD MOIRA.

[From Clarke and M'Arthur, vol. ii. p. 398.]

[No date ; probably towards the end of 1804, or early in 1805.]

A blow struck in Europe would do more towards making us respected, and of course facilitate a Peace, than the possession of Mexico or Peru ; in both of which, I am sure, we are perfectly ignorant of the disposition of the inhabitants ; and, above all, I hope we shall have no buccaneering expeditions. Such services fritter away our Troops and Ships, when they are so much wanted for more important occasions, and are of no use beyond enriching a few individuals. I know not, my dear Lord, if these sentiments coincide with yours ; but as glory, and not money, has through life been your pursuit, I should rather think you will agree with me, that in Europe, and not abroad, is the place for us to strike a blow, which would make the Corsican look aghast even upon his usurped throne. You may rely upon every attention in my power to Captain Austen.[5] I hope to see him alongside a French 80-gun Ship, and he cannot be better placed than in the Canopus, which was *once* a French Admiral's Ship, and struck to *me*. Captain Austen I knew a little of before ; he is an excellent young man. I hope soon, my dear Lord, to congratulate you upon the birth of a son who will emulate his father's manliness. In these days I see many people, but very few men. I am, &c.

NELSON AND BRONTE.

TO SIR ALEXANDER JOHN BALL, BART., MALTA.

[Autograph, in the possession of Sir William Keith Ball, Bart. The commencement of this letter has been lost.]

1st January, 1805.

By orders from home, brought out by a Mr. Cartwright, a new Consul for Algiers, I am restrained to demanding the *crew*, cargo, and Vessel called the Ape ; this complied with, all the rest is to be sunk in oblivion. Lord Camden laments the unhappy situation of these poor men, taken under the former

[5] Now Vice-Admiral Sir Francis William Austen, K.C.B.

Passports, but it cannot be made a subject of a National demand. Had I known of their sailing, I would most assuredly have followed your advice, so perfectly coinciding with my feelings. I have sent Keats, who will do everything which is possible, not absolutely to degrade us. We never should have given up the cause of Mr. Falcon. Mr. Cartwright you will see, for I do not expect that the Dey will now give up an *atom*. You will think with me that the two Consuls of Tripoli and Algiers might run in a curricle, and perhaps the new Consul to Tunis might be a spare animal: the French and Spanish Consuls are very able, both at Tunis and Algiers.

I fancy, my dear Ball, that Captain Shepherd, or any other Captain, would be precisely as tired as poor Schomberg,[6] of being cooped up at Malta. I have to thank you for the extracts of Colonel Lean's letters from Algiers. The Bey [?] of Constantinople is certainly beheaded; and I hope the Dey of Algiers is the same before this time. As I have an opportunity of writing from Madalena, I shall shorten my letter, as I have many to write, and am anxious not to keep Hirondelle. Gibraltar was to have pratique this day. I shall hardly hear from you again; but may every success attend you, and every comfort which you so eminently deserve, is the sincere wish of, my dear Ball, your most sincere and affectionate friend,

NELSON AND BRONTE.

Pray forward my letters to the East.

TO HIS HIGHNESS THE GRAND VIZIR.

[Autograph, formerly in the possession of the late William Upcott, Esq.]

Victory, off Toulon, January 2nd, 1805.

Sir,

Yesterday I was honoured by the receipt of your Highness's precious letter of October 30th, for the truly friendly expressions in which I feel much obliged; and for your Highness's good wishes for the recovery of my health, which has suffered very much from being one year and eight months constantly at sea, and preventing the designs of the French, who will

---

[6] Captain Schomberg, of the Madras.

certainly proceed to that place where they expect to find most friends at, the least resistance, and most plunder. In doing my utmost in preventing the Dominions of his Imperial Majesty from being invaded, I only fulfil the orders of the Great King, my Master, who has ever been, and I trust will ever continue, the most faithful Ally of the Sublime Porte. My inclination, your Highness will have the goodness to assure his Imperial Majesty, is ever alive to this important part of my duty. Mr. Stratton[7] will explain my sentiments respecting an additional force in the Adriatic, and my reasons will, I hope, satisfy your Highness. I have remained till this time, and shall stay some time longer; in hopes that I may be able to get hold of the French Fleet, and should I go home to get rest, I shall, if I recover, be ready to take this Command again. May health and every blessing attend your Highness, is the most sincere prayer of your Highness's most affectionate friend,

NELSON AND BRONTE.

TO COMMISSIONER OTWAY, MALTA.

[Autograph, in the possession of Rear-Admiral Inglefield, C.B.]

Victory, January 2nd, 1805.

My dear Sir,

I have to thank you for your obliging letters from Malta, and when the precise time is fixed for your leaving Malta, I will endeavour to give you either a Frigate, or a good Brig, to convey you safe to the Rock, where you will find plenty of work from the Squadron outside the Straits. Swiftsure has had a new fore-yard, Defence is to have a new mainmast, and St [andard?] topmasts, I hear, are sprung. It would not have done for my command, where till lately we had not a store.

I have wrote you a letter about the Ship timber. The Captors have nothing to do with sending it to England. You and the Dockyard Officers will judge whether it is fit for the Service, and wanted. If it is, to take it in charge, and send it home in Government Vessels; and if not wanted, the Agents will sell it. The valuation may either (if the King takes it) be made at Malta, or in England. Minorca, I should hope

---

⁵ Minister at Constantinople.

would be immediately taken; for I shall never send another
Ship to Malta. They are so far off, and act often so very different to my wishes that I will trust no more of my Frigates
there, and a Line-of-Battle Ship is out of the question; for
which reason I have wrote you for the Caulkers, and some
of the Artificers. I again strongly recommend either for
Minorca, or any other Yard, Mr. Bunce, Carpenter of the
Victory, who will be found a most valuable acquisition. The
Ventura will be an acquisition to our friend Ball's Squadron,
but she should be coppered with *thin* copper, and not the
thick, as is put upon our Ships; but I am ignorant if that
sort of copper is sent out. She is over-gunned, and so is
Hirondelle. Mr. Skinner[8] has very properly desired to get
rid of his two heavy ones. The Admiralty have approved of
my purchase of the Hirondelle, and I suppose the Storekeeper
will have orders to pay for her.

I agree perfectly with you respecting Mr. Eaton, and we
must watch what comes from him; for first samples are, with
knowing ones, always the best—witness Mr. James, of Naples,
and his beds. I thought I had taken all human precautions not
to be cheated, but if my plans are not followed up [*sic.*] But
the original fault was Mr. Taylor's not letting me know that
he had 1000 beds in store, whilst the Fleet was in the very
greatest distress. I sincerely hope that you will be able to
whitewash all the gentlemen. It is cruel in the Navy Board
not to do something about Mr. Lawson[9]—either confirm or
dismiss him. Sir Alexander Ball always recommended him
most strongly; and I hope he has not done anything to forfeit his good opinion. The Tribune is gone home, left her
Convoy and the Station, without any orders, but from his own
pleasure. What will the Admiralty say to such conduct?[1]
The excuse of carrying Sir Thomas Trigge appears to me very

---

[8] Lieutenant John Skinner, Commander of the Hirondelle.

[9] Mr. William Lawson, Master Attendant at Malta.

[1] Captain Richard Henry Alexander Bennett, of the Tribune, was tried by a
Court-Martial, at Portsmouth, on the 21st of February, 1805, by command of the
Admiralty, for returning to England from Gibraltar without orders. The sentence
was, that "the charge had been proved against Captain Bennett, but as it appeared to
the Court, that in deviating from their Lordships' order, he was actuated solely by
the purest motives for the good of his Majesty's Service, it did adjudge him to be
acquitted." He died the Senior Post Captain, between 1816 and 1820.

frivolous. General Fox was sent out in a Store Ship, and I suppose the Admiralty intended Sir Thomas to go home in one. Should any accident happen to the Convoy, it will be a very serious thing to Captain Bennett. I saw the French Fleet the 27th ultimo, but our reports say they are upon the eve of undertaking some Expedition. God send it soon! Reports say, and I believe them,[2] that I have leave to go home, and to leave Sir Richard Bickerton in the Command, during either my absence, or [until] another Commander-in-Chief comes out.

Sir John Orde has sent Niger home. Fisgard has sent into Gibraltar, a French Privateer—'Oncle Thomas,' eighteen nine-pounders, sails very fast, they say. The Spanish Manifesto[3] is dated December 14th, at Madrid. I have only one copy, or I would send it to Malta: it is full of abuse. I shall have an opportunity of writing from Madalena, to which place I shall proceed to-morrow morning. With every good wish, I am ever, my dear Commissioner, your most faithful, humble servant,

NELSON AND BRONTE.

TO CAPTAIN P. S. MOUAT, AGENT FOR TRANSPORTS AT
GIBRALTAR.

[From a Copy in the Admiralty.]

Sir,   Victory, at Sea, 4th January, 1805.

I have received your letter of the 22nd ultimo, together with the list of Transports, and of the ten Spanish prisoners of war ordered to be discharged (being non-combatants) by Sir Richard Bickerton. I am extremely displeased at the circumstance of the men being impressed from the Transports, as mentioned in your letter, and herewith transmit you an order to prevent a similar act from happening; and in case the Tribune should return to this Country, I enclose you an order for the discharge of the two men named in the margin from that Ship, that they may be sent to her by the first opportunity. I have also directed the Honourable Captain

---

[2] His leave to return to England had reached him some time before; but he kept it a "profound secret."—Vide p. 320, post.

[3] Vide p. 269, ante.

Boyle to discharge William Mowitt, Second Mate of the Berwick, freighted Transport, that he may join his proper Ship as soon as possible, being perfectly aware of the necessity of these Transports being manned agreeable to their Charter-party, and sufficiently to navigate them.   I am, Sir, &c.

NELSON AND BRONTE.

TO THE CAPTAINS OR COMMANDERS OF HIS MAJESTY'S SHIPS OR VESSELS BELONGING TO THE MEDITERRANEAN FLEET.

[From a Copy in the Admiralty.]

Victory, at Sea, 4th January, 1805.

Whereas it becomes the duty of every Officer to protect the Navy and Army Victuallers and Transports as much as possible, and to afford them every assistance in their power, when they shall be considered in want thereof, and on no account to impress their Mates or Seamen, who are required for their navigation, and who they are obliged to have agree-able to their Charter-party,—You are therefore hereby required and directed, on no account or consideration whatever, to impress either Mates, Seamen, or Boys from any of his Ma-jesty's regular or hired Army or Navy Transports, or Vic-tuallers, unless they shall be found drunk and rioting on shore, in which case I presume it may be proper to impress them for his Majesty's Ships of War.

NELSON AND BRONTE.

N.B. This order to remain with Captain Mouat, and to be shown when necessary.

TO CAPTAIN RICHARD H. A. BENNETT, H.M. SHIP TRIBUNE.

[From a Copy in the Admiralty.]

Victory, at Sea, 4th January, 1805.

Whereas it has been represented to me that the two men named in the margin, were impressed by the Officers of his Majesty's Ship Tribune, under your command, from the Active, regular Transport and Navy Victualler, by which means the said Vessel has been left in distress for men to navigate her; and being perfectly aware of the impropriety

of such a measure, and how detrimental it is to his Majesty's
Service, You are hereby required and directed to discharge
the said two men immediately, and deliver them to Captain
Mouat, Agent for Transports at Gibraltar, that they may be
sent to the Active Transport by the very first opportunity.

NELSON AND BRONTE.

TO WILLIAM MARSDEN, ESQ., ADMIRALTY.

[Original, in the Admiralty.]

Victory, at Sea, 4th January, 1805.

Sir,

I herewith transmit you an extract of a letter from Mr.
Richard Lewis, Garrison Apothecary at Gibraltar, who it
appears has acted as Surgeon of his Majesty's Naval Hospital
at that place, since the death of the late Mr. William Burd,[4]
and previous to that, as Dispenser, on the death of Mr. Christie,
by order from Mr. Burd, as stated in the accompanying certificate from Mr. Pownall, Naval Storekeeper, which I request
you will please to lay before the Lords Commissioners of the
Admiralty, for their information, and move their Lordships to
comply with Mr. Lewis's request, as I think him very justly
and fully entitled to the remuneration he requires. I am, &c.

NELSON AND BRONTE.

TO CAPTAIN ROBINSON, H.M. SHIP SWIFTSURE.

[Autograph, in the possession of Commander Robinson.]

Victory, January 7th, 1805.

Dear Sir,

As you must feel more comfortable to have an Officer on
board who has been at Madalena, I send you Lieutenant
Brown, of Victory. I sincerely hope that your gout is removed. We shall get a Westerly wind, and to-morrow forenoon be at anchor; and I beg that you will dine here if that
is the case, and believe me, dear Sir, yours most faithfully,

NELSON AND BRONTE.

---

[4] He died of the fever, at Gibraltar, on the 21st November 1804.

TO HIS EXCELLENCY HUGH ELLIOT, ESQ., NAPLES.

[Autograph, in the Elliot Papers. "January 12th [*i. e.*, 11th.] P.M. At 5, shortened sail and came to in the Straits of Bonifaccio. Squadron anchored as convenient. 12th. A.M. At 5, weighed and made sail. At 7 P.M., shortened sail and anchored. 13th. A.M. At 9, weighed and made sail for Agincourt Sound. At 1 P.M., anchored."—*Victory's Log.*]

Victory, Madalena, January 13th, 1805.

My dear Sir,

I am much pleased with your Excellency's letters of January 2nd, 3rd, and 4th, which put me in full possession of what is passing both in, and relative to, the Kingdom of Naples. Your Excellency will not expect from me that regular answer to every one of your dispatches which they deserve, as it would take up more time than either I or you, probably, have, to give to mere opinions. With respect to the French Fleet, I wish to God they were out; but I begin to despair of their putting to sea during the short time I shall probably be in the Mediterranean. I have stayed much longer than I ought to have done, if I had only considered myself; but I thought it very possible the short days might have tempted them to make a run. I saw them myself fourteen days ago, and the Frigates saw them the 6th; and since, the wind has been Easterly; therefore they could not go to Naples.

I am much pleased to hear that the Queen takes such a spirited part for the defence of Naples, but I would not have her Majesty depressed by hearing that the French are at sea; for if they never come out, how can she enjoy the spectacle of a Battle in the Bay of Naples? She may rely that nothing shall be wanting on my part to make it superior to the Nile, which it may be; and could anything add to my exertions against the Enemy, it would be the additional pleasure of knowing that I was fighting for the existence of the Monarchy of my benefactors. But let who will command this Fleet, they cannot go wrong: only get close enough. I wish her Majesty would cause some inquiry to be made at Messina. The Gun-boats are given up, and the provisions are selling out of the Citadel, upon an idea that they will spoil; and that may be true. But no orders are given to replace them, and I own I suspect much many of the Neapolitan Officers at that place; therefore, entreat her Majesty to keep one of her eyes fixed upon Messina, and do not be too late in calling for our Troops from Malta.   I am sure both King and Queen will take what I say in good part; for they have not a creature more sincerely attached to them, and their Royal Family, than their faithful Nelson.   With respect to Russia, I am clearly of opinion that she should not show her teeth, unless she is ready to bite, and the sending a few Troops would, perhaps, only expedite the plans of the French, unless they were ready to be supported by a large Army; but the distance of Russia is so great that all the mischief may be done before they get upon the scene of action.   I like the idea of English Troops getting into the Kingdom of Naples; and if they are well commanded, I am sure they will do well.   They will have more wants than us Sailors, but it will be nothing compared to those of the Russians, who will certainly fight well; but they are a scourge to the Country that unfortunately wants their assistance.   But when the French are turned out, I would recommend removing the others into places where they cannot plunder the people of the Country.

I now send you the Excellent, Captain Sotheron, to relieve the Renown, who will go to England; and you will find in Captain Sotheron every qualification of a complete gentleman and excellent Officer.   With respect to my making War upon Spain, and Sir John Orde not having done it, I believe you will think that I have acted not precipitately, but consistent with the firmness of John Bull.   I can't tell what schemes Ministers may have; but when I am without orders, and unexpected occurrences arise, I shall always act as I think the honour and glory of my King and Country demand. Upon the most mature and serious consideration I can give the subject, the present lays within the compass of a nut-shell. Our Ministers demand certain points to be conceded to them; they, to give a spur, detain the Spanish treasure.   Spain, the moment she hears of it, kicks your Minister out of Madrid; a plain proof they had not acceded to our propositions.   Indeed, Mr. Frere, you will see by his letter, did not believe it would have a favourable termination, even had not the Frigates been detained.   I send your Excellency his letters.   I feel I have done perfectly right. No desire of wealth could influence my conduct; for I had nothing to take worth twopence to me. Sir John Orde was sent, if it was a Spanish War, to take the money; but until he saw my orders, he did not act. I suppose he was fearful of that responsibility which I am ever ready to take upon me ; and now he is to wallow in wealth, whilst I am left a beggar. But such things are. I receive the kindest letters from Lord Melville and the Secretary of State, but they think the French Fleet is prize enough for me.

You will believe, my dear Sir, that if I had small Vessels, that one should be with you every month, or oftener, but I have them not. No, not half enough for the different services, and they are decreasing daily by Convoys going to England. Not one has arrived for these fifteen months. I will try and forward your letters to Lisbon, or it's possible the Renown may carry them to England. She will have orders to stay till the 20th instant at Naples, and I shall wait three or four days for her at this place. I hope both Austria and Prussia may be induced to oppose the upstart Emperor, and I think the ancient Monarchy nearer being established than since 1793. The Fleet, as Captain Sotheron will tell you, cannot be in better health. There has been much pains taken to make Europe believe that we were all dying of the fever. General Fox is arrived at Gibraltar, and the Rock was considered in pratique, and the yellow flag struck upon January 1st. But I fear the dead have been buried so very incautiously, that danger may be feared in the summer heats. Your Excellency will be so good as to present my humble duty to both the King and Queen, and believe me ever, with the highest respect, your most faithful, obliged, and obedient servant,　　　　　　　　　　　　NELSON AND BRONTE.

TO CAPTAIN MALCOLM, H.M. SHIP RENOWN.

[Autograph, in the possession of Rear-Admiral Sir Charles Malcolm.]

Victory, January 13th, 1805.

My dear Sir,

Long looked for is come at last. Captain Sotheron will relieve you. I hope you will be able to sail with all Mr.

Elliot's dispatches on the 20th, when he assures me he shall be ready. If you still keep in the mind to have an exchange into the Donegal, Sir Richard is ready for you, and I have given my consent, to oblige both him and you. I am ever, dear Sir, faithfully yours,

NELSON AND BRONTE.

I will take care of your Russians.[5]

TO HIS EXCELLENCY HUGH ELLIOT, ESQ., NAPLES.

[Autograph, in the Elliot Papers.]

Victory, January 13th, 1805.

Secret.

My dear Sir,

Sir John Orde brought me out my leave to go to England for the re-establishment of my health, and many suppose that, the moment I had passed the Straits, he would take upon him the command. Others suppose Sir John Colpoys will be my successor, and there are others that think I shall return, if my health permits, and that my services will continue to be acceptable. However, I have kept my permission a profound *secret* in the Fleet. Everybody expects that it will come; therefore do not mention my having received it, to either Captain Sotheron or Captain Malcolm, although you may to the King and Queen. I do assure you that nothing has kept me here, but the fear for the escape of the French Fleet, and that they should get to either Naples or Sicily in the short days; and that when I go I shall leave such instructions with Sir Richard Bickerton (who I am sure will follow them well up) to guard the Two Sicilies, as he would the apple of his eye; and nothing but gratitude to those good Sovereigns could have induced me to stay one moment after Sir John Orde's extraordinary Command, for his general conduct towards me is not such as I had a right to expect. Amazon is gone with my last dispatches to Gibraltar. I saw William for five minutes. He was to have dined here, but a fair wind came, and that cancels all invitations. I expected a much later letter from Mr. Jackson, at Rome, for I

5 The Russian young gentlemen before mentioned.

have wrote to him twice since the date of his letter. I am ever, my dear Sir, your very much obliged and faithful servant,

NELSON AND BRONTE.

You may trust Captain Sotheron with your confidence.

TO CAPTAIN FRANK SOTHERON, H.M. SHIP EXCELLENT.

[From a Copy in the Elliot Papers.]

Victory, Madalena Islands, Sardinia, 14th January, 1805.

Most secret and confidential.

You are hereby required and directed, on this order being delivered to you, to receive, or to convoy them, if they embark on board their own Ships, the King, Queen, and Royal Family of Naples, to Palermo, or such other place as the King may choose to proceed to; and you will afford every protection and assistance to all those who may wish to follow their Majesties, and that they approve of; and you will also receive his Majesty's Minister and suite, and afford such other protection as in your power to all British Subjects, and their property, as the urgency of the case may require.

NELSON AND BRONTE.

TO CAPTAIN KEATS, H.M. SHIP SUPERB.

[Autograph, in the possession of Mrs. Gatty.]

Victory, January 15th, 1805.

My dear Keats,

Many thanks for your Telegraph message, and I am sorry that, for form's sake, I must consider you, at least for one day, in Quarantine; but I think if Dr. Scott will go with one of your Officers to the shore, and state to the Governor and Officers of Health, that you have been as many days in Quarantine as you have been from Algiers, that the place is healthy, and you are healthy, with such winning ways as Dr. Scott knows so well how to use, I have no doubt but that you will have pratique; and let your Officer say that I have examined the state of the Ship, and find her proper to have pratique, &c. &c., which I am ready to certify if the Governor wishes it; then I shall hope to have you to dinner; but if they will not give you pratique, I shall to-morrow. Ever, my dear Keats, your much obliged,

NELSON AND BRONTE.

I send you some late Papers.

TO WILLIAM MARSDEN, ESQ., ADMIRALTY.

[Original, in the Admiralty.]

Victory, Madalena Islands, 16th January, 1805.

Sir,

It being my intention to send his Majesty's Ship Amphitrite (lately captured by the Donegal) to England, under charge of the Renown, in order to her being manned and completed for service, as their Lordships may think proper to direct, I have judged it necessary, for the good of his Majesty's Service, to appoint Sir William Bolton to be Captain of her, and herewith transmit you a copy of his Commission, and a copy of an acting order given to Lieutenant John Louis[6] to command the Childers, in the room of Sir William Bolton; also a copy of an order given to Mr. George Martin Sutherland[7] to act as Lieutenant of the Royal Sovereign, in the room of Captain Louis, which I request you will be so good as lay before the Lords Commissioners of the Admiralty for their information, and move their Lordships to confirm the said appointments. I am, Sir, &c.

NELSON AND BRONTE.

TO EARL CAMDEN, K.G., SECRETARY OF STATE FOR THE WAR DEPARTMENT.

[Autograph, in the Colonial Office.]

Victory, January 16th, 1805.

My Lord,

Yesterday his Majesty's Ship Superb, Captain Keats, returned from Algiers, having landed Mr. Cartwright, his Ma-

---

[6] Now Rear-Admiral Sir John Louis, Bart.

[7] Mr. George Martin Sutherland: he appears to have died a Lieutenant, between 1806 and 1809.

jesty's Consul-General to that place, who was received by the Dey, the Regency, and the Inhabitants, with much pleasure ; and I have no doubt but that our footing at Algiers is as a most favoured Nation. Your Lordship will not fail to observe that the conduct of Captain Keats merits those encomiums which would fall far short of his merits, were I to attempt to express what my feelings are upon this, as upon all other occasions where the services of Captain Keats are called forth. I shall, therefore, leave your Lordship to represent them to his Majesty, in the manner and language your Lordship's superior judgment shall point out as most proper for their having the fullest effect.

Captain Keats very handsomely attributes great credit to the services of the Reverend Mr. Scott, my confidential Secretary and Interpreter, and to the Reverend Mr. Evans, Chaplain of his Majesty's Ship Superb, and I beg leave to call your Lordship's attention to the merits of these gentlemen. They have, both in the last and present War, made themselves perfectly masters of all the European languages spoken in the Mediterranean, which has qualified them to be Interpreters on any important occasions, where confidence is required to be reposed. Our Navy Chaplains have not generally the good fortune to be in the road to promotion : their brethren ashore have all the advantage of being upon the spot (one exception, the present Lord Chancellor very handsomely having given my former Chaplain a Living,) I therefore presume to recommend both these gentlemen as proper candidates for Crown Livings; and it would be a great inducement for the Navy Chaplains to make themselves useful to the State, in a greater degree than they are at present, for we all want persons of learning and confidence to write our letters to Foreign Courts, which in the Mediterranean we are always in correspondence with.

The Dey having received the Consul, as he expressed himself at the time, ' I receive you without presents;' and our amity with Algiers being, perhaps more firmly established than for many years past, I submit to your Lordship's consideration, whether it would not at this moment cement the friendship, was some presents to be made to the Regency, not upon account of the Consul, but as a particular present from his Majesty. I have, &c.   NELSON AND BRONTE.

TO COMMISSIONER OTWAY, MALTA.

[Autograph, in the possession of Rear-Admiral Inglefield, C.B.]

My dear Sir,   Victory, January 18th, 1805.

I am much obliged by your favour of January 3rd, and as
the Camel will come direct to the Fleet, she will be by far
the most eligible conveyance you can have; and I hope to
reap another great advantage from your coming in that Ship,
that she will be much sooner unloaded, and reloaded, with
the stores wanted for the Fleet, by your presence. We want
an entire floating Arsenal. When we get you to the Fleet,
easy modes will be found to carry you to Gibraltar. As all
our Sloops will soon be wore out, if the Small Craft cannot
get men at Malta, I am afraid the Eastern part of the station
will be very badly off for the necessary protection; but if the
Admiralty will not give me Sloops, and Small Craft cannot
get men at Malta, I have no means of furnishing the means
of protection.

I send you a copy of Captain Malcolm's last letter to me.
You will see that Mr. Taylor has not been correct in saying
he had not given Mr. James any orders; it was enough
between man and man, where words were to be relied upon
more than the official forms. I can again repeat that Mr.
Bunce would be a most valuable acquisition to any Yard; and
should you find it proper to suspend Mr. Stocker, upon your
application I will send Mr. Bunce, for whose abilities and
good conduct I would pledge my head. The Excellent is
gone to relieve the Renown, who is going direct to England.
My staying or going seems at present very uncertain. With
every good wish, I am ever, my dear Sir, your much obliged,

NELSON AND BRONTE.

DIARY.

[From Clarke and M'Arthur, vol. ii. p. 393. " January 20th, [*i. e.*, 19th.] P.M.
Seahorse and Active rejoined. At 4·30, weighed and made sail out of Agincourt
Sound, through the Biche Channel. At 6·20, passed through the Biche Channel,
Squadron following."—*Victory's Log.*]

January 19th, 1805.

Hard gales N.W. At three, P.M. the Active and Seahorse
arrived at Madalena, with information that the French Fleet

put to sea from Toulon yesterday.[8] These Frigates were close to them at ten o'clock last night, and saw one of them until two o'clock this morning. Unmoored and weighed. At twenty-eight minutes past four, made the general signal for each Ship to carry a light, and repeat signals during the night, made by the Admiral. Ran through the Passage between Biche and Sardinia at six o'clock. At thirty-five minutes past six, burnt a blue light, and at forty-five minutes past, another. At seven the whole Fleet was clear of the Passage. Sent Seahorse round the Southern end of Sardinia, to St. Peters, to look out for them, but to prevent the Enemy, as much as possible, from seeing her ; and the moment Captain Boyle discovered them, to return to me. From their position when last seen, and the course they were steering, S. or S. b W., they could only be bound round the Southern end of Sardinia. At nine, P.M. bore away along that Island with the following Ships—Victory, Donegal, Superb, Canopus, Spencer, Tigre, Royal Sovereign, Leviathan, Belleisle, Conqueror, Swiftsure, and Active Frigate. During the night it was squally, unsettled

---

[8] Monsieur Thiers says, that the Fleet in Toulon, which had been increased from eight to eleven Ships of the Line, had required the whole month of December to get ready for sea; that General Lauriston, Napoleon's Aide-de-Camp, had been appointed to form a corps of 6000 picked men, with 50 cannon, and a battering train, and to embark the whole in the Toulon Fleet; that that Fleet, on its way, was to detach a division to St. Helena, to take possession of the Island, then to proceed to Surinam, retake the Dutch colonies, and then to join the Squadron under Admiral Missiessy, which, on its part, would have relieved the French West India Islands, and ravaged the English Colonies, and that both Squadrons, after having decoyed the English towards America, and liberated Ganteaume with the Brest Squadron, were to return to Europe. Monsieur Thiers then says, that Ganteaume had waited during the whole winter, until Missiessy and Villeneuve, running out of Toulon, should draw off the English ; that Missiessy sailed from Rochfort on the 11th of January, and, without being seen by the English, proceeded to the West Indies, with five Ships of the Line and four Frigates. After some very severe remarks on Admiral Villeneuve, Monsieur Thiers thus speaks of the sailing of the Squadron under Villeneuve's command from Toulon :—" Urged by Napoleon, by the Minister Decrès, and by General Lauriston, he got ready to weigh anchor towards the end of December. A head wind [un vent debout] detained him in Toulon Roads, from the end of December to the 18th of January. On the 18th, the wind having changed, he set sail, and by steering a wrong course, succeeded in evading the Enemy. [En faisant fausse route, à se soustraire à l'ennemi.] But in the course of the night a heavy tempest arose, and the inexperience of the crews, and the bad quality of the materials, exposed many of our Vessels [plusieurs de nos bâtiments] to serious accidents. The Squadron was dispersed. In the morning, Villeneuve found himself separated, with four Ships of the Line and one Frigate. Some had carried away their topmasts, others had sprung leaks, or had received damage not easily repaired at sea.

weather. At forty-eight minutes past eight, burnt a blue
light ; at half past ten, down topgallant yards, and struck top
gallant masts. At midnight, moderate breezes and clear. At
two, [A.M. 20th January] burnt a blue light, and at four burnt
another, and made more sail. At thirty-five minutes past seven,
Active made the signal for a Sail ; and immediately afterwards,
that the strange Sail was a Vessel of War, which proved to be
the Seahorse. At fifty minutes past seven, made the signal
that Spencer and Leviathan were to be a Detached Squadron;
delivered the Honourable Captain Stopford a letter to that
effect, directing him to keep on my weather-beam with them,
being fast-sailing Ships, to act as occasion might require. At
fifty-five minutes past eight, made Active's signal to close
nearer the Admiral, and at twenty minutes past nine, made
Swiftsure's to do the same. At twenty-five minutes past nine,
made the general signal to 'Prepare for Battle.' At twenty-
five minutes past eleven, made the same signal, to ' Form the
established Order of Sailing in two columns,' and the signal

Besides these misadventures, two English Frigates were watching us, and the
Admiral was afraid of the Enemy coming up with him [rejoint] at the moment
when he had but five Sail [vaisseaux] to oppose to him. He therefore determined
to put back to Toulon, although he was already seventy leagues distant from it ; and
notwithstanding the entreaties of General Lauriston, who, reckoning four thousand
and some hundreds of men on board the Vessels which still remained together, demanded to be taken to his destination, Villeneuve returned to Toulon on the 27th
[sic, but truly the 21st, i. e. " 1er pluviose, an xiii.," the date of Admiral Villeneuve's
dispatch, announcing his return], and succeeded in assembling his whole Squadron
there."—History of the Consulate and the Empire, translated by Campbell, vol. v.
pp. 157, 158; collated with the original edition. Upon this statement it is to be
observed, that the presence of our Squadron, rather than " un vent debout," seems
to have detained Admiral Villeneuve until after the 18th of January, because, in the
early part of the month, the wind was northerly; and as, on the 9th or 10th, Lord
Nelson quitted his station for Sardinia, Villeneuve, even if he was not aware of the
fact, must have known that the English Squadron had not been seen in the vicinity
of Toulon for upwards of a week, thus affording a presumption that they had, as
usual, either gone off Cape St. Sebastian, or to Sardinia for water and refreshments.
As on the 18th, the English Squadron was at anchor at Madalena, it is difficult to
understand how Admiral Villeneuve, by " faisant fausse route, à se soustraire à
l'ennemi;" inasmuch as by steering South or S. b E., instead of a course to take him
out of the Mediterranean, he did, in fact, approach Nelson's Squadron unnecessarily ;
and this is, no doubt, one reason for believing that he was not aware of its being at
Madalena, but supposed it was off Cape St. Sebastian. It is, however, obvious that
if the French really sailed with the intention of passing the Straits, their proceedings
completely deceived Lord Nelson, but whose usual sagacity, nevertheless displayed
itself in supposing that they were forced back to Toulon, in a crippled condition, by
the gale of the 19th.

to ' Keep in close Order.' Spencer and Leviathan separated from this Order, to be the readier to push at any detached Ships of the Enemy. [Noon, Mount Santo bore N.W., distance six leagues.—*Victory's Log.*] All night very hard gales from S.S.W. to S.W., which continued throughout the next day; during great part of the time we were under storm staysails.

TO CAPTAIN THOMAS, H.M. SHIP ÆTNA

[Autograph, in the possession of Rear-Admiral Thomas.

Sir,   Victory, January 19th, 1805.

The French Fleet put to sea yesterday, and were seen last night at twelve o'clock, steering South, or S. b W., then supposed in the latitude of Ajaccio, going ten or eleven miles per hour. They are therefore, from this account, bound round the South end of Sardinia. It is therefore my intention to proceed to the Southward, and endeavour to intercept them. If you do not hear of us in a few days, you must take the Transports to Malta, and then endeavour to join me, wherever you may hear I may be. I am, Sir, &c.

NELSON AND BRONTE.

TO HIS EXCELLENCY SIR JOHN ACTON, BART., PALERMO.

[From a Copy, in the Elliot Papers.]

My dear Sir John,   Victory, January 22nd, 1805.

The French Fleet sailed from Toulon on Friday last, the 18th. Our Frigates saw part of them all day, and were chased by some of the Ships. At ten o'clock the same night, they were in the French Fleet, then nearly in the latitude of Ajaccio, steering South, or S. b W., the direct course for the Island of Toro, South end of Sardinia, it blowing a strong gale at N.W., and a heavy sea. The French were then, by Captain Moubray's account, carrying a heavy press of sail. At three o'clock in the afternoon of the 19th, Captain Moubray made his report to me at Madalena, and at six the whole Fleet was at sea, with a fresh breeze at W.N.W., steering to the Southward along the Sardinian shore, intending to push for the South end of Sardinia, where I could have little fear but that I should meet them; for, from all I

have heard from the Captains of the Frigates, the Enemy
must be bound round the South end of Sardinia, but whether
to Cagliari, Sicily, the Morea, or Egypt, I am most completely in ignorance. I believe they have six or seven thousand Troops on board. On the 20th, we were taken with a
heavy gale at S.S.W., which has arrested our progress. It is
now (eight o'clock on the morning of the 22nd) at W. b S.,
and we are sixteen leagues East from Cape Carbonara, blowing fresh, with a heavy sea, so that I stand no chance of
closing with Sardinia to day. I have sent a Frigate to both
Cagliari and the Island of St. Pierres, to try and get information; and although I have only one Frigate with me, I send
her to your Excellency, that you may be put upon your
guard, in case the Enemy are bound to Sicily; and I beg
that you will send likewise to Naples, in case their passing
the South end of Sardinia should be a feint in order to
deceive me. But I rather think they believe I am off Cape
St. Sebastians, where I am often forced to take shelter. If
the French have had similar winds to us, it was impossible
they could be round Toro before the morning of the 20th;
and since that time, till this morning, they have had no winds
which would allow them to weather Maritimo, if they are destined for either Egypt or the Morea. It is almost impossible
they can have passed us and gone to Naples; and I am at this
moment in the best possible position for intercepting them,
should that be their destination.

I must be guided in all my future movements by information which I may receive; therefore I can only assure your
Excellency of my ardent desire to fall in with them, and that
no exertion of mine shall be wanting to annihilate them. I
ever, with the highest respect, your Excellency's most obedient
and faithful servant,   NELSON AND BRONTE.

TO SIR ALEXANDER JOHN BALL, BART., MALTA.

[Autograph, in the possession of Sir William Keith Ball, Bart.]

Victory, January 22nd, 1805, 8 A.M., 16 Leagues East of
Cape Carbonara.

My dear Ball,

I send you a copy of my letter to Sir John Acton, which
tells all I know, and I send you a copy of Captain Moubray's

Log, therefore all I have to request of you is, to advise Captain Schomberg, whom I have ordered to consult you, to send to every position you can think of to get information. If they are passed by Cape Bon, I should think they would know it at Tunis. What would I give to know where they are bound to, or to see them!—the result of a meeting I should be a wretch to doubt. I am naturally very anxious, therefore you must forgive my short letter.

11 A.M.—The Seahorse saw yesterday, at 3 P M, a French Frigate off Pula, but it was so thick that he could not see three miles distant, therefore could not make out the French Fleet. We have a dead foul wind and heavy sea. I cannot, for want of Frigates, send off this letter. I am ever, my dear Ball, yours most faithfully,

NELSON AND BRONTE.

DIARY.

[From Clarke and M'Arthur, vol. ii. p. 393.]

22nd January, 1805.

We had in the morning very heavy squalls from the Westward; Seahorse in sight coming down. At half-past nine, she made the signal that she had been chased by the Enemy's Frigates; and at ten, that she had ' Intelligence to communicate.' At eleven, Captain Boyle informed me, that yesterday afternoon, at three o'clock, he had seen a French Frigate standing in for Pula, but it was so thick he could not discern the French Fleet, and it blew a heavy gale of wind at S.S.W. I sincerely pray for a favourable wind; for we cannot be more than twenty leagues from them, and if Cagliari be their object, and the Sardes will but defend their Capital, we shall be in time to save them : pray God it may be so.

TO HIS EXCELLENCY HUGH ELLIOT, ESQ., NAPLES.

[Autograph, in the Elliot Papers.]

Victory, Gulf of Cagliari, January 25th, 1805.

My dear Sir,

I send your Excellency a copy of my letter to Sir John Acton, which will tell you all I know. If the French Fleet is gone to Naples, you will never get this letter. If they are not, it will be pleasant to know my position, and that I must cover Messina by my going to the Eastward. I shall probably push for the Morea, and heel of Italy, should they be destined to carry across the Adriatic the Army in the Kingdom of Naples. But God knows their intentions!—perhaps it may be Egypt again. Pray don't keep Captain Boyle one moment, for I have neither Frigates or small Vessels with me. Present me to their Majesties as most anxious to defend their Kingdoms. You will believe how anxious I must be. I am ever, my dear Sir, your most obliged and faithful servant,

NELSON AND BRONTE.

TO HIS EXCELLENCY SIR JOHN ACTON, BART., PALERMO.

[From a Copy, in the Elliot Papers.]

Victory, standing into the Gulf of Cagliari, January 25th, 1805.

My dear Sir John,

It has blown a heavy gale of wind from the S.S.W. until this morning, when I am off the Island of Serpentari. From the information of the French Frigates standing into the Gulf of Cagliari, I sent my two Frigates to watch the Enemy's motions, or to get me some information of their movements: one has just returned with *no* information, but as she has not communicated with Cagliari, I am obliged to send her back. If the Vice-Roy knows nothing of them, I shall push direct for Palermo, in case Sicily should be their object; and I shall, the moment I can get hold of any other Frigate, send her to Naples, with orders for her to join me off the Faro of Messina. I shall then be at hand to cover Messina, in case they should pass round Cape Passaro, or to proceed to Naples in case they are in that Bay. You will believe my anxiety. I have neither ate, drank, or slept with any comfort since last Sunday.

10 o'clock.—I have just spoke a Vessel which left the Gulf of Palma last night. The Enemy's Fleet was not there. I hope to have my answer from Cagliari by four o'clock, and I hope to be with you to-morrow. Pray, Sir John, tell the Captain all you know; Captain Bayntun is an excellent

Officer, and can tell you as much as I can.   Excuse my hasty scrawl; but I am ever your Excellency's most faithful and obliged friend and servant,

NELSON AND BRONTE.

I hope the Governor of Augusta will not give up the Post to the French Fleet; but if he does, I shall go in and attack them, for I consider the destruction of the Enemy's Fleet of so much consequence, that I would willingly have half of mine burnt to effect their destruction. I am in a fever. God send I may find them!

TO HIS EXCELLENCY THE VICE-ROY OF SICILY.

[Autograph draught, in the possession of Miss Bolton, of Burnham.]

Victory, at Sea, January 26th, 1805.

Sir,

The difficulties which some of his Majesty's Ships under my command have experienced in obtaining pratique in the Ports of Sicily, although they were clearly entitled to the most liberal pratique, render it necessary for me to demand, in the name of my Sovereign, that orders may be instantly given to all the Governors, &c., in the different Ports of Sicily, that all Ships having my Certificate of Health shall be instantly entitled to the most liberal pratique, and receive every hospitable reception which the close and intimate alliance between our most gracious Sovereigns so justly entitles them to expect; and I beg to be furnished with a duplicate copy of the Order.   I have the honour to be,

NELSON AND BRONTE.

PRIVATE DIARY.

[From Clarke and M'Arthur, vol. ii. p. 395.]

Victory, January 29th, 1805.

Stromboli burnt very strongly throughout the night. Passed round it at three in the morning. As we ran outside the Lipari Islands, we had been obliged to steer E. b N., and for two hours E.N.E. by compass, when, by the Spanish chart, E. and E. b S. were laid down as the proper course.

TO WILLIAM MARSDEN, ESQ., ADMIRALTY.

[Original, in the Admiralty, and Autograph draught, in the possession of Miss
Bolton, of Burnham.]

Victory, Faro of Messina, January 29th, 1805.

Sir,

From the middle of December, I had information from
various places, and amongst others, from the King of Sardinia,
that the French were assembling Troops near Toulon, and had
taken some of the best Troops and a corps of Cavalry from the
Riviere of Genoa. Captain Capel obtained information that
every Seaman was pressed and sent to Toulon. On the 16th,
the Active spoke a Vessel from Marseilles, who reported that
seven thousand Troops embarked on board the French Fleet.
The wind had been nearly fourteen days Easterly, from N.E.
to S.E.; therefore, if the Enemy had been bound to the
Westward, they could not have gone with a fair wind. On
the 18th,[9] the Enemy put to sea, steering for the South-end of
Sardinia. On the 19th, I was informed of it, and put to sea
from the Madalena Islands, that evening. On the 21st, a
French Frigate was seen off the South-end of Sardinia by the
Seahorse; but the weather was so thick and gale so strong,
that Captain Boyle could not see their Fleet, and he joined
me the 22nd with the information; but it was from heavy
gales the 26th, before I could communicate with Cagliari, at
which place they knew nothing of the Enemy. On the same
day, the Phœbe joined with information that a French Ship
of eighty guns had put into Ajaccio on the 19th, in the evening, with the loss of her topmasts, and otherwise much
crippled. The Seahorse was detached to Naples the 25th,
with information.

On the 28th, I was off Palermo and communicated with Sir
John Acton; and the news which the Court of Naples has
from Paris of January 5th, makes them fear that Sicily might
be the object of the Enemy's armament.

---

[9] On the 12th of February, 1805, Lord Nelson sent a duplicate of this dispatch,
to which he made the following addition:—" N.B. I now know that the Enemy's
Fleet came out of Toulon on the 17th of January, with a gentle breeze from the
N.W., and waited between that and the Hières Islands until the breeze freshened
on the 18th, when they proceeded with a strong gale.—NELSON AND BRONTE."

One of two things must have happened, that either the
French Fleet must have put back crippled, or that they are
gone to the Eastward, probably to Egypt, therefore, I find no
difficulty in pursuing the line of conduct I have adopted. If
the Enemy have put back crippled, I could never overtake
them, and therefore I can do no harm in going to the Eastward ; and if the Enemy are gone to the Eastward, I am right.
My future movements must be guided by such information as
I may be able to obtain, but their Lordships may rely that
every exertion shall be used to find them out and bring them
to Battle. I am, Sir, &c.

NELSON AND BRONTE.

TO SIR ALEXANDER JOHN BALL, BART., MALTA.

[Autograph, in the possession of Sir William Keith Ball, Bart.]

Victory, January 31st, 1805.

My dear Ball,

The French Fleet may possibly be severely crippled, and
put into various Ports. On the 22nd, in the evening, in a
gale W. S. W. the Hydra saw three large Ships running
along shore towards St. Fiorenzo ; but as Captain Mundy did
not know the Enemy's Fleet had sailed, he thought they might
be some of our Ships.

I have sent Morgiana to look into Elba and St. Fiorenzo,
then to drop a letter for me either at Madalena, St. Pierres,
or Cagliari, and proceed to Malta, Bittern to Tunis and
Pantalaria, then to Malta ; Seahorse round Cape Corse, or
through the Madalena Islands, off Toulon. Hydra round the
South end of Sardinia, or Madalena off Toulon. Active,
orders left at Messina, round either end of the Islands or
through Bonifaccio, off Toulon. Each ordered to send letters
for me to St. Pierres, Madalena, and Cagliari, and to Malta
—Termagant to cruize off Toro fourteen days. Phœbe
to Coron, round by Goza of Candia. I shall proceed as
winds, or information, or the getting no information may
make me judge proper ; you shall hear of me. If I return
I shall call perhaps off Malta, but that must be very uncertain.
Celerity in my movements may catch these fellows yet. By

reports of Vessels from Toulon, taken by Termagant, eleven Sail of the Line, and nine Frigates and Corvettes—twenty Sail of Ships in the whole. I shall only hope to fall in with them. I should be unworthy of my Command if I dared to doubt the event with such a fine Fleet as I have the happiness of commanding. God bless you, my dear Ball, and believe me ever your most sincere and faithful friend.

NELSON AND BRONTE.

TO . . . . . .

[Autograph draught, in the possession of the Reverend Henry Girdlestone.]

Victory, February 1st, 1805.

Sir,

As it is of the utmost importance that the Fleet should not be separated at this very important crisis, I rely that most particular attention will be paid in order to prevent it. But should such a circumstance unavoidably take place, it is absolutely impossible for me to point out precisely the place where the Fleet may be found, as my movements must depend upon such information as I may receive. My present intention is to proceed off Coron, where the Phœbe is gone for information; then off Goza of Candia; then probably to Alexandria; and not finding the Enemy in any of those places, then to return to the Westward.

You must therefore exercise your judgment, and, as a last resource, go off Valetta harbour, and remain there, until you hear from, or of me ; but you are not upon any consideration, short of absolute distress, to go into the harbour, but be ready to join me the first information you may be able to obtain where to find me. I am, Sir, &c.

NELSON AND BRONTE.

TO WILLIAM MARSDEN, ESQ., ADMIRALTY.

[Original, in the Admiralty.]

Victory, at Sea, 4th February, 1805.

Sir,

The Commissioners for taking care of Sick and Wounded Seamen, having requested that I would cause a further contract to be entered into with Mr. John Broadbent, Merchant at Messina, for twenty thousand gallons of lemon juice, in addition to the thirty thousand previously agreed for by Doctor Snipe at one shilling per gallon, cask included, I beg you will be so good as acquaint the Lords Commissioners of the Admiralty, that I sent Doctor Snipe, late Physician of the Fleet to Messina, with directions to contract with the said Mr. Broadbent for twenty thousand gallons of lemon juice for Home consumption, and ten thousand gallons for the use of the Fleet under my command, which he has with much attention and regard to the Public interest settled for at eighteen pence per gallon, instead of one shilling, formerly contracted for. This increased price is found, upon the most strict inquiry, to be just and necessary to cover the unavoidable expense attending the squeezing the lemons, which Mr. Broadbent was not aware of on his entering into the first Contract, and consequently will be a considerable loser by it.

I therefore judge it necessary to send you the copy of Mr. Broadbent's letter to Doctor Snipe, and also of the late Physician's letter to me on this subject, and request you will be pleased to lay them before their Lordships for their information, and move them to give the necessary directions to the Commissioners of the Sick and Hurt Board, to allow Mr. Broadbent sixpence more per gallon for the thirty thousand gallons at first contracted for, that he may not be a loser from the integrity of his conduct.

Mr. Broadbent, from every information I have received, is an honest upright man, and very justly entitled to their Lordships' consideration on the present occasion. Doctor Snipe, as he is going home, will furnish the Sick and Hurt Board with the Contracts, and such further information on this subject as the Commissioners may deem necessary. I am, Sir, &c.

NELSON AND BRONTE.

Victory, February 4th, 1805.

Sir,

If the French are arrived before me, you will, of course,
not receive this letter; if they are not arrived, it is my opinion
they are dispersed and crippled in the bad weather they have
experienced since their leaving Toulon. I have wrote the
Governor of Alexandria to be upon his guard against a
visit from those gentry; for, as a week ago they had not
either arrived in Sardinia, Naples, or Sicily, I still think
their destination is either Egypt or the Morea. I may chance
to fall in with them on my return; for I shall pursue the
route I think they will take; but, as the Governor is now
put upon his guard, I hope he will take every means in his
power for the defence of Alexandria; and in particular, to
have Vessels ready to sink, to prevent the entrance of the
French Fleet into the old Port, until the obstructions were
removed, which would give me time to get at them. The
French Fleet sailed on the 18th January, with from 8000 to
10,000 Troops embarked. On the 19th, they had a very
heavy gale of wind to the Westward of Corsica and Sardinia.
One Ship of 80 guns put into Ajaccio, crippled; three others
were seen steering for St. Fiorenzo. On the 21st, some of
them were seen off the South end of Sardinia. But I know
that, on the 28th, they had neither been in Sardinia or Naples,
and I was at Messina on the 30th; therefore, they are either
returned to Toulon, or are, I fear, arrived in Egypt. But
even in that case, if Alexandria is properly defended, it cannot have yet fallen into their hands, or their Fleet got into
the Port. If the Enemy is not here, I shall not remain one
moment on the Coast; you will, therefore, by the return of
the Boat, give me all the information you have. I shall be
much obliged to you to send my letter, when opportunity
efforts, to Major Misset, at Cairo. I am, Sir, with great respect, &c.

NELSON AND BRONTE.

TO SAMUEL BRIGGS, ESQ., BRITISH PRO-CONSUL AT ALEXANDRIA.

[Autograph, in the possession of Samuel Briggs, Esq.]

Victory, February 4th, 1805.

Dear Sir,

I sent a Frigate with my letters two days ago; but I see that she is still to leeward, and cannot get up, therefore, I send Duplicates. If nothing is known of the French Fleet at Alexandria, I shall instantly return to the Westward; therefore, I beg that the Boat may not be detained, nor must any communication be had with the Officer, so as to put the Ship in quarantine. The Officer is ordered not to wait more than thirty minutes; for you will readily believe my anxiety to find out the Enemy's Fleet. I am, dear Sir, with great respect, &c.

NELSON AND BRONTE.

There is very little news as to the active movements of the contending parties. A Continental War is looked upon as certain.

TO WILLIAM MARSDEN, ESQ., ADMIRALTY.

[Original, in the Admiralty. "February 8th [i. e., 7th.] P.M. At 6, the Pharos of Alexandria bore S.E. b S., distance 7 leagues."—*Victory's Log.*]

Victory, at Sea, 8th February, 1805.

Sir,

I herewith transmit you, for the information of the Lords Commissioners of the Admiralty, a letter from Captain Adair of the Marines belonging to the Victory, Inspecting Officer for raising Recruits in this Country for the Royal Marines, together with a List, Number 1, including those Recruits placed to the Companies of such as have died and deserted on this station, and of those placed to the respective Divisions, agreeable to their Lordships' instructions, communicated to me in your letter of the 14th September 1804. Number 2 contains the names of the Recruits sent home in the Kent and Triumph, agreeably to Sir Evan Nepean's letter to me, dated the 29th September 1803, an extract of which accompanies this, directing me to send to England by every

opportunity the surplus Recruits that might be raised more
than was necessary to complete the different Ships of the
Squadron; and in order to meet their Lordships' intentions,
(knowing that Marines were much wanted in England,) I
suffered the new raised Recruits on board the Kent and
Triumph to go to England in those Ships, although the
Ship's complements remaining on the station were not all
complete. And I beg, with due deference, to state, from my
experience in the Mediterranean, that Italians (who in any
other Country are faithful, steady men) are not good for
anything so near home, as they are constantly crying after
it; and, consequently, seek for opportunities to desert whenever the Ships go into Port. It will not, however, during the
period of contagion in the different Ports of the Mediterranean, (as great caution is necessary in receiving Foreigners
on board the Fleet,) be possible to raise so great a number as
otherwise would have been done, from the very [great] and
unremitted attention of Captain Adair to this service—most
probably not more than may be sufficient to keep the complements of the different Ships complete. Number 3 contains
the names of the new raised men serving on board the Ships
named in the margin,[1] who will be placed to vacant Companies
or Divisions the moment those Ships join, and the regular
Returns are made to Captain Adair, which shall afterwards be
transmitted to you for their Lordships' information. I am,
Sir, &c.

NELSON AND BRONTE.

TO SIR ALEXANDER JOHN BALL, BART., MALTA.

[Autograph, in the possession of Miss Collinson.]

Victory, off Gozo of Candia, February 11th, 1805.

My dear Ball,
Although I have not yet heard of the French Fleet, and
remain in total ignorance where they are got to, yet to this
moment I am more confirmed in my opinion, from communicating with Alexandria, that Egypt was the destination
of the French Armament from Toulon; and when I call all
the circumstances which I know at this moment, I approve

[1] Excellent, Juno, Phœbe, Active, Termagant.

(if nobody else does) of my own conduct, in acting as I have
done. We know the success of a man's measures is the
criterion by which we judge of the wisdom or folly of his
measures. I have done my best. I feel I have done right;
and should Ministers think otherwise, they must get somebody
else of more wisdom; for greater zeal I will turn my back on
no man. The following are the circumstances which made
me form my opinion; and the situation in which I found
Egypt, warrants the judgment I had formed. On these points
it is fair to judge me, and not upon what it is now known the
French Fleet have done. The winds had blown from N.E.
to S.E. for a fortnight before they sailed; therefore, it was
fair to presume they were not bound to the Westward. On
the 17th, they came out of Toulon with gentle breezes at
N.N.W., and lay between [Giens?] and the Hieres Islands till
the gale set in on the 18th, in the afternoon. Had they been
bound to Naples, it would have been better for them to have
gone to the Eastward, along their own Coast in fine weather,
with friendly ports open to them. If Cagliari was their
object, although I think of very great importance, yet their
Fleet ran the risk of a Battle, and the event, I fancy, they
hardly doubt. Almost as much might be said of Sicily; for
if the French Army took Naples, the King would, I think,
subscribe to such terms as Buonaparte would dictate: however, I did not choose to run that risk, but assured myself
they had neither gone to Sardinia, Naples, nor Sicily. The
French sailed with a strong gale at N.W. and N.N.W., steering
South or S.W., on the 19th. One of their Ships put into
Ajaccio, crippled. On the 21st, Boyle saw a French Frigate
off the South end of Sardinia, probably looking for stragglers;
they might have been crippled and dispersed in the very heavy
gale in which they left their own shore. On the 25th, I was
off Cagliari; on the 30th, the Seahorse joined from Naples;
the same day, I passed the Faro. On the 2nd of February,
was off the Morea; on the 7th, was off Alexandria, where we
found three Turkish Frigates, not more than 300 bad soldiers,
and, in short, not the least probability of making a defence
had they been so inclined; but 600 Troops would, without
any difficulty, have taken the place. The Consul told Captain
Hallowell, that, taking us for the French Fleet, the Governor

and Capitan Bey gave all up for lost. The Frigates intended to fire their guns. The works are precisely in the state we left them, and one week's work of the French would make it as strong as ever. The Turks and Mamelukes are at war in Upper Egypt; and the Albanians have left the Mamelukes, who would not pay them, and are now with the Turks. These Troops would certainly join, (at least, the greater number,) the French Army. Thus, the Mamelukes for their friends, (at least for the moment,) no Turkish Army which would oppose them—Cairo would fall as easily as Alexandria; and I calculate the French, with the junction of part of the Albanians, would, within a week, have an Army of 13,000 men; and we know there would be no difficulty for single Polaccas to sail from the shores of Italy with 300 or 400 men in each, (single Ships;) and that, in the Northerly winds, they would have a fair chance of not being seen, and even if seen, not be overtaken by the Russian Ships. Thus, 20,000 men would be fixed again in Egypt, with the whole people in their favour. Who would turn them out? Therefore, from the whole which I know, I have not a shade of doubt, but that Egypt was the original destination of the Toulon Fleet, when they sailed January 17th, 1805. You are tired of my reasoning; but I naturally am anxious that my friends should see fairly before them what has guided my proceedings; and, be I right or wrong, I have acted to the best of my judgment; and I am ever, my dear Ball, yours most faithfully,

NELSON AND BRONTE.

TO WILLIAM MARSDEN, ESQ., ADMIRALTY.

[Original, in the Admiralty, and Autograph Draught in the possession of Mrs. Hogarth, of Yarmouth.]

Victory, off the West End of Candia, February 12th, 1805.

Sir,

In addition to my letter of January 29th, off the Faro of Messina, I have to inform you, that on the 31st, the Seahorse joined me from Naples, at which place they had not heard of the Enemy's having sailed from Toulon. The same day, having detached the Seahorse, Hydra, Active, Bittern, Morgiana, and Termagant in all directions from Tunis to Toulon, both on the Italian shore, and to the Westward of Sardinia, the Fleet beat through the Faro—a thing unprecedented in nautical history; but although the danger from the rapidity of the current was great, yet so was the object of my pursuit; and I relied with confidence on the zeal and ability of the Fleet under my command. In the evening, I sent the Phœbe to Coron in the Morea for information, and on the 2nd of February, I was off the Morea; but no intelligence could be obtained of the French Fleet: but the Pacha told Captain Capel that the French Ambassador had left Constantinople on the 17th or 18th January.

On February 7th, I was off Alexandria; and from the information I received from the Pro-Consul, Mr. Briggs, there can be no doubt but six hundred men would, without assistance, occupy Alexandria. Three Turkish Frigates were in the Port, and not more than 300 bad Troops in the Town; indeed, nothing was less thought of than any resistance. The fortifications were precisely as left them by the British Army. Mr. Briggs further informed me, that the War still continued in Upper Egypt between the Turks and Mamelukes; that the former were in possession of Cairo, as the Albanians had left the Mamelukes, (they being no longer able to pay them,) and joined the Turks; and that Elfi Bey and Osman Bey had united together. From this information, with the knowledge that Lesseps, the French Consul in Egypt, had repeatedly told the Mamelukes, 'Whenever you want five thousand men to assist you, let me know, and in thirty days, the First Consul will land them in Egypt;' and when I take into consideration the importance of Egypt to France, and the injury we should sustain by her possessing that Country, I have not the smallest doubt but that the destination of the French Armament which left Toulon the 17th, and the Coast of France the 18th January, was Alexandria; and, under all the circumstances which I have stated, I trust their Lordships will approve of my having gone to Egypt in search of the French Fleet. I am, Sir, &c.,

NELSON AND BRONTE.

TO VISCOUNT MELVILLE, FIRST LORD OF THE ADMIRALTY.

[From Clarke and M'Arthur, vol. ii. p. 396.]

14th February, 1805.

Feeling, as I do, that I am entirely responsible to my King and Country for the whole of my conduct, I find no difficulty at this moment, when I am so unhappy at not finding the French Fleet, nor having obtained the smallest information where they are, to lay before you the whole of the reasons which induced me to pursue the line of conduct I have done. I have consulted no man, therefore the whole blame of ignorance in forming my judgment must rest with me. I would allow no man to take from me an atom of my glory, had I fallen in with the French Fleet, nor do I desire any man to partake of any of the responsibility—all is mine, right or wrong. Therefore, I shall now state my reasons, after seeing that Sardinia, Naples, and Sicily were safe, for believing that Egypt was the destination of the French Fleet; and at this moment of sorrow, I still feel that I have acted right.

1. The wind had blown from N.E. to S.E. for fourteen days before they sailed; therefore they might without difficulty have gone to the Westward. 2. They came out with gentle breezes at N.W. and N.N.W. Had they been bound to Naples, the most natural thing for them to have done would have been to run along their own shore to the Eastward, where they would have had Ports every twenty leagues of Coast to take shelter in. 3. They bore away in the evening of the 18th, with a strong gale at N.W. or N.N.W. steering S. or S. b W. It blew so hard that the Seahorse went more than thirteen knots an hour, to get out of their way. Desirable as Sardinia[2] is for them, they could get it without risking their Fleet, although certainly not so quickly as by attacking Cagliari . . . . . however, I left nothing to chance in that respect, and therefore went off Cagliari . . . . Having afterwards gone to Sicily, both to Palermo and Messina, and thereby given encouragement for a defence, and knowing all was safe

---

[2] " In a letter to Mr. Consul Magnon, Lord Nelson gave it as his opinion, that if the weather had been fine, he should have fallen in with the French Fleet off the Island of Toro."—*Clarke and M'Arthur*, vol. ii. p. 396.

at Naples, I had only the Morea and Egypt to look to: for
although I knew one of the French Ships was crippled, yet I
considered the character of Buonaparte ; and that the orders
given by him, on the banks of the Seine, would not take into
consideration winds or weather ; nor indeed could the accident
of even three or four Ships alter, in my opinion, a destination
of importance : therefore such an accident did not weigh in
my mind, and I went first to the Morea, and then to Egypt.
The result of my inquiries at Coron and Alexandria confirm
me in my former opinion ; and therefore, my Lord, if my ob-
stinacy or ignorance is so gross, I should be the first to recommend your superseding me ; but, on the contrary, if, as I flatter myself, it should be found that my ideas of the probable
destination of the French Fleet were well founded, in the
opinion of his Majesty's Ministers, then I shall hope for the
consolation of having my conduct approved by his Majesty ;
who will, I am sure, weigh my whole proceedings in the scale
of justice.　　The Pacha of Coron informed me, that the French
Ambassador was to leave Constantinople on the 17th or 18th
of January, which tallying with the sailing of the French Fleet,
might probably be a plan of Buonaparte not to subject himself
to the charge of invading the Country of a friendly Power, as
the French Government had been charged with, when he went
before to Egypt.　　I am, &c.

NELSON AND BRONTE.

TO WILLIAM MARSDEN, ESQ., ADMIRALTY.

[Original in the Admiralty.]

Victory, at Sea, 18th February, 1805.

Sir,

It being six years in April next since His Majesty's Ship
Royal Sovereign was coppered, and it being extremely foul
and worn off in many parts, I request you will be pleased to
communicate the same to the Lords Commissioners of the
Admiralty, and acquaint them that she has very much
retarded the Squadron in its pursuit of the Enemy to
Alexandria.　　I therefore submit to their Lordships the propriety of ordering her to England, and replacing her with

another Ship for the reception of Rear-Admiral Sir Richard Bickerton's flag, for it is perfectly clear in the event of falling in with the Enemy's Fleet, in a situation that would require a long chase to come up with them, the services of the Royal Sovereign would be entirely out of the question, as she could not keep company with the other Ships, but for a very short time, under a heavy press of sail, which she is constantly obliged to carry, and which naturally hurts and strains the Ship very much. I am, Sir, &c.

NELSON AND BRONTE.

TO WILLIAM MARSDEN, ESQ., ADMIRALTY.

[Original, in the Admiralty.]

Victory, at Sea, 21st February, 1805.

Sir,

I herewith transmit you for the information of the Lords Commissioners of the Admiralty, a letter from Captain Schomberg, dated the 13th February, giving an account of the capture of his Majesty's late Sloop Arrow, and Acheron, Bomb-Vessel, on the 4th of that month by two French Frigates,[3] together with the extract of the Log therein-mentioned; also a letter from Captain Schomberg, dated 19th February, with the one therein alluded to from Lieutenant Coggan, Agent for Transports, containing further particulars of the unfortunate loss of His Majesty's said late Vessels.

The circumstance of this misfortune can only be attributed to the very long and tedious passage of the Convoy which sailed from Malta on the 4th January, and the Enemy having no doubt gained intelligence of them, and knowing that I was in pursuit of their Fleet (which sailed from Toulon on the 17th ultimo) had sent two of their Frigates to the Westward for the purpose of intercepting them.

The two Frigates named in the margin[4] are to the Westward; and by the last accounts I had from the Fisgard, she was off Malaga, so that it was to be presumed the safety of the said Convoy was little to be doubted as far as Gibraltar. I am, Sir, &c.

NELSON AND BRONTE.

[3] Vide p. 263, ante.   [4] Fisgard, Amazon.

TO WILLIAM MARSDEN, ESQ., ADMIRALTY.

[Original, in the Admiralty. " At Noon, Maritimo N. b E. ¼ E., nine leagues."
—*Victory's Log.*]

Sir, Victory, at Sea, 22nd February, 1805.

Since my letter of the 12th of this month, I have to acquaint
you, for the information of the Lords Commissioners of the
Admiralty, that I arrived with the Fleet off Malta on the
morning of the 19th instant, and received information from
Captain Schomberg of the Enemy's Fleet having put back to
Toulon in a very crippled state ;[5] and yesterday, off Maritimo,
I received by the Bittern the accompanying letter from Mr.
Elliot, his Majesty's Minister at the Court of Naples, which
you will please to communicate to their Lordships, and acquaint them that all the Frigates and other Vessels are at
present detached to obtain intelligence of the Enemy's Fleet,
and that the moment I receive a more particular account of
their state, I shall send a Sloop of War with information
thereof to their Lordships.

The Fleet under my command is in excellent good health,
and the Ships, although we have experienced a great deal of
bad weather, have received no damage, and not a yard or
mast sprung or crippled, or scarcely a sail split. I am,
Sir, &c. NELSON AND BRONTE.

[5] On his return to Toulon, Admiral Villeneuve wrote a dispatch to the Minister of
Marine, dated, " 1er pleuviose, an. xiii," i. e. 21 January, 1805, in which he said:
" I declare to you, that Ships of the Line thus equipped, short-handed, encumbered
with troops, with superannuated or bad materials, vessels which lose their masts or
sails at every puff of wind, and which, in fine weather, are constantly engaged in
repairing the damages caused by the wind, or the inexperience of their sailors, are
not fit to undertake anything. I had a presentiment of this before I sailed ; I have
now only too painfully experienced it." And Monsieur Thiers adds, " Napoleon was
sensibly displeased on hearing of this useless sortie. ' What,' said he, ' is to be done
with Admirals who allow their spirits to sink, and determine to hasten home at the
first damage that they receive ? It would be requisite to give up sailing, and to remain
wholly inactive, even in the finest weather, if an Expedition is to be prevented by the
separation of a few Vessels. The whole of the Captains,' he added, ' ought to have
had sealed orders to meet off the Canary Islands. The damages should have been
repaired *en route*. If any Ship leaked dangerously, she should have been left at
Cadiz, her crew and the troops being transferred to L'Aigle, which was in that Port,
and ready for sailing. A few topmasts carried away, some casualties in a gale of
wind, were everyday occurrences. Two days of fine weather ought to have cheered
up the crews, and put everything to rights. But the great evil of our Navy is, that
the men who command it are unused to all the risks of command.' "—*Thiers' History of the Consulate and the Empire*, vol. v. p. 159.

TO REAR-ADMIRAL SIR RICHARD BICKERTON, BART.

[From Clarke and M'Arthur, vol. ii. p. 399. "February 28th [*i. e.* 27th.] P.M.
At 5·45, came to with the best bower anchor in Pula Roads, (Sardinia)."—*Victory's Log.*]

27th February, 1805.

What a dreadful thing, not either to get hold of the French Fleet, nor even to hear of them since their return, except from Naples: what weather! Did you ever see such in almost any Country? It has forced me to anchor here, in order to prevent being drove to leeward, but I shall go to sea the moment it moderates. I am, &c.

NELSON AND BRONTE.

TO WILLIAM MARSDEN, ESQ., ADMIRALTY.

[Original, in the Admiralty. "March 2nd [*i. e.* 1st.] P.M. At 5, arrived the St. Christopher, a Spanish Cartel, having on board the English Consul from Minorca." "March 2nd, A.M. At 6·20, weighed, and made sail out of Pula Roads. P.M. Fresh gales and heavy squalls. At 3·30, anchored in Pula Roads." "March 3rd. A.M. Light breezes. At 6·15, weighed, and made sail to the westward, Squadron in company. P.M. Strong gales and squally. At 3·30 anchored in Pula Roads—Squadron anchored as convenient." "March 4th. A.M. Light airs. At 3·30, weighed and made sail to the W.S.W. At noon, Squadron in company."—*Victory's Log.*]

Sir,   Victory, at Sea, 4th March, 1805.

I herewith transmit you, for the information of the Lords Commissioners of the Admiralty, copies of two Reports of survey held on the Officers named in the margin,[6] belonging to the Swiftsure and Spencer, together with copies of Orders given to Mr. Robert H. Barclay[7] and Mr. James Harris[8] to act in their room, which I request you will be pleased to lay before their Lordships for confirmation. And as the frequent Surveys upon Officers may appear strange, I judge it proper to acquaint you for their Lordships' information, that the most strict regard has been paid to prevent this measure as much as possible, and in no case where the least probability of recovery

[6] Lieutenant William Marcus Courtenay, Lieutenant James Proctor. The former of these Officers was made a Commander in 1810, and died between 1816 and 1820; and the latter died before 1814.

[7] Mr. Robert Heriot Barclay: he was made a Commander in 1813, Posted in 1824, and died in 1837.

[8] Mr. James Harris: he was wounded while Lieutenant of the Spencer, in Sir John Duckworth's Action, in 1806, and appears to have died a Lieutenant before 1809.

in this Country remained, has an Officer been condemned as
unserviceable ; but as you will observe from the different
Reports of Survey, that rheumatism and consumption (which
bring on general debility) are the prevailing complaints, and
from which there is no recovery in this Country, as clearly
established from experience, and confirmed by all the medical
opinions; I, therefore, trust their Lordships will be perfectly
satisfied that no countenance has been given to the Surveying
of Officers, and that my General Orders on this service are
most strict, a copy of which I also herewith enclose for their
Lordships' information, together with a list of Commissions,
Warrants, and Acting Appointments, which I have given to
the Officers therein mentioned, since the 16th August, 1804,
which you will be pleased to lay before their Lordships for
confirmation.   I am, Sir, &c.

                              NELSON AND BRONTE.

GENERAL ORDER.

[Enclosed and referred to in the preceding Letter.]

Whereas, Captain ———— , of His Majesty's Ship ———
has represented to me by letter of this date, that Lieutenant
A. B. of the said Ship is afflicted with rheumatism and
other complaints, which render him incapable of doing his
duty, and there being no prospect of his recovery in this
Country, has requested that I would order the said Lieutenant
to be surveyed.   You are therefore hereby required and
directed to repair immediately on board His Majesty's Ship
———, taking to your assistance the Captains of His Majesty's
Ships named in the margin, Doctor Gillespie, Physician of
the Fleet, together with your respective Surgeons; and as
great inconvenience may arise to the Service from Officers
quitting their Ships on Foreign Stations, and the Lords Commissioners of the Admiralty having very strongly marked
their disapprobation thereof, it is my positive directions that
you most strictly survey and examine into the state of health,
and nature of the complaints with which the said Lieutenant
A. B. is afflicted, reporting to me from under your hands
a very particular account of his complaints, and whether, in
your opinion there is any probable chance of his recovery in
this Country.   NELSON AND BRONTE.

TO SIR ALEXANDER JOHN BALL, BART.

[Autograph, in the possession of Sir William Keith Ball, Bart. "March 7th.
A.M. At 8·10 a Cartel came into the Squadron with Spanish Colours at the fore,
and Union-jack at the main, the Ship having American Colours at the mizen peak.
At 11·20, anchored in the Bay of Rousse, to the Eastward of Cape Favolaro.
Fresh gales and cloudy weather. Squadron in company, part of them at anchor.
March 8th. A.M. Moderate breezes and cloudy. At 10, weighed and made sail.
P.M. At 5·45, anchored in the Gulf of Palma."—*Victory's Log.*]

Victory, Gulf of Palma, March 8th, 1805.
My dear Ball,

From the 19th February to this day have we been beating,
and only going now to anchor here, as it blows a gale of wind
at N.W. It has been, without exception, the very worst
weather I have ever seen. In addition to my other mishaps,
(I must not call them misfortunes,) Captain Layman,[9] of his
Majesty's Sloop *late* Raven, arrived in a Flag of Truce from
Cadiz, where that Sloop was wrecked on the night of
January 29th, in a gale of wind. The humane and kind
attention of the Captain-General of Andalusia, the Marquis
of Solano, has been so great to these unfortunate people, and
his sending them to me, (I believe without the absolute condition of their being Prisoners of War,) that I cannot sufficiently return his kindness. I have wrote to Captain Lamb
to liberate instantly the Captain and Officers of the Ventura.
Captain Layman left Portsmouth January 21st. He had

---

[9] Captain Layman has been before mentioned. His narrative of the loss of his
Sloop will be found in the "Naval Chronicle," vol. xxxviii. p. 4, together with
honourable testimonies to his exertions and skill, from the Marquis de la Solano,
and Mr. Duff, the English Consul at Cadiz. A Court-Martial, however, considered
that "there appears to have been a great want of necessary caution in Captain Layman, in approaching the land, and the Court doth therefore adjudge the said Captain
Layman to be severely reprimanded, and put at the bottom of the List of Commanders." It is said that this severe Sentence was wholly unexpected by Lord
Nelson; and as he had, from humane consideration for the Officer of the Watch,
induced Captain Layman to omit a severe reflection upon him in his narrative, saying,
" If this is laid before the Court, they will hang the Officer of the Watch," his Lordship considered himself to have been, in some degree, the cause of that decision.
This fact, and his strong predilection for Captain Layman, explains the interest he
took in that Officer's behalf. See a long statement on the subject in the " Naval
Chronicle," vol. xxxviii., and in Marshall's " Naval Biography," vol. iii. p. 328,
et seq. This able and zealous, but not always judicious, Officer never recovered
his place on the Commander's List, and it is stated that he " terminated his existence in the year 1826."

dispatches for Sir John Orde, Gibraltar, and the mail for me, and dispatches for me and for Malta; but all are gone to the bottom, *I hope.* The Brig got into Cadiz, and the exertions of the Captain, Officers, and men, seem, by the accounts, to have been wonderful. He is to be tried to-morrow. I send you the King's speech, which Duff sent me from Cadiz.

You will suppose my misery; it is at its full, and must change: but I am ever, my dear Ball, your most obliged and faithful friend,

NELSON AND BRONTE.

Lord Cornwallis goes to India.
Sir J. Warren a Vice-Admiral, to India.

TO LADY HAMILTON.

[From " Lord Nelson's Letters to Lady Hamilton," vol. ii. p. 87.   " March 9th. A.M. At 8·15, weighed and made sail. At 9·10, Light airs, inclinable to calm— Anchored. Royal Sovereign made the signal for a Court-Martial. P.M. At 5, weighed and made sail. Standing between Vache and the main."—*Victory's Log.*]

Victory, March 9th, 1805.

I do assure you, my dearest Emma, that nothing can be more miserable, or unhappy, than your poor Nelson. From the 19th of February, have we been beating from Malta to off Palma; where I am now anchored, the wind and sea being so very contrary and bad. But I cannot help myself, and no one in the Fleet can feel what I do: and, to mend my fate, yesterday Captain Layman arrived—to my great surprise— not in his Brig, but in a Spanish Cartel; he having been wrecked off Cadiz, and lost all the dispatches and letters. You will conceive my disappointment! It is now from November 2nd that I have had a line from England. Captain Layman says, he is sure the letters are sunk, never to rise again; but, as they were not thrown overboard until the Vessel struck the rock, I have much fear that they may have fallen into the hands of the Dons.

My reports from off Toulon, state the French Fleet as still in Port; but I shall ever be uneasy at not having fallen in with them. I know, my dear Emma, that it is in vain to repine; but my feelings are alive to meeting those fellows, after near two years' hard service. What a time! I could not have thought it possible that I should have been so long absent ; unwell, and uncomfortable, in many respects. However, when I calculate upon the French Fleet's not coming to sea for this summer, I shall certainly go for dear England, and a thousand [times] dearer Merton. May heaven bless you, my own Emma. I cannot think where Sir William Bolton is got to ; he ought to have joined me before this time. I send you a trifle, for a birth-day's gift. I would to God, I could give you more ; but I have it not. I get no Prize-money worth naming; but, if I have the good fortune to meet the French Fleet, I hope they will make me amends for all my anxiety ; which has been, and is, indescribable.

How is my dear Horatia ? I hope you have her under your guardian wing, at Merton. May God bless her ! Captain Layman is now upon his trial. I hope he will come clear, with honour. I fear it was too great confidence in his own judgment that got him into the scrape ; but it was impossible that any person living could have exerted himself more, when in a most trying and difficult situation.

March 10th.

Poor Captain L. has been censured by the Court : but I have my own opinion. I sincerely pity him ; and have wrote to Lord Melville and Sir Evan Nepean, to try what can be done. Altogether, I am much unhinged.

To-morrow, if the wind lasts, I shall be off Toulon. Sir William Bolton is safe ; I heard of him this morning. I hear that a Ship is coming out for him ; but as this is only rumour, I cannot keep him from this opportunity of being made Post ; and, I dare say, he will cause, by his delay, such a tumble, that Louis's son, who I have appointed to the Childers, will lose his promotion; and then Sir Billy will be wished at the devil ! But I have done with this subject : the whole history has hurt me. Hardy has talked enough to him, to rouse his lethargic disposition. I have been much hurt at the loss of poor Mr. Girdlestone ! [2] He was a good man ; but there will be an end of us all. What has Charles Connor been about ? His is a curious letter ! If he does not drink, he will do very well. Captain Hillyar has been very good to him. Colonel

[2] Apparently the father of the Reverend Henry Girdlestone, who married Lord Nelson's niece, Miss Elizabeth Anne Bolton.

Suckling,[3] I find, has sent his son to the Mediterranean, taking him from the Narcissus, where I had been at so much pains to place him. I know not where to find a Frigate to place him. He never will be so well and properly situated again. I am more plagued with other people's business, or rather nonsense, than with my own concerns. With some difficulty, I have got Suckling placed in the Ambuscade, with Captain Durban, who came on board at the moment I was writing.

March 31st.

The history of Suckling will never be done. I have this moment got from him your letter, and one from his father. I shall say nothing to him; I don't blame the child, but those who took [him] out of the most desirable situation in the Navy. He never will get into such another advantageous Ship; but his father is a fool; and so, my dear Emma, that *ends.* The box which you sent me in May 1804, is just arrived in the Diligent Store-ship. I have sent the Arms[4] to Palermo, to Gibbs. The clothes are very acceptable. I will give you a kiss for sending them. God bless you! Amen. *

April 1st.

I am not surprised that we should both think the same about the kitchen; and, if I can afford it, I should like it to be done; but, by the fatal example of poor Mr. Hamilton, and many others, we must take care not to get into debt; for then we can neither help any of our relations, and [must] be for ever in misery. But of this we [will] talk more, when we walk upon the poop at Merton. Do you ever see Admiral and Mrs. Lutwidge? You will not forget me when you do. To Mrs. Cadogan, say everything that is kind; and to all our other friends; and be assured I am, &c.

NELSON AND BRONTE.

As I know that all the Mediterranean letters are cut and smoked, and perhaps read, I do not send you a little letter in this; but your utmost stretch of fancy cannot imagine more than I feel for my own dear Emma. God bless you. Amen.

---

[3] Vide, vol. iii. p. 1.
[4] To be recorded among those of the Nobility of Sicily.

TO VISCOUNT MELVILLE.

[From Clarke and M'Arthur, vol. ii. p. 397.]

[No date. Apparently about the 9th March, 1805.]

Those gentlemen are not accustomed to a Gulf of Lyons gale, which we have buffeted for twenty-one months, and not carried away a spar. I most sincerely hope they will soon be in a state to put to sea again. Everybody has an opinion respecting the destination of the Enemy, mine is more fully confirmed that it was Egypt : to what other Country could they want to carry saddles and arms? I yet hope to meet them before I go hence. I would die ten thousand deaths, rather than give up my command when the Enemy is expected every day to be at sea. I am, &c.

NELSON AND BRONTE.

TO WILLIAM MARSDEN, ESQ., ADMIRALTY.

[Original, in the Admiralty.]

Victory, at Sea, 10th March, 1805.

Sir,

I herewith transmit you the sentence of a Court-Martial, held on Captain Layman, the Officers, and Company of his Majesty's late Sloop Raven, for the loss of the said Sloop on the 30th of January last, which I request you will be pleased to lay before the Lords Commissioners of the Admiralty, for their information ; and, at the same time, acquaint their Lordships, that I feel it my duty, in justice to Captain Layman, to state, from the information I have received of this unfortunate circumstance from Mr. Duff, Consul at Cadiz, and also the Marquis de la Solano, Captain-General at that place, that the exertions of Captain Layman after the Raven was in a dangerous situation, were unequalled by anything they ever witnessed; and that, notwithstanding the heavy gale of wind which she encountered, the Raven would have twice got clear off, had she not, in the first instance, carried away her main-yard, and afterwards parted from her anchors. I have exceedingly to lament Captain Layman's misfortune, as I consider his present loss to the Service a very great one indeed, knowing from experience the abilities and exertions of that Officer. I am, Sir, &c.　　　　　　　NELSON AND BRONTE.

TO VISCOUNT MELVILLE.[4]

[From the " Naval Chronicle," vol. xxxviii. p. 18, the " Gentleman's Magazine," vol. lxxx. part ii. p. 102, and Marshall's " Naval Biography," vol. iii. p. 331.]

My dear Lord,　　　　　Victory, at Sea, 10th March, 1805.

I inclose some remarks made by Captain Layman whilst he was in Spain, after the very unfortunate loss of that fine Sloop, which your Lordship was so good as to give him the command of. Your Lordship will find the remarks flow from a most intelligent and active mind, and may be useful should any expedition take place against Cadiz ; and, my dear Lord, give me leave to recommend Captain Layman to your kind protection; for, notwithstanding the Court-Martial has thought him deserving of censure for his running in with the land, yet, my Lord, allow me to say, that Captain Layman's misfortune was, perhaps, conceiving that other people's abilities were equal to his own, which, indeed, very few people's are.

I own myself one of those who do not fear the shore, for hardly any great things are done in a small Ship by a man that is ; therefore, I make very great allowances for him. Indeed, his station was intended never to be from the shore in the Straits : and if he did not every day risk his Sloop, he would be useless upon that station. Captain Layman has served with me in three Ships, and I am well acquainted with his bravery, zeal, judgment, and activity ; nor do I regret the loss of the Raven compared to the value of Captain Layman's services, which are a National loss.

You must, my dear Lord, forgive the warmth which I express for Captain Layman ; but he is in adversity, and, therefore, has the more claim to my attention and regard. If I had been censured every time I have run my Ship, or Fleets under my command, into great danger, I should long ago have been *out* of the Service, and never *in* the House of Peers. I am, my dear Lord, most faithfully, your obedient servant,

　　　　　　　NELSON AND BRONTE.

---

[4] It was the perusal of this generous and characteristic letter, which, many years ago, suggested to the Editor the present publication.

TO ALEXANDER DAVISON, ESQ.

[Autograph, in the possession of Colonel Davison.]

Victory, March 11th, 1805.

My dear Davison,

You will readily believe that my heart is almost broke at not having got hold of those French folks. From January 19th to this day, I have not been to be envied. Had they not been crippled, nothing could have hindered our meeting them on January 21st, off the South end of Sardinia. Ever since, we have been prepared for Battle: not a bulk-head up in the Fleet. Night or day, it is my determination not to lose one moment in attacking them. To add to my sorrow, the Convoy has been intercepted. That would not have happened, could I have ordered the Officer off Cadiz to have sent Ships to protect them. But when I tell my tale of all the unpolite conduct, as reported to me, I pity the man. But it is impossible it can go on. I hear I am not to be allowed to send a Vessel even with my dispatches to Lisbon: I bear it patiently. When I see Lord Melville and Nepean, something will be decided.

The French Fleet are reported not to have disembarked their Troops, and I am in hourly hopes of getting at them; after which, I shall certainly return to England. But I shall never quit my post when the French Fleet is at sea, as a Commander-in-Chief of great celebrity once did. I would sooner die at my post, than have such a stigma upon my memory. To mend matters, poor Captain Layman came to me in a Cartel, having lost his fine Sloop, and I only hope that all dispatches are lost; but I much fear, as they were not thrown overboard till the Vessel struck, that they may wash on shore. Layman says it is impossible. He was tried by a Court-Martial the day before yesterday; and, to my great surprise, severely censured, for running uncautiously in with the land. The testimonies of his exertions to save the Sloop are uncontrovertible, and were never exceeded. I know too well to comment upon a Sentence; but if running in with the land, to rocks, passing narrow and dangerous passages, where my Ship, or Fleets intrusted to my care, might have been lost, is

a fault, I have been guilty of a thousand. I would employ
Layman to-morrow if I could ; and I beg that you will mention him with kindness to our friend Nepean, who I have
given Captain L. a letter to. I am, in truth, very, very
sad ; but ever, my dear Davison, your most faithful friend,.

NELSON AND BRONTE.

November 2nd, my last letters from England. I hope you
are entirely mistaken about the destination of the intended
Expedition. Ten thousand times more important are fifty other
places than if we were in the actual capture of Mexico or Peru.
We want a War that will make a Peace, and no Conquests there
will have that effect. You are, my friend, a man of business,
and I am not surprised at Lord Melville's attention to you.
He shows his discernment in that, as he does in everything
he undertakes. Remember me kindly to Nepean. I have
wrote to him about poor Captain Layman.

I am sensible of your goodness in paying all my bills for
the improvements at Merton, which I will, if I live, or have
as much property, repay with many thanks. But I fancy
dear Lady Hamilton wants some money to furnish the new
part. She will not be extravagant ; therefore, if you will let
her have the money for it, I shall feel much obliged. May
God bless my dear friend ; and be assured I am ever your
much obliged friend,

NELSON AND BRONTE.

TO CAPTAIN BAYNTUN, H. M. SHIP LEVIATHAN.

[Autograph, in the possession of Miss Bolton, of Burnham.]

Victory, 11th March, 1805.

Most Secret Memoranda.

In case the Fleet should not be able to get to Rendezvous
102, and Lord Nelson would have Captain Bayntun proceed
there, he wishes to give the directions hereafter mentioned.
The Fisgard to be left in the Command off Toulon, to watch
the Enemy, with such other Frigates—not to exceed three—
as shall be there. It is very desirable for a Frigate, or the
Bittern Sloop, to relieve the Thunder Bomb on Rendezvous
97, and the Thunder to be ordered to Rendezvous 98. The

Childers and Renown to be ordered to Rendezvous 98. The
Leviathan to proceed to Rendezvous 98, which is the General
Rendezvous. The Phœbe and Hydra are ordered to proceed to Rendezvous 102, and between that Rendezvous and
Toulon, to relieve Active and Seahorse, who must want water;
therefore, Captain Bayntun is desired to give them a present
supply of that article.

I shall, if possible, make my appearance off Barcelona, in
order to induce the Enemy to believe that I am fixed upon the
Coast of Spain, when I have every reason to believe they will
put to sea, as I am told the Troops are still embarked. From
off Barcelona I shall proceed direct to Rendezvous 98. Should
the Leviathan be at 98 before me, and find there either Termagant or Bittern, it would be very desirable to have a Vessel
fixed ten leagues West of St. Pierres, in case the French
Fleet should not steer close to the Island; for I think Egypt
is still their object. Captain Bayntun will keep this paper a
secret, and if not used, return it to me. Captain Bayntun
will be telegraphed when he is to proceed upon this service,
which will not be done whilst a hope remains of the Fleet's
getting, in any reasonable time, to Rendezvous 102.

NELSON AND BRONTE.

TO THE SURGEON, PURSER, AND CLERK[4] OF HIS MAJESTY'S LATE SLOOP RAVEN.

[From a copy in the Admiralty. "March 12th. A.M. Saw the high land over
Toulon, bearing N. b E."—*Victory's Log.*]

Sir,   Victory, at Sea, 12th March, 1805.

A Report having reached me that you have great reason to
believe that a paper produced by Mr. Edwards, late of His
Majesty's Sloop Raven, and sworn by him to be a copy of the
Raven's Log on the day and night alluded to, is a fabrication
and not copied, from the slate on which the Log was kept.[5]

---

[4] " N.B.—A separate letter was wrote to each."

[5] Captain Layman, in a letter to the Admiralty, requested their Lordships to take
into consideration various points stated therein, one of which was, " Whether the
paper from which the Commander received censure, produced by Mr. Edwards to
the Court, as a copy made in the prison from the Log-slate, does not appear invalid,
from the statements of Messrs. Bailey, Soden, and Horniton to the Commander-in-
Chief?"—*Naval Chronicle*, vol. xxxviii. p. 15.

If the report made to me has any truth in it, I desire that you will communicate the circumstances to me, that an inquiry may take place into so scandalous and infamous a proceeding. I am, Sir, &c.

NELSON AND BRONTE.

TO WILLIAM MARSDEN, ESQ., ADMIRALTY.

[Autograph, in the Admiralty.]

Victory, 18 leagues South from Toulon, March 13th, 1805.

Sir,

Their Lordships are fully aware of my reasons for not attending to my own health since I received their permission to return to England for its re-establishment. I do assure you that no consideration for Self could come into my mind when the Enemy's Fleet was sure of putting to sea, and they are now perfectly ready in appearance to put to sea again. Therefore, although I have suffered very much from anxiety and a very stormy winter, yet I shall either stay to fight them, which I expect every hour, or until I believe they will not come to sea for the summer, when I shall embrace their Lordships' permission and return to England for a few months for the re-establishment of a very shattered constitution. I am, Sir, &c.

NELSON AND BRONTE.

TO ALEXANDER DAVISON, ESQ.

[Autograph, in the possession of Colonel Davison.]

Victory, March 13th, 1805.

My dear Davison,

Everything by the Raven is gone. It is a sad loss, but I cannot help it. Your letter of January 7th, by the Amphion, I received last night, and I am glad to find that you can travel as far as Wimbledon, and before you receive this letter, you will again, thank God, be a freeman. No consideration should, was I in your situation, induce me to go into Parliament. You must soon take a part, and thus lose many of your present friends. Nothing has, or could keep me here one moment, but the sense of what I owe to myself, my King and Country. The business off Cadiz cannot go on, and the Admiralty will soon find it out. I attribute the loss of the Convoy to that cause, and we shall lose more if it is continued. Either Sir John Orde should command all, or myself; but I complain not. I shall mention it fully when I get home, which will be either the moment after the Battle, or that I believe the French Fleet will not come out for the summer. I am useless if I die ; and for what should I? No, I have wrote to the Admiralty my determination. I am now so hectic, that I run a great risk of never recovering; and, my dear Davison, your letter has hurt me not a little. It conveys to my mind an intimation, that *I* might have made you Agent for the Mediterranean Fleet. If I have that power, it is a power I am unacquainted with; nor do I see how it is possible. But we shall soon talk of this, and other matters; and, so far from having any such power, I do not believe that, if we were to take the whole French Fleet, the Agency would be offered to me *in toto*, and less I would not accept for you, with the proviso mentioned formerly.

There is nothing, my dear Davison, that I could do to meet your wishes, that I should not rejoice in doing; and I only regret that I cannot do impossibilities. I am at this moment very miserable, and am not to be envied. My friendship, regard, and affection for you is unalterable, and I am truly sensible of all the obligations I owe you. I am very glad to hear of the final distribution of the Copenhagen Prize-money. You cannot conceive the insinuations which have been made to me. I must not omit to mention that Sir Richard Strachan is the only Captain who, when stationed outside the Straits, wrote me, that he should, if he sent any Ship to England, make you his Agent. But I have done with this subject, which has much distressed me.[6]

---

[6] This letter was probably continued on another sheet, which has not been found.

TO VICE-ADMIRAL COLLINGWOOD.

[Autograph, in the possession of the Honourable Mrs. Newnham Collingwood.]

Victory, March 13th, 1805.

My dear Friend,

Many, many thanks for your kind remembrance of me, and for your friendly good wishes, which, from my heart, I can say are reciprocal. I am certainly near going to England; for my constitution is much shook, and nothing has kept me here so long but the expectation of getting at the French Fleet. I am told the Rochfort Squadron sailed the same day as that from Toulon. Buonaparte has often made his brags, that our Fleet would be worn out by keeping the sea—that his was kept in order, and increasing by staying in Port; but he now finds, I fancy, if *Emperors* hear truth, that his Fleet suffers more in one night, than ours in one year. However, thank God, the Toulon Fleet is got in order again, and, I hear, the Troops embarked; and I hope they will come to sea in fine weather. The moment the Battle is over, I shall cut; and I must do the same, if I think, after some weeks, that they do not intend to come out for the summer. We have had a very dull War; but I agree with you, that it must change for a more active one. We are in a sad jumble with Sir John Orde off Cadiz; but let him do as absurd things as he pleases about blockading the Ships under my command—even to be angry at my sending Ships to Lisbon with my dispatches, and angry at my sending Ships to a part of the station under my orders, before I knew of his arrival to take that lucrative part of my station from me—I shall never enter into a paper war with him, or any one else. We have lost one Convoy, I think, by it, and we shall lose more; *between two stools*, &c. &c. &c. I beg, my dear Coll., that you will present my most respectful compliments to Mrs. Collingwood; and believe [me] for ever, and as ever, your most sincere and truly attached friend,

NELSON AND BRONTE.

TO WILLIAM MARSDEN, ESQ., ADMIRALTY.

[Original in the Admiralty.]

Victory, at Sea, 14th March, 1805.

Sir,

You will be pleased to acquaint the Lords Commissioners of the Admiralty, that the Fleet under my command arrived off Toulon yesterday evening, and that by the information I have received from the Frigates stationed to watch the Enemy, their Fleet is all in the above harbour, apparently in perfect readiness to put to sea. Whether their Troops, who were disembarked on their late return, are again put on board, has not been learnt, but there is reason to believe they are. Their Lordships may rest assured, in the event of the Enemy putting to sea again, that I shall use every possible means to fall in with them, and bring them to Action.

I, at the same time, received their Lordships' duplicate order of the 14th December last, relative to the detention of all Spanish Ships and Vessels; and your several letters, &c. acknowledged under this date, brought out in the Amphion to Gibraltar, and from thence in the Fisgard, which sprung a leak, and was obliged to return to that place immediately, to have it stopped. Their Lordships' dispatches sent out in the late Raven, and Arthur [1] Cutter, have, with those unfortunate Vessels, been lost; the former, I have reason to believe from Captain Layman, were sunk when the Raven struck ; but the latter dispatches, brought by the Cutter, which was captured by the Enemy's Fleet on its return into Toulon, I fear may have fallen into their hands, as the Officer who commanded her, presuming, probably, that it was the Fleet under my command, may have been taken by surprise. This, however, is matter of conjecture, and may not be the case. I am, Sir,

NELSON AND BRONTE.

TO WILLIAM MARSDEN, ESQ., ADMIRALTY.

[Original, in the Admiralty.]

Victory, at Sea, 14th March, 1805.

Sir,

I herewith transmit you a copy of an appointment which I have this day given to Mr. William Bunce, Carpenter of his

---

[1] The Arthur, Hired Cutter, Lieutenant R. Cooban, of six guns.

Majesty's Ship Victory, to be Master-Shipwright of his Majesty's Yard at Gibraltar, in room of the late Mr. Burnett, which you will be so good as to lay before the Lords Commissioners of the Admiralty, for their information, and move their Lordships to confirm the appointment. I must, at the same time, request that you will be pleased to acquaint their Lordships, that Mr. Bunce is a very able and experienced Officer, of great abilities and quick resources; and that, from his long and faithful servitude, he is most deservedly entitled to their Lordships' patronage. I, therefore, hope this appointment will meet their approbation. I am, Sir, &c.　　　　　NELSON AND BRONTE.

TO WILLIAM MARSDEN, ESQ., ADMIRALTY.

[Original in the Admiralty.]

Victory, at Sea, 14th March, 1805.

Sir,

I have received your letter of the 21st November, relative to the French Prisoners of War at Malta, being sent to England in King's Ships, as opportunities may offer, from the reasons mentioned in your said letter; and you will please to acquaint their Lordships that I shall direct the Senior Officer at Malta, and Agent for Prisoners of War, to attend most strictly to these instructions, and send the French prisoners to England agreeably thereto; but I must desire to observe that the Ships leaving Malta with Convoys are in general so crowded with invalids (being Frigates and other small Vessels) that but very few prisoners can be accommodated: their Lordships' direction shall, however, be duly attended to. I am, Sir, &c.　　　　　NELSON AND BRONTE.

TO CAPTAIN SUTTON, H. M. SHIP AMPHION.

[Autograph, in the possession of Captain Ives Sutton.]

Victory, March 14th, 1805.

My dear Sutton,

I am much obliged by your kind letter, and return you many thanks for the good things which you was so good as to bring me from England, which will be most acceptable, for I have had nothing to eat but what my friends in the Fleet have supplied me with. Sir William Bolton has not yet joined; he has been sent to Madeira. The sheep, I hope, will come up in the first Frigate. I hope your expectations of gain by the Galleons will be realized; and I hope you will get enormously rich, for your own and good Captain Hardy's sake,[7] although an Admiral of more interest than I have, will take what ought to belong to me. I should think that the whole of this Fleet will be put under Sir John Orde's command; or, when he has made money enough, he will be removed, and the responsibility left where it was before.

We have had a long run to Egypt and back; but as the French Fleet are now ready for sea again, I fully expect we shall meet them; and then I would change with no man living. My health is but so-so; and the moment after the Battle, I shall go home for a few months. I think you will soon be drove off your Cruizing ground; the Rochfort Squadron will be with you before long, therefore make hay whilst the sun shines. I am sorry to hear George Martin[8] has quitted his Ship from ill-health. I wish I could have changed with you when you went to Merton; but I hope to see it very soon. Hardy is very well, and as good as ever; he hopes he will get something by the French Fleet, for your sake. If Sir John Orde condescends to ask after me, make my respectful compliments; and to George Hope.[9] And, believe me, dear Sutton, your much obliged and faithful friend, NELSON AND BRONTE.

TO WILLIAM MARSDEN, ESQ., ADMIRALTY.

[Original, in the Admiralty.]

Victory, at Sea, 14th March, 1805.

Sir,

I have received your letter of the 15th November, together with the copy of a letter from Mr. Hammond, and the several papers therein referred to in original, containing a representation from the Neapolitan Minister of violations committed by his Majesty's Ships in the Territory of the King of Naples. In answer to which, I herewith transmit you my letter to Captain Schomberg, dated the 11th November, directing an

[7] Vide p. 287, note 6, ante.
[8] Now Admiral Sir George Martin, G.C.B., G.C.M.G., Vice-Admiral of England.
[9] Captain George Hope, of the Defence.

inquiry into the conduct of Lieutenant Spencer, commanding
the Renard Schooner,[1] together with the inquiry, and several
other papers in original, relative to this circumstance, from
Number 1 to 7, which I request you will be pleased to lay
before the Lords Commissioners of the Admiralty for their
information; and acquaint their Lordships that the Neutrality
of his Sicilian Majesty's Dominions has been most shamefully
violated by the French Privateers and Row-boats, which have
been suffered to shelter themselves in the different Ports of
his Kingdom, from whence they have issued forth and captured our Coasting Trade under their Forts.

I am perfectly aware of the delicate situation of the King
of Naples, and, consequently, gave the most strict orders to
the Commanders of his Majesty's Ships on no account to
commit the least violation of Neutrality in any part of his
Kingdoms; but where French Privateers have so daringly and
piratically captured our Trade, his Majesty's Officers would
have been highly reprehensible to have witnessed it without
attempting to destroy the unwarrantable offenders. It is but
justice for me to repeat, what I have frequently mentioned,
that the Ships under my command have invariably adhered
to the strictest Neutrality, and that they cannot, without being
guilty of a breach of my most positive orders, commit the
least violation of Neutrality in any place.

It is worthy of remark, that the French Minister's complaint relative to the Bittern (even by his own account) has
no foundation, as no French Vessel was boarded by any of
her Boats. This circumstance would have been noticed by me
to Mr. Elliot, had I been in possession of Captain Corbet's
statement, which was perfectly correct, and shows his conduct
to have been Officer-like and regular, in the search for the
Seamen who had deserted from the Bittern at Naples, so that
the French Minister has taken up the affairs of those of other
Courts, which he had nothing to do with, and made the
concern his own. I am, Sir, &c.

NELSON AND BRONTE.

P.S.—I return the several papers which accompanied your
said letter.

[1] This Vessel, which has been so often mentioned, was afterwards called the
Crafty, and, still under the command of Lieutenant Spencer, was captured in March
1807 by three Spanish privateers, near Tetuan, after a gallant resistance.

TO WILLIAM MARSDEN, ESQ., ADMIRALTY.

[Original, in the Admiralty.]

Victory, at Sea, 14th March, 1805.

Sir,

I have received your letter of the 14th November, together with a copy of his Majesty's Order in Council, authorizing an increase to be made to the salaries of the Secretaries to Flag Officers; also, that no Secretary is to be allowed more than one Clerk as an assistant, and that no Purser of any of his Majesty's Ships in Commission shall be allowed to officiate at the same time as Secretary to a Flag Officer. In answer to which, I have transmitted to Rear-Admiral Sir Richard Bickerton a copy of his Majesty's said Order in Council, with that of your letter of the above date, and request you will be pleased to acquaint their Lordships that due attention shall be paid to the instructions therein contained, and that the name of my Secretary and that of Sir Richard Bickerton's are mentioned underneath. I am, Sir, &c.

NELSON AND BRONTE.

John Scott, Secretary to Vice-Admiral Lord Viscount Nelson.

J. D. Boyes, Secretary to Rear-Admiral Sir Richard Bickerton, Bart.

N.B.—Mr. Truppo's name in his Commission has, by mistake been inserted Peter Stuppo instead of Truppo; you will, therefore have the goodness to correct the mistake.

TO LIEUTENANT-GENERAL THE HONOURABLE HENRY EDWARD FOX, LIEUTENANT-GOVERNOR OF GIBRALTAR.

[Autograph, in the possession of John Bullock, Esq.]

Victory, March 14th, 1805.

Sir,

I have been honoured with your letters of February 5th, and I feel truly happy that all appearance of the epidemic has disappeared, and that a free communication with the Garrison is again permitted without danger. The cautions respecting the performance of Pratique are certainly very proper, although I am entirely at a loss to know where Vessels can lay their Quarantine with safety out of the Mole. With respect to the Naval force necessary for the protection of the Bullock Vessels going to Lisbon with your mails, and bringing them back to the Garrison, I hope the Admiralty will send me the proper Vessels for that service; for I do assure you, Sir, (and, I trust, my general attention towards the comfort of the Garrison will induce you to believe my assertion) that the care and comfort of the Garrison of Gibraltar is ever uppermost in my mind; and it is the cause of much regret to me, that the Officer down the Mediterranean is not under my command, as his instructions would be similar to that formerly given to Sir Richard Strachan and Captain Gore—viz., to take care and afford every assistance and comfort to the Garrison of Gibraltar, and I flatter myself it has been closely attended to. I have long ago presumed to recommend to Lord Melville that Gibraltar should be placed under the immediate care of the Officer commanding off Cadiz, and I hope, before this time, it has been attended to. The Raven was destined for the especial service of Gibraltar; and I lament the loss of her, and also of the services of Captain Layman, whose activity, zeal, and judgment, would have been of much use to the Garrison. I have the honour to remain, &c.

NELSON AND BRONTE.

TO WILLIAM MARSDEN, ESQ., ADMIRALTY.

[Original, in the Admiralty.]

Victory, at Sea, 14th March, 1805.

Sir,

In answer to your letter of the 17th December, relative to their Lordships being furnished with an account of the proceeds of the several Vessels captured by the different Ships of the Squadron, and sent to Malta for adjudication, being the property of the Subjects of the Ligurian and Italian Republics, I beg you will be pleased to acquaint the Lords Commissioners of the Admiralty, that I do not feel myself authorized to call upon the Judge of the Vice-Admiralty Court at Malta for the proceeds of the said Vessels, which, I

understand, was his Majesty's pleasure should be given to
the Captors immediately: their Lordships will, therefore, be
pleased to adopt such measures as to them may appear proper
on the occasion. It only remains with me to observe, that
the Captors have frequently applied to me on this subject. I
am, Sir, &c.

NELSON AND BRONTE.

TO ADMIRAL LORD RADSTOCK.

[Autograph, in the possession of Rear-Admiral Lord Radstock, C.B.]

Victory, March 15th, 1805.

My dear Lord,

I am sorry you should find a difficulty in getting your son
promoted. If he is to remain a Lieutenant I should rather
recommend him to be in a more active Ship than this. Promotion here, unless from the Admiralty, is out of the question.
Was I in this Command seven years, I could not expect to get
through the Admiralty recommendations which every Ship
increases. . . . I must not enter upon the business of Sir John
Orde's appointment, but I think whoever has that Command
should have this. They ought not have been divided, and so
much did I expect Orde to relieve me *in toto*, that all my
things were sent to the Superb, where they still remain. I
am ever, my dear Lord, yours most faithfully,

NELSON AND BRONTE.

TO EARL CAMDEN, K.G., SECRETARY OF STATE FOR THE WAR DEPARTMENT.

[Original, in the Colonial Office.]

Victory, March 15th, 1805.

My Lord,

Flattering as are the enclosed letters from their Sicilian
Majesties, yet I should not do them justice was I not (without
any consideration for my feelings) to transmit them to your
Lordship, and in your wisdom you will, if you think it proper,
communicate them to His Majesty. My wretched state of
health ought, long since, to have induced me to go to England
for its re-establishment: but I could never bring myself to

quit my post when the Enemy was coming to sea. This motive has induced me to remain, and I shall stay until after the Battle, or that I believe the French Fleet will not put to sea for the summer months. I have the honour to be, &c.

NELSON AND BRONTE.

TO WILLIAM MARSDEN, ESQ., ADMIRALTY.

[Original, in the Admiralty.]

Victory, at Sea, 17th March, 1805.

Sir,

Having understood that Mr. Peter Truppo,[1] Midshipman on board the Belleisle, had served his time and passed in England for a Lieutenant, I gave him a Commission for the Amphitrite; but on delivering it, and after my letter of the 14th instant, inclosing copy thereof, was sealed up in a packet with the other public letters, and sent on board the Renown in charge of Captain Layman, I discovered that the said Mr. Truppo had not served his time. I therefore request you will be so good as cancel the said Commission, and move their Lordships to confirm the one (a copy of which is herewith transmitted) which I have this day given to Mr. Peter Crawfurd,[2] Midshipman of the Victory. I am, Sir, &c.

NELSON AND BRONTE.

TO WILLIAM MARSDEN, ESQ., ADMIRALTY.

[Original, in the Admiralty.]

Victory, at Sea, 18th March, 1805.

Sir,

I herewith transmit you a copy of a duplicate letter from the Navy Board, dated the 22nd November last, together with a copy of my answer thereto; also an Account from Mr. Edward Gayner, Merchant of Rosas, of the expenses incurred by the late Hindostan's Officers and Company, together with Captain Le Gros' agreement for the hire of a Vessel sent out to me with an account of that misfortune off Toulon; also two certificates relative to the hire of a house, and of fifteen Deserters

---

[1] He died a Lieutenant, about 1823.   [2] Now a Retired Commander.

taken up by the Civil power at Gerona, and put on board the
Seahorse at Rosas, which I request you will be pleased to lay
before the Lords Commissioners of the Admiralty for their
information, and move their Lordships to order that the
impress which the Commissioners of the Navy have thought
proper to put against me, on this account, may be taken off.

I cannot help noticing to their Lordships, the objections
made by the Commissioners of the Navy to this Account,
as well as their calling for Vouchers, under the circumstances of the misfortune from Mr. Gayner, who had behaved
with so much friendship to the unfortunate sufferers, and
paid the money out of his pocket for their accommodation.
There are circumstances which justify the rigid forms of
Office being dispensed with, and the present I humbly conceive to be one. Their Lordships, I trust, will believe that
previous to my giving a bill to Mr. Gayner, I examined every
particular charge, and was satisfied from Captain Le Gros, and
also from Mr. Ford, Agent-Victualler, who was at Rosas purchasing wine, &c., for the Fleet at the time, consequently,
witnesses to the whole transaction, that Mr. Gayner was still
a loser on the occasion. It also strikes me particularly hard
that a Commander-in-Chief is liable to have his Accounts impressed for every disbursement that the Service imperiously
demands of him. I am, Sir, &c.

NELSON AND BRONTE.

TO CAPTAIN P. S. MOUAT, AGENT FOR PRISONERS OF WAR,
GIBRALTAR.

[From a Copy in the Admiralty.]

Victory, at Sea, 18th March, 1805.

Sir,

I have this morning received, by the Amazon, your letter
of the 28th ult., together with the lists from No. 1 to 18, of
the French and Spanish Prisoners of War received and exchanged ; also copies of Vice-Admiral Sir John Orde's letters,
and translations of General Castano's letters respecting the
exchange of Spanish Prisoners agreeable to the usual custom,
as mentioned in your said letter. I very much approve of
your having sent the Officers and Company of the late Raven

to me, as well as of your intentions of sending all English seafaring Prisoners to this Fleet, in the room of Spanish Prisoners taken by the Ships under my command.

I am perfectly satisfied with your exertions for the Public Service, and that everything in your department will meet with due and proper attention, and that you will afford Mr. Cutforth the necessary Transports for carrying the provisions on demand for the Fleet. Your sending the Officers and Seamen belonging to his Majesty's late Bomb-Vessel Acheron, &c. by the Amazon, meets my approbation; and with respect to the ten French Prisoners alluded to in your letter, as the Acheron's people have met with so ready a release, I would recommend their being immediately released and sent into Spain; and as the Spanish Government has behaved so handsomely to our Prisoners, I would also recommend, if there is no reasonable objection to the contrary, and it meets with the approbation of Lieutenant-General Fox, that they are all immediately released, agreeable to the usual custom, and your instructions on that head, and sent into Spain. This mutual accommodation to all parties, I would desire may be adopted on every future occasion, while Spain continues to act with the liberality she has done; and another very humane and strong reason for this line of conduct being carried into effect is, that there is no place for the accommodation of Prisoners at Gibraltar, nor is it safe or consistent with the health of that place, to keep them on board the Guerrier, as appears from the representation of the Surgeon of the Naval Hospital, which I have transmitted to the Admiralty for their Lordships' consideration. I am, Sir, &c.

NELSON AND BRONTE.

TO THE PRINCIPAL OFFICERS AND COMMISSIONERS OF HIS MAJESTY'S NAVY.

[From a Copy in the Admiralty.]

Victory, at Sea, 18th March, 1805.

Gentlemen,

I have received your duplicate letter of the 22nd November, acquainting me that you had ordered Mr. Gayner's bill for the amount of the expenses paid by him on account of

the Company of his Majesty's late Ship Hindostan, to be
honoured, and charged as an impress against me until regular
vouchers were received; and also requesting that some certificate, or other sufficient attestation (in lieu of vouchers)
should be transmitted to you, that the sums therein charged
were incurred and paid on his Majesty's Service, for the
services therein expressed; and that fuller information be
transmitted in respect to the following articles—viz., the
names of the Deserters on account of whom eighteen dollars
five reals were incurred, in conducting them from Gerona, &c.
to La Escala; and also the names of twenty-one Deserters
from La Escala to Rosas, that the amount may be charged
against their wages; also relative to the disposal of the stores
saved from the said late Ship; and likewise from where the
Express was sent by Captain Le Gros to me, for which three
hundred dollars was paid, and the manner in which he tra-
velled:

In answer to which, as I considered Mr. Gayner's Account,
transmitted you in my letter of the 17th September last, to
be perfectly just, and extremely moderate in every particular
charge, I did not judge it either necessary or consistent to
call upon an honest man, who had paid the principal part of
the sums stated in the said Account, in the presence of Captain
Le Gros, to produce vouchers for every trifling dollar he had
disbursed on the score of humanity, and for the accommodation of his Majesty's Subjects; and although Mr. Gayner did
not put his name immediately at the bottom of the said
Account, (which perhaps might have been more consistent
with the forms of your Office,) yet I considered his attached
receipt for the amount of the said Account, as fully sufficient,
and all that was necessary; and my transmitting it to you was
a most full approbation thereof. I was not a witness on the
spot, and therefore my signature to it did not appear necessary
or proper. With respect to a certificate or attestation, in lieu
of vouchers, that the sums charged in the said Account were
incurred and paid on his Majesty's Service, I shall not trouble
Mr. Gayner, whose conduct was so friendly and honourable
to the late Hindostan's people, (as acknowledged by the Admiralty, and for which he is to be presented with a silver cup,

value one hundred pounds,) by calling upon him for any
other voucher than has already been transmitted to your
Board, as I consider it would be injurious to his Majesty's
Service, in the event of a similar misfortune happening, and
am perfectly and most fully satisfied that his charges barely
covered his actual disbursements.

On the subject of transmitting you the names of the Deserters alluded to in your said letter, and for which eighteen
dollars five reals are charged, it is impossible to comply with
your request, as their names most likely were not known to
Mr. Gayner, or the people who brought them to him; and I
must here beg to observe to you, Gentlemen, that those poor
sufferers, more than probable, were not Deserters, but looking
about them for some friendly retreat after their misfortune,
which I trust the Sea-Officers of your Board, who are very
capable of judging its extent, as well as the hardship of charg-
ing any sum whatever against their wages, admitting it was
possible to ascertain their names, will perfectly agree with me.

The stores saved from the late Hindostan, were not worth
altogether ten pounds, although great exertions, as I understand from Captain Le Gros, were used by Mr. Gayner for
this purpose; they have consequently been charged to the
different Ships which received them, and will be accounted
for by the Officers into whose charge they were delivered in
the proper and usual manner. A list of them was not called
for, as they consisted chiefly of the ends of a few burnt Spars
and other trifling articles, and were kept by the Ships which
received them on the spot, except a Yawl that was afterwards
supplied to the Cameleon.

With respect to the distance and manner the Express came
to me with an account of this misfortune, I desire to acquaint
you that Mr. Gayner hired a Vessel, at the request of Captain
Le Gros, for which the sum of three hundred dollars was to
be given, and sent her from Rosas off Toulon in search of
me; and I further desire to observe that this sum was by no
means equal to the service required, and length of time the
Vessel was in search of the Squadron.

I have transmitted to Mr. Secretary Marsden, a copy of
your said duplicate letter, together with that of my answer;
likewise Mr. Gayner's Account, and Captain Le Gros's

agreement for the hire of the Vessel, together with two certificates from that Officer, relative to the hire of a house, and fifteen Deserters being taken up at Gerona, and put on board the Seahorse at Rosas, copies of which I also herewith transmit for your information; and must request, if you judge it necessary, that you will be pleased to apply to the Lords Commissioners of the Admiralty, for their authority to remove the impress from my Account. I am, Gentlemen, &c.

NELSON AND BRONTE.

TO WILLIAM MARSDEN, ESQ., ADMIRALTY.

[Original, in the Admiralty.]

Sir, Victory, at Sea, March 19th, 1805.

I herewith transmit you a copy of my letter, of yesterday's date, to Captain Mouat, Agent for Transports and Prisoners of War at Gibraltar, which I request you will be pleased to lay before the Lords Commissioners of the Admiralty for their information; and on the exchange and release of Prisoners of War therein mentioned, I beg to observe, for their Lordships' information, that every principle of humanity recommends Prisoners being released immediately, more particularly at Gibraltar, where no proper accommodation is for their security; and the keeping them crowded on board the Guerrier, as the warm season[4] sets in, may be attended with unpleasant consequences. I must also here observe that the great attention and ready release which our Prisoners have met with from the Spanish Government, deserve on our part a liberal return, and as much as possible, consistent with the rules of exchange, to cause it to be done immediately. I therefore hope their Lordships will approve of my recommendations to Captain Mouat, and be pleased to order his being furnished with further instructions on this head, if they shall judge it necessary. I am, Sir, &c.

NELSON AND BRONTE.

[4] Lord Nelson had received a letter from Mr. Magrath, Surgeon to the Naval Hospital at Gibraltar, stating that a malignant fever had made its appearance among the Prisoners on board the Guerrier, and that the accommodation in that Ship was not sufficient, which he transmitted to the Admiralty on the 19th of March.

TO WILLIAM MARSDEN, ESQ., ADMIRALTY.

[Original, in the Admiralty.]

Victory, at Sea, 20th March, 1805.

Sir,

Having received information that upwards of seventeen Sail of the Convoy, under the protection of the late Arrow, and Acheron Bomb Vessel, are at Gibraltar, and it being very unsafe, from the Enemy's numerous Gun-Boats and Fire-Vessels fitting out at Algesiras, that they should be left there unprotected, I have, contrary to my intentions, and their Lordships' instructions, directed Sir Richard Strachan of the Renown to take the whole of them, together with any other Vessels bound to the United Kingdom, under his protection, and convoy them in safety to Spithead, dropping such as are bound to Plymouth, and the different Ports in the Channel on his way up, which I hope will meet their Lordships' approbation.

I also herewith transmit you, for their Lordships' information, a copy of a list of the Convoy under the protection of his Majesty's late Sloop Arrow, and Acheron Bomb-Vessel, and beg to acquaint you, that those named in the margin[5] have arrived at Malta, and that the Adventure was sunk, being in a leaky state, to prevent her from falling into the hands of the Enemy, as mentioned in Lieutenant Coggan's[6] letter, transmitted in mine of the 21st ultimo. I have also great hopes that some of the said late Convoy have got into Algiers, and, consequently sent the Morgiana on the 10th instant to that place, for the purpose of convoying any that might be there to Malta, in order to their proceeding with the Anson and Convoy from that place, which is appointed to sail about the middle of next month for England. Three of the said Convoy were sunk by the Enemy after the Action on the 4th February; and I am led to believe that few, if any, others have either been destroyed, or fallen into their hands. The gallant resistance made by the late Arrow and Acheron in Action with the Enemy, for their own defence and the protection of

[5] Active, Elizabeth, Triad, Cora, Hope, Jupiter.

[6] Lieutenant Richard Coggan, (Agent for Transports,) who obtained that rank in 1794, and died a Lieutenant in 1828 or 1829.

the Convoy under their charge, so far as I have yet been informed, is highly meritorious, and much to their credit. It was unfortunate that the Fisgard, which, with the Wasp, were off Cape Pallas, and within a few leagues, perhaps miles, of the Convoy when the Action took place, did not arrive up with them, as mentioned in an extract from Lord Mark Kerr's letter to me, dated the 12th February, which is also herewith transmitted for their Lordships' information. I am, Sir, &c.

NELSON AND BRONTE.

TO WILLIAM MARSDEN, ESQ., ADMIRALTY.

[Original, in the Admiralty. " March 27th [i. e. 26th]. Off Toro, P.M. At 2, observed a Frigate standing out of Palma Bay, having a Rear-Admiral's flag (Blue) which proved H.M. Ship Ambuscade. At 2·50, the Ambuscade saluted with thirteen guns. At 3, returned the salute with eleven guns, which proved to be Rear-Admiral Louis from England. At 4·40, shortened sail and anchored in the Gulf of Palma. Squadron anchored here."—*Victory's Log.*]

Victory, in Palma Bay, Sardinia, 26th March, 1805.

Sir,

You will please to acquaint the Lords Commissioners of the Admiralty, that, on the Fleet's arrival here this evening, I was joined by Rear-Admiral Louis[7] in the Ambuscade, and that I have, agreeable to their Lordships' order of the 11th February, taken the said Rear-Admiral and Ambuscade under my command; and that, in obedience to their direction, communicated to me in your letter of the 31st January, I have directed Rear-Admiral Louis to hoist his Flag in the Canopus, which he will do to-morrow morning, and Captain Austen, who came out with him, [will] consequently supersede Captain Conn in the command of that Ship.

I take this opportunity to acquaint you for their Lordships' information, that a better or more zealous Officer than Captain Conn is not in his Majesty's Service, and beg to recommend him to their Lordships' patronage for immediate employment. I am, Sir, &c.

NELSON AND BRONTE.

[7] Rear-Admiral Thomas Louis, who commanded the Minotaur at the Battle of the Nile. Vide vol. iii. p. 90. He was created a Baronet in April 1806, and died in May 1807.

TO WILLIAM MARSDEN, ESQ., ADMIRALTY.

[Original, in the Admiralty.]

Victory, in Palma Bay, Sardinia, 26th March, 1805.

Sir,

I have just received your letter of the 5th ultimo, with the extract of the letter therein mentioned from Mr. Stanley, his Majesty's Consul at Trieste, to the Masters of Lloyd's Coffee-House, which shall be communicated to Captain Raynsford of the Morgiana. I have also to acknowledge your letter of the 15th ultimo, acquainting me that their Lordships intend ordering Captain Bennett of the Tribune to be tried by a Court-Martial, for his conduct in returning to England, and not putting himself under my command as he was directed. Their Lordships' duplicate order of the 12th January, relative to the seizing and destroying all Ships and Vessels belonging to Spain, together with their Lordships' printed Orders for that purpose, and likewise their printed Orders of the 4th February, with his Majesty's Orders in Council of the 1st of that month, relative to the importation of grain into Spain in Neutral bottoms being permitted, agreeable to the instructions therein contained, have been received, and shall be issued to the respective Captains and Commanders of the Fleet under my orders, and duly attended to, agreeably to their Lordship's direction. I am Sir, &c.

NELSON AND BRONTE.

TO HIS EXCELLENCY HUGH ELLIOT, ESQ., NAPLES.

[Autograph, in the Elliot Papers.]

Victory, Gulf of Palma, March 27th, 1805.

My dear Sir,

Your letters of January 19th, by Renown, with one from the King, and another from the Queen, I received on March 15th, when the Renown joined me off Toulon. Your others of the several dates from that time to March 1st, I received last night on my anchoring in this Bay, where I am come to clear the Transports with provisions. The Queen's letter[9] of

---

[9] The following is one of the letters written by the Queen of Naples, at that time, to Lord Nelson; and Mr. Elliot, in transmitting it, on the 20th of January, said,

January 29th I have received, but the one of February 21st is not arrived; but it will come forth when I next have the pleasure of hearing from you. The original destination of the French Fleet, I am every day more and more confirmed, was Egypt. To what other Country should they carry 5000 saddles, &c. &c., and flying artillery? The Commander of the Bomb, who was a prisoner on board the Hortensia (one of the Ships who *might*, but did *not*, take our Convoy—only six Sail being taken and destroyed) says, the Frigates had each 300 Troops, Swiss, on board. He could never learn their destination. However, they are ready for sea again, and I hope they will come forth; for, if they defer it one month from this time, they will not come forth this summer, unless the Brest Fleet comes into the Mediterranean. I shall, therefore, when I believe the danger from the Fleet is passed, take the opportunity of getting a few months rest, and return here before the next winter, which is the dangerous time for a run. Rear-Admiral Louis, who was in the Minotaur, and is known to

---

" I expect to receive a letter from the King to you upon the same subject to-morrow morning, after the Queen's return from Caserta":—

" J'ai reçu, mon digne Milord, votre lettre du mois de Decembre, et je profite de l'occasion du départ du Vaisseau pour vous écrire. Je ne puis vous dire assez, mon respectable et digne Général, combien le Roi et moi nous regardons comme une vraie calamité de plus aux malheurs qui nous accablent, votre depart du Commandement de la Méditerranée. Votre cœur, votre attachement, votre bravoure, votre nom inspirent cette confiance que l'expérience a justifiée, et qui ne se remplacera jamais. Ainsi je le regarde comme un vrai malheur, et me croirois bien heureuse si cela pouvoit se changer, ou au moins être retardé. Je suis convaincue que la crise doit bientôt arriver, ou l'asservissement de toute va l'Europe, être constaté, consolidé, ou qu'il va naitre de grands évenemens. L'ambition et le bonheur effréné du Corse venant de créer son frére Joseph Roi héréditaire de la Lombardie, ou pour dire vrai de l'Italie, ceci doit éveiller de l'assoupissement tous les Souverains, ou consolider leur esclavage. C'est dans ce moment de lutte et indécision, que nos dangers étant infiniment plus grands, s'augmente le vif désir de votre permanence auprès de nous, mon digne et respectable Général et vrai ami. Considérez avec votre sagesse, et surtout avec votre cœur, les circonstances actuelles, et vous trouverez justes mes souhaits; en un mot, mon digne et respectable ami, continuez à être notre sauveur, et comptez sur l'eternelle et sincere reconnoissance de gens qui sentent et meritent de vivre dans un autre siècle que celui de la boue actuelle. Le bon attaché Elliot vous expliquera mieux nos pénibles circonstances. Je me borne à vous exprimer notre vif souhait, que vous ne nous quittiez point, et que vous soyez encore une fois notre sauveur. Je sais que le Roi, mon innocente famille, et tous les gens bien pensans font les mêmes souhaits. Puissent-ils se réaliser. Cela augmentera la reconnaissance, avec laquelle je suis, et serai pour la vie votre bien attachée et reconnoissante amie,—CHARLOTTE."—From a Copy in the Elliot Papers.

their Majesties, is arrived in the room of Admiral Campbell.
I observe what you are pleased to tell me may, if necessary, be
your intentions.[1]   It is too delicate a subject for me to enter
into.   Your experience as a Diplomatic character will duly
appreciate the consequences which may attend leaving your
post.   If Acton had not gone, he might have stayed; but
once gone, never could be suffered to return.   May not that
be the case with you?   But I am sure I beg your pardon for in-
truding an opinion on a subject which you can so much [more]
ably determine than I can pretend to.   I write a line to their
Majesties to tell them that, from October, when I got my permission to go home for a few months' rest, I had, in consequence of my belief of the French Fleet intending to put to
sea, and afterwards their having come to sea, and my belief

[1] In a letter written on the 1st of March, Mr. Elliot informed Lord Nelson that,
on the 14th of February, an Aide de Camp of General St. Cyr arrived from the
French Army, demanding, within three days, a categorical answer to certain demands,
one of which was, that the British Minister, Mr. Elliot, should be obliged to quit
Naples ; and threatening hostilities if they were refused. In another letter, also dated
on the 1st of March, Mr. Elliot wrote to Lord Nelson: "In my preceding letter I have
acquainted you with the nature of the demand, relative to me, already made to this
Court by General St. Cyr, which has been withdrawn for some time, but which is
likely to be soon renewed. Had the French General insisted upon the dismission of the
whole of the British Mission, as well as upon my removal from Naples, this would
have amounted to an absolute act of hostility on the part of this Government against
Great Britain, and I could have taken no other step, than to have protested officially
against any measures which his Sicilian Majesty might have adopted, in order to
oblige me to quit this Court, without receiving orders from my own Sovereign. But
as I understand that the extent of General St. Cyr's demand at present is, that I
personally should absent myself from Naples, without otherwise breaking up the
Mission, it will remain to be determined by future considerations, whether I may
think it more eligible for the good of His Britannic Majesty's Service, and for the
benefit of the King of Naples to remain here, or to withdraw to some other situation
—as if in consequence of a leave of absence received from my own Court, naming
a Chargé d'Affaires to act here as is usual in such cases. The great object hitherto
recommended to my attention has been, to temporize as much as possible, in order
to gain time for the arrival of the foreign auxiliaries, Russian and English, which
have been so long promised to co-operate in the defence of his Sicilian Majesty's
Dominions. Should, therefore, their Sicilian Majesties secretly acquaint me, that
they are desirous of my departure from hence, as if upon leave of absence, upon the
condition of the French consenting to remain within their present limits, I may,
perhaps, in that case apply to Captain Sotheron for a passage in the Excellent, for
myself and my family, to Sicily, or to any other destination which I may think more
expedient."—*Original*, in the Elliot Papers. It may be here remarked that Mr.
Elliot appears to have obtained back the whole of his letters to Lord Nelson, as
they are now among the Elliot Papers.

that they may this spring put to sea again, deferred my departure through all the winter months, I can solemnly declare that nothing but my most particular gratitude to their Sicilian Majesties, with a due sense of what I owe to my own character, could have induced me to remain in the Mediterranean after my leave arrived; and I believe the French Fleet will not move until my return in the Autumn, should my health permit. I leave, my dear Sir, the finest Fleet in the world, with every Officer and man attached to me: therefore, you may easily believe that nothing but absolute necessity could induce me to go home for one instant. Sir Richard Bickerton will take a most active interest in the safety of their Majesties and their Kingdoms; and I feel confident that I may very essentially serve the good Cause by my personal communications in England. Wherever I am, be assured, my dear Sir, that I shall always feel your truly kind attentions for me. Your son is very well. He has received three hundred dollars Prize-money, and has as much more to receive, which I have begged Captain Parker to take from him. I am ever, my dear Sir, with the sincerest regard and esteem, your Excellency's most obliged and faithful Servant,

NELSON AND BRONTE.

P.S.—The Jalouse is arrived, and brought me duplicates of your letters and the letter of the Queen.

TO WILLIAM MARSDEN, ESQ., ADMIRALTY.

[Original, in the Admiralty.]

Victory, in Palma Bay, Sardinia, 27th March, 1805.

Sir,

I have received their Lordships' order dated the 1st ultimo, directing me, from the reasons therein mentioned, to send to England, under a proper Convoy, all such Spanish Vessels and cargoes as may have been detained by the Fleet under my command, prior to the 11th day of January, 1805, (the date of the King's Proclamation for granting reprisals against Spain) and which may be at Gibraltar, with the exception of such parts of the cargoes as it may be necessary, from their perishable state, to dispose of at that place, and for the sale of which to appoint an Agent who will be responsible to account for the proceeds of the same to the proper Officer of the Court of Admiralty in England:

In answer to which, you will please to acquaint the Lords Commissioners of the Admiralty that, in obedience to their order, I have appointed an Agent at Malta, and one at Gibraltar, both Agent-Victuallers; and as such, consequently, men of known integrity and public worth, and I must add of very high estimation in their private characters, to be responsible to account for the proceeds of such Ships and cargoes to the proper Officer of the Court of Admiralty in England. But from knowing the impossibility of manning the several detained Vessels, particularly those sent into Malta, as well as the danger and risk of sending them to England, many of them being in a bad state, I have judged it for the interest of the Crown and Captors to order all the Spanish Vessels and their cargoes, detained prior to the 11th day of January last, to be disposed of at public sale at Malta and Gibraltar, taking it for granted that the Vice-Admiralty Courts at those places will have received the necessary instructions to proceed against them; and herewith transmit you for their Lordships' information, a copy of the authority I have given to Mr. Patrick Wilkie at Malta, and Mr. James Cutforth at Gibraltar, which I hope will meet their Lordships' approbation.

I cannot here omit mentioning that to man the several detained Ships, upwards of three hundred Seamen would be required; and that under the many accidents which they would naturally be liable to during a long and tedious passage from Malta, I do not feel it would be right, or consistent with the interest of those concerned, to order them to England, and therefore hope, from the reasons before-mentioned, that their Lordships will agree with me in opinion. I am, Sir, &c.

NELSON AND BRONTE.

TO PATRICK WILKIE, ESQ., AGENT VICTUALLER, MALTA,
HEREBY APPOINTED SOLE AND ENTIRE AGENT FOR ALL
THE SPANISH SHIPS AND VESSELS, WITH THEIR CARGOES,
ETC., SENT INTO MALTA AS AFORESAID, PRIOR TO THE 11TH
DAY OF JANUARY, 1805.

[From a Copy in the Admiralty.]

Victory, in Palma Bay, 27th March, 1805.

Whereas the Lords Commissioners of the Admiralty have
directed me by their order, bearing date of the 1st February,
1805, to send to England all Spanish Ships and Vessels with
their cargoes, that have been detained at sea by his Majesty's
Fleet under my command prior to the 11th day of January
1805, (the date of the King's Proclamation for granting
reprisals against Spain,) in order to prevent abuses, and
to insure the said Ships and cargoes being disposed of to
their full value, (except such part of the cargoes as may,
from their perishable state, be necessary to dispose of at
Malta,) and having, at the same time, authorized me to appoint
an Agent, who will be held responsible to account for the
proceeds of the same to the proper Officer of the Court of
Admiralty in England: And whereas I think proper, from the
high and honourable character I have received of you, as well
as from the public confidence which Government reposes in you
as Agent Victualler, to appoint you to be the sole and entire
Agent for all the Spanish Ships and Vessels detained and sent
into Malta by the Fleet under my command, prior to the 11th
day of January 1805, as before mentioned:

I do, by virtue of the power and authority to me granted,
hereby nominate and appoint you sole and entire Agent, on
behalf of the Crown and Captors, for all the Spanish Ships and
Vessels detained and sent into Malta by the Fleet under
my command, prior to the said 11th day of January 1805;
and do hereby require and authorize you (from judging the
impracticability of sending the said Ships and Vessels with
their cargoes to England, as directed by their Lordships, as
aforesaid,) to enter upon, and immediately dispose of at public
sale, the said Spanish Ships and Vessels with their cargoes,
detained as aforesaid, prior to the 11th day of January 1805,
and sent into Malta; and to transmit a regular account of

their sales and amount, respectively, to the proper Officer of
the Court of Admiralty in England, to whom you are to hold
yourself accountable for the whole, and every particular transaction and amount of the said Vessels, and their cargoes; and
you will also, in like manner, transmit to me copies of the
accounts of sale, and the amounts thereof accordingly; and,
for so doing, this shall be your full and sufficient authority.

NELSON AND BRONTE.

N.B.—An order of the above tenor and date sent to Mr.
Cutforth, Agent-Victualler, Gibraltar.

TO CAPTAIN BRABAZON.[1]

[From Clarke and M'Arthur, vol. ii. p. 353.]

[Apparently towards the end of March, 1805.]

Although upwards of thirty years have passed away since
we met, yet I can never forget your great kindness; and
believe me, nothing could give me greater pleasure, than an
opportunity of being useful to any friend of yours. The loss
of that very fine Sloop the Raven, has consequently sent all
the Officers to England; and although it would not, probably,
have been in my power to promote your nephew at present,
yet you may rely that I shall bear him in my mind, and a
future occasion may offer. I hope some day, not very far
distant, that I shall enjoy the pleasure of having you under
my roof at Merton, where you shall have a most hearty wel-
come from, my dear Brabazon, your very old and much obliged
friend,   NELSON AND BRONTE.

TO WILLIAM MARSDEN, ESQ., ADMIRALTY.

[Original, in the Admiralty.]

Victory, in Palma Bay, Sardinia, 29th March, 1805.

Sir,

I herewith transmit you, for the information of the Lords
Commissioners of the Admiralty, the sentence of a Court-

[1] Captain Lambert Brabazon: he was Posted in 1782; for some years commanded the Dorset Yacht at Dublin; was passed over in Flag promotions, and died
the Senior Post Captain in April 1811. His nephew mentioned in this letter has
not been identified.

Martial,[2] held yesterday on board his Majesty's Ship Royal
Sovereign, on Captain Farquhar, the Officers, and Company
of his Majesty's late Bomb-Vessel Acheron, for the loss of the
same in Action with the Enemy on the 4th February last,
which leaves little for me to say on the gallant conduct of
Captain Farquhar, the Officers, and Company of the said late
Vessel in Action with an Enemy of such superior force, as
well as for the most able defence made for the security and
escape of the Convoy under their protection, which certainly
was effected by their judicious arrangements previous to the
Action; and the most gallant defence made by the Arrow and
Acheron in the unequal contest, which, from every information that I have received, reflects equal honour on Captain
Vincent, his Officers, and Company, and very justly entitles
those Commanders to their Lordships' patronage. I am,
Sir, &c.

NELSON AND BRONTE.

TO SIR ALEXANDER JOHN BALL, BART., MALTA.

[Autograph, in the possession of Sir William Keith Ball, Bart.]

Victory, March 29th, 1805.

My dear Ball,
Many, many thanks for all your truly kind letters, which I
received on my anchoring at Palma. I shall read with attention your paper upon Egypt; but till I dispatch off my letters

---

[2] The Court considered "that the conduct of Captain Farquhar on both days was
highly meritorious and deserving imitation, and that he was bravely supported by
the Officers and Ship's Company on the occasion, and doth most honourably acquit
Captain Farquhar, the Officers and Company of His Majesty's late Bomb-Vessel
Acheron of all blame ; and they are hereby most honourably acquitted accordingly."
On returning Captain Farquhar his sword, the President, Sir Richard Bickerton, said,
" I hope you will soon be called upon to serve in a Ship that will enable you to
meet L'Hortense upon more equal terms. The result of the contest may prove
more lucrative to you, but it cannot be more honourable."—*Marshall's Naval
Biography*, vol. ii. p. 931. Captain Vincent, of the Arrow, was tried at Portsmouth
on the 17th of June, and most honourably acquitted, by a sentence no less eulogistic
and flattering. Both these gallant Officers were immediately made Post Captains.
Of Captain Vincent, who became a Companion of the Bath and died in August 1831,
there is a Memoir in the *Naval Chronicle*, vol. xvii. Captain Farquhar died, a
Rear-Admiral of the White, a Knight Commander of the Bath, and a Knight Commander of the Guelphs, in October 1843.

for England, for which the Renown is waiting at Gibraltar, I have not a moment to myself. I am glad you approved of my voyage to Egypt, and that may be their future destination. I shall remain here a very few weeks longer, when, if the French do not put to sea, I think it very probable they will lay up for the summer, unless the Brest, or Ferrol, and Cadiz Fleet should come into the Mediterranean. I am fully aware that more Sloops of War are wanted for the service of Malta and the Convoys to the Eastward, than I have in the Mediterranean ; but none are sent me, and my force decreases every day. Gibraltar is in absolute distress; they have not force sufficient to convoy over their Bullock-Vessels. Fox has called upon Sir John Orde, who tells him he must refer to me, which he has done, and I have been forced to answer him, that I regretted the Officer at the Straits' Mouth was not junior to me, when I should order him to take care of Gibraltar. But this cannot go on. I have, on January 7th, wrote home of what would happen ; and I dare say, Orde has a trimmer before this time.[3] He will not be suffered to remain

---

[3] It is curious to find that, at the moment when Sir John Orde's conduct caused Lord Nelson such dissatisfaction, he should have been no less displeased with Nelson's proceedings towards him. The reply to the following letter from Sir John Orde to the First Lord of the Admiralty, was an immediate compliance with his request ; and he was desired, on the arrival of the Glory at Spithead, to strike his flag and come on shore. He was never again employed, and died an Admiral of the Red in February 1824. Sir John Orde, who was thus twice (*vide* vol. iii. 25) in collision with Lord Nelson, was one of the supporters of the pall at his funeral.

"TO LORD MELVILLE.

"My Lord,　　　　　　　　"Glory, off Cadiz, March 27th, 1805.

"Since writing the accompanying letter, I have received dispatches from the Board as late as the 26th February ; but no orders about the specie on board the Ships of War, nor any word that can satisfy my doubts respecting the propriety of my conduct in ordering the blockade of Cadiz.

"By these dispatches, I am made acquainted with the Admiralty having authorized Lord Nelson to appoint an Agent for the disposal of certain parts of the property detained *by my Squadron ;* and saw at Gibraltar an arrangement I should have thought myself entitled to complain of, had I been junior to his Lordship. I am also informed of its being their Lordships' opinion that it is an essential part of the duty of the Squadron under my command to protect the Trade of England to Gibraltar. This expectation, I must confess, I was not prepared to have satisfied, not only because of my general orders, but also because of the insufficiency of my Squadron for this duty, in addition to the many others it is called upon to perform.

"Some other Officer, my Lord, may possibly feel those circumstances less mortifying than I do ; and, possessing greater abilities, may be able to perform all that

much longer; he will go to the Channel: he will be the richest
Admiral that England ever had, and I one of the poorest.
Bravo! I can only touch upon different topics; for it would
take hours and hours to tell by mouth all I should like to do.
Mr. Elliot seems alarmed at Naples, and, I fear, will leave his
post. However, I have ventured to touch upon the importance
and probable consequences of such a measure; but I have done
it with delicacy,[5] and with all the deference and respect due to
his rank; but he is got frightened. The loss of the Raven
has been great, both as to Vessel and dispatches. I shall
have an opportunity of hearing and writing to you once
more before my departure ; therefore, I shall only assure you
that I am ever, my dear Ball, your most faithful and attached
friend,

NELSON AND BRONTE.

TO WILLIAM MARSDEN, ESQ., ADMIRALTY.

[Original, in the Admiralty.]

Victory, in the Gulf of Palma, Sardinia, 30th March, 1805.

Sir,

A report having reached me of its having been stated to
their Lordships, that the Ships under my command have been
frequently out of the Mediterranean, since the arrival of Vice-
Admiral Sir John Orde off Cadiz, I beg to assure their Lordships, upon my word of honour, that no Ship or Vessel under
my command was sent out of the Mediterranean, after I received official notice from him on the 15th December last,
except the Amazon, which was sent to Lisbon with my

seems expected by the Admiralty from me with the small force intrusted to my
command. No one, I will venture to say, can have shown more zeal and industry
than I have done in the execution of an arduous duty, which, I am sorry, notwithstanding, to say, I now feel myself unequal to perform with satisfaction to my em-
ployers, and to my own feelings, extremely hurt by recent treatment.

"May I, then, request of your Lordship permission to retire from a situation I owe
to your goodness, and which to hold any longer, would prove me unworthy the
protection I have received. In resigning my command into abler hands, possessing
the confidence of the Admiralty, I shall have the satisfaction to believe I am promoting his Majesty's Service, at the same time that I am discharging a duty I owe
to my Country, and to my own character. I remain, my Lord, with the strongest
sense of obligation, of consideration, and esteem, your Lordship's most faithful and
obedient servant.—J. ORDE."

[5] Vide p. 377, ante.

dispatches. A copy of my order[5] to Captain Parker for the performance of this service, is herewith transmitted for their Lordships' information. Not having received intimation from any quarter whatever, of Sir John Orde's being placed in the command of a Squadron off Cadiz, the instant our Minister left Madrid, I reinforced the Squadron then under Sir Richard Strachan, as much as the force under my command would permit, that the operations of the Enemy in that quarter might, as much as possible, be checked and frustrated. I am, Sir, &c.

NELSON AND BRONTE.

TO COMMISSIONER OTWAY, GIBRALTAR.

[Autograph, in the possession of Rear-Admiral Inglefield, C.B.]

Victory, March 30th, 1805.

My dear Commissioner,

I received, on the 26th, all your kind communications from Malta, for which I sincerely thank you, and I am very sorry that Captain ———— should have so far forgot himself, as to write you such an improper letter; but these young gentlemen sometimes think they have no superiors, and that their mandates are to be a law. I shall write him a public letter upon the subject, and you will receive a public letter[6] also from me upon it.

I hope you have had a safe and quick passage to Gibraltar. I hope long before this that the Admiralty have attended to my representations about giving Gibraltar that force, which is absolutely necessary to insure its supply of fresh provisions; and as I have not the pleasure of being known to General Fox, I wish you would tell of the absolute want of Small Craft at Malta, and that I have them not under my command, or Gibraltar should not have been neglected by me. If Sir John Orde was junior to me, I should instruct him as I have done formerly Sir Richard Strachan and Captain Gore.[7]

I have certainly had a long trip after the French Fleet, and now we have a report that their Troops embarked on Thurs-

---

[5] Vide p. 308, ante.
[6] The letters alluded to have not been found.   [7] Vide ante.

VOL. VI.   C C

day, March 21st. God send it may be true; but if they do not come forth very soon, I shall give up the hopes of meeting them, and then proceed to England. I sincerely hope that Gibraltar will escape the dreadful scourge of last autumn, and I hope General Fox has burnt down all the small houses at the back of the Town; and perhaps if half the Town went with them, it would be better for the Rock. With every good wish, I am ever, my dear Commissioner, your much obliged

NELSON AND BRONTE.

TO CAPTAIN KEATS, H.M. SHIP SUPERB.

[Autograph, in the possession of the Reverend Richard Keats.]

Victory, March 30th, 1805.

Most Private.

My dear Keats,

I felt most exceedingly last night, at finding your friend Admiral Murray so exceedingly hurt at some conversation which had passed between you and him, about hammocks. I can most solemnly assure you, that so far from Admiral Murray withholding any stores from the Superb, that he would stretch the point to comply with your wishes, well knowing that in our scanty supplies you would take no more than was absolutely necessary for present use. The Superb, upon every consideration, whether I consider the value of her Captain as an Officer, or the importance of preserving her Ship's company, ought to have every comfort which the Service will possibly allow. I have, therefore, desired that Admiral Murray will get from you an account of the number of hammocks wanted to complete the Superb for Channel Service, that I may send to Naples to purchase them; and I again assure you that Admiral Murray would stretch any length which you could desire, to meet your wants and wishes. The situation of first Captain is certainly a very unthankful Office, for if there is a deficiency of stores, he must displease, probably, the whole Fleet; for no Ship can have her demands complied with. I wish, my dear Keats, you would turn this in your mind, and relieve Admiral Murray from the uneasiness your conversation has given him; for I will venture to say, that if he could (or ought to) show a partiality, it would be to the Superb, because her Captain husbands the stores in a most exemplary manner. You will readily conceive what I must feel upon this occasion, being most truly your most obliged and faithful friend,

NELSON AND BRONTE.

TO WILLIAM MARSDEN, ESQ., ADMIRALTY.

[Original, in the Admiralty.]

Victory, in Palma Bay, Sardinia, 30th March, 1805.

Sir,

I have received your letter of the 31st January, (together with a copy of the instructions therein mentioned,) acquainting me that their Lordships had directed Major James Weir, of the Royal Marines, to proceed to Malta, with the party named in the margin of the said letter, for the purpose of enlisting Recruits towards completing the Detachments on board the Ships under my command, and to send the overplus (if any) to England ; and signifying their Lordships' direction to me to give such orders, as I may judge necessary from time to time, to carry their said instructions into effect. In answer to which, you will please to acquaint the Lords Commissioners of the Admiralty, that I shall pay due obedience to their instructions communicated to me in your said letter, and that I have directed Captain Adair, of the Royal Marines, belonging to the Victory, whom I had some time ago appointed Inspecting Officer for the raising Recruits for the Marine Service, to discontinue doing so ; but from the reasons stated in his letter herewith enclosed, I have permitted him to receive, from the different parts of the Mediterranean, such Recruits as his agents may have raised by his authority, and must beg you will be pleased to call their Lordships' attention to the very just statement he has made, in order that he may not only be entitled to the usual allowance made to Recruiting Officers in England, but also such remuneration for the loss he is likely to sustain by his prudent precaution, in providing such clothing for the new raised Recruits as they were likely to be in want of, immediately they were found fit for the Service, and attested. The several incidental expenses

mentioned in Captain Adair's said letter cannot escape their
Lordships' notice; and I must, in justice to this most excellent Officer, acquaint you, for their Lordships' information,
that his zeal for the Public Service has been very great, and his
exertions indefatigable, the number of Recruits he has raised,
amounting to one hundred and eighty-four, as mentioned in
the lists herewith transmitted, have been all stout, prime men;
and my considering his Appointment as permanent, has no
doubt led him to the most lively exertion, and recommended
the provision he has made for their future clothing, as necessary. I therefore feel his case particularly hard, and trust
their Lordships will take it into consideration, and order him
such remuneration and recompence as they shall deem him
entitled to. I am, Sir, &c.

NELSON AND BRONTE.

TO WILLIAM MARSDEN, ESQ., ADMIRALTY.

[Autograph, in the possession of Mrs. Leake.]

Victory, March 30th, 1805.

My dear Sir,

I have had the pleasure of seeing Mr. M——, who seems
a well-informed gentleman; but I do not think the situation
you have placed him in can be either lucrative or pleasant.
The arrival of Admiral Louis will enable me to get a little
rest, which I shall take as soon as I am satisfied in my own
mind that the French will not put to sea. On March 25th,
they either entirely disembarked their Troops, or re-embarked
them: I sincerely hope the latter, and, if so, I think a few
days will settle all my business in the Mediterranean. I am
truly sensible of all your kind attentions; and believe me,
with the highest respect, your most obliged,

NELSON AND BRONTE.

I beg my respectful compliments to Lord and Lady Spencer
when you see them.

TO DOCTOR SEWELL,[7] JUDGE OF THE VICE-ADMIRALTY COURT
AT MALTA.

[From Clarke and M'Arthur, vol. ii. p. 400.]

[About 30th March, 1805.]

I had hopes to have sent the French Fleet for condemnation; and although my hopes diminish, yet it is possible it may arrive before April is over, after which some other Admiral must have that great felicity. I am, &c.

NELSON AND BRONTE.

TO THE COMMISSIONERS OF THE TRANSPORT BOARD.

[Original, in the Record Office, Tower.]

Victory, in Palma Bay, Sardinia, 30th March, 1805.

Gentlemen,

I have to acknowledge your letter of the 29th January, with the List of Transports, therein mentioned, in the Mediterranean, and under orders for Gibraltar, and requesting that those upon the highest terms of hire, also such others as may not be wanted, are sent home, in order to their being discharged from the Service. In answer, I have to assure you that the Agents for Transports at Malta and Gibraltar have the most positive instructions from me, to send the Transports upon the highest terms of hire, and also such others as are not wanted for the service of Malta, and the Fleet under my command, by every opportunity of Convoy that offers; and I have reason to believe that my orders are most strictly attended to.

The Transports sent to Odessa by Sir Alexander Ball for corn for the Inhabitants of Malta, I cannot take upon me to account for, as, of course, he will have satisfied Government with the propriety of this measure. The misfortune that happened to the Convoy under the late Arrow and Acheron has, no doubt, detained the Transports intended for England under their protection; but they will soon arrive under the Anson and Convoy from Malta. I am, &c.

NELSON AND BRONTE.

[7] Afterwards Sir John Sewell, Knighted in May 1815.

TO ALEXANDER DAVISON, ESQ.

[Autograph, in the possession of Colonel Davison.]

Victory, March 30th, 1805.

My dear Davison,

Your kind letters of January 28th, February 11th, and 13th, I received by the Ambuscade, and I shall by this occasion do little more then thank you for them; for unless the Devil himself stands at the door, you will, perhaps, nearly as soon as this letter, see me in England. I have had a very hard fag. I shall not talk of Sir John Orde, who must be the richest Admiral that ever England saw. He will torment the Admiralty enough. '*How should he know* HOW *to behave: he never was at Sea ?*'[8] I only hope that I shall not be kept longer in Quarantine than is necessary. At this moment, we have not a sick man in the Fleet—I mean, beyond accidents. You will remember me kindly to Nepean, and I shall hope to see you in St. James's Square, and do *not* get into Parliament. I am ever, my dear Davison, yours most faithfully,

NELSON AND BRONTE.

TO VICE-ADMIRAL BLIGH.

[From Marshall's " Naval Biography," Supplement, part i. p. 431. " March 31st [*i. e.* 30th]. P.M. At 6·15, weighed and made sail to the Southward. Squadron weighed as convenient. April 1st [*i. e.* March 31st, P.M.] Squally. At 5·30, anchored in Pula Roads. Squadron anchored here as convenient."—*Victory's Log.*]

Victory, March 31st, 1805.

Many thanks for your constant and kind attention in sending me Newspapers. Your son is certainly upon the Admiralty list, but so far down, that nothing less than the French and Spanish Fleets being captured, can give him a reasonable chance ; however, it is good to be upon that list. I can assure

---

[8] Lord Nelson here alluded to an old anecdote, which, though well known to professional readers, may not be so to others. A sailor, seeing a young Prince of the Blood Royal on the quarter-deck with his hat on, while the Admiral, Captain, and other Officers were uncovered, expressed his astonishment to a shipmate, who replied, " Why, how should he know manners, seeing as how he's never been to sea !"

you that your son is an excellent young man. You must forgive my short letter, and only believe that I am ever, my dear Admiral, your most faithful servant,

NELSON AND BRONTE.

TO EARL CAMDEN, K.G.

[Original, in the Colonial Office.]

Victory, April 1st, 1805.

My Lord,

I have been honoured with your letter of December 3rd, inclosing a copy of one from your Lordship to General Villettes. I had very long ago wrote to the General, that those 2000 Troops were intended, unless called for, for other urgent occasions, for the service of Sicily, and that either Mr. Elliot or the Governor of Messina, or when his own judgment pointed out the necessity of sending, not upon any account to wait for any notice from me; and the Commander of H. M. Ships stationed there, has orders to give all the assistance in his power for getting them quickly to Messina.

I have a letter from Algiers of March 16th, from Mr. Cartwright, who states that the Regency seem very happy at our reconciliation, and that there is every probability of our remaining good friends. I am so near going to England to try and recruit myself, that I shall not at this moment intrude upon your Lordship any opinion of mine, relative to the Countries whose present situation and Government are not secure from one day to another. I have wrote to Sir John Acton to warn him of the state of Sicily from French intrigues. France will have both Sardinia and Sicily very soon, if we do not prevent it, and Egypt besides. I am, &c.

NELSON AND BRONTE.

TO ADMIRAL LORD RADSTOCK.

[Autograph, in the possession of Rear-Admiral Lord Radstock, C.B.]

Victory, April 1st, 1805.

My dear Lord,

Many thanks for your truly kind letter of February 14th, which I passed in a heavy gale of wind between the Morea and Candia. I owe much of my fame on that day[9] to your truly honourable mind; but for you it would hardly have [been] known that I was present.

As my station was to be lopped to give Sir John Orde a fortune, and to keep me poor, for that was sure to be the natural consequence of any Admiral being placed outside the Mediterranean, I wish it had fallen to you, for you had at least done as much service as Sir John Orde, or any other man in the Service. Report says that Sir John Orde will be the richest Admiral that England ever saw. It cannot be pleasing to me to have every person tell me this; but my soul soars above this consideration, although I cannot help thinking that I could have made as good a use of a large fortune as Sir John Orde, or any other Admiral. I should like to have tried. When opportunity offers, and a good Frigate offers, your son shall be put into a Frigate, and I am sure Sir Richard Bickerton will do whatever you wish him. I am very near my departure; the moment I make up my mind the French Fleet will not come out this summer, I embark in the Superb. My health does not improve; but, because I am not confined to my bed, people will not believe my state of health. Your son is very well and as good as ever, and I am always, my dear Lord, your most grateful and obliged friend,

NELSON AND BRONTE.

TO EARL CAMDEN, K.G.

[Original, in the Colonial Office. "April 3rd. A.M. At 5·30, weighed and made sail, as did the Squadron."—*Victory's Log.*]

Victory, April 3rd, 1805.

My Lord,

I send you a letter from Mr. Magnon, our Consul at Cagliari, by which you will form some further judgment of the state of the Island of Sardinia, whose fate is drawing fast to a close. I have, &c.

NELSON AND BRONTE.

[9] The Battle of the 14th of February, 1797.

TO CAPTAIN SIR RICHARD STRACHAN, BART., H. M. SHIP DONEGAL.

[Autograph in the possession of R. Watson, Esq. "April 4th. A.M. 10, Employed clearing Ship for Action. Phœbe rejoined with intelligence that the French Fleet were put to sea. (At 10·23, made the signal to Prepare for Battle.—*Signal Log.*) Passed through the Fleet a Spanish Cartel. Ætna parted at Noon. Squadron in company. Toro bore E. ¾ N. distance 6 leagues. P.M. 2, Active rejoined. 4, Active and Ambuscade parted. 6, Phœbe parted."—*Victory's Log.*]

Private.　　　　　　　　　　Victory, April 3rd, 1805.

My dear Sir Richard,

You know it was my wish to have sent you home with the Amphitrite, without being tacked to a Convoy, and indeed the wishes of the Admiralty, that the Line of Battle Ships should go home by themselves; but as I have received accounts that seventeen Sail of the Arrow's Convoy are at Gibraltar, I have been obliged to order you to protect them, but I still hope that you will fall in with a Galleon; and that you may, is the sincere wish, my dear Sir Richard, of your most faithful friend,

NELSON AND BRONTE.

TO CAPTAIN THOMAS, H. M. BOMB ÆTNA.

[Autograph, in the possession of Rear-Admiral Thomas.]

Victory, April 4th, 1805.

Sir,

The French Fleet is at sea,[8] steering to the Southward. Proceed off Cagliari, fire guns, and call out the Seahorse, and desire Captain Boyle to join me. I am now standing to the

---

[8] Napoleon's "plan was resolved upon early in March, and the orders accordingly given. In this plan, as in that of Surinam, the English were to be decoyed towards India and the West Indies, whither the Squadron of Admiral Missiessy, which had sailed on the 11th of January, already called their attention, and the French were then suddenly to return to the seas of Europe, with an assemblage of force superior to any Squadron the English could muster. It was in some degree the same project as that of the previous December, but increased and completed by the junction of the forces of Spain. Admiral Villeneuve was to sail with the first favourable wind, pass the Strait, call at Cadiz for Admiral Gravina, with six or seven Spanish Ships of the Line, besides the Eagle, then proceed to Martinique, and, if Missiessy were still there, join him, and wait for a further junction more considerable than all the others. This junction was that of Ganteaume. He, profiting by the

Westward, as I do not think the French will make Toro. I
can tell him no more, as my movements must be very uncertain; but, I believe, the French, if they do not make Toro,
will make Galita. I am, Sir, yours faithfully,

NELSON AND BRONTE.

first equinoctial gale which should disperse the English, was to sail from Brest with
twenty-one Ships, the best of this arsenal, steer for Ferrol, be joined by the French
division in Port there, and the Spanish division which would be ready to sail, and
then steer for Martinique, where Villeneuve would be awaiting him. After this
general assemblage, which presented but few real difficulties, there would be at
Martinique twelve Sail under Villeneuve, six or seven under Gravina, five under
Missiessy, and twenty-one under Ganteaume, besides the Franco-Spanish Squadron
of Ferrol, that is to say, about fifty to sixty Sail—an enormous force, the con-
centration of which had never been witnessed at any time, or on any sea. The plan
was now so complete, so well-calculated, that it necessarily produced in the mind
of Napoleon a rapture of hope. Even the Minister Decrès confessed that it presented the greatest chances of success. It was always possible to run out of Toulon
with the (*Mistral*) north-west wind, as the late sortie of Villeneuve showed.
The junction with Gravina at Cadiz, should Nelson be outwitted, was easy, for the
English had not yet thought it necessary to blockade that Port. The Toulon
Squadron, thus increased to seventeen or eighteen Sail, was almost certain to reach
Martinique. Missiessy had touched there without meeting anything during his
voyage, except some Merchantmen, which he captured. The most difficult point
was to get out of Brest Road. But in March there was every reason to expect some
equinoctial gale. Ganteaume, on arriving before Ferrol, which was only blockaded
by five or six English Ships of the Line, would, on presenting himself with twenty-
one, put all idea of fighting out of their minds, and, without striking a blow, succeed in adding to his force the French division commanded by Admiral Gourdon,
and those Spanish Vessels which were ready, and then proceed to Martinique.
It could not be suspected by the English that there was any design of assembling,
at a single point like Martinique, from fifty to sixty Sail of the Line at once. It was
probable that their ideas would turn towards India. At all events, Ganteaume,
Gourdon, Villeneuve, Gravina, and Missiessy, having once effected a junction, no
English Squadron that they might meet, and numbering at most only from twelve to
fifteen Sail, would venture to oppose fifty, and the return into the Channel was
consequently secured. All our forces, then, were to be assembled together between
the shores of England and France, at the moment when the Fleets of England
would be sailing towards the East, America, or in India. Events speedily proved
that this grand plan was practicable even with an inferior execution.

   " Every precaution was taken to preserve the most profound secrecy. The plan
was not confided to the Spaniards, who had engaged to follow with docility the
directions of Napoleon. Villeneuve and Ganteaume alone, of the Admirals, were to
be entrusted with the secret, and they were not to have it on sailing, but when
fairly at sea, and without opportunity of communicating with land. Then their
sealed orders, which they were only to open on reaching a certain latitude, would
instruct them what course to steer. None of the Captains of these Ships were
let into the secret of the expedition ; but they had certain fixed points at which to
rejoin each other in case of separation. None of the Ministers were acquainted
with the plan except Admiral Decrès. He was expressly instructed to correspond

TO CAPTAIN DURBAN, H. M. SHIP AMBUSCADE.

[From Clarke and M'Arthur, vol. ii. p. 401.]

4th April, 1805.

Proceed to Galita, communicate with the fishermen, and try and find out if they have seen the French Fleet. I shall lie-to all night, and drift for Galita, and I shall try to keep within Sardinia and Galita till you join. If I am led away by information, I shall endeavour to send a letter to Palma, St. Pierres, or Cagliari. I am, &c.

NELSON AND BRONTE.

TO WILLIAM MARSDEN, ESQ., ADMIRALTY.

[Original, in the Admiralty.]

Victory, at Sea, 4th April, 1805.

Sir,

In consequence of His Majesty's Sloop Childers not having joined the Fleet, and being desirous that the Renown and Convoy from Gibraltar should not be detained a moment, I have given a Commisson to Captain Corbet of the Bittern, to be Captain of the Amphitrite in the room of Sir William Bolton, and appointed the Purser of the Bittern also to that Frigate ; I have likewise given a Commission [to Lieutenant] Louis, who I had appointed to supersede Sir William Bolton in the Childers, to be Commander of the Bittern, and appointed Mr. George Voller Oughton[9] (who was intended to

directly with Napoleon, and to write his dispatches with his own hand. The report of an expedition to India was circulated in all the Ports. It was pretended that great numbers of Troops were embarked ; in reality, the Toulon Squadron was charged to take scarcely three thousand men, and the Brest Squadron six or seven thousand. The Admirals were instructed to land half that force in the West Indies, to reinforce the garrisons there, and to bring back four or five thousand of the best soldiers, to add to the force of Boulogne.

" By arranging matters thus, the Fleets would not be greatly encumbered, but free and comfortable. They were all victualled for six months, so that they might remain at sea a long time without putting into Port. Couriers were despatched to Ferrol and Cadiz, bearing orders to have everything prepared for weighing, because, at any moment, the blockade might be raised by an allied Fleet, without saying which or how."—*Ibid.* p. 166.

[9] Now a Knight of the Portuguese Order of the Tower and Sword ; he was not confirmed as Purser until December 1807.

supersede the Purser of the Childers) to be Purser of the Bittern; and herewith transmit you copies of the said two Commissions and Warrants, which I request you will be so good as lay before the Lords Commissioners of the Admiralty for their information, and move their Lordships to confirm the respective appointments. I am extremely concerned that the Childers has not joined, but trust their Lordships will approve of the arrangements I have made in consequence, and of the motives for not detaining the Renown and their public dispatches. I am, Sir, your most obedient, humble servant,

NELSON AND BRONTE.

TO WILLIAM MARSDEN, ESQ., ADMIRALTY.

[Original, in the Admiralty, and Autograph draught, in the possession of the Reverend Henry Girdlestone.]

Victory, at Sea, 5th April, 1805.

Sir,

The French Fleet put to sea in the night of Saturday, March 30th, and on Sunday morning the 31st, at eight o'clock, they were seen by the Active and Phœbe, with a light breeze at N.E., steering S.S.W., with all sail set; their force is supposed by the Frigates to be eleven Sail of the Line, seven Frigates, and two Brigs. At eight o'clock in the evening Captain Moubray detached the Phœbe, (Cape Sicie then bearing N. b E., true bearings, twenty leagues) to join me, which she did off Toro yesterday morning April the 4th, and the Active joined at three o'clock in the afternoon. Captain Moubray, the night of the 31st ultimo, having kept his wind, with fresh breezes from the W.N.W., lost sight of the Enemy; and therefore thinks they either bore away to the Eastward, or steered S.S.W., as they were going, when first seen. From the morning of April 1st, the winds have been very variable and mostly Southerly and Easterly, till the night of the 3rd, when it set in fresh at N.W. I have placed Frigates on the Coast of Barbary, and off Toro, and am laying half-way between Galita and Sardinia; for, I am sure, if they are bound this route that they could not pass before this day. The Minister of the Marine is said to command them, and I have nothing to wish for but to meet them: the Fleet I have the honour

to command is everything which I could wish in respect to
health and discipline, and their Lordships may rely that
nothing shall be left undone to get at them by, Sir, your
most obedient, humble servant,

NELSON AND BRONTE.

TO VISCOUNT MELVILLE.

[From Clarke and M'Arthur, vol. ii. p. 401.]

5th April, 1805, Midway between
the Coast of Barbary and Sardinia.

My dear Lord,

Although I feel so far comfortable that the French Fleet is
at sea, yet I must have a natural, and I hope a laudable anxiety
of mind, until I have the happiness of seeing them. However,
I have covered the Channel from Barbary to Toro, with
Frigates and the Fleet. The French could not pass before to-
day, if this be their route. I must leave as little as possible
to chance, and I shall make sure they are to the Eastward of
me, before I risk either Sardinia, Sicily, or Naples ; for they
may delay their time of coming even this distance, from an
expectation that I shall push for Egypt, and thus leave them
at liberty to act against Sardinia, Sicily, or Naples. I have
taken everything into my most serious consideration ; and
although I may err in my judgment, yet your Lordship may
rely, that I will do what I think is best for the honour of my
King and Country, and for the protection of his Majesty's
Allies. I will not say more. I am, &c.

NELSON AND BRONTE.

TO EARL CAMDEN, K.G.

[Original, in the Colonial Office. "April 5th. A.M. A Turkish Corvette came
into the Squadron and saluted with fifteen guns, which we returned with an equal
number. Amazon rejoined with three Transports. Bittern, Phœbe, and Moucheron
joined. P.M. Moucheron parted.— *Victory's Log.*]

Victory, April 5th, 1805.

My Lord,

Was the letter from the Grand Vizir only flattering to me,
I should, perhaps, not send it ; but it conveys such sentiments

of gratitude to our Sovereign,-that I feel I ought not to withhold it. I therefore inclose the translation sent from Constantinople, which I hope your Lordship will approve. I
have, &c.

NELSON AND BRONTE.

TO THE GRAND VIZIR.

[From Clarke and M'Arthur, vol. ii. p. 401. After assuring the Grand Vizir of
his inviolable attachment to the Sublime Porte, and to his Imperial Majesty; and
that in having recently pursued the Common Enemy to the Morea and Egypt,
believing that to have been their destination, he had only obeyed the orders of his
Sovereign, he added :]

5th April, 1805.

No particular merit is, I feel, due to an Officer for the performance of his duty. I think it is very possible that their
destination may be either to the Morea or Egypt. I have
placed his Majesty's Fleet in the narrow part between Sardinia
and the Coast of Africa, therefore it is scarcely possible for
them to pass without my seeing them, or receiving accounts
from the Frigates. . . . . . . I have only to hope that God
Almighty will deliver them into my hands, and give his blessing to my endeavours to serve the Public cause. I am, &c.

NELSON AND BRONTE.[1]

TO COMMISSIONER OTWAY, GIBRALTAR.

[Autograph, in the possession of Rear-Admiral Inglefield, C.B.]

Victory, 6 A.M., 6th April, 1805.

Sir,

The French Fleet sailed from Toulon on Monday [Sunday]
morning, March the 31st, at eight o'clock. When first seen,
Cape Sicie, bearing North by East ten leagues, the wind at
North East, light breezes. They were steering with their
steering-sails set, S.S.W. At sunset, when Phœbe left them,
their heads were to the South West, Cape Sicie N. b E., true,
twenty leagues. In the evening, the wind came fresh from
the W.N.W. The Active stood upon a wind to the S.W. all

----

[1] Statement of the two Fleets, as sent by Lord Nelson to Mr. Stratton, Minister
at Constantinople. French Fleet: Eleven Sail of the Line, seven Frigates, two
Brigs. English Fleet: Eleven Sail of the Line, four Frigates, two Corvettes.

night, and at daylight on Monday morning did not see them. Monday and Tuesday, was with the Frigates, light breezes Southerly and Easterly. On Thursday morning, Phœbe joined me off Toro, with fresh breezes N.W. At 3 P.M., the Active joined. On Friday, it was fresh breezes Northerly—to-day, calm. I have two Frigates on the Barbary Coast; have sent one off the Straits of Bonifaccio, on the East side of Sardinia; and am myself, till to-morrow, stationary, between Sardinia and Galita, when I shall stand to cover Naples and Sicily. You will, my dear Sir, readily conceive my anxiety at this moment; but I ever am your most obliged and faithful servant,

NELSON AND BRONTE.

TO SIR ALEXANDER JOHN BALL, BART., MALTA.

[Autograph, in the possession of Sir William Keith Ball, Bart.]

Victory, April 6th, 1805.

My dear Ball,

As Admiral Murray tells me that one of our Transports will be clear to-night, I shall let her take her chance of getting safely to Malta. The Cartel from Barcelona would have informed you of the French Fleets being at sea, and that Moubray lost sight of them on Sunday night. I shall repeat their position from the accounts of Capel and Moubray on the other side. I am, in truth, half dead; but what man can do to find them out, shall be done; but I must not make more haste than good speed, and leave Sardinia, Sicily, or Naples for them to take, should I go either to the Eastward or Westward, without knowing something more about them. Ambuscade has been sent to Galita; Active, to the Coast of Africa; and, last night, I sent Moucheron to cruize between Galita and the shore, and to go to Tunis for information; Seahorse and Ætna are off Toro; Hydra is gone along the East side of Corsica, to find out if they passed through the Straits of Bonifaccio; Ambuscade is now in sight, but not having any signal flying, of course has seen nothing; Amazon will go to Naples the moment Active joins, which I expect will be to-night or to-morrow morning; and if I still get no information, Phœbe will go off St. Sebastians, to speak my look-out Ship there, and try to find out where they are; .... [?] to examine Toulon. I shall take a position off Ustica, ready to communicate with the Vessels which will join me; and by this position, to be ready to push for Naples, should they be gone there, or to protect Sicily. I am very uneasy and unwell; therefore, I cannot write more. God bless you, my dear Ball, and believe me ever, most faithfully, your obliged friend,

NELSON AND BRONTE.

The French Fleet put to sea from Toulon on Sunday morning, the 31st of March. At ten o'clock, they were seen at Cape Sicie, bearing N. b E. ten leagues, the wind at N.E., and they steering with their larboard steering-sails set S.S.W. Light breezes. At noon, the wind came to the N.N.W., and they hauled to the Westward, as wishing not to let our Frigates near them. At sunset, Cape Sicie bore N. b E., true, twenty leagues. It came to blow fresh at W.N.W. Phœbe steered for Toro. Next day, Tuesday, and Wednesday, she had little winds Southerly and Easterly, and rain till Wednesday night, when it blew fresh at N.W. On Thursday morning, she joined me off Toro. At 3 P.M., the Active joined, having kept his wind to the S.W. all Sunday night, and seen nothing of the Enemy. Captain Mundy thinks they must have bore away to the Southward or Eastward.

5 P.M.—The Ambuscade is not in sight, which rather surprises me, as we are only five leagues from Galita. Can the French have chased her to the Eastward?

TO ALEXANDER DAVISON, ESQ.

[Autograph, in the possession of Colonel Davison.]

Victory, April 6th, 1805.

My dear Davison,

I have desired Captain Conn[1] to call upon you. He will tell you of all my present anxiety. I can neither eat, drink, or sleep. It cannot last long what I feel; but I am ever, my dear Davison, faithfully yours,

NELSON AND BRONTE.

You will tell Captain Conn, who is a most worthy man, whether Lady Hamilton is in Town, or at Merton, as he has a letter for her.

[1] He was superseded in the command of the Canopus, when she became the Flag-Ship of Rear-Admiral Louis, by Captain Austen.

TO CAPTAIN MUNDY, H. M. SHIP HYDRA.

[From the " Naval Chronicle," vol. xxxix. p. 11.]

Victory, April 6th, 1805.

Sir,

Proceed as expeditiously as possible along the Coast of
Sardinia, and off the Madalena Islands, but do not go into
the harbour or anchor; and send your Boat on shore to the
Town of Madalena, to inquire if the Governor has seen or
heard of the French Fleet having passed the Straits of
Bonifaccio. You will then join me off Palermo, which is my
next Rendezvous. After leaving Sardinia, should you see
the Termagant or Childers, you will direct them to join me.
As this is a service of great importance, I rely upon your exertions to execute it. I am, Sir, &c.

NELSON AND BRONTE.

TO HIS EXCELLENCY HUGH ELLIOT, ESQ., NAPLES.

[Autograph, in the Elliot Papers.]

Victory, South End of Sardinia, April 7th, 1805.

My dear Sir,

I send you a copy of my letter to the Commissioner at
Gibraltar; therefore, you will know all that I do of the French
Fleet. I am most unlucky, that my Frigates should lose sight
of them; but it is in vain to be angry, or repine: therefore, I
must do the best I can. I am this moment bearing up to go
off Palermo, and shall wait most anxiously the return of the
Amazon. I must be guided in my further movements by
such information as I may be able to obtain; but I shall
neither go to the Eastward of Sicily, or to the Westward of
Sardinia, until I know something positive. I am uneasy
enough; but I must bear it as well as I can. You must forgive a short letter; for I have nothing worth relating. I am
ever, my dear Sir, your Excellency's most faithful and obedient
servant,

NELSON AND BRONTE.

TO CAPTAIN SOTHERON, H. M. SHIP EXCELLENT, NAPLES.

[From a Copy in the Elliot Papers.]

Victory, South End of Sardinia, April 7th, 1805.

My dear Sir,

Don't keep Amazon one moment longer than my orders to Captain Parker; and if Termagant is still at Naples, send her to me; for I want all the Vessels I have under my command to send for information. I am entirely adrift by my Frigates losing sight of the French Fleet so soon after their coming out of Port. I am ever, my dear Sir, most faithfully yours,

NELSON AND BRONTE.

TO SIR ALEXANDER JOHN BALL, BART., MALTA.

[Autograph, in the possession of Sir William Keith Ball, Bart.]

Victory, April 10th, 1805, off Palermo.

My dear Ball,

I am most unfortunate, not having yet heard a word respecting the French Fleet; every Frigate is out upon the search, and I shall now stand towards Madalena and Cape Corse. I can hardly suppose that any Expedition would be sent to this Country, without my having some intimation, and I have not the most distant idea of such a thing.[1] If they are sent, they will be taken, for the French know everything which passes in England. However, I can do no more than I have done, for I am sorely vexed at the ignorance in which I am kept.

7, A.M.—Hallowell is just arrived from Palermo. He brings accounts that the great Expedition is sailed, and that seven Russian Sail of the Line are expected in the Mediterranean; therefore I may suppose the French Fleet are bound to the Westward. I must do my best. God bless you. I am very, very miserable, but ever, my dear Ball, [sic.]

[1] Vide pp. 406, 418, post.

TO WILLIAM MARSDEN, ESQ., ADMIRALTY.

[Original, in the Admiralty.]

Victory, at Sea, 11th April, 1805.

Sir,

I am extremely concerned to acquaint you, for the information of the Lords Commissioners of the Admiralty, that Lieutenant . . . . ., (son to that excellent and respectable Officer
Captain . . . . .,) from an unfortunate desire to travel, and
perhaps an imprudent attachment to an Italian female, quitted
the Hydra when she was last at Malta, without, I fear, the
smallest inclination of ever returning to his duty in that Ship.
I have, in consequence, removed the Honourable Lieutenant
Waldegrave,[2] of the Victory, into the Hydra, and appointed
Mr. William Ram,[3] of the Spencer, in his room, a copy of
which is herewith transmitted for their Lordships' approbation;
and also a copy of a Commission which I have given to Mr.
George Scott,[4] a former Admiralty recommendation, and also
of Admiral Lord Keith's, to be Lieutenant of the Childers, in
the room of the Honourable Lieutenant Maitland,[5] ordered to
England by their Lordships, which you will be so good as lay
before them for confirmation; and I must beg that you will
interest their Lordships in favour of this unfortunate young
Officer, Lieutenant . . . . ., whose youthful imprudence I trust
their Lordships will take into consideration, and, on account of
his worthy and respectable father, Captain . . . . ., allow his
name to remain on the list of Lieutenants.[6] Their Lordships
will readily conceive the feelings of Captain . . . . ., and, I
hope, enter into my wishes on this occasion. I am, Sir, &c.

NELSON AND BRONTE.

[2] Now Rear-Admiral Lord Radstock, C.B.

[3] Lieutenant William Ram was killed in the Victory, at Trafalgar.

[4] Promoted to the rank of Commander, in 1812, for his gallantry while Senior
Lieutenant of the Phœbe in action with an Enemy's Squadron off Madagascar, and
made a Post Captain in February 1830.

[5] Now Rear-Admiral the Honourable Sir Anthony Maitland, K.C.M.G., and C.B.

[6] Lord Nelson's intercession was successful. The Officer alluded to was, many
years afterwards, promoted, and is still living.

TO WILLIAM MARSDEN, ESQ., ADMIRALTY.

[Original, in the Admiralty.]

Victory, at Sea, 15th April, 1805.

Sir,

I have this moment received your letter of the 16th February, with the inclosures therein mentioned, from the Commissioners of Transports, and Captain Mouat, their Agent at Gibraltar, relative to the men impressed from the Transports by the Tribune and Seahorse, as therein stated.

In answer thereto, I herewith transmit you a copy of my letter of the 4th of January last, to Captain Mouat, with a copy of my order of that date, intended for Captain Bennett, and also of the one delivered to the Honourable Captain Boyle, together with a copy of a General Order, to remain with Captain Mouat, to prevent the impressing of men from Transports or Victuallers, which I request you will be pleased to lay before the Lords Commissioners of the Admiralty, for their information. I am, Sir, &c.

NELSON AND BRONTE.

P.S.—I conceive Captain Mouat's application to the Transport Board improper, as it implies a doubt of my putting a stop to the evil he complained of, and tending to give much trouble where none was necessary.

TO CAPTAIN THOMAS, H. M. BOMB ÆTNA.

[Autograph, in the possession of Rear-Admiral Thomas.]

Victory, April 16th, 1805.

Sir,

We have a report from the Vessel spoke by Leviathan, that the French Fleet (at least a Fleet) was seen on Sunday, the 7th April, off Cape de Gatte, with the wind Easterly, steering to the Westward; therefore you must tell any Ships in search of me, that I am going to ascertain that the French Fleet is not in Toulon, and then to proceed to the Westward, and this is all I can tell at present. I would have you continue, *until* further orders, on the station off Toro, to which place I shall send information, when I am sure where the French

Fleet is gone, or that I am likely to leave the Mediterranean after them; and I shall also, if possible, leave a Ship on Rendezvous 97. You may expect Phœbe, Seahorse, Ambuscade, and Termagant, upon the Rendezvous off Toro, and probably some Frigate from the Westward: you will, therefore, keep a very good look out for them. I am, Sir, &c.

NELSON AND BRONTE.

TO VICE-ADMIRAL DEANS.

[Autograph, in the possession of Captain Robert Deans, R.N.]

Victory, April 16th, 1805.

My dear Deans,

I had much pleasure in receiving your letter of March 10th, and if I can get hold of the French Fleet, you may rely that Mr. Gray shall be made a Surgeon; however, I have put him on my list, and if I go home, I shall leave him as a legacy to Sir Richard Bickerton, my successor. With respect to your son, if I live, and am in service, take you care to place him near me, and I will lose no opportunity of making him a Lieutenant. I do assure you, my dear Sir, that nothing gives me greater pleasure than being useful to the sons of brother Officers, and much more so to the sons of old and respected messmates. I gave your letter to Admiral Murray to read, and he thanks you for your remembrance of him, and desires his best respects and good wishes; and be assured, my dear Deans, that I am your most faithful friend and servant,   NELSON AND BRONTE.

Consider I write with a left hand. The last time I saw you, was just before you was commissioned for the Monmouth.

TO HIS EXCELLENCY HUGH ELLIOT, ESQ., NAPLES.

[Autograph in the Elliot Papers.]

Victory, April 16th, 1805.

My dear Sir,

The Decade,[8] with the Amazon, joined me yesterday. The Termagant, I fancy, has passed through the Straits of Boni-

---

[8] From England.

faccio. Your Excellency's notice about Troops being sent to
the Mediterranean is the first word I have ever heard of it;
nor have I an idea that any such thing could be in agitation
without the Admiralty telling me, in order that I might meet
and protect them. I have not yet heard of the French Fleet;
but as I have Frigates in every possible direction, I must soon
hear of them.

I am not sure whether, in your letter, you mean that Lord
Mulgrave says, that the Troops going to Malta are for a
service which *you* have been long acquainted with.[9] Does
your Excellency mean that *you* have, or that *I* have, been long
acquainted with [it]? If it is *you*, I dare say it is right; but
if I am meant as being in the secret of the destination of those
Troops, I most solemnly declare my entire ignorance as to the
force or destination, or even that *one* Soldier is intended for
the Mediterranean. I know certainly where many thousands
are wanted; but, as I said before, I never will believe that
any number of Troops will be risked inside Gibraltar, without
an assurance of my protection; and that I should be directed
to meet them upon some fixed station to the Westward of
Toulon, if not to the Westward of Carthagena. I am now
beating hard to get round the South end of Sardinia, blowing
strong Westerly, which does me no good. A Convoy of
Victuallers passed from England for Malta the 11th. They
saw nothing to the Westward. I am ever, your Excellency's
most obliged and faithful Servant,

NELSON AND BRONTE.

Noon: A Vessel just spoke says, that on Sunday, April
7th, he saw sixteen Ships of War, twelve of them large Ships,
off Cape de Gatte, steering to the Westward, with the wind at
East. If this account is true, much mischief may be apprehended. It kills me, the very thought.

---

[9] In a letter of the 9th of April, 1805, Mr. Elliot said: "Lord Mulgrave informs
me, in great secrecy, that a considerable body of Troops was upon the point of
sailing for Malta, for the purposes with which you have been long acquainted. Lieutenant Colonel Smith, Lord Mulgrave's Private Secretary, who has brought me secret
instructions upon this head, conceives that the Regiments will have left England a
few days after the departure of the Decade. Under this impression I think it highly
material that you should not be ignorant of a circumstance which, if known to the
French, may have some weight with them respecting the destination of the Toulon
Fleet."—*Original*, in the Elliot Papers. Lord Nelson received information from the
Admiralty of the approach of these Troops, on the 1st of May. Vide p. 418, post.

TO HIS EXCELLENCY HUGH ELLIOT, ESQ., NAPLES.

[Autograph, in the Elliot Papers.]

Victory, April 18th, 1805.

My dear Sir,

I am going out of the Mediterranean after the French Fleet. It may be thought that I have protected too well Sardinia, Naples, Sicily, the Morea, and Egypt, from the French; but I feel I have done right, and am, therefore, easy about any fate which may await me for having missed the French Fleet. I have left five Frigates, besides the Sloops, &c. stationed at Malta for the present service of the Mediterranean, and with the Neapolitan Squadron will, of course, be fully able to prevent any force the French have left to convoy Troops to Sicily. You will be so good as to present my humble duty to their Majesties, whose goodness I shall remember to the last moment of my life; and believe me, dear Sir, with the highest respect, your Excellency's most faithful Servant,

NELSON AND BRONTE.

TO WILLIAM MARSDEN, ESQ., ADMIRALTY.

[Autograph, in the Admiralty.]

Victory, off Toro, April 18th, 1805.

Sir,

Under the severe affliction which I feel at the escape of the French Fleet out of the Mediterranean, I hope that their Lordships will not impute it to any want of due attention on my part; but, on the contrary, that by my vigilance the Enemy found it was impossible to undertake any Expedition in the Mediterranean. I was obliged to come to Palma to meet the Transports with provisions, and by the report of the First Captain, I trust, it could not with propriety be longer deferred; however, I showed myself off Barcelona and the Coast of Spain, and the Islands of Majorca and Minorca, till the 21st of March. The Frigates, which I appointed to watch them, unfortunately lost sight of them the night of March 31st; and from April the 4th, when they joined, we have had nothing but strong, and sometimes hard gales of Westerly and

N.W. winds, (and, it appears, that the French Fleet must have had strong gales Easterly). After allowing forty eight hours for the possibility of the Enemy passing round the South end of Sardinia I proceeded off Sicily, sending Ships to Palermo and Naples for information.

On Tuesday the 9th, I made sail from the West end of Sicily for the Westward, but, to this moment, I have only advanced sixty-five leagues, being only off Toro, owing to very bad weather, and have just received the account of the Enemy having passed the Straits the 8th of April. I am pursuing my route to the Westward and must be guided by what I hear when I get off Gibraltar. I shall leave Captain Capel with five Frigates and the Small Craft stationed at Malta to protect our Commerce, and to prevent the French sending Troops by sea. I have the honour to be, Sir, &c.

NELSON AND BRONTE.

———————

TO CAPTAIN THE HONOURABLE THOMAS BLADEN CAPEL,
H. M. SHIP PHŒBE.

[From a Copy in the Admiralty, and Autograph draught, in the possession of Miss Bolton, of Burnham.]

Victory, at Sea, 18th April, 1805.

Whereas, from the information I have received that the Enemy's Fleet, which was seen off Cape de Gatte on the 7th instant, passed through the Straits on the day following, I am proceeding with the Fleet under my command as expeditiously as possible to the Westward in pursuit of them; and it being very probable that they may have left some Frigates and other Vessels of War at Toulon, for the purpose of convoying Troops either to Sardinia, Naples, Sicily, or Egypt, you are hereby required and directed to take his Majesty's Ships named in the margin [1] under your command, and station yourself off the Island of Toro, and between that and Maritimo, for the purpose of intercepting any Expedition which the Enemy may attempt against Sardinia, Sicily, or Egypt. With respect to Sicily, I should hope the Neapolitan Squadron will sufficiently protect that Island, and have written Mr. Elliot and Sir John Acton on this subject. With regard

---

[1] Hydra, Juno, Ambuscade, Niger, Thunder.

to the limitation of your Squadron between Toro and Maritimo, I only mention it as the most likely place to fall in with any Expedition which the Enemy may attempt against those places from Toulon, but must leave this important trust to your judgment, and to act as from certain circumstances of information you shall judge best, to prevent their effecting a landing at Sardinia, Sicily, or Egypt. As the Anson and Convoy are ordered to proceed to England, I have strengthened it with the Hydra as far as Carthagena, and then to return and join you; but must desire that you will cruize off Toro or Maritimo, for the purpose of falling in with it, and affording Captain Cracraft such further protection as he, from circumstances of information, shall judge necessary.

I have ordered the Ætna to proceed to Naples with my dispatches, and desire the moment you join her that you will send her away with them, and write Mr. Elliot and Captain Sotheron, who will give you all the information relative to the Enemy's intentions, which they may be in possession of. As the Thunder will be in want of provisions you will send her to Malta, and by that opportunity, or any other that may offer, you will communicate with Sir Alexander Ball, requesting him to furnish you, from time to time, with such information of the Enemy as he may obtain, sending it to Palma, where you will constantly leave a letter for any of his Majesty's Ships calling there, [stating] where you are to be found, in case the Enemy's movements with Troops should induce you to quit that Station. I have only to add, that the frustrating the Enemy's intentions in their attempt to invade either Sardinia, Sicily, or Egypt, is an object of the highest importance, and therefore deserves your utmost vigilance to prevent it. I am satisfied with your zeal for his Majesty's Service, and therefore shall only say, that there never was a greater occasion for your exertions than at this most important moment.

The instant I have obtained information of the Enemy, I shall send you an account thereof: at any rate a Vessel will be dispatched to you from Gibraltar. You will send orders to the Juno by the first opportunity going to Malta, to join you the moment Captain Richardson returns from Constantinople. The Victuallers and Coal-ships brought from Gibraltar to Rendezvous No. 97, by the Fisgard, are ordered to St. Vieves. [?]

You will therefore send them to Malta by the Thunder or Ætna, when she returns from Naples. They are to remain in Valetta Harbour for further orders.

NELSON AND BRONTE.

N.B.—A copy of the above Order was delivered to Rear-Admiral Sir R. Bickerton.

TO SIR ALEXANDER JOHN BALL, BART., MALTA.

[Autograph, in the possession of John Darlington, Esq.]

Victory, April 19th [1805], 10 leagues, West. [West from Toro.]

My dear Ball,

My good fortune seems flown away. I cannot get a fair wind, or even a side wind. Dead foul!—dead foul! But my mind is fully made up what to do when I leave the Straits, supposing there is no certain information of the Enemy's destination. The Officer who commands the Prize sent from Gibraltar will tell you all the news. I believe this ill luck will go near to kill me; but as these are times for exertions, I must not be cast down, whatever I feel. Ever, my dear Ball, yours faithfully,

NELSON AND BRONTE.

TO WILLIAM MARSDEN, ESQ., ADMIRALTY.

[Original, in the Admiralty.]

Victory, April 19th, 1805.

Sir,

Should their Lordships think it right to return any of this Fleet to the Mediterranean, or other place abroad, I beg leave to point out those Ships which want nothing from England: Victory, Spencer, Leviathan, Tigre, Conqueror, Swiftsure. If the Service presses, the other Ships, except the Superb, who must be docked, could stay out the summer months, but want coppering, more particularly the Royal Sovereign, who has been six years coppered. I am, Sir, &c.

NELSON AND BRONTE.

TO COMMISSIONER OTWAY, GIBRALTAR.

[Autograph, in the possession of Rear-Admiral Inglefield, C.B.]

Victory, April 19th, 1805.

My dear Sir,

You will guess at my uneasiness at not having met the French Fleet; but I could not quit my charge of Egypt, Morea, Sicily, Naples, and Sardinia, until I was sure that the Enemy were gone to the Westward; for any of these Countries would have been lost for ever if the French had twenty-four hours' start of me. We have been nine days coming sixty-five leagues. We have had nothing but gales of Westerly winds. I now hope that you will soon see us pass the Rock. I am ever, my dear Sir, with the greatest esteem, your much obliged friend,

NELSON AND BRONTE.

TO WILLIAM MARSDEN, ESQ., ADMIRALTY.

[Autograph, in the Admiralty.]

Victory, April 19th, 1805; 10 leagues West from Toro.　Wind N.W.

Sir,

The Enemy's Fleet having so very long ago passed the Straits, and formed a junction with some Spanish Ships from Cadiz, I think it my duty, which must be satisfactory to their Lordships, to know exactly my intentions. I have detached the Amazon to Lisbon for information, and I am proceeding off Cape St. Vincent as expeditiously as possible ; and I hope the Amazon will join me there, or that I shall obtain some positive information of the destination of the Enemy. The circumstance of their having taken the Spanish Ships which were for sea, from Cadiz, satisfies my mind that they are not bound to the West Indies, (nor probably the Brazils;) but intend forming a junction with the Squadron at Ferrol, and pushing direct for Ireland or Brest, as I believe the French have Troops on board ; therefore, if I receive no intelligence to do away my present belief, I shall proceed from Cape St. Vincent, and take my position fifty leagues West from Scilly,

approaching that Island slowly, that I may not miss any
Vessels sent in search of the Squadron with orders. My
reason for this position is, that it is equally easy to get to
either the Fleet off Brest, or to go to Ireland, should the
Fleet be wanted at either station. I trust this plan will meet
their Lordships' approbation; and I have the pleasure to say,
that I shall bring with me eleven[2] as fine Ships of War, as
ably commanded, and in as perfect order, and in health, as
ever went to sea. I have the honour, &c.

NELSON AND BRONTE.

I shall send to both Ireland and the Channel Fleet, an
extract of this letter, acquainting the Commander-in-Chief
where to find me.

TO WILLIAM MARSDEN, ESQ., ADMIRALTY.

[Original, in the Admiralty.]

Victory, at Sea, 19th April, 1805.

Sir,

The black General and Servant, named in the margin,[3]
having been sent from St. Domingo by the French, early in
1803, and captured in the Ambuscade by the Victory in June
following, on her passage to this Country, I request you will
be pleased to acquaint the Lords Commissioners of the Admiralty, that the said black General volunteered to serve with
me during my stay in the Mediterranean, or till I should have
an Action with the Enemy, when I promised him his discharge.
I have, in consequence, ordered him and his Servant to be
discharged from the Victory, and sent to England in the first

---

[2] The Squadron, on the 19th of April, consisted of the Victory, 110 guns, Vice-
Admiral Lord Nelson, Rear-Admiral George Murray, Captain of the Fleet, and
Captain Thomas Masterman Hardy; Royal Sovereign, 100, Rear-Admiral Sir
Richard Bickerton, Bart., Captain John Stuart; Canopus, 80, Rear-Admiral Thomas
Louis, Captain Austen; Spencer, 74, Captain the Honourable Robert Stopford;
Leviathan, 74, Captain William Bayntun; Tigre, 80, Captain Benjamin Hallowell;
Donegal, 74, Captain Pulteney Malcolm; Conqueror, 74, Captain Israel Pellew;
Superb, 74, Captain Richard Goodwin Keats; Belleisle, 74, Captain William
Hargood; and Swiftsure, 74; and the Active, Amazon, and Decade, Frigates.
Camel, Store-Ship; and Childers and Ariel, Sloops.

[3] Joseph Chrétien, General; Petit Désiré, servant.

Ship of War leaving the Fleet, and directed Captain Hardy to give them the proper and usual Pay-Tickets, to enable them to receive the wages due to them for the Victory. You will, therefore, be so good as move their Lordships to order the said General and Servant to be paid the wages due to them for the Victory, and such Ship as they may be sent on board of to England; and also to direct their being received on board any Ship at the Port they may arrive, until an opportunity offers, in any King's Ship, for their going to Jamaica or St. Domingo, when their Lordships will be pleased to order them a passage in such Ship. The particular attention shown the said General may have a good effect, and hereafter be of great advantage, in case of disturbances at Jamaica, or any other of our West India Islands. At any rate, it is but justice that he should receive his wages; and their Lordships will see the further propriety of granting him and his Servant a passage to St. Domingo or Jamaica. He is a very good orderly man, and has done his duty as a Seaman on board the Victory with great attention. I am, Sir, &c.

NELSON AND BRONTE.

TO ADMIRAL LORD GARDNER, COMMANDER-IN-CHIEF, IRELAND.

[Autograph, in the possession of Mr. Empson.]

Victory, April 19th, 1805.

My dear Lord,

If the Toulon Fleet, with that of Cadiz, is gone your road, the Ships under my command may be no unacceptable sight. If you do not want our help, tell us to go back again. I feel vexed at their slipping out of the Mediterranean, as I had marked them for my own game. However, I hope, my dear Lord, that now you will annihilate them, instead of, my dear Lord, your most faithful, humble servant,

NELSON AND BRONTE.

TO ADMIRAL LORD GARDNER, COMMANDER-IN-CHIEF, IRELAND.

[From a Copy in the Admiralty.]

Victory, April 19th, 1805.

My Lord,

I send you a copy of my letter to the Admiralty; therefore, if the Toulon and Cadiz Squadrons are gone to the Northward, you will know where to send information, that I may either join you, go to the Channel Fleet, or return to the Mediterranean, &c.   I have the honour to be, &c.

NELSON AND BRONTE.

TO LIEUTENANT-GENERAL FOX, GIBRALTAR.

[From Clarke and M'Arthur, vol. ii. p. 404.]

[About 20th April, 1805.]

Broken-hearted as I am, Sir, at the escape of the Toulon Fleet, yet it cannot prevent my thinking of all the points intrusted to my care, amongst which Gibraltar stands prominent.   I wish you to consider me as particularly desirous to give every comfort to the old Rock.   I am, &c.

NELSON AND BRONTE.

TO VISCOUNT MELVILLE.

[From Clarke and M'Arthur, vol. ii. p. 404.]

[About 20th April, 1805.]

I am not made to despair—what man can do shall be done. I have marked out for myself a decided line of conduct, and I shall follow it well up; although I have now before me a letter from the Physician of the Fleet, enforcing my return to England before the hot months.   Therefore, notwithstanding, I shall pursue the Enemy to the East or West Indies, if I know that to have been their destination, yet, if the Mediterranean Fleet joins the Channel, I shall request, with that order, permission to go on shore.   I am, &c.

NELSON AND BRONTE.

TO COMMISSIONER OTWAY, GIBRALTAR.

[Autograph, in the possession of Rear-Admiral Inglefield, C.B.]

Victory, April 26th, 1805.

My dear Commissioner,

From the 9th I have been using every effort to get down the Mediterranean, but to this day we are very little advanced. From March 26th, we have had nothing like a Levanter, except for the French Fleet. I believe Easterly winds have left the Mediterranean. I never have been one week without one, until this very important moment. It has half killed me ; but fretting is of no use.

I want, if I can, to give you the Moucheron, for the service of Gibraltar; but as she was sent out with dispatches, to carry to Trieste, I am delicate upon the subject of keeping her. However, if you and General Fox think you want a very fast-sailing Brig, I send you an order for Captain Hawes to remain upon the Gibraltar station until further orders. Malta is likewise in a dreadful state for want of Sloops of War, but I have not the means. I shall probably send you Termagant and Childers to be hove down, although they ought, at least the former, to go to England, and so ought the Bittern, but I have nothing sent me to replace them with.

I am very anxious to hear what is become of the French Fleet. I rather think, as the Spaniards went with them, they are destined first for Ferrol, and then either to Ireland, or to Brest. I can say nothing certain as to my movements, till I get intelligence ; but you will see my intentions from my letter to the Admiralty by the Active. I should think some of the Vessels with information could find me out to the Eastward of the Rock, standing towards Tetuan Bay, where, if I am detained by a West wind, I shall anchor to complete our water, and clear the Transports with wine. I shall send something to Malta, when I get outside the Mediterranean, and she shall call for any letters of yours. I am ever, my dear Sir, your much obliged friend and servant,

NELSON AND BRONTE.

TO WILLIAM MARSDEN, ESQ., ADMIRALTY.

[Original, in the Admiralty.]

Victory, at Sea, 26th April, 1805.

Sir,

In consequence of the loss of his Majesty's late Sloop
Raven, and the Cameleon's being ordered to England with
the Anson and Convoy, and Vessels of their description particularly wanted for the service of this Country, you will be
pleased to acquaint the Lords Commissioners of the Admiralty, that I have detained the Moucheron, and ordered Captain Hawes[4] to cruize in the Straits of Gibraltar for the protection of our Trade, and for affording the Garrison such
assistance as Lieutenant-General Fox may occasionally find
necessary, until he receives further orders; which I hope will
meet their Lordships' approbation. I am, Sir, &c.

NELSON AND BRONTE.

P.S.—I send you a copy of a letter from Captain Mundy,
of the Hydra, relative to Lieutenant . . . . ., late of that Ship,
which you will be so good as to communicate to their Lordships.

———

TO WILLIAM MARSDEN, ESQ., ADMIRALTY.

[Original, in the Admiralty.]

Victory, at Sea, 26th April, 1805.

Sir,

Having, on the 9th September 1804, found it necessary to
order some of the Madras's Seamen on board the Donegal to
be discharged from her into the Niger, as part of her complement, with their entry agreeable to the day they were lent
from the Madras, I directed Captain Schomberg to make out
the proper Remove-Tickets for the wages due to the said men,
and send them to the Niger, and, at the same time, to transmit
a list of the qualifications of those remaining on board the
Donegal, to Sir Richard Strachan, Captain of that Ship, in
case I should find it expedient to order their being entered as

---

[4] The Moucheron Brig of 16 guns, Captain James Hawes was lost some time in
1807 in the Mediterranean, and all her crew perished.

part of the Donegal's, or any other Ship's complement, that the
men might have their regular ratings, agreeable to the stations
they served on board the Madras, which was complied with;
and as they still were returned in the Donegal's Weekly
Account as Seamen, I took it for granted they were so, and
not composed of Petty Officers and Marines, consequently
directed Captain Schomberg to discharge them (thirty-eight
in number) from the Madras's Books on the day they were
lent (the 16th of May, 1803) into the Donegal, to serve as
part of her complement, and to send their Pay-Tickets to the
Navy Board by the first opportunity, and, at the same time,
gave an order to Captain Malcolm, of the Donegal, dated the
19th instant, to enter them from the Supernumerary List, as
part of that Ship's complement, on the 17th May 1803, who,
in consequence, informed me that the Petty Officers named
in the margin were amongst the said thirty-eight men, and
that there were not ratings to give them in the Donegal from
the above time, agreeable to those they had in the Madras.

I, therefore, as the said Petty Officers are very justly entitled to their wages, agreeable to their ratings in the Madras,
have to request that you will be pleased to move the Lords
Commissioners of the Admiralty, to give the necessary directions to the Navy Board for this purpose, as it would be a
very great hardship that the said men, who have been actively
employed in the Donegal, should be deprived of the wages
they would have been entitled to, had they remained in the
Madras. I am, Sir, &c.

NELSON AND BRONTE.

TO WILLIAM MARSDEN, ESQ., ADMIRALTY.

[Original, in the Admiralty.]

Victory, at Sea, 1st May, 1805.

Sir,

I herewith transmit you a letter from the Right Honourable
Lord Mark Kerr, Captain of his Majesty's Ship Fisgard,
acquainting me, that, in consequence of the Enemy's Fleet
from Toulon having passed through the Straits of Gibraltar
on the 9th ult, he intended to proceed off Ushant and Ireland,
with an account thereof, which you will be pleased to com-

municate to their Lordships; and acquaint them that I very much approve of Lord Mark's conduct on the occasion. I am, Sir, &c.

NELSON AND BRONTE.

TO WILLIAM MARSDEN, ESQ., ADMIRALTY.

[Original, in the Admiralty.]

Victory, at Sea, 1st May, 1805. 1 P.M.

Sir,

I have this moment received your letter of the 15th of April, acquainting me, by direction of the Lords Commissioners of the Admiralty, that Rear-Admiral Knight,[5] with the Queen and Dragon, were to sail, in a day or two after the date of the said letter, from Spithead, having under convoy Transports with 5000 Troops on board, part of which is to be landed at Gibraltar, and the remainder to be convoyed up the Mediterranean; and signifying to me their Lordships' direction to take such position with the Fleet under my command, as may be best calculated to protect the two Ships and the Troops, in their way from Gibraltar up the Mediterranean, against any force from Toulon.

As the Fisgard sailed from Gibraltar on the 9th ult., two hours after the Enemy's Fleet from Toulon passed the Straits, I have to hope she would arrive time enough in the Channel to give their Lordships information of this circumstance, and to prevent the Rear-Admiral and Troops, before mentioned, from leaving Spithead. I am at this moment in sight of Ceuta, endeavouring, against a contrary wind, to get to the Westward, and, consequently, will pass the Straits the moment the wind comes from the Eastward, and endeavour to get information of the Enemy, of whom I have as yet heard nothing. I am, Sir, &c.

NELSON AND BRONTE.

[5] Rear-Admiral, afterwards Admiral Sir John Knight, K.C.B., who died in June 1831. Vide vol. i. p. 307.

TO CAPTAIN KEATS, H.M. SHIP SUPERB.

[Autograph, in the possession of the Reverend Richard Keats.]

Victory, May 1st, 1805.

My dear Keats,

It is an age since I have had the pleasure of seeing you. I hope you will come on board after your breakfast that I may have some conversation with you. I am ever, my dear Keats, yours most faithfully,

NELSON AND BRONTE.

TO COMMISSIONER OTWAY, GIBRALTAR.

[Autograph, in the possession of Rear-Admiral Inglefield, C.B. " May 4th. A.M. At 10·30, Anchored in Mazri Bay, Tetuan. Squadron anchored here."—*Victory's Log.*]

Victory, off Tetuan, May 4th, 1805.

My dear Commissioner,

I believe my ill luck is to go on for a longer time, and I now much fear that Sir John Orde has not sent his Small Ships to watch the Enemy's Fleet, and ordered them to return to the Straits' Mouth, to give me information, that I might know how to direct my proceedings; for I cannot very properly run to the West Indies, without something beyond mere surmise; and if I defer my departure, Jamaica may be lost. Indeed, as they have a month's start of me, I see no prospect of getting out time enough to prevent much mischief from being done. However, I shall take all matters into my most serious consideration, and shall do that which seemeth best under all circumstances.

I am sending for a Collier, as we are in great want of fuel; and, as I am much hurried, I beg you will excuse my short letter. When I get out of the Straits, which I earnestly hope will not be much longer deferred, I shall write you of my further movements; and I beg that you will present my best compliments to General Fox; and believe me ever, my dear Commissioner, yours most faithfully,

NELSON AND BRONTE.

I have a letter of misery from Mr. King;[6] but the Admiralty seem to have fixed what he is to have, and I do not see that I can do anything.

---

[6] Mr. Joe King, the Boatswain, so often mentioned.

TO CAPTAIN KEATS, H. M. SHIP SUPERB.

[Autograph, in the possession of the Reverend Richard Keats. "May 5th. A.M. At 9·30, weighed and made sail to the N.E., Squadron in company."—*Victory's Log.*]

Victory, May 5th, 1805.

My dear Sir,

I send Mr. Ford[7] with dollars, but I have recommended him only to pay for what is *actually* embarked, for my movements must depend upon the wind, and I shall not lose a favourable appearance. When the Ships are complete with water, I shall recommend their anchoring nearer Tetuan, for the greater facility in getting cattle. Pray, do you get water. It is generally believed that the French and Spanish Ships are gone to the West Indies. As far as April 27th, nothing was known of them at Lisbon; therefore, I am likely to have a West India trip; but that I don't mind, if I can but get at them. Ever, my dear Keats, yours faithfully,

NELSON AND BRONTE.

I think you wrote Admiral Murray, that you would load the Superb with bullocks for us.

TO WILLIAM MARSDEN, ESQ., ADMIRALTY.

[Original, in the Admiralty.]

Victory, at Sea, 5th May, 1805.

Sir,

I herewith transmit you a letter from Captain Moubray of his Majesty's Ship Active, dated the 29th of April, with the log of that Ship on the 28th, relative to the Spanish Ships of War which he saw off Cape Pallas on the 27th ult., which you will be so good as to lay before the Lords Commissioners of the Admiralty, for their information. I am, Sir, &c.

NELSON AND BRONTE.

[7] Agent-Victualler to the Fleet.

TO CAPTAIN PEARSE, HIS MAJESTY'S SLOOP HALCYON.

[Original, in the Nelson Papers. It is doubtful if this letter was ever forwarded.]

Victory, at Sea, 5th May, 1805.

Sir,

I have received your letters of the 17th ultimo and 2nd instant, with the inclosures therein mentioned, and cannot help thinking the Halcyon particularly unfortunate, in carrying away, in the first instance, the bowsprit, and afterwards springing her gammoning-knee, at a moment when her services were so eminently wanted, and when every care and exertion became necessary. I hope her defects will soon be made good, and the Halcyon actively employed in the execution of my former orders. I am, &c.

NELSON AND BRONTE.

TO REAR-ADMIRAL SIR RICHARD BICKERTON, BART.

[From a Copy in the Admiralty.]

Victory, in Tetuan Bay, 5th May, 1805.

Whereas, the destination of the Enemy's Fleet (which, at this moment, I am perfectly unacquainted with) may probably lead me to the West Indies, and judging it necessary, under these circumstances, that an Officer of your rank and well-known experience in this Country should remain in the Mediterranean, for the purpose of carrying into effect the various important services of this Country, which, from your perfect and intimate knowledge of the intention of Government, and my sentiments, on every particular object of the Admiralty instructions for the protection and safety of their Sicilian, and their Sardinian Majesties' Dominions, as well as preventing the Enemy from effecting any Expedition against Egypt, You are therefore hereby required and instructed to shift your Flag from his Majesty's Ship Royal Sovereign, and hoist it on board any of his Majesty's Ships going into Gibraltar, and afterwards shift it at pleasure into any Ship or Vessel at that place, as you shall judge proper, for the purpose above-mentioned; and for carrying any further instructions which the Lords Commissioners of the Admiralty may send out to this Country into effect. You will herewith receive copies of several Admiralty orders, letters, and instructions, from No. 1 to No. 87, for your guidance and information, many of which, as you will observe, are obsolete, but will tend to show the line of conduct, intended at different times, to have been carried into effect. You will, consequently, make such use of them as you shall judge proper. From a perfect knowledge of your zeal for his Majesty's Service, and well known abilities, I feel it unnecessary to say anything more on this subject, as circumstances must naturally guide your future operations, with such additional force as may be sent to this Country and those left in it, named in the margin.[8]

Notwithstanding the orders which I have given to Captain Corbet, of the Amphitrite, to proceed to England if she can be manned and fitted for service in this Country, I would recommend, under the present scarcity of Ships, that she may be detained in the Mediterranean, as the active zeal of Captain Corbet will render her a valuable acquisition at this present moment.

NELSON AND BRONTE.

TO COMMISSIONER OTWAY, GIBRALTAR.

[Autograph, in the possession of Rear-Admiral Inglefield, C.B.]

Victory, Gibraltar Bay, May 6th, 1805.

Sir,

Mr. Joseph King not having received, since the Peace Establishment of 1802, the pay which was formerly paid him as Boatswain of the Yard, but only the pay as Boatswain of the Sheer Hulk, which seems to me to be very hard upon him, as he is by the Admiralty letter of March 1804 (at least, it appears so to me) told, that he is to be Boatswain of the Yard, and in consequence of his removal from afloat to the shore, is also to be allowed house-rent. It also enjoined him that in addition to his duty as Boatswain of the Yard, that he is to attend to the masting of Ships. From all these circumstances, I feel confident that Mr. King is intended by the Admiralty

---

[8] Phœbe, Hydra, Juno, Ambuscade, Niger, Bittern, Termagant, Halcyon, Sophie, Moucheron, Seahorse, Childers, Thunder, Ætna, Madras, Morgiana, Jalouse, Spider, Hirondelle, Renard, Ventura.

Board to be Boatswain of Gibraltar Yard, and not merely
Boatswain of the Sheer Hulk, although the duty of masting
Ships, &c., is attached to his other duty.

Therefore, with due submission, if you see no great irregularity in the proceeding, I think he should be entered as
Boatswain of Gibraltar Yard, and receive the same pay as the
Boatswain of Malta, Jamaica, or any other of the Foreign
Yards; and I feel so impressed with the justness of the
measure, that I shall feel myself responsible for any additional
pay to his present, as is equal to give him the same as the
Boatswain of Malta Yard, until you shall receive directions
from the Navy Board upon this subject.   I have the honour
to be, Sir, &c.

NELSON AND BRONTE.

TO WILLIAM MARSDEN, ESQ., ADMIRALTY.

[Original, in the Admiralty.]

Victory, in Gibraltar Bay, May 6th, 1805.

Sir,

Finding, on the perusal of their Lordships' order, dated the
1st day of February, 1805, relative to the sending to England
all Spanish Ships and Vessels detained and sent into Gibraltar, prior to the 11th January last, by his Majesty's Ships and
Vessels of War, and the appointment of an Agent to be held
responsible to the proper Officer of the Court of Admiralty in
England, for the amount thereof, that the spirit of their Lordships' said order is not fully carried into effect, as my authority to the Agents at Gibraltar and Malta only directs them
to take into their charge, and dispose of at public sale, all the
Spanish Vessels detained and sent into those places, prior to
the 11th of January last, by the Fleet under my command,
instead of all those detained and sent into Gibraltar by any
of his Majesty's Ships of War; I have, therefore, given Mr.
Cutforth and Mr. Wilkie new appointments of this date, to
take into their charge, and dispose of at public sale, all the
Spanish Vessels sent into these Ports, by any of his Majesty's
Ships or Vessels of War, prior to the 11th of January, 1805,
agreeably to their Lordships' said order; and herewith transmit
you, for their information, a copy of the said new appointments,

and letter which accompanied them, which I hope will meet
their Lordships' approbation, and that my reasons for not
sending them to England, as communicated to you in my
letter of the 27th of March last, and which at this moment
strikes me with greater force and propriety, will also meet
their Lordships' approval.   I am, Sir, &c.

                                        NELSON AND BRONTE.

————————

TO JAMES CUTFORTH, ESQ., AGENT VICTUALLER AT GIBRALTAR,
    HEREBY APPOINTED SOLE AND ENTIRE AGENT FOR ALL
    THE SPANISH SHIPS AND VESSELS, WITH THEIR CARGOES,
    DETAINED BY ANY OF HIS MAJESTY'S SHIPS OR VESSELS OF
    WAR, AND SENT INTO GIBRALTAR AS AFORESAID, PRIOR TO
    THE 11TH DAY OF JANUARY, 1805.

                [From a Copy in the Admiralty.]

                        Victory, in Gibraltar Bay, 6th May, 1805.

Whereas the Lords Commissioners of the Admiralty have
directed me by their order, bearing date the first day of
February, 1805, to send to England all Spanish Ships and
Vessels, with their cargoes, that have been detained at sea by
any of his Majesty's Ships or Vessels of War prior to the 11th
day of January, 1805, (the date of the King's proclamation for
granting reprisals against Spain,) in order to prevent abuses, and
to ensure the said Ships and cargoes being disposed of to their
full value, (except such parts of their cargoes as may, from
their perishable state be necessary to dispose of at Gibraltar;)
and having, at the same time, authorized me to appoint an
Agent, who will be held responsible to account for the proceeds of the same to the proper Officer of the Court of
Admiralty in England; And whereas I think proper, from
the high and honourable character I have received of you, as
well as from the public confidence which Government reposes
in you as Agent-Victualler, to appoint you to be the sole and
entire Agent for all the Spanish Ships and Vessels detained
and sent into Gibraltar by any of his Majesty's Ships or
Vessels of War prior to the 11th day of January, 1805, as
before mentioned; I do, by virtue of the power and authority
to me granted, hereby nominate and appoint you sole and

entire Agent, on behalf of the Crown, for all the Spanish
Ships and Vessels detained and sent into Gibraltar by any of
his Majesty's Ships or Vessels of War, prior to the 11th day
of January, 1805; and do hereby require and authorize you
(from judging the impracticability of sending the said Ships
and Vessels, with their cargoes, to England, as directed by
their Lordships, as aforesaid,) to enter upon, and immediately
dispose of, at public sale, all the said Spanish Ships and Vessels,
with their cargoes, detained, as aforesaid, prior to 11th day of
January, 1805, and sent into Gibraltar, and to transmit a
regular account of their sales and amount, respectively, to the
proper Officer of the Court of Admiralty in England, to whom
you are to hold yourself accountable for the whole and every
particular transaction and amount of the said Ships and their
cargoes; and you will also, in like manner, transmit to me
copies of the accounts of sale, and amount thereof accordingly;
and, for so doing, this shall be your sufficient authority.

NELSON AND BRONTE.

N.B.—An order of the above tenor and date sent to Mr.
Wilkie, Agent at Malta.

TO JAMES CUTFORTH, ESQ., SOLE AND ENTIRE AGENT FOR ALL
SPANISH VESSELS DETAINED AND SENT INTO GIBRALTAR BY
ANY OF HIS MAJESTY'S SHIPS OR VESSELS, PRIOR TO THE
11TH DAY OF JANUARY, 1805.

[From a Copy in the Admiralty.]

Victory, in Gibraltar Bay, 6th May, 1805.

Sir,

Observing that my authority to you, dated the 27th March
last, only directs you to take into your charge, and dispose of
at public sale, all Spanish Ships and Vessels, with their cargoes,
detained and sent into Gibraltar by the Fleet under my command, prior to the 11th day of January 1805, instead of all
the Spanish Ships and Vessels detained, prior to the said 11th
day of January, and sent into Gibraltar by any of his Majesty's
Ships or Vessels of War, as directed by the order from the
Lords Commissioners of the Admiralty, dated the 1st day of
February, 1805, I herewith transmit you a new appointment,
with full power and authority, agreeable to their Lordships' said

order.   A copy thereof also accompanies this, which I desire
you will present to the Judge of the Vice-Admiralty Court
at Gibraltar, with your new appointment, that both (if necessary) may be registered in the said Vice-Admiralty Court, and
their Lordships' instructions, through me, most fully carried
into effect.   I am, Sir, &c.

NELSON AND BRONTE.

N.B.—A letter of the above tenor and date sent to Mr.
Wilkie, Agent at Malta.

TO WILLIAM MARSDEN, ESQ., ADMIRALTY.

[Original, in the Admiralty, "May 6th. P.M. At 1·30, anchored in Rosia Bay,
Gibraltar. At 6, weighed and made sail out of the Bay to the Westward."—*Victory's
Log.*]

Victory, at Sea, 6th May, 1805.

Sir,

The Enemy's Fleet having quitted the Mediterranean, and
judging it probable that their route may lead me to the West
Indies, or some distant service, I have thought it proper
to leave Rear-Admiral Sir Richard Bickerton at Gibraltar,
in order that the important duties of the Mediterranean may
be duly attended to, and their Lordships' further instructions
carried into effect by that excellent Officer, whose zeal,
abilities, and perfect knowledge both of this Country, and my
sentiments upon every particular point of their Lordships'
instructions render him most fully competent to this charge,
and their expectations.   Inclosed you will receive for the
information of the Lords Commissioners of the Admiralty, a
copy of my order of the 5th instant, to Sir Richard Bickerton,
together with a copy of the schedule of unexecuted orders,
&c. left with him, which puts the Rear-Admiral in the perfect
possession of their Lordships' instructions, and of the various
circumstances which have presented themselves to me as necessary to adopt; and their Lordships may rely that they will
be duly followed up by that zealous Officer, and which I trust
will meet their approbation.   I am, Sir, &c.

NELSON AND BRONTE.

P.S.—A copy of their Lordships' letter of the 15th ultimo,
relative to the Troops given to Sir Richard Bickerton.

TO ALEXANDER DAVISON, ESQ.

[Autograph, in the possession of Colonel Davison.]

Victory, at Sea, May 7th, 1805.

My dear Davison,

God only knows, my dear friend, what I have suffered, by not getting at the Enemy's Fleet, and when I naturally consoled myself that, at least, time would be given for Sir John Orde's Frigates, who were naturally sent after them, to return to Gibraltar with information for me, I had the mortification yesterday to find that none had been sent there. Nor was it generally believed that Sir John Orde had sent after them; but this I cannot believe, and I must suppose that they have all been unfortunately captured. I think it more than probable I shall go to the West Indies; for, I believe, from what I have yet heard of their course, &c., that is their destination, and there I hope to get hold of them, and to save our valuable West India possessions, and then I shall immediately return to England. But my health, or even my life must not come into consideration at this important crisis; for, however I may be called unfortunate, it never shall be said that I have been neglectful of my duty, or spared myself.

The business of Merton still will call for your kind and friendly attention. The kitchen I hope will be built before even this letter reaches you, and I must trouble you, my friend, to pay the bills; but I hope soon to repay you with many, many kind thanks. I have just heard that Lord Melville has left the Admiralty,[9] owing to the Tenth Report of the Navy Inquiries. His Lordship was doing much for the Service, and now we have to look forward to some one else. I shall write a line to our friend Nepean, who must be harassed by these changes. God bless you, my dear Davison, and believe me ever, with the truest friendship, yours most faithfully and affectionately,　　　　NELSON AND BRONTE.

All my letters by Niger and Avenger are gone up the Mediterranean, and will never be received by me. But salt beef and the French Fleet, is far preferable to roast beef and champagne without them. May God prosper my exertions, I pray most fervently, and I think He will in the end.

---

9 Viscount Melville was succeeded as First Lord of the Admiralty on the 30th of April, 1805, by Admiral Charles Lord Barham. Sir Evan Nepean and all the other Lords remained.

TO WILLIAM MARSDEN, ESQ., ADMIRALTY.

[Original, in the Admiralty.]

Victory, at Sea, May 7th, 1805.

Sir,

After a heavy beat down the Mediterranean I reached Tetuan Bay on the 4th, and completed the water of the Fleet, and cleared a Transport with wine, and sailed on the 5th. Yesterday, at 2 P. M., we anchored in Gibraltar Bay, with fresh breezes Westerly, and began to clear Transports with fuel and provisions; but, before the whole Fleet had anchored, there was every appearance of a Levanter coming on. The Fleet was unmoored, the Transports taken in tow, and at 6 o'clock the whole Fleet was under sail, steering through the Gut. I was in great hopes that some of Sir John Orde's Frigates would have arrived at Gibraltar, from watching the destination of the Enemy, from whom I should have derived information of the route the Enemy had taken, but none had arrived. The Halcyon, which left Lisbon on April the 27th in the evening, reports to me, that nothing had been heard of them at Lisbon when the Halcyon sailed. I am now pushing off Cape St. Vincent's and hope that is the station to which Sir John Orde may have directed his Frigates to return from watching the route of the Enemy, and I shall also join the Amazon from Lisbon.

If nothing is heard of them from Lisbon or from the Frigates I may find off Cape St. Vincent's, I shall probably think the rumours which are spread are true, that their destination is the West Indies, and in that case think it my duty to follow them, or to the Antipodes, should I believe that to be their destination. I shall detach a Sloop of War to England, from off the Cape, when my mind is made up from either information, or the want of it. I am, Sir, &c.

NELSON AND BRONTE.

TO SIR EVAN NEPEAN, BART.

[From Clarke and M'Arthur, vol. ii. p. 406.]

7th May, 1805.

I still am as much in the dark as ever. I am now pushing off Cape St. Vincent, where I hope to be more fortunate; and I shall join the Amazon from Lisbon, from which place I

have accounts to April 27th, when they knew nothing of the
Enemy. If I hear nothing, I shall proceed to the West Indies.
I am, &c.

NELSON AND BRONTE.

TO CAPTAIN KEATS, H. M. SHIP SUPERB.

[Autograph, in the possession of the Reverend Richard Keats.]

Victory, May 8th, 1805.

My dear Keats,

I am very much pleased with the cheerfuluess with which
you are determined to share the fate of the Fleet.[1] Perhaps
none of us would wish for exactly a West India trip; but the
call of our Country is far superior to any consideration of self.
I will take care that Superb shall have neighbour's fare in
everything. I have wrote to the Admiralty that Superb
would be sent home before the hurricane months. I am
anxious to get off St. Vincent to meet Amazon from Lisbon,
when my route will be fixed. Will you dine here, if we
have little wind? And believe me ever, my dear Keats,
yours most faithfully,

NELSON AND BRONTE.

TO MRS. BOLTON.

[Autograph, in the possession of Miss Bolton, of Burnham. "May 9th. P.M.
At 9, anchored in Lagos Bay, Squadron and Transports anchored here. Employed
getting on board provisions from the Transports."—Victory's Log.]

Victory, May 9th, 1805.

My dear Sister,

God only knows where I may be on July first, and, therefore, I send you a bill for one hundred pounds; and when I
get home, I hope to be able to keep Tom[2] at College without
one farthing's expense to Mr. Bolton; and both you and him
may be assured, that I would do more, if in my power. I
should have been a very rich, instead of a poor man, if Lord
Melville had not given the Galleons to Sir John Orde.[3] God

---

[1] The Superb was so much in want of repair, that it was necessary she should
have gone to England.

[2] His nephew, Mrs. Bolton's eldest son, afterwards the second Earl Nelson.

[3] i. e. removed the Ships which captured the Galleons from his command to that
of Sir John Orde, who, consequently, obtained the share of Prize money that would
otherwise have belonged to him.

bless you, Mr. Bolton, and family; and believe me ever, your most affectionate brother,

NELSON AND BRONTE.

I have sent Sir William[3] a cruize, and I hope he will be more fortunate than he has hitherto been.

TO WILLIAM MARSDEN, ESQ., ADMIRALTY.

[Autograph, in the Admiralty.]

Victory, off Cape St. Vincent, May 9th, 1805.

Sir,

Having received from the Amazon, Captain Hill's[4] letter of yesterday's date, I shall wait here until Admiral Knight joins, and then proceed to Barbadoes, taking care that he is seen safely inside the Gut; and the Queen and Dragon, I am satisfied can protect them, and it is possible, upon a further consideration, I may add the Royal Sovereign, which would render it impossible for all the force at Carthagena to make an impression upon them. I am now clearing Transports, and victualling the Fleet to five months, and shall bear away the moment I can get hold of the Convoy. Should the Enemy not have gone to the West Indies, I shall return off Cape St. Vincent's, and then act as I may find orders; or, if I receive none, according to the best of my judgment, which I hope their Lordships will approve of. I am, Sir, &c.

NELSON AND BRONTE.[5]

The Royal Sovereign is ordered to join Admiral Knight.

---

[3] Her son-in-law, Captain Sir William Bolton, of the Amphitrite.

[4] Captain Henry Hill, of the Orpheus, now a Vice-Admiral of the Blue.

[5] The following was enclosed in the above letter:—

" The Louisa, of Baltimore, an American Brig, Peter Billings, Master, intelligence by whom is as follows:—' Left Cadiz on Thursday, the 2nd day of May, and informs that five Spanish Line-of-Battle Ships, a Spanish Frigate, a French 80-gun Ship, a French 20-gun Ship, and a French Brig of 16 guns, sailed from Cadiz between the 9th and 10th. There appeared off Cadiz, on the 9th, about eleven Sail of the Line and four Frigates, French; that a Spanish Line-of-Battle Ship sailed in the evening after the former, of great value, and touched the ground on going out. At noon of the 10th, there was no more to be seen of the combined Fleet. The reports of their destination were various; by some, it was supposed they were destined for Ireland; and by others, with great probability, for the West Indies, particularly Jamaica. Three thousand Spanish troops, amongst which there was a great number of Cavalry, embarked on board the Spanish Men-

TO SIR ALEXANDER JOHN BALL, BART.

[Autograph, in the possession of Sir William Keith Ball, Bart.]

Victory, May 10th, 1805, off Lagos.

My dear Ball,

My lot is cast, and I am going to the West Indies,[6] where, although I am late, yet chance may have given them a bad passage, and me a good one : I must hope the best. A number of Troops are now at Lisbon ; but, except that they are destined for the Mediterranean, I know nothing. I am still very unwell. May God bless you, my dear Ball ; and be assured I am, &c.　　　　　NELSON AND BRONTE.

TO REAR-ADMIRAL GEORGE CAMPBELL.

[From Clarke and M'Arthur, vol. ii. p. 408.]

May 10th, 1805.

Here we are, my dear Campbell, clearing Sir John Orde's Transports, which I found in Lagos Bay, completing ourselves to five months ; and to-morrow I start for the West Indies. Disappointment has worn me to a skeleton, and I am, in good truth, very, very far from well. Sir Richard Bickerton remains in the Mediterranean, and Admiral Knight, reports say, is to command at Gibraltar. He is at present off Lisbon

of-War, and there was great confusion attending their embarkation, and getting the Ships to Sea. The French Ships were supposed to contain from 7000 to 8000 French troops, which were said to be commanded by General Lauriston. The Spanish Squadron is said to be commanded by Admiral Gravina. There appears at present to be great activity in equipping the Ships at Cadiz : two Line-of-Battle Ships were apparently nearly ready for sea—viz., the St. Trinadad, of 130 guns, and the Glory, of 74 guns ; many Line-of-Battle Ships were also fitting with great expedition at the Caraccas. Provisions were in general plenty and cheap ; seamen were scarce, and were forced with great reluctance on board the Men-of-War. All the Officers of Government appeared to be extremely active and vigilant in forwarding their Squadrons.' A Copy.　　　　　NELSON AND BRONTE."

[6] Lord Nelson is said to have been informed that the French Fleet had gone to the West Indies, by Rear-Admiral Donald Campbell, of the Portuguese Service, who had commanded the Portuguese Squadron in the Mediterranean in 1799, (vide vol. iv. passim ;) and in a letter to Lord Nelson, dated Lisbon, 21st September 1805, he complained of having been deprived of his command by the Portuguese Government, at the instigation of the French Ambassador at Lisbon, on two grounds, one of which was " going on board your Lordship when you passed the Gut, and giving you information where the combined Fleets had gone."—*Clarke and M'Arthur*, vol. ii. p. 489.

with the Convoy of Troops. I wish he would come here; but he has been deceived by false information, that the Combined Squadrons were still in Cadiz—I wish they were; but I am sorry to believe they are now in the West Indies, or just off. I am, &c.   NELSON AND BRONTE.

TO THE COMMANDER OF ANY OF HIS MAJESTY'S SHIPS OR VESSELS IN SEARCH OF THE MEDITERRANEAN SQUADRON.

[From a Copy in the Admiralty.]

Most Secret.   Victory, in Lagos Bay, 10th May, 1805.

Sir,

I desire to acquaint you that I am proceeding with the Squadron,[6] under my command, to the West Indies, in search of the Enemy's Fleet; and request that you will, without a moment's loss of time, communicate the same to the Lords Commissioners of the Admiralty, and to the Commander-in-Chief of the Channel Fleet, in the event of your falling in with him. I am, Sir, &c.   NELSON AND BRONTE.

N.B.—Barbadoes will be the first place I shall call at.

TO WILLIAM MARSDEN, ESQ., ADMIRALTY.

[Autograph, in the possession of Mrs. Leake.]

Victory, May 10th, 1805.

My dear Sir,

I hope very soon to thank you in person for all your goodness to me; and that you will see me a Victor, shall be the exertion of, my dear Sir, your most obliged and faithful servant,   NELSON AND BRONTE.

I forgot to mention that the Martin Sloop[7] goes off this day

---

[6] The Squadron with which Lord Nelson pursued the Enemy's Fleet of eighteen Ships of the Line to the West Indies, consisted only of ten Sail of the Line—viz., Victory, Canopus, Superb, Spencer, Donegal, Tigre, Leviathan, Belleisle, Conqueror, and Swiftsure; and three Frigates, Decade, Amphion, and Amazon.

[7] The Martin, Captain R. H. Savage, conveyed a letter to Lord Seaforth, Governor of Barbadoes, "requesting him, in case Rear-Admiral Cochrane should not be at Barbadoes, to open and read his official letter, that had been sent to him, and would recommend its being forwarded as expeditiously as possible to the Rear-Admiral. He also earnestly begged that an embargo might be laid on all Vessels at Barbadoes, that the Enemy might not be apprised of his arrival, and thereby again escape from his Fleet."—Clarke and M'Arthur, vol. ii. p. 408.

for Barbadoes to Rear-Admiral Cochrane,[8] to tell him of my approach. Mention it to the Board.

N. AND B.

TO REAR-ADMIRAL KNIGHT.

[From Clarke and M'Arthur, vol. ii. p. 407. " May 11th. A.M. At 9·10, weighed under the staystails and jib: in launch and all boats. At 10·30, set the topsails and foresail. At Noon, Squadron in company. P.M. At 4, came into the Squadron H.M. Ship Queen, Rear-Admiral Knight, who saluted with eleven [Qy. 17] guns, which we returned with thirteen. H. M. Ship Dragon and a Convoy of Transports joined. Martin parted. Queen, Royal Sovereign, Dragon, and Transports parted. At 6·50, bore up and made sail. Cape St. Vincent N.W. by N., distance 7 leagues." —*Victory's Log.*]

May 11th, 1805.

My dear Admiral,

I have only to recommend, in order to make sure of your safe arrival, that you do not go near the land between Cadiz and Cape Trafalgar; but get, as soon as you can, into the latitude of Cape Spartel, before you run for the Strait's Mouth. And I must beg most seriously to call your attention, to carry the Convoy safe into Gibraltar from the numerous Gun-boats and Privateers which cover the Straits: I beg, therefore, to recommend, that the Convoy is not carried near Tariffa, or Cabrita Point, but kept in the middle of the Gut, until Gibraltar bears N.N.E. The being drove to the Eastward is of no consequence if it should be calm, any Vessel may work with ease round Europa Point. And there is only one thing more that I think it my duty to recommend, which is, that the Men-of-War are not suffered to anchor until every Vessel of the Convoy is anchored; for you may rely, that a serious attack will be made upon any stragglers, or on the last Ships of the Convoy, if there should be little wind. I am, &c.

NELSON AND BRONTE.

---

[8] Rear Admiral the Honourable (afterwards Admiral Sir) Alexander Forrester Inglis Cochrane, G.C.B., who died in June 1832.

Victory, off Cape St. Vincent, 11th May, 1805.

Sir,

In answer to your letter, this moment received, relative to
the Disposition of the Fleet under my command, not having
been transmitted to you since June last, I must desire to
acquaint you, for the information of the Lords Commissioners
of the Admiralty, that having expected permission to return
to England for the benefit of my health, about the latter end
of September last, or early in October, I intended forwarding
this paper on quitting the Mediterranean, that their Lordships
might see the Disposition of the Fleet at that period; that on
the 13th of October you were put in possession of the
Squadron placed under Sir Richard Strachan, outside the
Straits, and perfectly knew the force I had detained in the
Gut, for the protection of our Trade and comfort of the Garrison, as well as those placed at Malta, under the Senior
Officer, for the various duties of the Archipelago and Adriatic;
and that a Ship of the Line was at Naples for the protection
of that place. I, therefore, considering myself as constantly on
the eve of quitting the Mediterranean, for the time being withheld the Disposition above-mentioned, conceiving, [it] under
the circumstances before-stated, to be of little consequence.
Admiral Campbell's going home still procrastinated my return;
the sudden movement of the French Fleet from Toulon
having led me to Egypt, and the idea that they would again
put to sea, previous to the end of April, induced me on my
return to reserve the Disposition of the Fleet till it should be
transferred to Sir Richard Bickerton, about that time, when I
was satisfied they would not attempt any Expedition. And I
must here remark that, the Amphion having been taken to
England with the Treasure-Ships by Captain Graham Moore,
and the Medusa very properly sent home with the Spanish
Frigate Matilda by Sir Richard Strachan, the Niger afterwards sent to England by Sir John Orde, and other inter-
ferences at Gibraltar by Senior Captains of his Squadron, in
sending the Ships under my command on services not intended
for them by me, made the arrangements I had determined

upon in that quarter so uncertain, that it became a matter of doubt whether those Ships sent to Gibraltar would ever rejoin me. Under these uncertain and unpleasant circumstances, I trust their Lordships will not consider the Disposition of the Fleet's not being duly sent, as neglectful, but owing to the reasons before stated.

I herewith transmit you the Disposition of the Ships left in the Mediterranean, under Rear-Admiral Sir Richard Bickerton, on the 6th instant, which you will be pleased to lay before the Lords Commissioners of the Admiralty for their information, and acquaint them that I have sent the Rear-Admiral your letter on this subject, that due regard may be paid to it in future.

Inclosed is a copy of my order of the 18th of April, to the Honourable Captain Capel, which, together with the copy of my order of the 5th instant, and of the schedule that accompanied my letter to you of the 6th of this month, sent by the Wasp Sloop, will put their Lordships in the full possession of all the arrangements made by me in the Mediterranean, previous to my quitting it, which, I hope, will meet their approbation. I am, Sir, &c.

NELSON AND BRONTE.

TO WILLIAM MARSDEN, ESQ., ADMIRALTY.

[Original, in the Admiralty.]

Victory, off Cape St. Vincent, 11th May, 1805.

Sir,

I have this moment received your letter of the 20th of March last, transmitting me by direction of the Lords Commissioners of the Admiralty, a copy of the sentence of a Court-Martial held on Captain Bennett, of His Majesty's Ship Tribune, and also of the opinion of the Law Officers thereon. Your letter, also, of the above date, with fifty copies of a list containing the Names of the Ships and Vessels with their respective Numbers, which have been added to his Majesty's Navy since the 13th December last, has likewise been received, and shall be duly issued agreeably to their Lordships' direction. Your several other letters with the Commissions, &c. therein mentioned, I have sent by the Queen to Rear-

Admiral Sir Richard Bickerton, who will, consequently, acknowledge them, and put their Lordships' instructions into
effect. I am, &c.

NELSON AND BRONTE.

TO VISCOUNT SIDMOUTH.

[Autograph, in the Sidmouth Papers.]

Victory, off Cape St. Vincent, May 11th, 1805.

My dear Lord,

The Portuguese Admiral Campbell gave me a letter for you,
which I have put in the Admiralty packet; but I cannot allow
it to go without writing you a line. Notwithstanding my very,
very indifferent state of health, various other circumstances
(which I shall tell you when we meet) and my leave of
absence to go to England, I cannot forego the desire of getting,
if possible, at the Enemy; and, therefore, I this day steer for
the West Indies. My lot seems to have been hard, and the
Enemy most fortunate ; but it may turn,—patience and perseverance will do much.

I shall see you very soon, and, I hope, a Victor; that it shall
be so, nothing shall be wanting on the part of, my dear Lord,
your most faithful friend,

NELSON AND BRONTE.

TO WILLIAM MARSDEN, ESQ., ADMIRALTY.

[Autograph, in the possession of Mrs. Leake.]

Victory, May 14th, 1805. 38 leagues from Madeira.

My dear Sir,

I am very much obliged by your friendly letter of April
17th. Under the most serious consideration which I can
give from all I hear, I rather think that the West Indies must
be the destination of the Combined Squadrons. A trip to
England would have been far more agreeable, and more necessary for my state of health ; but I put self out of the question
upon these occasions. And, although it may be said I am
unlucky, it never shall be said that I am inactive, or sparing of
myself; and surely it will not be fancied I am on a party of
pleasure, running after eighteen Sail of the Line with ten,

and that to the West Indies. However, I know that patience and perseverance will do much; and if they are not there, the Squadron will be again off Cadiz by the end of June—in short, before the Enemy can know where I am gone to; and then I shall proceed immediately to England, leaving such a force as the Service requires; and as the Board will know where the Enemy are, I shall hope to receive their orders off Cape St. Vincent, should I return, from their not being in the West Indies. I shall trouble you with a few letters, and be assured that I am, my dear Sir, your most faithful and obliged, humble servant,

NELSON AND BRONTE.

TO EARL CAMDEN, K.G.

[Original, in the Colonial Office.]

Victory, May 14th, 1805.

My Lord,

I was honoured with your letter of March 29th,[9] in which your Lordship is pleased to acknowledge the receipt of my letter to the Dey of Algiers, and my instructions to Captain Keats, and to approve; but, from the shortness of my letter, think that a former one must have miscarried. I send your Lordship a copy of the one I wrote you a few days before the

---

[9] " TO VICE-ADMIRAL VISCOUNT NELSON, K.B.

" Downing Street, 29th March, 1805.
" My Lord,

" I have received your Lordship's letter of the 2nd of January, inclosing your instructions to Captain Keats, in consequence of the dispatch I wrote to your Lordship, under date the 29th day of October last, signifying his Majesty's pleasure respecting the conduct of his Highness the Dey of Algiers, and the provisional appointment of Mr. Cartwright to be Consul to that Regency. I entirely approve of the instructions you have given to Captain Keats, and can have no doubt but the Dey of Algiers will cheerfully acknowledge his Majesty's gracious condescension in the terms he has offered, unless the influence of hostile councils shall have persuaded him to reject every measure of reasonable accommodation.

" Your Lordship's letter is extremely concise, and limited to this sentence: ' I omitted to send my letter to the Dey of Algiers, and instructions to Captain Keats. I now beg leave to forward them.' It, therefore, naturally occurs to me, that some previous letter from your Lordship must have miscarried, as the sentence I have cited evidently alludes to some prior communication, which I have not received. I have the honour to be, &c., CAMDEN."—Original, in the possession of the Right Honourable John Wilson Croker.

one to which you allude, which I should think must have been received. I own, in sending inclosures which are to speak for themselves, I considered it would be a wanton waste of your Lordship's time to enter into any detail; for this reason I have not done more than sending you the last letters from Sardinia, having finished, to different Ministers, all that I can find to say upon the importance of Great Britain being in possession of it; and, as I expected to be at home very long before this time, I could have answered any questions which might have been asked me. I now, therefore, beg that your Lordship will not attribute my short letters to any other motive, than not taking up your time in reading a long letter upon nothing, than which, I know from experience, nothing can be more teasing.

I shall address myself in another letter upon the subject of General Sir James Craig's instructions, which I have sent to Sir Richard Bickerton. I have a report that another attempt has been made to assassinate the Dey of Algiers, and that he lost three of his fingers. He is, I fancy, very unpopular. I am, &c.

NELSON AND BRONTE.

I saw, for a moment, your nephew, Mr. James,[1] in his new coat. He says he likes his new profession.

TO EARL CAMDEN, K.G.

[Original, in the Colonial Office.]

Victory, May 14th, 1805.

My Lord,

In the afternoon of May 11th, I received your Lordship's letter of March 28th,[2] and a copy of Sir James Craig's in-

---

[1] Vide vol. v. p. 512.

[2] "TO THE RIGHT HONOURABLE ADMIRAL LORD VISCOUNT NELSON.

"Private.   "Arlington Street, March 28th, 1805.

"My Lord,

"Your lordship will receive, with the dispatches which will be forwarded to you from the Admiralty, the copy of my instructions to Sir James Craig, which will apprise your Lordship of the views with which that Officer is sent to take the command of his Majesty's Troops in the Mediterranean. I cannot, however, suffer

structions, which, after reading, I forwarded in ten minutes to
Rear-Admiral Sir Richard Bickerton, who I left at Gibraltar,
that he might be ready to co-operate with Sir James,[3] as I am
going to the West Indies in search of the Enemy's Fleet.
With respect to our taking possession of Messina, or any part
of the Island of Sicily, as it was not done when the first
French Soldier set his foot into the Neapolitan Dominions, it
would now cause the taking possession of the City of Naples
and the whole Kingdom; therefore, unless the French make
any movements for an attack upon Sicily, or are in the act of
taking possession of Naples, any interference of our Troops
will never be consented to by the King of Naples, as it would
hasten the downfal of so fine a portion of his Dominions; but
in the event of the French coming to Naples, our Troops would
be received in Sicily with much pleasure and gratitude, as
saving from the French Devils the Island of Sicily.   Sir John
Acton, I know, thinks Sicily perfectly safe against a coup,
and that Messina would be defended: so it might, very easily,
if the Officers are faithful to their Sovereign, which I very
much doubt is not the case with all of them.   The men will
do their duty if well commanded.

If I had not been in pursuit of the Enemy's Fleet, I should
have been, at this moment, in England, having had my leave
from October 6th, 1804; but self is out of the question when
I am after the Enemy.   I have only to again request that
Sardinia, its position, and importance, may be duly appreciated
before the French possess it; then we may lament, but in vain,
the loss of it.   I have, &c.,

NELSON AND BRONTE.

these dispatches to reach you, unaccompanied by a private acknowledgment from
myself, of the confidence I have in your Lordship's hearty co-operation with Sir
James Craig, in whatever may best conduce to the advantage of his Majesty's
Service.   Your Lordship's long experience in these seas, on the shores of which Sir
James is to act, and your intimate knowledge of Naples and Sicily will render your
advice and assistance most essential to him; and it is needless for me to inform
your Lordship, Sir James Craig will join you with every disposition and anxiety to
profit from them.   I have the honour to remain, &c.—CAMDEN."—*Autograph*, in
the possession of the Right Honourable John Wilson Croker.

[3] Lieutenant-General Sir James Craig, K.B., died a full General in January
1812.

TO ALEXANDER DAVISON, ESQ.

[Autograph, in the possession of Colonel Davison.]

Victory, May 14th, 1805—36 leagues E.N.E. from Madeira.

My dear Davison,

I received by Lieutenant M'Kenzie of the Queen, on May 11th, your letters of April 2nd and 10th, for which, and the newspapers, I thank you; and although I do not know when this letter may go, still I shall have it prepared, in case we meet any Vessel bound to England.

Your goodness in paying the bills for Merton, I am most truly sensible of, and I wish I had my account to any given period, that I might arrange and pay it off; or, at least, reduce it. But I have not got either it, or the account from the Banking-house. I don't clearly understand what you mean about the necessity of my signing a Power of Attorney to you, as Agent for the Orion. I believe I did sign the Power for the Amphion, if not for the Victory; but it is unnecessary, and not customary for Admirals to interfere in the Agents appointed by the Captors; at least, the Flag-Officers in the Mediterranean have never signed any Power of Attorney for particular Prizes. We have given to my Secretary, as the person who is customary, and knows all the captures made, a Power to receive the Flag eighth;. and he collects it from all the different Agents where the Prize may be sold, and he distributes it in proportion, according to the number of Flag-Officers on the station at the time of the capture. But I certainly intended that you should receive my proportion of Prize-Money for the Orion; and therefore, in case I have not signed the Power, I send an order for Marsh and Creed, if they have received it, to pay it to you, that it may help to reduce my account with you; and I, again and again, entreat that I may have it the moment of my arrival, in order that I may take measures to pay it off, which I shall do with much pleasure, and many, many thanks; and you ought to charge the interest. So much for business, which ought to be often settled between the dearest friends.

I believe Lord Melville would have been a good friend to the Navy; and, therefore, am sorry he is out. I have no idea of his pocketing the Public money. I sincerely hope these inquisitors will not find fault with your numerous Public Accounts; but I believe you are regular, and therefore, I hope, from my heart, may defy them. How is Nepean? Remember me to him. And, by this time, I congratulate you upon your return to St. James's Square, where I hope you will live many years; and that I shall often breakfast with you, is the sincere wish of, my dear Davison, your truly obliged and faithful friend,

NELSON AND BRONTE.

TO WILLIAM HASLEWOOD, ESQ.

[Autograph, in the possession of Earl Nelson.]

Victory, May 16th, 1805.

It is my desire that Mrs. Gibson[4] is given an annuity of twenty pounds a-year, when that she gives up my adopted daughter, Horatia Nelson Thompson, to the guardianship of my dear friend, Lady Emma Hamilton, and promises not to have anything more to do with the child, either directly or indirectly; and I leave my estate chargeable with this annuity.

NELSON AND BRONTE.

TO LADY HAMILTON.

[Autograph, in the possession of Earl Nelson.]

Victory, at Sea, May 16th, 1805.

My dearest Lady Hamilton,

As it is my desire to take my adopted daughter, Horatia Nelson Thompson, from under the care of Mrs. Gibson, and to place her under your guardianship, in order that she may be properly educated and brought up, I have, therefore, most earnestly to entreat that you will undertake this charge; and as it is my intention to allow Mrs. Gibson, as a free-will offering from myself, (she having no claim upon me, having been regularly paid for her care of the child,) the sum of twenty pounds a-year, for the term of her natural life; and I mean it should commence when the child is delivered to you. But

---

[4] Mrs. Gibson was the person to whose care Lord Nelson entrusted his child, and to whom he wrote several notes. See the next volume.

should Mrs. Gibson endeavour, upon any pretence, to keep my adopted daughter any longer in her care, then I do not hold myself bound to give her one farthing; and I shall, most probably, take other measures.

I shall write to Mr. Haslewood, upon your telling him that you have received the child, to settle the annuity upon Mrs. Gibson; and if you think Miss Connor disposed to be the governess of Horatia, I will make her any allowance for her trouble which you may think proper. I, again and again, my dearest friend, request your care of my adopted daughter, whom I pray God to bless. I am ever, for ever, my dear Lady Hamilton, your most faithful and affectionate,

NELSON AND BRONTE.

TO CAPTAIN KEATS, H. M. SHIP SUPERB.

[Autograph, in the possession of the Reverend Richard Keats.]

Victory, May 19th, 1805.

My dear Keats,

I am fearful that you may think that the Superb does not go so fast as I could wish. However that may be, (for if we all went ten knots, I should not think it fast enough,) yet I would have you be assured that I know and feel that the Superb does all which is possible for a Ship to accomplish; and I desire that you will not fret upon the occasion. I hope, and indeed feel confident, that very soon you will help me to secure the Majesteux.[5] I think we have been from Cape St. Vincent very fortunate, and shall be in the West Indies time enough to secure Jamaica, which I think is their object. Whatever may happen, believe me ever, my dear Keats, your most obliged and sincere friend,

NELSON AND BRONTE.

---

[5] The " Majesteux" does not, however, appear to have formed one of the French Squadron, which consisted of Le Bucentaur, 80, Vice-Admiral Villeneuve; Le Formidable, 80, Rear-Admiral Dumanoir; Le Neptune, 80; L'Indomptable 80; Le Pluton, 74; L'Atlas, 74; Le Swiftsure, 74; Le Mont Blanc, 74; L'Intrepide, 74; Le Scipion, 74; Le Berwick, 74; and L'Aigle, 74; several Frigates, and two Brigs: also the Spanish Ships—the Argonauta, 90, Admiral Gravina; La Firma, 80; Le Terrible, 80; San Raphael, 80; San Jago del America, 64; San Jago del Espana, 74; and one Frigate. Two more of the French Sail of the Line, the Algesiras and Achille, joined the Squadron about the 4th of June, off Martinique.

May 27th.—I have missed yesterday the opportunity of sending my letter, wrote long ago, as you will see. We shall be at Barbadoes the 3rd or 4th June; and I hope Cochrane will be able to give us every information about the Enemy. I still think Jamaica is their object; but many think that Surinam, Trinidada; and Bayntun, that they will land their Troops at the City of San Domingo. In short, every one has an opinion; but it will soon be beyond doubt. Our passage, although not very quick, has been far from a bad one. They started from Cadiz thirty-one days before we did from St. Vincent, and I think we shall gain fourteen days upon them in the *passage;* therefore, they will only arrive seventeen days before us at Martinico, for I suppose them bound there. I shall not anchor at Barbadoes. Martin, you know, is gone there; and I have prayed Lord Seaforth[6] to lay an embargo, that the French may not know of my approach, and thus again elude our vigilance. My mind is not altered that Egypt was their destination last January. Ever yours faithfully,

NELSON AND BRONTE.

PLAN OF ATTACK.

[From Clarke and M'Arthur, vol. ii. p. 427, who state that it was taken from the original in the St. Vincent Papers, and that it was drawn up by Lord Nelson during his pursuit of the French Fleet to the West Indies.]

The business of an English Commander-in-Chief being first to bring an Enemy's Fleet to Battle, on the most advantageous terms to himself, (I mean that of laying his Ships close on board the Enemy, as expeditiously as possible;) and secondly, to continue them there, without separating, until the business is decided; I am sensible beyond this object it is not necessary that I should say a word, being fully assured that the Admirals and Captains of the Fleet I have the honour to command, will, knowing my precise object, that of a close and decisive Battle, supply any deficiency in my not making signals; which may, if extended beyond these objects, either be misunderstood, or, if waited for, very probably, from various

---

[6] Francis Humbertone Mackenzie, created Lord of Seaforth, Baron Mackenzie, in October 1797, Governor of Barbadoes: he died in 1814.

causes, be impossible for the Commander-in-Chief to make: therefore, it will only be requisite for me to state, in as few words as possible, the various modes in which it may be necessary for me to obtain my object, on which depends, not only the honour and glory of our Country, but possibly its safety, and with it that of all Europe, from French tyranny and oppression.

If the two Fleets are both willing to fight, but little manœuvring is necessary; the less the better;—a day is soon lost in that business: therefore I will only suppose that the Enemy's Fleet being to leeward, standing close upon a wind on the starboard tack, and that I am nearly ahead of them, standing on the larboard tack, of course I should weather them. The weather must be supposed to be moderate; for if it be a gale of wind, the manœuvring of both Fleets is but of little avail, and probably no decisive Action would take place with the whole Fleet. Two modes present themselves: one to stand on, just out of gun-shot, until the Van-Ship of my Line would be about the centre Ship of the Enemy, then make the signal to wear together, then bear up, engage with all our force the six or five Van-Ships of the Enemy, passing, certainly, if opportunity offered, through their Line. This would prevent their bearing up, and the Action, from the known bravery and conduct of the Admirals and Captains, would certainly be decisive: the second or third Rear-Ships of the Enemy would act as they please, and our Ships would give a good account of them, should they persist in mixing with our Ships. The other mode would be, to stand under an easy but commanding sail, directly for their headmost Ship, so as to prevent the Enemy from knowing whether I should pass to leeward or windward of him. In that situation, I would make the signal to engage the Enemy to leeward, and to cut through their Fleet about the sixth Ship from the Van, passing very close; they being on a wind, and you going large, could cut their Line when you please. The Van-Ships of the Enemy would, by the time our Rear came abreast of the Van-Ship, be severely cut up, and our Van could not expect to escape damage. I would then have our *Rear* Ship, and every Ship in succession, wear, continue the Action with either the Van-Ship, or second Ship, as it might appear

most eligible from her crippled state; and this mode pursued,
I see nothing to prevent the capture of the five or six Ships
of the Enemy's Van. The two or three Ships of the Enemy's
Rear must either bear up, or wear; and, in either case,
although they would be in a better plight probably than our
two Van-Ships (now the Rear) yet they would be separated,
and at a distance to leeward, so as to give our Ships time to
refit; and by that time, I believe, the Battle would, from the
judgment of the Admiral and Captains, be over with the rest
of them. Signals from these moments are useless, when every
man is disposed to do his duty. The great object is for us to
support each other, and to keep close to the Enemy, and to
leeward of him.

If the Enemy are running away, then the only signals
necessary will be, to engage the Enemy as arriving up with
them; and the other Ships to pass on for the second, third,
&c. giving, if possible, a close fire into the Enemy in passing,
taking care to give our Ships engaged, notice of your intention.

TO WILLIAM MARSDEN, ESQ., ADMIRALTY.

[Autograph, in the Admiralty. "June 3rd. A.M. At 8·20, Amphion spoke two
English Merchant Ships, [from whom, according to Clarke and M'Arthur, Lord
Nelson learnt that the French Fleet was in the West Indies.] June 4th. A.M. At
6, saw the Island of Barbadoes, bearing West per compass, distance, six or seven
leagues. At 9, H. M. Ship Northumberland, Rear Admiral Cochrane, at anchor in
Carlisle Bay, who saluted with 13 guns, which was returned with 11. The Fort
(Needham) saluted with 15 guns, which was returned with an equal number. P.M.
At 4·50, anchored in Carlisle Bay, Barbadoes. H. M. Ship Spartiate joined."—
Victory's Log.]

Victory, off Carlisle Bay, June 4th, 1805.

Sir,

I arrived off here at noon this day, where I found Rear-
Admiral Cochrane in the Northumberland, and the Spartiate
is just joining. I send you some letters of information, which
the Rear-Admiral and Sir William Myers have received from
Dominica and from St. Lucia. There is not a doubt in any
of the Admirals' or General's minds, but that Tobago and
Trinidada are the Enemy's objects; and, although I am
anxious in the extreme to get at their eighteen Sail of the

Line, yet, as Sir William Myers[7] has offered to embark himself with 2000 Troops. I cannot refuse such a handsome offer; and, with the blessing of God on a just Cause, I see no cause to doubt of the annihilation of both the Enemy's Fleet and Army; and what man can do, shall be done by, Sir, your most obedient servant,

NELSON AND BRONTE.

I am now working to an Anchorage, and I hope that we shall have sailed before six hours, with the General and Troops.[8]

TO WILLIAM MARSDEN, ESQ., ADMIRALTY.

[Autograph, in the possession of Mrs. Leake.]

Private.　　　　　　　　　　　　Victory, June 4th, 1805.

My dear Sir,

Pray forward the inclosed; and I hope my next letter will be worth all I have hitherto wrote. Ever, my dear Sir, your much obliged,

NELSON AND BRONTE.

TO CAPTAIN HARDY, H. M. SHIP VICTORY.

MEMORANDUM.

Victory, in Carlisle Bay, Barbadoes, 5th June, 1805.

Whereas Lieutenant-General Sir William Myers, Commander-in-Chief of the Forces at Barbadoes and the Leeward

---

[7] Lieutenant-General Sir William Myers, Bart., Commander-in-Chief in the Leeward Islands: he died in July 1805.

[8] In this letter Lord Nelson enclosed the following Extract from a Letter from Brigadier-General Brereton to Lieutenant-General Sir William Myers, Bart., dated St. Lucia.

"Morning, 29th May, 11 o'clock, A M.

"P.S.—I have this moment received a report from the Windward side of Gros Islet that the Enemy's Fleet, of 28 Sail in all, passed there last night. Their destination, I should suppose, must be either Barbadoes or Trinidad.

"R. BRERETON."

To the above Extract, Lord Nelson added this Note, in his own hand:—

"Written by Major Myers, Sir William Myers's Secretary, and extracted from the General's letter; and Major Myers has no doubt but that the intelligence may be relied upon.　　　　　"NELSON AND BRONTE.

"Victory, June 4th, Carlisle Bay."

Islands, has very handsomely offered to embark himself, with two thousand Troops, on board the Fleet under my command, for the purpose of frustrating the Enemy's intentions, who, it appears have determined on an immediate attack on some of the Leeward Islands ; and, as our Troops have been very much harassed and fatigued in marching on so short notice from the different out-posts, for the purpose of embarking, conse-quently require every comfort which can be given them, and as any distinction in victualling them would, under the present circumstances, be, in my opinion, very improper, it is my intention, as we may soon be in Battle with the Enemy, and the stay of the Troops on board cannot be many days, that they shall be victualled the same as the respective Ships' Companies.

It is, therefore, my directions, that you cause the Troops who may be embarked from Barbadoes on board his Majesty's Ship, under your command, to be victualled at full allowance of all species of provisions, the same as your Ship's Company, during their continuance on board.

NELSON AND BRONTE.

N.B.—A similar Order given to the Captains of H. M. Ships, Northumberland, Canopus, Superb, Spencer, Belleisle, Conqueror, Tigre, Leviathan, Donegal, Swiftsure, Spartiate.

NELSON AND BRONTE.

TO WILLIAM MARSDEN, ESQ., ADMIRALTY.

[Original in the Admiralty. "June 5th. A.M. At 9·30, weighed, and made sail to the Southward : Squadron in company. P.M. 2·15, made the general signal to Prepare for Battle. June 6th. P.M. At 5·30, Mud Fort, at Tobago, saluted with 19 guns, which was returned by an equal number. [At 6·10, a Schooner made the signal for the Enemy being at Trinidada.—*Signal Log.*] At 6·20, bore up. June 7th. A.M. At 5, made sail to the Westward, towards the Bocaz of Trinidada. [At 9, observed Fort Abercrombie on fire, and the Troops to abandon it.—*Signal Log.*] P.M. At 5·30, anchored in the Gulf of Paria, near the West entrance of the Bocaz of Trinidada : Squadron anchored as convenient. June 8th. A.M. At 7, weighed and made sail."—*Victory's Log.* Clarke and M'Arthur state that—" On the 6th of June, the Fleet arrived off Great Courland Bay, Tobago ; and Captain Henderson of the Pheasant Sloop, was directed to proceed with all expedition to Port Toko in Trinidad, to send a boat on shore with Sir W. Myers' letters, for information whether the Enemy were in the Gulf of Paria, and to communicate by signal with the Admiral in the morning. At Tobago all was bustle and apparent uncertainty, when, in addition, the following singular occurrence took place. A Merchant, particularly anxious to ascertain whether the Fleet was that of a Friend or Enemy, had prevailed on his Clerk, with whom he had also agreed respecting signals, to embark in a Schooner, and to stand towards it; and it unfortunately happened, that the very signal made by the Clerk, corresponded with the affirmative signal which had been agreed on by Colonel Shipley, of the Enemy being at Trinidad. It was the close of the day, and no opportunity occurred of discovering the mistake. An American Merchant-brig also had been spoken with, the same day, by the Curieux, probably sent to mislead, whose Master reported that, he had been boarded a few days before by the French Fleet off Grenada, standing towards the Bocaz of Trinidad. No doubts were any longer entertained, the news flew throughout the British Squadron, the Ships were ready for Action before daybreak, and Nelson anticipated a second Aboukir in the Bay of Paria. If further confirmation was necessary, it appeared in the seeming conflagration of one of our outposts at daylight, and the party retreating towards the citadel. The Admiral and Officers of his Squadron, after such corroboration, felt it difficult to believe the evidence of their senses, when, on entering the Gulf of Paria on the 7th, no Enemy was to be seen, nor had any been there."—Vol. ii. p. 409.]

Victory, off Trinidad, 8th June, 1805.

Sir,

I herewith transmit you a copy of a letter from Captain Maurice, dated the 6th instant, acquainting me with the surrender of the Diamond Rock, late under his command, on the 2nd of this month, to the French Squadron of Ships and Gun-Boats therein mentioned, together with a copy of the terms of Capitulation that accompanied his said letter, which I request you will be pleased to lay before the Lords Commissioners of the Admiralty, for their information.

I also transmit you, for their Lordships' information, a copy of a letter from Captain Maurice, of the above date, informing me of his arrival at Barbadoes, and of the communication he received from the French Commodore, which I give but little credit to, as no Squadron or Ship, I understand, could arrive at Martinique but what must be seen from the Diamond Rock; and with respect to their future operations, they have only been mentioned, probably with a view to deceive. I am, &c.

NELSON AND BRONTE.

PRIVATE DIARY.

[From Clarke and M'Arthur, vol. ii. p. 410.]

8th June, 1805.

At daylight an Advice-Boat arrived in the Fleet from Barbadoes, with letters from Captain Maurice,[1] giving an account of the capture of the Diamond Rock; and also that the French and Spanish Squadrons had not sailed from Martinique, but that the French Commodore had told him, that the Ferrol Squadron, consisting of six Sail of French, and eight of Spaniards, had arrived in Fort Royal, June the 4th.

TO LORD SEAFORTH, GOVERNOR OF BARBADOES.

[From Clarke and M'Arthur, vol. ii. p. 410.]

8th June, 1805.

The information from St. Lucia of the Combined Squadron having been off that Island to Windward, must have been very incorrect. I have my doubts respecting the certainty of the arrival of the Ferrol Squadron, as I have always understood that nothing could pass in or out of Fort Royal without being seen; but, my Lord, powerful as their force may be, they shall not with impunity, make any great attacks. Mine is compact, theirs must be unwieldy; and although a very pretty fiddle, I don't believe that either Gravina or Villeneuve know how to play upon it. I am, &c.

NELSON AND BRONTE.

[1] Captain James Wilkes Maurice's account of his gallant defence of the Diamond Rock against a French Squadron of one Three-decker, four Seventy-fours, three Frigates, &c., under Rear-Admiral Missiessy, on the 20th of February 1805, will be found in the Memoir of that Officer in Marshall's Naval Biography, Supplement Part i. p. 439. He was tried by a Court-Martial, and "unanimously and most honourably acquitted" by a Sentence expressed in very eulogistic terms. It was not, however, until January 1809, that he obtained Post rank; and he subsequently distinguished himself by an equally gallant, but more successful, defence of the Island of Anholt.

[2] Vide vol. i. pp. 27, 79; ii. pp. 71, 131, 299.

TO CAPTAIN J. W. MAURICE.

[From Marshall's " Naval Biography," Supplement, part i. p. 441.]

Victory, at Sea, June 8th, 1805.

Sir,

I have received your letter of the 6th instant, acquainting me with the surrender of the Diamond Rock under your command on the 2nd of this month, to a Squadron of the Enemy's Ships and Gun-Boats therein mentioned, together with the terms of capitulation which accompanied your said letter. In answer to which, while I regret the loss of the Diamond, I have no doubt that every exertion has been used by yourself, and those under your command for its defence; and that its surrender has been occasioned from the circumstances you represent. It is particularly gratifying that so few lives were lost in the contest, and I have very fully to express my approbation of the terms of capitulation, as well as with your conduct personally, and that of the Officers and Men under your command, which I have to request you will be pleased to communicate to them. I am, &c.

NELSON AND BRONTE.

TO SIMON TAYLOR, ESQ., JAMAICA.

[From Clarke and M'Arthur, vol. ii. p. 412. "June 9th. A.M. 8·45, sent a Boat on board a Schooner. Saw the Island of Grenada N.N.W. P.M. At 12·15, hove to in George's Bay, Grenada, (a breast of Fort Royal.) The Garrison saluted us with 17 guns, which we returned with the same number. At 1·30 filled."—*Victory's Log.*]

10th June, 1805.

My dear Sir,

I was in a thousand fears for Jamaica, for that is a blow which Buonaparte would be happy to give us. I flew to the West Indies without any orders, but I think the Ministry cannot be displeased . . . . When I am satisfied that they are on their return, after sending some of the Spanish Ships to the Havanna, I shall push hard to get off the Straits' Mouth; and kind Providence, may some happy day, bless my endeavours to serve the Public weal, of which the West India Colonies form so prominent and interesting a part. I ever have been, and shall die, a firm friend to our present Colonial

system. I was bred, as you know, in the good old school,
and taught to appreciate the value of our West India possessions; and neither in the field, nor in the senate, shall their
just rights be infringed, whilst I have an arm to fight in their
defence, or a tongue to launch my voice. We are nearly, my
dear Mr. Taylor, thirty years' acquaintance; and I am, as
ever, your faithful and obliged friend,

NELSON AND BRONTE.

TO WILLIAM MARSDEN, ESQ., ADMIRALTY.

[Autograph, in the Admiralty. "June 11th. A.M. At 6, saw the Island of
Dominica, bearing East. Noon, saw the Island of Guadaloupe, bearing E. b. S.
Basseterre, Guadaloupe, bears S. 21 E., eight leagues. P.M. 6·50, North end of
Montserrat, E. ½ N., distant 6 miles."—*Victory's Log.*]

Victory, under Guadaloupe, June 11th, 1805.

Sir,

Having no reason to doubt the information from St. Lucia,
as sent by General Brereton,[6] sent to you in my letter of the
4th of June, the Fleet weighed early in the morning of the
5th, with Lieutenant-General Sir William Myers, and about
2000 Troops. On the 6th, at noon, we were off Tobago,
from whence I learnt that an American Ship had arrived there
the day before, who said that he had been *boarded* by one of
the Ships of the French Fleet, to windward of St. Vincent;
three days before; that they were standing to the Southward;
and he supposed they had passed the Island the night before.
In the evening, being off Sandy-Point, a Schooner to leeward made the signal established by Admiral Cochrane, that
the Enemy's Fleet was at Trinidada. On the 7th, in the
afternoon, we anchored in the Gulf of Paria, it being calm.
At daylight, on the 8th, as we were coming out of the Gulf, I
received information from Captain Maurice (late of the
Diamond Rock) that he heard the Enemy were to sail on the
evening of June 4th, for an attack upon Grenada and Dominica. On the 9th, at noon, we were in St. George's Bay,

6 Brigadier-General Robert Brereton, Commandant of St. Lucia. Lord Nelson,
in another letter, calls him his "old acquaintance," he having served as a Major at
the Sieges of Bastia and Calvi, (vide vol. i. pp. 399, 447; ii. p. 375.) He died a
Lieutenant-General.

Grenada, and received accounts from General Maitland[1] that all was safe at Grenada, St. Vincent's, and St. Lucia ; and that on the 4th, the Enemy had not moved from Martinico, proving all our former information to be false.

At 1, P. M., I received a letter from General Prevost by the Jason, Captain Champain,[2] of which, I enclose a copy. Captain Champain also being with General Prevost,[3] saw the Enemy's Fleet pass Prince Rupert's head on the 6th of June, consisting of eighteen Sail of the Line, six Frigates, and three Brigs and Schooners : in the evening they were under the Saints, standing to the Northward. Whether the Enemy's object is to attack Antigua, or St. Kitt's, or to return to Europe, time must show. I shall guide my movements according to the best of my judgment, for I have too [often?] unfortunately, been deceived by false intelligence. Not a moment has been lost in following them, and my final procedure shall be stated when the Vessel sails for England. I have the honour to be, &c.

NELSON AND BRONTE.

TO WILLIAM MARSDEN, ESQ., ADMIRALTY.

[Autograph, in the Admiralty. "June 12. A.M. At 6, saw Antigua, bearing S.E. b. E., seven or eight leagues. P.M. At 7, anchored, (in St. John's, Antigua.) Squadron anchored as convenient. Out all Boats, employed sending the Artillery Men and baggage on board the Northumberland. June 13. A.M. Fort St. John's saluted us with 17 guns, which we returned with the same number. At 11·50, weighed and made sail.]

Victory, June 12th, 1805, under Antigua.

Sir,

Yesterday afternoon the Fleet fetched under Monserrat, from which Island I only got vague and very unsatisfactory intelligence. On June the 8th they had seen sixteen Sail beating to windward under Guadaloupe. On Sunday an American came from Guadaloupe who told them the Fleet

---

[1] Afterwards Lieutenant-General the Honourable Sir Thomas Maitland, Governor of Malta and Lord High Commissioner in the Ionian Islands, Grand Master of the Order of St. Michael and St. George, G.C.B. : he died in January 1824.

[2] Captain William Burgundy Champain : he died a Post Captain in August 1818.

[3] Afterwards Lieutenant-General Sir George Prevost, Bart., and Commander-in-Chief in North America : he died in January 1816.

was gone, it was supposed, against Antigua; but they did not know, nor did it seem a matter of even curiosity to the good folks of Monserrat to inquire, very particularly. If I hear nothing of the Enemy from Antigua, I shall stand for Prince Rupert's Bay and form my judgment; but, I feel, having saved these Colonies, and two hundred and upwards of sugar-loaded Ships, that I must be satisfied they have bent their course for Europe before I push after them, which will be to the Straits' Mouth, when I shall leave the Command with Rear-Admiral Sir Richard Bickerton, and take their Lordships' permission to go to England, to try and repair a very shattered constitution. I am, Sir, &c.

NELSON AND BRONTE.

The French Fleet passed to leeward of Antigua on Saturday last, standing to the Northward. All their Troops and Stores which they took from Guadaloupe are re-landed there: therefore, I am pushing for the Anchorage at St. Johns, to land the Troops, and hope to sail in the morning after them for the Straits' Mouth.

NELSON AND BRONTE.

TO WILLIAM MARSDEN, ESQ., ADMIRALTY.

[Original, in the Admiralty.]

Victory, off Antigua, 8 o'clock P.M., 12th June, 1805.

Memorandum

Since closing my dispatches, I have received intelligence of importance, which I have directed Captain Bettesworth[4] to proceed with to the Admiralty, and communicate the same to their Lordships.

NELSON AND BRONTE.

TO ALEXANDER DAVISON, ESQ.

[Autograph, in the possession of Colonel Davison.]

Victory, June 12th, 1805.

My dear Davison,

I have only one moment to say I am going towards the Mediterranean after Gravina and Villeneuve, and hope to

⁴ Captain Bettesworth of Le Curieux.

catch them. At all events I shall soon take you by the hand. God bless you, my dear friend, and believe me ever your obliged, NELSON AND BRONTE.

I have saved these Colonies, and more than two hundred Sail of sugar-loaded Ships.

TO SIR ALEXANDER JOHN BALL, BART., MALTA.

[From Clarke and M'Arthur, vol. ii. p. 413.]

[About 12th June, 1805.]

I hear all, and even feel obliged, for all is meant as kindness to me, that I should get at them. In this diversity of opinions I may as well follow my own, which is, that the Spaniards are gone to the Havannah, and that the French will either stand for Cadiz or Toulon—I feel most inclined to the latter place ; and then they may fancy that they will get to Egypt without any interruption. I am, &c.

NELSON AND BRONTE.

TO THE RIGHT HONOURABLE EARL CAMDEN.

[From Clarke and M'Arthur, vol. ii. p. 411.]

[About 12th June, 1805.]

My Lord,

However unhappy I may feel at not having got up with the Enemy's Fleet, yet I should think myself very remiss if I failed to inform your Lordship, and to request you to inform his Majesty, of the very spirited conduct of Lieutenant-General Sir William Myers, who offered to embark on board the Fleet with 2000 Troops, in order to try and annihilate both the Enemy's Fleet and Army, had we fortunately found them in any of our Islands. The zeal of the Lieutenant-General and the whole body of Troops, was such as could not be exceeded ; and it is a matter of sincere regret that we have not met with the Enemy. But great merit is not less due to the Lieutenant-General, for the expedition with which the Troops were collected from different parts of Barbadoes, and to the Officers and Men for the cheerfulness with which they embarked. I am, &c.

NELSON AND BRONTE.

TO HIS ROYAL HIGHNESS THE DUKE OF CLARENCE.

[From Clarke and M'Arthur, vol. ii. p. 411.]

12th June, 1805.

Your Royal Highness will easily conceive the misery I am
feeling, at hitherto having missed the French Fleet; and entirely owing to false information sent from St. Lucia, which
arrived at Barbadoes the evening of June 3rd. This caused
me to embark Sir William Myers and 2000 Troops, and to
proceed to Tobago and Trinadad. But for that false information, I should have been off Port Royal, as they were putting
to sea; and our Battle, most probably, would have been fought
on the spot where the brave Rodney beat De Grasse. I am
rather inclined to believe they are pushing for Europe to get
out of our way: and the moment my mind is made up, I shall
stand for the Straits' Mouth. But I must not move, after
having saved these Colonies and 200 and upwards of sugar-
laden Ships, until I feel sure they are gone. We saw, about
200 leagues to the Westward of Madeira, a Vessel which I
took to be a French Corvette, that watched us two days; but
we could not take her. She, I hear, gave Gravina notice of
our approach, and that probably hastened his movements;
however, I feel I have done my duty to the very utmost of
my abilities. The Combined Squadron passed to the leeward
of Antigua on Saturday the 8th, standing to the Northward.
My heart is almost broke, and, with my very serious complaints, I cannot expect long to go on. I am, &c.

NELSON AND BRONTE.

TO THE RIGHT HONOURABLE LORD ROBERT FITZGERALD,
MINISTER AT LISBON.

[From Copies in the possession of the Right Honourable Sir George Rose,
G.C.H., and Captain Gambier.]

Victory, at Sea, June 15th, 1805.

My Lord,

The Combined Squadrons passed to leeward of Antigua on
the 8th, standing to the Northward, and when I left St. John's
Road, in that Island, on the 13th, nothing had been heard of
them; therefore I believe they are on their return to Europe.
As my trip to the West Indies must have greatly interested

your Lordship, I shall briefly run over the occurrences. I
arrived at Barbadoes June 4th, where I found Lieutenant-
General Sir William Myers, who the night before had received
information from Brigadier-General Brereton, at St. Lucia,
that twenty-eight Sail of the Enemy's Fleet had been seen to
windward of St. Lucia, steering to the Southward. As there
was no reason to doubt this information, the General offered
to embark himself, with 2000 Troops, for the relief of either
Tobago or Trinidada, which were supposed to be the intended
objects of the Enemy's attack. On the 6th, we were off
Tobago; on the 7th at Trinidada; on the 8th, I received an
account that the Enemy had not moved on the 4th from Port
Royal, but were expected to sail that night for the attack of
Grenada. On the 9th, I was at Grenada, when I received a
letter from General Prevost to say, that the Enemy had
passed Dominica on the 6th, standing to the Northward, to
the leeward of Antigua, and took that day a Convoy of fourteen Sail of sugar-loaded Ships, which unfortunately left St.
John's in the night, for England. On the 11th, I was at
Montserrat, and, at sunset of the 12th, anchored at St. John's,
Antigua, to land the Troops, which was done, on the morning
of the 13th, and at noon I sailed in my pursuit of the Enemy;
and I do not yet despair of getting up with them before they
arrive at Cadiz or Toulon, to which Ports I think they are
bound, or, at least, in time to prevent them from having a
moment's superiority. I have no reason to blame Dame Fortune. If either General Brereton could not have wrote, or his
look-out man had been blind, nothing could have prevented
my fighting them on June 6th; but such information, and
from such a quarter, close to the Enemy, could not be doubted.
The Frigate is directed to join me off Cape St. Vincent; and
if Sir John Orde, my Senior Officer, is not off Cadiz, I shall
anchor in Lagos Bay, and try to get both water and refreshments. If he has resumed his former station, I must go
inside the Mediterranean, as I know he is exceedingly displeased if any of the Mediterranean Ships are a moment upon
his station, and I have too great a respect for the wishes of
my superiors to act contrary to them. I am, with great
respect, &c.

NELSON AND BRONTE.

TO CAPTAIN MALCOLM, H. M. SHIP DONEGAL.

[Autograph, in the possession of Rear-Admiral Sir Charles Malcolm.]

Victory, June 16th, 1805.

My dear Sir,

I can give you little, for I got nothing except some trifles at Barbadoes; but accept the little I can offer you. Grieved as I am by the information from General Brereton at St. Lucia, which deprived us of a Battle, yet we must not despair of overtaking them. Whenever it is calm enough for a Boat to reach the Victory, I shall be truly glad to see you, being ever your most faithful servant,

NELSON AND BRONTE.

TO THE RIGHT HONOURABLE SIR EVAN NEPEAN, BART.

[From a Copy in the possession of Viscount Melville, K.T.]

Victory, June 16th, 1805.

My dear Sir Evan,

So far from being infallible, like the Pope, I believe my opinions to be very fallible, and therefore I may be mistaken that the Enemy's Fleet is gone to Europe; but I cannot bring myself to think otherwise, notwithstanding the variety of opinions which different people of good judgment form; but I have called every circumstance which I have heard of their proceedings before me—I have considered[5] the approaching season, the sickly state of their Troops and Ships, the means and time for defence which have been given to our Islands, and

---

[5] Clarke and M'Arthur, vol. ii. p. 413, give the following as part of one of Lord Nelson's " unreserved conversations" with his Captains, about the 16th June, 1805:—" I am thankful that the Enemy has been driven from the West India Islands with so little loss to our Country. I had made up my mind to great sacrifices; for, I had determined, notwithstanding his vast superiority, to stop his career, and to put it out of his power to do any further mischief. Yet do not imagine I am one of those hot-brained people who fight at immense disadvantage, without an adequate object. My object is partly gained. If we meet them, we shall find them not less than eighteen, I rather think twenty Sail of the Line, and therefore do not be surprised if I should not fall on them immediately: we wont part without a Battle. I think they will be glad to let me alone, if I will let them alone; which I will do, either till we approach the shores of Europe, or they give me an advantage too tempting to be resisted."

the certainty the Enemy must expect of our reinforcements'
arrival; and, therefore, if they were not able to make an
attack for the first three weeks after their arrival, they could
not hope for greater success after our means of resistance increased, and their means of offence were diminished; and it
is to be considered that the Enemy will not give me credit for
quitting the West Indies for this month to come. As this is
a letter of reasoning for my conduct, I may perhaps be prolix,
but I am anxious to stand well in your opinion; and if my
conduct is taken into consideration by Mr. Pitt, I will thank
you to show him this letter. A Frigate certainly arrived from
France, May 31st; from that moment all was hurry: on
June 1st, I believe, the Furet arrived with an account of my
being on the passage.—N.B. A Corvette watched us two
days, when 150 leagues to the Westward of Madeira. If
Barbadoes is the object of the Enemy's attack, a Fleet of Men
of War could get there, on the average, in four or five days
from Martinico; therefore why should they make a passage
of, at least, fifteen or sixteen days, by going to the Northward? If Tobago or Trinidad was their object, they had
only to weather St. Lucia, and they could fetch them with
ease; to St. Lucia, St. Vincent, and Grenada, they had a fair
wind, therefore it must be unnecessary to go to the Northward. If, therefore, any of those Islands are the objects of
their attack, as some people suppose, they are playing a game
which, I own, is incomprehensible to my weak understanding,
and I am completely deceived.

What impression could they expect to make upon Jamaica
with 4000 or 5000 men, and if that was their object, why not
steer direct from Martinico? Some think they may be going
to St. John's, Porto Rico, and wait to be joined there by reinforcements, but the season is passed; nor, if fifteen Sail of
the Line is coming out to join them, is there occasion to hide
themselves from our observations. My opinion is firm as a
rock, that some cause, *orders*, or *inability* to perform any service in these seas, has made them resolve to proceed direct
for Europe, sending the Spanish Ships to the Havannah.
Ever, my dear Sir Evan, yours faithfully,

NELSON AND BRONTE.

There would have been no occasion for opinions, had not

General Brereton sent his damned intelligence from St. Lucia; nor would I have received it to have acted by it, but I was assured that his information was very correct. It has almost broke my heart, but I must not despair.

TO THE CAPTAINS OF ANY OF HIS MAJESTY'S SHIPS CRUISING OFF THE WESTERN ISLANDS, OR NOT PROCEEDING ON MORE IMPORTANT SERVICE.

[From Clarke and M'Arthur, vol. ii. p. 414.]

17th June, 1805.

Sir,

As I believe the Enemy's Fleet is bound to Europe, and it being very uncertain whether they will go to Ferrol or Cadiz, I beg leave most strongly to recommend your proceeding off Ferrol, with this information, to the Admiral commanding off that Port, in order that he may be upon his guard against a surprise from a superior force. I am, &c.

NELSON AND BRONTE.

TO MAJOR-GENERAL VILLETTES, MALTA.

[From Clarke and M'Arthur, vol. ii. p. 415.]

18th June, 1805.

My dear General,

Unwell, and out of humour as I am by my disappointment, yet I will not let a letter go to Malta without writing you a line; and I am sure you will regret, with me, our old acquaintance Brereton's wrong information. Ball will show it to you, it could not be doubted, and, by following it, I lost the opportunity of fighting the Enemy. I am, &c.

NELSON AND BRONTE.

TO HIS EXCELLENCY SIR JOHN ACTON, BART.

[From a Press copy in the possession of the Right Hon. John Wilson Croker.]

Victory, June 18th, 1805—200 leagues North from Antigua.

My dear Sir John,

I am so far back on my way to the Mediterranean; for although I have not yet met the Enemy, I shall never allow them to get a superiority in the Mediterranean, so as to annoy Sicily, or the other Dominions of your good King. I am very, very unwell, and vexed. But for wrong information, I should have fought the Battle on June 6th. I send your Excellency an extract of a letter, giving an account of my trip. I feel I have done all that mortal man could do; therefore, I must try and be content. My *countryman*,[6] Gravina, has hitherto had a narrow miss of meeting me. I believe he is an honourable man; but they say, in the West Indies, that he has been most rudely treated by the French at Martinico. What a race I have run after these fellows; but God is just, and I may be repaid for all my moments of anxiety. God bless you, my dear Sir John; and with every good wish, be assured I am ever your most faithful friend,

NELSON AND BRONTE.

I have wrote a line to the King, to say I am on my return to the Mediterranean.

TO WILLIAM MARSDEN, ESQ., ADMIRALTY.

[Autograph, in the possession of Mrs. Leake.]

Victory, June 18th, 1805—200 leagues from Antigua.

My dear Sir,

Pray send the inclosed. I am, as you may readily believe, very, very unhappy at not having got at the Enemy: they were missed by General Brereton's unlucky information; but I shall be close after them in Europe, and when I have housed them I shall certainly instantly return to England: I want rest. I am ever, my dear Sir, your most obliged friend,

NELSON AND BRONTE.

[6] Admiral Gravina, was born at Naples in April 1747, and is said to have been a natural son of King Charles the Third. Nelson, from the honours and favours he had received from the King of the Two Sicilies, sometimes called his Majesty's subjects his *countrymen*.

TO HIS EXCELLENCY HUGH ELLIOT, ESQ.

[Autograph, in the Elliot Papers.]

Victory, June 18th, 1805—200 leagues North from Antigua.

My dear Sir,

I am so far on my way to the Mediterranean, and, I believe, following the French Fleet. You will lament the unfortunate intelligence from General Brereton, which led me a wrong road, or June 6th would have been a fighting day for me, and, I trust, a glorious one for our Country. However, I must not despair of getting up with them before they enter the Straits. At least, they will have no time to carry any of their future plans into execution, and do harm to any of the Countries under my charge. I send you a brief account of my trip to the West Indies, and General Brereton's intelligence, which was not, nor could be doubted. It has made me very sorrowful; but I feel that mortal man could not do more to serve my Country, and the common Cause more faithfully. Your son is very well, and improves every day in his profession : Captain Parker likes him very much. If I am able, I will write a line to either the good King or Queen; but if I do not, I beg you will present my humble duty; and believe me ever, my dear Sir, your most obliged and faithful servant,

NELSON AND BRONTE.

TO COMMISSIONER OTWAY, GIBRALTAR.

[From a Press-copy in the possession of the Right Hon. John Wilson Croker.]

Victory, June 18th, 1805.

My dear Commissioner,

I am sure that you who have always taken a lively interest in the success of this Fleet, will be sorry to find that we have not yet had our Battle, and much more so to find that it has been occasioned by wrong information. I send you the unfortunate information, and an extract of a letter giving a brief account of our West Indies trip. Cochrane had but just arrived from Jamaica, where Dacres[7] had kept all his Ships, except

---

[7] Rear, afterwards Vice-Admiral James Richard Dacres, Commander-in-Chief at Jamaica. He is mentioned in vol. ii. pp. 334, 393; and a Memoir of his services may be found in the *Naval Chronicle*, vol. xxvi. He died in January 1810.

Spartiate, which I have brought with me; for I believe the Enemy's force to be fourteen French Sail of the Line, and one or two Spanish. The Diamond Rock was taken June 2nd, and, if our Merchants had not most imprudently sent away their Ships from Antigua on the night of the 7th, this would have been all the mischief that the Combined Fleets would have done by their expedition. We are as healthy as usual, and I hope you continue so at Gibraltar. You will be so good as to communicate our history to General Fox and Admiral Knight, and be assured I am, my dear Commissioner, your most obliged and faithful servant,

NELSON AND BRONTE.

TO WILLIAM MARSDEN, ESQ., ADMIRALTY.

[From a Press-copy in the Croker Papers.]

Victory, June 19th, 1805.

Sir,

I send you[8] a report of a Vessel spoke, which, with the circumstances attending it, can leave me no room to doubt but that I am hard upon the heels of the Enemy's Fleet. In addition, Captain Parker reports to me that there was a note in the American's log, that they supposed them the French Fleet from Martinico. The Master was anxious to know if the French had taken Antigua, as he was bound there, and had traded to that Island many years. The remark of seeing this Fleet in the log of the Vessel, with the difference of the course the Master and Mate supposed the Fleet to be steering, satisfies my mind that there could be no intended deceit in the information, (which sometimes happens;) nor did the Vessel see our Fleet until she had been spoken by the Amazon. I think we cannot be more than eighty leagues from them at this moment, and by carrying every sail, and using my utmost efforts, I shall hope to close with them before they get to either Cadiz or Toulon—to accomplish which most desirable object, nothing shall be wanting on the part of, Sir, your most obedient servant,

NELSON AND BRONTE.[9]

---

[8] " 19th June. Noon. Decade and Martin parted."—*Victory's Log.*

[9] The following was enclosed in the above letter; and a fuller Report is in p. 474, post:—" ' The Vessel Sally, of North Carolina, bound to Antigua, boarded on the

TO CAPTAIN KEATS, H. M. SHIP SUPERB.

[Autograph.]

Victory, June 19th, 1805.

My dear Keats,

I can offer you but little; for, to say the truth, I have been unlucky in not getting anything but a few sheep in the West Indies, of which I beg that you will accept one. I should be very glad to see you when the weather is such as to allow your Gig to pass; but we have been so far fortunate as not to get calms. As the Telegraph told you yesterday, a Fleet of Ships of War were seen on Saturday evening last, standing to the Northward. It was noted in the log of the day by Jonathan, or I should have doubted; and their supposition has noted that it was the French Fleet from Martinico. He wanted to know if they had taken Antigua, as he was bound there. I calculate that we cannot be more than eighty leagues from them; and I think they will keep well to the Southward of the Western Islands, to avoid being seen by our Cruizers. I am ever, my dear Keats, yours most faithfully,

NELSON AND BRONTE.

I think the Superb is improved in her sailing.

TO CAPTAIN SAMUEL SUTTON, H. M. SHIP AMPHION.

[Autograph, in the possession of Captain Ives Sutton.]

My dear Sutton, Victory, June 20th, 1805.

If we have little wind perhaps you will come on board. Your Gunner will be removed to the Donegal—he is spoken of as a very good man—therefore, he must have his stores ready for survey. I wish you had wrote a line in telegraph figures to Admiral Cochrane to say our information about the French Fleet. Many thanks for the papers. Ever, my dear Sutton, yours faithfully,

NELSON AND BRONTE.

17th June, 1805, by Captain Parker, H. M. S. Amazon, 17 days out, gave the following intelligence:—'At 7 P.M., on Saturday evening last, saw about 22 Sail of large Ships steering, Master's account, N.N.E.; Mate's account, N.N.W., in latitude, on Saturday noon, 27° 28', longitude, 60° 58' W.—W. PARKER.' (A Copy.) NELSON AND BRONTE."—"17th June. P.M. At 3, the Amazon examined a Schooner; and on joining the Fleet, the Captain of the Ship was signalled on board the Victory."— *Signal Log.*

PRIVATE DIARY.

[From Clarke and M'Arthur, vol. ii. p. 415.]

21st June, 1805.

Midnight, nearly calm, saw three planks, which I think came from the French Fleet. Very miserable, which is very foolish.

NELSON AND BRONTE.

TO WILLIAM MARSDEN, ESQ., ADMIRALTY.

[Original, in the Admiralty.]

Victory, at Sea, June 26th, 1805.

Sir,

I herewith transmit you for the information of the Lords Commissioners of the Admiralty, a copy of an order issued on the 5th instant, to the Captains of His Majesty's Ships named in the margin,[1] directing them for the reasons therein mentioned to victual the Troops at full allowance of provisions, instead of two-thirds, as is usually the custom. The cheerfulness with which they embarked, and the fatigue of marching all night from the different out-posts, deserved my particular notice; and therefore considering that we should soon be in Action with the Enemy, and that the Troops, at any rate, would only be on board the Fleet a few days, I thought it advisable to order them to be victualled the same as the Seamen, judging that a distinction (under the above circumstances, when unanimity and a hearty joint co-operation were necessary) would have been detrimental to the Service. I therefore trust their Lordships will approve of my having done so, and be pleased to give the necessary directions to the Victualling-Board, that the respective Pursers may be allowed credit for the same on passing their Accounts. I am, Sir, &c.

NELSON AND BRONTE.

[1] Victory, Northumberland, Canopus, Superb, Spencer, Belleisle, Conqueror Tigre, Leviathan, Donegal, Swiftsure, Spartiate. Vide p. 446, ante.

TO CAPTAIN SUTTON, H.M. SHIP AMPHION.

[Autograph, in the possession of Captain Ives Sutton.]

Victory, June 30th, 1805.

Sir,

As it is of the very utmost importance that I should know, as speedily as possible, if the Enemy's Fleet from the West Indies have entered the Mediterranean, I have, therefore, to desire that you will proceed, (when I shall make the signal for that purpose,) without one moment's loss of time, to Tangier Bay, sending a Boat on shore for information to Mr. Matra, the British Consul, to know from him if the Enemy have entered the Straits, or are gone into Cadiz; and such other information as may be important for me to be acquainted with. You will keep my near approach as secret as you can, desiring the Officers to say they left me at sea, and that they do not know which way I was going. And you will also request Mr. Matra to keep my near approach a secret; that if the Enemy's Fleet is gone up the Mediterranean, no Vessels may be sent with information. You will delay as little time as possible at Tangier; and I rely on your zeal, activity, and attention to this very important service; and that I shall find the Amphion from seven to sixteen leagues West from Cape Spartel. Should you hear that I am gone to any other place after the Enemy, you will follow me, as I have not a single Frigate with me. I am, Sir, with the highest esteem, your most obliged and faithful servant,

NELSON AND BRONTE.

It will be desirable for every Frigate and Vessel you may meet between St. Vincent's and Cape Spartel, to join me on the afore-mentioned Rendezvous, unless they are upon very important service.   N. AND B.

TO WILLIAM MARSDEN, ESQ., ADMIRALTY.

[Original, in the Admiralty.]

Victory, at Sea, 30th June, 1805.

Sir,

I herewith transmit you, for the information of the Lords Commissioners of the Admiralty, a Report of Survey held

this day on Lieutenant Thomas Wing,[2] of his Majesty's Ship
Amazon, and beg to acquaint you, for their information, that
I have appointed Mr. Philip Horn,[3] Midshipman of the Victory, to act as Lieutenant of the said Ship, in Mr.
Wing's room, and herewith transmit you a copy of his acting order,
which you will be pleased to lay before their Lordships for
confirmation. Mr. Horn is an Admiralty recommendation,
an *elève* of the late Captain Riou's, and was, while with him,
severely wounded in the thigh, on board the Amazon, in the
Battle at Copenhagen. In addition to these circumstances,
he is a very promising and deserving young man. I am, &c.

NELSON AND BRONTE.

TO J. M. MATRA, ESQ., H. M. CONSUL AT TANGIERS.

[From a Press-copy in the possession of the Right Hon. John Wilson Croker.]

Victory, June 30th, 1805.

Sir,

I have sent the Amphion, Captain Sutton, to Tangier-Bay,
in order to receive such intelligence of the Enemy's Fleet as
you may be able to give him. It is a very interesting moment
for me to know if the Enemy have entered the Mediterranean,
or are gone to Cadiz: therefore, I shall thank you to tell
Captain Sutton all you know relative to the Enemy's Fleet,
and such other information as you may be so good as to give
him. I have further to request that my near approach may
be kept as great a secret as is possible. Should the Enemy's
Fleet not have passed the Straits, it is very possible that I may
anchor the Fleet in Tangier Bay, and therefore should be glad
to know if I can procure bullocks, onions, lemons, and oranges'
for the Ships' Companies, for which will be paid dollars.
Upon all these points your kind information will most truly
oblige, Sir, your most obedient Servant,

NELSON AND BRONTE.

The Combined Fleet passed to the Northward of Antigua
on June 8th.

---

[2] Lieutenant Thomas Wing: he died a Lieutenant in 1837.

[3] Mr. Phillip Thicknesse Horn: his Commission, as Lieutenant, was dated 7th
October 1805; and having been First Lieutenant of the Superb at Algiers, in 1816,
when he was severely wounded, he was promoted to be a Commander in September
of that year, in which rank he died in 1825 or 1826.

TO CAPTAIN PARKER, H. M. SHIP AMAZON.

[From a Press Copy in the possession of the Right Hon. John Wilson Croker.]

Victory, June 30th, 1805.

Sir,

As information is at this moment of the very utmost importance respecting the Enemy's Fleet, I have therefore to desire that you will make the best of your way, when I shall make the signal for the Amazon to proceed upon this service, by Cape St. Vincent, Cape St. Mary's and off Cadiz, that I may be informed, as expeditiously as possible, if the Enemy's Fleet from the West Indies have entered the Port of Cadiz, or gone into the Mediterranean; and you will join me directly off Cape Spartel, from seven to twelve leagues West from it, where I shall expect your arrival with the greatest anxiety. If, before you get so far as Cadiz, that you can get information, which may be depended upon, you will go to the above-mentioned Rendezvous, and wait my arrival; and should you hear of either my having followed the Enemy into the Mediterranean, or gone to any other place in pursuit of them, you will endeavour to join me with all expedition. I know with what confidence I may rely upon your activity, zeal, and attention to this service, so highly important to our Country, and be assured, I am, with the highest regard, your most obedient, humble servant,

NELSON AND BRONTE.

Should you meet Frigates or Sloops, not employed upon very important service, it is of the greatest consequence that they should join me on the above Rendezvous.

N. AND B.

TO REAR-ADMIRAL LOUIS.

[Autograph, in the possession of the Reverend Dr. Raffles. "July 1st. Noon. Light breezes and clear. St. Mary's (Azores) S. 89 E., distance 175 leagues.' — Victory's Log.]

Victory, July 1st, 1805.

My dear Admiral,

I think you may with great safety venture to dine on board the Victory to-day, for I too much fear that we shall not have a wind to move us faster than Boats can pass. I can tell you no news, but Amazon[4] may bring us some. Ever, my dear Louis, yours most faithfully,

NELSON AND BRONTE.

TO CAPTAIN HARGOOD, H.M. SHIP BELLEISLE.

[From the " Memoir of the Life and Services of Admiral Sir William Hargood, G.C.B., G.C.H.," p. 112.]

Victory, July 1st, 1805.

My dear Hargood,

As the day is very fine, I was in hopes that you would have come on board, and dined. From winds, and the expectation of wind, I have been afraid to ask my friends to dinner; but I need not, I hope, assure you, how glad I am always to see you, being, my dear Hargood, yours most faithfully,

NELSON AND BRONTE.

PRIVATE DIARY.

[From Clarke and M'Arthur, vol. ii. p. 415. "8th July. A.M. At 11·30, saw the Island of St. Michael's E.S.E. per compass, distance 17½ leagues."—*Victory's Log.*]

8th July, 1805.

We crawled thirty-three miles the last twenty-four hours ; my only hope is, that the Enemy's Fleet are near us, and in the same situation. All night light breezes, standing to the Eastward, to go to the Northward of St. Michael's. At times squally with rain. On examining the Spanish log and chart we had taken in a Bark from La Guira,[6] I find that the Combined Squadrons went in sight of Cape Blanco, and passed close to the Salvages.

---

[4] At 5, A.M. on the 1st of July, the Amazon made the signal for a strange sail, S.S.W., which she proceeded to examine, but nothing more occurs in the Victory's Log, or Signal Log, on the subject.

[5] June 28th. " P.M. At 5·45, observed the Amazon to hoist French colours. 7, Amazon fired a gun. 29th June, A.M. 6·40, observed the Amazon with her chase in tow."—*Signal Log.* " Daylight, observed the Amazon having a Settee in tow, which proved to be Spaniard from La Guira. Noon, St. Mary's (Azores) N 85° E., distance 210 leagues."—*Victory's Log.*

TO CAPTAIN KEATS, H.M. SHIP SUPERB.

[Autograph, in the possession of the Reverend Richard Keats.]

Victory, July 10th, 1805.

My dear Keats,

I send you the last Papers; they seem rather worse for wear. I hope our present wind will last us to Cape Spartel. When the weather is fine, and you feel so inclined, I trust I need not repeat how happy I am at all times to see you, feeling myself your much obliged,

NELSON AND BRONTE.

TO COMMISSIONER OTWAY, GIBRALTAR.

[Autograph, in the possession of Rear-Admiral Inglefield, C.B.]

Victory, July 10th, 1805.

My dear Commissioner,

Be so good as to order a fore-yard to be prepared for the Canopus; hers is rotten. Whether the Fleet will anchor at Gibraltar, or pass up the Mediterranean, must depend upon what the Enemy may have done, and when they passed Gibraltar; for if there is a hope of getting up with them before they get to Toulon, I shall not anchor. I have ordered no letters to be received for Gibraltar, as I do not wish it to be known, at the Rock, my intention of anchoring. You will be so good as to mention my intentions and wishes for secrecy, to General Fox. If I pass up the Mediterranean, I shall write you a line relative to stores, &c. &c. I am always, my dear Commissioner, your much obliged, humble servant,

NELSON AND BRONTE.

TO REAR-ADMIRAL KNIGHT, GIBRALTAR.

[From a Press-copy in the possession of the Right Hon. John Wilson Croker.]

Victory, July 10th, 1805.

My dear Admiral,

I wish the probability of the Fleet's anchoring at Gibraltar to be kept as secret as possible, for everything which is known on the Rock gets into Spain. If the Enemy's Fleet has

passed up the Mediterranean, (unless it has been such a length
of time that there is no chance of my getting up with them
before they get into Toulon,) I shall not anchor at Gibraltar,
but have the Transports convoyed after the Fleet; but on
this subject I shall write, if I do not stop. Be so good as to
mention these circumstances to General Fox. I have wrote to
the Commissioner to prepare a fore-yard for Canopus, as hers
is rotten. I am ever, my dear Admiral, your most faithful,
humble servant,

NELSON AND BRONTE.

TO WILLIAM MARSDEN, ESQ., ADMIRALTY.

[Original, in the Admiralty.]

Victory, at Sea, 10th July, 1805.
Sir,

You will be pleased to acquaint the Lords Commissioners
of the Admiralty that Mr. James Marguette, (a man of colour,)
who has for these many years piloted his Majesty's Ships, in
Squadrons and otherwise, from Barbadoes to the different
Leeward Islands, came on board the Victory off that Island,
on the 4th ult., for the purpose of piloting the Fleet under
my command to any of the Leeward Islands in pursuit of the
Enemy; and that on the 13th June, when the Fleet sailed
from Antigua, I judged it proper to take him with me, that I
might (in case of certain information after we left that place,
that the Enemy had gone to Porto Rico or Jamaica,) have a
person with me who was perfectly acquainted with the pilotage of those places; and as Mr. Marguette is a very clever,
able man, and had been at the former place with Sir Henry
Harvey,[6] and several other Admirals; he is, therefore, now
on board the Fleet; and it is my intention to send him to
England by the first opportunity, in order that their Lordships may direct him a passage to Barbadoes by the first Ship
of War going there.

I shall furnish Mr. Marguette with a letter, when he
quits the Victory, that due attention may be paid to this

[6] Admiral Sir Henry Harvey, K.B., who died in December 1810.

valuable man, who very cheerfully offered his services to pilot the Fleet. I, therefore, beg leave to recommend him to their Lordships' notice, and trust they will be pleased to approve of my having taken him with me, for the reasons before mentioned. I am, Sir, &c.

NELSON AND BRONTE.

TO CAPTAIN PARKER, H.M. SHIP AMAZON.

[From a Press-copy in the possession of the Right Hon. John Wilson Croker.]

July 10th, 1805.

Sir,

If you find[7] off Cape *Spartel* any Vessel which can convey your intelligence to me, on my arrival off that Cape, you will proceed to Gibraltar, and complete your water, provisions, and stores with all possible expedition, and join me, unless I send you further orders. I am, Sir, &c.

NELSON AND BRONTE.

PRIVATE DIARY.

[From Clarke and M'Arthur, vol. ii. p. 415.]

Wednesday, 17th July, 1805.

Our whole run from Barbuda, day by day, was 3459 miles: our run from Cape St. Vincent to Barbadoes was 3227 miles, so that our run back was only 232 miles more than our run out—allowance being made for the difference of the latitudes and longitudes of Barbadoes and Barbuda; average, per day, thirty-four leagues, wanting nine miles.

18th July, 1805.

Cape Spartel in sight,[8] but no French Fleet, nor any information about them: how sorrowful this makes me, but I cannot help myself!

---

[7] Though this Note was dated on the 10th of July, the Amazon did not leave the Squadron until the forenoon of the 13th of that month, when Cape St. Vincent bore S. 89° E., distance about 183 leagues.—*Signal Log.*

[8] " 18th July. Noon. Cape Spartel S. 75° E., distance 12 leagues."—*Victory's Log.*]

TO VICE-ADMIRAL COLLINGWOOD.[8]

[Autograph, in the possession of the Honourable Mrs. Newnham Collingwood.
" 18th July. Noon. Several Men of War in sight."—*Signal Log.*]

Victory, July 18th, 1805.

My dear Collingwood,

I am, as you may suppose, miserable at not having fallen in with the Enemy's Fleet; and I am almost increased in sorrow, in not finding them. The name of General Brereton will not soon be forgot. But for his false information, the

[8] On the 18th of May, 1805, Vice-Admiral Collingwood was appointed to command a Squadron on Foreign Service : he arrived off Cape Finisterre, on the 27th of that month, and fell in with Sir Richard Bickerton, which induced him to take his station off Cadiz.

On the 18th of July, Vice Admiral Collingwood wrote the following letter to Lord Nelson :

"Dreadnought, July 18th, 1805, off Cadiz.

" My dear Lord,

" I congratulate your Lordship on your return from the long chase you have had to the West Indies, and wished sincerely I could have had the pleasure of seeing you, and of telling you how truly dear you are to my friendship. We approached you with caution, not knowing whether we were to expect your Lordship, or the Frenchmen first.

" I had been for some time under orders for Foreign Service before the Toulon Ships sailed, and my Ships were increased or diminished as the apparent service seemed to require. The sailing of the Toulon Ships determined my route. But I have always had an idea that Ireland alone was the object they have in view, and still believe that to be their ultimate destination—that they will now liberate the Ferrol Squadron from Calder, make the round of the Bay, and, taking the Rochefort people with them, appear off Ushant—perhaps, with thirty-four Sail, there to be joined by twenty more. Admiral Cornwallis collecting his out Squadrons may have thirty and upwards. This appears to be a probable plan ; for unless it is to bring their great Fleets and Armies to some point of service—some rash attempt at conquest—they have been only subjecting them to chance of loss, which I do not believe the Corsican would do, without the hope of an adequate reward. This summer is big with events. We may all, perhaps, have an active share in them, and sincerely I wish your Lordship strength of body to go through—and to all others, your strength of mind.

" I have a letter from Calder to-day by the Pickle. He complains of his health : the constant anxiety of his situation is wearing him down. He tells me, that Cotton, dissatisfied with something, is likely to leave the Fleet ; and instead of the old ones, Sterling has a Squadron off Rochfort, and Nugent is First Captain to Admiral Cornwallis. I hope my worthy friend Admiral Murray is well, and beg my kind regards to him, and Admiral Louis. When I found you had only ten Ships, I sent Pickmore and the Illustrious—our best sailers, to join at Barbadoes ; but as they were for the purpose of joining your Lordship only, and to follow wherever you were, I conclude they are on their way home again. This day the Pickle brought me your Lordship's letter of March, for which I am much obliged. All my family are well, and only

Battle would have been fought where Rodney fought his, on June 6th. I must now only hope that the Enemy have not tricked me, and gone to Jamaica; but if the account, of which I send you a copy, is correct, it is more than probable they are either gone to the Northward, or, if bound to the Mediterranean, not yet arrived. The Spaniards, or the greatest part of them, I take for granted, are gone to the Havannah, and I suppose, have taken fourteen Sail of Antigua sugar loaded Ships with them. The moment the Fleet is watered, and got some refreshments, of which we are in great want, I shall come out, and make you a visit; not, my dear friend, to take your Command from you, (for I may probably add mine to you,) but to consult how we can best serve our Country, by detaching a part of this large force. God bless you, my dear friend, and believe me ever most affectionately yours,

NELSON AND BRONTE.

Admiral Murray desires to be kindly remembered.

TO WILLIAM MARSDEN, ESQ., ADMIRALTY.

[Autograph, in the Admiralty. "19th July. A.M. At 7·30, anchored in Rosia Bay, Gibraltar. Squadron anchored as convenient. Found riding here H. M. Ships Decade and Amazon, and Rear-Admiral Knight's Flag on board the Guerrier Sheer-hulk in the Mole."—*Victory's Log.*]

Victory, July 20th, 1805, Gibraltar.

Sir,

By a Brig which sails for England this day, I have to acquaint you that I anchored in this Bay yesterday morning, without having obtained the smallest intelligence of the Enemy's Fleet, except what is contained in the enclosed paper. The Squadron is in the most perfect health, except

lamenting this long War should keep me for ever from home. God bless you, my dear Lord, with health and every happiness. I am ever, with a most affectionate regard, your Lordship's faithful and most humble servant and friend,

"CUTHBERT COLLINGWOOD.

"I am exceedingly pleased with Captain Mundy of the Hydra. His vigilance and activity are exemplary; he is a clever young man. I must send him in for water, &c.; but I want two or three Frigates very much."—*Autograph*, in the Nelson Papers. A very imperfect copy of this letter occurs in the "Correspondence and Memoir of Lord Collingwood," (Vol. i. p. 150,) where it is erroneously said to have been dated on the 21st of October.

some symptoms of scurvy, which I hope to eradicate by bullocks and refreshments from Tetuan, to which I shall proceed to-morrow. Having completed the Fleet to four months' provisions, and with stores for Channel Service, I shall get outside the Mediterranean, leaving a sufficient force to watch Carthagena, and proceed as upon a due consideration, on reading Vice-Admiral Collingwood's orders, and those which Rear-Admiral Sir Richard Bickerton may have received during my absence, may suggest to be most proper, or waiting until their Lordships' orders may arrive from England, for the distribution of this very large force of Line-of-Battle Ships, unless I should hear that the Enemy have gone for some of the Ports in the Bay, when I shall join the Squadron off Ferrol, or off Ushant, as I think the case requires. When I know something certain of the Enemy's Fleet, I shall embrace their Lordships' permission to return to England for a short time, for the re-establishment of my health. The Prévoyante, Store-Ship will sail in a few days, by which Ship I shall write further of my intended proceedings; and I beg, through you, to assure their Lordships, that however erroneous my judgment may be, that I am anxious to act as I think their Lordships would wish me, was I near enough to receive their orders. I am, Sir, &c.

NELSON AND BRONTE.[9]

[9] The following intelligence was enclosed in the above letter:—" Intelligence received from the American Schooner Sally, Dempsey Wade, Master, from New Burn (North Carolina), bound to Antigua, laden with lumber: boarded at 6 P.M., June the 18th, 1805, by his Majesty's Ship Amazon. Extract from the Sally's Log-book:

'H.	K.	F.	Courses.	Winds.	Remarks: Sunday, 16th June, 1805.
P.M.	7		S. b E.	E. b S.	Saw twenty-two Sail of large Ships to the Eastward, standing to the Northward: supposed them to be the French Fleet from Martinique, going home.'

(A true Copy.) " RICHARD SEYMOUR, Lt.

" At noon, the Schooner was in Latitude 27° 28" N., Longitude 60° 58" W., and ran only 12 miles S.S.E. to the time the strange Fleet was seen: from that time until the Amazon boarded the Schooner she made little way, having the wind very light from the S.E. On asking the Master and Mate why they supposed the Fleet seen by them were French? the Master replied that an American Brig from Martinique spoke him eight days before, and informed him that a Squadron had arrived at Martinique from France; he therefore supposed the Fleet seen to be that Squa-

PRIVATE DIARY.

[From Clarke and M'Arthur, vol. ii. p. 415.]

20th July, 1805.

I went on shore for the first time since the 16th of June, 1803; and from having my foot out of the Victory, two years, wanting ten days.

NELSON AND BRONTE.

TO THE RIGHT HONOURABLE LORD BARHAM, FIRST LORD OF THE ADMIRALTY.

[Autograph, in the possession of Charles J. Middleton, Esq.]

Victory, July 20th, 1805.

My Lord,

It was not until my return to the Mediterranean, that I knew who was appointed First Lord of the Admiralty, in the room of Lord Melville, or I should have wrote you whenever opportunities offered for sending letters; for there must be, your Lordship well knows, many things which may be said to the First Lord, which would be improper to address to a Public Board; and in presuming to offer any opinions, I trust that your Lordship will not think that I offer my opinions with a presumptuous expectation that they ought to be followed, but rather to enable the First Lord to become an accurate judge of the present situation of the Mediterranean. Not having seen either Admiral Collingwood, who is off Cadiz, or Sir Richard Bickerton, who is off Carthagena, I know not what orders they have received, or the reasons on which their present mode of acting is followed; but I have sent for Sir Richard Bickerton, and shall go to Admiral Collingwood, to be better informed.

dron returning home. The Master's opinion of the course steered by the strange Fleet was, N.N.E.; the Mate thought, about N.N.W. Both of them went to the mast-head of the Schooner, and were positive that the Ships seen were Men-of-War, having royals, stay-sails, and all sails set, showing them as low as the lower yards. On referring back to the Schooner's Log, I found entered on it the intelligence obtained by him from the Brig (as before stated) from Martinique.

"RICHARD SEYMOUR.

(Copy.)

"NELSON AND BRONTE."

I find the Admiral at Gibraltar without any Naval force under his orders, which, from the orders of the Admiralty to Admiral Knight, does not seem to be the Board's intention. Gibraltar, between the two Admirals, seems (if I may be allowed the expression) almost abandoned. Some regular and proper force must be thought of, and it should be permanent; besides which, if the Town of Gibraltar and the Garrison is to be saved from the harassing and distress occasioned by the Gun-boats, something of the Praam kind must be adopted, and a Marine Brigade, to man from ten to twenty Gun-Boats. Nobody in our Service can have more knowledge on this subject than my friend Sir Roger Curtis. It is generally believed that a very formidable annoyance by red-hot shot from Gun-Boats is intended.

I hear, indeed see, by Admiral Collingwood's orders to Admiral Knight, that several of the Frigates are drawn from the upper part of the Mediterranean. Unless Russia takes this service upon herself, the French will, whenever they please, convey an Army to Sardinia, Sicily, the Morea, or Egypt, all which points I have been instructed to guard, and for which service I have repeatedly applied for *many, many* more Frigates and Sloops of War. The consequence of our abandoning this service will be the loss of our influence in this Country, which has hitherto (I mean Sardinia, Naples, and Turkey) considered themselves as protected by Great Britain.

Your Lordship will, I trust, pardon my remarks; and I could enlarge very much upon those important subjects, but I will not intrude more upon your time, than to assure you that I am, with the highest respect, your Lordship's most faithful and obedient servant,

NELSON AND BRONTE.

TO VICE-ADMIRAL COLLINGWOOD.[1]

[Autograph, in the possession of the Honourable Mrs. Newnham Collingwood.]

Victory, July 20th, 1805.

My dear Collingwood,

The Martin Sloop arrived this morning, and, as Captain Savage[2] says that the Pickle Schooner left the Fleet before him, for Gibraltar, I fear that some accident has happened to her. I shall be in Tetuan on the 22nd; and twenty-four hours will then complete us for an East India voyage; and I shall see you as soon as possible. I have sent for Sir Richard Bickerton, as I am in total ignorance of the intentions of the Admiralty, and I find that the Frigates are ordered from aloft to join you, and at a moment when I have fancied that at least double the number are wanted; but the orders of the Admiralty must be obeyed. I only hope Officers will not be blamed for the events which it is not difficult to foresee will happen. God bless you, my dear friend, and believe me ever, yours most faithfully,　　　NELSON AND BRONTE.

[1] On the 19th of July, Vice-Admiral Collingwood replied to Lord Nelson's letter of the 18th. (Vide p. 472, ante.)

"Dreadnought, July 19th, 1805.

"My dear Lord,

"I well know what your Lordship's disappointment is, and share the mortification of it. It would have been a happy day for England, could you have met them; small as your force was, I trust it would have been found enough. Truly glad will I be to see you, my dear friend, and to give you my best opinion on the present state of affairs, which are in the highest degree intricate; but reasoning on the policy of the present French Government, who never aim at little things while great objects are in view, I have considered the invasion of Ireland as the real mark and butt of all their operations. The flight to the West Indies was to take off the Naval Force, which is the great impediment to their undertaking. The Rochfort Squadron's return confirmed me. I think they will now collect their force at Ferrol, which Calder tells me are in motion—pick up those at Rochfort, who, I am told, are equally ready, and will make them above thirty Sail; and then, without going near Ushant, or the Channel Fleet, proceed to Ireland. Detachments must go from the Channel Fleet to succour Ireland, when the Brest Fleet—twenty-one, I believe, of them, will sail, either to another part of Ireland, or up the Channel—a sort of force that has not been seen in those seas, perhaps, ever.

"The Martin has just arrived here; and by her, I shall send all the letters, &c., for Gibraltar. I send your Lordship a packet which Admiral Knight transmitted to me to go to England for the Secretaries of State. I have the honour to be, &c.,

"CUTHBERT COLLINGWOOD.

"Is not your Lordship surprised to find Vice-Admiral Nugent, First Captain to the Commander-in-Chief, Channel Fleet?"—Autograph, in the Nelson Papers.

[2] Captain R. S. Savage appears to have died a Commander, between 1806 and 1809

TO WILLIAM MARSDEN, ESQ., ADMIRALTY.

[Autograph, in the possession of Mrs. Leake.]

[About 20th July, 1805.]

I am, my dear Mr. Marsden, as completely miserable as my greatest enemy could wish me; but I neither blame fortune or my own judgment. Oh, General Brereton! General Brereton! Pray forward the inclosed, I shall see and thank you very soon. Ever your obliged,

NELSON AND BRONTE.

TO HIS EXCELLENCY HUGH ELLIOT, ESQ., NAPLES.

[Autograph, in the Elliot Papers.]

My dear Sir,   Victory, Gibraltar, July 21st, 1805.

I arrived here a day before the Martin Sloop; therefore, I can only tell you, that I heard nothing since of the Enemy's Fleet—therefore, whether they are bound for the Mediterranean, Cadiz, or some Port in the Bay, I am ignorant. I shall sail to-morrow to watch for them outside the Straits, and to act as circumstances shall render necessary.

I have only, from public rumour, not having seen either the Admirals off Cadiz, or off Carthagena, [heard] of what is passing at Naples, except some extracts of letters sent by Sir Alexander Ball, which Admiral Knight has sent off Cadiz. But I see too clearly that matters seem drawing to a conclusion respecting Naples; but I hope the Allies of Naples will not suffer those Kingdoms to be seized by Buonaparte.

I can say nothing more. The Admiralty, I hear, have ordered three Frigates from up the Mediterranean outside the Straits. It is past my comprehension, when I have wrote that *many, many* more than are there at present are wanted. I shall direct a Ship to relieve the Excellent as soon as the destination of the Enemy's Squadron is ascertained; and if it is true that the Line-of-Battle Ship[2] is anchored at Genoa, I must send, and try and take her. When these things are arranged, I shall proceed to England. Your son is very well. I am ever, my dear Sir, your Excellency's most faithful and obedient servant,   NELSON AND BRONTE.

[2] A French Ship of the Line building at Genoa. Vide p. 488, post.

TO HIS EXCELLENCY SIR JOHN ACTON, BART.

[From a Press-copy in the possession of the Right Hon. John Wilson Croker.]

Victory, Gibraltar Bay, July 21st, 1805.

My dear Sir John,

I arrived here [the day before] yesterday, and shall sail to-morrow morning; for having got not even a drop of water in the West Indies, we had nothing in the Fleet. I may, if it is possible, be yet ahead of the Enemy; but I almost despair of their coming this road. I know scarcely anything of what is passing up the Mediterranean; for I have seen neither the Admiral from Carthagena or Cadiz, who have between them all the letters; but public rumour says here, that Buonaparte has threatened Naples with his vengeance. I hope the Allies of our good Sovereign will not any longer be deterred from acting an honourable and vigorous part. When the destination of the Enemy's Fleet is fixed, I shall proceed to England, to try and recruit myself; and nothing shall be wanting on my part there to be useful to the Two Sicilies. I am ever, my dear Sir John, your Excellency's most obliged and faithful servant,

NELSON AND BRONTE.

TO SIR ALEXANDER JOHN BALL, BART., MALTA.

[From a Press-copy in the possession of the Right Hon. John Wilson Croker.]

Victory, Gibraltar, July 21st, 1805.

My dear Ball,

I arrived here before the Martin, (on Friday.) I have little to add to my letter by her, having heard nothing of the Enemy's Fleet; but it is possible I may be ahead of them, for I have carried every rag, night and day. We have lost neither Officer or man by sickness since we left the Mediterranean. The Enemy's Squadrons have been very sickly. I shall sail at daylight for outside the Straits, to try and meet, or be ready to pack after, them, if they are gone to the Bay, which many think, and that Ireland is the great object. I hear the Admiralty—indeed, I have seen it—have ordered all *your* Sloops of War from the service of Malta. I am all astonishment, and shall send them up again. I fancy the folks at home have lost their recollection. God bless you, my dear Ball, and believe me ever your most attached friend,

NELSON AND BRONTE.

TO HER MAJESTY THE QUEEN OF NAPLES.

[From a Press-copy in the possession of the Right Hon. John Wilson Croker.]

Victory, Gibraltar, July 21st, 1805.

Madame,

I was only nine days in my tour round the West India Leeward Island; therefore, I had not an opportunity of getting any of the produce of those Islands, which might be acceptable, except a few tamarinds, and a little preserved ginger, which I beg your Majesty to accept from your faithful Nelson. The Fleet having received not the smallest refreshment, or even a cup of water in the West Indies, I have been obliged to put in here for a few hours; but I sail to-morrow, and it is still possible I may be sure of [*a line is illegible.*]

I rather think most of the Spanish Ships are gone to the Havannah. Both French and Spaniards are dreadfully sickly. They landed 1000 sick when they arrived at Martinico, and buried full that number during their stay. The Fleet under my command, thank God, has lost neither Officer or Man by sickness since I left the Mediterranean.

When I think of the situation of my benefactors, and their Kingdoms, I shudder; but God is good, and he may do much by driving a spirit of firmness into the councils of many of the Sovereigns of Europe. Your Majesty will readily perceive that I mean more than I choose to commit to paper. I write Mr. Elliot a line; but as I have seen none of the Admirals since my arrival here—one being off Cadiz, and the other off Carthagena—I know nothing but from public rumour. I shall only assure your Majesty that I am, as I have ever been, and shall be, your and the King's most devoted, grateful, and attached,

NELSON AND BRONTE.

TO REAR-ADMIRAL SIR RICHARD BICKERTON, BART.

[From a Press-copy in the possession of the Right Hon. John Wilson Croker.]

Victory, July 21st, 1805.

My dear Sir Richard,

If the orders of the Admiralty force you to remain off Carthagena, with all your Squadron, and that the Queen cannot be spared from that service, then I must desire (as I am ignorant of what orders the Admiralty have given since my departure) that you will proceed and join me in the Amphion, calling at Gibraltar for any orders I may have left with either Admiral Knight, or the Commissioner. And as it is of the greatest consequence that they should be acquainted at Naples and Malta of my return into the Mediterranean, you will send some Ship with my letters for Naples, Sicily, and Malta. I am ever, my dear Sir Richard, your most faithful servant,

NELSON AND BRONTE.

TO REAR-ADMIRAL SIR RICHARD BICKERTON, BART.

[From a Press-copy in the possession of the Right Hon. John Wilson Croker.]

Victory, July 21st, 1805.

My dear Sir Richard,

I would have you turn in your mind the probability of falling in with me, should you come outside the Straits after me. I intend, in case I cannot get to Tetuan to-morrow, to get clear of the Gut, and join Collingwood. From thence, probably, I shall go to, or towards Lagos Bay, until I think all chance is past of the Enemy's Fleet coming towards the Mediterranean, when, if I hear nothing from Lisbon or Ferrol of the arrival of the Enemy's Fleet in the Bay, I shall, if I cannot water at Lagos, come to Tetuan Bay. I wish to see you, that I may arrange a proper force for the service of the Mediterranean, when I go off, unless Collingwood is, in that case, to take the command.

I am surprised at the orders for drawing all our Sloops from Malta. The Island must starve, besides the other distresses which the Army and Island must suffer. I shall make arrangements for all these services, and the Admiralty may censure me if they please. I am ever, my dear Sir Richard, with the greatest regard, your most faithful friend,

NELSON AND BRONTE.

TO REAR-ADMIRAL KNIGHT, GIBRALTAR.

[From a Press-copy in the possession of the Right Hon. John Wilson Croker.]

Victory, July 21st, 1805.

My dear Admiral,

When the Pickle is refitted send her to me, if in Tetuan Bay : if I am out of the Mediterranean, send her to Admiral Collingwood. You will, of course, signify to the Governor, that she will proceed to England, and receive the mails and dispatches. Admiral Cornwallis certainly commands the Fleet, and they say *Nugent* is First Captain ; but this I cannot believe. I see, in an Admiralty Order to Collingwood, that you are to hoist your Flag in a Frigate ; but all these matters I shall fully and clearly arrange, and I hope to your satisfaction, and the good of the Public Service. I am, my dear Admiral, your faithful servant,

NELSON AND BRONTE.

As the Pickle goes home, the Prévoyante need not wait for my letters.

TO CAPTAIN KEATS, H. M. SHIP SUPERB.

[From a Copy.]

Victory, July 21st, 1805.

The Superb will be the first Line-of-Battle Ship, which proceeds to England ; but that may not take place for one month, and it may take place in a few days : therefore, if the Merchants choose to send money to the Superb under these circumstances, they will be acquainted with all that may happen.

NELSON AND BRONTE.

TO WILLIAM MARSDEN, ESQ., ADMIRALTY.

[Original, in the Admiralty.]

Victory, in Gibraltar Bay, July 21st, 1805.

Sir,

I herewith transmit you, for the information of the Lords Commissioners of the Admiralty, a copy of an Acting-Order, which I have given to Mr. John Chrystie,[3] Midshipman of the Victory, to act as Lieutenant of his Majesty's Ship Guerrier, in the room of Lieutenant William Tiller,[4] invalided. Mr. Chrystie is an Admiralty recommendation, and received a severe wound in his left cheek in an Action between the Anson and La Loire,[5] by having a musket-ball shot through it. He is also a very deserving young man. I am, Sir, &c.

NELSON AND BRONTE.

TO CAPTAIN BAYNTUN, H. M. SHIP LEVIATHAN.

[From a Press-copy in the possession of the Right Hon. John Wilson Croker.]

Victory, July 21st, 1805.

Sir,

If the Fleet cannot water at Tetuan, I would have you go off Tetuan, take the Amazon under your orders, and receive all the bullocks and refreshments which Mr. Ford may have procured for us, and join me off Cadiz. I am, Sir, &c.

NELSON AND BRONTE.

---

[3] Mr. John Chrystie. His Commission was dated on the 27th of December, 1805, and he died a Lieutenant about 1834.

[4] He died a Lieutenant in 1814.

[5] On the 18th of October, 1798, the Anson of 44 guns, Captain Philip Charles Durham, in company with the Kangaroo Sloop, off the Coast of Ireland, captured La Loire of 46 guns. The Anson had two Seamen killed, a Lieutenant of Marines, and two Marines; nine Seamen, and two Marines wounded.—*London Gazette*, 30th October, 1798. It is remarkable that Mr. Chrystie's name is not among the wounded; but he may have been wounded in the Action of the 12th, between Sir John Borlase's Squadron and that of Commodore Bompard, when the Anson and La Loire were engaged.

TO REAR-ADMIRAL KNIGHT, GIBRALTAR.

[From a Press-copy in the possession of the Right Hon. John Wilson Croker.
" 22nd July. A.M. At 9·30, weighed and made sail. Noon, Squadron in Company.
P.M. At 7·30, anchored (in Mazri Bay, Tetuan). Squadron anchored as convenient.
H. M. Ship Amazon anchored here."—*Victory's Log.*]

Victory, July 22nd, 1805.

My dear Admiral,
Be so good as to allow the Gun-Brig to bring over to
Tetuan 3000lbs. of onions, which I have desired Mr. Cutforth
to put on board her for the Pursers, as I find we shall get no
onions for the people's broth at Tetuan. The Brig shall not
anchor, or be detained one moment. This will much oblige
yours faithfully, NELSON AND BRONTE.

TO REAR-ADMIRAL KNIGHT, GIBRALTAR.

[From a Press-copy in the possession of the Right Hon. John Wilson Croker.]

Victory, July 22nd, 1805.

My dear Admiral,
As far as my humble judgment goes, it appears that the
Gibraltar station (which I shall in my Order define), probably
from Malaga to some leagues outside Cape Spartel, is intended
by the Admiralty to be left to your charge, and that whatever
happens within the limits of the Gibraltar station, I shall of
course look to you for an account: therefore, it is my duty as
far as I can, to appoint a proper force for this very important
service, and for the neglect of which Admiral Collingwood
sent me yesterday a complaint from the Merchants to the
Admiralty, respecting the capture of two American Ships in
the Gut, with cargoes valued at £100,000, which were carried
into Algesiras.

If the wind is Westerly, I shall go to Tetuan: if Easterly,
out of the Straits. Collingwood thinks the Enemy is gone to
the Bay: therefore I long for water, that I may be able to
follow them, which I shall do, if to Madras. I send you a
copy of the complaint of the Merchants. Yours faithfully,
NELSON AND BRONTE.

TO . . . . . .[6]

[From a Press-copy in the possession of the Right Hon. John Wilson Croker.]

Victory, July 22nd, 1805.

Sir,

I have been honoured with your letter of yesterday respecting Signals. It is certainly desirable that the Enemy should not know all our Signals; but Admirals are restricted by the Admiralty from altering the Flags, or, indeed, meddling with the Signals, as they intend that all Fleets and Ships which may meet, should perfectly understand each other. The Number of the Ship is only a part of our signal, for knowing whether the Ships are friends when they meet at sea. I am much obliged by your good wishes, and am, Sir, your very obedient servant,

NELSON AND BRONTE.

TO J. CUTFORTH, ESQ.

[From a Press-copy in the possession of the Right Hon. John Wilson Croker.]

Victory, July 22nd, 1805.

Dear Sir,

Be so good as to purchase, and put on board the Gun-Brig, whose Lieutenant will deliver you this letter, 3000lbs. of onions, for the use of the Pursers; and I find none will be procured at Tetuan. The price, I hear, will probably be twopence, or twopence half-penny per lb., but send the price. Mr. Ford shall receive the money from the Pursers. Pray, have this done as soon as possible. Captain Hardy saw a Spanish Boat with about that quantity laying at the old Mole, and you can send one of your people, to see them weighed into the Brig. I am, dear Sir, your obliged, humble Servant,

NELSON AND BRONTE.

[9] The address is illegible.

PRIVATE DIARY.

[From Clarke and M'Arthur, vol. ii. p. 417.]

22nd July, 1805.

Bring the Tower on the Cape at the Western side of the Bay, [of Mazri, near Tetuan] to bear from W.N.W. to W. b S. and abreast of the Bay, from half a mile to one and a half mile distant, where there is from ten to twenty fathom water. The River runs inside a sandy beach and parallel to it, so that Boats may lay alongside the beach the whole extent of the Bay, and roll their casks over to the River, and fill them.

NELSON AND BRONTE.

TO WILLIAM MARSDEN, ESQ., ADMIRALTY.

[Autograph, in the Admiralty. "July 23rd. Noon. Weighed, and made sail." —*Victory's Log.*

Victory, Tetuan Bay, July 23rd, 1805.

Sir,

I have seen in their Lordships' orders to Vice-Admiral Collingwood, that the Frigate and Sloops upon the Malta Station are ordered to put themselves under his command; and, as he has ordered them to join him, I take for granted, for services outside the Mediterranean, and as I have not heard that any force is stationed in the environs of Malta, to give protection to the Convoys required for that Island, to and from the Archipelago, Adriatic, Sicily, and Naples, and to Barbary for cattle, I beg leave to apprise their Lordships that Malta cannot more than exist, and that our Troops would be placed in a situation of great distress, without a Naval force to ensure their necessary supplies; and for these services and carrying the Ships from England up the Archipelago and Adriatic, there ought always to be (and my losses have been occasioned by my never having had sufficient means for their protection) two Vessels with each Convoy, to protect them from the swarms of Row-boats, Privateers; and, I am now informed, the Enemy have a Ship-Privateer of twenty-two guns, one hundred and seventy men, and a large Brig of sixteen guns and one hundred men. The force which, always when I had it, I judged it necessary to keep to the Eastward of Sicily was—

and not less is wanted now—one Frigate, 12-pounders; four Sloops of War; the Spider, Renard, and Ventura Schooners, and Hirondelle Cutter, to which I often added Anson Frigate, and Cameleon, and other Sloops.

The Station of Gibraltar, and to watch the French Ship in Cadiz was always (except for a few weeks when I recalled the Donegal) never without a Line-of-Battle Ship, three Frigates, two Sloops; and more when I had them.

The watching Toulon and Genoa at this moment will require more Frigates than when the Fleet was up the Mediterranean, or the French Frigates and Sloops will convoy their Troops to their destination. A Ship of the Line has always been stationed at Naples, not only for the protection of our Merchants and their property, but also with secret orders for the reception of the Royal Family of Naples. His Majesty, through the Secretary of State, has always approved of this precaution; and his Minister has been ordered to declare that the personal safety of their Sicilian Majesties was an object always near his heart: in short, the pledge I believe has been given that a Ship of the Line should always be in Naples Bay—at least, I have understood it so; and by their Lordships' orders of 31st May and 28th August, 1804, I am directed to have a Frigate at the disposal of his Sardinian Majesty, and to protect the Island of Sardinia. These services I have endeavoured to perform, and left all the force of Frigates and Sloops in my power for the services ordered by the Board when the Fleet came down; and I must beg leave to refer Lord Barham to a secret letter of the Cabinet for these and other important services expected from me, signed by Lord Melville. I herewith transmit you a statement of the force which I think necessary to the Eastward of Carthagena for performing the services intrusted to my care; and when I get the lists of Frigates and Sloops, I shall apportion them as far as their number will allow, and my judgment will admit. I have the honour to be, &c.

NELSON AND BRONTE.

Force[7] necessary for the different Stations in the Mediterranean:—

[7] An autograph of this paper is in the possession of Earl Nelson.

MALTA STATION.

One (twelve-pounder,) Frigate.

Four . . . . . Sloops.

Spider ⎫
Ventura ⎬ Schooners.
Renard ⎭

Hirondelle . . Cutter.

NAPLES.

One Ship of the Line.

To watch Toulon, Genoa, Leghorn, to prevent the removal of Troops by sea, to guard Sardinia, and occasionally to call at Palermo, in Sicily—Four Frigates.

N.B.—If the French Line-of-Battle Ship is *launched*, and at sea from Genoa, then two Sail of the Line, two Frigates, and one Sloop.

To WATCH CARTHAGENA.

Line-of-Battle Ships.

Two Frigates.

One Sloop, or three Frigates in lieu.

GIBRALTAR STATION—extent, from Old Malaga, to ten leagues West of Cape Spartel—at least, the number of

Two Frigates,

Two Ship Sloops,

One Brig,

Two Gun-Brigs.

N.B.—The Gun-Brigs, singly, are not considered equal to four Gun-Boats, as their shot never reach the Gun-Boats, which always keep at long shot. Perhaps it would be better to have them at Malta; and two Sloops might perhaps then be drawn from thence, unless these Brigs can be fitted with one eighteen pounder on each side, and one at the head and stern.

OFF CAPE ST. VINCENT.

One Frigate.

WITH ADMIRAL COLLINGWOOD, OFF CADIZ.

Two Frigates.

Two Bombs; Childers Sloop.

WITH LORD NELSON'S SQUADRON.

Two Frigates.

N.B.—A Frigate and a Sloop wanted for the Convoy from Malta, ordered by their Lordships to sail every two months.

NELSON AND BRONTE.

TO THE RIGHT HONOURABLE LORD BARHAM.

[From a Press-copy in the possession of the Right Hon. John Wilson Croker.]

Victory, Tetuan, July 23rd, 1805.

My Lord,

The Fleet is complete, and the first Easterly Wind, I shall pass the Straits. I have yet not a word of information of the Enemy's Fleet: it has almost broke my heart. But the name of General Brereton will never be forgot by this generation; but for him our Battle would have been fought on June 6th. The event would have been in the hands of Providence; but we may without, I hope, vanity, believe that the Enemy would have been fit for no active service after such a Battle. All our losses which have happened, or may happen, are entirely to be attributed to his information. I shall take my position most convenient for receiving intelligence; and if I find the Enemy gone to the Bay, I shall go off Ferrol, or Ushant, as the case appears to me to require.

Your Lordship will observe, in my letter to the Board, that I am taking part of the Small Craft, which they directed to be under Admiral Collingwood, unless other Vessels are in the Mediterranean for the different stations, not one of which can with propriety be given up; and I hope the Board will consider it as not wishing to alter any arrangement of theirs, but as a measure absolutely necessary. I shall return to England the moment I know that the Enemy's Fleet is in Port, and out of my reach; and I shall with pleasure give your Lordship every information which twelve years experience has given me of the Mediterranean. I shall add a Postscript[8] when I get out of the Straits: therefore shall only assure you that I am, with great respect, your Lordship's most obedient Servant,

NELSON AND BRONTE.

[8] No Postscript appears to have been added.

TO THE HON. CAPTAIN CAPEL, H.M. SHIP PHŒBE.

[From a Press-copy in the possession of the Right Hon. John Wilson Croker.]

Private.　　　　　　　　　　Victory, July 23rd, 1805.

My dear Capel,

It is not my intention that you should remain any great length of time on the Gibraltar Station ; but whilst you stay, I beg that you will show an active attention to the important service, which will be an example to those who will follow you. Five miles from Cape Spartel you are sure of taking Spanish Barks from, and to the West Indies, and perhaps a Ship from Lima. Be active, and I will ensure you success. I am ever, my dear Capel, your sincere friend,

NELSON AND BRONTE.

TO WILLIAM MARSDEN, ESQ., ADMIRALTY.

[Autograph, in the Admiralty.]

Victory, Tetuan Bay, July 23rd, 1805.

Sir,

Referring you to my letter of July the 20th, by the Thomas Merchant Brig (of which I send a duplicate) for my arrival at, and proceedings to Gibraltar, I have now only to inform you that, having completed the Fleet to four months' provisions, except bread, of which there was not a sufficient quantity in store, and completed the stores of the Ships to Channel Service, I came over here yesterday ; and, by night, the Fleet will be complete with water, and, I hope, have on board a fortnight's fresh provisions, of which, and refreshments, we were much in want, every Ship having much of the scurvy, but, thank God, not the smallest symptom of any other complaint. I shall pass the Straits the moment the wind comes from the Eastward, and take such a position between Cape St. Vincent and Spartel, that I may receive the earliest information of the Enemy's Fleet, and regulate my proceedings accordingly. I should not have come within the Straits for several days after my arrival off Spartel, but the want of water and refreshments rendered it a measure absolutely necessary, for the Fleet could not have gone even off Ferrol without water, &c.; and now, if the case requires, ten Sail of us can go to Madras, or round Cape Horn. Their Lordships will, I trust, give me full credit that it is not my wish for a moment to get out of the track of the Enemy, but that I am anxious to have the fine Fleet I have the happiness to command, ready to follow them, to whatever place they may proceed.

Respecting the alteration I may think it necessary to make in arranging the proper force off Cadiz, Carthagena, the Gibraltar station, the Malta station, the stationing a Squadron to prevent the sailing of Troops from Genoa and Toulon, which I am informed are ready, I beg to refer you to another letter.[9] I only entreat that, as I may have appeared to have removed some of the Frigates and Sloops from stations, to which I think their Lordships have directed their services, nothing but the present urgency of the case having required it [sic.] I trust I am the last Officer in the Service who would not follow up closely the orders, and even wishes, of the Board, as far as I can collect them. I am, Sir, &c.

NELSON AND BRONTE.

TO WILLIAM MARSDEN, ESQ., ADMIRALTY.

[Original, in the Admiralty.]

Sir,　　　　　Victory, in Tetuan Bay, 23rd July, 1805.

I herewith transmit you, for the information of the Lords Commissioners of the Admiralty, a copy of an order which I have given to Rear-Admiral Knight, respecting the force which I have placed under his command, for the comfort of the Garrison and protection of the Trade in the Straits, as therein mentioned, which I hope will meet their Lordships' approbation. I am, Sir, &c.

NELSON AND BRONTE.

TO REAR-ADMIRAL JOHN KNIGHT, GIBRALTAR.

[From a Copy in the Admiralty.]

Victory, in Tetuan Bay, 23rd July, 1805.

Whereas the Lords Commissioners of the Admiralty have judged it expedient for the better Naval protection of the

[9] Vide p. 488, ante.

Garrison at Gibraltar, its comforts, and the perfect security of
our Commerce, passing to, and from thence, through the Straits,
that you should hoist your Flag on board the Guerrier, or
any Frigate under your orders; and their Lordships having,
by their order, dated the 28th March 1805, directed you to
put yourself under my command, and it also being their intention that a sufficient force shall be attached to the Straits
of Gibraltar, for the purposes above mentioned; and whereas
I am fully aware of the very great importance of the services
entrusted to your charge, and the necessity of an adequate
force being put under your orders for these purposes,—

You are hereby required and instructed to take his Majesty's Ships, Sloops, and Gun-brigs, named in the margin,[8]
under your command, and such others as I may hereafter
find necessary, and employ them as you shall judge best for
the service of the Garrison, the protection of our Commerce
in Gibraltar Bay, and also of our Trade passing to, and from
that place through the Straits, for which purpose you will
place a Vessel of War either at Tangier, or to the Westward of
Cape Spartel, that she may at all times be ready, not only to
give you intelligence of the approach of an Enemy, but also
to protect the Commerce from being captured by their numerous Gun-boats in the Straits. You are to consider the
limits of your command from Old Malaga to ten leagues to
the Westward of Cape Spartel, that our Trade coming from
Malta, &c., may have certain security from your Cruizers on
their arrival off the former place, and the Commerce from
the United Kingdom, bound into the Mediterranean, may be
sure of meeting some Vessel of War, on its approaching the
Straits' Mouth. The recent capture of two valuable American
Ships from Liverpool in the Gut, laden with English property,
strongly points out the very great necessity for the most active
and zealous exertions being used to prevent the capture of our
Trade; nor is it, I trust, (from your zeal, and perfect knowledge of the important service committed to your charge,)
necessary for me to do more than observe, that there never
was a season when more constant and active attention was

---

[8] Guerrier, Phœbe, Decade, Martin, Termagant, Halcyon, Dexterous Gun-Brig,
Fervent Gun-Brig.

required at Gibraltar, and in the Straits, than the present, in order to prevent our Trade from being captured. I, therefore, shall only add, that I consider the Garrison and Commerce, within the limits of your command, as properly protected and freed from annoyance or capture by the Enemy's Gun-boats, as is possible for a Naval force to accomplish. I have also the most full confidence in your indefatigable exertions to frustrate the intentions of the Enemy on all occasions. You will, in addition to these important services, bear in mind their Lordships' intentions relative to the sending and bringing the mails to, and from Lisbon; and so soon as a greater force can be spared, I shall place them under your command, for the more perfect protection of our Commerce, and for securing supplies of provisions from the Coast of Barbary, intended for the comfort of the Garrison, and also for the purpose of getting the mails to and from Lisbon, or communicating with the Squadron off Carthagena. Rear-Admiral Sir Richard Bickerton, who, it is probable, I shall soon leave in the temporary command of the Mediterranean Fleet, (under whose command you will, of course be,) will do everything in his power to strengthen your force, and enable you to carry my instructions into full effect.

You are at liberty to shift your Flag from the Guerrier on board any of the Ships or Vessels under your command; and it is recommended by their Lordships always to have one in the Bay ready to man the Gun-boats. You will inform Rear-Admiral Sir Richard Bickerton of your proceedings, from time to time, during my absence from the Mediterranean, in order that he may be a judge of what further force may be necessary, or for changing any Ships or Vessels under your orders; and you will also, when it may be necessary, communicate with the Admiralty direct, as it might very much retard your correspondence to send your letters through the Rear-Admiral; but you will, as early after as possible, transmit Sir Richard copies thereof, that he may be in full possession of every information relative to Gibraltar. I must also desire to recommend that you frequently consult with General Fox, the Lieutenant-Governor, in what manner the Squadron under your command may be made most serviceable for the real comforts of the Garrison, and to prevent

it from being annoyed by the Enemy's Gun-boats; and also,
as a most essential advantage to his Majesty's Service, that
the most perfect harmony and good understanding is preserved between you and the Governor, that a mutual and
cordial co-operation may at all times take place for the defence
of the Garrison. I must also desire that you transmit a copy
of this order as early as possible to Vice-Admiral Collingwood,
and to Rear-Admiral Sir Richard Bickerton, for their information.

NELSON AND BRONTE.

TO ALEXANDER DAVISON, ESQ.

[Autograph, in the possession of Colonel Davison.]

Victory, July 24th, 1805.

My dear Davison,

As all my letters have been sent to England, I know nothing
of what is passing; but I hope very, very soon to take you
by the hand. I am as miserable as you can conceive. But
for General Brereton's damned information, Nelson would
have been, living or dead, the greatest man in his Profession
that England ever saw. Now, alas! I am nothing—perhaps
shall incur censure for misfortunes which may happen, and
have happened. When I follow my own head, I am, in
general, much more correct in my judgment, than following
the opinion of others. I resisted the opinion of General
Brereton's information till it would have been the height of
presumption to have carried my disbelief further. I could
not, in the face of Generals and Admirals, go N.W., when it
was *apparently* clear that the Enemy had gone South. But
I am miserable. I now long to hear that they are arrived in
some Port in the Bay; for until they are arrived somewhere, I
can do nothing but fret. Then I shall proceed to England.
I can say nothing, or think of anything, but the loss my
Country has sustained by General Brereton's unfortunate,
ill-timed, false information. God bless you; and believe me
ever, my dear Davison, your most faithful and affectionate
friend,

NELSON AND BRONTE.

TO CAPTAIN PARKER, H. M. SHIP AMAZON.

[From a Copy, in the Nelson Papers. " 25th July. A.M. 3·30, hove to, and
spoke H.M. Ship Termagant."—*Victory's Log.*][9]

Victory, July 25th, 1805.

My dear Parker,

Make haste and join me. If all places fail, you will find
me at Spithead. Yours most truly,

NELSON AND BRONTE.

TO CAPTAIN PARKER, H. M. SHIP AMAZON.

[From a Copy in the Admiralty.]

Victory, off Cadiz, 25th July, 1804.

Having received information that the Combined Fleet was
seen on the 19th ultimo, steering to the Northward, I am
proceeding with the Fleet in pursuit of them with all dispatch,
You are, therefore, hereby required and directed to repair
immediately in search of me off Cape St. Vincent; or, not
finding me there, you will make the best of your way off
Ferrol, if you shall judge, from information, that I have gone
there; otherwise, you will proceed DIRECT off Ushant or
IRELAND, where you will fall in with me, or gain intelligence
where I am gone to. But, in the event of not gaining information of me, or, on your arrival at either of those places, you
should learn that I am returned into Port, it is my direction
that you immediately repair to Spithead, and acquaint the
Secretary of the Admiralty thereof. As the Amazon is the
only Frigate attached to the Squadron, I have no occasion
to request that you will use your utmost endeavours to join
me.

NELSON AND BRONTE.

[9] "On the 24th of July, the Decade joined from Admiral Collingwood, yet still no
information of the Enemy. The Fleet weighed at Noon and stood for Ceuta: during
the night they remained in the Gut with variable winds and a thick fog. On [*i. e.*
in] the next day, the 25th, the Termagant joined with an account that the Combined
Fleet had been seen by the Curieux Brig, on the 19th, standing to the Northward.
Having passed the Straits and communicated with Admiral Collingwood, the
Squadron under Lord Nelson bore away to the Westward, and then proceeded off
Cape St. Vincent, with a view to go more Northward, or to act as circumstances of
intelligence might render necessary."—*Clarke and M'Arthur.* vol. ii.

TO WILLIAM MARSDEN, ESQ., ADMIRALTY.

[Autograph, in the Admiralty.]

Victory, July 25th, 1805, off Cape Spartel.

Sir,

At four o'clock this morning I received from Lisbon, through a newspaper, an account of the arrival of the Curieux, and of her having fallen in with the Enemy's Fleet from the West Indies, and I know it's true from my words being repeated: therefore, I shall not lose a moment, after I have communicated with Admiral Collingwood, in getting to the Northward to either Ferrol, Ireland or Ushant, as information or circumstances may point out to be proper. I shall wish to bring eleven Sail of the Line with me, although, when a junction is formed, two Sail of the Line will be wanted for the Mediterranean service, and one or two off Cadiz, if the Ramilies and Illustrious[1] do not return here from the West Indies. I have pointed out to Vice-Admiral Collingwood and Rear-Admiral Sir Richard Bickerton, my ideas of the services required of them, particularly the latter, inside the Mediterranean. I will not detain the Pickle one moment longer than to say that I am, Sir, &c.

NELSON AND BRONTE.

Victory—Fit for service.

Canopus—Ditto, but would be better docked before the winter.

Spencer—Fit for service.

Superb—Must be docked, and a new fore-mast.

Belleisle—Wants docking.

Donegal—Wants docking; but not so much as Belleisle.

Conqueror ⎞
Tigre ⎪
Spartiate ⎬ Fit for service.
Leviathan ⎪
Swiftsure ⎠

The whole of the Ships are complete to bear four months, and in perfect health.

---

[1] Vice-Admiral Collingwood had sent those Ships, on the 27th of May, to reinforce Lord Nelson in the West Indies.

TO VICE-ADMIRAL COLLINGWOOD.

[Autograph, in the possession of the Hon. Mrs. Newnham Collingwood.]

Victory, July 25th, 1805.

My dear Collingwood,

We are in a fresh Levanter. You have a Westerly wind; therefore I must forego the pleasure of taking you by the hand until October next, when, if I am well enough, I shall (if the Admiralty please) resume the Command. I am very far from well; but I am anxious that not a moment of the services of this Fleet should be lost. Amazon is the only Frigate I take with me, and she has not joined from Gibraltar: I send her orders. I feel disappointed, my dear friend, at not seeing you: so does Admiral Murray and many, I am sure, in this Fleet. May God bless, and send you alongside the Santissima Trinidada; and let me see you in perfect health, and ever believe me, my dear Collingwood, your most faithful and affectionate friend,

NELSON AND BRONTE.

Termagant came to me at four o'clock this morning, off Tariffa. It turns out he had all my things from Gibraltar; but as I fancied he came from Lisbon, I would not allow him to stop, except to deliver your letters; and he has carried all, even to my last shirt, back again.

TO VICE-ADMIRAL COLLINGWOOD.

[From a Copy in the Admiralty.]

Victory, off Cadiz, July 25th, 1805.

Sir,

I am proceeding with the Squadron which I brought with me from the West Indies to the Northward, in search of the Combined Squadron. I have therefore to desire that you will continue on the service you have hitherto been employed on, off Cadiz. But I must beg leave to submit to your consideration a paper containing my ideas of the number of stations necessary to be occupied inside the Mediterranean, which I have sent to the Admiralty,[2] and to Rear-Admiral Sir Richard Bickerton. You will observe that I have only left for your Squadron the Ships stationed off Cape St. Vincent, two Frigates, Childers Brig, and the two Bombs; the others ordered by the Admiralty to be under your command are, in some measure, unnecessary, as I have appointed a Squadron for Rear-Admiral Knight (a copy of which order he is directed to transmit you) at Gibraltar, whereby the safety of the Gut is, as far as a Naval force can do it, secured to our Commerce.

I submit the propriety of sending, without loss of time, to Rear-Admiral Sir Richard Bickerton, the Frigates and Sloops above what I have before mentioned as necessary, in my opinion, for your station off Cadiz, whom I have instructed how to dispose of them for the necessary services ordered by the Admiralty; and I am persuaded that you will agree with me in the propriety of attending duly to the services of Malta, and the other stations in the Mediterranean, and that the force I have appointed is barely equal to the very arduous services required of it, and any diminution of which must prove detrimental to the interest of his Majesty in these seas. Your judgment on these points, and zeal for the Service, promise everything that can be expected, and no one more highly estimates both, than he who has the honour to be, Sir, &c.

NELSON AND BRONTE.

TO REAR-ADMIRAL SIR RICHARD BICKERTON.

[From a Copy in the Admiralty.]

Victory, July 25th, 1805.

Sir,

Having received information that the Combined Fleet from the West Indies has gone to the Northward, I am proceeding in pursuit of it. The charge, therefore, of watching the Spanish Squadron at Carthagena, and of executing the other important services inside the Mediterranean, will devolve upon you; and as you are already in possession of copies of all my orders, it is only necessary for me, in conse-

* Vide p. 438, ante.

quence of orders which have been sent to Vice-Admiral Collingwood, respecting the removal of many Frigates and Sloops from stations to which I had thought it proper to appoint them; and as I am totally ignorant if their Lordships have appointed others in their room, I send you a copy of my ideas of the force which is necessary for the different stations, which I have sent to the Lords Commissioners of the Admiralty; and as you are as fully sensible as I am, of the necessity of keeping the force on those stations, and most particularly that of Malta, (without which force the Island could have no commerce, or even communication with any place, from the numerous French Privateers in that neighbourhood, and both the Inhabitants and Troops would be reduced to a very disagreeable, if not distressing situation,) I shall only take the Amazon Frigate with me; and as soon as I get to any force which may render my present one unnecessary, I shall detach, or recommend it to my Superior Officer, two Sail of the Line to reinforce you. I will not presume to say anything further on the duties of the Commanding Officer in the Mediterranean station, as you have, before my arrival, and since my departure for the West Indies, filled the post with so much ability and honour to yourself, and advantage to your King and Country. I am, I do assure you, Sir, with the highest respect and esteem, your most humble servant,

NELSON AND BRONTE.

TO WILLIAM MARSDEN, ESQ., ADMIRALTY.

[Original, in the Admiralty. "26th July. Noon. Squadron in company, Cape St. Mary's N. 45 W., distance, 17½ leagues.—*Victory's Log.* Admiral Collingwood's Squadron in sight to the Eastward."—*Signal Log.*]

Victory, at Sea, July 26th, 1805.

Sir,

Not having had an opportunity of seeing, or hearing from Rear-Admiral Sir Richard Bickerton, during my short stay inside the Straits, I am totally ignorant of the orders he may have received from their Lordships during my absence, and having yesterday morning, at four o'clock, received information from Vice-Admiral Collingwood, by the Termagant, (through the channel of a newspaper from Lisbon,) that the

Enemy's Squadron from the West Indies had gone to the Northward, induced me to avail myself of the Easterly wind ; consequently, as the Vice-Admiral was considerably to leeward of Cadiz, I did not wait to see him, but from the copies of their Lordships' orders, &c. which he sent me on the 20th inst., I have been enabled to judge the force in my opinion necessary for blockading Cadiz, &c. as well as for watching the Enemy's Squadron at Carthagena, and the other important services within the Mediterranean, and therefore wrote Vice-Admiral Collingwood, and Rear-Admiral Sir Richard Bickerton, copies of which are herewith transmitted, together with a copy of a paper containing my ideas of the force necessary for the station off Cadiz, and for the several and very important ones within the Mediterranean, which I trust their Lordships will be pleased to approve of; at any rate, to do me the justice to believe that the arrangements I have made, have been done upon the most mature deliberation, and to the utmost of my abilities. I am, Sir, &c.

NELSON AND BRONTE.

TO ADMIRAL THE HONOURABLE WILLIAM CORNWALLIS.

[From a Press-copy in the possession of the Right Hon. John Wilson Croker.]

Victory, off Cape St. Mary's, July 27th, 1805.

My dear Friend,

The Enemy's Fleet from the West Indies being certainly gone to some Port in the Bay, I am proceeding to the Northward, with eleven Sail of the Line. I shall either call off Cape Clear, or proceed direct off Ushant, to form a junction with you, as circumstances may, in my judgment, (from intelligence,) require. I shall only hope, after all my long pursuit of *my* Enemy, that I may arrive at the moment they are meeting you ; for my very wretched state of health will force me to get on shore for a little while. I am ever, my dear friend, your most faithful and attached,

NELSON AND BRONTE.

TO   .   .   .   .   .   .

[From a Press-copy in the possession of the Right Hon. John Wilson Croker.]

Victory, off Cape St. Mary's, July 27th, 1805.

Sir,

If you should fall in with any of the Cruizers belonging to the Irish station, you will submit to the Captain the propriety of receiving my letter for the Right Honourable Lord Gardner, or the Commander-in-Chief in Ireland ; and should you fall in with one of the Honourable Admiral Cornwallis's Cruizers, you will deliver to him my letter for the Commander of the Channel Fleet, and show both the Captains my letter to them, and this one to you. I am, Sir, &c.

NELSON AND BRONTE.

Should you fall in with no Vessel, you will send the letters to the Port-Admiral.

TO THE RIGHT HONOURABLE ADMIRAL LORD GARDNER.

[From a Press-copy in the possession of the Right Hon. John Wilson Croker.]

Victory, off Cape St. Mary's, July 27th, 1805.

My Lord,

I am proceeding to the Northward, as I have no doubt that the Enemy's Fleet from the West Indies are gone into some Port in the Bay. Should I receive any information which may lead me to suppose the destination of the Enemy is Ireland, I shall form a junction with you; and it is most probable that I shall, if [I] receive no intelligence, make Cape Clear ; therefore, I shall be obliged if you will order some of your Cruizers to look out for me, with such information as may enable me to direct my further proceedings. I have with me eleven Sail of the Line. I cannot be many days after the Pickle Schooner, who is directed to put this letter on board any Frigate of your Squadron, or any one looking out for information near the Channel, which she may fall in with. I have the honour to be, with the highest respect, &c.   NELSON AND BRONTE.

TO THE COMMANDERS OF ANY FRIGATES OR VESSELS ON THE
IRISH OR CHANNEL STATION.

[From a Press-Copy in the possession of the Right Hon. John Wilson Croker.]

Victory, off Cape St. Mary's, July 27th, 1805.

Sir,

I submit to you the propriety of carrying my letter to the Commander-in-Chief on the Irish station, or to the Commander-in-Chief of the Channel Fleet, as you may belong to one station or the other. It is of very great importance the knowledge of my very near approach; but I cannot say of what importance the service you are employed upon—being of more or less importance, that I must leave to your judgment. I am, Sir, &c.

NELSON AND BRONTE.

END OF VOL. VI.

.